CANADIAN POLITICAL THOUGHT

CANADIAN POLITICAL THOUGHT

EDITED BY H.D. FORBES

Toronto
OXFORD UNIVERSITY PRESS

Oxford University Press, 70 Wynford Drive, Don Mills, Ontario, M3C 1J9

Toronto   Oxford   New York   Delhi   Bombay   Calcutta   Madras   Karachi
Petaling Jaya   Singapore   Hong Kong   Tokyo   Nairobi   Dar es Salaam
Cape Town   Melbourne   Auckland

and associated companies in
Berlin   Ibadan

CANADIAN CATALOGUING IN PUBLICATION DATA
Main entry under title:
Canadian political thought

Bibliography: p.
ISBN 0-19-540457-2

1. Political science – Canada – Addresses, essays, lectures. 2. Canada —
Intellectual life – History – Addresses, essays, lectures. I. Forbes, Hugh
Donald, 1942–
   JL31.C36 1985   320.5′0971   C84-098328-X

Acknowledgements

ANONYMOUS. 'Letter from a Nationalist' originally appeared as 'Lettre d'un nationaliste' *Cité libre*, No. 35 (1961). English translation © Sally Livingston. SALEM GOLDWORTH BLAND. 'The New Christianity' from *The New Christianity, Or the Religion of the New Age* (1920), The Social History of Canada Series © University of Toronto Press 1973, used by permission. HENRI BOURASSA. 'The French-Canadian in the British Empire' used by permission of Anne Bourassa and Marie Bourassa. 'The Spectre of Annexation' from *The Spectre of Annexation and the Real Danger of National Disintegration* (1912) used by permission of Le Devoir. ALBERT BRETON *et al.* 'An Appeal for Realism in Politics' *Canadian Forum*, May 1964, used by permission. PAUL CHAMBERLAND. 'Cultural Alienation and National Revolution' originally appeared as 'Aliénation culturelle et révolution nationale' (*parti pris*, No. 2, November 1963). Used by permission of L'Hexagone. English translation © Craig Thomas. JOHN DALES. 'Protection, Immigration and Canadian Nationalism' used by permission of Professor David P. Shugarman. GEORGE GRANT. 'The Minds of Men in the Atomic Age' used by permission of George Grant. 'Teaching What Nietzsche Taught: Part I' from *Time as History*. Canadian copyright © CBC Enterprises/les Entreprises Radio-Canada, a division of the Canadian Broadcasting Corporation, Toronto. 'Teaching What Nietzsche Taught: Part II' from 'Nietzsche and the Ancients: Philosophy and Scholarship' *Dionysius*, 3 (1979). Used by permission. LIONEL GROULX. 'Tomorrow's Tasks' originally appeared as 'Labeurs de demain' in *Directives*, Montreal, Les Éditions du Zodiaque, 1937. Used by permission of Juliette Remillard and the Fonds Lionel-Groulx. English translation © Sally Livingston. 'Methods of Education' from *Mes Mémoires* Vol. 1, Montreal, Éditions Fidès, 1970. Used by permission of Juliette Remillard and the Fonds Lionel-Groulx. English translation © H.D. Forbes. GAD HOROWITZ. 'Mosaics and Identity' from *Canadian Dimension* (Dec.-Jan. 1965-66). Reprinted by permission. 'On the Fear of Nationalism' from *Canadian Dimension* (May-June 1967). Reprinted by permission. 'Tories, Socialists and the Demise of Canada' from *Canadian Dimension* (May-June 1965). Reprinted by permission. ANDRÉ LAURENDEAU. 'The Conditions for the Existence of a National Culture' originally appeared as 'Les conditions d'existence d'une culture nationale' *L'Action nationale*, 37 (1951). Used by permission. English translation © Sally Livingston. STEPHEN LEACOCK. 'Greater Canada. An Appeal' (1907) from *The Social Criticism of Stephen Leacock* edited by Alan Bowker © University of Toronto Press, 1973. Used by permission. 'The Apology of a Professor: An Essay on Modern Learning' from *Essays and Literary Studies* by Stephen Leacock. Used by permission of The Canadian Publishers, McClelland and Stewart Limited, Toronto. RENÉ LÉVESQUE. 'A Country That Must be Made' from *An Option for Quebec* by René Lévesque. Used by permission of The Canadian Publishers, McClelland and Stewart Limited, Toronto. KARI LEVITT. 'Silent Surrender' from *Silent Surrender: The Multinational Corporation in Canada* (1970). Used by permission of Macmillan of Canada (A Division of Gage Publishing Limited). DAVID LEWIS. 'A Socialist Takes Stock' from *A Socialist Takes Stock* (1955). Used by permission of Michael Lewis. W. L. MORTON. 'Canadian Conservatism Now' from *Contexts of Canada's Past: Selected Essays of W. L. Morton*, edited by A. B. McKillop. Used by permission of Carleton University Press Inc. LOUIS-JOSEPH PAPINEAU. 'Papineau on Constitutional Reform' English translation © Sally Livingston. ÉTIENNE PARENT. 'The Importance of Studying Political Economy' originally appeared as 'Importance de l'étude de l'économie politique' (1846). English translation © Sally Livingston. MGR JOSEPH-OCTAVE PLESSIS. 'Sermon on Nelson's Victory at Aboukir'. English translation © H.D. Forbes. ADOLPHE-BASILE ROUTHIER *et al.* 'The Programme Catholique: The Next Elections' originally appeared as 'Programme Catholique: les prochaines élections' (1871). English translation © H.D. Forbes. JULES-PAUL TARDIVEL. 'On Liberalism'. English translation © H.D. Forbes. CHARLES TAYLOR. 'The Agony of Economic Man' from *Essays on the Left* edited by Laurier LaPierre *et al.*, used by permission of The Canadian Publishers, McClelland and Stewart Limited, Toronto. PIERRE EL-LIOTT TRUDEAU. 'Advances in Politics' from *Approaches to Politics* translated by I.M. Owen. Used by permission of Oxford University Press Canada. 'Nationalist Alienation' originally appeared as 'L'aliénation nationaliste' *Cité libre*, No. 35 (1961). English translation © Sally Livingston. FRANK H. UNDERHILL. 'O Canada' from *Canadian Forum* (December 1929). Used by permission. 'Some Reflections on the Liberal Tradition in Canada' from *In Search of Canadian Liberalism* © Ruth Underhill. PIERRE VADEBONCOEUR. 'Gentle Genocide' from *Un génocide en douce: Écrits polémiques* (L'Hexagone/parti pris, 1976). Used by permission of L'Hexagone. English translation © Craig Thomas. J.S. WOODSWORTH. 'Thy Kingdom Come' from 'Sermons for the Unsatisfied' *Grain Grower's Guide* (30 June 1915).

Contents

Preface

This anthology is meant to serve as an introduction to the study of Canadian political thought. It provides materials ranging from party platforms to philosophical essays, the earliest from 1799 and the most recent from 1979, that cover many points on the political spectrum. They have been selected from a much greater number of possibilities because they are useful in teaching an historically oriented survey of the subject. Readers will find the standard pieces—Mgr Pless̗s on divine providence, Baldwin on responsible government, Macdonald on federalism, the Quebec Bishops on ultramontanism, Laurier on liberalism, Bland on the social gospel, Lewis on socialism, Morton on conservatism, Trudeau on functionalism and multiculturalism, and Lévesque on separatism, along with the Six Counties Address, Mackenzie's Draft Constitution, the Nationalist League Program, the Regina Manifesto, the Waffle Manifesto, and one or two others. They will also find samplings from some of our best political writers—Joseph Howe, Goldwin Smith, Henri Bourassa, Stephen Leacock, Frank Underhill, André Laurendeau, Pierre Vadeboncoeur, and George Grant—as well as a few pieces a different anthologist might hardly have considered. I hope the book may be of interest to a wider audience than those who will be required to read it as part of a university course on Canadian politics.

In making my selections I have tried to highlight individuals whose writings throw a clear light on the main course of our history. Consequently I have emphasized the themes of authority and nationality. Corporatism, feminism, Gompersism, and many varieties of Marxism and social credit, important though they undoubtedly were and are, have had to be ignored. I considered and decided against making excerpts from two key books—Mackenzie King's *Industry and Humanity* and George Grant's *Lament for a Nation*—that can be neither abridged nor ignored. Once I had decided to centre Part III on Grant's lament, I was forced to make some hard decisions about a number of his contemporaries. Some of these decisions will be contested. Still, the anthologist must ultimately be guided by his own experience of different writers, and if he wrongly slights certain figures, stubbornly resisting the good advice of friends and colleagues, he can offer the consolation that his errors reflect badly on him, not them. Finally, I did not want to duplicate anything in Ramsay Cook's excellent *French-Canadian Nationalism*, an anthology that in some ways is a companion volume to this one.

Two years ago, when I began this project, I intended to follow Cook's severe rule: only complete texts. No snippets to illustrate a favourite theme; no reworkings to bring out more clearly what the author really had in mind or to fit him into a favourite scheme. Let the readers decide for themselves how the pieces should fit together and what they mean. But these high ideals have fallen by the wayside and the secret desire of every anthologist to sketch an argument has triumphed. Only about half of the following selections are offered complete; the remainder have been edited to save space or to make a point.

I assume that the national factor is fundamental: that what we need is not a class analysis of Canadian politics but a national analysis. By a national analysis, I mean one that treats the fact of two nations as fundamental. The selections are in rough chronological order. Readers may group them as they please—for example, under the usual heads of Conservatism, Liberalism, Socialism, and Nationalism.

A lengthy introduction would be needed to explain at all adequately the relation between these isms and our pervasive Americanism—our tendency to see ourselves through American eyes. This tendency is a natural consequence of American power and can be seen for what it is only by those who neither rage against that power nor bend to its demands.

Brief introductions to the selections are provided by the headnotes. I have also added some editorial notes, marked by symbols in the text, to explain some allusions to contemporary events and to provide references that may be of interest to scholars and essay writers. These notes are collected at the end of the book.

I have received advice and assistance from a number of people whom I wish to thank. Jack McLeod stands at the head of the list. His generosity and good nature gave me the chance to put this anthology together. He gave me his outlines and drafts for a similar anthology he had planned ten years ago and made detailed comments and suggestions in response to my early proposals. Without his contribution, this book would never have taken the shape that it has. He is obviously not to be blamed for whatever faults remain in it, and he certainly deserves much of the credit for whatever good it may do. I am also very grateful to Donald LePan of Oxford University Press for seeing the need for an anthology, drawing up a rough outline of what it might contain, constructively criticizing my own attempts, and collating helpful comments from many authorities. My colleagues at the University of Toronto and elsewhere have been generous in offering advice. Among them I wish to mention Ed Andrew, Carl Berger, Rainer Knopff, Ken McRae, Ken McRoberts, Cliff Orwin, Jone Schoeffel, and Nelson Wiseman. My editor, Sally Livingston, has been a model of painstaking discretion, and the book has been much improved by her efforts. Finally, special thanks are due Gad Horowitz, not only for his useful suggestions, but for twenty years ago providing, for me as for many others engaged in the study of Canadian politics, a clear theory that was a stimulus to thought.

H. D. FORBES

November 1984

I
FROM COLONIES
TO NATION

MGR JOSEPH-OCTAVE PLESSIS

One of the architects of French Canada's accommodation to the Conquest, Joseph-Octave Plessis (1763-1825) was Bishop of Quebec from 1806 until his death. Under Sir James Craig's 'reign of terror' he combined firmness with deference, preaching submission to established authority and decrying the sovereignty of the people while skilfully resisting the governor's efforts to bring the Church to heel. He enjoyed easier relations with Craig's successor, Sir George Prevost, and during the war of 1812 played an important part in ensuring the loyalty of the Canadiens. In 1817 he was appointed to the Legislative Council of Lower Canada.

Plessis's best-known writing is this sermon preached on 10 January 1799, a day set aside for public celebrations of Nelson's surprising victory over Napoleon the previous August. It is a fine example of persuasive speech in which Plessis explains that the Conquest may have been a blessing in disguise, since Britain is a conservative and monarchical nation, wholeheartedly in support of Throne and Altar. Thus French Canada's most precious treasure, its religious faith and form of Church government, will be safer under British sovereignty than in any connection with revolutionary France or republican America. Plessis was the first to elaborate the elements of a nationalism that made sense of French Canada's past and pointed the way to a possible future. His sermon shows toryism without its usual blush.

Sermon on Nelson's Victory at Aboukir

Thy right hand, O Lord, shattered the enemy.
EXODUS 15

[INTRODUCTION]

Nothing occurs here below without the command or permission of God. To credit men—their cleverness, valour, or expertise—with the success or failure of their enterprises is to fail to recognize the Sovereign Wisdom that, from the height of the Eternal Throne, decides, as it pleases, the fate of States and Empires, and rarely grants them anything fixed and certain except the very turmoil and instability by which they are continually perturbed. If the Pharaoh and his army are engulfed in the Red Sea, if Sennacherib is obliged suddenly to abandon the siege of Jerusalem, if the troops of Holophernes draw back in disgrace from Bethulia, it is not to Moses, nor Ezekiel, nor Judith that the credit for these happy events should go. The hand of God alone effects all these wonders: *Thy right hand, O Lord, shattered the enemy.* Thus to the Rear Admiral Horatio Nelson belongs the glory of having been the instrument used by the Lord to humble a proud and unjust power.* But who among us, my brothers, knows so little of the principles of his religion that he does not attribute to God all the success in arms of this expert and celebrated warrior?

It is to you, therefore, Lord, that we ought to direct our praise and thanksgiving. It is in your Temple that our cries of relief and our hymns of victory will resound today. *Vota mea Domino reddam in atriis domus Domini.*†

Far be it from us, Christians, to indulge in that profane and worldly glee to which the unregenerate may abandon themselves today. Rather let us rejoice in the Lord. Let us give thanks for the benefits won for us by Nelson's brilliant success. Let us not look on indifferently when news reaches us of a great event so closely connected to all of our interests.

For whoever will consider in its true light the victory won early last August by the naval forces of His Majesty must recognize, first of all, that this victory humbles and discomfits France; second, that it heightens the glory of Great Britain and crowns its generosity; and, third, that it assures the happiness of this Province in particular. Let us reflect on these three points, and let us once again say with thanksgiving, that it is your hand, Lord, that has struck down our enemy. *Dextera tua, Domine, percussit inimicum.*

CONFIRMATION

First Point.—Does it not seem a hard thing, my brothers, to have to call those people *enemy* from whom this Colony originated; those who were so long united to us by ties of blood, of friendship, of commerce, of language, and of religion; who gave us our fathers, protectors, governors, pastors, our models of all the virtues, our dear Sovereigns whose wise and moderate government ensured our happiness and merited our affection and gratitude?

Such was, in fact, the France we knew—loved by its own people, formidable to its enemies, attached to its religion, respected by all the nations of the world. Thus, surely, she deserved the sorrow you felt when you left her and the unstinting efforts you made to maintain yourselves under her domination. But since God in his mercy has made us pass under the domination of another empire, great Heaven! what baneful changes have overwhelmed this unfortunate kingdom! The enemy of our eternal salvation, envious at seeing the reign of God so firmly established there, came by night—I mean with the dark, sinister cunning of a deceitful philosophy—to sow over the whole of this rich and fertile country the tares of impious entertainments and incendiary books. These tares flourished: impiety and dissoluteness took root: hearts and minds let themselves be swept away by the seductive appeals of a religion without dogmas and a morality without commandments. Enchanting words like reason, liberty, philanthropy, fraternity, equality, and tolerance have been avidly seized upon and now are in every mouth. Under their cover private judgement and unbelief have established their fatal empire. The sovereign authority of the Prince has been called tyranny; religion, fanaticism; its holy practices, superstitions; its ministers, imposters; and God himself, a figment of the imagination!

What becomes of man, my brothers, when he casts off these restraints? Left to his own depraved reason, is there any aberration he is not capable of? Consider the behaviour of our fellow citizens who have had the misfortune to yield to the monstrous principles of the Diderots, Voltaires, Merciers, Rousseaus, Volneys, Raynals, d'Alemberts, and other deists of this century. Has it made them better husbands, more devoted fathers, more obedient sons, more upright citizens, more sincere friends, more loyal subjects? Certainly not, my brothers in Christ. Such trees can produce only worthless and wretched fruit. But if individuals infatuated with these fashionable ideas become such a menace to society, what frightful ravages must France not have suffered from that godless mob that rose up, so to speak, *en masse* against the peaceful existence of religion and royalty and that conceived the horrible design of exterminating and annihilating both the one and the other.

No, Gentlemen, for the immediate and effective cause of the French revolution, let us look nowhere else than to the plots of impiety. There is the damned instrument that slowly and carefully prepared the way for it, that nurtured it craftily and cleverly, and that finally made it burst upon us so tumultuously. A terrible explosion! It has astonished the world, infected the air with its pestilential vapours, and shaken all the thrones and threatened all the churches of the world with its sulphureous flames.

A sudden revolution! Somehow, in a single moment, it had the fatal capacity to galvanize all minds. Scarcely had it broken out in Paris than it had already travelled to the depths of the most remote provinces. Everywhere the cry was raised against despotism. Everywhere the bonds of allegiance disappeared. The people of middle rank rose against the great, the better to oppress the little people beneath them; the authority of the laws was scorned; property was pillaged; force took the place of the most ancient and the most legitimate rights.

A conquering revolution. At first it was supposed to keep its so-called reforms within the boundaries of France. But like a torrent breaking through the dikes, it was soon inundating all the surrounding region. One after another, the low countries, Holland, Spain, Switzerland, Italy, and Germany have become the theatres of a frightful war—against despots, if we listen to its leaders, but in fact led by the most cruel and pernicious tyrants.

A bloody revolution. It started with shooting and continued with massacres, inventing, to speed them along, a new instrument of execution. How many heads, alas! have fallen its unhappy victims! Princes, priests, nobles, royalists— all have tested its fatal effectiveness. And among the revolutionaries themselves— how many factional leaders have left with it their criminal heads?

A patricidal revolution. It has seen the most devout and peaceful Sovereign as an object of implacable hatred. Heaven forbid! To have put him beneath his own subjects by means of a constitution that was as bizarre and illegal in its form as it was monstrous in its principles—was this not enough? Was it really necessary to tear him away from the palace of his ancestors, to put him on display in the Tuileries, to imprison him in the Temple, to try him like a political prisoner, to bring him to the scaffold, and to ignominiously decapitate him for imaginary crimes? Oh Louis XVI! Oh King, you who were worthy of a longer life, had not such a premature death been a happier fate than to live only for bitter tribulations! But God, my brothers, had resolved to reward the sublime virtues of this truly Christian Prince, and that, without any doubt, is why he turned against him the rage of the usurpers of his sovereign authority.

A sacrilegious revolution. No excess of this sort has been beyond it. Witness the centres of devotion it has proscribed; the religious monuments it has torn down; the priests it has slaughtered before the very altars they were attempting to defend; the Mass it has suppressed; the Sacred Mysteries it has trampled underfoot; the solemn holy days it has abolished; the idol it has put in the temple of the true God; the holy Virgins it has chased from their cloisters; the head of the Universal Church, the worthy and venerable successor of the Apostles, whom it has cruelly evicted from his see and obliged, in his extreme old age, to wander from city to city, waiting till it please God to reward his life full of virtue, effort and merit with the crown of eternal glory.* This, my brothers, is but a faint sketch of the atrocities committed by those who propagated the French revolution. How long, Lord, will you suffer that they insult you in such a way? *Usquequo, Domine, improperabit inimicus?*† What! will you not put a stop to their audacity? Lift at last your Almighty hand to put them down. *Leva manus tuas in superbias eorum in finem.*°

The time for this punishment has come, my brothers. This proud Pharaoh, this ambitious Nebuchadnezzar, this insolent Goliath is starting to lose the upper hand. Plunge on, you people reputed invincible. Assemble a powerful fleet. Undertake the conquest of the East. Boast in advance of the victories you will never win. Glory in the strength of your ships and the number of your troops. God has made use of you as a scourge to chastise the world, and He will not hesitate to let you feel how heavy weighs His arm on all the impious. You will be taken by surprise, surrounded, and conquered in your turn, and in the most striking way, most fitted to give heart to Africa and Asia whose overthrow you have anticipated. Whatever resources you still pretend to have, you cannot hide the disgrace brought upon you by this immense and unexpected loss.

What purpose did Providence have, my brothers, in thus ruining France's Mediterranean fleet? Was it simply to disconcert and perplex our enemies? Was it meant, in addition, to reassure the good citizens who for almost ten years have secretly bemoaned the blindness of their unfortunate fatherland? In vain would we hazard any guesses on these matters. One thing, however, seems certain: that Providence has deigned by this brilliant success to heighten the glory of Great Britain and to reward its generosity. This is the second point on which I will now reflect.

Second Point.—For a long time Britain remained merely an attentive spectator of the barbaric scenes afflicting France. Prudently, it hesitated before deciding what part it should take in a quarrel whose issue was impossible to foresee. Those in revolt were doing everything possible to destroy legitimate authority; but there was also a Sovereign seeking by voluntary concessions to calm the rage of these wild men. On the one hand, there were innumerable decrees, all tending to establish a monstrous system of anarchy; on the other hand, silence and a compliance that seemed to betray the good cause and to concur in making changes. On the one hand, cry after cry of *Vive le Roi*; on the other, measures tending to strip him of all his powers and to destroy him personally. On the one hand, promises of unlimited liberty for all the citizens of France; on the other, innumerable massacres, on the most frivolous pretexts, which betrayed only too well the spirit of the revolution. In the midst of all this, the king went on living, though a captive, and there were some grounds for hope, in the diversity of opinions to be found among his subjects, that order might be restored at any moment.

You have not willed it so, almighty God! The sins of this unhappy people have been too notorious; too long have they provoked your anger. But while You were making the wicked cities of France feel the effects of Your anger, You were preparing, through the generosity of a neighbouring state, a safe and hospitable refuge for the just, who are still there. It appears that this, Gentlemen, was the first active step taken by England in the French revolution, and in all likelihood the real cause of the war that she had soon to undertake against the perfidious revolutionaries. Without regard for the consequences, this charitable people welcomed the refugees. Come, they said, come, precious remnants of a nation always our rival, but whose courage and virtue we have always honoured and respected. Come, venerable prelates, edifying ministers of a religion we no longer know. Come, descendants of the ancient heroes of France, subjects of all classes, unhappy victims of your love of duty, who have renounced your offices, your titles, your great houses, and your lands, rather than betray your consciences in consenting to the overthrow of Throne and Altar. Come, for we offer you a new fatherland in a foreign country. Come, share our homes, our wealth, our work, our abundance. You may not find among us all that you have lost, but at least you will be compensated by our efforts to comfort you in your exile and your misfortune. The Prophet said it long ago: I have never seen the just abandoned. *Non vidi justum derelictum.** French émigrés, today you know that this is so. But what help did Providence employ to provide you such abundant relief? The help of a people who had always competed with you, whom interests of State had made your enemy, and who seemed to hate you quite openly, but who in your misfortunes saw in you only brothers who were suffering. *Salutem ex inimicus nostris et de manu omnium qui oderunt nos.*†

Furthermore, Gentlemen, England did more than lend a helping hand to the victims of the revolution, loading them with kindness and bounty; she also put a stop to some of the disorders threatening the entire Universe. I see her wise leaders taking steps to keep peace within the country and to ward off the perversion of revolutionary thinking, and then I see her eagerly accepting the war offered in 1793 by those who had usurped the sovereign authority in France. What ardour, what strength, what energy she has displayed in upholding her honour! Formidable armaments; great numbers of soldiers on the continent; fearsome fleets on the sea; money sent to her allies; new taxes throughout the kingdom; voluntary contributions from individuals; quick promotions in the army and navy—nothing has been neglected that could serve this noble end.

Great Powers of Europe, States and Provinces of America, rich possessions of the East Indies, well it is that you should turn your eyes towards England. She is the great bulwark of your hopes. If she triumphs, her glory will be your safety and will assure your peace. But if she succumbs, so much for your peace and your governments. The deadly liberty tree will be planted in the middle of your towns;° the rights of man will there be proclaimed; new taxes will burden your finances; your laws will become the laughing-stock and plaything of the arrogant enemies of humankind; you will have to share all the ills which France now suffers; you will be free, but oppressively so, having taken for masters the dregs of the Citizens and having ruined the respectable leaders who have your confidence now and your love.

But what am I saying? No, almighty God! You will not permit our arms to falter. And since it is your cause we are defending, arise, Lord; disperse your enemies; put to flight those who hate you. Let them disappear like smoke; let them melt like wax before fire. *Sicut fluit cera a facie ignis, sic pereant peccatores a facie Dei.* *

Such, Gentlemen, will be the ultimate outcome. Great Britain, abandoned by her strongest allies, will almost alone shoulder the full weight of this enormous war. Look at her, multiplying her fleets and flaunting them on the oceans with the air of superiority that befits her alone. One moment she is bringing them all together; the next, she is dividing them up; soon, with incredible speed and intelligence, she is moving them from one hemisphere to another. One protects the coasts of America; another aids in the conquest of the Cape of Good Hope; this one accompanies the ships transporting the rich products of the Indies; that one keeps watch on the coasts of Ireland; another, having defeated the Spanish fleet, holds it captive in one of its ports; another blockades all the harbours of the enemy, never letting them reach the open sea; still another wins a glorious victory over the Dutch. If successes are heartening, my brothers, here are some that no one can dispute, and that will do much to fortify the English. But lastly a still more decisive blow, a more memorable victory has been reserved for the arms of this empire. Heaven would put off no longer the recompense for its generosity, the repayment for its countless efforts. The intrepid Admiral Nelson, with a squadron weaker in men and in ships but bold enough to attack the whole French Mediterranean fleet, has just won one of the most complete victories in the annals of naval history. Nine French warships captured, one sunk, three burned to cinders, the rest dispersed, many transport ships run aground and lost: such is the memorable event that we celebrate today. Is it not fitting that a day be devoted expressly to giving thanks to the God of battles?

Where is the good patriot, the loyal subject, I say, and more, even the true Christian, whose heart has not been gladdened by these happy tidings? Great Britian's command of the seas is assured; her colours fly majestically on all the oceans; her enemies are humbled and perplexed; the peace the whole world longs for is approaching. Do these considerations alone not suffice to bring cheer to all hearts? But here let us add that we have a special reason for rejoicing in this victory, for by consolidating Great Britain's power, it guarantees the peace and happiness of this Province. This will be my last point.

Third Point.—What sort of government, Gentlemen, is the best suited for our happiness? Is it not the one marked by moderation, which respects the religion of those it rules, which is full of consideration for its subjects, and gives the people a reasonable part in its administration? Such has always been the British government in Canada. To say this is in no way to practise the flattery that cowards use to bless the powers that be. God forbid, my brothers, that I should profane this holy pulpit by base adulation or interested praise. This testimony is demanded by truth as well as gratitude, and I have no fear of being contradicted by anyone who knows the spirit of the English government. It always proceeds with wise deliberation; there is nothing precipitous in its methodical advance. Do you see in its operations any of the delusive enthusiasm, the thoughtless love of novelty, the liberty without limits or restraints that, before our very eyes, is destroying certain malconstituted states? What care it takes for the property of its subjects! What skillful efforts are made to arrange the public finances so that its subjects are scarcely aware of the burden! Have you heard any complaints, these past forty years under their rule, of the poll-taxes, the tariffs, the head taxes under which so many other nations groan? What of those arbitrary requisitions of immense sums that unjust conquerors arrogantly impose on the unhappy conquered? Have you been reduced, by their lack of foresight, to those famines that formerly afflicted our Colony, which we still recall with horror and shuddering? Have you not seen, on the contrary, that in years of scarcity the government wisely prohibits the export of grain until enough has been put aside for your own needs? Have you been subjected to military service since the Conquest, obliged to leave your wives and children destitute in order to go to some far-off place to attack or repulse some enemy of the State? Have you contributed a penny to the expenses of this costly war that Great Britain has been waging for almost six years? Almost the whole of Europe has been given over to carnage and destruction, the holiest cloisters have been violated, virgins dishonoured, mothers and children slaughtered in several places. Is it not evident, and can it not be said, that at the height of this war you enjoy all the advantages of peace? To whom, my brothers, aside from God, do you owe these favours, if not to the paternal vigilance of an Empire which, in peace as in war, I dare to say, has your interests closer to its heart than its own? In every field I see evidence of this partiality.* Your criminal code, for example, was too severe; it provided no sufficiently reliable rule for distinguishing the innocent from the guilty, and it exposed the weak to the oppression of the strong. It has been replaced by the criminal law of England, that masterpiece of human intelligence, which checks calumny, which recognizes as crimes only those actions that violate the law, which convicts only those whose guilt is obvious, which gives the accused every means of legitimate defence, and which, leaving nothing to the discretion of the judge, punishes only in accordance with the precise provisions of the law. Finally, what about the common law? While in France all is in disorder, while every Ordonnance bearing the stamp of Royalty is proscribed, is it not wonderful to see a British Province ruled by the common law of Paris and by the Edicts and declarations of the kings of France? To what are we to attribute this gratifying peculiarity? To the fact that you wanted to maintain these ancient laws; to the fact that they seemed better adapted to the nature of real property in this country. There they are, then, preserved without any alterations except those that provincial Legislation is free to make. And in that Legislation you are represented to an infinitely greater degree than the people of the British Isles are in the Parliaments of England or Ireland.

Do such benefits, Gentlemen, not demand from us some return? A lively feeling of gratitude towards Great Britain; an ardent desire never to be separated from her; a deep conviction that her interests are no different from our own; that our happiness depends upon hers; and that if sometimes it has been necessary to grieve over her losses, we must, by the same principle, rejoice today in the glory she has won and regard her latest victory as an event no less consoling for us than it is glorious for her.

Where do we stand, Christians, if we add to these political considerations another that, above all else, makes this empire worthy of your gratitude and praise? I mean the liberty left our religion and guaranteed by law; the respect shown to those in our monasteries; the unbroken succession of Catholic Bishops, who have so far enjoyed the favour and confidence of the King's Representatives; the unfailing support our curés have enjoyed in the villages and countryside in their efforts to conserve faith and morals. If this faith is growing weaker among us, my brothers, if morality is becoming more lax, it is not because of any change of government; it is to you yourselves that this disorder must be attributed; to your lack of submission to the teaching of the Gospels; to your foolish pursuit of a liberty you already enjoy without knowing it; to the poisonous harangues of those dishonest and unprincipled men, those perpetual grumblers who are offended by order, humiliated by obedience, and outraged by the very existence of religion.

Alas! Where would we be, my brothers, if such men should ever get the upper hand, if their desires should be fulfilled, if this country, by a grievous misfortune, should return to its former masters? This house of God, this august temple, would soon be converted to a den of thieves! Ministers of religion—you would be displaced, banished, and perhaps decapitated! Fervent Christians—you would be deprived of the ineffable consolations you enjoy in the accomplishment of your religious duties! Your land, consecrated by the sweat and tears of so many virtuous missionaries who have planted the faith here, would, to a religious eye, display nothing but a vast, melancholy solitude. Catholic fathers and mothers, under your very eyes, in spite of yourselves, you would see your beloved children nursed on the poisoned milk of barbarism, impiety, and dissoluteness! Tender children, whose innocent hearts still manifest only virtue, your piety would become prey to these vultures, and a savage education would soon obliterate the pleasing sentiments that humanity and religion have engraved on your souls!

Conclusion.—But what am I saying? Why dwell on such sad reflections on a day when all ought to be joy? No, no, my brothers. Fear not that God will abandon us if we remain faithful. What he has just done for us should inspire only comforting thoughts for the future. He has struck down our perfidious enemies. Let us rejoice in this glorious event. Everything that weakens France tends to draw us away from it. Everything that separates us from her assures our lives, our liberty, our peace, our property, our religion, and our happiness. Let us give everlasting thanks to the God of victories. Let us pray that He will long preserve the bountiful and august Sovereign who governs us, and that he will continue to lavish on Canada his most abundant blessings.

Te deum laudamus, etc.

THE RIGHT REV.
JOHN STRACHAN

John Strachan (1778-1867) was Upper Canada's outstanding Tory. Arriving in Kingston from Scotland on 31 December 1799 (having almost perished of the winter journey from New York), he moved to Cornwall in 1803, and finally to Toronto in 1812. He had been trained at Aberdeen for the Scottish Church but, being poor, had received no call for his services. Strachan was also enterprising, however, and he seized the opportunity to become tutor to the children of two rich merchants in Kingston. When an opportunity arose to fill a vacancy in the Established (Anglican) Church in Cornwall, he accepted ordination from Bishop Jacob Mountain in 1803. During the 1820s and 1830s he was the central figure in the Family Compact and was deeply involved in all aspects of educational and religious politics as a Legislative and Executive Councillor, founder of King's College (later the University of Toronto), and first President of the Board for the General Superintendence of Education. In 1839 he became the first Bishop of Toronto.

Although Strachan wrote a great deal, he left no single outstanding work systematically presenting his views on the questions of the day. Two selections are reprinted here: part of a sermon preached in 1825 on the death of Bishop Mountain, the first Protestant Bishop of Quebec, and a draft written in 1828 or 1829 for an essay that was never published. In the first Strachan makes clear his toryism; in the second he sketches our first lament for a vanishing nation.

On Church Establishment

I

On dividing the Province of Quebec into two distinct Governments, our late venerable Sovereign signified to Parliament his intention of making provision for a Protestant Clergy, according to the Church of England, by which the people might enjoy all the benefits of religious instruction—rightly judging that the establishment of an enlightened Clergy in the Colony would contribute more than any other measure to its happiness and prosperity.* To follow up this pious and benevolent measure, and to meet the wants of the rising Church with more ease & convenience, by rendering it unnecessary for young men, desirous of entering her ministry, to proceed to England for Holy Orders, as well as to perform those Episcopal functions, which are necessary to her very existence, a Bishop was appointed, retaining the former name of the colony, that both Provinces might be included in the Diocese. For this arduous charge Dr Mountain, then a Dignitary in the Church of England, was most judiciously selected. This gentleman had taken his degrees at the University, with great distinction, and from his elegance of taste, extensive literary acquirements, and private worth, had been rapidly preferred. The friend of the great Mr Pitt, and of the present Bishop of Winchester so justly revered as the champion of the true faith, the brightest prospects were opened to his view, and when it appeared expedient to constitute an Ecclesiastical establishment in the Province of Quebec, he was nominated Bishop, and consecrated in 1793. This appointment, or rather the Ecclesiastical establishment of which the late Bishop was the head, is remarkable, not only in the history of this Province, but in that of the British Empire, as being the first step ever taken by the Imperial Legislature, towards a recognition of that obvious, but still unacknowledged principle, that the Colonies of a Country have as good a right to receive moral and religious instruction from the Parent state, as her laws and Government. . . .

When the late Bishop was appointed, about thirty-two years ago, to diffuse the light of the Gospel through this extensive portion of his Majesty's dominions, it was even a greater spiritual, than a natural wilderness. . . . The majority of the inhabitants of Lower Canada, where his Lordship determined to reside, belonged to the Roman Catholic persuasion and looked upon [him] as the head of a rival Ecclesiastical establishment. The Protestant dissenters, who composed a considerable number of the remainder, envied and opposed him, because the Church over which he presided, was the religion of the state, and was therefore more immediately under its protection. To soften the asperity of the opposition of these two classes and the undisguised hatred of inferior sects, and to shew them the real excellence of the Church of England, happily placed in the true medium between extravagant and dangerous extremes, could only be the work of time. His Lordship had also the mortification to find that many of the Protestant inhabitants, imbibing the levelling opinions of the times, declaimed against the appointment of a Bishop and against all religious establishments, as inconsistent with the spirit of true religion and the peace of society. Had not Christianity been revealed, then had mankind been left to follow their own imaginations, as they did before the coming of Christ, but as the Supreme Being has been pleased to communicate his will, it is the duty of every Christian Government, to support such a religious establishment, as may best secure the benefits of this revelation to all their subjects. Now, as this divine revelation is intended to promote among all men true morality and purity of life, to become the mother of good works, our cordial in affliction, and our comfort in death, to bring us daily into the presence of God and our Saviour that we may believe in his holy name, love him with all our hearts, and by making him the object of our imitation and the foundation of our faith, resemble him on earth, and follow him to heaven; an establishment which produces these excellent effects ought to be cherished by every good Government, in its own defence, as the guardian and nourisher of the purest social, and domestic virtues. Indeed the very appointment of Parochial instructors of the people, in the duties of morality and the doctrines of revelation, is so eminently wise and beneficial, that it may not only be adduced as a collateral evidence of the Divine origin of Christianity, but of the necessity of a public establishment, to render it truly efficacious. Accordingly the most eminent friends of the Gospel have considered an Ecclesiastical establishment, so necessary to the moral and religious improvement of the people, and so essential to give permanent effect to the most pure and sublime principles that can direct the understanding, and influence the heart, that they have declared a regular Clergy, and those authorities which appoint and superintend them, important branches of the Church of Christ. Experience has justified this declaration. The religious establishments of England and Scotland have, under the Divine blessing, been the great promoters of all that is great and good, in those happy Countries. The mass of the population are taught their duty to God and man—to attend to a law, not to be obtained in books, nor to be engraven on tablets of brass—a law which always subsists, which is every moment forcing itself into notice, and which condemns every species of wrong. Hence the British nation is the most intellectual, and moral in Europe—The world's centre of arts, commerce and civilization. Here the light of freedom burns with the brightest radiance, and the rights and liberties of man are the best understood and most abundantly enjoyed; and here a lofty sense of independence is of universal growth. From this nation, the cherisher and supporter of religious establishments, have come almost all the lights that exalt modern times. She takes the lead in those mighty efforts, which are changing the face of the world. To the able administration of her excellent laws, and the wisdom of her political institutions, all nations turn their eyes not only to admire, but to imitate. She stands aloft like the sun in the Heavens, dispensing her charities wherever distress is to be found, without regard to difference of language, climate, or complexion. Not satisfied with shewing the way, she compels by entreaties and donations, other nations to pursue her virtuous course. It is to religion that she owes her pre-eminence—it is this that throws a holy splendour round her head, makes her the hope of every land, and urges her to achieve the evangelization of mankind. Never without a religious establishment could she have soared so high above other nations—it is this that diffuses through her whole population, the most sublime and disinterested principles, which, refining the sentiments and elevating the affections, enable them to subdue selfish passions and appetites, and to pant after the felicity of doing good. Indeed a Christian nation without a religious establishment is a contradiction, and notwithstanding the praiseworthy exertions of a few denominations in the neighbouring States, more especially the Episcopal Church, Christianity except in a few large towns is found to languish, and seldom in the country pervades the mass of the people. Let the candid opponents of Ecclesiastical establishments, if any such there be, compare the people who have no standing ministry, not merely in towns, where a spark of Christianity may exist, but through the country, with a people possessing this inestimable advantage, and they will acknowledge that no country can be called Christian, which does not give public support to Christianity, and that no other Religion but that of Jesus could have suggested an idea so grand and affecting as that of placing a public Teacher of Righteousness in every small Society throughout the world.

On his first visitation the Bishop found things very different from what he had anticipated. Nothing which he had seen could enable him to form any conception whatever of the nature of the country in which he was to constitute a Religious establishment. . . . In Lower Canada some associations might be found, but the Western part of the Diocese, in regard to Religion and education presented a dreary waste. The people were scattered over a vast surface, and had the means been furnished of building Churches, and Schools, which ought always to go together, there was little or no chance of their being supported. . . . The people would speak of their inclination, but the site of the Church was too distant—how could they with their families go through roads almost impassable, and over brooks without bridges. It was easy to see that the taste of many had become vitiated, and that they were disposed to exaggerate difficulties, and to calculate the benefit rather with a tendency to refuse than to assist. Settlers in a wilderness are often found greatly changed in a few years—at first they lament their distance from Churches and Schools, but by degrees such lamentations die away, as well as the generous and noble dispositions from which they emanated—and when the accommodations for public worship are provided, bad weather, bad roads, or any other trifling cause, prevents any thing like a regular attendance. Living without restraint, and without the eye of those whom they respect, a sense of decency and Religion frequently disappears. Here the disinclination to holy things presents itself in all its deformity, a distaste for divine worship, and neglect of every thing sacred, and a total estrangement from God, and although from their situation, crimes against Society are few, the heart becomes entirely dead to true piety and virtue. Were it not for the mothers, nothing engaging or amiable would remain in many of the back settlements; but they, lamenting their separation from civilized society, are still anxious to cherish and inculcate some of the principles of social life. . . .

In regard to Education, something has been done by the Provincial Legislature; but to build Churches, and to place Clergymen is a work of greater difficulty. Even when Churches are erected, the persons who give regular attendance are so few as greatly to discourage the Minister, and his influence is frequently broken or injured by numbers of uneducated itinerant Preachers, who, leaving their steady employment, betake themselves to preaching the Gospel from idleness, or a zeal without knowledge, by which they are induced without any preparation, to teach what they do not know, and which, from their pride, they disdain to learn.* Under such circumstances, the Minister placed in the first Church, or Settlement where in all probability he will have several Churches to attend, has many difficulties to encounter—his people live scattered on their farms, cut off from that daily intercourse, which softens and polishes the manners. Confined to family circles, their ideas become selfish and contracted, and they are little disposed to trouble themselves about any other thing than what contributes immediately to their own comfort. Among such a population, social intercourse is very rare, and they seldom meet unless to bargain and traffic. Consequently the social affections sleep or expire—their deportment becomes rough and forbidding—at one time, forward and impudent, at another time awkward & sheepish. From all which, the first Clergyman finds himself not only engaged to preach the gospel, but also to preach civilization. Such was the picture, which the Diocese presented to the Lord Bishop on his first visitation, and though now in many places much changed such is still the picture of some of the remote settlements, and must continue to be so till the whole country is filled with inhabitants. . . .

Should the future historian feel inclined to find fault with the little that has been done by the first Protestant Bishop of Quebec, I request him to pause before pronouncing judgment, in order to examine the many obstacles in his Lordship's way during the whole of his Episcopacy, and how little his efforts were seconded by those who were able to command success, and indeed how little disposition the people of Great Britain manifested, till lately, towards the religious instruction of their Colonies. That extensive Settlements, composed of British subjects whose loyalty has stood the most bitter trials, and whose unaffected devotedness to the constitution of the Mother Country is above all praise, should be left comparatively destitute of religious instruction, and without an efficient Ecclesiastical establishment to watch over their spiritual interests, is altogether incomprehensible. Can any thing attach Colonies to the Parent State so strongly as a community of religious feeling? How then comes it that Great Britain, conspicuous among the nations for her high moral, and intellectual qualities, and deriving much of her power, wealth, and political importance from her Foreign possessions, should be so culpably deficient in what should be the first care of a Christian nation? Is it not evident that the Canadas, as well as the other Colonies, have been left in a great measure to grope their way as they could through the darkness which surrounds them, almost totally unaided by the Parent State? Does not the greater part of the population of this Diocese, notwithstanding the meritorious exertions of the late Bishop, his scattered Clergy, and many individuals, remain unimproved, and sadly destitute of religious instruction? What can 53 Clergymen do, scattered over a Country of greater extent than Great Britain? Is it to be wondered at that under such circumstances, the religious benefits of the Ecclesiastical establishment of England are little known or felt, and that Sectaries of all descriptions are increasing on every side? And when it is considered that the religious teachers of the other denominations of Christians, a very few respectable Ministers of the Church of Scotland excepted, come almost universally from the Republican States of America, where they gather their knowledge and form their sentiments, it is quite evident, that if the Imperial Government does not immediately step forward with efficient help, the mass of the population will be nurtured and instructed in hostility to our Parent Church, nor will it be long till they imbibe opinions any thing but favourable to the political Institutions of England.

Convinced that the attachment of Colonies to the Metropolis, depends infinitely more upon moral and Religious feeling, than political arrangement, or even commercial advantage, I cannot but lament that more is not done to instil it into the minds of the people. . . . It is [by] reasoning, by early instruction and example, that the unity of the Empire is to be maintained—all other methods will be found vain. The Church establishment must be made efficient, and commensurate with the wants of the people—it must no longer be thought a matter of indifference in Colonial policy, nor even of secondary consideration. It must take the lead of all others, if their preservation be of importance; and can it be doubted, that it is only through the Church and its Institutions, that a truly English character and feeling can be given to, or preserved among the population of any Foreign possession? . . .

To form Colonies under the guidance of Christian principles, is one of the noblest and most beneficial purposes which Governments can fulfil. It is thus, that uninhabited countries are peopled—an asylum found for a redundant population—where want is exchanged for plenty—independence for slavery— and the purposes of creation accomplished in conferring happiness upon a greater number of rational beings. It is thus that deserts may be reclaimed, and the idolatrous inhabitants of distant regions, taught to exert the mighty energies of their minds, and to worship their Creator in spirit, and in truth. Now this is a field of glory more in the power of Great Britain, than in that of all the rest of the world combined. The slightest inspection of the Globe presents her vast possessions as a belt around it, and opens an unbounded theatre for the exercise of an enlightened policy as regards their government and laws, and what is of infinitely more consequence of infusing into their minds the truths of eternal life. What are the triumphs of victory to the dissemination of the Gospel? In vain shall Great Britain confer upon her Colonies the free government and liberal principles of legislation, for which she is distinguished, if she do not carry with her the revelations of God. Till she does this, she is unjust to her high station—to her splendid reputation and birth-right among the nations.—Every other crown she has earned, and worn. Every other sort of glory has faded in her possession, but this the most glorious of all remains to be won. Let her therefore no longer leave to individuals or associations the labour of evangelizing her Colonies, or even the whole world—their means are inadequate, and acting without concert, their progress must be slow and uncertain. But let England, as she has the means and requires only the will, with the divine blessing put forth her strength. At an expense trifling indeed, compared to what she frequently spends upon unprofitable contests, she might place the moral world on a new foundation, and rise to the pinnacle of moral glory. By adopting a uniform system of religious instruction for all her Colonies in the East, as well as in the West, and following it up with energy and skill, she will establish an Empire more absolute than any, which unhallowed power can hold in subjection, and which will rest on the affections and opinions of more than two hundred millions of men. Nor would such a policy, sublime and affecting as it is, and pregnant with happiness and peace, increase her expenditure; for as the influence of Christian principles extended, the charge for physical coercion would become less—murmurs would give way to blessings and praise; and one fourth of the human race being thus reclaimed, the remainder would gradually follow, and thus the whole earth become the garden of the Lord. . . .

II

Believing it to be the duty of every State to provide for the religious instruction of its people I feel it my duty to defend the Establishment by every lawful means in my power but the progress of liberalism is bringing everything into disorder

Appearances here are verging to what they formerly were in America which in this country is the more appalling as the Inhabitants have peculiar claims to the Protection of the Govt. They were driven from their homes by rebellion and they have the painful spectacle before them of the commencement of Similar proceedings—the causes of the American Revolution are again rising before them—The enemies of British Principles and of the Church of England are acting upon the same system as they did in 1774 a system deeply laid widely spread—and made energetic by malignity falsehood deception calumny and slander

The statements of the Friends of good order & the Constitution thrown aside & those of the enemies of both adopted. The friends of the Church unassisted by the advice and encouragement of the Parent Church are without Union combination or interest and are continually & habitually overlooked disregarded & unattended to

The ark is with us let us preserve it—and it will preserve us No virtue no piety no zeal screen the Friends of the Church from their Revilers—and all this not that they may have any religion but that they may rise to power. The spirit of religion is immortal & communicates immortality to the subjects in which it resides tho' of themselves of a Transitory nature. Is it a thing to be lamented that the members of the Church of England should be educated with prepossessions in favour of their own Church—Or is it want of Candour in a Professor who after the examination of other Systems can discover none which he thinks so good as his own—to show more regard to it than to any other

Can it be blameable at a season when every exertion is making by the very means of education—by education conducted both openly and privately to alienate the rising generation from the Established Church—it is [is it?] not our bounden duty at such a season to call forth our energies in making education on our part subservient to the Established Church

Who would live in a Colony who possesses English feeling and had been brought up with reverence for the British Constitution

Of late years there appears in England a merit in giving up all principles. Instead of gaining credit for an uncompromising adherence to what we have been in the habit of believing to be the true pillars of that form of Govt which has raised G Britain so high we are laughed to Scorn

The Church of England is assailed on the one side by Roman Catholics and on the other by Dissenters and both parties accuse her of bigotry persecution & intolerance

In regard to Canada this state of things suggests the most melancholy reflexions to those who when they left the Shores of G Britain did not conceive that they left their birthright behind them and who had a right to expect that in passing to a British Colony they were not depriving themselves of the Privileges of the British Constitution nevertheless they find that in as far as the Church is concerned they are sure to be losers The Protestant Church in Church & State which used to be the glory of our Ancestors is now considered an antiquated thing. That Establishment for which so much English blood has been spilt for which one King was expelled and a distant branch of the same called to the Succession has become the subject of animosity to many Colonists and these have been supported by many Members and by a select Committee of the House of Commons*

How the Ministry can expect to Govern their distant colonies by the policy which has been pursued for the last two or three years is beyond my conjecture. If they think that by breaking down the Constitution which used in former days to be the envy of the World the model for Politicians the theme of the Eloquent & the meditation of the Philosopher in every part of the world

As for Englishmen till the lights of liberalism dawned upon us it was their pride & consolation. By it they lived & for it they were ready to die

Now all the Excellencies of that most cherished & endearing part of it from which we can alone separate our political System by the necessary destruction of both are forgotten. Its faults are forcibly dragged into day and exaggerated by every artifice of misrepresentation. Its Bishops & Ministers are fully calumniated and abused. Its doctrines are held up to ridicule as contradictory and intolerant

It is sickening to the heart to read the language of Ministers of State & Members of the House of Commons

CANADIAN VOICES OF REFORM AND REVOLT

The reformers and revolutionaries of the 1830s represent the mainstream of Canadian liberalism—local self-government, a democratic constitution, the voluntary principle, and a tendency to admire the American model. The first selection is an abridgement of a speech by Louis-Joseph Papineau (1786-1871) delivered in the Legislative Assembly of Lower Canada in January 1833. It presents the standard criticisms of the Constitutional Act of 1791 and suggests a constitutional convention on the American model to reform it. Robert Baldwin (1804-58) is represented by excerpts from the letter he wrote to Lord Glenelg, the Colonial Secretary, in July 1836, warning him of the potential for revolution in the colonies and recommending that responsible government be granted. The Six Counties Address, our best approximation to the Declaration of Independence, was adopted at a mass meeting in St Charles on 24 October 1837: Papineau had addressed the gathering the previous day, but the leading Patriote at that point was Wolfred Nelson (1791-1863). The final selection is the draft constitution that William Lyon Mackenzie (1795-1861) published on 15 November 1837, three weeks before his ill-fated march on Toronto.

Papineau on Constitutional Reform

There is no discussion more important, on which the country's attention is more wholly concentrated, than the one to which the Chamber ought to devote itself at this time. It would be a great mistake to believe that, because the petitions submitted to the Chamber today—which set out, clearly and reasonably, the burden of wrongs this province is suffering—come from only a few regions of Lower Canada, they do not express the feelings of the great majority of the people. Only a calamity as disastrous as the one that has so ravaged our population,* bringing desolation to all hearts, affliction and mourning to all families; only a time of terror and danger this serious could have dispersed the inhabitants of this country, isolated them and prevented them from gathering to make this chamber ring with their universal complaints against the defects of our constitutional act. . . .

The government of Lower Canada is corrupt in its head and its members; the constitution is flawed in most of its provisions except for those relating to the constitution of the Legislative Assembly. In every other branch it is at fault; it is a baneful experiment for this colony itself and for Upper Canada; it has brought us only hardship, and virtually nothing good. . . .

We were told: 'You enjoy the English constitution, the freest of any in Europe. Your public bodies are organized in the same fashion as those that have brought Great Britain such greatness and glory.' This is an illusion that the majority have taken for reality; a false and lying argument that a few hypocritical partisans have upheld in order to exploit misapprehension to their profit; an untruth that is revealed the moment one stops to reflect on the history of England and compare the state of our society with that of the mother country. And even if we did in fact have this much-acclaimed constitution of the parent state, who could maintain that it is right for us? Institutions suitable to an old country, where laws, customs, and practices differ from our own; where the distribution of wealth is unequal; where, more than anywhere else in the world, one finds on the one hand the pride of opulence, and on the other the degradation of beggary—these cannot be right for a new country, where the inhabitants are scattered over a vast territory, where hard work is the only way for anyone to attain some degree of comfort, where luxury is unheard of. Such people need institutions different from those of Europe; and those who would maintain the contrary should also tell us in what respects the ones they favour have worked and can work to our benefit. Those who would argue in this way are the unprogressive types who would say that their constituents are as happy and satisfied as they ought to be, who would not wish a better future for them, and who would say that they aspire to nothing better. . . .

In 1774 all previous arrangements were declared null and void: the [Quebec] act revoked and annulled all proclamations, ordinances, and commissions of public officers; for the first time England published legislative acts for us; and we had a new and curious form of government. The act also suspended the introduction of the representative system. It is neither necessary nor prudent to go back to first principles; to examine whether this new experiment in legislation was strictly legal. The province submitted to this regime at the time and it has since ceased to exist. Whether the authorities [*la métropole*] encroached on our rights or not, at least their intentions were blameless. The first time they legislated for Canada they proclaimed, in conformity with the modern rules of public law among Christian people, that the inhabitants of the said province had enjoyed 'a system of laws by which their persons and property had been protected, governed, and ordered for a long series of years from the first establishment of the said Province of Canada', that all earlier acts contrary to the present one would be 'revoked, annulled, and made void', 'that all His Majesty's Canadian subjects within the Province of Quebec, the religious orders and communities only excepted, may also hold and enjoy their property and possessions, together with all customs and usages relative thereto, and all others their civil rights, in as large, ample, and beneficial manner as if the said Proclamation, Commissions, Ordinances, and other Acts and Instruments had not been made, and as may consist with their allegiance to his Majesty, and subjection to the Crown and Parliament of Great Britain; and that in all matters of controversy relative to property and civil rights, resort shall be had to the laws of Canada as the rule for the decision of the same; and that all causes that shall hereafter be instituted in any of the courts of justice, to be appointed within and for the said Province by his Majesty, his heirs and successors, shall with respect to such property and rights be determined agreeably to the said laws and customs of Canada, until they shall be varied or altered by any Ordinance that shall from time to time be passed in the said Province by the Governor, Lieutenant-Governor, or Commander-in-Chief for the time being, by and with the advice and consent of the Legislative Council of the same, to be appointed in manner [specified in this act].'*

These principles were wise and correct. But the political system provided to defend and protect them was inadequate. It gave the people no guarantee that they could fend off the aggressions of the governors and counsellors who had been made masters of their fate, when they had no part whatever in their nomination. With a new form of constitution, the people nevertheless continued to suffer the burden of injustice and oppression. This system was arbitrary; everything depended on the personal character of the governor. . . .

After long and urgent appeals, the country at last obtained the representative system. What are the advantages of this system, if not that the people will obey only their own laws, and will not lose a penny of their property without having consented to it through a law they have had a say in passing? This is how it was, more or less, in Greek and Roman times. In those days they let the majority of the citizens' votes decide. But as it became impossible to gather an entire people in one place to make its decision, the idea was introduced of turning to representatives instead.

Going back to first principles, what were the primary considerations that led to the adoption of this form of government? What are the fundamental maxims it enshrines? That no one is obliged to acquiesce in the law without having the opportunity, personally or through his representative, to discuss the reasons behind it. That if all the people who make up the state could conveniently be gathered in a single place, the numbers standing on the right and left would show which was the majority; the latter makes the law. Certainly the majority would not choose from the ranks of the minority the magistrate entrusted with the faithful execution of the law he has just opposed. At every level in representative government, therefore, the magistrate should belong to the majority. It is this principle that animates all departments in the English government; and its neglect that brings corruption in this province.

They sought the political arrangement best-suited to make known the expression of the general will that is the law. A representation without influence on the conduct of government and the choice of its agents is nothing but a fraud against a people and a trap set for those who defend its rights.

Is there any similarity between the actual state of this country and the principles that derive from the [English] government? No. We have only a misleading shadow of the English constitution; we have none of the advantages that ought to derive from it.

By natural law, half a million people situated as we are should have a local legislature. It is English positive law that colonists should, wherever practicable, enjoy the representative system, and that one of the essential parts constituting this legislature should be a large elected assembly that meets frequently and is frequently renewed. It is not English positive law that in its other parts the legislature should be modelled after that of Great Britain. In no other British colony, until the fatal attempt of 1791, had they ever dreamed of constituting any body whatever of persons appointed to public office for life. In none had they dreamed of anything analogous to the British aristocracy, because none of them contained necessary elements—except for a laughable attempt in Carolina. Its nobility lasted less than three years, even though it was conceived by a man of transcendant genius,* but being a European, he was incapable of really understanding social conditions in America. Nowhere have we seen this system established. By what fluke should it prevail in Canada alone? To find out the reason, we must go back to the events and recall the circumstances that gave rise to this aberration. Not only has a lifetime magistrature been established here, but folly and conceit have been tempted by the lure of a hereditary titled nobility. Canada—a country impoverished by its harsh climate, whose laws and customs have always encouraged the equal division of property, rejected entailment, and condemned the privileges of primogeniture—should have been the last place to try such an absurd measure. One can hardly conceive that those who had never offered these titles, so sought-after by vain Europeans, to the rich planters of the southern colonies, or to the rich merchants that the republican institutions of New England had made such industrious and enlightened millionaires—that they should have decided to lavish them on poor provinces just when they were losing rich ones.

The provinces they lost had been well governed, had prospered, and at the first stirrings of discontent had separated. This was the natural result of the strength acquired by two million men. The first injustice on the part of the parent country showed them they were capable of governing themselves better through their representatives than through far-away masters. Instead of learning moderation from this potent lesson, England took offence; its pride piqued by the loss of those colonies, it apparently feared the freedom and growth of those that remained, and therefore resorted to this system.

The collapse of the French monarchy had fanned the fears of the privileged classes, who wanted to prevent the idea of liberty from taking hold in America. Burke, the most eloquent writer of the period, who deserted the cause of freedom in order to become one of Pitt's pensioners, was frightened by the crimes that had accompanied the French revolution.* Ignoring the fact that it was a monarchist education that had formed the perpetrators of these crimes, he made himself the persuasive champion of the nobility's privileges, and introduced them for the first time into the English colonial regime. . . .

The trial run at creating a titled nobility could have been offered to those proud southern planters. Thus it was a matter of chance: the coming together of circumstances, none of them having anything whatever to do with the situation of the Province of Quebec, that subjected it to these baneful endeavours; to these fumbling trials of political novelties; that inevitably made us the victims of European Theorists' research into the best ways of keeping the remaining colonies chained to the parent country, whether they be governed well or ill. The bitterness at having lost other colonies, the English aristocracy's shock at witnessing the collapse of the French monarchy, and the culpable madness of fomenting certain conflicts which in the first years following the American revolution agitated some of the parties involved (a result of the misfortunes a civil war always brings)—these, I fear, were the ignoble inspirations that had their influence in the drafting of our constitutional act. Indeed, how else is one to explain the fact, unique in all of English colonial history, that neither before 1791 nor since has anything analogous to our Legislative Council been granted to any other British colony? Tomorrow's Legislative Council will be no more respected than today's. Do they think they have corrupted the common sense of the country to the point of making it believe there is the slightest resemblance between this Council and the House of Lords? Calling an individual to the Council gives him no more respectability than he had before entering it. He is neither a greater nor a lesser man the day after his nomination than he was the day before. When the reason for his being called is not public service, when some petty merchant suddenly moves from private life to this post—so important by reason of its prerogatives, and so diminished by the majority of its occupants—all he is granted is the right quietly to flatter himself that he is distinguished from the crowd from which he has been drawn and put before the world. He becomes more vain; more inflexible towards those he has left behind; more compliant towards whoever discovered in him a merit of which the public was not aware, since he had never made use of it. He concludes that he owes his sudden aggrandizement to his eagerness and skill at paying court to the governor. The more he puffs himself up and rises, the more the public brings him down, and in the end one finds that the copy is a bad parody of the original, a failed imitation of the House of Lords, and that the distance between the obscure individual chosen here by blind favour and the man chosen in England by the will of the people, on the grounds of public service, is as great as the distance between man and ape.

There are no fortunes great enough here, no historic names, no illustrious persons, no ancient memories, to give their possessors privileges—respect, esteem, a life magistrature—that would be fortified by the opinion and gratitude of the public. A law confined to the books and not engraved in hearts is a bad law.

Those who obstinately oppose any change in the constitution and the composition of the council, on the pretext that this would mean acting against the English constitution, are deluding themselves. They are the ones who favour the innovations conceived and contrived for the Canadas alone. At the sight of the word *Convention* they fancy, because it is possible that it might want to make everything elective, that it would introduce an entirely new system that would lead to nothing but evil. It is because they have not studied carefully enough—indeed, know shamefully little about—the history of the former colonies that they regard these proposals as practically criminal.

But England should be neither surprised nor offended if we tell her it is in our mutual and reciprocal interest that she grant us just as many liberties, privileges, and freedoms as she has granted other colonies. . . .

There is no diversity of opinion on the necessity of a reform in the Council; the only differences concern the best way of reaching that goal and what to replace it with. The petitioners whose demands we are examining believe that it is the elective system, extended as far as possible, that should replace the existing one.

The great fear that certain persons have regarding the elective system comes from their imagining that in a country governed by this system everything is transient and precarious, that nothing is stable. Their assumptions are belied by the history of the colonies. . . .

Of all [the colonial] governments, those in which the regime has produced the happiest fruits, beyond comparison, have been the purely or only very slightly modified republican governments of the New England states. Republicanism achieved an improvement in the customs of the people that remains palpable and visible to this day. All travellers will tell you, unanimously, that everywhere in the southern and western states they recognize the true Yankee who has gone there to settle and who by his merit most often succeeds in placing himself at the head of public affairs, business, the universities, workshops, and factories, by reason of his superiority over his compatriots in the rest of the union in terms of activity, industry, and education. And since all come from the same origins, such a strongly marked distinction can only derive from the difference in political institutions that governed them in the early years of their social existence. These distinctions will soon be erased, now that the regime is the same for all, at least in those states not condemned to the irreparable misfortune of having among their institutions domestic slavery: the principle reason that prevented the republicanism of the ancient world, to which Europe owes the superiority of its civilization over that of Asia, from achieving the great and happy results for humanity that will be achieved by the modern republicanism of the Americans. . . .

Some may object that the great liberty enjoyed by the English colonies of New England weakened their bonds to the mother country. But it was the legislatures of the royal governments that were the first to resist, courageously, the unjust provisions of certain Acts of the British Parliament: the Assembly of Virginia, in the case of the stamp act; that of New York, regarding the supply of certain goods for the use of troops. Connecticut and Rhode Island were the last to follow the general movement. In other possessions, in effect, quarrels were frequent between the representatives and the governors sent from England; and often the bitterness against the employee could not but extend to the authority that had chosen him. Until the fatal day when it was destroyed by the attempt to impose taxes, the affection for Great Britain was stronger and, until that day, better established in New England than anywhere else. Nevertheless, this attachment to the land and laws of their ancestors was not blind. When they organized themselves in separate governments, they had been raised in the administration of English institutions that were perfectly well adapted to the situation, customs, and needs of the parent country; but all of them believed these to be inapplicable to their own situation. No commentator, neither in America nor in Europe, dreamt that they were obliged, in their own interest or in the interest of humanity, to adopt a constitution the same as that of Great Britain.

It is the good government granted the country, not the extent of patronage possessed and exercised by the executive, that must determine the strength and durability of the bond to the parent country. A small council, named for life by an executive empowered to distribute lucrative jobs, will always be a venal body. Such it was, such it will be, in the majority of its members; almost all our administrations have been, by turns, either violent and detested, or scheming and despised. . . .

A governor sent to a colony takes his prejudices with him, and is accompanied by his favourites. These royal governors [in the American colonies] often came into conflict with the people when they attempted to do there what is now being done here; but their efforts never succeeded; the people always emerged victorious. These colonies offer us instructive lessons, which should be more widely studied than they are; models from which we can learn how to resist infringements on our rights, through perseverance in the constitutional channels of systematic resistance to every plan that would strengthen and concentrate power in the hands of the few.

Our reasons for attachment to the mother country are to be found above all in the powerful protection she offers us against aggression from outside; and in the advantageous outlet she offers our products through reciprocally useful exchange. It is to this end that she should multiply her colonial possessions, not in order to transplant aristocratic institutions where they are not wanted. Whatever will bring contentment to the people will strengthen their attachment to England. Our interests will be in harmony with our duties if we are well governed. . . .

The question is whether a change in the legislative council promises us better fortune than we have had in the past.

In the colonies the people need democratic institutions because they are less expensive and less burdensome than more costly institutions. In order to exploit the forests, a new country needs men who are robust, accustomed to work, privation, and economy. It is in the customs, the nature, and the common interest of both the colony and the parent country that governmental institutions be economical, for everything that is not wasted on luxuries will serve to endow new families, who will marry younger; to clear new acres of land; to create new productive capital, which will buy useful manufactured goods of cloth and iron, rather than silks and liqueurs.

Making all offices elective would cause this primary and fertile source of conflict to dry up. The intervention—frequent, niggling, and meddlesome—of the Colonial Office in interests too widely scattered all over the globe for it to understand them [means that] the complaints proclaimed by the people are secretly denied, and the facts coloured by prevaricators who always have the last word, the protection of connections unknown to the country, and the expedient of schemes that escape even the sharpest eyes. Under the elective system, the mother country would say: we have only to count the votes [?] in those extremely rare cases where it would be necessary to call the government's attention to a few passing difficulties. And there would be this advantage: local interests would be debated and judged knowledgeably. Free and easy relations between the parent country and its former colonies would rapidly increase both their profits and its own; this would be the same in every case where she placed industry in the best circumstances for it to develop. And it is not from monopoly of lands, nor from any other European weakness—for entailment, primogeniture, vast inequality of condition, the pomp of palaces and their schemes to multiply jobs in favour of beribboned counsellors and hangers-on—that love of country springs, nor love of work, study, and application to business.

Give us institutions in which there are no motives for sycophancy, and national distinctions will cease. In the present situation, the Government is reaping what it sowed. It says it needs a Council to defend a part of the population that cannot form a majority in the Assembly. It needs a party in the Chamber to support the Council: and so from one scheme to another, the government has found it necessary to intervene directly, in even the smallest details. . . .

This country's complaints against the flaws in the constitution of the Council are too unanimous to require further elaboration. The Constitutional Act gave the Council a disastrous preponderance, which has allowed it to paralyse all the operations of the Chamber of Assembly. The latter was intended to have some influence, since the Province of Quebec had been divided so that the old population of Lower Canada could protect its own institutions. But the Constitutional Act provided an easy means of destroying that hope: by bringing Upper Canada into the Legislative Council of Lower Canada. And come it has. Such contrivances were introduced into the Act that it has become the subject of constant complaints. Out of the fifty clauses it contains, there are 15 or 16 on the organization of the Legislative Council. The idea of creating a nobility in Canada was so far-fetched that it took a great deal of work to arrive at a very meagre result. Everyone is aware that the effects achieved by these 15 or 16 clauses are in no way beneficial. Seven or eight clauses are devoted to setting aside one-seventh of the [Crown] lands for the Protestant clergy.

If there is one part of the government's operations that has slowed the progress of the country to a greater degree and provoked more just complaints than any other, it is this. A proposal has just been made to put an end to this wrong; we do not know whether it was intended to create another monopoly, even more speculative than the first. I believe the danger has passed, but it was imminent. It may reappear at any moment, until we have a better regime that will protect us from all these secret plots to serve the supposed good of the province by any way other than that of petitions to the local legislature and its decisions based on discussion and persuasion. It was the Constitutional Act that provided these reserves for the clergy—this territorial revenue from Crown lands that has revived the difficulties we thought we had escaped. It was also this Act that established our court of appeal, [and] our mysterious and irresponsible Executive Council. Surely no one can say that this is right. Certain parts of the Act, therefore, are notable for their defects. What is good is contained in two of its fifty clauses: one stating that, almost universally, the people will elect its representatives, the other that they will meet every year.

Let us ask the farmers where their attachment lies. If we say to them: is it advantageous for you to be subject to laws made by the men of your choice? would it not be equally advantageous to extend your influence to the choice of your representatives in another body? Will they be easy to fool? Will they not all answer in the affirmative?

Those who fear the reform of wrongs will not say so openly, but they will tell you that a convention is a frightening idea; that it is not fitting; that it can only lead to danger. And they will cite you the misfortunes of those who have reversed wrongs by force of arms, and often succumbed in these attempts and made things worse than before by rushing to take these criminal measures. Yes, changes made by violence have most often been dangerous; rarely have they led to a happy ending. But changes demanded in legal ways, under the direction and protection of the parent country, are within reach if, on the one hand, we examine the list (all too accurate) of the divisions suffered by this Province; and if, on the other, we state with unanimity and force that the People itself must indicate the appropriate remedies—not some authority that, for lack of understanding, has already subjected it to two unfortunate experiments and considered—and almost subjected it to—others that would have been more baneful still. As for the pride that suggested we ourselves prepare this third constitution, we were not sent here by our constituents to do so, but to prevent wrongs and, when we can lead the Council to think as we do, to effect a little good—and to give up this hope when the Council remains attached to its old policies. Let us turn a deaf ear to those false friends who used to say: 'Continue in the path you have been following: the day will come when the Council will recognize its error.'

The wrongs caused by procrastination have already made themselves too deeply felt; such a course could not re-establish peace in this country.

By means of the proposed convention, the Electors would give closer attention to this choice. It would give men of talent and merit—who, because they are in the Council, are now excluded from participating in these serious deliberations—the advantage of being able to be delegates. They would be as eligible as the rest, and they could take part in the debates on the country's constitution, whereas at present they are disenfranchised, in a way, belonging to a body in which, if they were left in a majority today, a new governor would make their voice powerless tomorrow by an infusion of antagonistic elements. The remedy suggested seems to me the best suited to do away with them and to content the people. If it is not good, the petitioners have the incontestable right to take their demand to the government of England, which can grant it or refuse it.

Only two alternatives remain: to say that everything is fine and change nothing; or to agree that much is wrong, and remedy it. If the remedy proposed is not good, one has only to suggest and outline a better, more effective one.

Baldwin on Responsible Government

MY LORD:

. . . I am deeply impressed with the responsibility which the present state of Upper Canada necessarily throws upon every man connected with it—As my native Country its prosperity is necessarily to be an object of the most intense Anxiety.—Educated in the warmest attachment to the monarchical form of Government, believing it to be best adapted to secure the happiness of the people, and fully sensible that it can be maintained in Upper Canada only by means of the connexion with the Mother Country, I have always been most earnestly anxious for the continuation of that Connexion: I believe it to be now endangered. I sincerely believe the crisis to have arrived, which is to decide the ultimate destiny of Upper Canada as a dependancy of the British Crown.—I feel therefore that it would be criminal in me to refuse compliance with Your Lordship's request to communicate with you in writing on the subject of the present state of that Province, and the events which have recently taken place there—At the same time I cannot but feel, that altho' there may be some advantages in this mode of communication where Principles are merely to be laid down; they are more than counterbalanced by the disadvantages attendant upon it, where principles are not only to be laid down, but discussed, and the details connected with them, and the political situation of a country in a state of high and dangerous excitement, to be enlarged upon, and disposed of.—*

I shall however as clearly as I can, state to Your Lordship my view of the present state of the Province, with reference to the principle contended for in the recent memorial from the House of Assembly,† to the Imperial House of

Commons, and the value and importance of that principle in producing harmony among the several Branches of the Provincial Legislature, and inspiring the people with confidence in the Home and Provincial Governments and will conclude with most respectfully submitting my opinion as to the course which, with all deference for the opinion of others, it appears to me absolutely necessary should be promptly taken for preserving the connexion of that Colony with the Mother Country.—

If it is the desire of the Mother Country, which I of course assume it to be, to retain the Colony it can only be done either by force, or with the consent of the People of Upper Canada themselves. I take it for granted that Great Britain cannot desire to exercise a Government of the sword, and that she will therefore only govern the Canadas so long as she can do so with the concurrence of the People—For the purpose therefore of continuing the connexion upon this footing it is absolutely necessary; First—That the political machinery of the Provincial Government should be such, as shall work harmoniously within itself, without collision between any of its great wheels; And secondly, That it should be such as that the People may feel that they have an influence upon it sufficiently powerful to secure attention, not only to their abstract rights, but to their feelings and Prejudices; without regard to these you can govern no people satisfactorily or successfully—That the Constitution of Upper Canada administered upon the principles heretofore applied to it, has failed to accomplish either of these objects a very cursory view of the history of the Colony, without reference to Your Lordship's late dispatch,* will sufficiently demonstrate.—It may however be well to state that the differences alluded to are of a much earlier date than appears to be generally known in this Country, or until lately to have been recollected even in the department over which Your Lordship presides. As early as in the Provincial Parliament of 1820 an opposition respectable if not formidable both in talents, and numbers existed,—some of the leading Members of which not only expressed their entire want of confidence in the Provincial Executive, but adopted the principle now contended for as a part of their political creed, and assumed it as necessarily pertaining as much to the provincial Constitution as to that of the Mother Country.—During the whole of that Parliament however the opposition were generally in a minority.—In the parliament of 1824 and in that of 1828 the Executive were uniformly in an inconsiderable minority.—In that of 1830, owing to Circumstances to which it is not worth while now to allude the Executive obtained a Majority; but in that 1834 they were again in a minority; so that taking the twelve Years from 1824 to 1836, the Provincial Executive have been in the minority for eight Years and three Parliaments, and have had a Majority only for four Years and one Parliament; during the whole of this time also the House of Assembly were constantly passing Bills which the Legislative Council as uniformly threw out. As therefore the present Constitution administered, upon the principles heretofore applied to it, has failed in both particulars, I mean in working smoothly itself or satisfying the People, it necessarily follows that something must be done to accomplish the objects desired.—To this end four remedies have been proposed; first to make the Legislative Council elective; Secondly, to abolish it; Thirdly to concede certain isolated points, which have been earnestly called for by the Representatives of the People, and fourthly, to put the Executive Council permanently upon the footing of a local Provincial Cabinet, holding the same relative position with reference to the representative of the King and the Provincial Parliament, as that on which the King's Imperial Cabinet stands with respect to the King and the Parliament of the Empire, and applying to such provincial Cabinet both with respect to their appointment to, and continuation in, office; the same principles as those which are acted upon by His Majesty with respect to the Imperial Cabinet in this Country.—

The two first remedies, if not inexpedient, I look upon as at least wholly insufficient to accomplish the objects desired:—the third, as equally insufficient of itself to do so; and the last as the only remedy by the application of which those objects can be attained and upper Canada preserved to the Mother Country—

First, the making the Legislative Council elective I look upon as inexpedient; among other reasons because I am of opinion that the institutions of every Colony ought as nearly as possible to correspond with those of the Mother Country—The Upper House of the Imperial Parliament not being elective I would therefore not have the Upper House of the Provincial Parliament elective unless under the pressure of an absolute necessity.—I moreover disapprove of the adoption of such a measure at all events at present,—because it is as a general principle inexpedient to make an alteration in the forms of the constitution of any Country, until the necessity for such change has been demonstrated, by putting into full and efficient operation, the existing constitution in all its details; which cannot be said to have been done with that of Upper Canada, until the Executive Council is practically converted into a provincial Cabinet for the local and internal Affairs of the Province:—Had this been done ten or twelve Years ago when the Executive first found themselves in a decided and uniform minority in the Provincial Parliament, I am satisfied that an elective legislative Council would not now have been thought of, and I am not without hopes, although they may prove fallacious, that it is not yet too late by the adoption of this principle to render such change in the constitution unnecessary. But at all events as a remedy amounting merely to the application of an English principle to the constitution as it stands, it ought yet to be tried fully and fairly, previous to resorting to the more violent measure of a legislative change in the Charter. It is but right however to inform Your Lordship that altho' my opinion of the inexpediency of such a change in the organization of the Legislative Council is concurred in by many I believe, a considerable majority of the Reformers of the Province (which every day's delay is increasing) think that such a change will ultimately be found necessary.—After the intimation contained in Your Lordship's despatch and out of regard to the opinions entertained by us, who in this point differ from them, they were however willing to drop the question of an elective Legislative Council until the Constitution as it is should have been fully and fairly tested by the application of those principles which have been found so valuable and so necessary in the successful working of that of the Mother Country;—And whatever may be the opinion entertained as to the expediency or inexpediency of making the Legislative Council elective, I believe no doubt exists of such change being found wholly insufficient of itself to accomplish the two objects desired—The making the legislative Council elective might convert that body into an additional engine of hostility against the executive Government, but could never supersede the necessity for the concession of the Principle [of responsibility] contended for.—Resistance to the concession of this Principle may drive the Reformers into Unanimity in the call for an Elective legislative Council, but it will only be as a means and not as an end—And when this state of things arrives, be assured that England will have lost the last hold upon the *Affections* of the great mass of the people of Upper Canada—That such change in the constitution of the Legislative Council would not be found to produce harmony between the three branches of the Provincial Government, will be readily admitted when it is remembered that the Collision which has produced so much evil has not been merely between the Representative Branch of the Government and the Legislative Council, but between the Representative Branch and the Executive Government; the complaint has always been of the influence of the Executive upon the Legislative Council, and not of the influence—of the Legislative Council upon the Executive Government.—It were idle therefore to expect unanimity while you leave untouched the main source of discord.

Secondly—To the proposal to abolish the Legislative Council altogether, most of the reasons against making it elective will equally apply: it may in addition be urged that a second chamber of some kind has, at least in modern constitutional legislation, been deemed essential to good Government; It has not been dispensed with in any of the new constitutions of any of the neighbouring Republics; and has I believe in more instances than one been not long since adopted as an improvement to the political machinery of Government where the previous constitution had contained no such provision. And moreover, the abolition of the Legislative Council has not been asked for, by any portion of the Canadian People.—

As to the third remedy proposed, that of conceding certain isolated points as they arise, and are called for; I will only say, that the whole history, not only of the Canadas but of the Colonies in general shews that such course as a means of producing permanent satisfaction and harmony, has wholly failed; —nor indeed does it appear to me to require much consideration to convince any one of the insufficiency of this as a permanent remedy—In the first place such concessions are never made, and under the present system never will be made, until after such a prolonged struggle, that when they come, they are always felt to have been wrung from the Government, and not to have proceeded from a sense of justice or expediency of granting them.—They never remove the distrust which is felt of the Provincial Executive Government. —They leave untouched the great evil of the disadvantageous comparison which is constantly before the eyes of the people when they look at the administration of the Imperial Government, by the King and that of the Provincial Government by his representative—They see the former always so far consulting the wishes of his people as never to keep in his Councils persons who have not the confidence of their Representatives; while in the administration of their own Government they see the mere Representative of that Sovereign constantly surrounded by those very individuals, of whom sometimes with reason, and perhaps sometimes without they have become distrustful and jealous: And they very naturally ask the question, why are not our Representatives to be paid as much attention to by the King's Deputy, as the Representatives of our fellow Subjects in England by the King himself?—Astute reasonings may no doubt be framed, and fine distinctions drawn upon the subject but this is a plain common sense and practical view of it; out of which be assured it will be impossible ultimately to persuade the Yeomanry of Upper Canada—You may indeed, by strenuously insisting on the inapplicability of this principle to their situation, drive them to insist on a more extended system of elective institutions.— By refusing what no one can deny to be an English principle— the same upon which Your Lordship, and Your Colleagues were selected to fill the high and important situations which you hold in His Majesty's Councils; the same by which you at this moment continue to retain those places—you may indeed divert their attention to another Quarter, and drive them to call for the power of electing their own Governor, and their own Executive; but you never can persuade them to abandon the object of obtaining more influence than they now possess, through their Representatives, in the administration of the Executive Government of the Colony.—

I now come to the consideration of the fourth remedy, which consists of nothing more than having the provincial Government as far as regards the internal affairs of the Province, conducted by the Lieutenant Governor (as Representative of the paramount Authority of the Mother Country) with the advice and assistance of the Executive Council, acting as a Provincial Cabinet, and composed of Men possessed of the public confidence, whose opinions and policy would be in harmony with the opinions and policy of the Representatives of the People. This, as I have before said, I look upon not only as an efficient remedy, but as the only efficient one that can be applied to the evils under which the Province is at present suffering.—

I shall avoid troubling Your Lordship with any observations upon the construction of the Constitutional Act [of 1791]; because not only has the subject been already fully entered into, in the Report of the Select Committee of the House of Assembly; but I sincerely believe matters to have arrived at that point when it really signifies nothing whether it be or be not *required* by the Charter. The only question worth discussing is, whether it is or is not *expedient* that the principle should be applied to it: And for this purpose all that it is necessary to ascertain in the first instance is, that there is nothing in the Charter which forbids the application of such a principle. That this is the case, as it has never been denied, and as the principle in its practical application consists in fact merely in the ordinary exercise of the Royal Prerogative will, I take it for granted, be readily admitted.—The Concession of the principle therefore calls for no legislative interference;—It involves no sacrifice of any constitutional principle,—It involves no sacrifice of any branch of the Royal Prerogative,—It involves no diminution of the paramount Authority, of the Mother Country; It produces no such embarrassment to the Home Government, as in the present state of the Imperial Parliament, the attempt to grant an Elective Legislative Council would be almost certain to do:—From being an English Principle, it would strengthen the Attachment of the People to the connexion with the Mother Country; and would place the Provincial Government at the head of Public opinion, instead of occupying its present invidious position of being always in direct opposition to it.

But in addition to these Advantages, which this remedy possesses in an eminent degree over all others, that have been suggested, it would be found effectual for the purposes desired.—

Permit me to restate those objects,—they were first, that the different branches of the Provincial Government should be brought to act in harmony with each other; and secondly, that the People should feel that they had sufficient influence upon their Government to secure attention to their rights,—and respect for their feelings and prejudices: I am of opinion that this principle if fully and fairly acted upon, would affect both those objects.—An Executive Council constituted upon this principle, would from their situation as confidential advisers of the Lieutenant Governor necessarily have great influence in the House of Assembly: Their weight in the Country, as well as their confidential situation, about the person of the Lieutenant Governor, would give them great weight in the Legislative Council: And they would of course from both circumstances possess great weight with the Lieutenant Governor. They would generally if not uniformly be in one or other House of Parliament, and would there form a centre of Union, and in fact act as a sort of balance Wheel to the constitution. The measures which they brought forward, as they would necessarily have the previous sanction of the Lieutenant Governor, would come recommended on the one hand by all the weight of executive influence, and on the other by the support of those to whom the people both from habit and principle had been accustomed to look with confidence.—The people would therefore be predisposed to receive their Measures with satisfaction and confidence, as the fruit of the advice of their friends; and the Legislative Council as recommended by the servants of the Crown, whose interests as well as duty it was, to recommend nothing but what was safe, as well as satisfactory to the Public.—What was not deemed wise or prudent to adopt, instead of being suffered to pass heedlessly through the Assembly, and left to be thrown out by the Legislative Council or negatived by the Veto of the Lieutenant Governor would be met in the first instance and resisted; because every step that such proposal advanced would increase the probability of ultimate embarrassment to the Executive Council, and to those whose confidence they enjoyed; who would of course be always the most powerful Party in Parliament.—Such an Executive Council would necessarily feel a moral as well as a political responsibility for the success of their Measures.—Their permanent connexion with the Country as well as a sense of duty and natural desire to retain office, would necessarily insure their utmost exertions, not only to procure harmony but to produce good government.—The People when they saw that the King's Representative would not retain Men in his Councils who have forfeited their confidence, would be the more careful in the exercise of the Elective Franchise, and far less likely to withdraw their confidence from those in whom they had once found reason to place it.—

That the adoption of this principle would without vesting the Election of the Executive Council in the People place in their hands such an indirect influence upon it, as would be sufficient to secure attention to their rights, feelings, and prejudices, is sufficiently evident; because if such attention were not paid by those in the confidence of the Lieutenant Governor, the people have only to return to the next Parliament, men who would not give them parliamentary support, and they would necessarily have to resign; and the

Lieutenant Governor to appoint others who possessed the confidence of the Representatives of the People.—A, B and C would go out of office, and D, E and F would come in; the Lieutenant Governor always retaining the Power of calling into Action his superintending control with respect to the measures of both the one and the other: and the effect produced upon the interests of the Mother Country, being none other than that the change would give satisfaction, and, at least most probably, insure good government in the management of the internal affairs of the Colony.—

But it will be said that even under this system, collision may arise.—The Lieutenant Governor may disapprove of the measures recommended by his Council, and find it impossible to form an Executive Council which would secure parliamentary support upon any other terms than concession; or the Executive Council may find it impossible to bring the two houses to an Understanding upon every Measure:—To which I reply, that the practical working of the principle would be sure to postpone such collision to the latest possible period: That the intermediate steps of a change of the Executive Council, and of appealing to the people by a dissolution, would at all events give the Home Government the great advantage of not itself coming in collision with the People till the last moment, and of ascertaining the exact point where the question of Concession would become one merely of expediency; . . .

It is objected that the concession of this principle is inconsistent with the preservation of the paramount Authority of the Mother Country. With respect to this, I would remark that it does not appear to be more so than the concession of the power of legislation; in the one case you vest the power of legislating on the internal Affairs of the Colony in a local Parliament with the consent of the King's Representative; in the other, you leave the Executive Power in the hands of the King's Representative requiring only that it should be exercised with the advice of persons named by himself but possessed of weight and influence with the people whose local Affairs, he is deputed to administer.—

It is objected, that it would interfere with the patronage of the Lieutenant Governor; this also appears to me to be an error; the power of appointment to office would remain in the Lieutenant Governor as at present. The right of advising is all that is claimed for the Executive Council: If such be considered an interference, it is such as can be exercised, alone to prevent mischief. But suppose that it actually deprived the Lieutenant Governor of every vestige of patronage; the simple question is, is the patronage in the hands of the Lieutenant Governor the great object for which England desires to retain Upper Canada. If this be, indeed the chief or only object, let it be candidly avowed: I will only remark that the People have been hitherto induced to believe that the Home Government were actuated by other and loftier motives.—

It is objected that it would lessen the responsibility of the Lieutenant Governor to the Home Government: this is a mistake, every Act of the Provincial Government would be the Act of the Lieutenant Governor requiring his full consent quite as much as at present.—How would he be less responsible then to the King and Parliament of the Empire because he acted upon the advice of those who had the confidence of the People? The Lieutenant Governor is the connecting link between the Government of the two Countries.—You cannot make him responsible to the People of the Province, such would be wholly inconsistent with the respect due to the sovereign whom he represented, and fatal to the connexion between the two Countries.—The proper place for his responsibility to rest is, in England.—But you must give the people such an influence upon their Executive Government as will prevent the constant jealousy to which it is at present exposed.—You can do so only either by permitting a direct influence, by vesting the election in the hands of the people, which I look upon as inexpedient and unsafe; or you must give them that indirect influence, which they see constantly exercised by their fellow subjects through their Representatives in this Country. . . .

To conclude my Lord, I most earnestly recommend not only as *expedient,* but *necessary* for the preservation of the Connexion between this Country and Upper Canada:—First, That His Majesty's Imperial Government should at once adopt the final determination, that the Provincial Government as far as respects the internal Affairs of the Province, should be conducted by the Lieutenant Governor, with the Advice and Assistance of the Executive Council, acting as a Provincial Cabinet;—And that the same Principle on which His Majesty's Cabinet in this Country is composed, should be applied and acted upon in the formation, continuance in office and removal, of such local Provincial Cabinet:—Secondly that this Resolution of the Home Government should be inserted in the shape of a Specific Clause in the general Royal Instructions for the Government of the Province, and formally communicated to both houses of the Provincial Parliament; And Thirdly—That Sir Francis Head should be recalled, and a Successor appointed who shall have been practically acquainted with the working of the Machinery of a free Representative Government. . . .

The Six Counties Address

FELLOW CITIZENS:

WHEN a systematic course of oppression has been invariably harrassing a People, in despite of their wishes expressed in every manner recognized by constitutional usage; by popular assemblies, and by their Representatives, in Parliament, after grave deliberation; when their rulers, instead of redressing the various evils produced by their own misgovernment, have solemnly enregistered and proclaimed their guilty determination to sap and subvert the very foundations of civil liberty, it becomes the imperative duty of the People to betake themselves to the serious consideration of their unfortunate position—of the dangers by which they are surrounded—and by well-concerted organization, to make such arrangements as may be necessary to protect, unimpaired, their rights as Citizens and their dignity as Freemen.

The wise and immortal framers of the AMERICAN DECLARATION OF IN-DEPENDENCE, embodied in that document the principles on which alone are based the RIGHTS OF MAN; and successfully vindicated and established the only institutions and form of government which can permanently secure the prosperity and social happiness of the inhabitants of this Continent, whose education and habits, derived from the circumstances of their colonization, demand a system of government entirely dependent upon, and directly responsible to, the People.

In common with the various nations of North and South America who have adopted the principles contained in that Declaration, we hold the same holy and self-evident doctrines: that GOD created no artificial distinctions between man and man; that government is but a mere human institution formed by those who are to be subject to its good or evil action, intended for the benefit of all who may consent to come, or remain under, its protection and control; and therefore, that its form may be changed whenever it ceases to accomplish the ends for which such government was established; that public authorities and men in office are but the executors of the lawfully-expressed will of the community, honoured because they possess public confidence, respected only so long as they command public esteem, and to be removed from office the moment they cease to give satisfaction to the People, the sole legitimate source of all power.

In conformity with these principles, and on the faith of treaties and capitulations entered into with our ancestors, and guaranteed by the Imperial Parliament, the People of this Province have for a long series of years complained by respectful petitions, of the intolerable abuses which poison their existence and paralyse their industry. Far from conceding our humble prayers, aggression has followed aggression, until at length we seem no longer to belong to the British Empire for our own happiness or prosperity, our freedom or the honour of the British Crown or people, but solely for the purpose of fattening a horde of useless officials, who not content with enjoying salaries enormously disproportioned to the duties of their offices, and to the resources of the country, have combined as a faction, united by private interest alone, to oppose all reforms in the Province, and to uphold the iniquities of a Government inimical to the rights and liberties of this colony.

Notwithstanding the universally admitted justice of our demands, and the wisdom and prudence of remedying our complaints, we still endure the misery of an irresponsible Executive, directed by an ignorant and hypocritical Chief; our Judges, dependent for the tenure of their office on the mere will and pleasure of the Crown, for the most part the violent partizans of a corrupt administration, have become more completely the tools and mercenaries of the Executive, by accepting the wages of their servility, in gross violation of every principle of Judicial independence, from foreign authority, without the intervention of the people to whom, through their Representatives, belongs the sole right of voting the salaries of their public servants; the office-holders of the Province devour our revenues, in salaries so extravagant as to deprive us of the funds requisite for the general improvement of the Country, whereby our public works are arrested, and the navigation of our rivers [remains] obstructed; a Legislative Council appointed by men resident three thousand miles from this country, and systematically composed so as to thwart and oppose the efforts of our freely-chosen Representatives in all measures for the promotion of the public good, after continuing unchanged during the present administration, thereby depriving the country of the advantages of domestic legislation, has at length been modified in a manner insulting to all classes of society, disgraceful to public morality, and to the annihilation of the respect and confidence of all parties in that branch of the Legislature, by the introduction of men for the most part notorious only for their incapacity, and remarkable alone for their political insignificance,* thus making evident, even to demonstration, to all, whatever may be their preconceived ideas, the propriety and urgent necessity of introducing the principle of election into that body, as the only method of enabling the Provincial Legislature to proceed beneficially to the despatch of public business.

Our municipalities are utterly destroyed; the country parts of the Province, as a disgraceful exception to the other parts of this Continent, are totally deprived of all power of regulating, in a corporate capacity, their local affairs, through freely elected Parish and Township Officers; the rising generation is deprived of the blessings of education, the primary schools, which provided for the instruction of 40,000 children, having been shut up by the Legislative Council, a body hostile to the progress of useful knowledge, and instigated to this act by an Executive inimical to the spread of general information among the people—the Jesuits' College founded and endowed by the provident government which colonized this Province for the encouragement and dissemination of learning and the sciences therein, has, with a barbarism unworthy the rulers of a civilized state, disgraceful to the enlightened age in which we live, and unparalleled even among the Goths and Vandals, been converted into, and is still retained, as a barrack for soldiery, whilst the funds and property devoted to the support of this and similar institutions have been, and continue to be, squandered and mal-administered for the advantage of the favourites, creatures and tools of the Government; our citizens are deprived of the benefits of impartially chosen juries, and are arbitrarily persecuted by Crown officers, who to suit the purposes of the vindictive Government of which they are the creatures, have revived proceedings of an obsolete character, precedents for which are to be found only in the darkest pages of British history. Thus our Judiciary being sullied by combined conspiracies of a wicked Executive, slavish Judges, partizan Law Officers, and political Sheriffs, the innocent and patriotic are exposed to be sacrificed, whilst the enemies of the country, and the violators of all law, are protected and patronized, according as it may please the administration to crush and destroy; to save and protect. Our commerce and domestic industry are paralysed; our public lands alienated, at a nominal price, to a company of speculators, strangers to the country, or bestowed upon insolent favourites, as a reward for their sycophancy; our money is extorted from us without our consent, by taxes unconstitutionally imposed by a foreign Parliament, to be afterwards converted into an instrument of our degradation by being distributed among a howling herd of officials, against our will, without our participation, and in violation of all principles of constitutional law.

In the midst of their honest and unwearied efforts to procure a redress of the foregoing grievances, our fellow citizens have been insolently called on to give an account of their public conduct, for which they were responsible to no individual, least of all to the person whom chance or ministerial partonage may place for a season at the head of our Provincial Government. They have been harrassed and annoyed by dismissals from offices of mere honour, held for the benefit and at the request of their own immediate neighbours, because they vindicated the rights of their country, like American Freemen; and as an index of further intended aggression, armed troops are being scattered in time of profound peace throughout the country, with the presumptuous and wicked design of restraining by physical force the expression of public opinion, and of completing by violence and bloodshed our slavery and ruin, already determined upon beyond the seas.

Such an aggression as this might justify the recourse, on the part of an outraged people, to all and every means to preserve the last of their insulted privileges—the right to complain. But, thanks to the blindness of the aggressors, the wickedness of the measure will be providentially neutralized by its folly. The regiments about to be quartered among us are composed of men sprung from, and educated with, the Democracy of their country. They, for the most part, entered on their present profession, not from choice, but because they could not find any other employment in their native land. Instead of being stimulated to good conduct by the hope of promotion, too poorly paid, they are exposed to every sort of petty tyranny, and if a murmur escape their lips, they are subjected, like the bonded slave, to the ignoble punishment of the lash. Contrasting this hard fate with the freedom, content, employment and high wages to be obtained in the United States, and certain that the inhabitants of these Counties lying near and bordering upon the [boundary] Lines will not impede the efforts which these soldiers may make to emigrate to the neighbouring Republic, it will become morally impossible to keep in Her Majesty's Province, whilst scattered in detachments, the men who are now about to be made the vile instruments of our slavery and their own dishonor.

The long and heavy chain of abuses and oppressions under which we suffer, and to which every year has only added a more galling link, proves that our history is but a recapitulation of what other Colonies have endured before us. Our grievances are but a second edition of their grievances. Our petitions for relief are the same. Like theirs, they have been treated with scorn and contempt, and have brought down upon the petitioners but additional outrage and persecution. Thus the experience of the past demonstrates the folly of expecting justice from European authorities.

Dark, however, and unpromising as may be the present prospects of this our beloved country, we are encouraged by the public virtues of our fellow-citizens to hope that the day of our regeneration is not far distant. Domestic manufactures are springing up amongst us, with a rapidity to cheer us in the contest. The impulse given but a few short months ago by the example of generous and patriotic minds, of wearing domestic cloths, has been generally followed, and will shortly be universally adopted. The determination not to consume duty-paying merchandise, and to encourage Free Trade with our neighbours, matters of vital importance, is daily becoming more general, resolute and effective. The people are every where being duly impressed with the conviction that the sacrifices to be made must bear some proportion to the glorious object to be achieved, and that personal inconvenience for the good cause must therefore be not only freely, but readily, endured.

FELLOW-COUNTRYMEN! Brothers in affliction! Ye, whatsoever be your origin, language or religion, to whom Equal Laws and the Rights of Man are dear; whose hearts have throbbed with indignation whilst witnessing the innumerable insults to which your common country has been exposed, and who have often been justly alarmed whilst pondering over the sombre futurity [being prepared] by misgovernment and corruption for this Province and for your posterity; in the name of that country, and of the rising generation, now having no hope but in you, we call upon you to assume, by systematic organization in your several Townships and Parishes, that position which can alone procure respect for yourselves and your demands. Let Committees of Vigilance be at once put in *active* operation throughout your respective neighbourhoods. Withdrawing all confidence from the present administration, and from such as will be so base as to accept office under it, forthwith assemble in your Parishes and elect Pacificator Magistrates [*magistrats pacificateurs*], after the example of your brother Reformers of the County of Two Mountains, in order to protect the people at once from useless and improvident expense, and from the vengeance of their enemies. Our Young Men, the hope of the country, should everywhere organize themselves, after the plan of their brothers, 'The Sons of Liberty' in Montreal, in order that they may be prepared to act with promptitude and effect as circumstances may require; and the brave Militiamen, who by their blood and valour have twice preserved this country for ungrateful rulers, should at once associate together, under officers of their own choice, for the security of good order and the protection of life and property in their respective localities. Thus prepared, Colonial Liberty may haply be yet preserved.

In this hope, and depending, for a disenthralment from the misrule under which we now groan, on the Providence of GOD, whose blessing on our disinterested labours we humbly implore; relying on the love of liberty which the free air and impregnable fastnesses of AMERICA should inspire in the hearts of the People at large, and upon the sympathy of our Democratic neighbours, who in the establishment of arbitrary rule on their borders, wisely and clearly [will foresee] the uprearing of a system which might be made a precedent and instrument for the introduction of the same arbitrary rule into other parts of the American Continent, and who can never consent that the principles for which they successfully struggled in the Eighteenth, shall, in our persons, be trampled in the dust in the Nineteenth century, WE, the DELEGATES of the Confederated Counties of Richelieu, St Hyacinthe, Rouville, L'Acadie, Chambly and Verchères, hereby publicly register the solemn and determined resolution of the People whom we represent, to carry into effect, with the least delay possible, the preceding recommendations, and never to cease their patriotic exertions until the various grievances of which they now complain shall have been redressed; and We hereby invite our fellow-citizens throughout the Province to unite their efforts to ours to procure a good, cheap and responsible system of government for their common country.

Signed for, and on behalf of, the Confederation of the Six Counties, this 24th day of October, 1837.

WFD. NELSON, President

J. T. DROLET,
F. C. DUVERT, | Vice Presidents

A. GIROD,
J. P. BOUCHER-BELLEVILLE | Secretaries

Mackenzie's Draft Constitution

WHEREAS the solemn convenant made with the people of Upper and Lower Canada, and recorded in the statute book of the United Kingdom of Great Britain and Ireland, as the thirty-first chapter of the Acts passed in the thirty-first year of the reign of King George III, hath been continually violated by the British government, and our rights usurped, *And Whereas* our humble petitions, addresses, protests, and remonstrances against this injurious interference have been made in vain—We, the people of the State of Upper Canada, acknowledging with gratitude the grace and beneficence of God, in permitting us to make choice of our form of government, and in order to establish justice, ensure domestic tranquility, provide for the common defence, promote the general welfare, and secure the blessings of civil and religious liberty to ourselves and our posterity, do establish this constitution.

1. Matters of religion and the ways of God's worship are not at all intrusted by the people of this State to any human power, because therein they cannot remit or exceed a tittle of what their consciences dictate to be the mind of God, without willful sin. Therefore the Legislature shall make no law respecting the establishment of religion, or for the encouragement or the prohibition of any religious denomination.

2. It is ordained and declared that the free exercise and enjoyment of religious profession and worship, without discrimination or preference, shall forever hereafter be allowed within this State to all mankind.

3. The whole of the public lands within the limits of this State, including the lands attempted, by a pretended sale, to be vested in certain adventurers called the Canada Company (except so much of them as may have been disposed of to actual settlers now resident in the State), and all the land called Crown Reserves, Clergy Reserves, and rectories and also the school lands, and the lands pretended to be appropriated to the use of the University of King's College, are declared to be the property of the State, and at the disposal of the Legislature, for the public service thereof. The proceeds of one million of acres of the most valuable public lands shall be specially appropriated to the support of Common or Township schools.

4. No Minister of the Gospel, clergyman, ecclesiastic, bishop or priest of any religious denomination whatsoever, shall, at any time hereafter, under any pretense or description whatever, be eligible to, or capable of holding a seat in the Senate or House of Assembly, or any civil or military office within this State.

5. In all laws made, or to be made, every person shall be bound alike—neither shall any tenure, estate, charter, degree, birth, or place, confer any exemption from the ordinary course of legal proceedings and responsibilities whereunto others are subjected.

6. No hereditary emoluments, privileges, or honours, shall ever be granted by the people of this State.

7. There shall neither be slavery nor involuntary servitude in this State, otherwise than for the punishment of crimes whereof the party shall have been duly convicted. People of Colour, who have come into this State, with the de-

sign of becoming permanent inhabitants thereof, *and are now resident therein*, shall be entitled to all the rights of native Canadians, upon taking an oath or affirmation to support the constitution.

8. The people have a right to bear arms for the defence of themselves and the State.

9. No man shall be impressed or forcibly constrained to serve in time of war, because money, the sinews of war, being always at the disposal of the Legislature, they can never want numbers of men apt enough to engage in any just cause.

10. The military shall be kept under strict subordination to the civil power. No soldier shall, in time of peace, be quartered in any house without the consent of the owner, nor in time of war but in a manner to be prescribed by law.

11. The Governor, with the advice and consent of the Senate, shall choose all militia officers above the rank of Captain. The people shall elect their own officers of the Rank of Captain, and under it.

12. The people have a right to assemble together in a peaceful manner, to consult for their common good, to instruct their representatives in the Legislature, and to apply to the Legislature for the redress of grievances.

13. The printing presses shall be open and free to those who may wish to examine the proceedings of any branch of the government, or the conduct of any public officer, and no law shall ever restrain the right thereof.

14. The trial by jury shall remain for ever inviolate.

15. Treason against this State shall consist only in levying war against it, or adhering to its enemies, giving them aid and comfort. No person shall be convicted of treason unless on the testimony of two witnesses to the same overt act, or on confession in open court.

15A. No ex post facto law, or any law impairing the validity of legal compacts, grants, or contracts, shall ever be made; and no conviction shall work corruption of blood or forfeiture of estate.

16. The real estate of persons dying without making a will shall not descend to the oldest son to the exclusion of his brethren, but be equally divided among the children, male and female.

17. The laws of Entail shall be forever abrogated.

17A. There shall be no lotteries in this State. Lottery tickets shall not be sold therein, whether foreign or domestic.

18. No power of suspending the operation of the laws shall be exercised except by the authority of the Legislature.

19. The people shall be secure in their persons, papers, and possessions, from all unwarrantable searches and seizures; general warrants, whereby an officer may be commanded to search suspected places, without probable evidence of the fact committed, or to seize any person or persons not named, whose offences are not particularly described, and without oath or affirmation, are dangerous to liberty, and shall not be granted.

20. Private property ought, and will ever be held inviolate, but always subservient to the public welfare, provided a compensation in money be first made to the owner. Such compensation shall never be less in amount than the actual value of the property.

22. The Legislative authority of this State shall be vested in a General Assembly, which shall consist of a Senate and House of Assembly, both to be elected by the People.

24. The Senate shall consist of twenty-four members. The Senators shall be freeholders and be chosen for four years. The House of Assembly shall consist of seventy-two members, who shall be elected for two years.

30. In order to promote the freedom, peace, and quiet of elections, and to secure, in the most ample manner possible, the independence of the poorer classes of the electors, it is declared that all elections by the people, which shall take place after the first session of the Legislature of this State, shall be by ballot, except for such town officers as may by law be directed to be otherwise chosen.

37. In each House the votes shall, in all cases when taken, be taken openly, and not by ballot, so that the electors may be enabled to judge of the conduct of their representatives.

40. Any bill may originate in either House of the Legislature; and all bills passed by one House may be amended or rejected by the other.

42. Every bill, which shall have passed the Senate and Assembly, shall before it becomes law, be presented to the Governor. If he approve, he shall sign it; but if not, he should return it with his objections to that House in which it shall have originated, which shall enter the objections in its Journal, and proceed to reconsider it. If, after such reconsideration, two-thirds of the members present shall agree to pass the bill, it shall be sent, together with the objections, to the other House, by which it shall likewise be reconsidered, and if approved by two-thirds of the members present it shall become a law. In all such cases, the votes of both Houses shall be determined by yeas and nays, and the names of the persons voting for and against the bill shall be entered on the Journals of each House respectively. If any bill shall not be returned by the Governor within ten days (Sundays excepted) after it shall have been presented to him, the same shall be a law, in like manner as if he had signed it, unless the Legislature shall, by its adjournment, prevent its return, in which case it shall not be a law.

43. No member of the Legislature, who has taken his seat as such, shall receive any civil appointment from the Governor and Senate, or from the Legislature, during the term for which he shall have been elected.

44. The assent of the Governor, and of three-fourths of the members elected to each branch of the Legislature, shall be requisite to authorize the passage of every bill appropriating the public moneys or property for local or private purposes, or for creating, continuing, altering, or renewing any body politic or corporate, and the yeas and nays shall be entered on the Journals at the time of taking the vote on the final passage of any such bill.

52. Gold and silver shall be the only lawful tender in payment of debts.

56. There shall never be created within this State any incorporated trading companies, or incorporated companies with banking powers. Labor is the only means of creating wealth.

58. The Executive power shall be vested in a Governor. He shall hold his office for three years. No person shall be eligible to that office who shall not have attained the age of thirty years.
59. The Governor shall be elected by the people at the times and places of choosing members of the Legislature. . . .

62. The Governor shall nominate by message, in writing, and, with the consent of the Senate, shall appoint the Secretary of State, Comptroller, Receiver General, Auditor General, Attorney General, Surveyor General, Postmaster General, and also all Judicial Officers, except Justices of the Peace and Commissioners of the Courts of Request, or local Courts.

65. The Judicial power of the State, both as to matters of law and equity, shall be vested in a Supreme Court, the members of which shall hold office during good behaviour, in District or County Courts, in Justices of the Peace, in Courts of Request, and in such other Courts as the Legislature may from time to time establish.
66. A competent number of Justices of the Peace and Commissioners of the Courts of Request shall be elected by the people, for a period of three years, within their respective cities and townships.
67. All courts shall be open, and every person for any injury done him in his lands, goods, person or reputation shall have remedy by the due course of law; and right and justice shall be administered without delay or denial.
68. Excessive bail shall not be required; excessive fines shall not be imposed, nor shall cruel and unusual punishments be inflicted.
69. All persons shall be bailable by sufficient sureties, unless for capital offences, where the proof is evident or the presumption is great, and the privilege of the writ of Habeas Corpus shall not be suspended by any act of the Legislature, unless, when in cases of actual rebellion or invasion, the public safety may require it.
70. In all criminal prosecutions, the accused hath a right to be heard by himself and his Counsel, to demand the nature and cause of the accusation against him, and to have a copy thereof; to meet the witnesses face to face; to have compulsory process for obtaining witnesses in his favour; and in prosecutions by indictment or presentment a speedy public trial, by an impartial and fairly selected jury of the County, District, or Division in which the offence shall be stated to have been committed; and shall not be compelled to give evidence against himself—nor shall he be twice put in jeopardy for the same offence.
71. In prosecutions for any publication respecting the official conduct of men in a public capacity, or when the matter published is proper for public information, the truth thereof may always be given in evidence, and in all indictments for libel, the jury shall have a right to determine the law and the fact.

72. No person arrested or confined in jail shall be treated with unnecessary rigor, or be put to answer any criminal charge except by presentment, indictment, or impeachment.

78. All powers not delegated by this Constitution remain with the people.

80. The Senators and Members of the House of Assembly, before mentioned, and all Executive and Judicial Officers within this State, shall, before entering upon the duties of their respective offices or functions be bound, by an oath or solemn affirmation, to support the Constitution; but no religious test shall ever be required as a qualification to any office or public trust under this State.

81. This Constitution, and the laws of this State, which shall be made in pursuance thereof, and all treaties, made, or which shall be made under the authority of this State, shall be the supreme law of the land, and the judges shall be bound thereby.

Several clauses for the carrying of a Constitution like the above into practice are omitted, the whole being only given in illustration of, and for the benefit of a comparison in detail, with other systems.

We have not entered upon the questions, whether any, and if so, what restrictions ought to be laid upon the right of voting, or as to residence in the State, taxation, performance of militia duty, &c. These matters, however, might be advantageously discussed by the public press.

HENRY GRATTAN,
JOHN LOCKE,
ALGERNON SYDNEY,
BENJN. FRANKLIN.*

Committee Room, Royal Oak Hotel,
13th Nov., 1837.

ÉTIENNE PARENT

Perhaps the most philosophical of the Reformers was Étienne Parent (1802-74). He was born in Beauport, a few miles from Quebec, where his family farmed land that had been granted to their ancestors on their arrival in New France in 1634. Little is known of his early years except that he received a classical education at the Collège de Nicolet and the Séminaire de Québec. During his twenties and thirties he edited Le Canadien *and held various minor positions connected with the Assembly. In 1837 he counselled moderation and the avoidance of violence, but was nonetheless imprisoned for four months following the second rebellion in 1838. In 1841 he was elected to the Assembly with LaFontaine on the platform of co-operation with the Upper Canadian Reformers that eventually won responsible government.*

What would such a collaboration with the English really mean? Among the liberals of his generation, Parent alone seems to have thought seriously about this question and written on it. Between 1846 and 1852 he delivered seven lengthy 'lectures publiques', the main theme of which was educational reform. He projected a vast new system of public schools and colleges designed to produce a mandarinate ('Classe des Lettrés') that would be charged, through popular elections, with the government of the country. In the second lecture of the series, reprinted below, Parent teaches what Trudeau learned: the importance of social science.

The Importance of Studying
Political Economy

GENTLEMEN:

At the beginning of this year, I had the honour of addressing you on a subject that is important because of its relation to our national as well as our personal interests.* Being ever more persuaded that, of all the objects of our affection, the one that is at once the most threatened and the most incumbent on our honour to defend is our nationality, I intend, if you will permit me—and in so doing I believe I could make no better response to your invitation to address you a second time—I intend, as I was saying, to follow the same train of thought and to deal with a subject of great concern to this nationality we hold so dear, without losing sight of the material interests of our people—which are in any case so closely linked to the former as to be inseparable, being the body of which the other is the soul. The subject on which I am going to speak is simply the continuation or complement of the one I spoke on last time, when I endeavoured to show how the unfortunate mania that is driving our educated young people almost *en masse* towards the so-called liberal professions was sapping our strength and providing legitimate grounds for alarm regarding our political and national existence, inasmuch as all the intellectual energy of our race was draining away, from generation to generation, in the unprofitable struggles of an overcrowded arena.

If, through your kind recommendation, this idea had made some impression, and induced some of our educated young men to enter the broad and fruitful paths of industry, we would have done no more than lay the foundations for our work; it would still remain to build and consolidate the edifice of our national power. We would indeed have many excellent candidates for agriculture, commerce, and all other branches of industry, and hence a means of attracting wealth and spreading it amongst us; in short, we would have all the components of the social power and influence that should be ours. But these great concerns that we have just created must be preserved and augmented; they must keep abreast of rival interests, in our own midst as well as beyond our borders, within as well as without. But more—they must be advanced, protected against the prejudices, the biases, the false and mistaken ideas that have come down to us from the days when the principles of the science that governs all these important social interests were unknown. Now gentlemen, this we cannot do unless we have amongst us men steeped in the study of political economy and in the enlightened application of the principles it teaches. And this science is a new one everywhere: since it was only in 1776 that it appeared for the first time, as a complete body of doctrine, in England, in Dr Smith's *Wealth of Nations*; and in France only in 1803, in Jean-Baptiste Say's *Traité d'économie politique*. In 1785 Quesnay did publish the work entitled 'Tableau économique et maximes générales du gouvernement économique'—under the influence of which the school of economists or physiocrats was formed in France. McCulloch, a distinguished economist of our time, even credits Quesnay with being the first to give a systemic form to political economy, raising it to the rank of a science, and he acknowledges that the works of the French economists have helped significantly to accelerate the development of economic science. But their theory founded on the axiom that 'land is the only source of wealth' has been rejected by more modern economists. Today, therefore, for the oracles of this science we look back no further than to Smith in England and Say in France. However, we must do Italy the justice of recognizing her initiative in political economy; for as early as the sixteenth century Botero was concerned with this science, and several other Italian writers followed his path.

It would therefore be surprising if a science as new and as vast as political economy—and one that, judging by the complaints and remonstrances of those who have written about it, still has few adepts even in Europe, the cradle, storehouse, and dispensary of all the sciences—it would be surprising if this science were widespread in a young country like our own, which in order to arrive where it is, has had to go through so many trials of so many different kinds. Thus it must be confessed that, for reasons of which we will speak in the course of this lecture, our knowledge and experience with regard to political economy are very limited, especially in the most important branches of the science, those dealing with finances, commerce, and related subjects. Moreover, gentlemen, we must make this confession at a time and under circumstances in which our need for deep knowledge of this little-known science has never been so pressing or vital: no doubt many others have had similar thoughts before me. So what is to be done? Lose hope, leave it to our neighbours to look out for our interests, to state and to discuss the great economic questions that are going to arrive all at once before the parliamentary tribunal? No, indeed! the children, the nephews of the men who always made sure that Lower Canada marched at the head of the colonial troops in the long struggle for political liberty will know how to keep their race in the same position in the discussions about to take place on the field of material interests. We managed to find Burkes and Mirabeaus when we needed them, and now that we need Cobdens and Peels we will be able to find them too. We will find them among our fair youth, aflame with patriotism, hungry for useful knowledge, inspired to noble emulation. We will see them disdain frivolities, reading simply for pleasure, even useful studies that are less urgent, in order to devote themselves entirely to the great study of the day, the study imperiously demanded not only by the interest of our province, but by that of our nation and of each of the individuals of which it is composed.

It is with ever-increasing pleasure that I see appearing in the columns of the *Revue canadienne* the excellent and useful articles written by one of our compatriots[1] to initiate Canadian readers into the truths and mysteries of political economy: this work should earn its author the gratitude of his compatriots. My only regret is that publication of this work is not proceeding swiftly enough, at a pace equal to the pressing demands of the situation. I am also sorry that none of our Canadian newspapers are reprinting these articles or devoting part of their space to analyses of or extracts from good works on political economy. Such material, in my humble opinion, would be just as valuable as the more or less frivolous novels and stories that fill their pages. A population like ours, situated as ours is, needs useful and instructive reading material. And since the periodical has become the book of the people, practically the only means they have of clarifying their material interests, is it not deplorable to see our press filled with snippets of light literature, fodder for the lazy and jaded minds of a civilization that has had its day? What good can a population like ours derive from the work of these European scribblers, a population with forests to clear, fields to improve, manufacturing of all kinds to establish, improvements of all kinds to accomplish; one, in short, whose mission it is to make of its heritage on the North American continent what the English and French have made of England and France, and what our neighbours are now doing so well on this same American continent? Admit it, journalists, you will not help us to accomplish this great work of civilization with the thin trash of European serials. Quite the contrary, these impressive productions, sparkling with wit and erudite style, decked out in all the charms of the imagination, will only intoxicate us and halt us by the wayside, like the sirens in the fable whose enchanting voices paralysed the imprudent traveller who ventured too near their retreat.

Indeed, by filling themselves with this ephemeral literature, our papers cannot help but inspire a taste for it: it is the rage of the salons, sometimes even going so far as to overshadow the marriage column. It is the same with any-thing—*vires acquirit eundo*; appetite comes with eating. Soon the papers will no longer be enough for the readers' appetites; they will have to go to the bookstore to find satisfaction. And all the leisure of our youth, if not a more precious time, will be taken up with reading of the kind that sweeps the imagination away in exaltation, and leaves the mind empty and starving. When we open our papers to look for some examples of native literature, what do we usually find (apart from local quarrels)?—attempts to imitate French fiction; sweet nothings, sometimes quite prettily turned out, in the French fashion; just what is required for social success, but also just what is required to make the thoughtful man, who feels the needs of his country and his race, lament the abuse, the waste of fine talents and of time that is precious for authors and readers alike.

Journalists, join together to repair the damage you have done. Make our educated youth understand, in their own interest as much as in the interest of the country, that the time for light literature has not yet arrived in Canada, and that it will not for some time to come; and that at the risk of both individual and national ruin, we must devote ourselves entirely and exclusively to serious studies, instructive reading, and heavy mental exercise. Europe is old and rich—its people are free to abandon themselves to works of imagination; in them they find fortune, often even fame, at least for their lifetime. Then too, Europe has such an abundance of enlightened men in all the sciences that there are enough for all society's needs; so that in embracing the career of imagination, the European can be assured that he is not leaving any social interest to suffer; on the contrary, he is in the order of things, for he is simply putting the finishing touches on a civilization that has reached its apogee. But is this the case in our country, here where we are still laying the foundations? What we need are labourers; the time for painters and sculptors will come later. What young Canadian, therefore, picking up a popular novel to read, can lay his hand on his heart and honestly swear to himself that he knows of no more useful way to spend his time, both for himself and for his country? Indeed, what will it teach him? What will he find in it—moral lessons, perhaps? His catechism has already told him all that there is to know on that subject, and a good deal better than Eugène Sue or Alexandre Dumas can. Descriptions of manners and morals? When a true picture is presented, it will refer to a state of society so different from our own that in practice it can only set him on the wrong track, and that would be a great pity. But most often he will simply be transported into a fantasy world, where everything is so exaggerated, over-done and caricatured, that even a European reader would not recognize himself.

There is thus nothing useful to be gained from reading current fiction except relaxation from serious, instructive reading. Yes; but challenge me if you dare, young readers, I will maintain—and call on your conscience to witness—that this reading is work for you; tiring work, in fact, which takes up all your days and nights; that once you have started a novel you cannot stop reading until you have found out how it ends—or sleep closes your eyes and the book falls from your hands. I have seen people start a book and go on reading right through a meal. Is that relaxation? And tell me how many times that has happened with your Domat, your de Lolme, your Jean-Baptiste Say? What am I talking about, your Jean-Baptiste Say? Shall I tell you a little story about that celebrated author of the best treatise on political economy ever to appear in French, if not in any language? The story is true, and I was present when it took place.

Recently, then, I was in a bookstore in this city [Montreal], the capital of Canada, seat of the representative government, when someone asked to purchase Say's *Traité*, assuming it to be one of those works that one should find in any bookstore, especially in a country with a representative government. At first the bookseller seemed not to have understood, then he recovered. 'Ah!' said he, 'you mean M. Say's treatise on political economy? We do not have it.' 'Well, when will you have it?' asked the customer. 'The fault is mine for waiting so long. You must sell a great many copies, of course; it must be hard to keep stock on your shelves.' 'I beg your pardon,' replied the bookseller, 'but that book does not sell; we only get it in on special order.'

The shelves were well-stocked, on the other hand, with all the fashionable novelists. No special orders for them; they sell.

I shall not describe the astonishment of our political-economy man, to learn that a work that should be in the hands of every educated man, young or old, the essential *vade mecum* of anyone wishing to take part in the public affairs of his country, is a work that does not sell.

Until then, for reasons I will explain in a moment, I had thought that the study of political economy must necessarily have been seriously neglected here; but I am forced to admit that I did not think the neglect was as serious as the anecdote I have just told you reveals. And I will confess that since then I have more than once considered taking advantage of the first available opportunity to disturb, as much as it is in my feeble power to do so, the extreme indifference that until now seems to have prevailed here regarding the study of political economy. Under your auspices, gentlemen, that is what I am attempting to do today; and I hope that your patronage and sanction will give my words an authority I could [not] give them myself.

If I had a studious young friend endowed with all the right talents, brimming with the enthusiasm and noble aspirations that lead to great things, who had both the desire and the means to devote himself to the happiness of his compatriots in a political career, all the while working for his own individual honour and advantage, and if he asked me what above all he should choose to study, I think I would parody the answer they attribute to the celebrated Marshal Saxe, when asked what was required to wage a successful war. I would tell my young friend to study, first, political economy; second, political economy; and third, political economy. Marshal Saxe said that to wage war successfully one needed, first, money; second, money; and third, money. That was the most effective way he could find of saying that with money you can do anything in war, and that without money you can do nothing. Similarly, I believe that, having carefully considered the position and circumstances in which we find ourselves, each of us will agree that a man or a political party can do anything in this country with a solid understanding of political economy, and that without it neither can do anything worthwhile.

The day is past when to maintain the struggle with honour or advantage, it was enough for our public figures to have courage, devotion, eloquence, and a broad understanding of natural, political, and constitutional law. The day is past, furthermore, when by our numbers alone we could hold off the social and political forces opposed to us in a struggle over the very principles of government. Our governmental machine is now properly organized; that is, the principles that should regulate its operation have been agreed upon and recognized—which is not to say that all is well in the current political arrangement. But as far as the government itself is concerned, no further theoretic or organizational questions are likely to arise; given its present organization, it should function in harmony with the will of the people as expressed through their representatives. Everyone is agreed on this point. But the struggle is not over; in fact it will never end, under our system of government; only the battleground has changed. From elevated governmental theories it has come down to questions of material interest, which for the mass of people are often more important. For half a century we have fought over the form that our common dwelling should have; and now that that point is settled, each one will endeavour to occupy the best place in it he can. The thousand and one different interests that make up society will set to work to make each individual position better and better, or less and less bad. And the talents and knowledge required for this new struggle will be no less than those required in the past; they will simply have to be of a different order, in some respects, from those required for the previous struggle. And we must hasten to acquire them, for in the new arena as in the old—even more so, perhaps—victory will go to the most clever; again, as much and more than before, we must be doubly right, and doubly capable of proving it. Thus has the Providence willed that put us in this corner of the globe, to live in the midst of foreign peoples from whom we cannot expect much sympathy. Let us not grumble, however; for who can plumb the secrets of Providence? Who can say that Providence does not have great plans for us, that the trials to which we are subject in adolescence are not preparing our manhood for a glorious future on this continent? For the rest, whatever fate the future has in store for us, if it is good, let us make ourselves worthy of it; and if it is bad, let us ensure that we have not deserved it; such is the duty of every generation, and of each individual. We will fulfil this duty if we keep alive in our hearts the sacred flame of noble emulation to sustain us in all things and at all times on a level equal to that of the peoples around us.

Now, these people come from a race of men that appear to have undertaken the conquest and renewal of the world by material interest. Their god is *Plutus*; their children are born and live their lives only for gain; for them the only dreams are dreams of fortune, quick and colossal fortune; no *aurea mediocritas* [golden mean] for them. And in the service of this passion they put all the ardour, energy, constancy, and persistence that men ordinarily devote to the pursuit of the most lively and insatiable passions.

This is no satire that I am presenting; on the contrary, I am merely pointing out a fact that seems to me providential; and I am led to believe that this avidity for gain in the Anglo-Saxon race—an avidity, we might note in passing, that has only increased in the American branch of the race—is destined to form a link in the historical chain of humanity, an age of industry, of material improvement, the age of positivism, the age of the glorification of labour. Without the persistent, unceasing work of the industrious nations, the world would enjoy far fewer material and intellectual pleasures than it does. Far from envying them, therefore, we owe them a debt of gratitude. If we are not to let ourselves be overrun, absorbed, and crushed by them, let us do as they do; work as they do, with ardour, intelligence, and constancy. In earlier times the slack, stupid nations were prey to the warriors; now the indolent and ignorant peoples will be exploited by the industrious and intelligent ones. That is the law of humanity; or rather, the law of all creation applied to humanity and tempered, if you will, among humans by the religion that is capable of counteracting the egoism of human inclinations with the sublime precept of universal charity, and the sway of temporal interests with the consideration of eternal wealth.

But avidity for gain, an excess of acquisitiveness, as the phrenologists would say, must often lead one to be less than scrupulous, or to blind oneself to the means used to satisfy it. For this reason, those who must discuss common interests with people so inclined must be able to put forward the arguments and considerations best suited to make an impression on them and command their respect. The most eloquent speech delivered by a Demosthenes, a Burke, a Mirabeau, would be no more to them than a futile waste of rhetoric if it did not touch the chord of material interests, and did not rest on the recognized principles of the science that deals specifically with those interests: only for these do they have eyes and ears. Even in the case of a patent injustice, you will have to be able to show that it is detrimental to general interests; which, fortunately, you will always be able to do with the aid of political economy, for it will enable you to show that the whole social body must necessarily suffer the afflictions of any one of its members. 'For', as Say puts it, 'a people who steal from one another will soon have no one left to rob.'

I said earlier that the study of political economy had become more indispensable to us than ever before. We held our own in the solution of the questions of governmental theory that formerly absorbed the attention of all parties in this country. But with these settled, attention will turn to measures or questions concerning material interests, and on this new terrain we are going to meet adversaries, or if you wish, competitors, better prepared than ourselves. It is necessary that we prepare ourselves for this at the risk of losing all influence, and thus perhaps all advantage, in the settlement of these new questions.

No doubt you recall the remark made by one of our young representatives in the last session, regarding the senior members' silence on certain important commercial and financial measures. If that gentleman merely wanted to express his regret, let us hope that he and the rest of his generation will not give their successors cause to express the same regret in regard to them. If he meant to reproach the public figures who have gone before him, I must tell you that that reproach is unjust.

In speaking a moment ago of the sharp and uninterrupted political struggle that lasted until 1840, and that resulted in our current governmental arrangements, I think I have said enough to suggest that until the present time it was hardly possible for our public figures to devote themselves to lengthy and sustained studies in political economy. Since [17]91, I would tell the new generation, your predecessors have had to fight for political liberty, for the practical consequences of the representative government that until very recently existed only in name. They created, developed, and organized the power of the people, gaining for them the degree of influence and participation in government they enjoy today: a degree of participation and influence that, compared to what they were in the old order of things, constitutes a genuine revolution in our political condition. This, you realize, is the fruit of hard, ceaseless effort, which must have exhausted all the moral and intellectual energy your elders had to give. How then could one of them have devoted himself to the study of a science that requires a great deal of time, and still more tranquillity of spirit, if it is to be studied in depth? Even had they been able to steal the time for study from the ordinary occupations of daily life, the state would have lacked the tranquillity that must exist before one can apply the truths this science teaches. Besides, the field of the economist was far more restricted at that time, when the mother country still kept control of our commerce: yet another reason, another excuse, for our elders not to have been particularly concerned with studies in economics.

No reproaches therefore, gentlemen of the younger generation; be lenient, be fair. Thanks to the long hard work of your elders, you have reached the promised land; they have done their part; now it is up to you to do yours. They sacrificed their time, energy, and intelligence to this great conquest—now it is up to you to make it worthwhile. They had to be tribunes; you must be statesmen, enlightened economists. In this way you will enter the arena with the right armour, and will not be at a disadvantage in the struggle with competitors who, as I noted earlier, are at present better prepared than we—there would be foolish pride, even danger, in not recognizing this fact. The first condition, the surest guarantee of success in any situation in which one finds oneself is to know and appreciate the forces of one's adversary.

The superiority of your competitors in matters of political economy is easily explained. Do they not belong to the most industrious, most mercantile race of men in the world? This has led a distinguished economist of our day to remark that 'England is the birthplace of political economy.'* The English, a nation of merchants and manufacturers, must quite naturally have been led to study and observe more closely than others the formation, distribution, and consumption of wealth, the phenomena that constitute the subject of political economy. Without a solid study of this science, from books as much as from observation and reflection, England would never have attained the degree of wealth and power she has. One important proof of the English nation's broad, healthy economic understanding is the resounding triumph recently scored by the principle of free trade over the principle of restriction, prohibition, or protection.† The interests opposed to this measure were so powerful that what Sir Robert Peel did astonished the world; yielding heroically to the voice of public opinion as much as to honest conviction, this great man, a new Samson, had to bury himself as a political leader under the ruins of the shattered monopoly. But the [repeal of the] Corn Laws made a glorious shroud; and should Sir Robert Peel never recover from his recent fall, he has done enough for his fame in assuring the victory of a beneficent principle whose consequences for the whole of humanity are incalculable. Is it not evident that the old prohibitive and protectionist system had the effect of turning every people against every other and made them see one another as enemies, each seeking the other's ruin? The new system, on the contrary, will tend to give all peoples an interest in one another's prosperity, and thus eliminate the cause of the ruinous wars so frequently and foolishly undertaken for supposed commercial interests, which existed only in the erroneous theories of the time. Certainly, if there is one thing that should aid in the realization of the universal peace dreamt of by the good Abbé de St Pierre°—that dream someone once called the dream of an honest man—it is the universal free trade toward which Sir Robert Peel's [repeal of the] Corn Laws [is] the first step—first but decisive, one of those steps, like Atlas's, that will shake and affect the whole world.

Now, gentlemen, this great commercial revolution that the bells of Westminster have just announced has opened a path that we will be the first to enter. By withdrawing the protection she used to extend to our products, our mother country will give us the right to withdraw on our own part the protection she used to ensure for her own products in our market; at the same time she will open all the markets in the world to us and allow the whole world to come here. In short, we ourselves will have to regulate our commercial relations with the world in our own interests; take over a responsibility that until now the metropolis reserved for itself and exercised in the interests of the empire. (There is no need for me to discuss a few points of restriction that apparently have not yet been settled, which will no doubt be the subject of negotiations between the mother country and the colony.) This is an occupation as serious as it is novel for our public figures, which is going to require considerable knowledge of political economy to protect us from the consequences of blunders, which are all the more to be feared in that our first steps may determine the future of our country in more than one respect. We are now about to sow our social body with the seeds of either wretchedness or prosperity, of life or of death; we are going to have to debate not only our regional and class interests, but to settle our provincial interests with foreign peoples. And surely our race will feel it is to its advantage as well as its honour to bring to the discussion of these important issues as much enlightenment, knowledge, and experience as we have always been able to provide in public discussions. And this, once again, we cannot do except through serious studies in political economy. On this point, shall I quote you a passage from the *Discourse* on political economy by Professor McCulloch?

> It is a profound and intimate, not a superficial and general, knowledge of the just principles and conclusions of economical science, that can alone enable the statesman to appreciate the bearings and effect of different institutions and measures, and consequently to adopt those that are most for the national advantage. A person may be able to declaim with spirit and eloquence on the advantages of free trade, and unrestricted competition in all the departments of industry, and yet be miserably ignorant of many fundamental and most important principles. It is a vulgar error to suppose that these principles all lie on the surface: many of them eluded the observation of Quesnay and Smith; and these, we may be assured, are not to be understood without serious study and patient attention.*

Elsewhere he reveals the danger of legislators' ignorance in matters of political economy:

> In financial and commercial legislation, it is impossible to make a single false step,—to impose a single injudicious tax or restriction,—without materially affecting the interests of every individual, and actually endangering the subsistence of many families. Rectitude of intention affords no security against error; and measures intended to hasten the progress of improvement will, if not founded on sound principles, prove productive only of disaster and disgrace.†

Now gentlemen, would you not agree with me that a legislator should approach questions of political economy only in fear and trembling? Would you not agree with me that those able to do so, who neglect the means that would enable them to speak with some knowledge of the subject, bear an immense responsibility? But do not think that this responsibility weighs only on those directly involved in legislation. The study of political economy is necessary and hence obligatory for all of us. On this point, let us listen to Say, in his preliminary discourse: 'For a long time,' he writes, 'it was believed that political economy was a matter only for the handful of men who direct the affairs of state. I know that it is important that the men elevated to power be more enlightened than the rest; I know that the mistakes of private individuals can never ruin more than a handful of families, whereas those of princes and ministers spread desolation throughout an entire country. But can princes and ministers be enlightened when private individuals are not? In countries with the good fortune to have a representative government, each citizen has an even stronger obligation to teach himself the principles of political economy, since each is called upon to deliberate on the affairs of state. Finally,' Say goes on, 'supposing that all those who participate in government, in whatever degree, could be competent without the nation being so—which is quite unlikely—would their best plans not meet with tremendous resistance? Would they not encounter obstacles in the prejudices even of those most favourably inclined towards their operations? In order for a nation to enjoy a sound economic system, it is not enough for the leaders to be capable of adopting the best plans; in addition, the nation must be capable of accepting them.'*

It would be as easy to multiply the quotations on this point as it is to find examples in the history of societies that support what we have just read. I will cite you one notable example, which leaves nothing to be desired. In 1773, Sir Robert Walpole proposed a financial plan intended to introduce the bonding system, which would have made London the biggest market in the world—which today it in fact is. Unfortunately, the science of economics was then still in its infancy in England as well as the rest of Europe; the English nation was not yet ready for its minister's plan, admirable though it was; the mere proposal nearly turned the country upside-down, and it was with great celebrations that the people welcomed the abandonment of the measure. And such was the strength of the prejudice that it was not until 1803, thirty years later, that the bonding system could be safely adopted—'perhaps the greatest improvement,' McCulloch says, 'ever made in a country's financial and commercial policy.'†

Ignorance and prejudice in matters of political economy not only cause good legislative measures to be rejected; they also cause bad ones to be imposed.

Anyone studying political economy for the first time is astonished to discover the monstrous errors, drawn to his attention on every page, that have been made by the most advanced nations and the most enlightened men. You will find Egypt compelling children to follow their father's trades, as if nature necessarily gave men the aptitudes required for the station in which they were born; not to mention the danger of overcrowding certain industries and leaving others without enough workers, according to the varying needs of society. You will find certain states in ancient Greece absolutely forbidding their citizens—

who roughly corresponded to today's noblemen—to engage in any kind of industry. In Rome this law presented itself in the form of a prejudice, but it was one so deeply entrenched that Cicero himself, for all his philosophy, could not avoid it. In his view retail trade was sordid and dishonourable, and the best he could say for high commerce was that it was not altogether so contemptible— *nonadmodum vituperanda*. Given such notions, Greece and Rome could never have existed without slavery. Among modern nations, you will see Spain falling prey to the misconception that gold and silver are the only source of wealth, a misconception formerly so common that all the states in Europe passed laws prohibiting the export of these metals—reasoning on a par with that of the miser who starves to death sitting on his treasure. The operations of the famous East India Company in England were long hampered for this reason, and it was only after sixty-three years of discussion that it obtained, both for itself and for private trade, full and complete freedom in this regard. Which means that for sixty-three years England rejected a measure that in the end helped as much and more than anything else to gain it two million subjects in Asia. Finally, to cite a few famous modern names, we find Montesquieu and Voltaire commending luxury as a blessing, almost a virtue. Louis XIV used to say that a king gave alms by spending lavishly, but some sixty years later the people of Paris began a terrible revolution by demanding bread. Another monarch closer to us than that great king, Frederick II—also known as the Great—found war an admirable way of distributing among the provinces the subsidies with which the people supplied the government. Surely, however, the people would have been better off had they been allowed to keep the subsidies.

Let us end these examples, chosen from among thousands of others in foreign lands, with a very recent one drawn from our own country. A fairly remarkable example is what we call the agriculture protection act,* which has not protected agriculture in any way whatsoever; for if we examine the accounts presented to Parliament in the last session, we see that in the previous year this act produced £1,587 in claims, which when divided among the masses of Canadian producers comes to nothing apiece. Thus our producers have not enjoyed any protection, and the act has cost several times £1,500 to implement. But even if it had put a considerable sum in the farmer's pocket in the first place, the act would have meant a proportionate increase in the cost of living for all groups that do not produce agricultural products; and these groups would have been forced to charge more for their services; thus either the farmer would be giving away with one hand what he had taken with the other; or else protection would have attracted labour and capital towards agriculture, and the competition would have swiftly reduced prices to their natural level. But when prices are below this natural level—then by virtue of the same law, labour and capital go elsewhere, and since the competition is less, prices necessarily rise. Thus it is one of the fundamental principles of political economy that protection is an absurd and disastrous system, except perhaps in certain very special cases, when it is a question of assisting the development of a new industry—provided it is suited to the country's soil, climate, and situation—or of cushioning the decline of an old industry that has ceased to enjoy those same conditions. Then it is a temporary tax that society as a whole imposes on itself to strengthen a growing industry and hasten the moment when it will be able to sustain itself. Likewise in the second case, society comes to the aid of a declining industry, not to bring it back to life, but to prevent the ruin of thousands of families, and allow time for the capital and labour committed to it to be diverted into more favourable areas.

But I will stop now, for I suspect that I am getting away from my thesis, and your patience must be nearly exhausted even if my subject is not. In fact, among my notes I find some pertaining to two subjects that are closely linked to political economy; I will simply mention them in passing. One is the introduction in college programmes of the elements of political economy; the other is the establishment in this country of chairs of political economy such as have been established in other countries where the need has been less than it is here. I believe that the college of St-Hyacinthe, which under its current professors has gained such an eminent rank among our institutions of higher learning, has begun to take an interest in political economy; if so, that institution will have earned itself the credit of being the first to recognize an important and pressing social need. Let us urge it to pursue this useful endeavour, and let us urge the rest of our colleges to follow its example. Let us also urge our legislators to provide our young students with the means of perfecting their studies in this science that they have begun in our colleges. Everyone knows that teachers save the student considerable time and effort; they show him the direction to follow, point out the shoals, smooth over the obstacles, keep him from going astray. In a young country like ours, where the division of labour has not reached the point it has in older ones, there is so much to be learned that one could never save students too much time. And there could be no more profitable use of the money that would be spent to this end. A few hundred louis a year voted to establish chairs of political economy, over a certain period, would be worth hundreds of thousands to the province, whether in losses avoided or in gains brought about by the spread of economic knowledge.

Before leaving you, allow me to address a word of encouragement to this fine Canadian youth whose élite I see crowded around this rostrum. Youth is the time of strong and pure patriotic virtues. At your age considerations of personal interest do not freeze the impulses of the heart, nor do wrongful passions, excited by prolonged political struggles, mislead or obscure the judgement. Oh, how powerful youth would be, with all its superabundance of strength and vitality, were experience not the fruit of long years of apprenticeship. Well, you can hasten the acquisition of that experience prodigiously through study; books—good books—are the depositary of the experience of the past centuries. There in a very short time you find the means to become fathers of your country, your brothers' protectors, apostles of progress. I see your eyes light up at the word *country*, I hear your hearts beating at the word *brothers*; your imaginations catch fire at the word *progress*. Do you want to ensure that your youthful aspirations will not prove fruitless and vain? Then hasten to master the science that deals with the wealth of nations. Thereby you will give our work, the source of all our wealth, the right direction, and at the same time you will assure us of all the profit we are entitled to expect from our labour. Man comes to life and delights in his work when he receives proper recompense for it. As for myself, I have never understood the notion that God could have imposed work on man as a punishment, although I believe I understand how our artificial societies, more or less tainted with privilege and monopolies, have managed to make one of the All-Powerful's most admirable decrees resemble a punishment. Does work not bring man closer to God, by making him a creator himself? Did not God himself labour for six days and rest on the seventh? And in creating matter and leaving men responsible for giving, or creating, its value, or utility, does God not appear to have called on man to complete the task he started, to have made man in a way his associate in his six days' labour? Oh, gentlemen, such an association is worth all the noble titles passed down through generations of do-nothings. The worker, the industrious man, would be very mistaken to feel ashamed of his station; he alone truly fulfils the design of the Creator. All he needs is that he reap the fruit of his labour: this fruit is wealth and well-being; and for man well-being is progress and development [*le perfectionnement*].

Thus, gentlemen, you see that the science of political economy, which presides over wealth, is the science of progress *par excellence*. Let the truths it teaches be well understood, well applied, and the sad moralists weeping today over the wretchedness of man, who indeed appears to be suffering under the blows of a divine condemnation, will perhaps find that the creator has in the end destined the king of creation for a quite royal fate, and that God deserves from us not endless lamentations, but endless thanks. Why would we, as it were, reproach God for the ills that seem to attach to humanity, when he has given us all the means required to be happy? It is also true that he created us free to use his gifts for good or for ill. But how could he have done otherwise, without creating us either angels or brutes? Let us therefore endeavour to use our freedom well. Let us work with a good heart, as it is the nature of intelligent creatures to do; but let us at the same time learn to leave each man the fruit of his labour; for if we do not we will cover the earth with misery and desolation. As under most of our current social systems, you may well have privileged classes who will get fat at the expense of the exploited masses; but this wrongly acquired gain, you may be sure, serves only to fuel searing worries in these people—and perhaps gnawing remorse, as they wait for God's justice to pass over entire generations. This is what the history of past times teaches us, and political economy, by explaining how it happens, teaches us to prevent it. Yes, gentlemen, political economy can do even that. Its proofs support the precepts of the most wholesome morality and make us see that to give or leave to each man what belongs to him, is the surest way for nations to attain prosperity and happiness, just as it is for individuals the surest way of achieving a better world.

AUTHOR'S NOTE

[1] M. Amédée Papineau.

JOSEPH HOWE

The most famous of the Reformers was Joseph Howe (1804-73), 'the tribune of Nova Scotia'. As a journalist and member of the House of Assembly he led the struggle for responsible government and was victorious, without bloodshed, in February 1848. His four public letters to Lord John Russell, published in 1839, are the classic colonial statement of the case for self-government.

The selection below shows a less familiar side of Howe. For most Canadians today it takes some effort to understand that Nova Scotia was once a separate country that did not want to be part of Confederation. It had a different, perhaps grander, vision than that of a new Dominion, a mari usque ad mare. It dreamed of ruling the seas—of linking arms across the seas with Great Britain and the other maritime colonies to rule the world, rather than across a thousand miles of barren or French and Catholic land to join with those perplexing strangers, the English of Upper Canada. Nova Scotia's greatest dreamer was Joseph Howe. His pamphlet on the Empire, published in London in 1866, shows his sense of power.

The Organization of the Empire

Under the Providence of God, after centuries of laborious cultivation, the sacrifice of much heroic blood, and the expenditure of a vast amount of treasure, the British Empire, as it stands, has been got together, and the question which is presented to us, in some form of parliamentary or newspaper disputation almost every week, is, what is now to be done with it?

Two opinions appear to prevail. A great many persons are content to drift on without forethought or statesmanlike provision for the future, but others hold that it is the duty of the parent state to prepare the outlying provinces for independence—to so group and organize as to inspire them, at the earliest possible period, with the ambition and the desire to dissolve the national connection and set up for themselves.* They think that Great Britain, regardless of her own interests, should be content with the glory of founding, peopling and setting great provinces adrift; that they will prosper by the separation, and that she will share their prosperity and be secure of a moral and political influence, without care or cost, in proportion to the liberality of her conduct and to the sacrifices she has made. This party is reinforced from time to time by those who take a lower and more sordid view of the question—who think that Great Britain would hardly want an army or a navy, arsenals or dockyards, if she had no colonies; who charge them with sums borne on the estimates, but never credit them with their consumption, or with the sacrifices they make to defend the interests and to uphold the dignity of the empire. The parental relation is assumed to sanction this policy. Young men grow, and, when they are of age, marry and set up for themselves, and why should not the colonies do the same? But the analogy is not perfect. One house would not hold all the married members of a large family, nor one estate maintain them. They scatter that they may live. They are kept in friendship by the domestic affections and personal ties which, in respect of distant communities, do not exist, and at the death of the founder of the family there is an estate to divide.

Not so with colonies. Their life begins at a distance from the homestead. There are few personal attachments. There is no estate to divide and no security that when they separate they may not drift into antagonism to each other and to the parent country. The policy then of rearing them with the thought of separation ever in their minds, of prematurely preparing them for separation, or of rudely casting them off, appears to me an unsound policy. The idea to be cultivated, instead of that of the parental relation, with its inevitable termination at the close of a very limited period, should rather be that of a partnership, which may last for centuries, and need not terminate at all, so long as it is mutually advantageous.

That colonies have the right to break away and set up for themselves, if they are oppressed, will not at the present day be denied. That they will do this, if kindly and fairly dealt by, I hold to be at least 'not proven'. I would act as though it could not be proved. I would discountenance the idea of separation. I would have faith in the future—in our common brotherhood (which ought to count for something) even less than in the conviction, founded on our daily experience, that it is our interest to keep together.

It is sometimes thought that the empire was weakened by conceding to the colonies the system of responsible government. The very reverse is true. They would inevitably have been dispersed sooner or later, had it not been conceded. This was a great conservative measure, as well as a substantial reform. . . .

England has not been weakened by those municipal and parochial organizations which assume and exercise authority within certain well-defined limits, and do a vast amount of valuable work which the general government could never overtake, or do so well if it could; nor will the empire be weakened by throwing upon the provincial legislatures and colonial municipalities all the responsibilities and labour of government that do not conflict with the general laws and regulations which can only be wisely framed and administered by some central authority. This division of labour is now universally recognized and appreciated, and if all the outlying possessions of the Crown were peopled with English-speaking inhabitants, capable of self-government, the system might be extended to every part of the empire. The presence of a foreign population, as in India and elsewhere, will for a long time make it doubtful to what extent political franchises can be conferred, but I can hardly imagine any state of society in which the people might not be gradually trained to the exercise of municipal privileges with great advantage. Assuming then that the powers conferred upon the English-speaking colonies leave them, as respects domestic administration, nothing to desire; and that, as regards Crown colonies and foreign possessions and dependencies, our present system, subject to modifications from time to time, is the best that can be devised, it is apparent that but for external pressure, and danger from without, we might go on as we are without any material change. The Maori question in New Zealand, the land question in Prince Edward Island,* and the 'tacking' question in Melbourne, are but ripples on the surface of the general tranquillity, and may soon be set right by a little firmness and discretion. As a general rule we may rest upon the assurance that the outlying portions of the empire are prosperous and contented;

and if peace could be maintained, the people of England, annually enlarging their trade and reducing their taxation, might be content to keep up, as they have hitherto done, the ordinary armaments necessary for national police, and the security of the seas, without calling upon the colonies to aid them.

But we have no security for peace, or if there be any, it is only to be sought in such an organization and armament of the whole empire as will make the certainty of defeat a foregone conclusion to any foreign power that may attempt to break it.

This conviction was forced upon my mind, while endeavouring, under instructions from Her Majesty's Government in 1855, to draw a few thousand soldiers from the United States, while not a man was moved of the millions that we had to spare, in every quarter of the globe, to reinforce, it might have been to save, the gallant little army fighting and perishing before Sebastopol. This subject has occupied many a leisure hour since, and I have never dwelt upon it without feeling that the question of questions for us all, far transcending in importance any other within the range of domestic or foreign politics, is, not how the empire can be most easily dismembered, not how a province or two can be strengthened by a fort, or by the expenditure of a million of dollars, but how the whole empire can be so organized and strengthened as to command peace or be impregnable in war.

Many people have, since 1855, been driven to think of this question. Passing over all the second- and third-rate powers, which possess no navies and whose armies may always be neutralized by being balanced or broken against each other by skilful diplomacy, France, Russia and the United States grow with our growth, and loom up before the mind of every thoughtful British subject, as standing menaces, warning him to prepare for any eventuality.

Prussia is now coming forward as a fourth great power, and will presently control an extensive sea-board, behind which there will be a warlike population of twenty or thirty millions. In estimating her influence as well as her strength, it may be wise to remember that the German emigration to the United States has been as extensive as the Irish, that Germans swarm in the sea-board cities and in the western States, that Frankfort was the chief mart for national securities during the civil war, and that the sympathy between the great republic and the fatherland is an element too apparent to be overlooked by diplomatists in any prudent calculation of forces.

A very distinguished person said, at the outbreak of the Crimean war, that our free institutions were about to be put upon their trial. Our free institutions were really in no danger; what was upon its trial was the mode in which we organize the physical force of the empire, and that, as we have all since been compelled to acknowledge, was found to be sadly defective.

Combined with France, we could only bring Russia to terms with half the fortresses in the Crimea frowning defiance at us; but the question naturally arises, what would we do were France and Russia combined against us? or should that combination so familiar to the American mind be formed between the fleets and armies of Russia and the United States for the humiliation of England. With France as an ally we might still have nothing to fear, but we ought to have something more secure to rely upon than the eccentricities of French politics or the life of a single man. . . .

Now I would lift this question above the range of doubt or apprehension, and prepare for all eventualities, by such an organization of the empire as would enable the Sovereign to command its entire physical force. If Russia, France or the United States is involved in war to-morrow, the revenue and the manhood of the whole territory are at the disposal of the Executive; while, if we go to war, the whole burthen of sustaining it falls upon the people of these two small islands. This is not fair, and, what is worse, our unprepared condition makes war at all times possible, sometimes imminent.

But, it may be asked, suppose this thing to be desirable, how is it to be done? And I answer, as all other good things are done in this free country, by propounding the policy, by discussion and argument, to be followed, when the public sentiment is prepared for it, by wise legislation.

I foresee the difficulties: in this as in all other cases there is a certain amount of indifference, of ignorance and of selfishness, to be overcome, but I rely upon the general intelligence of the empire to perceive the want, and upon its patriotism and public spirit to supply it. Surely if a Russian serf can be got to march from Siberia to the Crimea to defend his empire, the Queen's subjects can be educated to know and feel that it is alike their duty and their interest to march anywhere to defend their own.

The young men of Maine and Massachusetts rushed to protect their capital from rebellious fellow-citizens, and I am sure, when once the possibility of a requisition is made familiar to the colonial mind, that the youths in our outlying provinces would rush as eagerly to defend London from a foreign foe. But it may be said the Russian obeys a central authority that it would be vain to dispute, and that the American fights for his perfect citizenship, which includes the control of his foreign policy and representation in the national council. This is the weak point in our case, but let us see if it cannot be met by such reasonable concessions and appeals to the good sense of our people as suit their practical turn of thought, and would give to the colonies prepared for it a direct influence in the national councils, without disorganizing the political machinery already working so well.

The House of Commons, whatever may be its defects, enjoys the respect of the empire, and I assume that, whatever may come hereafter, nobody wishes to see its composition and character very materially changed. How far representation in Parliament can be safely conceded to the outlying portions of the empire, by what modes these members should be selected and distributed, to what extent they should be permitted to interfere, are questions beset with difficulties which I need not linger to state, but which have been pondered with some anxiety during the last ten years. I can see no solution of them all more simple and easy than this:

To treat all the colonies which have legislatures, and where the system of responsible government is in operation, as having achieved a higher political status than Crown colonies or foreign dependencies, and to permit them to send to the House of Commons one, two, or three members of their cabinets, according to their size, population, and relative importance.

The advantages gained by this mode of selection, assuming the principle of any sort of representation to be sanctioned, are various:

1. We get rid of all questions about franchise and the modes of election,

which might or might not correspond to those which obtain in England.

2. We are secure of men truly representing the majority in each colony, because they would speak in the name and bring with them the authority of the cabinets and constituencies they represented.

3. We have no trouble about changing them, as they would sit till their successors, duly accredited, announced the fact of a change of administration.

4. We have no contested elections or questions about bribery and corruption to waste the time of Parliament.

5. We are secure by this mode of obtaining the best men, because only the best can win their way into these colonial cabinets, of whom the flower would be selected by their colleagues to represent the intellect and character of each Province on the floor of Parliament.

6. We do nothing more in fact than permit colonial ministers to defend their policy, and explain their conduct before Parliament, as British ministers do now, thus training them in the highest school of politics for the better discharge of their duties at home.

Technical difficulties of all sorts may be urged against the adoption of this proposition, but, for the present, I will assume that these may be overcome, if it is seriously entertained. To one or two objections, involving principle, I would for a moment invite attention.

It may be said that the introduction of these men by this mode would destroy the symmetry and violate the general principles upon which imperial legislation is based; but I would respectfully submit that all our legislation springs out of a series of compromises. That this would only be another, and one quite in accordance with the general spirit of all the rest.

In the House of Lords the three kingdoms are variously represented, and the dissenting interests are without any spiritual representation at all. The House of Commons presents but little simplicity of outline, but is the result of a series of compromises, between those already in possession of the seats and the growing wealth, population and intelligence outside. To distribute a certain number of seats among great Provinces, peopled by Englishmen, prepared to discharge all the duties of loyal subjects, would seem to be only a move in the same direction as all the others, by which a working legislature, representing all interests but the colonial, has been secured; and surely the millions who are now claiming an extension of the franchise will hardly think it right that the millions beyond the seas, who are bound by British legislation, should have, in the Parliament which can at any moment plunge them into a war, no representation at all.

But it may be asked, would you allow these men to speak and vote on English, Scottish and Irish questions? This is a matter of detail of easy adjustment. If I were a resident of these islands I would say yes, let us hear what such men as Mr Verdon of Victoria, Mr Galt from Canada, or Mr Tilley from New Brunswick have to say even on domestic topics, because their testimony would be all the more valuable, as they would have no interest in the matter. But if permitted to express their opinions, good taste would probably restrain colonial gentlemen from mingling but upon rare occasions in purely local controversies. They would probably confine themselves to the exposition and defence of those measures for which they were at once responsible to the

Provinces they represented, and to the august assembly which must then form, as it does now, the high court of review for all colonial questions.

Matters of foreign policy, they should not only be permitted, but invited to debate, because upon the wise adjustment of these depends the preservation of peace, in any breach of which the Provinces would be directly compromised. What more appropriate theme for British Americans to discuss than the relations between Great Britain and the United States? And I am quite sure that an earnest-minded man, speaking good sense upon any of the varied questions that these relations involve, would be listened to with respect by the House of Commons, and would not be without influence in the great country which it might be sound policy to conciliate.

But take a purely provincial question, and I select one at random because it often attracts a good deal of public attention. There are 60,000 Englishmen in the colony of New Zealand, who hold a portion of the islands by what has often appeared to be a most precarious tenure. The Maoris hold all the rest, under some agreement with the British Government, and are said to have the patronage and protection of certain worthy people in England, whose philanthropy seriously embarrasses the local government. When war breaks out, nobody in this country can get at the merits of the controversy. The colonists are accused of provoking it, that they may despoil the Maoris of their land or profit by military expenditure; and the policy is seriously entertained of leaving these 60,000 Englishmen, thousands of miles from home, to fight and slay these savages at their own cost and charges. Then matters become complicated by disputes between the Executive and the Commander-in-chief, and nobody knows who is to blame. We rarely get out of these entanglements without a good deal of bloodshed and a large expenditure. And scarcely anybody in England can tell, even when the war is over, why it was begun. Now I would simplify all this by saying to the New Zealanders, send over here the best man you have got, clothed with the authority of office and sustained by the public confidence, and let him explain your case before the Parliament of the empire. If you are right you shall be sustained, if wrong, you must give way or change your policy. A single night's discussion in the House of Commons, with the New Zealand minister there, would do more for the peace and order of the colony than a year's debate without him. No man would come here with a bad case, and if he did, and if it broke down, no wise man would persist in a line of policy which had been patiently reviewed and condemned by the House of Commons, in his own presence, after a fair discussion in which he had been heard at large.

But it may be asked, would the colonists value this privilege? Would they send these members? I think they would, but if they did not, their mouths would be closed: and the offer of free consultation, not only on such local concerns as from their pressure on the imperial treasury challenged the investigation of Parliament, but on the great questions of peace or war, having been freely tendered to them, they could not complain if the British Government took such measures for the preservation of domestic tranquillity and the general defence of the empire as in its wisdom seemed politic and discreet. It is not probable that all the colonies would send these members, to waste their time in the House of Commons, when they had no special grievances to discuss, or policy to represent, because their leading men, in the absence of these, would be better employed at home; but when they had, the privilege would be much esteemed, and the conviction that they had the right to send them at all times would add a new element of strength and cohesion to the empire.

But it may be asked, might not these colonial representatives combine and form a brigade, embarrassing governments and obstructing public business in pursuit of anti-British or other unworthy objects? There is no danger of this. These men would represent communities wide as the poles asunder, with climates, soils, productions, interests, as varied as the skies under which they were bred. They would know less of each other and of each other's interests than the body of Englishmen, among whom they were thrown, would perhaps know of them all. These men would bring with them stores of accurate information, often invaluable in parliamentary inquiries, and they might sometimes throw into debates the fruits of long experience and the subtle vivacity of very accomplished minds; but I cannot conceive with what designs, or under what leadership, they could possibly combine for objects that were not legitimate. The effect of this concession would not only be to supply the House of Commons, at first hand, with much valuable information, but to raise the standard of qualification, and to elevate the tone of public instruction and debate, in all the colonies.

The Crown colonies and foreign populations are not included in this scheme. Her Majesty's ministers may devise some mode by which they can be provided for. I pass them by, because I do not see the way clear to admit them until they have achieved the status of self-governing Provinces with responsible ministers to send; but if they were made to feel that, by qualifying themselves for rational self-government, they might ultimately enjoy the full privileges of British citizenship, the effect even upon those portions of the empire, still treated as territories are treated in the United States, might not be without its value in exciting to emulation and improvement.

Having made this step in advance, I would proceed to treat the whole empire as the British Islands are treated, holding every man liable to serve the Queen in war, and making every pound's worth of property responsible for the national defence. . . .

If the general principle be admitted, we need not waste time with the details, which actuaries and accountants can adjust. Fair allowance being made, under these two heads, I can see no reason why the colonies should not contribute in peace and war their fair quotas towards the defence of the empire.

As respects the mode in which this contribution should be levied, there are many reasons why a tax on imports should be preferred. Direct taxes are easily collected in a densely peopled country like England, where everybody can be got at, and where every acre of land has a marketable value. In the Provinces direct taxes often cost more than they come to, because the scarcity of money in new settlements, the distance to be travelled by the collectors, and the difficulty of enforcing payment if there is evasion or resistance, renders this by far the least satisfactory mode of collecting revenue. But, added to their *ad valorem* duties, the tax for national defence could, if fairly adjusted, be paid by all the colonies without restricting their commerce or being burthensome to their industry.

But the question may now be asked, and everything turns upon the answer that may be given to it, will the colonies consent to pay this tax, or to make any provision at all for the defence of the empire? It must be apparent that no individual can give an answer to this question; that the cabinet, were they to propound this policy even after the most anxious inquiry and full deliberation, could only wait in hope and confidence for the response to be given by so many communities, so widely dispersed, and affected by so many currents of thought. There is enough of doubt to perplex and almost to deter them from trying the experiment, yet it is so hopeful, there is so little to be lost by failure, and so much to be gained by success, that, with all respect, I would urge Her Majesty's Government to give the question their grave consideration.

That it is the duty, and would be for the interest, of all Her Majesty's subjects in the outlying Provinces, fairly admitted to the enjoyment of the privileges indicated, to make this contribution, I have not a shadow of doubt. Without the protection of the fleets and armies of England, they are all defenceless. Without efficient organization, they cannot lean upon and strengthen each other, or give the mother country that moral support which in peace makes diplomacy effective, and in war would make the contest short, sharp and decisive. Besides, the overflow of labour and of capital into the colonies is to some extent checked by doubts as to the security of their future. If once organized and consolidated, under a system mutually advantageous and universally known, there would be an end of all jealousies between the taxpayers at home and abroad. We would no longer be weakened by discussions about defence or propositions for dismemberment, and the irritation which is now kept up by shallow thinkers and mischievous politicians would give place to a general feeling of brotherhood, of confidence, of mutual exertion, dependence and security. The great powers of Europe and America would at once recognize the wisdom and forethought out of which had sprung this national combination, and they would be slow to test its strength. We should secure peace on every side by the notoriety given to the fact, that on every side we were prepared for war.

Now let us see if Her Majesty's subjects, making these sacrifices and giving these aids, would be worse off or would stand on a lower level than the people of any other great empire, with whom our pride might tempt us to challenge equality. We would have, in all the Provinces, responsible governments, independent courts and legislatures, a free press, municipal institutions, the entire control of our own revenues (the defence contribution being deducted), and the regulation of our trade, foreign and domestic; and we should have the right of free discussion of international and intercolonial questions in the House of Commons. What privileges are enjoyed by Russians or Frenchmen, or by the subjects of any European sovereign, that can be compared with these? Turning to the United States, and admitting the entire success of their political experiments it must be confessed that, from the moment that the colonies are permitted to send their accredited ministers, representing their parliamentary majorities, to the national council, we shall have attained a status that will leave us little or nothing to desire that they have achieved. In a pecuniary point of view we shall be better off. The whole of the import duties in all the States now go into the national treasury to sustain the general government. We should still retain ours (less the contribution for national defence), and have, in all the Provinces, a large fund available for local services and internal improvements.

But suppose this policy propounded and the appeal made, and that the response is a determined negative. Even in that case it would be wise to make it, because the public conscience of the mother country would then be clear, and the hands of her statesmen free, to deal with the whole question of national defence, in its broadest outlines or in its bearing on the case of any single province or group of provinces, which might then be dealt with in a more independent manner.

But I will not, for a moment, do my fellow-colonists the injustice to suspect that they will decline a fair compromise of a question which involves at once their own protection and the consolidation and security of the empire. At all events, if there are any communities of British origin anywhere who desire to enjoy all the privileges and immunities of the Queen's subjects without paying for and defending them, let us ascertain where and who they are—let us measure the proportions of political repudiation now, in a season of tranquillity, when we have leisure to gauge the extent of the evil and to apply correctives, rather than wait till war finds us unprepared and leaning upon presumptions in which there is no reality.

But it may be asked, can such an empire as this, wanting the compactness of France, Russia or the United States, ever be kept together, and so brought to yield to the guidance and control of any central authority, as to be strong in war, and in peaceful times mutually interested in a common name and in a simultaneous development? We may save our pains if this question cannot be answered; but, after much reflection on the subject, I think it can, with as much certainty as any question can be answered that includes so many elements of speculation to which no positive test can be applied.

A nation of soldiers, like the Romans or the French, would hardly have known what to do with such an empire as ours had Providence bestowed it as a gift. But to a nation of merchants, manufacturers, planters, fishermen and sailors, its very extent, expansion, and diversity of production and consumption are its chief attractions. All that the sun ripens or the seas produce is ours without going beyond our own boundaries. If a *Zollverein*, such as the Germans have, or free trade between states such as the great republic enjoys, be advantageous, we have them on the widest scale, and with a far larger population. The seas divide our possessions it is true, but out of this very division grow our valuable fisheries, our mercantile marine, our lines of ocean steamers; and out of these our navy and the supremacy upon the sea, which, if we hold together, with cheaper iron, coal, timber and labour than almost any maritime country, no other power can dispute.

Besides, though in some respects our distant possessions are a source of weakness, on the whole they give great strength and power. Through India we command the trade and almost control the policy of Asia; and even in America, which at this moment is held to be our weakest point, while we possess half the continent with the provinces of British America and the West Indies, we control the North Atlantic and the Gulf of Mexico, and have a power of offence as well as the duty of defence, all along a frontier which no surveillance can possibly close against our trade; and so it is in every quarter of the globe, the risks and the costs of empire are counterbalanced by the possession of political power and of great commercial advantages. While we act in concert these are the common property of us all, and I cannot believe that there is in a single province of the empire, in which British settlers form a majority, a disposition to break away from the honourable compact under which these advantages are mutually shared, or an indisposition to contribute towards their perpetual guardianship and protection. . . .

SIR JOHN A. MACDONALD

John A. Macdonald (1815-91) and George-Etienne Cartier (1814-73) founded the Liberal-Conservative party and the Canada we know today. Macdonald, who came from Scotland to Kingston with his parents in 1820, was first elected to the Legislative Assembly in 1844 and first held office in 1847. In 1867, having dominated the 'Great Coalition', he was chosen to be the first Prime Minsiter of the new country. He is represented here by the complete text of his speech on Confederation—the first of a series of six Ministerial speeches to the Legislative Assembly of Canada in February 1865.

Speech on the Quebec Resolutions

Mr Speaker, in fulfilment of the promise made by the Government to Parliament at its last session, I have moved this resolution.* I have had the honor of being charged, on behalf of the Government, to submit a scheme for the Confederation of all the British North American Provinces—a scheme which has been received, I am glad to say, with general, if not universal, approbation in Canada. The scheme, as propounded through the press, has received almost no opposition. While there may be occasionally, here and there, expressions of dissent from some of the details, yet the scheme as a whole has met with almost universal approval, and the Government has the greatest satisfaction in presenting it to this House.

This subject, which now absorbs the attention of the people of Canada, and of the whole of British North America, is not a new one. For years it has more or less attracted the attention of every statesman and politician in these provinces, and has been looked upon by many far-seeing politicians as being eventually the means of deciding and settling very many of the vexed questions which have retarded the prosperity of the colonies as a whole, and particularly the prosperity of Canada. The subject was pressed upon the public attention by a great many writers and politicians; but I believe the attention of the Legislature was first formally called to it by my honorable friend the Minister of Finance [Alexander Galt]. Some years ago, in an elaborate speech, my hon. friend, while an independent member of Parliament, before being connected with any Government, pressed his views on the Legislature at great length and with his usual force.† But the subject was not taken up by any party as a branch of their policy, until the formation of the CARTIER-MACDONALD Administration in 1858, when the Confederation of the colonies was announced as one of the measures which they pledged themselves to attempt, if possible, to bring to a satisfactory conclusion. In pursuance of that promise, the letter or despatch, which has been so much and so freely commented upon in the press and in this House, was addressed by three of the members of that Administration to the Colonial Office.°

The subject, however, though looked upon with favor by the country, and though there were no distinct expressions of opposition to it from any party, did not begin to assume its present proportions until last session. Then, men of all parties and all shades of politics became alarmed at the aspect of affairs. They found that such was the opposition between the two sections of the province, such was the danger of impending anarchy, in consequence of the irreconcilable differences of opinion, with respect to representation by population, between Upper and Lower Canada, that unless some solution of the difficulty was arrived at, we would suffer under a succession of weak governments,—weak in numerical support, weak in force, and weak in power of doing good. All were alarmed at this state of affairs. We had election after election,—we had ministry after ministry,—with the same result. Parties were so equally balanced, that the vote of one member might decide the fate of the Administration, and the course of legislation for a year or a series of years. This condition of things was well calculated to arouse the earnest consideration of every lover of his country, and I am happy to say it had that effect. None were more impressed by this momentous state of affairs, and the grave apprehensions that existed of a state of anarchy destroying our credit, destroying our prosperity, destroying our progress, than were the members of this present House; and the leading statesmen on both sides seemed to have come to the common conclusion, that some step must be taken to relieve the country from the dead-lock and impending anarchy that hung over us.—With that view, my colleague, the President of the Council [George Brown], made a motion founded on the despatch addressed to the Colonial Minister, to which I have referred, and a committee was struck, composed of gentlemen of both sides of the House, of all shades of political opinion, without any reference to whether they were supporters of the Administration of the day or belonged to the Opposition, for the purpose of taking into calm and full deliberation the evils which threatened the future of Canada. That motion of my honorable friend resulted most happily. The committee, by a wise provision,—and in order that each member of the committee might have an opportunity of expressing his opinions without being in any way compromised before the public, or with his party, in regard either to his political friends or to his political foes,—agreed that the discussion should be freely entered upon without reference to the political antecedents of any of them, and that they should sit with closed doors, so that they might be able to approach the subject frankly and in a spirit of compromise. The committee included most of the leading members of the House,—I had the honor myself to be one of the number,—and the result was that there was found an ardent desire—a creditable desire, I must say,—displayed by all the members of the committee to approach the subject honestly, and to attempt to work out some solution which might relieve Canada from the evils under which she labored. The report of that committee was laid before the House, and then came the political action of the leading men of the two parties in this House, which ended in the formation of the present Government.

The principle upon which that Government was formed has been announced, and is known to all. It was formed for the very purpose of carrying out the object which has now received to a certain degree its completion, by the resolutions I have had the honor to place in your hands.

As has been stated, it was not without a great deal of difficulty and reluctance that that Government was formed. The gentlemen who compose this Government had for many years been engaged in political hostilities to such an extent that it affected even their social relations. But the crisis was great, the danger was imminent, and the gentlemen who now form the present Administration found it to be their duty to lay aside all personal feelings, to sacrifice in some degree their position, and even to run the risk of having their motives impugned, for the sake of arriving at some conclusion that would be satisfactory to the country in general. The present resolutions were the result. And, as I said before, I am proud to believe that the country has sanctioned, as I trust that the representatives of the people in this House will sanction, the scheme which is now submitted for the future government of British North America. (Cheers).

Everything seemed to favor the project, and everything seemed to shew that the present was the time, if ever, when this great union between all Her Majesty's subjects dwelling in British North America, should be carried out. (Hear, hear.) When the Government was formed, it was felt that the difficulties in the way of effecting a union between all the British North American Colonies were great—so great as almost, in the opinion of many, to make it hopeless. And with that view it was the policy of the Government, if they could not succeed in procuring a union between all the British North American Colonies, to attempt to free the country from the dead-lock in which we were placed in Upper and Lower Canada, in consequence of the difference of opinion between the two sections, by having a severance to a certain extent of the present union between the two provinces of Upper and Lower Canada, and the substitution of a Federal Union between them. Most of us, however, I may say, all of us, were agreed—and I believe every thinking man will agree—as to the expediency of effecting a union between all the provinces, and the superiority of such a design, if it were only practicable, over the smaller scheme of having a Federal Union between Upper and Lower Canada alone.

By a happy concurrence of events, the time came when that proposition could be made with a hope of success. By a fortunate coincidence the desire for union existed in the Lower Provinces, and a feeling of the necessity of strengthening themselves by collecting together the scattered colonies on the sea-board, had induced them to form a convention of their own for the purpose of effecting a union of the Maritimes Provinces of Nova Scotia, New Brunswick, and Prince Edward Island, the legislatures of those colonies having formally authorized their respective governments to send a delegation to Prince Edward Island for the purpose of attempting to form a union of some kind. Whether the union should be federal or legislative was not then indicated, but a union of some kind was sought for the purpose of making of themselves one people instead of three. We, ascertaining that they were about to take such a step, and knowing that if we allowed the occasion to pass, if they did indeed break up all their present political organizations and form a new one, it could not be expected that they would again readily destroy the new organization which they had formed,—the union of the three provinces on the sea-board,—and form another with Canada. Knowing this, we availed ourselves of the opportunity, and asked if they would receive a deputation from Canada, who would go to meet them at Charlottetown, for the purpose of laying before them the advantages of a larger and more extensive union, by the junction of all the provinces in one great government under our common Sovereign. They at once kindly consented to receive and hear us. They did receive us cordially and generously, and asked us to lay our views before them. We did so at some length, and so satisfactory to them were the reasons we gave; so clearly, in their opinion, did we shew the advantages of the greater union over the lesser, that they at once set aside their own project, and joined heart and hand with us in entering into the larger scheme, and trying to form, as far as they and we could, a great nation and a strong government. (Cheers.)

Encouraged by this arrangement, which, however, was altogether unofficial and unauthorized, we returned to Quebec, and then the Government of Canada invited the several governments of the sister colonies to send a deputation here from each of them for the purpose of considering the question, with something like authority from their respective governments. The result was, that when we met here on the 10th of October, on the first day on which we assembled, after the full and free discussions which had taken place at Charlottetown, the first resolution now before this House was passed unanimously, being received with acclamation as, in the opinion of every one who heard it, a proposition which ought to receive, and would receive, the sanction of each government and each people. The resolution is, 'That the best interests and present and future prosperity of British North America will be promoted by a Federal Union under the Crown of Great Britain, provided such union can be effected on principles just to the several provinces.'

It seemed to all the statesmen assembled—and there are great statesmen in the Lower Provinces, men who would do honor to any government and to any legislature of any free country enjoying representative institutions—it was clear to them all that the best interests and present and future prosperity of British North America would be promoted by a Federal Union under the Crown of Great Britain. And it seems to me, as to them, and I think it will so appear to the people of this country, that, if we wish to be a great people; if we wish to form—using the expression which was sneered at the other evening—a great nationality, commanding the respect of the world, able to hold our own against all opponents, and to defend those institutions we prize: if we wish to have one system of government, and to establish a commercial union, with unrestricted free trade, between people of the five provinces, belonging, as they do, to the same nation, obeying the same Sovereign, owning the same allegiance, and being, for the most part, of the same blood and lineage: if we wish to be able to afford to each other the means of mutual defence and support against aggression and attack—this can only be obtained by a union of some kind between the scattered and weak boundaries composing the British North American Provinces. (Cheers).

The very mention of the scheme is fitted to bring with it its own approbation. Supposing that in the spring of the year 1865, half a million of people were coming from the United Kingdom to make Canada their home, although they brought only their strong arms and willing hearts; though they brought neither skill nor experience nor wealth, would we not receive them with open arms, and hail their presence in Canada as an important addition to our strength? But when, by the proposed union, we not only get nearly a million of people to join us—when they contribute not only their numbers, their physical strength, and their desire to benefit their position, but when we know that they consist of old-established communities, having a large amount of realized wealth,—composed of people possessed of skill, education and experience in the ways of the New World—people who are as much Canadians, I may say, as we are—people who are imbued with the same feelings of loyalty to the Queen, and the same desire for the continuance of the connection with the Mother Country as we are, and at the same time, have a like feeling of ardent attachment for this, our common country, for which they and we would alike fight and shed our blood, if necessary. When all this is considered, argument is needless to prove the advantage of such a union. (Hear, hear.)

There were only three modes,—if I may return for a moment to the difficulties with which Canada was surrounded,—only three modes that were at all suggested, by which the dead-lock in our affairs, the anarchy we dreaded, and the evils which retarded our prosperity, could be met or averted.

One was the dissolution of the union between Upper and Lower Canada, leaving them as they were before the union of 1841. I believe that that proposition, by itself, had no supporters. It was felt by every one that, although it was a course that would do away with the sectional difficulties which existed, —though it would remove the pressure on the part of the people of Upper Canada for the representation based upon population,—and the jealousy of the people of Lower Canada lest their institutions should be attacked and prejudiced by that principle in our representation; yet it was felt by every thinking man in the province that it would be a retrograde step, which would throw back the country to nearly the same position as it occupied before the union,—that it would lower the credit enjoyed by United Canada,—that it would be the breaking up of the connection which had existed for nearly a quarter of a century, and, under which, although it had not been completely successful, and had not allayed altogether the local jealousies that had their root in circumstances which arose before the union, our province, as a whole, had nevertheless prospered and increased. It was felt that a dissolution of the union would have destroyed all the credit that we had gained by being a united province, and would have left us two weak and ineffective governments, instead of one powerful and united people. (Hear, hear.)

The next mode suggested, was the granting of representation by population. Now, we all know the manner in which that question was and is regarded by Lower Canada; that while in Upper Canada the desire and cry for it was daily augmenting, the resistance to it in Lower Canada was proportionably increasing in strength. Still, if some such means of relieving us from the sectional jealousies which existed between the two Canadas, if some such solution of the difficulties as Confederation had not been found, the representation by population must eventually have been carried; no matter though it might have been felt in Lower Canada, as being a breach of the Treaty of Union, no matter how much it might have been felt by the Lower Canadians that it would sacrifice their local interests, it is certain that in the progress of events representation by population would have been carried; and, had it been carried—I speak here my own individual sentiments—I do not think it would have been for the interest of Upper Canada. For though Upper Canada would have felt that it had received what it claimed as a right, and had succeeded in establishing its right, yet it would have left the Lower Province with a sullen feeling of injury and injustice.

The Lower Canadians would not have worked cheerfully under such a change of system, but would have ceased to be what they are now—a nationality, with representatives in Parliament, governed by general principles, and dividing according to their political opinions—and would have been in great danger of becoming a faction, forgetful of national obligations, and only actuated by a desire to defend their own sectional interests, their own laws, and their own institutions. (Hear, hear.)

The third and only means of solution for our difficulties was the junction of the provinces either in a Federal or a Legislative Union. Now, as regards the comparative advantages of a Legislative and a Federal Union, I have never hesitated to state my own opinions. I have again and again stated in the House, that, if practicable, I thought a Legislative Union would be preferable. (Hear, hear.) I have always contended that if we could agree to have one government and one parliament, legislating for the whole of these peoples, it would be the best, the cheapest, the most vigorous, and the strongest system of government we could adopt. (Hear, hear.) But, on looking at the subject in the Conference, and discussing the matter as we did, most unreservedly, and with a desire to arrive at a satisfactory conclusion, we found that such a system was impracticable.

In the first place, it would not meet the assent of the people of Lower Canada, because they felt that in their peculiar position—being in a minority, with a different language, nationality and religion from the majority,—in case of a junction with the other provinces, their institutions and their laws might be assailed, and their ancestral associations, on which they prided themselves, attacked and prejudiced; it was found that any proposition which involved the absorption of the individuality of Lower Canada—if I may use the expression—would not be received with favor by her people.

We found too, that though their people speak the same language and enjoy the same system of law as the people of Upper Canada, a system founded on the common law of England, there was as great a disinclination on the part of the various Maritime Provinces to lose their individuality, as separate political organizations, as we observed in the case of Lower Canada herself. (Hear, hear.)

Therefore, we were forced to the conclusion that we must either abandon the idea of Union altogether, or devise a system of union in which the separate provincial organizations would be in some degree preserved. So that those who were, like myself, in favor of a Legislative Union, were obliged to modify their views and accept the project of a Federal Union as the only scheme practicable, even for the Maritime Provinces. Because, although the law of those provinces is founded on the common law of England, yet every one of them has a large amount of law of its own—colonial law framed by itself, and affecting every relation of life, such as the laws of property, municipal and assessment laws, laws relating to the liberty of the subject, and to all the great interests contemplated in legislation; we found, in short, that the statutory law of the different provinces was so varied and diversified that it was almost impossible to weld them into a Legislative Union at once. Why, sir, if you only consider the innumerable subjects of legislation peculiar to new countries, and that every one of those five colonies had particular laws of its own, to which its people have been accustomed and are attached, you will see the difficulty of effecting and working a Legislative Union, and bringing about an assimilation of the local as well as general laws of the whole of the provinces. (Hear, hear.)

We in Upper Canada understand from the nature and operation of our peculiar municipal law, of which we know the value, the difficulty of framing a general system of legislation on local matters which would meet the wishes and fulfil the requirements of the several provinces. Even the laws considered the least important, respecting private rights in timber, roads, fencing, and innumerable other matters, small in themselves, but in the aggregate of great interest to the agricultural class, who form the great body of the people, are regarded as of great value by the portion of the community affected by them. And when we consider that every one of the colonies has a body of law of this kind, and that it will take years before those laws can be assimilated, it was felt that at first, at all events, any united legislation would be almost impossible. I am happy to state—and indeed it appears on the face of the resolutions themselves—that as regards the Lower Provinces, a great desire was evinced for the final assimilation of our laws. One of the resolutions provides that an attempt shall be made to assimilate the laws of the Maritime Provinces and those of Upper Canada, for the purpose of eventually establishing one body of statutory law, founded on the common law of England, the parent of the laws of all those provinces.

One great objection made to a Federal Union was the expense of an increased number of legislatures. I will not enter at any length into that subject, because my honorable friends, the Finance Minister and the President of the Council, who are infinitely more competent than myself to deal with matters of this kind—matters of account—will, I think, be able to show that the expenses under a Federal Union will not be greater than those under the existing system of separate governments and legislatures. Here, where we have a joint legislature for Upper and Lower Canada, which deals not only with subjects of a general interest common to all Canada, but with all matters of private right and of sectional interest, and with that class of measures known as 'private bills', we find that one of the greatest sources of expense to the country is the cost of legislation. We find, from the admixture of subjects of a general, with those of a private character in legislation, that they mutually interfere with each other; whereas, if the attention of the Legislature was confined to measures of one kind or the other alone, the session of Parliament would not be so protracted and therefore not so expensive as at present. In the proposed Constitution all matters of general interest are to be dealt with by the General Legislature; while the local legislatures will deal with matters of local interest, which do not affect the Confederation as a whole, but are of the greatest importance to their particular sections. By such a division of labor the sittings of the General Legislature would not be so protracted as even those of Canada alone. And so with the local legislatures, their attention being confined to subjects pertaining to their own sections, their sessions would be shorter and less expensive. Then, when we consider the enormous saving that will be effected in the administration of affairs by one General Government—when we reflect that each of the five colonies have a government of its own with a complete establishment of public departments and all the machinery required for the transaction of the business of the country—that each have a separate executive, judicial and militia system—that each province has a separate ministry, including a Minister of Militia, with a complete Adjutant General's Department—that each have a Finance Minister with a full Customs and Excise staff—that each Colony has as large and complete an administrative organization, with as many Executive officers as the General Government will have—we can well understand the enormous saving that will result from a union of all the colonies, from their having but one head and one central system.

We, in Canada, already know something of the advantages and disadvantages of a Federal Union. Although we have nominally a Legislative Union in Canada—although we sit in one Parliament, supposed constitutionally to represent the people without regard to sections or localities, yet we know, as a matter of fact, that since the union in 1841, we have had a Federal Union; that in matters affecting Upper Canada solely, members from that section claimed and generally exercised the right of exclusive legislation, while members from Lower Canada legislated in matters affecting only their own section. We have had a Federal Union in fact, though a Legislative Union in name; and in the hot contests of late years, if on any occasion a measure affecting any one section were interfered with by the members from the other—if, for instance, a measure locally affecting Upper Canada were carried or defeated against the wishes of its majority, by one from Lower Canada,—my honorable friend the President of the Council, and his friends denounced with all their energy and ability such legislation as an infringement of the rights of the Upper Province. (Hear, hear, and cheers.) Just in the same way, if any act concerning Lower Canada were pressed into law against the wishes of the majority of her representatives, by those from Upper Canada, the Lower Canadians would rise as one man and protest against such a violation of their peculiar rights. (Hear, hear.)

The relations between England and Scotland are very similar to that which obtains between the Canadas. The union between them, in matters of legislation, is of a federal character, because the Act of Union between the two countries provides that the Scottish law cannot be altered, except for the manifest advantage of the people of Scotland. This stipulation has been held to be so obligatory on the Legislature of Great Britain, that no measure affecting the law of Scotland is passed unless it receives the sanction of a majority of the Scottish members in Parliament. No matter how important it may be for the interests of the empire as a whole to alter the laws of Scotland—no matter how much it may interfere with the symmetry of the general law of the United Kingdom, that law is not altered, except with the consent of the Scottish people, as expressed by their representatives in Parliament. (Hear, hear.) Thus, we have, in Great Britain, to a limited extent, an example of the working and effects of a Federal Union, as we might expect to witness them in our own Confederation.

The whole scheme of Confederation, as propounded by the Conference, as agreed to and sanctioned by the Canadian Government, and as now presented for the consideration of the people, and the Legislature, bears upon its face the marks of compromise. Of necessity there must have been a great deal of mutual concession. When we think of the representatives of five colonies, all supposed to have different interests, meeting together, charged with the duty of protecting those interests and of pressing the views of their own localities and sections, it must be admitted that had we not met in a spirit of conciliation, and with an anxious desire to promote this union; if we had not been impressed with the idea contained in the words of the resolution—'That the best interests and present and future prosperity of British North America would be promoted by a Federal Union under the Crown of Great Britain', —all our efforts might have proved to be of no avail. If we had not felt that, after coming to this conclusion, we were bound to set aside our private opinions on matters of detail, if we had not felt ourselves bound to look at what was practicable, not obstinately rejecting the opinions of others nor adhering to our own; if we had not met, I say, in a spirit of conciliation, and with an anxious, overruling desire to form one people under one government, we never would have succeeded. With these views, we press the question on this House and the country.

I say to this House, if you do not believe that the union of the colonies is for the advantage of the country, that the joining of these five peoples into one nation, under one sovereign, is for the benefit of all, then reject the scheme. Reject it if you do not believe it to be for the present advantage and future prosperity of yourselves and your children. But if, after a calm and full consideration of this scheme, it is believed, as a whole, to be for the advantage of this province—if the House and country believe this union to be one which will ensure for us British laws, British connection, and British freedom—and increase and develop the social, political and material prosperity of the country, then I implore this House and the country to lay aside all prejudices, and accept the scheme which we offer. I ask this House to meet the question in the same spirit in which the delegates met it. I ask each member of this House to lay aside his own opinions as to particular details, and to accept the scheme as a whole if he think it beneficial as a whole.

As I stated in the preliminary discussion, we must consider this scheme in the light of a treaty.* By a happy coincidence of circumstances, just when an Administration had been formed in Canada for the purpose of attempting a solution of the difficulties under which we laboured, at the same time the Lower Provinces, actuated by a similar feeling appointed a Conference with a view to a union among themselves, without being cognizant of the position the government was taking in Canada. If it had not been for this fortunate coincidence of events, never, perhaps, for a long series of years would we have been able to bring this scheme to a practical conclusion. But we did succeed. We made the arrangements, agreed upon the scheme, and the deputations from the several governments represented at the Conference went back pledged to lay it before their governments, and to ask the legislatures and people of their respective provinces to assent to it. I trust the scheme will be assented to as a whole. I am sure this House will not seek to alter it in its unimportant details; and, if altered in any important provisions, the result must be that the whole will be set aside, and we must begin de novo. If any important changes are made, every one of the colonies will feel itself absolved from the implied obligation to deal with it as a Treaty, each province will feel itself at liberty to amend it ad libitum so as to suit its own views and interests; in fact, the whole of our labours will have been for nought, and we will have to renew our negotiations with all the colonies for the purpose of establishing some new scheme.

I hope the House will not adopt any such a course as will postpone, perhaps for ever, or at all events for a long period, all chances of union. All the statesmen and public men who have written or spoken on the subject admit the advantages of a union, if it were practicable: and now when it is proved to be practicable, if we do not embrace this opportunity the present favorable time will pass away, and we may never have it again. Because, just so surely as this scheme is defeated, will be revived the original proposition for a union of the Maritime Provinces, irrespective of Canada; they will not remain as they are now, powerless, scattered, helpless communities; they will form themselves into a power, which, though not so strong as if united with Canada, will, nevertheless, be a powerful and considerable community, and it will be then too late for us to attempt to strengthen ourselves by this scheme, which, in the words of the resolution, 'is for the best interests, and present and future prosperity of British North America.'

If we are not blind to our present position, we must see the hazardous situation in which all the great interests of Canada stand in respect to the United States. I am no alarmist. I do not believe in the prospect of immediate war. I believe that the common sense of the two nations will prevent a war; still we cannot trust to probabilities. The Government and Legislature would be wanting in their duty to the people if they ran any risk. We know that the United States at this moment are engaged in a war of enormous dimensions—that the occasion of a war with Great Britain has again and again arisen, and may at any time in the future again arise. We cannot foresee what may be the result; we cannot say but that the two nations may drift into a war as other nations have done before. It would then be too late when war had commenced to think of measures for strengthening ourselves, or to begin negotiations for a union with the sister provinces. At this moment, in consequence of the ill-feeling which has arisen between England and the United States—a feeling of which Canada was not the cause—in consequence of the irritation which now exists, owing to the unhappy state of affairs on this continent, the Reciprocity Treaty [of 1854], it seems probable, is about to be brought to an end—our trade is hampered by the passport system, and at any moment we may be deprived of permission to carry our goods through United States channels—the bonded goods system may be done away with, and the winter trade through the United States put an end to. Our merchants may be obliged to return to the old system of bringing in during the summer months the supplies for the whole year. Ourselves already threatened, our trade interrupted, our intercourse, political and commercial, destroyed, if we do not take warning now when we have the opportunity, and while one avenue is threatened to be closed, open another by taking advantage of the present arrangement and the desire of the Lower Provinces to draw closer the alliance between us, we may suffer commercial and political disadvantages it may take long for us to overcome.

The Conference having come to the conclusion that a legislative union, pure and simple, was impracticable, our next attempt was to form a government upon federal principles, which would give to the General Government the strength of a legislative and administrative union, while at the same time it preserved that liberty of action for the different sections which is allowed by the Federal Union. And I am strong in the belief—that we have hit upon the happy medium in those resolutions, and that we have formed a scheme of government which unites the advantages of both, giving us the strength of a legislative union and the sectional freedom of a federal union, with protection to local interests.

In doing so we had the advantage of the experience of the United States. It is the fashion now to enlarge on the defects of the Constitution of the United States, but I am not one of those who look upon it as a failure. (Hear, hear.) I think and believe that it is one of the most skillful works which human intelligence ever created; is one of the most perfect organizations that ever governed a free people. To say that it has some defects is but to say that it is not the work of Omniscience, but of human intellects. We are happily situated in having had the opportunity of watching its operation, seeing its working from its infancy till now. It was in the main formed on the model of the Constitution of Great Britain, adapted to the circumstances of a new country, and was perhaps the only practicable system that could have been adopted under the circumstances existing at the time of its formation. We can now take advantage of the experience of the last seventy-eight years, during which that Constitution has existed, and I am strongly of the belief that we have, in a great measure, avoided in this system which we propose for the adoption of the people of Canada, the defects which time and events have shown to exist in the American Constitution.

In the first place, by a resolution which meets with the universal approval of the people of this country, we have provided that for all time to come, so far as we can legislate for the future, we shall have as the head of the executive power, the Sovereign of Great Britain. (Hear, hear.) No one can look into futurity and say what will be the destiny of this country. Changes come over nations and peoples in the course of ages. But, so far as we can legislate, we provide that, for all time to come, the Sovereign of Great Britain shall be the Sovereign of British North America. By adhering to the monarchical principle, we avoid one defect inherent in the Constitution of the United States. By the election of the President by a majority and for a short period, he never is the sovereign and chief of the nation. He is never looked up to by the whole people as the head and front of the nation. He is at best but the successful leader of a party. This defect is all the greater on account of the practice of re-election. During his first term of office, he is employed in taking steps to secure his own re-election, and for his party a continuance of power. We avoid this by adhering to the monarchical principle—the Sovereign whom you respect and love. I believe that it is of the utmost importance to have that principle recognized, so that we shall have a Sovereign who is placed above the region of party—to whom all parties look up—who is not elevated by the action of one party nor depressed by the action of another, who is the common head and sovereign of all. (Hear, hear and cheers.)

In the Constitution we propose to continue the system of Responsible Government, which has existed in this province since 1841, and which has long obtained in the Mother Country. This is a feature of our Constitution as we have it now, and as we shall have it in the Federation, in which, I think, we avoid one of the great defects in the Constitution of the United States. There the President, during his term of office, is in a great measure a despot, a one-man power, with the command of the naval and military forces—with an immense amount of patronage as head of the Executive, and with the veto power as a branch of the legislature, perfectly uncontrolled by responsible advisers, his cabinet being departmental officers merely, whom he is not obliged by the Constitution to consult with, unless he chooses to do so. With us the Sovereign, or in this country the Representative of the Sovereign, can act only on the advice of his ministers, those ministers being responsible to the people through Parliament.

Prior to the formation of the American Union, as we all know, the different states which entered into it were separate colonies. They had no connection with each other further than that of having a common sovereign, just as with us at present. Their constitutions and their laws were different. They might and did legislate against each other, and when they revolted against the Mother Country they acted as separate sovereignties, and carried on the war by a kind of treaty of alliance against the common enemy. Ever since the union was formed the difficulty of what is called 'State Rights' has existed, and this had much to do in bringing on the present unhappy war in the United States.

They commenced, in fact, at the wrong end. They declared by their Constitution that each state was a sovereignty in itself, and that all the powers incident to a sovereignty belonged to each state, except those powers which, by the Constitution, were conferred upon the General Government and Congress.

Here we have adopted a different system. We have strengthened the General Government. We have given the General Legislature all the great subjects of legislation. We have conferred on them, not only specifically and in detail, all the powers which are incident to sovereignty, but we have expressly declared that all subjects of general interest not distinctly and exclusively conferred upon the local governments and local legislatures, shall be conferred upon the General Government and Legislature.—We have thus avoided that great source of weakness which has been the cause of the disruption of the United States. We have avoided all conflict of jurisdiction and authority, and if this Constitution is carried out, as it will be in full detail in the Imperial Act to be passed if the colonies adopt the scheme, we will have in fact, as I said before, all the advantages of a legislative union under one administration, with, at the same time the guarantees for local institutions and for local laws, which are insisted upon by so many in the provinces now, I hope, to be united.

I think it is well that, in framing our Constitution—although my honorable friend the member for Hochelaga (Hon. Mr DORION) sneered at it the other day, in the discussion on the Address in reply to the speech from the Throne—our first act should have been to recognize the sovereignty of Her Majesty. (Hear, hear.) I believe that, while England has no desire to lose her colonies, but wishes to retain them, while I am satisfied that the public mind of England would deeply regret the loss of these provinces—yet, if the people of British North America after full deliberation had stated that they considered it was for their interest, for the advantage of the future of British North America to sever the tie, such is the generosity of the people of England, that, whatever their desire to keep these colonies, they would not seek to compel us to remain unwilling subjects of the British Crown. If therefore, at the Conference, we had arrived at the conclusion, that it was for the interest of these provinces that a severance should take place, I am sure that Her Majesty and the Imperial

Parliament would have sanctioned that severance. We accordingly felt that there was a propriety in giving a distinct declaration of opinion on that point, and that, in framing the Constitution, its first sentence should declare, that 'The Executive authority or government shall be vested in the Sovereign of the United Kingdom of Great Britain and Ireland, and be administered according to the well understood principles of the British Constitution, by the Sovereign personally, or by the Representative of the Sovereign duly authorised.' That resolution met with the unanimous assent of the Conference. The desire to remain connected with Great Britain and to retain our allegiance to Her Majesty was unanimous. Not a single suggestion was made, that it could, by any possibility, be for the interest of the colonies, or of any section or portion of them, that there should be a severance of our connection. Although we knew it to be possible that Canada, from her position, might be exposed to all the horrors of war, by reason of causes of hostility arising between Great Britain and the United States—causes over which we had no control, and which we had no hand in bringing about—yet there was a unanimous feeling of willingness to run all the hazards of war, if war must come, rather than lose the connection between the Mother Country and these colonies. (Cheers.)

We provide that 'the Executive authority shall be administered by the Sovereign personally, or by the Representative of the Sovereign duly authorized.' It is too much to expect that the Queen should vouchsafe us her personal governance or presence, except to pay us, as the heir apparent of the Throne, our future Sovereign has already paid us, the graceful compliment of a visit. The Executive authority must therefore be administered by Her Majesty's Representative. We place no restriction on Her Majesty's prerogative in the selection of her representative. As it is now, so it will be if this Constitution is adopted. The Sovereign has unrestricted freedom of choice. Whether in making her selection she may send us one of her own family, a Royal Prince, as a Viceroy to rule over us, or one of the great statesmen of England to represent her, we know not. We leave that to Her Majesty in all confidence. But we may be permitted to hope, that when the union takes place, and we become the great country which British North America is certain to be, it will be an object worthy the ambition of the statesmen of England to be charged with presiding over our destinies. (Hear, hear.)

Let me now invite the attention of the House to the provisions in the Constitution respecting the legislative power. The sixth resolution says, 'There shall be a general legislature or parliament for the federated provinces, composed of a Legislative Council and a House of Commons.' This resolution has been cavilled at in the English press as if it excluded the Sovereign as a portion of the legislature. In one sense, that stricture was just—because in strict constitutional language, the legislature of England consists of King, Lords and Commons. But, on the other hand, in ordinary parlance we speak of 'the King and his Parliament,' or 'the King summoning his Parliament,' the three estates—Lords spiritual, temporal Lords, and the House of Commons, and I observe that such a writer as Hallam occasionally uses the word Parliament in that restricted sense. At best it is merely a verbal criticism. The legislature of British North America will be composed of King, Lords, and Commons. The Legislative Council will stand in the same relation to the Lower House, as the

House of Lords to the House of Commons in England, having the same power of initiating all matters of legislation, except the granting of money. As regards the Lower House, it may not appear to matter much, whether it is called the House of Commons or House of Assembly. It will bear whatever name the Parliament of England may choose to give it, but 'The House of Commons' is the name we should prefer, as shewing that it represents the Commons of Canada, in the same way that the English House of Commons represents the Commons of England, with the same privileges, the same parliamentary usage, and the same parliamentary authority.

In settling the constitution of the Lower House, that which peculiarly represents the people, it was agreed that the principle of representation based on population should be adopted, and the mode of applying that principle is fully developed in these resolutions.

When I speak of representation by population, the House will of course understand, that universal suffrage is not in any way sanctioned, or admitted by these resolutions, as the basis on which the constitution of the popular branch should rest.*

In order to protect local interests, and to prevent sectional jealousies, it was found requisite that the three great divisions into which British North America is separated, should be represented in the Upper House on the principle of equality.

There are three great sections, having different interests, in this proposed Confederation. We have Western Canada, an agricultural country far away from the sea, and having the largest population who have agricultural interests principally to guard. We have Lower Canada, with other and separate interests, and especially with institutions and laws which she jealously guards against absorption by any larger, more numerous, or stronger power. And we have the Maritime Provinces, having also different sectional interests of their own, having, from their position, classes and interests which we do not know in Western Canada.

Accordingly, in the Upper House,—the controlling and regulating, but not the initiating, branch (for we know that here as in England, to the Lower House will practically belong the initiation of matters of great public interest), in the House which has the sober second-thought in legislation—it is provided that each of those great sections shall be represented equally by 24 members. The only exception to the condition of equality is in the case of Newfoundland, which has an interest of it own, lying, as it does, at the mouth of the great river St Lawrence, and more connected, perhaps, with Canada than with the Lower Provinces. It has, comparatively speaking, no common interest with the other Maritime Provinces, but has sectional interests and sectional claims of its own to be protected. It, therefore, has been dealt with separately, and is to have a separate representation in the Upper House, thus varying from the equality established between the other sections.

As may be well conceived, great difference of opinion at first existed as to the constitution of the Legislative Council. In Canada the elective principle prevailed, in the Lower Provinces, with the exception of Prince Edward Island, the nominative principle was the rule. We found a general disinclination on the part of the Lower Provinces to adopt the elective principle; indeed, I do not think there was a dissenting voice in the Conference against the adoption of the nominative principle, except from Prince Edward Island. The delegates from New Brunswick, Nova Scotia and Newfoundland, as one man, were in favor of nomination by the Crown. And nomination by the Crown is of course the system which is most in accordance with the British Constitution. We resolved then, that the constitution of the Upper House should be in accordance with the British system as nearly as circumstances would allow.

An hereditary Upper House is impracticable in this young country. Here we have none of the elements for the formation of a landlord aristocracy—no men of large territorial positions—no class separated from the mass of the people. An hereditary body is altogether unsuited to our state of society, and would soon dwindle into nothing. The only mode of adapting the English system to the Upper House, is by conferring the power of appointment on the Crown (as the English peers are appointed), but that the appointments should be for life.

The arguments for an elective Council are numerous and strong; and I ought to say so, as one of the Administration responsible for introducing the elective principle into Canada. (Hear, hear.) I hold that this principle has not been a failure in Canada; but there were causes—which we did not take into consideration at the time—why it did not so fully succeed in Canada as we had expected. One great cause was the enormous extent of the constituencies and the immense labor which consequently devolved on those who sought the suffrages of the people for election to the Council. For the same reason the expense—(laughter)—the legitimate expense was so enormous that men of standing in the country, eminently fitted for such a position, were prevented from coming forward. At first, I admit, men of the first standing did come forward, but we have seen that in every succeeding election in both Canadas there has been an increasing disinclination, on the part of men of standing and political experience and weight in the country, to become candidates; while, on the other hand, all the young men, the active politicians, those who have resolved to embrace the life of a statesman, have sought entrance to the House of Assembly.

The nominative system in this country, was to a great extent successful, before the introduction of responsible government. Then the Canadas were to a great extent Crown colonies, and the upper branch of the legislature consisted of gentlemen chosen from among the chief judicial and ecclesiastical dignitaries, the heads of departments, and other men of the first position in the country. Those bodies commanded great respect from the character, standing, and weight of the individuals composing them, but they had little sympathy with the people or their representatives, and collisions with the Lower House frequently occurred, especially in Lower Canada.

When responsible government was introduced, it became necessary for the Governor of the day to have a body of advisers who had the confidence of the House of Assembly which could make or unmake ministers as it chose. The Lower House in effect pointed out who should be nominated to the Upper House; for the ministry, being dependent altogether on the lower branch of the legislature for support, selected members for the Upper House from among their political friends at the dictation of the House of Assembly. The Council was becoming less and less a substantial check on the legislation of the Assembly; but under the system now proposed, such will not be the case. No ministry can in future do what they have done in Canada before,—they cannot, with the view of carrying any measure, or of strengthening the party, attempt to over-rule the independent opinion of the Upper House, by filling it with a number of its partisans and political supporters. The provision in the Constitution, that the Legislative Council shall consist of a limited number of members—that each of the great sections shall appoint twenty-four members and no more, will prevent the Upper House from being swamped from time to time by the ministry of the day, for the purpose of carrying out their own schemes or pleasing their partisans. The fact of the government being prevented from exceeding a limited number will preserve the independence of the Upper House, and make it, in reality, a separate and distinct chamber, having a legitimate and controlling influence in the legislation of the country.

The objection has been taken that in consequence of the Crown being deprived of the right of unlimited appointment, there is a chance of a dead-lock arising between the two branches of the legislature; a chance that the Upper House being altogether independent of the Sovereign, of the Lower House, and of the advisers of the Crown, may act independently, and so independently as to produce a dead-lock. I do not anticipate any such result.

In the first place we know that in England it does not arise. There would be no use of an Upper House, if it did not exercise, when it thought proper, the right of opposing or amending or postponing the legislation of the Lower House. It would be of no value whatever were it a mere chamber for register-ing the decrees of the Lower House. It must be an independent House, having a free action of its own, for it is only valuable as being a regulating body, calmly considering the legislation initiated by the popular branch, and preventing any hasty or ill-considered legislation which may come from that body, but it will never set itself in opposition against the deliberate and understood wishes of the people. Even the House of Lords, which as an hereditary body, is far more independent than one appointed for life can be, whenever it ascertains what is the calm, deliberate will of the people of England, it yields, and never in modern times has there been, in fact or act, any attempt to overrule the decisions of that House by the appointment of new peers, excepting, perhaps, once in the reign of Queen Anne. It is true that in 1832 such an increase was threatened in consequence of the reiterated refusal of the House of Peers to pass the Reform Bill. I have no doubt the threat would have been carried into effect, if necessary; but every one, even the Ministry who advised that step, admitted that it would be a revolutionary act, a breach of the Constitution to do so, and it was because of the necessity of preventing the bloody revolution which hung over the land, if the Reform Bill had been longer refused to the people of England, that they consented to the bloodless revolution of over-riding the independent opinion of the House of Lords on that question. (Hear, hear.) Since that time it has never been attempted, and I am satisfied it will never be attempted again. Only a year or two ago the House of Lords rejected the Paper Duties Bill, and they acted quite constitutionally, according to the letter and as many think, according to the spirit of the Constitution in doing so. Yet when they found they had interfered with a subject which the people's house claimed as belonging of right to themselves, the very next session they abandoned their position, not because they were convinced they had done wrong, but because they had ascertained what was the deliberate voice of the representatives of the people on the subject.

In this country, we must remember, that the gentlemen who will be selected for the Legislative Council stand on a very different footing from the peers of England. They have not like them any ancestral associations or position derived from history. They have not that direct influence on the people themselves, or on the popular branch of the legislature, which the peers of England exercise, from their great wealth, their vast territorial possessions, their numerous tenantry and that prestige with which the exalted position of their class for centuries has invested them. (Hear, hear.) The members of our Upper House will be like those of the Lower, men of the people, and from the people. The man put into the Upper House is as much a man of the people the day after, as the day before his elevation. Springing from the people, and one of them, he takes his seat in the Council with all the sympathies and feelings of a man of the people, and when he returns home, at the end of the session, he mingles with them on equal terms, and is influenced by the same feelings and associations, and events, as those which affect the mass around him. And is it, then, to be supposed that the members of the upper branch of the legislature will set themselves deliberately at work to oppose what they know to be the settled opinions and wishes of the people of the country? They will not do it. There is no fear of a dead-lock between the two houses. There is an infinitely greater chance of a dead-lock between the two branches of the legislature, should the elective principle be adopted, than with a nominated chamber—chosen by the Crown, and having no mission from the people. The members of the Upper Chamber would then come from the people as well as those of the Lower House, and should any difference ever arise between both branches, the former could say to the members of the popular branch—'We as much represent the feelings of the people as you do, and even more so; we are not elected from small localities and for a short period; you as a body were elected at a particular time, when the public mind was running in a particular channel; you were returned to Parliament, not so much representing the general views of the country, on general questions, as upon the particular subjects which happened to engage the minds of the people when they went to the polls. We have as much right, or a better right, than you to be considered as representing the deliberate will of the people on general questions, and therefore we will not give way.' (Hear, hear.)

There is, I repeat, a greater danger of an irreconcilable difference of opinion between the two branches of the legislature, if the upper be elective, than if it holds its commission from the Crown.

Besides, it must be remembered that an Upper House, the members of which are to be appointed for life, would not have the same quality of permanence as the House of Lords; our members would die; strangers would succeed them, whereas son succeeded father in the House of Lords. Thus the changes in the membership and state of opinion in our Upper House would always be more rapid than in the House of Lords. To show how speedily changes have occurred in the Upper House, as regards life members, I will call the attention of the House to the following facts:—At the call of the House, in February, 1856, forty-two life members responded; two years afterwards, in 1858, only thirty-five answered to their names; in 1862 there were only twenty-five life members left, and in 1864, but twenty-one. (Hear, hear.) This shows how speedily changes take place in the life membership. But remarkable as this change has been, it is not so great as that in regard to the elected members. Though the elective principle only came into force in 1856, and although only twelve men were elected that year, and twelve more every two years since, twenty-four changes have already taken place by the decease of members, by the acceptance of office, and by resignation. So it is quite clear that, should there be on any question a difference of opinion between the Upper and Lower Houses, the government of the day being obliged to have the confidence of the majority in the popular branch—would, for the purpose of bringing the former into accord and sympathy with the latter, fill up any vacancies that might occur, with men of the same political feelings and sympathies with the Government, and consequently with those of the majority in the popular branch; and all the appointments of the Administration would be made with the object of maintaining the sympathy and harmony between the two houses. (Hear, hear.)

There is this additional advantage to be expected from the limitation. To the Upper House is to be confided the protection of sectional interests; therefore is it that the three great divisions are there equally represented, for the purpose of defending such interests against the combinations of majorities in the Assembly. It will, therefore, become the interest of each section to be represented by its very best men, and the members of the Administration who belong to each section will see that such men are chosen, in case of a vacancy in their section. For the same reason each state of the American Union sends its two best men to represent its interests in the Senate. (Hear, hear.)

It is provided in the Constitution that in the first selections for the Council, regard shall be had to those who now hold similar positions in the different colonies. This, it appears to me, is a wise provision. In all the provinces, except Prince Edward [Island], there are gentlemen who hold commissions for the Upper House for life. In Canada, there are a number who hold under that commission; but the majority of them hold by a commission, not, perhaps, from a monarchical point of view so honorable, because the Queen is the fountain of honor,—but still, as holding their appointment from the people, they may be considered as standing on a par with those who have Her Majesty's commission. There can be no reason suggested why those who have had experience in legislation, whether they hold their positions by the election of the people or have received preferment from the Crown—there is no valid reason why those men should be passed over, and new men sought for to form the Legislative Council of the Confederation. It is, therefore, provided that the selection shall be made from those gentlemen who are now members of the upper branch of the Legislature in each of the colonies, for seats in the Legislative Council of the General Legislature. The arrangement in this respect is somewhat similar to that by which Representative Peers are chosen from the Peers of Scotland and Ireland, to sit in the Parliament of the United Kingdom. In like manner, the members of the Legislative Council of the proposed Confederation will be first selected from the existing Legislative Councils of the various provinces.

In the formation of the House of Commons, the principle of representation by population has been provided for in a manner equally ingenious and simple. The introduction of this principle presented at first the apparent difficulty of a constantly increasing body until, with the increasing population, it would become inconveniently and expensively large. But by adopting the representation of Lower Canada as a fixed standard—as the pivot on which the whole would turn—that province being the best suited for the purpose, on account of the comparatively permanent character of its population, and from its having neither the largest nor least number of inhabitants—we have been enabled to overcome the difficulty I have mentioned. We have introduced the system of representation by population without the danger of an inconvenient increase in the number of representatives on the recurrence of each decennial period. The whole thing is worked by a simple rule of three. For instance, we have in Upper Canada 1,400,000 of a population; in Lower Canada 1,100,000. Now,the proposition is simply this—if Lower Canada, with its population of 1,100,000, has a right to 65 members, how many members should Upper Canada have, with its larger population of 1,400,000? The same rule applies to the other provinces—the proportion is always observed and the principles of representation by population carried out, while, at the same time, there will not be decennially an inconvenient increase in the numbers of the Lower House. At the same time, there is a constitutional provision that hereafter, if deemed advisable, the total number of representatives may be increased from 194, the number fixed in the first instance. In that case, if an increase is made, Lower Canada is still to remain the pivot on which the whole calculation will turn. If Lower Canada, instead of sixty-five, shall have seventy members, then the calculation will be, if Lower Canada has seventy members, with such a population, how many shall Upper Canada have with a larger population?

I was in favor of a larger House than one hundred and ninety-four, but was overruled. I was perhaps singular in the opinion, but I thought it would be well to commence with a larger representation in the lower branch. The arguments against this were, that, in the first place, it would cause additional expense; in the next place, that in a new country like this, we could not get a sufficient number of qualified men to be representatives. My reply was that the number is rapidly increasing as we increase in education and wealth; that a larger field would be open to political ambition by having a large body of representatives; that by having numerous and smaller constituencies, more people would be interested in the working of the union, and that there would be a wider field for selection for leaders of governments and leaders of parties. These are my individual sentiments,—which, perhaps, I have no right to express here—but I was overruled, and we fixed on the number of one hundred and ninety-four, which no one will say is large or extensive, when it is considered that our present number in Canada alone is one hundred and thirty. The difference between one hundred and thirty and one hundred and ninety-four is not great, considering the large increase that will be made to our population when Confederation is carried into effect.

While the principle of representation by population is adopted with respect to the popular branch of the legislature, not a single member of the

Conference, as I stated before, not a single one of the representatives of the government or of the opposition of any one of the Lower Provinces was in favor of universal suffrage. Every one felt that in this respect the principle of the British Constitution should be carried out, and that classes and property should be represented as well as numbers. Insuperable difficulties would have presented themselves if we had attempted to settle now the qualification for the elective franchise. We have different laws in each of the colonies fixing the qualification of electors for their own local legislatures; and we therefore adopted a similar clause to that which is contained in the Canada Union Act of 1841, viz., that all the laws which affected the qualification of members and of voters, which affected the appointment and conduct of returning officers and the proceedings at elections, as well as the trial of controverted elections in the separate provinces, should obtain in the first election to the Confederate Parliament, so that every man who has now a vote in his own province should continue to have a vote in choosing a representative to the first Federal Parliament. And it was left to the Parliament of the Confederation, as one of their first duties, to consider and to settle by an act of their own the qualification for the elective franchise, which would apply to the whole Confederation.

In considering the question of the duration of Parliament, we came to the conclusion to recommend a period of five years. I was in favor of a longer period. I thought that the duration of the local legislatures should not be shortened so as to be less than four years, as at present, and that the General Parliament should have as long a duration as that of the United Kingdom. I was willing to have gone to the extent of seven years; but a term of five years was preferred, and we had the example of the New Zealand carefully considered, not only locally, but by the Imperial Parliament, and which gave the provinces of those islands a general parliament with a duration of five years. But it was a matter of little importance whether five years or seven years was the term, the power of dissolution by the Crown having been reserved. I find, on looking at the duration of parliaments since the accession of George III to the Throne, that excluding the present parliament, there have been seventeen parliaments, the average period of whose existence has been about three years and a half. That average is less than the average duration of the parliaments in Canada since the union, so that it was not a matter of much importance whether we fixed upon five or seven years as the period of duration of our General Parliament.

A good deal of misapprehension has arisen from the accidental omission of some words from the 24th resolution. It was thought that by it the local legislatures were to have the power of arranging hereafter, and from time to time of readjusting the different constituencies and settling the size and boundaries of the various electoral districts. The meaning of the resolution is simply this, that for the first General Parliament, the arrangement of constituencies shall be made by the existing local legislatures; that in Canada, for instance, the present Canadian Parliament shall arrange what are to be the constituencies of Upper Canada, and to make such changes as may be necessary in arranging for the seventeen additional members given to it by the Constitution; and that it may also, if it sees fit, alter the boundaries of the existing constituencies of Lower Canada. In short, this Parliament shall settle what shall be the different constituencies electing members to the first Federal Parliament. And so the other provinces, the legislatures of which will fix the limits of their several constituencies in the session in which they adopt the new Constitution. Afterwards the local legislatures may alter their own electoral limits as they please, for their own local elections. But it would evidently be unproper to leave to the Local Legislature the power to alter the constituencies sending members to the General Legislature after the General Legislature shall have been called into existence. Were this the case, a member of the General Legislature might at any time find himself ousted from his seat by an alteration of his constituency by the Local Legislature in his section. No, after the General Parliament meets, in order that it may have full control of its own legislation, and be assured of its position, it must have the full power of arranging and re-arranging the electoral limits of its constituencies as it pleases, such being one of the powers essentially necessary to such a Legislature. (Hear, hear.)

I shall not detain the House by entering into a consideration at any length of the different powers conferred upon the General Parliament as contra-distinguished from those reserved to the local legislatures; but any honorable member on examining the list of different subjects which are to be assigned to the General and Local Legislatures respectively, will see that all the great questions which affect the general interests of the Confederacy as a whole, are confided to the Federal Parliament, while the local interests and local laws of each section are preserved intact, and entrusted to the care of the local bodies.

As a matter of course, the General Parliament must have the power of dealing with the public debt and property of the Confederation. Of course, too, it must have the regulation of trade and commerce, of customs and excise. The Federal Parliament must have the sovereign power of raising money from such sources and by such means as the representatives of the people will allow. It will be seen that the local legislatures have the control of all local works; and it is a matter of great importance, and one of the chief advantages of the Federal Union and of local legislatures, that each province will have the power and means of developing its own resources and aiding its own progress after its own fashion and in its own way. Therefore all the local improvements, all local enterprizes or undertakings of any kind, have been left to the care and management of the local legislatures of each province. (Cheers.) It is provided that all 'lines of steam or other ships, railways, canals and other works, connecting any two or more of the provinces together or extending beyond the limits of any province', shall belong to the General Government, and be under the control of the General Legislature. In like manner 'lines of steamships between the Federated Provinces and other countries, telegraph communication and the incorporation of telegraph companies, and all such works as shall, although lying within any province, be specially declared by the Acts authorizing them, to be for the general advantage', shall belong to the General Government. For instance, the Welland Canal, though lying wholly within one section, and the St Lawrence Canals in two only, may be properly considered national works, and for the general benefit of the whole Federation.

Again, the census, the ascertaining of our numbers and the extent of our resources, must, as a matter of general interest, belong to the General Government. So also with the defences of the country.

One of the great advantages of Confederation is, that we shall have a united, a concerted, and uniform system of defence. (Hear.) We are at this moment with a different militia system in each colony—in some of the colonies with an utter want of any system of defence. We have a number of separate staff establishments, without any arrangement between the colonies as to the means, either of defence or offence. But, under the union, we will have one system of defence and one system of militia organization. In the event of the Lower Provinces being threatened, we can send the large militia forces of Upper Canada to their rescue. Should we have to fight on our lakes against a foreign foe, we will have the hardy seamen of the Lower Provinces coming to our assistance and manning our vessels. (Hear, hear.) We will have one system of defence and be one people, acting together alike in peace and in war. (Cheers.)

The criminal law too—the determination of what is a crime and what is not and how crime shall be punished—is left to the General Government. This is a matter almost of necessity. It is of great importance that we should have the same criminal law throughout these provinces—that what is a crime in one part of British America, should be a crime in every part—that there should be the same protection of life and property [in one part] as in another. It is one of the defects in the United States system, that each separate state has or may have a criminal code of its own,—that what may be a capital offence in one state, may be a venial offence, punishable slightly, in another. But under our Constitution we shall have one body of criminal law, based on the criminal law of England, and operating equally throughout British America, so that a British American, belonging to what province he may, or going to any other part of the Confederation, knows what his rights are in that respect, and what his punishment will be if an offender against the criminal laws of the land. I think this is one of the most marked instances in which we take advantage of the experience derived from our observations of the defects in the Constitution of the neighboring Republic. (Hear, hear.)

The 33rd provision is of very great importance to the future well-being of these colonies. It commits to the General Parliament the 'rendering uniform all or any of the laws relative to property and civil rights in Upper Canada, Nova Scotia, New Brunswick, Newfoundland and Prince Edward Island, and rendering uniform the procedure of all or any of the courts in these provinces.' The great principles which govern the laws of all the provinces, with the single exception of Lower Canada, are the same, although there may be a divergence in details; and it is gratifying to find, on the part of the Lower Provinces, a general desire to join together with Upper Canada in this matter, and to procure, as soon as possible, an assimilation of the statutory laws and the procedure in the courts, of all these provinces. At present there is a good deal of diversity. In one of the colonies, for instance, they have no municipal system at all. In another, the municipal system is merely permissive, and has not been adopted to any extent. Although, therefore, a legislative union was found to be almost impracticable, it was understood, so far as we could influence the future, that the first act of the Confederate Government should be to procure an assimilation of the statutory law of all those provinces, which has, as its root and foundation, the common law of England. But to prevent local interests from being over-ridden, the same section makes provision, that, while power is given to the General Legislature to deal with this subject, no change in this respect should have the force and authority of law in any province until sanctioned by the Legislature of that province. (Hear, hear.)

The General Legislature is to have power to establish a general court of

Appeal for the Federated Provinces. Although the Canadian Legislature has always had the power to establish a Court of Appeal, to which appeals may be made from the courts of Upper and Lower Canada, we have never availed ourselves of the power. Upper Canada has its own Court of Appeal, so has Lower Canada. And this system will continue until a General Court of Appeal shall be established by the General Legislature. The Constitution does not provide that such a court shall be established. There are many arguments for and against the establishment of such a court. But it was thought wise and expedient to put into the Constitution a power to the General Legislature, that, if after full consideration they think it advisable to establish a General Court of Appeal from all the Superior Courts of all the provinces, they may do so. (Hear, hear.)

I shall not go over the other powers that are conferred on the General Parliament. Most of them refer to matters of financial and commercial interest, and I leave those subjects in other and better hands.

Besides all the powers that are specifically given, the 37th and last item of this portion of the Constitution confers on the General Legislature the general mass of sovereign legislation, the power to legislate on 'all matters of a general character, not specially and exclusively reserved for the local governments and legislatures.' This is precisely the provision which is wanting in the Constitution of the United States. It is here that we find the weakness of the American system—the point where the American Constitution breaks down. (Hear, hear.) It is in itself a wise and necessary provision. We thereby strengthen the Central Parliament, and make the Confederation one people and one government, instead of five peoples and five governments, with merely a point of authority connecting us to a limited and insufficient extent.

With respect to the local governments, it is provided that each shall be governed by a chief executive officer, who shall be nominated by the General Government. As this is to be one united province, with the local governments and legislatures subordinate to the General Government and Legislature, it is obvious that the chief executive officer in each of the provinces must be subordinate as well. The General Government assumes towards the local governments precisely the same position as the Imperial Government holds with respect to each of the colonies now: so that as the Lieutenant Governor of each of the different provinces is now appointed directly by the Queen, and is directly responsible, and reports directly to Her, so will the executives of the local governments hereafter be subordinate to the Representative of the Queen, and be responsible and report to him.

Objection has been taken that there is an infringement of the Royal prerogative in giving the pardoning power to the local governors, who are not appointed directly by the Crown, but only indirectly by the Chief Executive of the Confederation, who is appointed by the Crown. This provision was inserted in the Constitution on account of the practical difficulty which must arise if the power is confined to the Governor General. For example, if a question arose about the discharge of a prisoner convicted of a minor offence, say in Newfoundland, who might be in imminent danger of losing his life if he remained in confinement, the exercise of the pardoning power might come too late if it were necessary to wait for the action of the Governor General. It must be remembered that the pardoning power not only extends to capital cases, but to every case of conviction and sentence, no matter now trifling—even to the case of a fine in the nature of a sentence on a criminal conviction. It extends to innumerable cases, where, if the responsibility for its exercise were thrown on the General Executive, it could not be so satisfactorily discharged. Of course there must be, in each province, a legal adviser of the Executive, occupying the position of our Attorney General, as there is in every state of the American Union. This officer will be an officer of the Local Government; but, if the pardoning power is reserved for the Chief Executive, there must, in every case where the exercise of the pardoning power is sought, be a direct communication and report from the local law officer to the Governor General. The practical inconvenience of this was felt to be so great, that it was thought well to propose the arrangement we did, without any desire to infringe upon the prerogatives of the Crown, for our whole action shews that the Conference, in every step they took, were actuated by a desire to guard jealously these prerogatives. (Hear, hear.) It is a subject, however, of Imperial interest, and if the Imperial Government and Imperial Parliament are not convinced by the arguments we will be able to press upon them for the continuation of that clause, then, of course, as the over-ruling power, they may set it aside. (Hear, hear.)

There are numerous subjects which belong, of right, both to the Local and the General Parliaments. In all these cases it is provided, in order to prevent a conflict of authority, that where there is concurrent jurisdiction in the General and Local Parliaments, the same rule should apply as now applies in cases where there is concurrent jurisdiction in the Imperial and in the Provincial Parliaments, and that when the legislation of the one is adverse to or contradictory of the legislation of the other, in all such cases the action of the General Parliament must overrule, *ex-necessitate*, the action of the Local Legislature. (Hear, hear.)

We have introduced also all those provisions which are necessary in order to [ensure] the full working out of the British Constitution in these provinces. We provide that there shall be no money votes, unless those votes are introduced in the popular branch of the Legislature on the authority of the responsible advisers of the Crown—those with whom the responsibility rests of equalizing revenue and expenditure—that there can be no expenditure or authorization of expenditure by Address or in any other way unless initiated by the Crown on the advice of its responsible advisers. (Hear, hear.)

As regards the financial features of the scheme, the arrangements made as to the present liabilities of the several provinces, and the future liabilities of the Confederation, on these and kindred matters, I have no doubt that my honorable friends, the Finance Minister [Galt] and the President of the Council [Brown], will speak at full length, and that they will be able to shew you that this branch of the subject has received the fullest consideration. I feel I would be intruding myself unnecessarily on the House if, with my inferior knowledge of those subjects I were to detain you by venturing to speak of them, when I know that they will be so ably and fully gone into by my two honorable friends.

The last resolution of any importance is one which, although not affecting the substance of the Constitution, is of interest to us all. It is that 'Her Majesty the Queen be solicited to determine the rank and name of the federated provinces.' I do not know whether there will be any expression of opinion in this House on this subject—whether we are to be a vice-royalty, or whether we are still to retain our name and rank as a province. But I have no doubt Her Majesty will give the matter Her gracious consideration, that She will give us a name satisfactory to us all, and that the rank She will confer upon us will be a rank worthy of our position, of our resources, and of our future. (Cheers.)

Let me again, before I sit down, impress upon this House the necessity of meeting this question in a spirit of compromise, with a disposition to judge the matter as a whole, to consider whether really it is for the benefit and advantage of the country to form a Confederation of all the provinces; and if honorable gentlemen, whatever may have been their preconceived ideas as to the merits of the details of this measure, whatever may still be their opinions as to these details, if they really believe that the scheme is one by which the prosperity of the country will be increased, and its future progress secured, I ask them to yield their own views, and to deal with the scheme according to its merits as one great whole. (Hear, hear.)

One argument, but not a strong one, has been used against this Confederation, that it is an advance towards independence. Some are apprehensive that the very fact of our forming this union will hasten the time when we shall be severed from the mother country. I have no apprehension of that kind. I believe it will have the contrary effect. I believe that as we grow stronger, that, as it is felt in England we have become a people, able from our union, our strength, our population, and the development of our resources, to take our position among the nations of the world, she will be less willing to part with us than she would be now, when we are broken up into a number of insignificant colonies, subject to attack piece-meal without any concerted action or common organization of defence. I am strongly of [the] opinion that year by year, as we grow in population and strength, England will more see the advantages of maintaining the alliance between British North America and herself. Does any one imagine that, when our population instead of three and a-half, will be seven millions, as it will be ere many years pass, we would be one whit more willing than now to sever the connection with England? Would not those seven millions be just as anxious to maintain their allegiance to the Queen and their connection with the Mother Country, as we are now? Will the addition to our numbers of the people of the Lower Provinces, in any way lessen our desire to continue our connection with the Mother Country? I believe the people of Canada East and West to be truly loyal. But, if they can by possibility be exceeded in loyalty, it is by the inhabitants of the Maritime Provinces. Loyalty with them is an overruling passion. (Hear, hear.) In all parts of the Lower Provinces there is a rivalry between the opposing political parties as to which shall most strongly express and most effectively carry out the principle of loyalty to Her Majesty, and to the British Crown. (Hear, hear.) When this union takes place, we will be at the outset no inconsiderable people. We find ourselves with a population approaching four millions of souls. Such a population in Europe would make a second, or at least, a third rate power. And with a rapidly increasing population—for I am satisfied that under this union our population will increase in a still greater ratio than ever before—with increased credit—with a higher position in the eyes of Europe—with the increased security we can offer to immigrants, who would naturally prefer to seek a new home in what is known to them as a great country, than in any one little colony or another—with all this I am satisfied that, great as has been our increase in the last twenty-five years since the union between Upper and Lower Canada, our future progress, during the next quarter of a century, will be vastly greater. (Cheers.) And when, by means of this rapid increase, we become a nation of eight or nine millions of inhabitants, our alliance will be worthy of being sought by the great nations of the earth. (Hear, hear.) I am proud to believe that our desire for a permanent alliance will be reciprocated in England. I know that there is a party in England—but it is inconsiderable in numbers, though strong in intellect and power—which speaks of the desirability of getting rid of the colonies; but I believe such is not the feeling of the statesmen and the people of England. I believe it will never be the deliberately expressed determination of the Government of Great Britain. (Hear, hear.)

The colonies are now in a transition state. Gradually a different colonial system is being developed—and it will become, year by year, less a case of dependence on our part, and of overruling protection on the part of the Mother Country, and more a case of a healthy and cordial alliance. Instead of looking upon us as a merely dependent colony, England will have in us a friendly nation—a subordinate but still a powerful people—to stand by her in North America in peace or in war. (Cheers.) The people of Australia will be such another subordinate nation. And England will have this advantage, if her colonies progress under the new colonial system, as I believe they will, that, though at war with all the rest of the world, she will be able to look to the subordinate nations in alliance with her, and owning allegiance to the same Sovereign, who will assist in enabling her again to meet the whole world in arms, as she has done before. (Cheers.) And if, in the great Napoleonic war, with every port in Europe closed against her commerce, she was yet able to hold her own, how much more will that be the case when she has a colonial empire rapidly increasing in power, in wealth, in influence, and in position. (Hear, hear.)

It is true that we stand in danger, as we have stood in danger again and again in Canada, of being plunged into war and suffering all its dreadful consequences, as the result of causes over which we have no control, by reason of [this] connection. This, however, did not intimidate us. At the very mention of the prospect of a war some time ago, how were the feelings of the people aroused from one extremity of British America to the other, and preparations made for meeting its worst consequences. Although the people of this country are fully aware of the horrors of war—should a war arise, unfortunately, between the United States and England, and we all pray it never may—they are still ready to encounter all perils of that kind, for the sake of the connection with England. There is not one adverse voice, not one adverse opinion on that point.

We all feel the advantages we derive from our connection with England. So long as that alliance is maintained, we enjoy, under her protection, the privileges of constitutional liberty according to the British system. We will enjoy here that which is the great test of constitutional freedom—we will have the rights of the minority respected. (Hear, hear.) In all countries the rights of the majority take care of themselves, but it is only in countries like England, enjoying constitutional liberty, and safe from the tyranny of a single despot or of an unbridled democracy, that the rights of minorities are regarded. So long, too, as we form a portion of the British Empire, we shall have the example of her free institutions, of the high standard of the character of her statesmen and public men, of the purity of her legislation, and the upright administration of her laws. In this younger country one great advantage of our connection with Great Britain will be, that, under her auspices, inspired by her example, a portion of her empire, our public men will be actuated by principles similar to those which actuate the statesmen at home. These although not material, physical benefits, of which you can make an arithmetical calculation, are of such overwhelming advantage to our future interests and standing as a nation, that to obtain them is well worthy of any sacrifices we may be called upon to make, and the people of this country are ready to make them. (Cheers.)

We should feel, also, sincerely grateful to beneficent Providence that we have had the opportunity vouchsafed us of calmly considering this great constitutional change, this peaceful revolution—that we have not been hurried into it, like the United States, by the exigencies of war—that we have not had a violent revolutionary period forced on us, as in other nations, by hostile action from without, or by domestic dissensions within. Here we are in peace and prosperity, under the fostering government of Great Britain—a dependent people, with a government having only a limited and delegated authority, and yet allowed, without restriction, and without jealousy on the part of the Mother Country, to legislate for ourselves, and peacefully and deliberately to consider and determine the future of Canada and of British North America. It is our happiness to know the expression of the will of our Gracious Sovereign, through Her Ministers, that we have her full sanction for our deliberations, that Her only solicitude is that we shall adopt a system which shall be really for our advantage, and that She promises to sanction whatever conclusion after full deliberation we may arrive at as to the best mode of securing the well-being,—the present and future prosperity of British America.—(Cheers.) It is our privilege and happiness to be in such a position, and we cannot be too grateful for the blessings thus conferred upon us. (Hear, hear.)

I must apologize for having detained you so long—for having gone perhaps too much into tedious details with reference to the questions bearing on the Constitution now submitted to this House.—(Cries of 'no, no' and 'go on.')—In conclusion, I would again implore the House not to let this opportunity to pass. It is an opportunity that may never recur. At the risk of repeating myself, I would say, it was only by a happy concurrence of circumstances, that we were enabled to bring this great question to its present position. If we do not take advantage of the time, if we show ourselves unequal to the occasion, it may never return, and we shall hereafter bitterly and unavailingly regret having failed to embrace the happy opportunity now offered of founding a great nation under the fostering care of Great Britain, and our Sovereign Lady, Queen Victoria. (Loud cheers, amidst which the honorable gentleman resumed his seat.)

ULTRAMONTANISM

At the time of Confederation French Canadians had been debating radicalism and religion for a generation. The radicals had failed miserably in the political arena in 1837, but had cut a better figure in the intellectual life of the Union period. They echoed the doctrines of advanced nineteenth-century liberalism, a movement regarded by the Church as a mortal threat. Its defence was ultramontanism, best represented in Canada by Ignace Bourget (1799-1885), Bishop of Montreal from 1840 to 1876. The first selection below is the Programme Catholique of 1871, written by Adolphe-Basile Routhier (1839-1920), François Trudel (1838-90), and their friends, Catholic laymen under the influence of Bishop Bourget. The second is a pastoral letter from the Catholic bishops of Quebec to their parishioners in 1875. In the background at that time was the case of Joseph Guibord, a liberal printer who had died excommunicate in Montreal in 1869. Refused burial in the graveyard of Notre Dame cathedral, his body had been interred in a Protestant cemetery for five years while his widow and liberal friends fought to have the courts compel burial in consecrated ground; eventually, at the command of the Judicial Committee of the Privy Council, his remains were moved (under an armed guard of more than 1200 soldiers) from the one graveyard to the other, only to have the ground in which they were laid—encased in concrete and scrap iron—promptly deconsecrated by Bishop Bourget.

The Programme Catholique: The Next Elections

Our country, in accordance with its constitutional regime, will soon have to choose its representatives. This simple fact necessarily raises a question that as Catholic journalists we are duty-bound to resolve, and that question can be posed as follows: What part should Catholic voters play in the battle that is brewing and what should be their policy in choosing between the candidates who will be soliciting their votes? We think that we can answer this question satisfactorily by developing somewhat further the ideas expressed by His Highness the Bishop of Three Rivers [Mgr Laflèche] in his most recent pastoral letter.

This is what we find there: 'The men you send as your representatives to the Legislature are charged as much with protecting and defending your religious interests according to the understanding of the Church as with promoting and safeguarding your temporal interests. For at many points the civil laws necessarily touch on the sphere of religion. This is what your Bishops clearly say in their decree. You must therefore be careful to ensure that the candidate for whom you vote is duly qualified from both points of view, and that, as regards morality, he offers all the appropriate guarantees for the protection of these grave interests. We should no doubt give thanks to God for the full and entire liberty that the constitution of our country accords, as a matter of right, to the Catholic religion to rule and govern itself in conformity to the laws of the

Church. It is by choosing your legislators carefully that you can guarantee the conservation and future enjoyment of this liberty, the most precious of all, which gives your leading clergymen the immense advantage of being able to govern the Canadian Church simply according to the prescriptions and directives of the Holy See and the Roman Church, the mother and mistress of all churches.'*

We hope that all Catholic voters of this province will understand this wise advice. No one can deny that politics and religion are inextricably related, and that the separation of Church and State is an absurd and impious doctrine. This is particularly true of the constitutional regime that, by granting the Parliament complete legislative power, puts in the hands of its members a double-edged and potentially terrible weapon. This is why it is necessary that those who exercise the legislative power be in perfect accord with the teachings of the Church. This is why it is the duty of Catholic voters to choose for their representatives men whose principles are perfectly sound and dependable. Full and complete acceptance of Roman Catholic doctrines on religion, politics, and economics must be the first and most important qualification that Catholic voters will have to require of the Catholic candidate. It is the surest criterion for them to use in judging men and events.

Clearly, there can be no question here of [the duties of] Protestants, to whom we grant the same liberty that we demand for ourselves.

Once these premises are admitted, the consequences that will serve to guide voters are easy to deduce. But to derive practical rules, easily applied, one must take into account the special circumstances of our country, the political parties that have developed here, and their past history.

In principle we belong to the Conservative party, that is to say, to the party that has made itself the defender of social authority.† By the *Conservative party*, it hardly need be said, we do not mean any collection of men having no other bond than that of interest and personal ambition, but a group of men sincerely professing the same principles of religion and nationality [and] upholding in their integrity the traditions of the old Conservative party, which can be summed up as an inviolable attachment to Catholic doctrine and an absolute devotion to the national interests of Lower Canada.

In the political situation of our country, with the Conservative party the only one that offers serious guarantees for religious interests, we regard it as a duty loyally to support its leaders.

But this loyal support must be subordinate to the religious interests that we must never lose from sight. Thus if there are in our laws any deficiencies, ambiguities, or other provisions that endanger Catholic interests, we must demand of our candidates a formal promise to work towards rectifying these flaws in our legislation.

Thus the religious press has reason to complain that our laws on marriage, on education, on the erection of parishes, and on the registration of civil status are defective inasmuch as they infringe on the rights of the Church, limit its liberty, hamper its administration, or are open to a hostile interpretation. Such being the case, it is the duty of Catholic deputies to make whatever changes or modifications may be demanded by our Lords the Bishops of the Province in order to bring them into harmony with the doctrines of the Roman

Catholic Church. Now, to ensure that the deputies are more diligent in their discharge of this duty, the voters must make it a condition of their support. It is the duty of voters to grant their support only to those candidates who are willing to conform completely to the teachings of the Church relative to these matters.

Let us conclude, therefore, by adopting the following general rules to be applied to the given cases.

1. If the struggle is between two Conservatives, it goes without saying that we shall support the one who will accept the programme we have just outlined.

2. If, on the contrary, it is between a Conservative of whatever kind and an adept of the liberal school, our active sympathies will be given to the former.

3. If the only candidates competing for our votes in a constituency are all Liberals or oppositionists, we must choose the one who will subscribe to our conditions.

4. Finally, should the contest be between a Conservative rejecting our programme and an oppositionist who nonetheless accepts it, the situation would be more delicate. To vote for the first would be to contradict the doctrine we have just set out; to vote for the second would be to imperil the Conservative party that we wish to see strong. What choice are we to make between these two dangers? In such a case we would advise Catholic electors to abstain.

It should nevertheless be understood that these rules still leave the voters a certain freedom of action depending upon the special circumstances of each county and the background of each candidate. We have striven above all to bring to light the religious convictions and qualifications that voters ought to demand of those seeking their votes. It is worth adding that intelligence and education are essential in deputies if they are to make their religious convictions prevail. After making sure of the candidates' religious principles, it is thus necessary to endeavour, secondly, to send to Parliament the greatest possible sum of intelligence and of education. We would thus condemn any ministerial action that would tend to eliminate from the parliamentary arena men capable of serving the Catholic and national cause, under the pretext that they would get in the way of certain ambitious men. For our representatives to consist of docile and impotent nonentities would certainly be a great evil, which must be avoided.

In two words, we wish to safeguard both the honour of the Fatherland and the liberty of the Church, and our whole programme can be summed up in these words: Religion and Fatherland.

Pastoral Letter of the Bishops
of the Ecclesiastical Province of Quebec

WE, BY THE MERCY OF GOD AND THE FAVOUR OF THE HOLY APOSTOLIC SEE, ARCHBISHOP, BISHOPS, AND ADMINISTRATOR OF THE DIOCESES OF THE ECCLESIASTICAL PROVINCE OF QUEBEC.

To the Clergy, Secular and Regular, and to all the Faithful of the said Province, Greeting and Benediction in Our Lord.

Our Dearly Beloved Brethren,—We deem it our duty as Your Pastors, to address you on many most important subjects to which divers circumstances have given rise.

I
POWERS OF THE CHURCH

'Whosoever will be saved,' says the creed of St Athanasius, 'before all things it is necessary that he hold the Catholic faith.' *Quicumque vult salvus esse, necesse est ut teneat catholicam fidem.* And to obtain a certain knowledge of this faith, 'without which faith it is impossible to please God', *sine fide impossibile est placere Deo* (Heb. xi, 6), it is necessary to listen to the Church in which Jesus Christ himself taught, and out of which one can find only error, doubt and uncertainty, for it 'is the Church of the living God, the pillar and support of the truth;' *Ecclesia Dei vivi, columna et firmamentum veritatis* (1 Tim. iii, 15). It has received a mission 'to teach to all nations the commandments of Jesus Christ'; *Docete omnes gentes servare omnia quaecumque mandavi vobis* (Matt. xxviii, 20).

To fulfil this sublime and difficult mission it was necessary that the Church be constituted by its Divine founder in the form of a Society perfect in itself, distinct and independent of civil society.

No society whatever can exist without laws, and consequently, without law-givers, judges and a power to make the laws respected; the Church has, therefore, necessarily received from its founder authority over its children to maintain order and unity. To deny this authority would be to deny the wisdom of the Son of God. To subordinate this authority to the civil power, would be to side with a Nero and a Diocletian against those millions of Christians who preferred death to betraying their faith; it would be to side with Pilate and Herod against Jesus Christ himself.

Not only is the Church independent of civil society, but it is superior to it by its origin, by its extent, and by its end.

Without doubt civil society has its root in the will of God, who has decreed that men would live in society; but the forms of civil society vary with times and places; the Church is born from the blood of a God on Calvary, has received direct from His mouth its unchangeable constitution, and no power on earth can alter it.

A civil society embraces but one people; the Church has received dominion over all the earth; Jesus Christ himself has given the mission 'to teach all nations', *docete omnes gentes* (Matt. xxviii, 20); the State, then, is in the Church, and not the Church in the State.

The aim of the Church is the eternal happiness of souls, the supreme and last aim of man; civil society has for its aim the temporal happiness of peoples. Even by the nature of things, civil society finds itself *indirectly* but in truth subordinate, for not only ought it to abstain from putting any obstacle in the way of that supreme and last aim of man, but it ought also to assist the Church in its divine mission and if need be to protect and defend it. And besides, is it not evident that even the temporal happiness of peoples depends on truth, justice and morality, and consequently, on all those truths the keeping of which is confided to the Church? The experience of the last hundred years teaches us there is no longer either peace or security for nations who have thrown off the yoke of religion, of which the Church is the only true guardian.

This subordination in no way prevents these societies [civil and religious] from being distinct, because of their aims, and independent, each in its proper sphere. But the moment a question touches on faith, morals or the divine constitution of the Church, on its independence or on what it needs to fulfil its spiritual mission, it is for the Church alone to judge, for Jesus Christ has said to it alone, 'All power is given me in heaven and on earth. . . . As my Father has sent me, so I send you. . . . Go then, teach all nations. . . . Who hears you hears me, and who contemns you contemns me, and who contemns me contemns Him that sent me. . . . Who does not listen to the Church deserves to be considered as a heathen and a publican', that is to say, as unworthy to be called His child. (Matt. xxviii, 18, 19; John xx, 21; [Luke x, 16;] Matt. xviii, 17.)

But in thus claiming the rights of the Catholic Church over its children, by no means do we intend to usurp or fetter the civil rights of our brothers who differ from us, with whom we will always be happy to be on the best of terms in the future as we have been in the past. The principles we expound are not new; they are as old as the Church itself. If we repeat them today, it is because certain Catholics appear to have forgotten them.

II
CONSTITUTION OF THE CHURCH

The power of legislating and judging in the Church exists in the highest degree in the Sovereign Pontiff, the successor of St Peter, to whom Christ confided the keys of the Kingdom of Heaven and whom He ordered to confirm his brethren.

The general Councils, summoned, presided over and confirmed by the Pope, have this same power.

'The Bishops have been appointed by the Holy Spirit to govern the Church of God'; *Spiritus Sanctus posuit Episcopos regere Ecclesiam Dei* (Acts xx, 28). In their respective dioceses they have the power of teaching, commanding and judging; a power nevertheless subordinate to that of the Head of the Church in whom alone is centred the fulness of the Apostolic power and doctrinal Infallibility.* Priests and laymen owe to the Bishops submission, respect and obedience.

Each priest, in his turn, when he has received from his Bishop authority to preach and administer spiritual comfort [*secours*] to a certain number of the faithful, has a strict right to the respect, love and obedience of those whose spiritual interests are confided to his pastoral care.

Such is the divine plan of this Catholic Church which Jesus Christ has clothed with his power; such is this Ecclesiastical Hierarchy which, in its admirable harmony, shows us a body perfectly organized and capable of surely reaching its end, which is the eternal salvation of every one of its innumerable children 'of all tribes, languages, peoples and nations', *ex omni tribu et lingua et populo et natione* (Apoc. v, 9).

III
CATHOLIC LIBERALISM

Catholic liberalism, says Pius IX, is the most ruthless and dangerous enemy to the divine constitution of the Church.* Like a serpent that glides through the terrestrial paradise to entice and destroy the human race, it presents to the children of Adam the deceptive bait of a certain liberty and of a certain knowledge of good and evil, a liberty and knowledge which leads to death. It endeavours to slip imperceptibly into the most holy places; it charms the most perspicacious eyes; it poisons the simplest hearts, if one wavers ever so little in faith in the authority of the Sovereign Pontiff.

The followers of this subtle error concentrate all their strength to burst the bonds which unite the people to the Bishops and the Bishops to the Vicar of Jesus Christ. They applaud civil authority every time it invades the sanctuary; they seek by every means to induce the faithful to tolerate, if not approve, of iniquitous laws.—Enemies so much the more dangerous that often, without even being conscious of it, they favour the most perverted doctrines, which Pius IX has so well described in calling them *a fanciful reconciliation of truth with error*.

The Catholic liberal reassures himself, because he still has some Catholic principles, certain pious practices, a certain background [*fond*] of faith and attachment to the Church; but he carefully shuts his eyes to the rent made in his heart by the error which silently devours it. He still boasts to all about his religious convictions, and is angry when warned that he has dangerous principles; he is perhaps sincere in his delusion; God alone knows it! But, beside all these fine appearances, there is a great depth [*fond*] of pride which lets him believe he has more prudence and wisdom than those to whom the Holy Spirit gives authority [*mission*] and grace to teach and govern the faithful people. He will be seen censuring without scruple the acts and writings of the highest religious authority. Under pretence of removing the cause of dissensions and of reconciling with the Gospel the progress of present-day society, he puts himself in the service of Caesar and of those who invent pretended laws in favor of a false liberty; as if darkness could exist with light, and as if truth did not cease to be truth when one violated it, therein turning it aside from its true meaning and despoiling it of that immutability inherent in its nature.

In the presence of five Apostolic Briefs denouncing *Catholic liberalism* as absolutely incompatible with Church doctrine, although it may not be yet formally condemned as heretical, it can no longer be permitted in conscience to be *a Catholic liberal*.

IV
CATHOLIC POLITICS

One of the greatest geniuses who ever lived on this earth, St Thomas Aquinas, defines *law* in general. '*Quaedam rationis ordinatio ad bonum commune et ab eo qui euram communitatis habet, promulgata.*' 'Law is a rule dictated by reason for the common good, and promulgated by he who has the care of society.'* The Catholic Church recognizes in this short definition all the features of a Christian politics.

The common good is the only and supreme end.

Reason is to be the source of law. Reason, that is to say, the conformity of the means employed, not only with the end to be attained, but also with justice and morality; reason, and not the spirit of party, not the intention of holding on to power, not the wish to cripple the opposed party.

The authority which imposes the law is here admirably defined. The Holy Spirit often represents it to us as bearing a sword and ready to strike whoever refuses to render it honor, fear and homage; it is thus it ought to appear to peoples, 'as minister of the vengeance of God on those who do evil'; *Dei minister est, vindex in iram ei qui malum agit* (Rom. xiii, 4). But our Holy Doctor, considering the authority in the person clothed with it, shows him his duties at the same time that he defines his rights. 'To you, oh princes, oh legislators, has been confided the care of society; *qui curam societatis habet*; it is not to satisfy your ambition, your thirst for honors and riches, that authority has been given you; it is a charge, an obligation, a duty, that has been imposed upon you.'

Truly, a Divine politics! Oh, it leaves far behind it that false and utterly unreasonable politics which treats the most serious interests of a people like a child's toy with which blind partisans seek to amuse and enrich themselves, and to mutually supplant one another.

Far be it from us not to recognize the advantages of the constitutional regime considered in itself, and consequently, the usefulness of its distinctions of party, which hold one another in check, in order to signal and stop the errors of power. What we deplore, what we condemn, is the abuse of it; it is the pretension that politics, reduced to the mean and ridiculous proportions of party interests, becomes *the supreme rule* of every public administration, that *everything* may be *for the party* and nothing for *the common good*; nothing for *that society of which one has the charge*. What we condemn once again, is that one is allowed to say and to dare all that can tend to the triumph of a party. 'Listen to my words,' says the Holy Spirit (Wisdom of Solomon vi), 'you who govern the people, consider you have received the power from the Most High, who will examine your works, scrutinize even your thoughts; because being the ministers of His kingdom, you have not guarded the law of justice nor walked according to His will. He will also come to you in a terrible manner to judge you with extreme severity.'

V
THE ROLE OF THE CLERGY IN POLITICS

Men who would lead you astray, Our Dearly Beloved Brethren, tell you repeatedly that religion has nothing whatever to do with politics; that it is not necessary to take any account of religious principles in the discussion of public affairs; that the clergy have no functions except within the Church and the sacristy; and that the people should practice moral independence in politics.

Monstrous errors, Our Dearly Beloved Brethren; and woe to the country in which they take root. In excluding the clergy, the Church is excluded; and in putting aside the Church, one is deprived of all that is salutary and unchangeable it contains—God, morality, justice, truth, and when one has swept away all the rest, one has nothing left to rely upon except force!

Every man who has his salvation at heart should govern his actions according to Divine law, of which religion is the expression and guardian. Who cannot understand what justice and rectitude would reign everywhere, if governments and peoples had always before their eyes that Divine law which is equity itself, and the formidable judgement which they will have to undergo one day before Him from whose hands no one can possibly escape? The greatest enemies of the people are, therefore, those who wish to banish religion from politics; for, under the pretext of freeing the people from what they call *the tyranny, the undue influence of the priest*, they are preparing for this people the heaviest chains and the ones that will be the most difficult to throw off; they place might above right, and take from the civil power the only moral check which can prevent it from degenerating into despotism and tyranny!

They wish to shut the priest up in the sacristy! Why? Is it because during his studies he has acquired certain and salutary knowledge of the rights and duties of each of the faithful confided to his care? Is it because he sacrifices his resources, his time, his health, even his life, for the benefit of his fellow creatures?

Is he not a citizen with the same rights as others? What! any newcomer may write, speak and act; you sometimes see an influx of strangers into a parish or a county, who came there to impose their own political opinions: and the priest alone will be unable to speak or to write! Any one who wishes will be permitted to come into a parish and to promulgate all sorts of principles and the priest, who in the midst of his parishioners is like a father amongst his children, will have no right to speak, no right to protest against the enormities which are submitted to them!

Those who today are shouting that the priest has nothing whatever to do in politics, not long ago were finding his influence salutary; those who now deny the competency of the clergy in these questions formerly used to praise the steadiness of principles that the study of Christian morality gives a man. Whence this change of mind, if not from sensing that this influence, which they are aware they no longer merit, now acts against them?

Without doubt, our Dearly Beloved Brethren, the exercise of all the rights of citizenship by a priest is not at all times opportune; it may even have its dangers and disadvantages: but it must not be forgotten that to the Church alone belongs the right to give to its ministers the instructions which she may deem appropriate, and to reprimand those who may go astray; and the Bishops of this Province have not failed to do their duty on this point.

Up to the present we have considered the priest as a citizen, and as speaking of politics in his own name, like any other member of civil society.

Are there questions in which the Bishop and the priest may, and some-times even must, interfere in the name of religion?

We answer without hesitation: Yes, there are political questions in which the clergy may and even must interfere in the name of religion. The principle governing this right and duty is found in the very distinction we have already indicated, between the Church and the State.

There are, in effect, political questions which touch on the spiritual interests of souls, either because they relate to faith and morals, or because they can affect the liberty, independence or existence of the Church, even from a temporal point of view.

A candidate may present himself whose programme is hostile to the Church, or whose antecedents are such that his candidature threatens these same interests.

Likewise, a political party may be judged dangerous, not only because of its programme and antecedents, but also because of the particular programmes and antecedents of its leaders, of its principal members, and of the press which represents it, unless this party explicitly disavow them and separate itself from them, assuming they are persisting in their error after having been warned about it.

In this case a Catholic cannot, without denying his faith, show himself hostile to the Church of which he is a member, refuse to the Church the right of defending itself, or rather defending the spiritual interests of the souls confided to its safekeeping! But the Church speaks, acts, and fights through its clergy, and to refuse these rights to them is to refuse them to the Church.

Thus, the priest and the bishop may in all justice, and must in all conscience, raise their voices, point out the danger, declare authoritatively that to vote in a particular way is a sin, and that to do such a thing makes one liable to the censure of the Church. They may and must speak, not only to the electors and the candidates, but also to the constituted authorities, for the duty of every man who wishes to save his soul is traced out by divine law; and the Church, as a good Mother, owes to all her children, regardless of their station in life, love and, consequently, spiritual vigilance. It is not, therefore, converting the pulpit into a political platform [when the clergy] enlighten the conscience of the faithful on all those questions in which salvation is involved.

Doubtless, Our Dearly Beloved Brethren, such questions do not come up for discussion everyday; but the right [of the clergy] is no less certain for all that.

It is evident, by the very nature of the question, that to the Church alone must belong the right of judging the circumstances under which it must raise its voice in favour of Christian faith and morality.

It will perhaps be objected that the priest is liable, like every man, to go beyond the limits assigned to him, and that then it is up to the State to make him return to his duties.

To this we will reply, firstly, that it is a gratuitous insult to the entire Church to suppose that there is not in its hierarchy a remedy for the injustice or error of one of its ministers. In fact, the Church has its regularly constituted tribunals; and if any one thinks he has reason to complain of a minister of the Church, he should cite him, not before the civil tribunal, but rather before the ecclesiastical tribunal, which is alone competent to judge the doctrine and the conduct of the priest. That is why Pius IX, in his bull *Apostolicae Sedis*, in October 1869, declares major excommunication against those who, either directly or indirectly, require lay judges to summon ecclesiastical personages before their courts, against the provisions of canon law.

Secondly, when the state invades the rights of the Church, and tramples under foot its most sacred privileges, as to-day happens in Italy, France and Switzerland, would it not be the height of derision to give to this same state the right to gag its victim?

Thirdly, if we establish as a principle that a power does not exist because it may happen that somebody abuses it, it will be necessary to deny the existence of all the civil powers, because all persons in whom these powers are vested are fallible.

VI
THE PRESS AND ITS DUTIES

In our day, the press plays a role, for good as well as for evil, the importance of which cannot be concealed. The Church cannot remain an indifferent spectator to these journalistic struggles which occur either in books or in newspapers. These writings which the press eternalizes, as it were, and scatters to the winds are far more productive, either in a constructive way or scandalously, than a talk forgotten almost as soon as it is heard by a small number of listeners. Honor and glory to those Catholic writers who make it their primary duty to propagate and defend the truth; and who examine with scrupulous care the questions they are called upon to discuss! But what answers will they give to the Sovereign Judge, those writers for whom politics as they understand it means above all serving the interests of their party—who take no account of the Church, who would make of that spouse of Jesus Christ the slave of Caesar; and who neglect, or even scorn, the advice of those whom Jesus Christ has charged with teaching the truths of religion?

The duties of the press, as laid down by our last Council at Quebec,* may be summed up as follows:—Firstly, always to treat one's opponents with charity, moderation and respect, because zeal for the truth cannot excuse any excess of language; secondly, to judge one's opponents with impartiality and justice, as one would wish to be judged oneself; thirdly, not to hasten to condemn before having carefully examined every thing [relevant]; fourthly, to put the best construction on what is ambiguous; fifthly, to avoid raillery, sarcasm, conjectures injurious to the reputation [of one's opponents], ill-founded accusations, and the imputation of intentions which God alone knows.

It is allowed to combat what the Church has not condemned, but not to bring it into improper publicity [*mais non pas le mal noter*].

In matters connected with the ecclesiastical or civil authorities, the language should always be proper and respectful.

Establishments of which the Bishops are the natural protectors and judges, must not be brought before the incompetent tribunal of public opinion.

Let us add that the priest, and with stronger reason, the Bishop, in the exercise of his ministry, is not under the jurisdiction of public opinion, but under that alone of his hierarchical superiors. If any person thinks he has a right to complain, he can always do so before those who have the power to do him justice; from the priest an appeal can be made to the Bishop, from the

Bishop to the Archbishop, and from the Archbishop to the Sovereign Pontiff; but it can never be permitted to broadcast through the press the thousand rumors which political disturbances causes to spring up like the waves on a stormy sea.

It must not be forgotten that if particular laws made by a Bishop are not binding upon those outside his diocese, the principles which he makes known in his pastoral letters are for all times and all places. If any person, ecclesiastic or lay, believes he has a right not to listen to the voice of a pastor who is not his own, he has not for that reason any right to criticise or judge him.

VII
CONCERNING OATHS

'The name of God is holy and terrible' (Psalms cx, 9); it ought not to be uttered except with the most profound respect, and 'the Lord will not hold him innocent who takes the name of the Lord his God in vain' (Exodus xx, 7).

It is further written in our holy books: 'You will make oath, saying: Long live the Lord; but that it may be with truth, with discretion, with justice' (Jeremiah iv, 2).

The oath is an act of religion, and, consequently, it pertains above all to the Church, which alone has authority to define and make known its nature and conditions.

There are two distinct parts to every oath: 1st, *The affirmation* of any fact or wish; 2nd, *The invocation of God* as witness to the truth of this fact or wish. The affirmation is called the *formula* when its terms are determined by authority, but this difference of name changes nothing in the nature even of that part of the oath.

All depends on the conformity of that affirmation or formula with the truth as known by him who takes the oath. If the affirmation or formula is true in all its parts, the oath is good and true.

There is perjury the moment the affirmation or formula contains something false, known as such by him who takes the oath. Even when there might be a thousand truths in your affirmation or formula, if you knowingly mix with them a single word which is not true, that single lie is sufficient to make you guilty of perjury.

From all this two very important conclusions result:—1st, Before taking an oath it is necessary to examine and understand the formula one is called to swear to, lest there be something there contrary to the truth as one knows it; if there is anything there one does not thoroughly understand, if there is any doubt, one must have it explained and refuse to take the oath until one's conscience is satisfied on the subject; otherwise one risks perjuring oneself, and consequently one commits a grave sin; 2nd, One must never speak of the formula of an oath as a matter *of little importance*: and we condemn absolutely the distinction that some would make between different formulae in order to slight some of them, or to give them a sense that the expressions they contain cannot bear. Words clear in themselves allow no interpretation whatever, just as light requires no other light to be seen. When a formula says clearly and formally that some particular thing exists, no possible interpretation can make it say that this thing does not exist.

Upon taking up their responsibilities, public officials take what is known as an *oath of office*. They promise solemnly in the presence of Almighty God to fulfil faithfully [*avec exactitude*] certain duties imposed on them. This is no empty formula, a promise devoid of sense, but among the most serious obligations, which lasts as long as one is in office. This ought to be the object of a strict and serious examination of the conscience when preparing to receive the sacraments.

If one must respect one's own oaths, one must respect no less those of others. We seize this occasion to condemn as impious and scandalous the practice of certain legal men who, for the sake of their cause, do not hesitate to cross-examine witnesses even to the point of confusing them and making them contradict and perjure themselves. It is not enough that a cause be good; it is necessary that the means employed to make it prevail be in conformity with the unalterable rules of truth, justice and charity.

VIII
ON ECCLESIASTICAL BURIAL

Ecclesiastical burial has not, doubtless, the same degree of sanctity as the sacraments, but it nevertheless belongs entirely and solely to the judgement of the Church. We wish to speak of *ecclesiastical burial* as defined and ordained by canon law; that is to say, not only the prayers and religious rites which accompany the interment, but also the ground sanctified and consecrated by prayers and benedictions for the burial of those who die in the peace of the Catholic Church.

No temporal power can oblige the Church to pray over the tomb of a dead person whom the Church has judged unworthy of its prayers; it is an assault upon the Church [*un attentat sacrilège*] to violate by force the sanctity of ground consecrated by the prayers and benediction of the Church.

It will perhaps be said that the privation of the honors of ecclesiastical burial brings with it disgrace and infamy, and that it thus comes within the province of the civil authority, which is responsible for protecting the honor of the citizens.

We answer that the dishonor and the infamy are found rather in the revolt of a child against its mother, and that nothing can wipe out a grievous disobedience persevered in at the hour of death. All the trials, appeals and sentences of the world will only serve to publicize the transgression and render the disgrace and infamy more notorious and more deplorable in the eyes of all true Catholics.

'Jesus Christ', said the Apostle St Paul, 'loved His Church and gave himself up for it' (Eph. v, 25). Following the example of our Divine Master and Model, nothing should be dearer to us in this world than that same Church, of which we are members under the same Head who is Jesus Christ. She is our Mother, since she has awakened us to the life of grace; we should have for her a tender, filial love, rejoice in her triumphs, share her sorrows, and when necessary raise our voice in her defence. When, therefore, we see her dignity and liberty denied, her children, and still less her pastors, cannot be permitted a silence that would be equivalent to treason.

The Holy Catholic Church, faithful to the teachings of her Divine Master, teaches her children 'to give unto Caesar the things that are Caesar's, and to God the things that are God's' (Matt. xxii, 21). She repeats, with the great Apostle, 'Render to each one his due, tribute to whom tribute; taxes to whom taxes; fear to whom fear; and honor to whom honor' (Rom. xiii, 7). This duty of justice and respect which she never stops proclaiming, she has a stronger right than anyone to expect will be fulfilled on her own behalf, and that what belongs to the Church of God will be given to the Church of God.

Now, our Dearly Beloved Brethren, sorrowfully we have to say that a case unfortunately renowned* shows us that the Catholic Church in Canada is threatened in its liberty and most precious rights, and what makes our affliction more keen is that the Church can say with the Prophet, 'I have nourished my children and loaded them with benefits, and they have despised me'; *filios enutrivi et exaltavi, ipsi autem spreverunt me* (Isaiah i, 2)! The first authors of this assault were brought up on the knees of a Christian mother; in their youth they knelt at the holy table; they received the ineffaceable mark of confirmation; and to-day, notwithstanding their revolt, they call themselves Catholics, in order to have the right to force open the gates of a cemetery consecrated by the prayers of the Church and destined by her for the burial of her faithful children.

In order to disguise this criminal usurpation, the so-called *Gallican liberties*† were invoked, as if Catholic unity, founded by Jesus Christ on the supreme authority of St Peter and his successors, were but a vain and empty title. And, in fact, what else would an authority be against which subjects were permitted to appeal in the name of *their liberties*! What prince, what republic, would willingly recognize a like principle invoked by a province, notwithstanding the express declarations, a hundred times repeated, of the constitution and of the supreme tribunals of the state?

Let those who are outside the Church consider such principles good and admirable if they will, for they do not believe in that authority which is the foundation of the Catholic Church. But that some men still dare to call themselves children of the Church, while denying to that degree its teachings and its hierarchy, is an incomprehensible error.

Those who have commenced, sustained or encouraged by their subscriptions this unqualified assault against the just rights of the Church, we hold guilty of an open revolt against the Church, and of a grievous injustice, for which they cannot obtain pardon, unless they strive to repair [the injury] by all means in their power.

We invite all the true children of the Church to pray the Divine Heart of Our Lord to have pity on those who have thus strayed from the path of faith and justice, that they may recognize their sin, make reparation, and obtain mercy.

CONCLUSION

Such, Our Dearly Beloved Brethren, is the important advice we deem it our duty to give you under the present circumstances.

Beware, above all, of this *liberalism* which hides itself under the beautiful name of *Catholic*, the more surely to accomplish its criminal work. You will easily recognize it from the picture the Sovereign Pontiff has so often drawn of it. 1st, Efforts to subjugate the Church to the State. 2nd, Incessant attempts to divide the bonds which unite the children of the Church amongst themselves and to the clergy. 3rd, Monstrous alliance of the truth with error under the pretence of resolving all differences and avoiding conflicts. 4th, Lastly, delusion and sometimes hypocrisy, which, under a religious exterior and fine protestations of submission to the Church, hide a boundless pride.

Remember that true Christian politics has but one aim, which is the *public good*; but one *means*, which is the perfect conformity of the laws with truth and justice.

Respect the oath as an important religious act; before taking it, examine carefully if the formula is true in all points, to the best of your knowledge; scrupulously fulfil the duties of your oath of office and take care not to lead your neighbour into perjury.

The present *mandement* shall be read and published at the Prone [i.e., during the time for the sermon] of all churches and chapels, parochial and mission, where public service is performed, on the first Sunday after its reception.

Given under our signatures, the seal of the archdiocese and the counter-signature of the secretary of the archiepiscopal palace of Quebec the twenty-second of September, one thousand eight hundred and seventy-five.

E.A. Arch. of Quebec.
Ig. Bish. of Montreal.
L.F. Bish. of Three Rivers.
Jean, Bish. of S.G., of Rimouski.
E.C. Bish. of Gratianopolis.
Antoine, Bish. of Sherbrooke.
J. Thomas, Bish. of Ottawa.
L.Z. Moreau, Pst. Adm. of St Hyacinthe.
By Messeigneurs,
  C.O. Collet, Priest,
  Secretary

GOLDWIN SMITH

Goldwin Smith (1823-1910) made his acquaintance with our politics as a mature man, when he moved to Toronto in 1871, after a distinguished career at Oxford as Regius Professor of Modern History. Describing himself as 'a liberal of the old school', he believed it was of immense importance for the future of mankind that the family feuds within the English-speaking world be overcome and that antagonism between Britain, Canada, and the United States give way to practical union. For more than a generation Smith was our most interesting essayist, and his work remains our most distinguished contribution to the definition of liberalism.

The passages from his Reminiscences *(1910) are intended to help the reader locate Smith in relation to his times. They are followed by the first half of a lengthy essay, published in 1877, that discusses Darwin's* Descent of Man *(1871). The last selection, another essay published in 1877, outlines the analysis of Canadian politics that Smith developed in his well-known book,* Canada and the Canadian Question *(1891).*

From His *Reminiscences*

The great man of Canadian politics, when first I came to Canada, was Sir John Macdonald, who ruled the country for many years. A very curious and notable character he was. The study of his life from his earliest years had been the manipulation of human nature for the purposes of party. In that craft he was unrivalled. A statesman in the higher sense he was not, nor an administrator. His principles, his economical principles especially, were the shifts of the hour. Only in his attachment to the British Crown, and in his determination, as he said, to die a British subject, could he be said to be firm. He was personally very attractive, bright, good-humoured, versatile, capable of being all things to all men, of talking well on serious and even on literary subjects to the guests at one end of the table, and cracking rough jokes or telling *risqué* anecdotes to the guests at the other end. He was said to be like Disraeli. There may have been a slight likeness in face. The dark Highland face has something of Jewish cast. Other likeness there was none. Macdonald had nothing of Disraeli's imagination. He more resembled Palmerston as a tactician and a speaker whose object was not oratorical effect, but the capture of votes. He was not himself corrupt. It was for the game more than for the stakes that he cared. But he was unscrupulous in corrupting other men. He decidedly did not love Spartans. He was credited with saying that the perfection of a ministry would be twelve men, each of whom, if you liked, you could put into the penitentiary. He spoke in jest, no doubt; but in the jest there was a grain of truth. On the eve of a general election it was pointed out to him that some of his men were talking Protectionism, which, whatever might be its effect in such a country as the United States, with their vast area of production and home trade, would not do for Canada. 'No,' was his reply, 'you need not think I am going to get into that hole.' Scarcely two months had passed when into that hole he got. Rallied by his friend on his change, he jauntily replied, 'Yes, Protection has done so much for me, that I must do something for Protection.' He was a survivor of the times in which whiskey played an important part in politics, and he had not put off the habits of his jovial generation.

Macdonald was not delicate in the choice of his instruments. An incident which I am going to mention showed this and at the same time a certain sensitiveness which he retained after a life which it might have been supposed would have thoroughly steeled his nerves. He came to my house [in 1876?] for the wedding of his son [Hugh John Macdonald]. On the evening of his arrival he was in his usual spirits. Next morning as we drove to the church a cloud seemed to have come over him. At the wedding breakfast he sat perfectly silent. When his health was drunk, he disappointed the company by merely stumbling through two or three disjointed sentences. He was called up to reply to another toast, with no happier result. On my return home I found the Chief of Police waiting at my door and desiring to see Sir John Macdonald. Those were the days of Fenianism, and I fancied that this was some alarm from that quarter. It turned out, however, that an American who had served Sir John in some secret and probably associated with him in some political business, had quarrelled with him, and having demanded $3000 of him was trying to indict him for perjury and had chosen the day of the marriage for the service of the writ. The attempt, of course, came to nothing, but the apprehension of it had evidently been enough to upset Sir John Macdonald. . . .

The professions of George Brown, the head of the Grit party and Macdonald's mortal enemy, were far more moral than those of Macdonald. Whether he was a better man may be questioned, while he unquestionably was far less attractive and amusing. A Liberal he might call himself; but it could be only in a party sense. Of liberality of character and sentiment, of breadth of view or toleration of difference of opinion, no human being was ever more devoid. Master of *The Globe*, which then, unhappily for the country, was the only powerful paper, he used it without scruple or mercy to crush everybody who would not bow to his will. . . . The best of Brown was his fidelity to the cause of the North during the American war of Secession. On the other hand, he traded long on the antipathy of the British and Protestant to the French and Catholic Province, a very mischievous and unpatriotic line. . . . In his large and burly body dwelt a strong but thoroughly coarse mind. When pitted against Sir John Macdonald in the Confederation Government he soon felt his own inferiority and withdrew to his despotic reign in the office of *The Globe*. . . .

Another Canadian politician of mark with whom I came into contact was Joseph Howe, the favourite son and renowned orator of Nova Scotia. He came to England when I was there to demand the liberation of Nova Scotia from Federation, into which they had been inveigled by the black arts of Sir Charles Tupper. Applying to Lord Campbell, Howe was by him introduced to me. He attended a dinner at which the chiefs of the Liberal party were present, and made a speech somewhat too eloquent for a rather unimpressionable audience of old politicians, threatening bloodshed if his Province were not set free. The Liberals accordingly moved in Parliament. But scarcely had they done this when the news came that Mr Howe was in a Confederation Government. His apologists say that he yielded to destiny. But destiny, if it requires submission, hardly requires acceptance of place. About Howe's eloquence, it seems, there could be no doubt, though when I heard him it was rather overstrained. . . .

Sir Charles Tupper was a man of extraordinary force and a thunderer of the platform, though the staple of his oratory was purely exaggeration, with a large measure of rather vulgar invective. Unwearied, undaunted, and unabashed, while he served as the shield-bearer of Sir John Macdonald, he was very useful to his chief, whose apparently lost cause he did much to redeem after the catastrophe of the Pacific Railway scandal.

Of the few people in England who thought about colonial subjects in my day, the general opinion was that the destiny of the colonies was independence. I brought that opinion, certainly not one disparaging either to the colonies or to the Mother-country, with me to Canada. It drew me to a set of Canadian youths strongly imbued with it. . . . a movement called 'Canada First', the tendency, if not the avowed object, of which was to make Canada an independent nation linked by affection to the Mother-country.* This was my own idea, as it was that of the British statesmen from whom my opinions had been imbibed, and indeed of British statesmen generally in my day. It seemed desirable that there should be two experiments in Democracy on this continent. I was, besides, attracted by genuine patriotism and fresh hope. . . . But the guiding star, the hero of the party, was Mr Edward Blake,† an advocate and politician of the highest promise, whose 'Aurora speech' had seemed to open a new political era and given a terrible shock to the orthodox and senile Liberalism of Mr George Brown and the *Globe*. . . . But [the next year] Mr Edward Blake suddenly left his following, let *The Liberal* die, surrendered to *The Globe*, took office in the Mackenzie Government, which was formed under the auspices of George Brown, and left his adherents to the vengeance of the enemy. That was the end of 'Canada First', and, as it turned out, of the hope of making Canada a nation.

Mr Edward Blake was a man of the highest character, a powerful advocate, a jurist of repute, and a strong though prolix speaker. But his career has shown that he mistook his vocation when he undertook to be a leader of men. Too much is said about the necessity of magnetism. A leader may be, as some of the most powerful leaders—Pitt and Peel—have been, destitute of magnetism, and yet have devoted followers if he is unselfish and true at heart to his cause, and to his friends.

The Ascent of Man

Science and criticism have raised the veil of the Mosaic cosmogony and revealed to us the physical origin of man. We see that, instead of being created out of the dust of the earth by Divine fiat, he has in all probability been evolved out of it by a process of development through a series of intermediate forms.

The discovery is, of course, unspeakably momentous. Among other things it seems to open to us a new view of morality, and one which, if it is verified by further investigation, can hardly fail to produce a great change in philosophy.

Supposing that man has ascended from a lower animal form, there appears to be ground at least for surmising that vice, instead of being a diabolical inspiration or a mysterious element of human nature, is the remnant of the lower animal not yet eliminated; while virtue is the effort, individual and collective, by which that remnant is being gradually worked off. The acknowledged connection of virtue with the ascendency of the social over the selfish desires and tendencies seems to correspond with this view; the nature of the lower animals being, so far as we can see, almost entirely selfish, and admitting no regard even for the present interests of their kind, much less for its interests in the future. The doubtful qualities, and 'last infirmities of noble minds', such as ambition and the love of fame, in which the selfish element is mingled with one not wholly selfish, and which commend themselves at least by their refinement, as contrasted with the coarseness of the merely animal vices, may perhaps be regarded as belonging to the class of phenomena quaintly designated by some writers as 'pointer facts', and as marking the process of transition. In what morality consists, no one has yet succeeded in making clear. Mr Sidgwick's recent criticism of the various theories leads to the conviction that not one of them affords a satisfactory basis for a practical system of ethics.* If our lower nature can be traced to an animal origin, and can be shown to be in course of elimination, however slow and interrupted, this at all events will be a solid fact, and one which must be the starting-point of any future system of ethics. Light would be at once thrown by such a discovery on some parts of the subject which have hitherto been involved in impenetrable darkness. Of the vice of cruelty, for example, no rational account, we believe, has yet been given; it is connected with no human appetite, and seems to gratify no human object of desire; but if we can be shown to have inherited it from animal progenitors, the mystery of its existence is at least in part explained. In the event of this surmise being substantiated, moral phantasms, with their mediaeval trappings, would for ever disappear; individual responsibility would be reduced within reasonable limits; the difficulty of the question respecting free will would shrink to comparatively narrow proportions; but it does not seem likely that the love of virtue and the hatred of vice would be diminished; on the contrary, it seems likely that they would be practically intensified, while a more practical direction would certainly be given to the science of ethics as a system of moral training and a method of curing moral disease.

It is needless to say how great has been the influence of the doctrine of Evolution, or rather perhaps of the method of investigation to which it has given birth, upon the study of history, especially the history of institutions. Our general histories will apparently have to be almost rewritten from that point of view. It is only to be noted, with regard to the treatment of history, that the mere introduction of a physical nomenclature, however elaborate and apparently scientific, does not make anything physical which before was not so, or exclude from human actions, of which history is the aggregate, any element not of a physical kind. We are impressed, perhaps, at first with a sense of new knowledge when we are told that human history is 'an integration of matter and concomitant dissipation of motion; during which the matter passes from an indefinite incoherent homogeneity to a definite coherent heterogeneity, and during which the retained motion undergoes a parallel transformation.'†

But a little reflection suggests to us that such a philosophy is vitiated by the assumption involved in the word 'matter', and that the philosophy of history is in fact left exactly where it was before. The superior complexity of high civilization is a familiar social fact which gains nothing in clearness by the importation of mechanical or physiological terms.

We must also be permitted to bear in mind that evolution, though it may explain everything else, cannot explain itself. What is the origin of the movement, and by what power the order of development is prescribed, are questions yet unsolved by physical science. That the solution, if it could be supplied, would involve anything arbitrary, miraculous, or at variance with the observed order of things, need not be assumed; but it might open a new view of the universe, and dissipate for ever the merely mechanical accounts of it. In the meantime we may fairly enter a caveat against the tacit insinuation of an unproved solution. Science can apparently give no reason for assuming that the first cause, and that which gives the law to development, is a blind force rather than an archetypal idea. The only origination within our experience is that of human action, where the cause is an idea. Science herself, in fact, constantly assumes an analogous cause for the movements of the universe in her use of the word 'law', which necessarily conveys the notion, not merely of observed co-existence and sequence, but of the intelligent and consistent action of a higher power, on which we rely in reasoning from the past to the future, as we do upon consistency in the settled conduct of a man.

Unspeakably momentous, however, we once more admit, the discovery is, and great is the debt of gratitude due to its illustrious authors. Yet it seems not unreasonable to ask whether in some respects we are not too much under its immediate influence, and whether the revolution of thought, though destined ultimately to be vast, may not at present have somewhat overpassed its bounds. Is it not possible that the physical origin of man may be just now occupying too large a space in our minds compared with his ulterior development and his final destiny? With our eyes fixed on the 'Descent', newly disclosed to us, may we not be losing sight of the *Ascent* of man?

There seems in the first place, to be a tendency to treat the origin of a being as finally decisive of its nature and destiny. From the language sometimes used, we should almost suppose that rudiments alone were real, and that all the rest was mere illusion. An eminent writer on the antiquities of jurisprudence intimates his belief that the idea of human brotherhood is not coeval with the race, and that primitive communities were governed by sentiments of a very different kind.* His words are at once pounced upon as a warrant for dismissing the idea of human brotherhood from our minds, and substituting for it some other social principles, the character of which has not yet been definitely explained, though it is beginning in some quarters pretty distinctly to appear. But surely this is not reasonable. There can be no reason why the first estate of man, which all allow to have been his lowest estate, should claim the prerogative of furnishing his only real and indefeasible principles of action. Granting that the idea of human brotherhood was not aboriginal—granting that it came into the world at a comparatively late period, still it has come, and having come, it is as real and seems as much entitled to consideration as inter-tribal hostility and domestic despotism were in their own day. That its advent has not been unattended by illusions and aberrations is a fact which does not cancel its title to real existence under the present conditions, and with the present lights of society, any more than it annuls the great effects upon the actions of men and the course of history which the idea has undeniably produced. Human brotherhood was not a part of a primaeval revelation; it may not have been an original institution; but it seems to be a real part of a development, and it may be a part of a plan. That the social principles of certain anti-philanthropic works are identical with those which governed the actions of mankind in a primaeval and rudimentary state, when man had only just emerged from the animal, and have been since worked off by the foremost races in the course of development, is surely rather an argument against the paramount and indefeasible authority of those principles than in favour of it. It tends rather to show that their real character is that of a relapse, or, as the physiologists call it, a reversion. When there is a vast increase of wealth, of sensual enjoyment, and of the selfishness which is apt to attend them, it is not marvellous that such reversions should occur.

Another eminent writer appears to think that he has put an end to metaphysical theology, and perhaps to metaphysics and theology altogether, by showing that 'being', and the cognate words, originally denoted merely physical perceptions.* But so, probably, did all language. So did 'spirit', so did 'geist', so did 'power', so did even 'sweet reasonableness', and 'the not us which makes for righteousness'. Other perceptions or ideas have gradually come, and are now denoted by the words which at first denoted physical perceptions only. Why have not these last comers as good a claim to existence as the first? Suppose the intellectual nature of man has unfolded, and been brought, as it conceivably may, into relations with something in the universe beyond the mere indications of the five bodily senses—why are we bound to mistrust the results of this unfolding? We might go still further back, and still lower, than to language denoting merely physical perceptions. We might go back to inarticulate sounds and signs; but this does not invalidate the reality of the perceptions afterwards expressed in articulate language. It seems not very easy to distinguish, in point of trustworthiness of source, between the principles of metaphysics and the first principles of mathematics, or to say, if we accept the deductions in one case, why we should not accept them in the other. It is conceivable at least, we venture to repeat, that the development of man's intellectual nature may have enabled him to perceive other things than those which he perceives by means of his five bodily senses; and metaphysics, once non-existent, may thus have come into legitimate existence. Man, if the doctrine of evolution is true, was once a creature with only bodily senses; nay, at a still earlier stage, he was matter devoid even of bodily sense; now he has arrived—through the exercise of his bodily senses it may be—at something beyond bodily sense, at such notions as *being, essence, existence*: he reasons upon these notions, and extends the scope of his once merely physical vocabulary so as to comprehend them. Why should he not? If we are to be anchored hard and fast to the signification of primaeval language, how are we to obtain an intellectual basis for 'the not us which makes for righteousness'? Do not the anti-metaphysicists themselves unconsciously metaphysicize? Does not their fundamental assumption—that the knowledge received through our bodily senses alone is trustworthy—involve an appeal to a mental necessity as much as anything in metaphysics, whether the mental necessity in this case be real or not?

Again, the great author of the Evolution theory himself, in his *Descent of Man*, has given us an account of morality which suggests a remark of the same kind. He seems to have come to the conclusion that what is called our moral sense is merely an indication of the superior permanency of social compared with personal impressions. Morality, if we take his explanation as complete and final, is reduced to tribal self-preservation subtilized into etiquette; an etiquette which, perhaps, a sceptical voluptuary, wishing to remove the obstacles to a life of enjoyment, might think himself not unreasonable in treating as an illusion. This, so far as appears, is the explanation offered of moral life, with all its beauty, its tenderness, its heroism, its self-sacrifice; to say nothing of spiritual life with its hopes and aspirations, its prayers and fanes. Such an account even of the origin of morality seems rather difficult to receive. Surely, even in their most rudimentary condition, virtue and vice must have been distinguished by some other characteristic than the relative permanency of two different sets of impressions. There is a tendency, we may venture to observe, on the part of eminent physicists, when they have carefully investigated and explained what seems to them the most important and substantial subjects of inquiry, to proffer less careful explanations of matters which to them seem secondary and less substantial, though possibly to an intelligence surveying the drama of the world from without the distinctly human portion of it might appear more important than the rest. Eminent physicists have been known, we believe, to account summarily for religion as a surviving reminiscence of the serpent which attacked the ancestral ape and the tree which sheltered him from the attack, so that Newton's religious belief would be a concomitant of his remaining trace of a tail. It was assumed that primaeval religion was universally the worship of the serpent and of the tree. This assumption was far from being correct; but, even if it had been correct, the theory based on it would surely have been a very summary account of the phenomena of religious life.

However, supposing the account of the origin of the moral sense and of moral life, given in *The Descent of Man*, to be true, it is an account of the origin only. Though profoundly significant, as well as profoundly interesting, it is not more significant, compared with the subsequent development, than is the origin of physical life compared with the subsequent history of living beings. Suppose a mineralogist or a chemist were to succeed in discovering the exact point at which inorganic matter gave birth to the organic; his discovery would be momentous and would convey to us a most distinct assurance of the method by which the governing power of the universe works: but would it qualify the mineralogist or the chemist to give a full account of all the diversities of animal life, and of the history of man? Heroism, self-sacrifice, the sense of moral beauty, the refined affections of civilized men, philanthropy, the desire of realizing a high moral ideal, whatever else they may be, are not tribal self-preservation subtilized into etiquette; nor are they adequately explained by reference to the permanent character of one set of impressions and the occasional character of another set. Between the origin of moral life and its present manifestation has intervened something so considerable as to baffle any anticipation of the destiny of humanity which could have been formed for a mere inspection of the rudiments. We may call this intervening force circumstance, if we please, provided we remember that calling it circumstance does not settle its nature, or exclude the existence of a power acting through circumstance as the method of fulfilling a design.

Whatever things may have been in their origin, they are what they are, both in themselves and in regard to their indications respecting other beings or influences the existence of which may be implied in theirs. The connection between the embryo and the adult man, with his moral sense and intelligence, and all that these imply, is manifest, as well as the gradual evolution of the one out of the other, and a conclusive argument is hence derived against certain superstitions or fantastic beliefs; but the embryo is not a man, neither is the man an embryo. A physiologist sets before us a set of plates showing the similarity between the embryo of Newton and that of his dog Diamond. The inference which he probably expects us to draw is that there is no essential difference between the philosopher and the dog. But surely it is at least as logical to infer, that the importance of the embryo and the significance of embryological similarities may not be so great as the physiologist is disposed to believe.

So with regard to human institutions. The writer on legal antiquities before mentioned finds two sets of institutions which are now directly opposed to each other, and between the respective advocates of which a controversy has been waged. He proposes to terminate that controversy by showing that though the two rival systems in their development are so different, in their origin they were the same. This seems very clearly to bring home to us the fact that, important as the results of an investigation of origins are, there is still a limit to their importance.

Again, while we allow no prejudice to stand in the way of our acceptance of Evolution, we may fairly call upon Evolution to be true to itself. We may call upon it to recognise the possibility of development in the future as well as the fact of development in the past, and not to shut up the hopes and aspirations of our race in a mundane egg because the mundane egg happens to be the special province of the physiologist. The series of developments has proceeded from the inorganic to the organic, from the organic upwards to moral and intellectual life. Why should it be arrested there? Why should it not continue its upward course and arrive at a development which might be designated as spiritual life? Surely the presumption is in favour of a continued operation of the law. Nothing can be more arbitrary than the proceeding of Comte, who, after tracing humanity, as he thinks, through the Theological and Metaphysical stages into the Positive, there closes the series and assumes that the Positive stage is absolutely final. How can he be sure that it will not be followed, for example, by one in which man will apprehend and commune with the Ruler of the Universe, not through mythology or dogma, but through Science? He may have had no experience of such a phase of human existence, nor may he be able at present distinctly to conceive it. But had he lived in the Theological or the Metaphysical era he would have been equally without experience of the Positive, and have had the same difficulty in conceiving its existence. His finality is an assumption apparently without foundation. . . . .

We do not presume, of course, in these few pages to broach any great question, our only purpose being to point out a possible aberration or exaggeration of the prevailing school of thought. . . .

The Political Destiny of Canada

Ignorance of the future can hardly be good for any man or nation; nor can forecast of the future in the case of any man or nation well interfere with the business of the present, though the language of colonial politicians seems often to imply that it may. No Canadian farmer would take his hand from the plough, no Canadian artisan would desert the foundry or the loom, no Canadian politician would become less busy in his quest of votes, no industry of any kind would slacken, no source of wealth would cease to flow, if the rulers of Canada and the powers of Downing Street, by whom the rulers of Canada are supposed to be guided, instead of drifting on in darkness, knew for what port they were steering.

For those who are actually engaged in moulding the institutions of a young country not to have formed a conception of her destiny—not to have made up their minds whether she is to remain for ever a dependency, to blend again in a vast confederation with the monarchy of the mother country, or to be united to a neighbouring republic—would be to renounce statesmanship. The very expenditure into which Canada is led by her position as a dependency in military and political railways, in armaments and defences, and other things which assume the permanence of the present system, is enough to convict Canadian rulers of flagrant improvidence if the permanency of the present system is not distinctly established in their minds.

To tax forecast with revolutionary designs or tendencies is absurd. No one can be in a less revolutionary frame of mind than he who foresees a political event without having the slightest interest in hastening its arrival. On the other hand, mere party politicians cannot afford to see beyond the hour. Under the system of party government, forecast and freedom of speech alike belong generally to those who are not engaged in public life.

The political destiny of Canada is here considered by itself, apart from that of any other portion of the motley and widely scattered 'Empire'. This surely is the rational course. Not to speak of India and the military dependencies, such as Malta and Gibraltar, which have absolutely nothing in common with the North American colonies (India not even the titular form of government, since its sovereign has been made an empress), who can believe that the future of Canada, of South Africa, of Australia, of the West Indies, and of Mauritius will be the same? Who can believe that the mixed French and English population of Canada, the mixed Dutch and English population of the Cape, the negro population of Jamaica, the French and Indian population of Mauritius, the English and Chinese population of Australia, are going to run for ever the same political course? Who can believe that the moulding influences will be the same in arctic continents or in tropical islands as in countries lying within the temperate zone? Among the colonies, those, perhaps, which most nearly resemble each other in political character and circumstances are Canada and

Australia; yet the elements of the population are very different; and still more different are the external relations of Australia, with no other power near her, from those of Canada, not only conterminous with the United States, but interlaced with them, so that at present the road of the Governor-General of Canada, when he visits his Pacific province, lies through the territory of the American republic. Is it possible to suppose that the slender filament which connects each of these colonies with Downing Street is the thread of a common destiny?

In studying Canadian politics, and in attempting to cast the political horoscope of Canada, the first thing to be remembered, though official optimism is apt to overlook it, is that Canada was a colony not of England but of France, and that between the British of Ontario and the British of Nova Scotia and New Brunswick are interposed, in solid and unyielding mass, above a million of unassimilated and politically antagonistic Frenchmen. French Canada is a relic of the historical past preserved by isolation, as Siberian mammoths are preserved in ice. It is a fragment of the France before the Revolution, less the monarchy and the aristocracy; for the feeble parody of French feudalism in America ended with the abolition of the seigniories [in 1854], which may be regarded as the final renunciation of feudal ideas and institutions by society in the New World. The French Canadians are an unprogressive, religious, submissive, courteous, and, though poor, not unhappy people. They would make excellent factory hands if Canada had a market for her manufactures; and, perhaps, it is as much due to the climate as to their lack of intelligent industry that they have a very indifferent reputation as farmers. They are governed by the priest, with the occasional assistance of the notary; and the Roman Catholic Church may be said to be still established in the province, every Roman Catholic being bound to pay tithes and other ecclesiastical imposts, though the Protestant minority are exempt. The Church is immensely rich, and her wealth is always growing, so that the economical element which mingled with the religious causes of the Reformation may one day have its counterpart in Quebec. The French Canadians, as we have said, retain their exclusive national character. So far from being absorbed by the British population, or Anglicized by contact with it, they have absorbed and Gallicized the fragments of British population which chance has thrown among them; and the children of Highland regiments disbanded in Quebec have become thorough Frenchmen, and prefixed Jean Baptiste to their Highland names. For his own Canada the Frenchman of Quebec has something of a patriotic feeling; for France he has filial affection enough to make his heart beat violently for her during a Franco-German war; for England, it may be safely said, he has no feeling whatever. It is true that he fought against the American invaders in the revolutionary war, and again in 1812; but then he was animated by his ancient hostility to the Puritans of New England, in the factories of whose descendants he now freely seeks employment. Whether he would enthusiastically take up arms for England against the Americans at present, the British War Office, after the experience of the two Fenian raids, can no doubt tell. With Upper Canada, the land of Scotch Presbyterians, Irish Orangemen, and ultra-British sentiment, French Canada, during the union of the two provinces, led an uneasy life; and she accepted confederation, on terms which leave her nationality untouched, rather as a severance of her special wedlock with her unloved consort than as a measure of North American union. The unabated antagonism between the two races and the two religions was plainly manifested on the occasion of the conflict between the French half-breeds and the British immigrants in Manitoba, which presented a faint parallel to the conflict between the advanced posts of slavery and anti-slavery in Kansas on the eve of the civil war; Quebec openly sympathizing with Riel and his fellow-insurgents, while Ontario was on fire to avenge the death of Scott. Sir George Cartier might call himself an Englishman speaking French; but his calling himself so did not make him so; much less did it extend the character from a political manager, treading the path of ambition with British colleagues, to the mass of his unsophisticated compatriots. The priests hitherto have put their interests into the hands of a political leader, such as Sir George himself, in the same way in which Irish priests used to put their interests into the hands of O'Connell; and this leader has made the best terms he could for them and for himself at Ottawa. Nor has it been difficult to make good terms, since both the political parties bid emulously for the Catholic vote, and, by their interested subserviency to those who wield it, render it impossible for a Liberal Catholic party, or a Liberal party of any kind, to make head against the priestly influence in Quebec. By preference the priests, as reactionists, have allied themselves with the Tory party in the British provinces, and Canada has long witnessed the singular spectacle, witnessed for the first time in England at the last general election, of Roman Catholics and Orangemen marching together to the poll. Fear of contact with an active-minded democracy, and of possible peril to their overweening wealth, has also led the priesthood to shrink from Annexation, though they have not been able to prevent their people from going over the line for better wages, and bringing back with them a certain republican leaven of political and ecclesiastical unrest, which in the end may, perhaps, lead to the verification of Lord Elgin's remark, that it would be easier to make the French Canadians Americans than to make them English. Hitherto, however, French Canada has retained, among other heirlooms of the *Ancien Régime,* the old Gallican Church, the Church of Louis XIV and of Bossuet, national, quiet, unaggressive, capable of living always on sufficiently good terms with the State. But now the scene is changed. Even to French Canada, the most secluded nook of the Catholic world, Ultramontanism has penetrated, with the Jesuit in its van. There is a struggle for ascendancy between the Jesuits and the Gallicans, the citadel of the Gallicans being the Sulpician seminary, vast and enormously wealthy, which rises over Montreal. The Jesuit has the forces of the hour on his side; he gains the day; the bishops fall under his influence and take his part against the Sulpicians; the Guibord case marks, distinctly though farcically, the triumph of his principles; and it is by no means certain that he, a cosmopolitan power playing a great game, will cling to Canadian isolation, and that he will not prefer a junction with his main army in the United States. Assuredly his choice will not be determined by loyalty to England. At all events, his aggressive policy has begun to raise questions calculated to excite the Protestants of the British provinces, which the politicians, with all their arts, will hardly be able to smother, and which will probably put an end to the long torpor of Quebec. The New Brunswick

School case points to education as a subject which can scarcely fail soon to give birth to a cause of war. *

Besides the French, there are in Canada, as we believe we have good authority for saying, about four hundred thousand Irish, whose political sentiments are generally identical with those of the Irish in the mother country, as any reader of their favourite journals will perceive. Thus, without reckoning a considerable German settlement in Ontario, which by its unimpaired nationality in the heart of the British population attests the weakness of the assimilating forces in Canada compared with those in the United States, or the Americans, who, though not numerous, are influential in the commercial centres, we have at once to deduct one million four hundred thousand from a total population of less than four millions in order to reduce to reality the pictures of universal devotion to England and English interests which are presented by the speeches of official persons or of persons professing to know Canada, but deriving their idea of her from the same source.

Confederation, so far, has done nothing to fuse the races, and very little even to unite the provinces. . . . From the composition of a cabinet to the composition of a rifle team sectionalism is the rule. Confederation has secured free trade between the provinces; what other good it has done it would not be easy to say. Whether it has increased the military strength of Canada is a question for the answer to which we must appeal once more to the British War Office. Canadians have shown, on more than one memorable occasion, that in military spirit they are not wanting; but they cannot be goaded into wasting their hardly-earned money on preparations for a defence which would be hopeless against an invader who will never come. Politically, the proper province of a federal government is the management of external relations, while domestic legislation is the province of the several states. But a dependency has no external relations; Canada has not even, like South Africa, a Native question, her Indians being perfectly harmless; and consequently the chief duty of a federal government in Canada is to keep itself in existence by the ordinary agencies of party, a duty which it discharges with a vengeance. English statesmen bent on extending to all the colonies what they assume to be the benefits of confederation, should study the Canadian specimen, if possible, on the spot. They will learn, first, that while a spontaneous confederation, such as groups of states have formed under the pressure of a common danger, develops mainly the principles of union, a confederation brought about by external influence is apt to develop the principles of antagonism in at least an equal degree; and, secondly, that parliamentary government in a dependency is, to a lamentable extent, government by faction and corruption, and that by superadding federal to provincial government the extent and virulence of those maladies are seriously increased. If an appeal is made to the success of confederation in Switzerland, the answer is that Switzerland is not a dependency but a nation.

It is of Canada alone that we here speak, and we speak only of her political destiny. The ties of blood, of language, of historical association, and of general sympathy which bind the British portion of the Canadian people to England, are not dependent on the political connection, nor is it likely that they would be at all weakened by its severance. In the United States there are millions of Irish exiles, with the wrongs of Ireland in their hearts, and the whole nation retains the memories of the revolutionary war, of the war of 1812, and of the conduct of the British aristocracy towards the United States during the rebellions of the South—conduct which it is difficult to forgive, and which it would be folly to forget. Yet to those who have lived among the Americans it will not seem extravagant to say that the feelings of an Anglo-American towards his mother country are really at least as warm as those of the natives of dependencies, and at least as likely to be manifested by practical assistance in the hour of need. A reference to the history of the opposition made to the war of 1812 will suffice at least to bring this opinion within the pale of credibility.

The great forces prevail. They prevail at last, however numerous and apparently strong the secondary forces opposed to them may be. They prevailed at last in the case of German unity and in the case of Italian independence. In each of those cases the secondary forces were so heavily massed against the event that men renowned for practical wisdom believed the event would never come. It came, irresistible and irrevocable, and we now see that Bismarck and Cavour were only the ministers of fate.

Suspended of course, and long suspended, by the action of the secondary forces, the action of the great forces may be. It was so in both the instances just mentioned. A still more remarkable instance is the long postponement of the union of Scotland with England by the antipathies resulting from the abortive attempt of Edward I, and by a subsequent train of historical accidents, such as the absorption of the energies of England in continental or civil wars. But the union came at last, and, having the great forces on its side, it came for ever.

In the case before us, it appears that the great forces are those which make for the political separation of the New from the Old World. They are—

1. The distance, which may be shortened by steam and telegraph for the transmission of a despot's commands, but can hardly be much shortened for the purposes of representative government. Steam increases the Transatlantic intercourse of the wealthier class, but not that of the people, who have neither money nor time for the passage. Everything is possible in the way of nautical invention; fuel may be still further economized, though its price is not likely to fall; but it is improbable that the cost of shipbuilding or the wages of seamen will be reduced; and the growth of manufactures in the New World, which we may expect henceforth to be rapid, can hardly fail to diminish the intercourse dependent on Transatlantic trade. A commonwealth spanning the Atlantic may be a grand conception, but political institutions must after all bear some relation to nature and to practical convenience. Few have fought against geography and prevailed.

2. Divergence of interest, which seems in this case to be as wide as possible. What has Canada to do with the European and Oriental concerns of England, with her European and Oriental diplomacy, with her European and Oriental wars? Can it be conceived that Canadian traders would allow her commerce to be cut up by Russian cruisers, or that Canadian farmers would take arms and pay war taxes in order to prevent Russia from obtaining a free passage through the Dardanelles? An English pamphlet called 'The Great Game' was reprinted the other day in Canada; but the chapter on India was omitted as having no interest for Canadians. For English readers that chapter had probably more interest than all the other chapters put together. On the

other hand, whenever a question about boundaries or mutual rights arises with the United States, the English people and the English government betray, by the languor of their diplomacy and the ease with which they yield, their comparative indifference to the objects in which Canada is most concerned. A Canadian periodical some time ago had a remarkable paper by a native writer, showing that the whole series of treaties made by Great Britain with the United States had been a continuous sacrifice of the claims of Canada. It was not, assuredly, that Great Britain wanted either force or spirit to fight for her own rights and interests, but that she felt that Canadian rights and interests were not her own. Her rulers could not have induced her people to go to war for an object for which they cared so little, and had so little reason to care, as a frontier line in North America. . . . With regard to economical questions, the divergence is, if possible, still clearer than with regard to diplomatic questions. The economic interests of Canada must evidently be those of her own continent, and to that continent, by all the economic forces, she must be and visibly is drawn. Her currency, whatever may be the name and superscription on the coin, is American, and it is the sure symbol of her real connection. In the British manufacturer the Canadian manufacturer sees a rival; and Canada at this moment is the scene of a Protectionist movement led, curiously enough, by those 'Conservative' politicians who are loudest in their professions of loyalty to Great Britain.

3. More momentous than even the divergence of interest is the divergence of political character between the citizen of the Old and the citizen of the New World. We speak, of course, not of the French Canadians, between whom and the people of Great Britain the absence of political affinity is obvious, but of the British communities in North America. The colonisation of the New World, at least that English portion of it which was destined to give birth to the ruling and moulding power, was not merely a migration, but an exodus; it was not merely a local extension of humanity, but a development; it not only peopled another continent, but opened a new era. The curtain rose not for the old drama with fresh actors, but for a fresh drama on a fresh scene. A long farewell was said to feudalism when the New England colony landed with the rough draft of a written constitution, which embodied a social compact and founded government not on sacred tradition or divine right, but on reason and the public good. The more one sees of society in the New World, the more convinced one is that its structure essentially differs from that of society in the Old World, and that the feudal element has been eliminated completely and for ever. English aristocracy, fancying itself, as all established systems fancy themselves, the normal and final state of humanity, may cling to the belief that the new development is a mere aberration, and that dire experience will in time bring it back to the ancient path. There are people, it seems, who persuade themselves that America is retrograding towards monarchy and Church establishments. No one who knows the Americans can possibly share this dream. Monarchy has found its way to the New World only in the exceptional case of Brazil, to which the royal family of the mother country itself migrated, and where after all the Emperor is rather an hereditary president than a monarch of the European type. In Canada, government being parliamentary and 'constitutional', monarchy is the delegation of a shadow; and any attempt to convert the shadow

into a substance, by introducing a dynasty with a court and civil list, or by reinvesting the Viceroy with personal power, would speedily reveal the real nature of the situation. [In 1791] Pitt proposed to extend to Canada what as a Tory minister he necessarily regarded as the blessings of aristocracy; but the plant refused to take root in the alien soil. No peerage ever saw the light in Canada; the baronetage saw the light and no more; of nobility there is nothing now but a knighthood very small in number, and upon which the Pacific Railway scandal has cast so deep a shadow that the Home Government, though inclined that way, seems shy of venturing on more creations. Hereditary wealth and the custom of primogeniture, indispensable supports of an aristocracy, are totally wanting in a purely industrial country, where, let the law be what it might, natural justice has always protested against the feudal claims of the firstborn. To establish in Canada the State Church, which is the grand buttress of aristocracy in England, has proved as hopeless as to establish aristocracy itself. The Church lands have been secularised; the university [of Toronto], once confined to Anglicanism, has been thrown open; the Anglican Church has been reduced to the level of the other denominations, though its rulers still cling to the memories and to some relics of their privileged condition. As a religion, Anglicanism has little hold upon the mass of the people: it is recruited by emigration from England, and sustained to a certain extent by a social feeling in its favour among the wealthier class. More democratic churches far exceed it in popularity and propagandist force: Methodism especially, which, in contrast to Episcopacy, sedulously assigns an active part in church work to every member, decidedly gains ground, and bids fair to become the popular religion of Canada. Nor is the militarism of European aristocracies less alien to industrial Canada than their monarchism and their affinity for State Churches. The Canadians, as we have already said, can fight well when real occasion calls; so can their kinsmen across the line; but among the Canadians, as among the people of the Northern States, it is impossible to awaken militarism—every sort of galvanic apparatus has been tried in vain. Distinctions of rank, again, are wanting; everything bespeaks a land dedicated to equality; and fustian, instead of bowing to broadcloth, is rather too apt, by a rude self-assertion, to revenge itself on broadcloth for enforced submissiveness in the old country. Where the relations of classes, the social forces, and the whole spirit of society are different, the real principles and objects of government will differ also, notwithstanding the formal identity of institutions. It proved impossible, as all careful observers had foreseen, to keep the same political roof over the heads of slavery and anti-slavery. To keep the same political roof over the heads of British aristocracy and Canadian democracy would be an undertaking only one degree less hopeless. A rupture would come, perhaps, on some question between the ambition of a money-spending nobility and the parsimony of a money-making people. Let aristocracy, hierarchy, and militarism be content with the Old World; it was conquered by the feudal sword; the New World was conquered only by the axe and plough.

4. The force, sure in the end to be attractive, not repulsive, of the great American community along the edge of which Canada lies, and to which the British portion of her population is drawn by identity of race, language, religion, and general institutions; the French portion by its connection with

the Roman Catholic Church of the States; the whole by economic influences, against which artificial arrangements and sentiments contend in vain, and which are gathering strength and manifesting their ascendancy from hour to hour.

An enumeration of the forces which make in favour of the present connection will show their secondary and, for the most part, transient character. The chief of them appear to be these:—

(a) The reactionary tendencies of the priesthood which rules French Canada, and which fears that any change might disturb its solitary reign. Strong this force has hitherto been, but its strength depends on isolation, and isolation cannot be permanent. Even the 'palaeocrystallic' ice which envelops French Canada will melt at last, and when it does French reaction will be at an end. We have already noted two agencies which are working towards this result—the leaven of American sentiment brought back by French Canadians who have sojourned as artisans in the States, and the ecclesiastical aggressiveness of the Jesuits.

(b) 'United Empire Loyalism', which has its chief seat in Ontario. Every revolution has its reaction, and in the case of the American Revolution the reaction took the form of a migration of the Royalists to Canada, where lands were assigned them, and where they became the political progenitors of the Canadian Tory party, while the 'Reformers' are the offspring of a subsequent immigration of Scotch Presbyterians, mingled with wanderers from the United States. The two immigrations were arrayed against each other in 1837, when, though the United Empire Loyalists were victorious in the field, the political victory ultimately rested with the Reformers. United Empire Loyalism is still strong in some districts, while in others the descendants of Royalist exiles are found in the ranks of the opposite party. But the whole party is now in the position of the Jacobites after the extinction of the House of Stuart. England has formally recognized the American Revolution, taken part in the celebration of its centenary, and through her ambassador saluted its flag. Anti-revolutionary sentiment ceases to have any meaning, and its death cannot be far off.

(c) The influence of English immigrants, especially in the upper ranks of the professions, in the high places of commerce, and in the press. These men have retained a certain social ascendancy; they have valued themselves on their birth in the imperial country and the superior traditions which they supposed it to imply; they have personally cherished the political connection, and have inculcated fidelity to it with all their might. But their number is rapidly decreasing; as they die off natives take their places, and Canada will soon be in Canadian hands. Immigration generally is falling off; upper-class immigration is almost at an end, there being no longer a demand for anything but manual labour; and the influence of personal connection with England will cease to rule. The press is passing into the hands of natives, who are fast learning to hold their own against imported writing in literary skill, while they have an advantage in their knowledge of the country.

(d) While the British troops remained in Canada, their officers formed a social aristocracy of the most powerful kind, and exercised a somewhat tyrannical influence over opinion. The traces of this influence still remain; but, with the exception of the reduced garrison of Halifax, the military occupation has ceased, and is not likely to be renewed.

(e) The Anglican Church in Canada clings to its position as a branch of the great State Church of England, and, perhaps, a faint hope of re-establishment may linger in the breasts of the bishops, who still retain the title of 'lords'. We have already said that the roots of Anglicanism in Canada do not appear to be strong, and its chief source of reinforcement will be cut off by the discontinuance of upper-class emigration. It is rent in Canada, as in England, by the conflict between the Protestants and the Ritualists; and in Canada, there being no large endowments or legal system to clamp the hostile elements together, discord has already taken the form of disruption. As to the other churches, they have a connection with England, but not with England more than with the United States. The connection of Canadian Methodism with the United States is very close.

(f) Orangism is strong in British Canada, as indeed is every kind of association except the country. It retains its filial connection with its Irish parent, and is ultra-British on condition that Great Britain continues anti-papal. Old Irish quarrels are wonderfully tenacious of life, yet they must one day die, and Orangism must follow them to the grave.

(g) The social influence of English aristocracy and of the little court of Ottawa over colonists of the wealthier class. With this, to dismiss at once a theme more congenial to the social humorist than to the political observer, we may couple the influence of those crumbs of titular honour which English aristocracy sometimes allows to fall from its table into colonial mouths. If such forces cannot be said to be transient, the tendencies of human nature being perpetual, they may at least be said to be secondary; they do not affect the masses, and they do not affect the strong.

(h) Antipathy to the Americans, bred by the old wars, and nursed by British influences, military and aristocratic, not without the assistance of the Americans themselves, who in the case of the Fenian raids, and in other cases, have vented on Canada their feelings against England. This antipathy, so far as it prevails, leads those who entertain it to cling to an anti-American connection. But generally speaking it is very hollow. It does not hinder young Canadians from going by hundreds to seek their fortunes in the United States. It does not hinder wealthy Americans who have settled in Canada from finding seats at once in the Canadian Parliament. It never, in fact, goes beyond talk. So far as it partakes of the nature of contempt it can hardly fail to be modified by the changed attitude of the British aristocracy, who have learned to exhibit something more than courtesy towards the victorious republic; while the Americans, it may be reasonably presumed, now that the cause of irritation is removed, will not think it wise to make enemies of a people whose destinies are inextricably blended with their own.

(i) The special attachment naturally felt by the politicians as a body to the system with reference to which their parties have been formed, and with which the personal ambition of most of them is bound up. Perhaps of all the forces which make for the present connection, this is the strongest; it has proved strong enough, when combined with the timidity and the want of independence which lifelong slavery to a faction always breeds, to prevent any Canadian politician from playing a resolute part in such efforts as there have been to make Canada a nation. In some cases it is intensified by commercial connections with England, or by social aspirations, more or less definite, which have England for their goal. In this respect the interest of the politicians, as a class, is distinct from, and is liable to clash with, the real interest of the community at large. So in the case of Scotland, it was the special interest of the politicians to resist the union, as, without special pressure and inducements, they would probably have persisted in doing: it was the interest of the people to accept the union, as the flood of prosperity which followed its acceptance clearly showed. In the case of Scotland the interest of the people triumphed at last; and it will probably triumph at last in Canada.

Such, we say, are the chief forces that make for the existing connection; and we repeat that they appear to be secondary and for the most part transient. United, all these strands may make a strong cable; but one by one they will give way, and the cable will cease to hold. This conviction is quite consistent with the admission that the connectionist sentiment is now dominant, especially in Ontario; that in Ontario it almost exclusively finds expression on the platform and in the press; and that the existence of any other opinions can only be inferred from reticence, or discovered by private intercourse. A visitor may thus be led to believe and to report that the attachment of the whole population to the present system is unalterable, and that the connection must endure for ever. Those who have opportunities of looking beneath the surface, may at the same time have grounds for thinking that, on economical subjects at least, the people have already entered on a train of thought which will lead them to a different goal.

What has been the uniform course of events down to the present time? Where are the American dependencies of Spain, Portugal, France, and Holland? Those on the continent, with unimportant exceptions, are gone, and those in the islands are going; for few suppose that Spain can keep Cuba very long. Of the English colonies on the continent, the mass, and those that have been long founded, have become independent; and every one now sees, what clear-sighted men saw at the time, that the separation was inevitable, and must soon have been brought about by natural forces apart from the accidental quarrel. If Canada has been retained, it is by the reduction of imperial supremacy to a form. Self-government is independence; perfect self-government is perfect independence; and all the questions that arise between Ottawa and Downing Street, including the recent question about appeals, are successively settled in favour of self-government. Diplomatic union between two countries in different hemispheres with totally different sets of external relations, common responsibility for each other's quarrels, and liability to be involved in each other's wars—these incidents of dependence remain, and these alone. Is it probable that this last leaf can continue to flutter on the bough for ever? . . .

It is, perhaps, partly the recoil of feeling from a severance felt to be imminent, as well as the temporary influence of Conservative reaction in England, that has led to the revival in certain quarters, with almost convulsive vehemence, of the plan of imperial confederation. Certainly if such a plan is ever to be carried into effect, this is the propitious hour. The spirit of aggrandisement is in the ascendant, and the colonies are all on good terms with the mother country. Yet of the statesmen who dally with the project and smile upon its advocates, not one ventures to take a practical step towards its fulfilment. On the contrary, they are accessory to fresh inroads upon imperial unity, both in the judicial and in the fiscal sphere. Colonial governors talk with impressive vagueness of some possible birth of the imperial future, as though the course of events, which has been hurrying the world through a series of rapid changes for the last century, would now stand still, and impracticable aspirations would become practicable by the mere operation of time; but no colonial governor or imperial statesman has ventured to tell us, even in the most general way, to what it is that he looks forward, how it is to be brought about, or even what dependencies the confederation is to include. It is therefore needless to rehearse all the arguments against the feasibility of such a scheme. The difficulties which beset the union under the same parliamentary government of two countries in different parts of the world, with different foreign relations and differing internally in political spirit, would of course be multiplied in the case of a union of twenty or thirty countries scattered over the whole globe, bound together by no real tie of common interest, and ignorant of each other's concerns. The first meeting of such a conclave would, we may be sure, develop forces of disunion far stronger than the vague sentiment of union arising from a very partial community of descent and a very imperfect community of language, which would be the sole ground of the federation. . . . That England would allow questions of foreign policy, of armaments, and of peace and war to be settled for her by any councils but her own, it is surely most chimerical to suppose. . . .

Supposing such a confederation to be practicable, of what use, apart from the vague feeling of aggrandisement, would it be? Where would be the advantage of taking from each of these young communities its political centre (which must also be, to some extent, its social and intellectual centre), and of accumulating them in the already overgrown capital of England? Does experience tell us that unlimited extension of territory is favourable to intensity of political life, or to anything which is a real element of happiness or of greatness? Does it not tell us that the reverse is the fact, and that the interest of history centres not in megalosaurian empires, but in states the body of which has not been out of proportion to the brain? Surely it would be well to have some distinct idea of the object to be attained before commencing this unparalleled struggle against geography and nature. It can hardly be military strength. Military strength is not gained by dispersion of forces, by presenting vulnerable points in every quarter of the globe, or by embracing and undertaking to defend communities which, whatever may be their fighting qualities, in their policy are thoroughly unmilitary, and unmilitary will remain. . . .

In all these projects of Pan-britannic empire there lurks the assumption of a boundless multiplication of the Anglo-Saxon race. What are the grounds for this assumption? Hitherto it has appeared that races, as they grow richer, more luxurious, more fearful of poverty, more amenable to the restraints of social pride, have become less prolific. There is reason to suppose that in the United States the Anglo-Saxon race is far less prolific than the Irish, who are even supplanting the Anglo-Saxons in some districts of England, as the Home-Rule compliances of candidates for northern boroughs show. But the Irish element is small compared with the vast reservoir of industrial population in China, which is now beginning to overflow, and seems as likely as the Anglo-Saxon race to inherit Australia, where it has already a strong foothold, as well as the coast of the Pacific. . . .

It is taken for granted that political dependence is the natural state of all colonies, and that there is something unfilial and revolutionary in proposing that a colony should become a nation. But what is a colony? We happen to have derived the term from a very peculiar set of institutions, those Roman colonies which had no life of their own, but were merely the military and political outposts of the Imperial republic. With the Roman colonies may be classed the Athenian cleruchies and, substituting the commercial for the political object, the factories of Carthage. But colonies generally speaking are migrations, and, as a rule, they have been independent from the beginning. Independent from the beginning, so far as we know, were the Phoenician colonies, Carthage herself among the number. Independent from the beginning were those Greek colonies in Italy which rapidly outran their mother cities in the race of material greatness. Independent from the beginning were the Saxon and Scandinavian colonies, and all those settlements of the Northern tribes which founded England herself with the other nations of modern Europe. So far as we can see, the original independence in each case was an essential condition of vigour and success. No Roman colony, Athenian cleruchy, or Carthaginian factory ever attained real greatness. New England, the germ and organizer of the American communities, was practically independent for a long time after her foundation, the attention of the English government being engrossed by troubles at home; but she retained a slender thread of theoretic dependence by which she was afterwards drawn back into a noxious and disastrous subordination. That thread was the feudal tie of personal allegiance, a tie utterly irrational when carried beyond the feudal pale, and by the recent naturalisation treaties now formally abolished; yet probably the main cause of the continued subjection of the Transatlantic colonies, and of the calamities which flowed both to them and to the mother country from that source.

It is natural that British statesmen should shrink from a formal act of separation, and that in their brief and precarious tenure of power they should be unwilling to take the burden and possible odium of such a measure upon themselves. But no one, we believe, ventures to say that the present system will be perpetual; certainly not the advocates of imperial confederation, who warn us that unless England by a total change of system draws her colonies nearer to her, they will soon drift further away.

Apart from lingering sentiment, it seems not easy to give reasons, so far as Canada is concerned, for struggling to prolong the present system. The motives for acquiring and holding dependencies in former days were substantial if they were not good. Spain drew tribute directly from her dependencies. England thought she drew it indirectly through her commercial system. It was also felt that the military resources of the colonies were at the command of the mother country. When the commercial system was relinquished, and when self-government transferred to the colonies the control of their own resources, the financial and military motives ceased to exist. But the conservative imagination supplied their place with the notion of political tutelage, feigning—though, as we have seen, against all the evidence of history—that the colony, during the early stages of its existence, needed the political guidance of the mother country in order to fit it to become a nation. Such was the language of colonial statesmen generally till the present Conservative reaction again brought into fashion something like the old notion of aggrandisement, though for tribute and military contingents, the solid objects of the old policy, is now substituted 'prestige'. That the political connection between England and Canada is a source of military security to either, nobody, we apprehend, maintains. The only vulnerable point which England presents to the United States is the defenceless frontier of Canada; the only danger to which Canada is exposed is that of being involved in a quarrel between the aristocracy of England and the democracy of the United States. . . .

'Commerce follows the flag', is a saying which it seems can still be repeated by a statesman; but, like the notion that dependencies are a source of military strength, it is a mere survival from a departed system. Commerce followed the flag when the flag was that of a power which enforced exclusive trading. But exclusive trading has given way, as an imperial principle, to free trade, and the colonies, in the exercise of their fiscal power of self-government, have dissolved the commercial unity of the empire. They frame their independent tariffs, laying, in some cases, heavy duties on English goods. . . . As to Canada, what she needs, and needs most urgently, is free access to the market of her own continent, from which, as a dependency of England, she is excluded by the customs line. With free access to the market of her own continent, she might become a great manufacturing country; but manufactures are now highly specialised, and to produce with advantage you must produce on a large scale. Nor is the evil confined to manufactures; the farm products of Canada are depreciated by exclusion from their natural market and the lumber trade, which is her great industry, will be in serious jeopardy, since, by the fall of wages in the States, the production of lumber there has been rendered nearly as cheap as it is in Canada, while Canadian lumber is subject to a heavy duty. The projects for opening markets in Australia merely serve to show how severely Canada feels the want of a market close at hand. Cut off any belt of territory commercially from the continent to which it belongs, industry will be stunted, the inflow of capital will be checked, and impoverishment will follow isolation. The Canadians will find this out in time, and the discovery will be the first step towards a change of system. . . .

That emigration is favourably influenced by political dependency is another lingering belief which seems now to have no foundation in fact, though it had in the days when emigration was a government affair. The stream of emigration, in ordinary times, sets, as has often been proved, not towards Canada, but towards the United States; and of the emigrants who land in Canada a large proportion afterwards pass the line, while there is a constant exodus of French Canadians from their own poor and overpeopled country (overpeopled so long as it is merely agricultural) to the thriving industries and high wages of the States. Emigrants, whose object is to improve their material conditions, are probably little influenced by political considerations; they go to the country which offers the best openings and the highest wages; but English peasants and artisans would be likely, if anything, to prefer the social elevation promised them in a land of equality to anything like a repetition of the social subjection in which they have lived at home, while by the Irishman escape from British rule is deemed escape from oppression. . . .

Most readers of the *Fortnightly* are probably prepared to regard with tolerance the proposition that figments and hypocrisies do no more good in politics than they do in general life.* In Canadian politics they do much evil by blinding public men and the people generally to the real requirements of the situation. The hereditary principle was dead at its root; its work was done, and its age had passed away in the more advanced portion of humanity when the communities of the New World were founded. It lingers on, as things do linger on, in its native soil; but it can furnish no sound basis for government in the soil of reason and equality. The only conceivable basis for government in the New World is the national will; and the political problem of the New World is how to build a strong, stable, enlightened, and impartial government on that foundation. That it is a very difficult problem, daily experience in Canada, as well as in the neighbouring republic, shows, and to be successfully resolved it must be seen in its true bearings, which the ostensible retention of the hereditary principle as the security for good and stable government obscures. Canada, though adorned with the paraphernalia of eight constitutional monarchies (one central and seven provincial), is a democracy of the most pronounced kind; the Governor-General was not wrong in saying that she is more democratic than the United States, where the President is an elective king, and where the Senate, which though elective is conservative, possesses great power, whereas the nominated Senate of Canada is a cypher. Demagogism and the other pests of democratic institutions are not to be conjured away by forms and phrases; they can be repressed and prevented from ruining the State only by developing remedial forces of a really effective kind, and by adjusting the actual machinery of the constitution so as to meet the dangers which experience may reveal. The treason law of the Plantagenets with which, as well as with the Lord Chamberlain's code of precedence, Canada is endowed, is not of much use to her while she is left without any legal means of repressing her real cancer, political corruption. Loyalty to the *fainéant* deputy of a distant Crown may be in a certain sense real; it may be felt by those who profess it; but it probably does not often prompt to a good political action, and it certainly never restrains from a bad one. Among Canadians, as among American politicians, the most 'truly loyal' are often the most unscrupulous and corrupt. They are often, through the whole course of their public lives, disloyal to everything that represents public honour and the public good. A provincial court adds flunkeyism to demagogism without making the demagogue less profligate, less dangerous, or less vile. It does not even make him less coarse. No refining influence can really be exercised by a few dinners and receptions even over the small circle which attends them; while the social expenditure and display which are imposed on the Governor-General as the condition of his popularity in the colony, and of the maintenance of his reputation at home, are anything but a wholesome example for colonial society, which on the contrary needs an example of hospitality and social enjoyment cultivated in an easy and inexpensive way.

At present the bane of Canada is party government without any question on which parties can be rationally or morally based. The last question of sufficient importance to form a rational and moral basis for a party was that of the Clergy Reserves and the Church Establishment, since the settlement of which there has been absolutely no dividing line between the parties or assignable ground for their existence, and they have become mere factions, striving to engross the prizes of office by the means which faction everywhere employs. The consequences are the increasing ascendency of the worst men, and the political demoralisation of a community, which, if a fair chance were given it, would furnish as sound a basis for good government as any community in the world. Of course, England cannot be charged with introducing the party system into Canada; but she does fling over it the glamour of British association, and beguile a country really abandoned to all the instability and all the degrading influences of government by faction with the ostensible stability and dignity of the hereditary Crown. Indeed, the provision in the draught of confederation that both the parties should be considered in the first nomination of senators is, perhaps, the only authoritative recognition which the party system has ever received. In common with the other colonies, Canada is deemed happy in being endowed with a counterpart of the British Constitution. The British Constitution, putting aside the legal forms and phrases, is government by party; and whatever government by party may be in England, where there are some party questions left, in Canada it is a most noxious absurdity, and is ruining the political character of the people.

When Canadian Nationalists say that patriotism is a good thing, they are told to keep their wisdom for the copy-books; and the rebuke would be just if those who administer it would recognise the equally obvious truth, that there can be no patriotism without nationality. In a dependency there is no love of country, no pride in the country; if an appeal is made to the name of the country no heart responds as the heart of an Englishman responds when an appeal is made to the name of England. In a dependency every bond is stronger than that of country, every interest prevails over that of country. The province, the sect, Orangism, Fenianism, Freemasonry, Odd Fellowship are more to the ordinary Canadian than Canada. So it must be while the only antidote to sectionalism in a population with strongly marked differences of race and creed is the sentiment of allegiance to a distant throne. . . .

[Though Canada is not a nation], there were reasons which, not only to patriotic Canadians, but to patriotic Americans, if they took a comprehensive view of the interests of their country, seemed strong for wishing that Canada should remain politically separate from the United States. Democracy is a great experiment, which might be more safely carried on by two nations than by one. By emulation, mutual warning and correction, mutual supplementation of defects, they might have helped each other in the race and steadied each other's steps; a balance of opinion might have been established on the continent, though a balance of power cannot; and the wave of dominant sentiment which spreads over that vast democracy like the tide running in over a flat, might have been usefully restricted in its sweep by the dividing line. Nor was there any insurmountable obstacle in the way. Canada is wanting in unity of race; but not more so than Switzerland, whose three races have been thoroughly welded together by the force of nationality. She is wanting in compactness of territory, but not more so, perhaps, than some other nations—Prussia for instance—have been. In this latter respect, however, the situation has been seriously altered by the annexation of Manitoba and British Columbia, which in their present raw condition have no influence beyond that of distant possessions, but which, when peopled and awakened to commercial life, will be almost irresistibly attracted by the economical forces to the States which adjoin them on the south, and will thus endanger the cohesion of the whole confederacy. The very form of the Dominion indeed, drawn out and attenuated as it is by these unnatural additions, apart from the attractive influence of Minnesota and California, would seriously imperil its political unity, as will be seen, if, instead of taking Canada as it is presented by the political map, the boundary line is drawn between the habitable portion and that which belongs only to Arctic frosts. In the debate on confederation it was urged by the advocates of the measure that seven sticks, though separately weak, when bound together in a faggot would be strong. 'Yes,' was the reply, 'but not so seven fishing rods tied together by the ends.' . . .

The question of military security has reference solely to the danger to be apprehended on the side of the United States; and danger on the side of the United States, supposing Canada disentangled from English quarrels, we believe that there is none. The Americans, as has been repeatedly observed, have since the fall of slavery given every proof of an unambitious disposition. They disbanded their vast armaments immediately on the close of the civil war, without waiting even for the Alabama question to be settled; they have refused to annex St Domingo; they have observed a policy of strict non-intervention in the case of Cuba, which they might have made their own with the greatest ease; they have declined to take advantage of the pretexts furnished them in abundance, by border outrages, of conquering Mexico; it is very doubtful whether they would even have purchased Alaska, if Mr Seward had not drawn them by secret negotiations into a position from which they could not well retreat. Slavery wanted conquest for the creation of new slave states, but with slavery the spirit of aggression appears to have died. Welcome Canada into the Union, if she came of her own accord, the Americans no doubt would. They would be strangely wanting in wisdom if they did not; for she would bring them as her dower not only complete immunity from attack and great economical advantages, but a political accession of the most valuable kind in the shape of a population, not like that of St Domingo, Cuba, or Mexico, but trained to self-government, and capable of lending fresh strength and vitality to republican institutions. It is true that, slavery having been abolished, the urgent need of adding to the number of the Free States in order to counterbalance the extension of slavery in the councils of the Union no longer exists; but there are still in the population of the United States large elements essentially non-republican—the Irish, the emigrants from Southern Germany, the negroes—to which, perhaps, may be added a considerable portion of Southern society itself, which can hardly fail to retain something of its old character while it continues to be composed of a superior and inferior race. Against these non-republican elements, the really republican element still needs to be fortified by all the reinforcements which it can obtain. Welcome Canada therefore into the Union the Americans no doubt would. But that they have the slightest inclination to lay violent hands upon her, that such a thought ever enters their minds, no one who has lived among them, and heard the daily utterances of a by no means reticent people, can believe. Apart from moral principle, they know that though a despotic government may simply annex, a republic must incorporate, and that to incorporate four millions of unwilling citizens would be to introduce into the republic a most dangerous mass of disaffection and disunion. That the Americans have been litigious in their dealings with Canada is true; but litigiousness is not piracy; and as we have already said the real object of their irritation has not been Canada, but England. The Monroe doctrine was held by Canning as well as by Monroe; and, irrespectively of any desire of aggrandisement, the intrusion of an American power here would probably give as much umbrage to England as the intrusion of the English power in their own continent gives to the people of the United States. That the Americans would feel pride in behaving generously towards a weaker State, will appear credible only to those who have seen enough of them to know that, though supposed to care for nothing but the dollar, they have in reality a good deal of pride.

As an independent nation, Canada would, of course, be at liberty to negotiate freely for the removal of the customs line between herself and the United States, and for her admission to all the commercial advantages of her own continent. At present not only is she trammelled by imperial considerations, but it can hardly be expected that the American government will place itself on a lower international level than that of England by treating with a dependency as a nation, especially as there are constant intimations that the dependency is retained, and is being nursed up, with the view of making it a rival power to the United States, and thus introducing into the continent the germs of future jealousy, and possibly of war.

That Canada can ever be made a rival power to the United States—that, if she is only kept long enough in a state of dependence, there will be an indefinite increase of her population and her strength—seems to be little better than a rhetorical fancy. The barrier of slavery being removed, the set of population is likely to be, not towards the frozen north, where the winter, besides suspending labour and business, eats up the produce of the summer in the cost of fuel, but towards those countries in which warmth is provided by the sun, and work may be carried on during the whole year. The notion that the north is the natural seat of empire seems to have no more solid foundation. It is apparently a loose generalisation from the success of the northern tribes which conquered the Roman empire. It is forgotten that those northern warriors had not only been hardened by exposure to the full severity of the northern climate, but picked by the most rigorous process of natural selection. Stove heat is not less enervating than the heat of the sun. But a nation Canada, so far as we can see, might have been, had the attempt been vigorously made at the propitious moment, when, owing to the effects of the civil war in the United States, the balance of prosperity was decidedly in her favour, when her financial condition appeared immensely superior to that of her neighbour, and when the spirit of her people had been stirred by confederation. That opportunity was allowed to pass, and, in all probability, it will never return.

A movement in favour of nationality there was—one which had a twofold claim to sympathy, because it was also a movement against faction and corruption, and which, though it has failed, has left honourable traces on public life. But it was not strong enough to make head against the influences which have their centre in the little court of Ottawa and the attacks of the lower class of politicians, who assailed it with the utmost ferocity, seeing clearly that the success of the higher impulse would not suit their game. Moreover, the French province interposed between the British provinces of the east and west, is a complete non-conductor, and prevents any pulsation from running through the whole body. It must further be owned that in industrial communities the economical motives are stronger than the political, and that the movement in favour of Canadian nationality had only political motives on its side. Perhaps the appearance of a great man might after all have turned the scale; but dependencies seldom produce great men.

Had the movement in favour of nationality succeeded, the first step would have been a legislative union, which would in time have quelled sectionalism and made up for the deficiency of material size and force by moral solidity and unity of spirit. Canada, as was said before, is hardly a proper subject for federal government, which requires a more numerous group of states and greater equality between them. Confederation as it exists, we repeat, has done little more than develop the bad side of democratic government. . . . That there would have been opposition to a legislative union of the whole of Canada on the part of Quebec is more than probable; but Quebec, if she had been handled with determination, would most likely have given away.

Canadian nationality being a lost cause, the ultimate union of Canada with the United States appears now to be morally certain; so that nothing is left for Canadian patriotism but to provide that it shall be a union indeed, and not an annexation; an equal and honourable alliance like that of Scotland with England, not a submission of the weaker to the stronger; and at the same time that the political change shall involve no change of any other kind in the relations of Canada with her mother country. The filaments of union are spreading daily, though they may be more visible to the eye of one who sees Canada at intervals than to that of a constant resident. Intercourse is being increased by the extension of railways; the ownership and management of the railways themselves is forming an American interest in Canada; New York is becoming the pleasure, and, to some extent, even the business, capital of Canadians; American watering-places are becoming their summer resort; the periodical literature of the States, which is conducted with extraordinary spirit and ability, is extending its circulation on the northern side of the line; and the Canadians who settle in the States are multiplying the links of family connection between the two countries. To specify the time at which a political event will take place is hardly ever possible, however assured the event itself may be; and in the present instance the occurrence depends not only on the circumstances of Canada, where, as we have seen, there is a great complication of secondary forces, but on the circumstances of the United States. If the commercial depression which at present prevails in Canada continues or recurs, if Canadian manufactures are seen to be dying under the pressure of the customs line; if, owing to the depression or to overcostly undertakings, such as the Pacific Railway, financial difficulties arise; if, meantime, the balance of prosperity, which is now turning, shall have turned decisively in favour of the United

States, and the reduction of their debt shall have continued at the present rate—the critical moment may arrive, and the politicians, recognising the voice of Destiny, may pass in a body to the side of Continental Union. . . .

To Canada the economical advantages of continental union will be immense; to the United States its general advantages will be not less so. To England it will be no menace, but the reverse: it will be the introduction into the councils of the United States, on all questions, commercial as well as diplomatic, of an element friendly to England, the influence of which will be worth far more to her than the faint and invidious chance of building up Canada as a rival to the United States. In case of war, her greatest danger will be removed. She will lose neither wealth nor strength; probably she will gain a good deal of both. As to glory, we cannot do better than quote in conclusion the words of Palmerston's favourite colleague, and the man to whom he, as was generally supposed, wished to bequeath his power:—

There are supposed advantages flowing from the possession of dependencies, which are expressed in terms so general and vague, that they cannot be referred to any determinate head. Such, for example, is the glory which a country is supposed to derive from an extensive colonial empire. We will merely remark upon this imagined advantage, that a nation derives no true glory from any possession which produces no assignable advantage to itself or to other communities. If a country possesses a dependency from which it derives no public revenue, no military or naval strength, and no commercial advantages or facilities for emigration, which it would not equally enjoy though the dependency were independent, and if, moreover, the dependency suffers the evils which (as we shall show hereafter) are the almost inevitable consequences of its political condition, such a possession cannot justly be called glorious.*

SIR WILFRID LAURIER

Wilfrid Laurier (1841-1919) founded the Liberal party that has governed our country for sixty-six of the past eighty-eight years. He was trained as a lawyer, mixed law with journalism and politics as a young man, was first elected to the House of Commons in 1874, succeeded Blake as Liberal leader in 1887, and served as prime minister from 1896 to 1911. Laurier combined Macdonald's tactical skills with a clearer understanding of his country and his time to weld together the coalition of promoters, Grits, Bleus, and Rouges that is the Liberal party.

Laurier was a great orator. It is remarkable evidence of our lack of interest in our own political tradition that no collection of his speeches is currently available. His most famous speech, reprinted below, was a defence of liberalism against the charge of irreligion, which he delivered to a packed hall in Quebec City in 1877. Laurier appeals to his audience to recognize that French-Canadian liberalism is not the anti-Catholic and anti-clerical liberalism of Europe, but the tolerant variety of Great Britain. He shows a clear grasp of the main issues, and the attentive reader will see that he concedes little to the Catholic hierarchy.

Political Liberalism

MR CHAIRMAN, LADIES AND GENTLEMEN:

I cannot conceal the fact that it was with a certain feeling of pleasure that I accepted the invitation to come before you to explain the doctrines of the Liberal party and what this word 'liberalism' connotes for the Liberals of the province of Quebec.

I say that it was not without a certain feeling of pleasure that I accepted; but I would certainly have refused had I looked only to the difficulties of the task, for they are numerous and delicate. Yet, on the other hand, I am so imbued with the importance for the Liberal party of clearly defining its position, before the public opinion of the province, that this consideration weighed more heavily with me than all the others.

Indeed, I do not deceive myself with regard to the position of the Liberal party in the province of Quebec, and I say at once that it occupies a false position from the perspective of our public opinion. For a large number of our compatriots, I know, the Liberal party is a party composed of men of perverse doctrines and dangerous tendencies, pressing knowingly and deliberately towards revolution. For some of our compatriots, I know, the Liberal party is a party of men with upright intentions, perhaps, but victims and dupes of principles that are leading them unconsciously, but inevitably, towards revolution. For another portion, and not the least considerable portion, perhaps, of our people, I know finally that liberalism is a new form of evil, a heresy carrying with it its own condemnation.

I know all this, and it is because I know it that I have accepted your invitation to come here. I have not the presumption to believe that anything I might say here tonight will dissipate any of the prejudices that exist at present against us; my only ambition is to lead the way in the hope that it will be followed by others and that the work thus begun will be fully carried out; my pretensions go no farther than this.

And let no one say that this manifestation is useless or untimely. It is neither useless nor untimely to combat the prejudices that have been raised like a barrier everywhere between us and public opinion. It is neither useless nor untimely clearly to define our position as it really is.

It is true that we have been before public opinion long enough already for it to know us and appreciate us. But it is equally true that, if we have had our enemies, like every political party, we have been attacked more than any political party. Among the enemies we have, some have systematically blackened us; others have in good faith calumniated us. Both the former and the latter have represented us as professing doctrines, the effect of which, foreseen and calculated by some of us, not foreseen by others, but inevitable nonetheless, would be the overthrow of our society, the revolution with all its horrors. To reply to these charges and to defend our position is the object of tonight's demonstration organized by the *Club Canadien*.

To my mind, the most efficacious, the only way, in fact, to defeat these charges, to defend our ideas and principles, is to make them known. Yes, I am convinced that the mere statement of our principles will be their best and most eloquent vindication.

And when we shall have made ourselves known as we are, when we shall have made known our principles as they are, we shall have gained, I believe, two results. The first will be to rally to our side all the friends of liberty, all those who, before 1837 or after it, laboured to secure responsible government for us, government of the people by the people, and who, once that form of government was established, drew away from us for fear that we were in reality what we were represented to be, and for fear that the realization of the ideas ascribed to us would lead to the destruction of the government which they had had so much trouble establishing. The second result will be to force our real enemies—all those who at heart are enemies, more or less disguised, of liberty—to stop appealing to prejudice and fear against us, and to come before the people frankly as we do with their ideas and their acts.

And when the fight turns on pure questions of principle, when acts are judged according to the thinking which inspires them, and this thinking according to its inherent value—when people are no longer afraid to accept the good and reject the bad under the impression that, in accepting the one and rejecting the other, they would be strengthening a party of perverse doctrines and dangerous tendencies—little does it matter to me which side is then victorious. When I say that it matters little to me which side is victorious, I do not mean to say that I am indifferent to the result of the struggle. I mean this: if the struggle turns against us, the opinion expressed will be the free expression of the people. But I am convinced that a day will come when our ideas, cast on the ground, will germinate and bear fruit, if the seed is sound and just.

Yes, I am confident, I am certain that if our ideas are just, as I believe they are, if they are an emanation of the eternal and immutable truth, as I believe they are, they will not perish. They may be rejected, reviled, persecuted, but a day will come when they will germinate, spring up and grow, as soon as the sun has done its work and prepared the ground.

I have already noted some of the charges that are made against us, and I shall return to the subject, for it is the most important point. All the charges brought against us, all the objections to our doctrines, can be summed up in the following propositions: (1) liberalism is a new form of error, a heresy already virtually condemned by the head of the Church; (2) a Catholic may not be a liberal.

This is what our adversaries proclaim.

Mr Chairman, all who honour me with their attention at this moment will do me the justice of recognizing that I put the question as it is and that I exaggerate nothing. All will do me the justice of admitting that I reproduce faithfully the reproaches that day after day are being addressed to us. All will acknowledge that this is well and truly the language of the Conservative press.

I know that Catholic liberalism has been condemned by the head of the Church.* I will be asked: What is Catholic liberalism? On the threshold of that question I stop. It does not come within the bounds of my subject; moreover, it is not within my competence. But I know and I say that Catholic liberalism is not political liberalism. If it were true that the ecclesiastical condemnation of Catholic liberalism should apply to political liberalism, this fact would constitute for us, French by origin, Catholic by religion, a state of affairs, the consequences of which would be as strange as they would be painful.

In fact, we French Canadians are a conquered race. This is a melancholy truth to utter, but it is, in short, the truth. But if we are a conquered race, we have also made a conquest: the conquest of liberty. We are a free people; we are a minority, but we have retained all our rights and all our privileges. Now, what is the cause to which we owe this liberty? It is the constitution that was won for us by our fathers and that we enjoy today. We have a constitution that bases the government on the suffrage of the citizens and that was granted to us for our own protection. We have no more rights, no more privileges, but we have as many rights and as many privileges, as the other elements that go to make up the Canadian family. Now it must not be forgotten that the other members of the Canadian family are divided into two parties, the Liberal party and the Conservative party.

If we who are Catholics were not to have the right to have our preferences, if we were not to have the right to belong to the Liberal party, one of two things would happen: either we would be obliged to abstain completely from taking any part in the management of the affairs of state, and then the constitution—that constitution that was granted to us for our protection—would no longer have any significance for us; or else we would be obliged to take part in the management of the affairs of state under the direction of and for the profit of the Conservative party, and then, our action no longer being free, the constitution would again be a dead letter for us and, to boot, we would have the ignominy of being nothing more, for the other members of the Canadian family in the Conservative party, than tools and extras.

Do these absurd consequences, the strict accuracy of which nobody can question, not show conclusively how false is the assertion that a Catholic cannot belong to the Liberal party?

Since Providence has brought together in this remote land populations of different origins and creeds, is it not manifest that these populations must share some common and identical interests, and that in all that affects his interests, each person is free to follow either the Liberal party or the Conservative party, according to the dictates of his conscience?

For my part, I belong to the Liberal party. If it be wrong to be a Liberal, I accept the reproach; if it be a crime to be a Liberal, then I am guilty of it. For my part, I ask only one thing, that we be judged according to our principles. I would be ashamed of our principles if we were afraid to give expression to them, and our cause would not be worth our efforts on its behalf if the best way to secure its triumph were to conceal its nature. The Liberal party has been in Opposition for twenty-five years, and let it remain there for another twenty-five years, if the people have not yet come to accept its ideas, but let it march proudly, with its banners displayed, hiding nothing from the country!

It is most important, however, to come to an understanding about the meaning, value and bearing of this word 'liberal', and of that other word 'conservative'.

I maintain that there is nothing so little understood in this country by its assailants as liberalism, and that there are several reasons for this.

It was only yesterday that we were introduced to representative institutions. The English element understands the working of these institutions as if by instinct as well as by long experience. By contrast, our people as yet hardly understand them at all. Education is only beginning to spread amongst us, and in the case of the well educated, our French education leads us naturally to study the history of modern liberty, not in the classic land of liberty, not in the history of old England, but among the peoples of the continent of Europe, among the peoples of the same origin and faith as ourselves. And there, unfortunately, the history of liberty has been written in letters of blood on what are perhaps the most harrowing pages in the annals of human history. In all classes of educated society you can see loyal souls, frightened by these mournful pages, who regard the spirit of liberty with terror, imagining that it must produce here the same disasters and the same crimes as in the countries I have mentioned. In the eyes of such well-meaning people, the very word 'liberalism' is fraught with national calamity.

Without condemning altogether these fears, but without allowing ourselves to be frightened by them, let us go back to the fountainhead itself and calmly examine what is at the bottom of these two words, *liberal* and *conservative*. What idea is hidden under this word *liberal* that it should have called down upon us so many anathemas? What idea is hidden under the word *conservative* that it should be modestly applied to everything that is good? Is the one, as is alleged, and in fact asserted every day, the expression of a new form of error? Is the other, as it seems to be constantly insinuated, the definition of good under all its aspects? Does the one mean revolt, anarchy, disorder, and is the other the only stable principle of society? There you have some of the questions that people are asking themselves every day in our country. These subtle distinctions, which are found again and again incessantly in our press, are nevertheless not new [news]. They are only repetitions of the musings of certain French journalists who, shut up in their studies, see only the past and bitterly criticize everything that exists today, for the simple reason that what exists today bears no resemblance to what existed formerly.

These writers say that the liberal idea is a new idea, and they are mistaken.

The liberal idea is no more a new idea than is the contrary idea. It is as old as the world and is found written on every page of the world's history. But it is only in our own day that we have become acquainted with its force and its laws and have understood how to use it. Steam existed before Fulton, but it has only been since Fulton that we have learned the full extent of its power and how to make it produce its marvellous effects. The combination of tube and piston is the instrument employed to put steam to work; the system of representative government has brought the two principles, liberal and conservative, to light, and it is the instrument which has made them yield all their effects.

Upon any subject whatever, in the domain of human things, the truth does not manifest itself equally to all intellects. There are some whose gaze pierces further into the unknown, but takes in less at a time; there are others whose gaze, even if it be less penetrating, perceives more clearly within the sphere that it embraces. This primordial distinction at once explains to a certain extent the liberal and conservative ideas. For this reason alone, the same object will not be seen under the same aspect by different eyes; for this reason alone, some will take a route that others will avoid, although all propose to arrive at the same end. But there is a conclusive account that clearly explains the nature, the end, and the justification of the two different ideas. Macaulay, in his history of England, sets forth this account with admirable clearness. Speaking of the meeting of the Houses for the second session of the Long Parliament, under Charles I, the great historian says:

> From that day dates the corporate existence of the two great parties which have ever since alternately governed the country. In one sense, indeed, the distinction which then became obvious had always existed and always must exist; for it has its origin in diversities of temper, of understanding, and of interest, which are found in all societies and which will be found until the human mind ceases to be drawn in opposite directions by the charm of habit and by the charm of novelty. Not only in politics, but in literature, in art, in science, in surgery and mechanics, in navigation and agriculture, nay, even in mathematics, we find this distinction. Everywhere there is a class of men who cling with fondness to whatever is ancient and who, even when convinced by overpowering reasons that innovation would be beneficial, consent to it with many misgivings and forebodings. We find also everywhere another class of men sanguine in hope, bold in speculation, always pressing forward, quick to discern the imperfection of whatever exists, disposed to think lightly of the risks and inconveniences which attend improvements and disposed to give every change credit for being an improvement.*

The former are the conservatives, the latter are the liberals. Here you have the real meaning, the true explanation, of both the liberal principle and the conservative principle. They are two attributes of our nature. As Macaulay has admirably expressed it, they are to be found everywhere: in the arts, in the sciences, in all the branches open to human speculation; but it is in politics that they are most apparent.

Consequently, those who condemn liberalism as a new idea have not reflected upon what is happening every day under their eyes. Those who condemn liberalism as an error have not reflected that, in so doing, they condemn an attribute of human nature.

Now, it must not be forgotten that our form of government is a representative monarchy. This is the instrument that clarifies and brings into action the two principles, liberal and conservative. We are often accused, we liberals, of being republicans. I do not note this reproach for the purpose of taking it up for discussion, for it is not worth taking up. I merely state that the form matters little; whether it be monarchical or republican, the moment the people exercise the right to vote, the moment they have a responsible government, they have the full measure of liberty. Still, liberty would soon be nothing more than an empty word, if those in power were left unchecked. A man whose astonishing sagacity has formulated the axioms of governmental science with undeviating accuracy, Junius, has said: 'Eternal vigilance is the price of liberty.'* Yes, if a people wish to remain free, they must like Argus have a hundred eyes and be always on the alert. If they slumber, or relax, each moment of indolence loses them a particle of their rights. Eternal vigilance is the price they have to pay for the priceless blessing of liberty. Now, the form of a representative monarchy lends itself marvellously—better, perhaps, than the republican form—to the exercise of this necessary vigilance. On the one hand, you have those who govern, and on the other hand, those who keep an eye on them. On the one hand, you have those who are in power and who have an interest in remaining there, and on the other hand, those who have an interest in getting there themselves. What is the bond of cohesion to hold each of these different groups together? What is the principle, the sentiment, to range the different elements of the population, either among those who govern or those who keep watch? It is the liberal principle and the conservative principle. You will see grouped together those who are attracted by the charm of novelty and on the other side those who are attracted by the charm of habit. You will see together those who are attached to all that is ancient, and you will see together those who are always disposed to reform.

Now I ask, between these two ideas which are the basis of parties, can there be a moral difference? Is the one radically good and the other radically bad? Is it not evident that both are what in moral philosophy we call *indifferents*, that is to say, that both are susceptible of being appreciated, pondered, and chosen? Would it not be as unfair as it would be absurd to condemn or approve either the one or the other as absolutely bad or good?

Both are susceptible of much good, as both are also of much evil. The conservative who defends his country's old institutions may do much good, just as he may also do much evil, if he is obstinate in maintaining abuses that have become intolerable. The liberal who contends against these abuses and who, after long efforts, succeeds in extirpating them, may be a public benefactor, just as the liberal who lays a rash hand on hallowed institutions may be a scourge not only for his own country, but for humanity at large.

Certainly, I am far from blaming my adversaries for their convictions, but for my part, as I have already said, I am a liberal. I am one of those who think that everywhere, in human affairs, there are abuses to be reformed, new horizons to be opened up, and new forces to be developed.

Moreover, liberalism seems to me in all respects superior to the other principle. The principle of liberalism lies in the very essence of our nature, in that thirst for happiness which is always with us in life, which follows us everywhere, though it never be completely satisfied this side of the grave. Our souls are immortal, but our means are limited. We constantly gravitate towards an ideal which we never attain. We dream of an absolute, but never attain more than a comparative good. We reach the goal we had set for ourselves only to discover new horizons opening up that we had not before even suspected. We rush on towards them, and those horizons, explored in their turn, reveal to us others which lead us on ever further and further.

And thus it will be as long as man is what he is, as long as the immortal soul inhabits a mortal body; his desires will always be vaster than his means and his actions will never come up to his conceptions. He is the real Sisyphus of the fable; his work is always finished only to be begun again.

This condition of our nature is precisely what makes the greatness of man, for it dooms him, as his fate, to movement and to progress: our means are limited, but our nature is perfectible, and we have the infinite for our arena. Thus there is always room for the improvement of our condition, for the perfecting of our nature, and for the accession of a greater number to an easier life. Here again is what, in my eyes, constitutes the superiority of liberalism.

Besides, experience has established that insensibly, imperceptibly, abuses will creep into the life of society and end by seriously obstructing its upward march, if not endangering its existence.

Experience has further established that institutions useful at the outset because they were appropriate to the state of society into which they were introduced, will end by becoming intolerable abuses, owing to the simple fact that everything around them will change. Such has been [the course of] seigneurial tenure amongst us. It is unquestionable that this system, in the infancy of the colony, greatly facilitated the settling of the land. But by 1850 everything had changed so much amongst us that the system would have ended in deplorable complications, if our Legislature, upon the initiative of the liberals, had not had the wisdom to abolish it.*

As a consequence of the law that I have pointed to as the determining cause of the liberal and conservative ideas, men will always be found who will attach themselves lovingly to these abuses, who will defend them to the bitter end, and who will be terrified by any attempt to strike them down. Woe to such men if, having the power, they know not how to sacrifice their own preferences! They will draw down upon their country disturbances that will be all the more terrible the longer justice has been refused. History, alas! proves only too clearly that very few of those who govern have been able to understand these aspirations of humanity and to do them justice. More revolutions have been caused by conservative obstinacy than by liberal exaggeration.

The supreme art of government consists in guiding and directing, while controlling, these aspirations of human nature. The English are the supreme masters of this art. Look at the work of the great Liberal party of England! How many reforms it has brought about, how many abuses it has done away with, without shock, disturbance, or violence! It has understood the aspirations of the oppressed and the new needs created by new situations, and under the law, without any instrument except the law, it has brought about a series of reforms that have made the English people the freest, the most prosperous, and the happiest of Europe.

See how different are the continental governments. Most of them have never been able to understand the aspirations of their peoples. They met the stirrings of their poor with brutal repression, and rather than allowing the wretches a few breaths of air and freedom, they pushed them back into an ever more tightly confined existence.

But a day came when the impediments were shattered, when these peoples, no longer paralysed by their restraints, stampeded, and then the most frightful crimes were committed in the holy name of liberty. Should we be astonished at this?

Are we astonished when the storm clouds gathering over our heads break out in hail and lightning? Are we surprised when the steam bursts the boiler whose safety valve the engineer in charge has neglected to open, and which is supposed to release its excessive pressure? No, because we see there the working of an inevitable law which always has the same effect, in the moral as well as in the physical order. Wherever there is compression, there will be explosion, violence and ruin. I do not say this to excuse revolutions; I hate revolutions; I detest all attempts to win the triumph of opinions by violence. What is more, I am less inclined to cast the responsibility on those who make revolutions than on those who provoke them by their blind obstinacy. I say this to explain the superiority of liberalism, which understands the aspirations of human nature, and instead of doing violence to them, seeks to direct them.

Do you believe, for instance, that if England had persisted in refusing emancipation to the Catholics; if it had persisted in refusing the fullness of their civil and political rights to the Catholics, the Jews, and the other Protestant denominations not forming part of the Established Church; if it had persisted in keeping the suffrage limited to a small number; if it had persisted in refusing free trade in grain; if it had persisted in refusing the right to vote to the working classes—do you think that a day would not have come when the people would have risen in arms to obtain for themselves the justice obstinately denied them? Do you think that riot would not have raised its hideous head under the windows of Westminster and that the blood of civil war would not have reddened the streets of London as it has so often reddened the streets of Paris? Human nature is everywhere the same, and there, as elsewhere, compression would have produced explosion, violence, and ruin. These terrible calamities, however, were avoided by the initiative of the liberals who, understanding the evil, proposed and applied the remedy.

What is finer than the history of the great English Liberal party during the present century? On its threshold looms the figure of [Charles James] Fox, the wise, the generous Fox, defending the cause of the oppressed, wherever there are oppressed to be defended. A little later comes [Daniel] O'Connell, the great O'Connell, claiming and obtaining for his co-religionists the rights and privileges of English subjects. He is helped in this work by all the Liberals of the three kingdoms, [Charles, the second Earl] Grey, [Henry Peter, the first Baron] Brougham, [Lord John] Russell, [Lord Francis] Jeffrey and a host of others. Then come, one after the other, the abolition of the ruling oligarchy, the repeal of the corn laws, the extension of the suffrage to the working classes, and, lastly, to crown the whole, the disestablishment of the Church of England as the state religion in Ireland. And note well: the Liberals who carried out these successive reforms were not recruited only from the middle classes—some of their most eminent leaders were recruited from the peerage of England. I know of no spectacle that reflects greater honour on humanity than the spectacle of these peers of England, these rich and powerful nobles, stubbornly fighting to eradicate a host of venerable abuses and sacrificing their privileges with calm enthusiasm to make life easier and happier for a larger number of their fellow beings. While on this subject, let me cite a letter of Macaulay's written to one of his friends on the day after the vote on the famous Reform Bill [of 1832], which put an end to the system of *rotten boroughs*. This letter, to my mind, makes admirably clear what an English liberal is. Here it is. I ask your pardon for making this quotation, as it is somewhat long:

Such a scene as the division of last Tuesday I never saw, and never expect to see again. If I should live fifty years, the impression of it will be as fresh and sharp in my mind as if it had just taken place. It was like seeing Caesar stabbed in the Senate house, or seeing Oliver [Cromwell] taking the mace from the table; a sight to be seen only once, and never to be forgotten. The crowd overflowed the House in every part. When the strangers were cleared out, and the door locked, we had six hundred and eight members present—more by fifty-five than ever were on a division before. The ayes and noes were like two volleys of cannon from opposite sides of a field of battle. When the Opposition went out into the lobby, an operation which took up twenty minutes or more, we spread ourselves over the benches on both sides of the House; for there were many of us who had not been able to find a seat during the evening. When the doors were shut we began to speculate on our numbers. Everybody was desponding. 'We have lost it. We are only two hundred and eighty at most. I do not think we are two hundred and fifty. They are three hundred. Alderman Thompson has counted them. He says they are two hundred and ninety-nine.' This was the talk on our benches. The House, when only the ayes were in it, looked to me a very fair House—much fuller than it generally is even on debates of considerable interest. I had no hope, however, of three hundred. As the tellers passed along our lowest row on the left-hand side the interest was insupportable—two hundred and ninety-one—two hundred and ninety-two—we were all standing up and stretching forward, telling with the tellers. At three hundred there was a short cry of joy—at three hundred and two another—suppressed, however, in a moment, for we did not yet know what the hostile force might be. We knew, however, that we could not be severely beaten. The doors were thrown open, and in they came. Each of them, as he entered, brought some different report of their numbers. It must have been impossible, as you may conceive, in the lobby, crowded as they were, to form any exact estimate. First we heard that they were three hundred and three; then that number rose to three hundred and ten; then went down to three hundred and seven. We were all breathless with anxiety, when Charles Wood, who stood near the door, jumped up on a bench and cried out, 'They are only three hundred and one.' We set up a shout that you might have heard to Charing Cross, waving our hats, stamping against the floor, and clapping our hands. The tellers scarcely got through the crowd; for the House was thronged up to the table, and all the floor was fluctuating with heads like the pit of a theatre. But you might have heard a pin drop as Duncannon read the numbers. Then again the shouts broke out, and many of us shed tears. I could scarcely refrain. And the jaw of Peel fell; and the face of Twiss was as the face of a damned soul; and Herries looked like Judas taking his neck-tie off for the last operation. We shook hands, and clapped each other on the back, and went out laughing, crying, and huzzaing into the lobby. And no sooner were the outer doors opened than another shout answered that within the House. All the passages and the stairs into the waiting-rooms were thronged by people who had waited till four in the morning to know the issue. We passed through a narrow lane between two thick masses of them; and all the way down they were shouting and waving their hats, till we got into the open air. I called a cabriolet, and the first thing the driver asked was, 'Is the bill carried?' 'Yes, by one.' 'Thank God for it, sir!'

And Macaulay concludes with a sentence strongly indicative of the Liberal: 'And so ended a scene which will probably never be equalled till the reformed Parliament wants reforming.'*

The man who wrote in these cheery terms had just come from voting the abolition of the system by virtue of which he held his own seat. Macaulay owed his seat to the generosity of an English peer, Lord Lansdowne, who had him returned for the rotten borough of Calne. I know of few pages that do more honour to humanity than this simple letter which shows us these English natures, calm and unyielding in the struggle, but who become emotional finally, laughing and crying at the same time, when the battle has been won, because justice has been done and an abuse uprooted from the soil of old England.

Members of the *Club Canadien*, Liberals of the Province of Quebec, there are our models! there are our principles! there is our party!

It is true that there exists in Europe, in France, in Italy and in Germany, a class of men who give themselves the title of Liberals, but who have nothing about them that is liberal except the name, and who are the most dangerous of men. They are not liberals, they are revolutionaries; in their principles they are such fanatics that they aim at nothing less than the destruction of modern society. With these men we have nothing in common; but it is the tactic of our adversaries always to assimilate us to them. Such accusations are beneath our notice, and the only answer we can with dignity give them is to proclaim our real principles and to conduct ourselves in such a way that our acts will always conform to our principles.

Now, at this stage of my discourse, I shall review the history of the Liberal party of this country. I am one of those who do not fear to scrutinize the history of my party. I am one of those who think there is more to be gained by frankly stating the truth than by trying to deceive ourselves and others. Let us have the courage to tell the truth! If our party has sometimes gone astray, our denials will not keep things from having been what they were. Besides, if our party has sometimes erred, we shall always find in the other party enough transgressions to balance ours, and even if the other party were immaculate, our principles would be neither better nor worse for all that. Let us have the courage to tell the truth, and let the truth told about our past errors keep us from falling into the same ones in the future.

Down to 1848, all the French Canadians had formed but one party, the Liberal party [i.e., the *Patriotes* and Reformers]. The Conservative, or rather the *Tory* party, as it was called, represented only a tiny minority. But from 1848 date the first traces of the two parties that have since then disputed power. M. Lafontaine had accepted the regime established in 1841. When M. Papineau returned from exile, he assailed the new order of things with his great eloquence and all his elevation of mind. I shall not here undertake to review the respective policies of these two great men. Both loved their country ardently, passionately; both devoted their lives to it; both, in different ways, had no other ambition than to serve it; and both were pure and disinterested. Let us be content with these souvenirs, without seeking which of the two was right and which wrong.

During this period there was a generation of young men of great talent and still greater impetuosity of character. Disappointed at having come on the scene too late to risk their lives in the events of 1837, they threw themselves with blind enthusiasm into the political movement of the day. They were among the foremost of M. Lafontaine's partisans in his glorious struggle against Lord Metcalf. They afterwards abandoned him for the more advanced policy of M. Papineau, and although they ranged themselves behind his leadership, as was natural, they had soon gone beyond him.

Emboldened by their own success and carried away by their enthusiasm, they one day founded [a newspaper,] *L'Avenir*, in which they posed as reformers and regenerators of their country. Not satisfied with attacking the political situation, they boldly attacked the social situation. They issued a programme containing no less than twenty-one articles, commencing with the election of justices of the peace and ending with annexation to the United States, and taken as a whole, practically amounting to a complete revolution.* If it had been possible, by the wave of some magic wand, to realize the twenty-one articles of this programme in a single night, the next morning the country would no longer have been recognizable. The person who left it the evening before and returned the next day, would not have known where he was.

The only excuse for these Liberals was their youth; the oldest of them was not yet twenty-two years of age.

Gentlemen, I am stating facts. I have no intention of reproaching anyone. Talent and sincere convictions are always entitled to respect. Moreover, who amongst us, assuming he had been living at that time, can flatter himself that he would have been wiser and that he would not have fallen into the same errors? Everything at the time favoured such exaggerations, the situation of our own country and the situation of Europe.

The country had not yet recovered from the wounds of the insurrection. We had been granted, true, a free constitution, but it was not being applied in good faith by the Colonial Office. In the depths of every heart there were nasty grumblings kept down only by the memory of the vengeance let loose by the insurrection. Moreover, the germs of democracy and revolt came pouring in upon us from all sides. Society was already shivering in the first blasts of that great storm which a few years later was to break over the whole civilized world and which for a moment made society totter on its foundations. The years preceding 1848 are frightful to contemplate. One is horrified to note the sinister work underway everywhere that drew into revolt, at one time, upwards of eighty millions of men.

This state of things must have made a powerful impression on young, ardent, and inexperienced imaginations. And so, our young reformers—not satisfied with striving to revolutionize their own country—greeted ecstatically each new revolution in Europe.

Scarcely had they taken two steps in life, however, when they perceived their immense error. Starting in 1852 they brought out a new newspaper. They abandoned *L'Avenir* to the fanatics, and in the new paper, *Le Pays*, they sought—though admittedly without always finding it—the new path that the friends of liberty were to follow under the new constitution.

One cannot help smiling today on rereading *L'Avenir*'s programme; one cannot help smiling at finding, mixed in now and then with such good sense, so many absurd or impossible propositions. It would be idle to review one by one all the incongruous propositions it contained. I shall take one of them at random: annual parliaments. I am sure that every one of the young reformers of that time who is today in Parliament, is firmly convinced that an election every five years is quite sufficient. And moreover, is it not obvious that annual parliaments would be a constant impediment to all serious legislation and a permanent source of agitation?

Still, the harm was done. The clergy, alarmed by this behaviour, which reminded them of the revolutionaries of Europe, at once declared unrelenting war on the new party. The English population, friendly to liberty, but friendly too to the maintenance of order, also ranged themselves against the new party, and for twenty-five years that party remained in opposition, although it deserves the honour of having taken the initiative in all the reforms accomplished during that period. In vain did it demand and obtain the abolition of seigneurial tenure; in vain did it demand and obtain judicial decentralization; and in vain was it the first to give an impetus to the work of colonization—it was not credited with these wise reforms. It was in vain that those youngsters, now grown into men, disavowed the rashness of their youth; it was in vain that the Conservative party made mistake after mistake—the generation of the Liberals of 1848 had almost entirely disappeared from the political scene before the dawn of a new day began to break for the Liberal party. Since that time, the party has received new adherents; calmer and more thoughtful ideas have prevailed in its councils; and as for the old programme, nothing whatever remains of its social part, and of its political part, there remain only the principles of the English Liberal party.

During all this time, what was the other party doing? When there had been a complete split between M. Papineau and M. Lafontaine, the fraction of the Liberal party that followed M. Lafontaine wound up, after some groping, by allying themselves with the Tories of Upper Canada, and then to the title Liberal that they still could not or dared not acknowledge, they added that of Conservative. The new party took the name Liberal-Conservative. Some years elapsed and fresh modifications ensued: the new party abandoned altogether the title Liberal and no longer called itself anything but Conservative. Again some years elapsed; more modifications occurred; I no longer know by what name we call this party. Those who today seem to occupy its leading positions will themselves call it the Ultramontane party, the Catholic party. Its principles, like its name, have been changed. If M. Cartier were to come back to earth today, he would not recognize his party. M. Cartier was devoted to the principles of the English constitution. Those who today take the lead among his old partisans openly reject the principles of the English constitution as a concession to what they call the spirit of evil. They understand neither their country nor their time. All their ideas are copied from those of the French reactionaries, just as the ideas of the Liberals of 1848 were copied from those of the French revolutionaries. They go into ecstacies over Don Carlos or the Comte de Chambord, just as the Liberals admired Louis Blanc and Ledru-Rollin. They shout: long live the King! just as the Liberals shouted: long live the Republic! In speaking of Don Carlos and the Comte de Chambord, they affect never to say anything except His Majesty the *King*, Charles VII, and His Majesty the *King*, Henry V, just as the Liberals, in speaking of Napoleon III, always used to say 'Mister Louis Bonaparte'.

I have too much respect for the opinion of my adversaries ever to insult them, but I reproach them with understanding neither their time nor their country. I accuse them of judging the political situation of our country, not according to what is happening here, but according to what is happening in France. I accuse them of wanting to introduce ideas here that cannot be applied in our state of society. I accuse them of laboriously, and unfortunately only too efficaciously, working to reduce religion to the simple proportions of a political party.

In our adversaries' party, it is the habit to accuse us, Liberals, of irreligion. I am not here to parade my religious sentiments, but I declare that I have too much respect for the faith in which I was born ever to use it as the basis of a political organization.

You wish to organize a Catholic party. But have you not considered that, if you had the misfortune to succeed, you would draw down upon your country calamities, of which the consequences are impossible to foresee?

You wish to organize all the Catholics into one party, with no other bond, with no other basis, than a common religion; but have you not reflected that, in so doing, you organize the Protestant population as a single party, and then, instead of the peace and harmony now prevailing between the different elements of the Canadian population, you throw open the door to war, religious war, the most terrible of all wars?

Once again, Conservatives, I accuse you publicly of understanding neither your country nor your time.

[But] our adversaries are still reproaching us: they reproach us with loving liberty, and they term the spirit of liberty a dangerous and subversive principle.

Is there any justification for these attacks? None whatever, unless it be that in France there is a group of Catholics who curse liberty wherever they find it. To be sure, there are in France not only enemies of liberty who regard it with terror. The most ardent friends of liberty often contemplate it with the same feeling. Recall Madame Rolland's last words. She had warmly loved liberty; she had ardently prayed for it; and her last, heart-rending words were these: 'O Liberty! how many crimes are committed in thy name!' How often have these same words been just as sincerely uttered by just as sincere friends of liberty!

I can readily conceive, though without sharing them, the feelings of those Frenchmen who, seeing how much liberty has cost them in tears, blood and ruin, have sometimes favoured a vigorous despotism for their country. I can understand their anathemas, but that these anathemas should be repeated in our own midst is a thing I know not how to understand.

Stop and think: Really! Is it for us, a conquered race, to execrate liberty?

What would we be without liberty? What would we be today if our fathers had cherished the same sentiments as the Conservatives of the present time? Would we be anything but a race of pariahs?

I frankly admit that liberty, as it has been generally understood and practised in France, has nothing very attractive about it. The French have had the name of liberty, but they have not yet had liberty itself. One of their poets, Auguste Barbier, has given us a pretty correct idea of the kind of liberty which is sometimes in vogue in France, and which was last seen at work in 1871. [In 'La Curée'] he represents it as a woman:

> A la voix rauque, aux durs appas
> Qui, du brun sur la peau, du feu dans les prunelles,
>   Agile et marchant à grands pas,
> Se plaît aux cris du peuple, aux sanglantes mêlées,
>   Aux longs roulements des tambours,
> A l'odeur de la poudre, aux lointaines volées,
>   Des cloches et des canons sourds;
> Qui ne prend ses amours que dans la populace,
>   Et ne prête son large flanc
> Qu'à des gens forts comme elle, et qui veut qu'on l'embrasse
>   Avec des bras rouges de sang.*

If liberty were well and truly this sinister virago, I could understand the anathemas of our adversaries, and I would be the first to join in them. But such is not liberty. An English poet, Tennyson, has sung about liberty, the liberty of his country and ours. In his poem 'On a Mourner', Tennyson addresses himself to a friend who enquires why he does not seek a milder climate in the South Sea islands and why, notwithstanding his impaired health, he persists in remaining under the foggy skies of England. The poet replies:

> It is the land that freemen till,
> That sober-suited Freedom chose,
> That land where, girt with friends or foes,
> A man may speak the thing he will;
>
> A land of settled government,
> A land of just and old renown,
> Where Freedom broadens slowly down,
> From precedent to precedent;
>
> Where faction seldom gathers head
> But by degrees to fulness wrought,
> The strength of some diffusive thought
> Hath time and space to work and spread.

Such is the liberty we enjoy and defend and such is the liberty our adversaries, while sharing in its benefits, attack without understanding. Jean Baptiste Rousseau, in one of his odes, speaks of barbarous tribes that one day, in a moment of inconceivable folly, took to insulting the sun with their cries and curses. The poet briefly characterizes this stupid piece of impiety:

> Le Dieu poursuivant sa carrière,
> Versait des torrents de lumière
> Sur ses obscurs blasphémateurs.*

So it is amongst us with those who attack liberty. Liberty covers them, surrounds them, protects them, and defends them even in their cursing.

> Le Dieu poursuivant sa carrière,
> Versait des torrents de lumière
> Sur ses obscurs blasphémateurs.

But while our adversaries reproach us with being friends of liberty, they further reproach us with an inconsistency that would be very serious were the charge true—with denying the Church the freedom to which it is entitled. They reproach us with seeking to silence the administrative body of the Church, the clergy, and of trying to prevent it from teaching the people their duties as citizens and electors. They reproach us—to use the standard phraseology—with wanting to keep the clergy from meddling in politics and with relegating them to the sacristy.

In the name of the Liberal party and of Liberal principles, I repel this assertion!

I maintain that there is not a single Canadian Liberal who wants to prevent the clergy from taking part in political affairs, if the clergy wants to do so.

In the name of what principle would the friends of liberty seek to deny the priest the right to take part in political affairs? In the name of what principle would the friends of liberty seek to deny the priest the right to have and express political opinions, the right to approve or disapprove public men and their acts, and to instruct the people in what he believes to be their duty? In the name of what principle would he not have the right to say that, if I am elected, religion will be endangered, when I have the right to say that if my adversary is elected, the State will be endangered? Why would the priest not have the right to say that, if I am elected, religion will be inevitably destroyed, when I have the right to say that, if my adversary is elected, the State will go straight into bankruptcy? No, let the priest speak and preach as he thinks best, for it is his right. Never will this right be challenged by a Canadian Liberal.

Our constitution invites all citizens to take part in the direction of political affairs; it makes no exceptions. Each person has the right, not only to express his opinion, but to influence, if he can, by the expression of his opinion, the opinions of his fellow citizens. This right exists for all, and there can be no reason why the priest should be deprived of it. I am here to speak my whole mind, and I would add that I am far from finding opportune the kind of intervention by the clergy in politics that we have seen for some years past. I believe, on the contrary, that from the standpoint of the respect due his character, the priest has everything to lose by getting mixed up in the ordinary questions of politics. Still his right to do so is indisputable, and if he thinks it proper to use it, our particular duty as Liberals, is to guarantee it to him against all denial.

This right, however, is not unlimited. We have no absolute rights amongst us. The rights of each man, in our state of society, end precisely at the point where they encroach upon the rights of others.

The right of intervening in politics ends at the point where it encroaches on the independence of the elector.

The constitution of the country is based upon the freely expressed will of each elector. It intends that each elector shall cast his vote freely and voluntarily, as he deems best. If the bulk of the electors at a particular time and place are of a particular opinion, and if as a result of the influence over them of one or more men—as a result of words they have heard or writings they have read—their opinion changes, all this is perfectly legitimate. Although the opinion they express is different from the one they would have expressed without such influence, still the opinion they express is really the one they want to express, the one they truly hold, and the requirements of the constitution are being met. But if, despite all reasonable efforts to change their opinion, their opinion remains unchanged, but then you force them, through intimidation or fraud, to vote differently, the opinion they express is no longer their opinion, and from that point the constitution is being violated. The constitution intends, as I have already said, that the opinion of each one shall be freely expressed as he understands it, at the moment that he gives it, and that the aggregation of all these individual opinions, freely expressed, shall determine the government of the country.

The law watches with so jealous an eye the free expression of the elector's opinion, as it really is, that if the opinion expressed by a single one of the electors in a constituency is not his real opinion, but an opinion forced from him by fear, fraud or corruption, then the election must be annulled.

It is therefore perfectly within the law to alter the elector's opinion by reasoning and all other means of persuasion, but never by intimidation. After all, persuasion changes the elector's conviction; intimidation does not. When, by persuasion, you have changed the elector's conviction, the opinion he expresses is his own opinion; but when, by terror, you force him to vote [your way], the opinion he expresses is your opinion; remove the cause of his fear and he will then express another opinion, which is his own.

One understands at once, that if the opinion expressed by the majority of the electors is not their real opinion, but an opinion extracted from them by fraud, by threats or by corruption, the constitution is violated and you do not have the government of the majority, but the government of a minority. Now, if such a state of things continues and is repeated, if, after each election, the will expressed is not the real will of the country, once more you fetter the constitution, and responsible government becomes no more than an empty name, and sooner or later, here as elsewhere, compression will lead to explosion, violence, and ruin.

But people are not wanting who say that the clergy have a right to dictate to the people what their duties are. I answer simply that we are here under the government of the Queen of England, under the authority of a constitution that was granted to us as an act of justice, and that if the exercise of the rights that you claim were to have the effect of fettering this constitution, and of exposing us to all the consequences of such an act, then the clergy itself would not want it.

I am not one of those who parade themselves as friends and champions of the clergy. However, I say this: like most of my young compatriots, I was brought up by priests and among young men who have become priests. I flatter myself that I have among them some sincere friends, and to them at least I can and I do say: see if there is a country under the sun happier than ours; see if there is a country under the sun where the Catholic Church is freer or more privileged than it is here. Why, then, would you, by claiming rights incompatible with our state of society, risk exposing this country to agitations, the consequences of which it is impossible to foresee?

But I address myself to all my fellow countrymen without distinction and I say to them:

'We are a happy and a free people; and we are happy and free thanks to the liberal institutions that govern us, institutions which we owe to the exertions of our fathers and the wisdom of the mother country.

'The policy of the Liberal party is to protect these institutions, to defend and spread them, and under the sway of these institutions, to develop our country's latent resources. Such is the policy of the Liberal party; it has no other.'

Now, to appreciate the full value of the institutions that govern us today, let us compare the state of the country at present with what it was before they were granted to us.

Forty years ago this summer the country was in a state of feverish commotion, prey to an agitation which, a few months later, broke out in rebellion. The British crown was maintained here only by the force of arms. And yet what were our predecessors seeking? They were asking for nothing more than the institutions that we have at present. Those institutions were granted to us; and they have been worked loyally; and see the result: the British flag floats over the old citadel of Quebec, it floats tonight over our heads, and not a single English soldier is to be found in the entire country to defend it; its sole defence is the recognition we owe it for the liberty and security we have found under its shadow.

Where is the Canadian who, comparing his country with even the freest countries, would not feel proud of the institutions which protect him?

Where is the Canadian who, passing through the streets of this old city and reaching the monument raised a few steps from here to the memory of the two brave men who died on the same field of battle while contending for empire in Canada, would not feel proud of his country?

In what other country under the sun can you find a similar monument reared to the memory of the conquered as well as of the conqueror? In what other country under the sun will you find the names of the conquered and the conqueror equally honoured and occupying the same place in the respect of the population?

Gentlemen, when in that last battle, which is recalled by the monument to Wolfe and Montcalm, the hail of bullets was spreading death in the ranks of the French army; when the old heroes, who had so often been victorious, at last saw victory escaping them; when, stretched on the ground, feeling their blood trickling out and their life ebbing away, they saw, as the consequence of their defeat, Quebec in the hands of the enemy and the country lost forever, their final thoughts must doubtless have concerned their children, those they were leaving without protection and without defence; no doubt they saw them persecuted, enslaved, and humiliated, and then, one may believe, they breathed their last breath in a cry of despair. But if, [we may suppose,] Heaven had lifted the veil of the future from their dying eyes; if, before they closed forever, Heaven had allowed their gaze to penetrate the unknown; if they could have seen their children free and happy, striding with head held high in every walk of life; if they could have seen the first pew in the old cathedral, which used to be occupied by the French governors, now taken by a French governor; if they could have seen the church steeples rising in every valley from the shores of the Gaspé to the prairies of the Red River; if they could have seen this old flag, which reminds us of the finest of their victories, triumphantly shown in all our public ceremonies; if they could have seen, finally, our free institutions—is one not allowed to believe that their last breath expired in a murmur of gratitude to Heaven, and that they died consoled?

If the shades of these heroes still hover over this old city, for which they laid down their lives; if their shades hover tonight over the hall in which we are now assembled, we are allowed to believe, we Liberals—at least we cherish the fond illusion—that their sympathies are all with us.

JULES-PAUL TARDIVEL

Four months after Laurier's 1877 speech, the Quebec bishops advised their clergy to beware of excessive partisanship and informed the faithful that they had never intended, in condemning Catholic liberalism, to condemn any particular political party. But it would be wrong to infer that Laurier had succeeded in reconciling liberalism with ultramontanism.

Jules-Paul Tardivel (1851-1905), best known today as the author of an extravagant separatist novel, Pour la patrie *(1895), was in his own day the leading ultramontane journalist in French Canada. The following selections on liberalism are taken from a series of articles written in 1882 for his newspaper,* La Vérité, *and from a book, published in 1890, about his European tour of the previous year.*

On Liberalism

What is a liberal? Ninety-nine per cent of those who call themselves liberals would have as much difficulty answering this question as the bulk of the so-called conservatives would have in answering the [same] question [about conservatism] we discussed in our first article. According to some, a liberal is a progressive man; for others he is a broadminded man; for still others, someone who wants certain reforms.

Progress, broadmindedness, reform—so many rather vague terms that can signify something or nothing at all, not enough or too much. Everyone wants progress; everyone thinks his own outlook broader than that of his neighbour; and no human institution exists so perfect that it could not and ought not to be perfected and reformed. To speak of liberalism in this way is idle talk and nonsense. All those who call themselves liberals, and who sincerely believe that liberalism comprises nothing but progress, openmindedness, and reform, would do well to keep these things, but to renounce the name that by no means signifies these things and which, for good reason, is in very bad repute.

We will not embark on a long philosophical dissertation about liberalism, its origin, and its fundamental causes here. This aspect of the question is dealt with learnedly in the lectures of Father Paquin, which are now being published.

What is understood, and what must be understood, by *liberalism* is the exclusion of God from politics, or, to use the definition of Father Ubald, 'the suppression of the rights of God in the civil and political order'. To be sure, there are also godless liberals who seek to suppress the rights of God, not only in the civil and political order, but everywhere; who wish not only to banish Jesus Christ from the earth, but to drive him out of heaven itself. Here we shall not be concerned with this absolute liberalism, which is nothing but atheism.

The liberalism to be combatted here is that network of seductive doctrines that professes a great respect for the rights of God but wishes to restrict their exercise and limit them to certain subjects—as if God were not the sovereign Master of everything, societies as well as individuals; as if His holy laws did not bind every man here below, in whatever station he finds himself, whether he be king, prince, legislator, or common citizen; as if politics, which is the art of guiding peoples towards their end in life, were withdrawn from His almighty jurisdiction!

Such is liberalism. There is no other. And take careful note that by nature this liberalism we have just defined resembles godless liberalism and atheism, to which it inevitably leads. In effect, one begins by excluding God from politics; one contends that He has nothing to do with elections, laws, and public policy; that electors, deputies, and ministers owe Him no account of their public acts. Then one goes a step further: one says that the good Lord has no place in school; then that He has no place in the family; and finally, that He is superfluous everywhere, even in the Church and in the conscience of individuals. Such is the slippery slope taken by those who begin by denying the rights of God in the civil order, and it is a slope that leads to the abyss, to hell.

Once again we entreat all those who by *political liberalism* wish to designate only true love of progress, useful reforms, and a wise administration of public business, to renounce this term so that there will no longer be any equivocation.

There are a certain number of political men who loudly proclaim their belief in the exclusion of any idea of God from politics and who tell you boldly that the Church has nothing to do with the affairs of this world. These are the open Liberals. But there are a still greater number who do not *profess* this doctrine, but who *practise* it every day, who reject the name of *Liberal* or who presume to couple it with *Conservative*, and who are deeply infected with the liberal virus. These are the hidden liberals, and they are the ones we are going to unmask today.

To recognize these liberals in disguise, it suffices to follow their public acts. Pay no attention to the name they give themselves; ignore the cloak in which they masquerade. More than one good-for-nothing villain has a fine name, and rich clothing often covers a wretched body. Rather follow what they do in the political arena. It is by their fruits, by their acts, that you will know them, and not by their words. *Ex fructibus eorum cognoscetis eos.**

If they are ordinary voters, at election time you will see them resorting to all kinds of dishonest tricks. They stop at nothing. If they can carry an election by violence, intimidation, corruption, drunkenness, or fraud, they will do it. Or if they do not do it themselves, they will let it be done and they will rejoice in the victory obtained at that price. They will say, to excuse themselves, that their adversaries do the same thing, as if the sin of one's neighbour could justify one's own failings.

Flee such men, whatever name they give themselves; they are the true liberals, in the worst sense of the word. They have no conscience; they do not recognize the rights of God in elections; they act as if they would not one day have to give an account to the Sovereign judge of every bad vote they cast or have cast, of every conscience they corrupt, and of every fraud they commit.

If they are candidates, they will be guilty of all the crimes just mentioned and in addition they will use lies and calumny; they will make formal agreements knowing well that they will not fulfil them; they will make false promises; they will obtain the mandate they covet under 'false pretenses'.

Flee such men. There is no morality for them in politics; in their eyes only success is worth anything.

[If they get to] Parliament these *liberals in disguise* hold to the same line of conduct. There they behave as true atheists. Never do they ask for the slightest illumination from Above; never does the thought cross their minds that each of their votes, each of the motives behind their actions, is being inscribed in the Great Book of God, on the basis of which the world will be judged. *Unde mundus judicetur.* They have only one thought: that they have a mandate that will last five years, and at the end of that time they will perhaps be able to have it renewed by again resorting to the same illicit means they have already employed. Thus you see them advancing their own private interests or the interests of their friends at the expense of the common interest; you see them trampling upon the oath they swore on entering Parliament; you see them selling themselves; you see them approving laws or deals that they *know* to be baneful, that they *admit* are disastrous; you see them sanctioning injustice, some from party spirit, others from motives still more shameful. And whatever you may say, they will claim to owe a reckoning to no one except to the people who are so easy to fool.

If they are Ministers, these *liberals in disguise* will stop at nothing provided they can obtain the support of the majority, support they obtain by buying votes, by threats, and by intrigues of every kind. In the House, in the press, on the hustings, these men have neither faith, nor morals, nor principles, nor honour, nor honesty. They have only one goal, which is to satisfy their ambition, to attain power, to stay in power, to serve their personal interests. They know only one way of acting, which is to live by their wits. As for the Church, they imagine that it is an institution invented expressly for them, to help them attain their personal goals, a sort of political club. But the teachings of the Church they do not respect. The rights of the clergy they combat as soon as the exercise of these rights gets in the way of their little intrigues.

Such is liberalism in action.

[Finally,] let us say a few words about that *English liberalism* we hear so much about. Canadian Liberals, with M. Laurier in the lead, are always asserting that they profess only *English liberalism* which, according to them, is a purely political and perfectly harmless liberalism. In passing, let us note first of all that several of our Canadian Liberals, while claiming to favour nothing but English liberalism, have great difficulty hiding their sympathy and admiration for French liberalism. But the important point is the following one. Does there exist, as is claimed, an essential difference between *English liberalism* and other *liberalisms*? I say definitely not. Fundamentally, every liberalism, whether it be called English, French, Italian, Belgian, Spanish, or Canadian, commits the same error. The differences one notes between the manifestations of liberalism in England and on the continent derive exclusively from differences in circumstances and milieux; they are accidental differences. To be convinced of this it suffices to reflect for a moment on the true nature of the liberal error. First, there is not, properly speaking, a purely political liberalism. To prefer representative institutions over monarchy is to be a republican, not a *liberal*. Garcia Moreno was a partisan of the republican form [of government], yet no one ever thought of giving him the title of *liberal*.* On the other hand, the most absolute king imaginable could be a wildly extreme liberal. Liberalism is a *politico-religious* error that can appear under all forms of government. It is, in two words, the *secularization* of politics, its *laicization*, to use a new term. The true liberal wishes to see every religious idea excluded from the practice of government; he wishes to see laws drafted and public affairs administered without taking into account any positive doctrine or any revelation—only the light of human reason. This is why liberalism puts all religions on a footing of equality before the law. True religion and the different sects are to it merely *private opinions* about which the State need not concern itself in any way, so long as they do not openly disturb the public peace. Such is true *liberalism*, which must not be confused with *radicalism*, that is to say, openly proclaimed hatred of the Church and legal persecution of Catholics. No doubt liberalism prepares the way for radicalism, but the two errors are different.

Now, is it not easy to see that liberalism in England has set itself the same goal as in France, in Spain, in Italy, or in Belgium? This goal is the *secularization* of politics. In Catholic countries liberalism comes into conflict with the Church, which makes it easy for us to grasp all that is dangerous and subversive in it. In England it aims its blows against a sect, which is the State religion, to beat it down and to put all the other sects, and even the true religion, on a footing of equality before the law. As the attacks of English liberalism favour the liberty and development of the Catholic Church in England, one may admire and support it *in a relative way*. If I were English I would be tempted to back Gladstone and his party with all my efforts, not only because they are sympathetic to the aspirations of Ireland, but because they are constantly seeking to destroy the supremacy of the sect created by the dreadful Henry VIII. But while English Catholics may, *in England*, use that terrible battering-ram called liberalism—since it is always permitted to make the best of something evil—one must nonetheless recognize that liberalism in England rests, as does liberalism in every other country, on the false principles of *naturalism* and the *laicization* of politics. Thus for someone in Canada to say that he professes only *English liberalism* makes no sense. In reality, there are not several liberalisms: there is only one liberalism, which has different manifestations in different countries.

SIR GEORGE PARKIN

One of the great public controversies of the period from 1890 to 1914 was the question of imperialism vs. nationalism. Imperialists wanted to consolidate Canada's ties with the Empire; nationalists wanted Canada to become an independent nation. One legacy from that great conflict is our current assumption that it is impossible to be both a nationalist and an imperialist. But this whole phase of our history was initiated by men who were both Canadian nationalists and British imperialists: nationalists within the Empire, and imperialists when they looked outside the Empire from its perspective. This double nationalism is as tenable today as it was a century ago, when its outstanding representative was George Parkin (1846-1922), one of the patriarchs of Canadian political thought.

Born on a farm in New Brunswick, educated in the local schools and at Oxford, headmaster of the Collegiate School in Fredericton and of Upper Canada College in Toronto, Parkin called himself 'a wandering Evangelist of Empire'. In 1902 he became the first head of the Rhodes Scholarship Trust, a position he retained until his death. Between 1892 and 1912 he produced six books, some of which sold tens of thousands of copies; yet perhaps his most interesting work was this essay on the reorganization of the British Empire ('a vaster Empire than has been'), which was published in an American monthly in 1888.

The Reorganization of the British Empire

The development of the Anglo-Saxon race, as we rather loosely call the people which has its home in the British Isles, has become, within the last century, the chief factor and central feature in human history. The flux of population, by which new and great centers of human activity are created, has been so overwhelmingly Anglo-Saxon that nearly all minor currents are absorbed and assimilated by it. In the new continents over which the race is spreading, the offshoots of other European families for the most part lose their identity, and tend to disappear in the dominant mass. Since it has found space on which to expand it has increased with great rapidity, and seems destined ultimately to surpass, in mere mass of numbers, any other branch of the human stock, while its comparative influence is indefinitely increased by the singular individual energy of its members and the collective energy of its communities. Add to this the fact that it embodies the most aggressive moral forces and the most progressive political and social forces of the world, and we have sufficient grounds on which to predict for it a future of supreme interest, and infinitely greater than its past.

The bifurcation of Anglo-Saxon national life which was caused by the American Revolution is now, after a hundred years, fully recognized as the most important political event in modern history. Hitherto, the fact that it led to the foundation of the American republic has been considered an adequate measure of its vast significance. But immense though that fact is, it is now beginning to be clearly seen that the American Revolution has had another effect of at least equal significance and probable influence upon the world's future. It compelled Great Britain, by the stern teaching of experience, to master the true principles of colonial government, and, as a consequence, to acquire the art of bringing her colonies into essential harmony with the national life. The folly of so-called statesmen, which reft from Great Britain her first great offshoot, left untouched the nation-building energy of her people, and around her has since grown up, in every quarter of the globe, a vast system of dependencies, occupying an eighth of the earth's surface and embracing even now a considerable portion of the world's population, with a capacity for enormous expansion. National development on such a scale is unparalleled in history, and must be pregnant with results. Already, as the process of expansion goes on, it has become manifest that this aggregation of states is slowly but surely outgrowing the system under which it was created. The question of its reconstruction or adaptation to new conditions is undoubtedly one of the greatest of the world-problems now coming up for solution.

In one of his most striking poems ['Heine's Grave'] Matthew Arnold speaks of England as

> The weary Titan, with deaf
> Ears, and labor-dimmed eyes,
> Staggering on to her goal,
> Bearing, on shoulders immense,
> Atlantean, the load
> Well-nigh not to be borne
> Of the too vast orb of her fate.

It is not the poet's mind alone which is profoundly moved by this fact of Great Britain's vast expansion; by the question of whether she will continue able to bear her enormous burden of empire. Statesmen have to face the fact in all its gravity; nations in every quarter of the globe know that their future history depends, more than on anything else, on the answer given to the question. For the world at large, civilized and uncivilized, there is not at present, in the whole range of possible political variation, any question of such far-reaching significance as whether Great Britain shall remain a political unit, with effective energy equal to her actual and increasing greatness, or, yielding to some process of disintegration or dismemberment, shall abdicate her present position of world-wide influence, and suffer the great current of her national life to be broken up into many separate channels.

The growing influence, immense interests, and widening aspirations of the greater colonies—the commercial, legislative, and even social exigencies of the whole national system—make it clear that an answer to this great political problem cannot long be delayed. A profound movement of thought upon the subject has for the past few years been going on among British people in every part of the world. More recently, a great stimulus to discussion has been given by the formation of the Imperial Federation League, a society unofficial in its character, but guided or supported by many of the best minds of the empire, and apparently destined to become a rallying-point for a strong national enthusiasm.*

Within a short time a remarkable change has come over public opinion in the British Isles themselves. Twenty years ago it almost seemed as if Great Britain was ready voluntarily to throw away her vast colonial empire. A whole school of politicians favored the idea, and seemed to have gained the public ear. *The Times*, supposed to reflect public opinion, claimed that England was paying too high a price for enjoying the luxury of colonial loyalty, and warned the colonies to prepare for the separation that was inevitable.

John Bright's eloquence and Goldwin Smith's literary skill were alike employed in the same direction. Under such guidance, intoxicated by the success of free trade, and indulging in dreams of a cosmopolitan future which it was to produce for the nations, the British people seemed for a time to look upon the colonies as burdens which entailed responsibilities without giving any adequate return. All this has now been changed. John Bright in England and Goldwin Smith in Canada still harp on the old string, but get no response from the popular heart, nor even from political parties. Great Britain has found that she still has to fight for her own hand, commercially and politically, and cannot afford to despise her natural allies. The vigor of colonial life, the expansion of colonial trade and power, the greatness of the part which the colonies are manifestly destined to take in affairs, have impressed even the slow British imagination. The integrity of the empire is fast becoming an essential article in the creed of all political parties. The idea appeals to the instincts of Great Britain's new democracy even more strongly than to the pride of her aristocracy, and with better reason, for the vast unoccupied areas of the empire in the colonies offer to the workingman a field of hope when the pressure at home has become too severe. Statesmen of the first rank, such as Earl Rosebery and the late W. E. Forster, have grasped the idea that national consolidation should form the supreme object of national policy, and have done what they could to develop the public sentiment which alone can make it such. The range of the national vision is widening; there is a tendency to look beyond the old ruts of European diplomacy to the nobler work and larger destiny opened up in the Greater Britain beyond the sea.

To the development of this wider view the growth of the United States has contributed largely. It has illustrated on a large scale the expansive energy of our race where the conditions are favorable. It has enlarged our conception of Anglo-Saxon self-governing capacity. It has shown that an unparalleled impulse to a nation's life may be given by vast breadth of territory with variety of climate and production. On the other hand, the British people see in the American Union proof that immense territorial extent is not incompatible, under modern conditions, with that representative system of popular government which had its birth and development in England and its most notable adaptation in America. They are beginning to believe that their political system will safely bear the strain of still further adaptation to wider areas, if the welfare or necessities of the empire demand a change. That they will demand it is a proposition now become so evident that it scarcely requires proof. The home population of Great Britain, which alone exercises national functions in their broadest sense, and bears the full burden of national responsibilities, is about thirty-five millions. This number has practically reached its outside limit of expansion. The Anglo-Saxon population of the empire abroad is already about eleven millions, and is increasing rapidly. It is a population which has already grouped itself into communities of national extent, self-governing, self-reliant, progressive, and with a clear sense of the large place which they are destined to fill in the world. The time cannot be very far distant when, by the flux of population and the process of growth, their numbers will equal or surpass those of the people of the British Isles. There can be no question that long before that period has arrived a readjustment of functions and responsibilities will be essential to the maintenance of the empire as a political unit. The British people at home cannot continue to bear alone the increasing burden of imperial duties. Great communities like Australia or Canada would disgrace the traditions of the race if they remained permanently content with anything short of an equal share in the largest possible national life. For both mother land and colonies that largest life will unquestionably be found in organic national unity. The weight of public sentiment throughout the empire is at present strongly in favor of such unity, and national interest recommends it.

It is perhaps hard for Americans, imbued with traditions of the struggle by which their country threw off the yoke of an oppressive English government, to understand how completely, and for what strong reasons, the relations between Great Britain and her present colonies are those of profound sympathy and warm affection. The mother land regards with natural pride the energy which is planting free political institutions and extending civilization in so many quarters of the globe; which is opening up such vast areas of virgin soil for British occupation, and which, by so doing, is preparing for her a solution of the difficult problem pressing upon her at home from dense population and limited land—a solution such as no other of the overcrowded nations of Europe can hope for. To the richness of her own past the colonies open a boundless vista of hope for the future. The colonies, on the other hand, feel equally proud of their unbroken connection with the grand traditions of the mother land. Little has occurred to mar the strength of this sentimental attachment. They have enjoyed the advantages of being members of a great empire without, as yet, bearing the severer weight of its burdens. All the perfect freedom of self-government for which they have asked has been ungrudgingly allowed. The population which is flowing into their waste lands comes chiefly from the mother country—not driven out by religious persecution or political tyranny, but the overflow of a fecund race, impelled by the spirit of enterprise, or in search of the larger breathing-space of new continents. In almost every case they come to strengthen the loyalty of the colony. The emigrant is encouraged or even assisted in leaving the old Britain; he is heartily welcomed in the new Britain beyond the seas. For generations afterwards his descendants speak of 'going home' without feeling it necessary to explain that by 'home' they mean England, Scotland, or Ireland. Great Britain's new colonial policy has thus given a new cohesion to the empire. Even in the case of a distinct race, with strong race instincts, it has achieved a marked success. French-Canadians are not only content with their political condition, but warmly loyal to British connection. Their greatest statesman emphasized, but scarcely exaggerated, this attitude of mind when he described himself as an Englishman speaking French.* So high an authority as Cardinal Manning told me not long since that French-Canadian bishops and clergy had over and over again assured him that their people were practically a unit in preferring British to French connection. There is no doubt that in respect of either religious freedom or political security the preference is justified. The lapse of years brings into stronger relief the truth of Montalembert's remark, that the Frenchmen of Canada had gained under British rule a freedom which the Frenchmen of France never knew.

With this sentiment, which makes unity possible, the national interest coincides. For the colonies the alternative is independence, when, as small and struggling nationalities, they will have to take their place in a world which has developed distinct tendencies towards the agglomeration of immense states, and where absorption or comparative insignificance can alone await them. For Great Britain the choice is between amalgamating permanently in some way her strength and resources with those of the colonies, or abdicating the relatively foremost place which she now holds among the nations. The growth in population of the United States and the expansion of Russia are already beginning to dwarf by comparison all other nations. Those confined to Europe will, within the next fifty years, be out of the first rank. Great Britain alone, with unlimited room for healthful expansion on other continents, has the possibility of a future equal to the greatest; has the chance of retaining her hegemony as a ruling and civilizing power. Should she throw away the opportunity, her history will be one of arrested development. The process by which her vast colonial empire has come to her has been one of spontaneous growth, the outcome of a decisive national tendency. By inherent inclination the Anglo-Saxon is a trader. The character is one of which we need not feel ashamed. It has been found to consist in our history, with all the fighting energy of the Roman and much of the intellectual energy of the Greek. It does not seem incompatible with the moral energy of Christianity, and furnishes the widest opportunity for its exercise.

It has been under the impulse of this trading instinct that Great Britain has founded empire; to satisfy it, she must maintain empire. Among all the nations of the earth she stands in the unique position of owning by undisputed right immense areas of territory under every climate on the globe, and hence produces, or can produce, within her own national boundaries, all the raw materials of commerce. As civilization becomes more complex and more diffused, the products of every clime are, in an increasing ratio, laid under contribution to supply its manifold wants. Every step towards the complete national assimilation of so widespread an empire must favor the free exchange of commodities, with the necessary result of stimulating productive energy and developing latent resources. Every expansion of trade makes the security of trade a matter of increasing importance. For a race of traders, scattered over all quarters of the globe, peace, made secure by resting on organized power, is a supreme interest. The best guarantee of permanent peace that the world could have would be the consolidation of a great oceanic empire, the interests of whose members would lie chiefly in safe commercial intercourse. For filling such a place in the world Great Britain's position is absolutely unique among the nations of history. She holds the chief key to the commerce of the East in the passes of the Mediterranean and the Red seas. She commands an alternative route by the Cape of Good Hope. Across Canada she has yet a third, giving her for many purposes a still closer connection with the extreme East than do the other two. The geographical distribution of the coal areas under her control, and the defended or defensible harbors suitable for coaling stations contiguous to them, are among the most remarkable elements in her incomparable resources for prosecuting or protecting commerce in an age of steam. Already in electric connection with almost every important point in her dominions, her telegraph system only awaits the laying of the proposed cable from British Columbia to Australasia to make that connection complete without touching on foreign soil.

Her widely separated provinces and outlying posts of vantage are thus effectively in touch for mutual support, more than the parts of any of the great nations of the past. She thus unites the comprehensiveness of a world-wide empire with a relative compactness secured by that practical contraction of our planet which has taken place under the combined influences of steam and electricity. No other nation has ever had—it is well-nigh impossible to believe that any other nation ever will have—so commanding a position for exercising the functions of what we have called an oceanic empire, interested in developing and able to protect the commerce of the world. The question of whether she shall permanently retain this position is one of profound international as well as national concern. Above all, for the United States, as a great trading community, kindred in race, language, and, speaking very broadly, in national purpose, it must have a deep and abiding interest.

The political writers of the past century, from De Tocqueville onward, have been accustomed to draw from the American Revolution the confident inference that the natural tendency of colonies is towards separation from the mother land; that the growth of local interests and feelings of independence make new communities detach themselves, like ripe fruit, from the parent stem. If the birth of the American republic gave strength to this inference, its growth has done much to dissipate the idea. The development of the United States has proved that the spread of a nation over vast areas, including widely separated States with diverse interests, need not prevent it from becoming strongly bound together in a political organism which combines the advantages of national greatness and unity of purpose with jealously guarded freedom of local self-government. This is in part due to the amazing change which has been effected in the mutual relation of the world's inhabitants by improved means of speedy intercourse. Steam and electricity have re-created the world, and on a more accessible scale. Canada, or even Australia, is now much closer to the center of the British Empire for all practical purposes than were the Western and Pacific States to Washington forty years ago; nearer even than Scotland was to London one hundred years ago. Under these new conditions there is no sufficient reason for doubting that an empire like that of Great Britain can be held together in bonds as secure as those which bind together great continental states like the United States and Russia, provided that the elements of true national life are present, as they certainly are in this case.

The federation of Great Britain and her colonies would only be an extension of what has already been done on a large scale. The United States are a federation, Germany is a federation, each designed by its framers to obviate the difficulties incident to the administration of a congeries of small states, and for great ends to secure unity of national action. The problem before Great Britain is different, but would seem to be incomparably less difficult than that involved in either of the two cases referred to. In Germany, dynasties and states whose individual existence had been carefully preserved and fondly cherished for centuries long presented an apparently insuperable barrier to union, effected at last only under the strong pressure of external danger and in the enthusiasm of a great and successful struggle for race supremacy. Every student of American history knows the violent prejudices which had to be overcome and the extraordinary effort which it required to organize and gain acceptance for the Federal Constitution, even after the War of Independence had demonstrated the necessity for united action on the part of the various States. Sectional jealousies and rivalries have never been developed to a corresponding extent in the various provinces of the British Empire. For them federation would only be recasting and making more permanent a union which already exists, though under imperfect conditions. Besides this, the operation of the federal principle is now more thoroughly understood; its advantages have been gauged and its difficulties grappled with. The freedom of self-government long enjoyed by the great colonies has developed a strong feeling of local independence; but it has also been the best of all preparations for a wider political organization. Canada and Australia are to-day as jealous of imperal interference with local legislation as is any State in the Union of unjustified Federal assumptions. But as their autonomy in the control of their own affairs has become admitted and assured, they look without suspicion on the idea of combination having for its purpose the accomplishment of great national ends. These ends have become more manifest with the spread of their commerce to every part of the world, and with the manifold multiplication of national interests. Questions of peace and war: the safety of the great ocean routes; the adjustment of international differences; the relations of trade, currency, communication, emigration—in all these their concern is already large, and becomes larger from year to year. In dealing with all such questions their voice, as component parts of a great empire, will be far more efficient than as struggling independent nationalities. That voice is, in a measure, given to them now by courtesy, and as a necessary concession to their growing importance; but for permanent nationality it must be theirs by ordinary right of citizenship, through full incorporation into the political system of the state, so far as relations with other states are concerned. Those who believe it impracticable to give unity of this kind to the empire underestimate the strength of the influences which make for the continuity of national life. On this continent we see to-day a sufficiently striking illustration of this strength. We can easily understand that it requires no very marked natural boundary to form a permanent line of separation between nations which differ in language, religion, and descent, as in the case of European states. But in America an almost purely arbitrary line of division has for more than a century served sharply to separate into two nationalities, and across the breadth of a continent, two peoples who are of the same origin, speak the same language, study the same literature, and are without any decisive distinctions of religious creed. The admitted present loyalty of Canada has deepened and matured through a long series of years when the United States were sweeping past them in a career of prosperity almost without example in history, and when union with them seemed as if it would secure for Canada an equal share of all the prosperity that they enjoyed. The bias of national life has been so strong that neither geographical facts nor commercial tendencies have weakened the national bond. Nor are they more likely to do so now that Canada has, by the opening up of her great western provinces, manifestly entered upon a like period of development.

In spite of this evidence of a century's history Mr Goldwin Smith still argues that trade interests will ultimately draw Canada into political connection with the United States, and apparently does not understand why his opinion is rejected with indignation by the vast majority of Canadians. Yet it seems impossible to conceive how, without a debasement of public sentiment quite unparalleled in history, a people whose history began in loyalty to British institutions, who through a hundred years have been sheltered by British power, who under that rule have attained and enjoyed the most complete political and religious liberty, who have constantly professed the most devoted regard for a mother land with which they are connected by a thousand ties of affectionate sympathy, should deliberately, in cold blood, and for commercial reasons only, break that connection and join themselves to a state in whose history and traditions they have no part. They would incur, and unquestionably would deserve, alike the contempt of the people they abandon and of the people they join. In a Great Britain reorganized as a federation, or union, or alliance, Canada would hold an honorable place, gained on lines of true national development; in annexation to the United States she could have nothing but a bastard nationality, the offspring of either meanness, selfishness, or fear.

What is thus true of Canada is true of the other British colonies as well. The forces which make for unity and continuity of national life are not only strong, but noble and natural.

The argument for unity may be carried to still higher ground. A strong impulse has unquestionably been given to national effort and earnestness, both in Great Britain and the United States, by the prevailing conviction that Anglo-Saxon civilization is a thing distinct in itself and with a mission in the world. Granting the truth of this, we must also grant that any hindrance to the safe and free development of that civilization in either of its two great currents would be to the world's loss. In the United States, through its isolation, it seems comparatively secure to deal with the complex problem, weighted with grave anxieties, which it has to solve in the assimilation and elevation of confluent races. Great Britain's task, more diversified and world-wide, seems burdened with even greater responsibilities, and not free from great dangers. The enormous expansion and persistent ambition of at least one great despotic power, the possibility of combinations against her such as she has had to face before but may not be able again to cope with single-handed, point to the necessity for national consolidation if she is to have that prestige of national power which commands peace, or if she is to form a sufficient bulwark for the free institutions to which she has given birth in many lands.

Great Britain, again, has assumed vast responsibilities in the government of weak and alien races—responsibilities which she cannot now throw off, even if she wish to, without a loss of national honor. With increasing force the public conscience insists that her rule shall be for the good of the ruled; none deny that the removal of her sway, in Asia and Africa at least, would result in wide-spread anarchy. But her task is herculean.

An empire which has leaning upon it an Indian population of two hundred and forty millions over and above the native races of Australia, New Zealand, South Africa, and many minor regions must require, if stability and equilibrium are to be permanently maintained, an immense counterbalancing weight of that trained, intelligent, and conscientious citizenship which is the backbone of national strength.

Standing face to face, as she does to-day, with almost every uncivilized and unchristian race on the globe, Great Britain needs to concentrate her moral as well as her political strength for the work she has to do. Neither British statesmen nor British Christians can afford to lose one fraction of the moral energy which is becoming centralized in the great colonies. Great Britain's political unity and dominance are to the spread of religion in Africa, Asia, and the Pacific now what Rome's political unity and dominance were to the spread of religion in the days of St Paul. The fact that the flag of a firmly organized oceanic state will everywhere give the greatest safety to the missionary will, without doubt, ultimately throw the whole weight of Christian thought throughout the British world towards the support of permanent national unity. The sympathy of Christian thought in America ought to and will reënforce this influence.

Working out on separate and yet parallel lines the great problems of liberty and of civil and religious progress, the United States and Great Britain have the strongest reasons for sympathizing with each other's efforts to consolidate and perfect the national machinery by which their aims are to be accomplished. Great Britain now understands and respects the motives which actuated the resolute and successful struggle of the American people against disruption. A nation which suffered and sacrificed so much for unity as did the United States [in the Civil War] can assuredly understand and sympathize with the strong desire for national consolidation which is now spreading throughout the British Empire.

It has long been a Saxon boast that while other races require to be governed, we are able to govern ourselves. To this kingly power, in every stage of our development, new and more comprehensive tests have been applied. From the organization of the parish or county to that of States which span a continent this self-governing capacity has not yet failed to find the political device adapted to the political necessity. It would now seem that the British people stand face to face with the ultimate test to which this ability can be put. Have they the grasp of political genius to establish permanently on a basis of mutual benefit and organic unity the empire which they have had the energy to create?

When a great nation ceases to advance, or loses control of the problems involved in its own growth, we can safely say that decadence has begun. Nations as well as individuals find their true place when challenging their highest destiny, provided this be along the lines of natural development. But beyond these general reasons there are others of present and pressing weight which will soon compel the British people to grapple resolutely with this great political problem. The increasing pressure and unequal distribution of national burdens, the inability of Parliament to unite the management of imperial affairs with local legislation, the immense strides in arts or arms made by rival nations, the widening aspirations of the great colonies—these are but a few among many influences by which is being developed that weight of opinion which forces questions forward into the sphere of practical politics, compels statesmen to find some form of expression for the public will, and for the attainment of great ends makes masses of people willing to forget minor differences.

ADAM SHORTT

Adam Shortt (1859-1931) must be regarded as the founder of the Canadian political economy tradition. He held the Sir John A. Macdonald Chair of Political Science at Queen's University from 1892 to 1908, when he resigned to become the first chairman of the Civil Service Commission, a post he held until 1917. He was an outstanding authority on the economic history of Canada, particularly banking and currency under the French regime. Here, however, we see him discussing, not the details of economic history, but the broad principles of political economy.

In Defence of Millionaires

There is at present [1899] a decided attitude of hostility on the part of many respectable organs of public opinion towards men of great wealth and consequent power, commonly styled millionaires. In the thorough conviction that this attitude is largely based on mistaken ideas, however natural, that it is obstructive of progress and injurious to many of the best interests of society, I have ventured to make the following observations on the position of millionaires and popular opinions regarding them.

There can be no reasonable objection to a criticism of millionaires, or any other element in the community, provided the criticism is fair and enlightened. On the contrary such criticism accomplishes much, for, even if outwardly resented at the time, it cannot be conscientiously ignored by the objects of it. Even to prove it inapplicable to themselves they must remedy the defects pointed out. But ignorant, unreasonable, or merely envious criticism is simply resented and despised with a fortified conscience. Such criticism by arousing in those who are the objects of it a strong sense of injustice suffered, tends to close their eyes to those real weaknesses and defects which properly call for reform.

Again, in meeting attacks based upon ignorance or malice, those attacked feel justified in using whatever means of defence are available; suiting the weapons of defence to those of attack, meeting reckless and unscrupulous action with like action, and offsetting vexatious legislative attacks by legislative bribery.

In the interest of the common good what seems to be called for is a better understanding of the place and function in society of men of great wealth, and of the true grounds upon which they may be judged either beneficial or injurious to the best social interests.

A characteristic feature of the Anglo-Saxon element, and of its assimilated immigrants in North America, is the setting forth of equality as a great social and political ideal. In some respects the ideal is admirable and has done good service. But for this very reason, among others, its importance has been greatly exaggerated and its limitations ignored.

As a practical ideal it was first directed against the stereotyping class-distinctions of Europe. Those distinctions, it was thought, chiefly accounted for the historic inequality among men. With their removal and the consequent throwing open of every occupation to every individual it was fondly hoped that a general equality would be secured, and with it an introduction to something like the millennium. The results, though truly beneficial, were not what were expected. A new form of inequality simply took the place of the old.

In America all things were made possible for all men, but this very speedily brought to light the fact that all men are not capable of all things. It is true, that, under the circumstances, every dormant ambition tended to be awakened. But the lines in which these ambitions were to be gratified were naturally determined by the social atmosphere of the country, and this was of narrower range than that of Europe. The freedom of making trial brought many competitors, and the resulting inequality has been in some ways more pronounced and more keenly felt than that of Europe.

Thus the original expectations from the freedom and equality of America have been justified only in this particular, important though it is, that the general average of comfort and intelligence is higher here than in Europe, though in some respects the cultured classes of Europe may have attained to a more complete life than is yet common in America.

But while the American has abolished the outward accident of birth, as determining the station to which the individual is called, he has strongly emphasized the inner accident of birth, or natural capacity, which determines the station to which the individual can raise himself. Thus, in abolishing inequality of one kind we have simply promoted inequality of another and much more permanent kind. Ignoring this fact, a great many people still cling to the belief in equality as something that ought to be; and, in the teeth of all experience and the very structure of human nature, they still persist in coupling equality and freedom in popular social ideals. Ignoring also many other forms of inequality, popular interest is centered chiefly upon the growing inequality in the possession of wealth. The forces which were formerly directed against birth and privilege, are now directed against ability and success where they find expression in increase of wealth.

The millionaire is by no means in danger of being abolished by these attacks; because, in the first place, his forthcoming is in the line of economic progress; and, secondly, the very persons who preach, write and legislate against him, when it comes to practical everyday business, not only foster him but even go very much out of their way to do so. So little have many of them rationalized their action, that is, connected what they think and say with what they do, that, not content with giving men of wealth the same rights and privileges as other citizens, they grant them special favours, afterwards not unfrequently cursing liberally those who make successful use of them.

As I have said, the millionaire is the normal outcome, in business life, of that freedom to seek self-realization regardless of social status, which is one of the chief characteristics of America. It is, however, a popular fallacy that free competition permits of the fullest possible realization for each individual. As a matter of fact, all that free competition expresses is the opportunity to make trial of one's powers; but the success of some means the failure of others, comparative or absolute. In America all may enter in every race. This accounts for the fact that America is at once the most speculative of countries, and yet the one where mere luck counts for least and ability for most. Fortune may account for isolated successes, but in modern life success must be sustained, and fortune is capricious, while ability backed by experience is certain.

These conditions, again, account for the remarkable proportion of successful men in America who have risen from humble beginnings and made their way against those who started with the advantage of acquired wealth and position which, in other parts of the world, represent an immense handicap.

This peculiarly fluid economic condition gives great scope for the operation of natural selection. It greatly stimulates division of labour, or specialization of function, which again calls for more perfect organization of the specialized parts. In highly developed organization, both in mechanism and human agency, we have the most characteristic development of modern business, shared in most completely by the Anglo-Saxon world, and particularly America.

But increased organization permits the individual to operate with larger and larger forces over an ever-widening field. Here we have at once the opportunity and the necessity for the millionaire. The men who successfully manage such a system must have at their command millions of capital, and even small percentages, above or below the line which divides success from failures, mean immense gains or ruinous losses.

Here it may be observed that it is one thing to have command over millions of capital, and quite another to lavishly consume wealth in gratifying one's personal desires. A man becomes a millionaire by recapitalizing the greater part of his income. As far as personal expenditure goes, the capital which the millionaire accumulates and invests might more properly be said to belong to the men who are employed by it, than to the nominal owner, whose relation to it is practically only that of accumulator and manager. The contrast, therefore, so commonly drawn, between the millionaire as a man suffocated with wealth and luxury, and his employees as having nothing but their incomes, is utterly fallacious. When it comes to income for personal enjoyment the invested millions do not count. They are simply the common fund from which alike employer and employed obtain the means of living, and in many cases it will be found that the personal expenditure of employees is greater than that of the employer. A man might be a multi-millionaire in GTR [Grand Trunk Railway] ordinary stock and yet not enjoy an income from it equal to that of a common section man on the road.

That the capital fund stands in the name of the employer or stock-owner, merely indicates that he has the right to manage or dispose of it, a right which must be vested in some one. If anyone cares to say that capital would have been accumulated, invested and managed quite as well under the direction of the employed or their delegates, the only reply which can be made here is that that system has had equal opportunity for development with the present, and has been frequently tried by picked groups, but has not as yet proved itself equal, much less superior to the prevailing system. The real question is not how much wealth stands in this or that man's name, but how does he manage or dispose of it; for while his position is fortunately not due to popular suffrage, yet he is none the less responsible for his use of it.

Destructive as speculation is commonly supposed to be, there is in it little loss of wealth to the community. It is simply passed from one control to another, and, in the long run, it usually reaches the most capable hands. The millionaire who buys and sells stocks or produce is popularly looked upon as a kind of gambler. But those who succeed on the stock or produce exchange are, in proportion to their success, the least speculative of all. Everything that man attempts from philanthropy to war is speculative, in that the results are more or less uncertain. But while mere speculation may occasionally succeed, yet in the long run the operations based upon a close study of the facts and the most accurate information obtainable, will be successful. The millionaire in this region, instead of being the speculator, is the one who profits at the expense of the speculator, and this is no loss to the community as it tends to discourage the mere gambling spirit.

A really great and serious loss of wealth, both to the individual and to the community, occurs where the public usually looks for great benefit, namely in the process of competition.

Under free competition, where the lists are open to all, where great quantities of wealth are available for investment, there is required extensive organization, great outlay in preparation and considerable time for a test to be made. It is not possible to know what the result is to be until vast quantities of raw material and human energy are cast in moulds from which they cannot be withdrawn without losing the greater part of their value. Competition is the very antithesis of co-operation. Co-operation means the economizing of means towards a definite end. Competition means the striving of several independent units to serve the same end or secure the same object.

In days of simpler economic structure and isolated action, the unsuccessful competitors simply withdrew, with slight loss, and tried their fortunes elsewhere. But in these advanced times, with the steady growth of business corporations, and the organization of industry on the grand scale, the number of competitors has narrowed while the interests involved in each have enormously increased. Failure now means loss to hundreds, even thousands, and great waste of capital, which is none the less to be deplored because wealth is more easily reproduced than formerly.

Being brought face to face with the growing disadvantages of competition and the increasing advantages of organization, the narrowing list of competitors, containing men of insight and foresight, perceived the advantage of agreeing to merge competitive businesses in a still higher and more wide-reaching organization.

At first they sought the end without sacrificing the independent existence of the original competitors. But this being found unworkable, the movement passed through the various stages of agreements, pools, combines, trusts, and has now reached the stage of practically all-embracing companies, in which the identity of the individual business is finally lost in an absolute corporation with shares and bonds open to public subscription.

The last eighteen months have shown the remarkable spectacle of all the world rushing to become shareholders in these Midas-gifted trusts, so called, most of whose stocks have been thoughtfully expanded to meet a crying public want. Thus does the foolish public gratuitously prepare bait for the millionaires by representing the trusts as industrial monsters capable of gaining no end of proft. Then many of the same foolish public eagerly swallow this very bait, straining the nets of the millionaires in landing their catch. When afterwards they begin to realize where they are—but, of course, that time has not yet arrived. Still, we shall hear from them in the course of the next year or so, when their opinions of millionaires and trusts will be abundantly recorded in terms of wisdom and righteousness.

Apart from these incidentals, the whole growth of economic organization, the subsequent development of the millionaire, and the final effort to avoid the ruinous waste of independent competition, are simply stages in the economic triumph of man over nature. This victory secures the supply of an increasing number of wants with a decreasing proportion of human effort. In promoting this development the millionaire may not have been actuated to any great extent by philanthropic motives, but he was for the most part sufficiently enlightened to see that his interest in the development of his enterprises lay in the direction of the public interest. Thus has the rise of millionaires and the rise in the standard of living for the average citizen gone hand in hand. Wherever there is a country with few or no millionaires there is a country with heavy taxation in proportion to means, of ill-developed industries, low wages, exorbitant profits, extortionate rates of interest, and, quite generally, of little return for human effort.

But it may be asked: What, then, becomes of the selective process of competition, of the free trial by which men of capacity are discovered and brought to the front? In reply, it may be pointed out that the removal of competition between highly developed corporations does not imply the abolition of competition between individuals. The intensity of competition may indeed be lessened—a point to which I shall return immediately—but the competitive selective process, even before the movement to abolish competition between industries, had been in process of transfer from competition between businesses to competition within businesses. Competition for promotion within industrial corporations under business management differs from competition in all establishments based upon popular suffrage, in that the element of personal or extraneous influence has little place in the one, while it is a predominant element in the other.

Again, there is no reason to suppose that when men are confined within the limits of great organizations they will never be able to find that outlet which the millionaires themselves found before outward competition came to be suppressed. Millionaires, as a rule, have not obtained their millions in independent action, but in co-operation with others. In every great enterprise certain individuals are leaders. This is to the advantage not only of the leader but of his associates as well. Moreover, leadership in such extensive enterprises is possible only when the organization is so perfect as to give a large measure of freedom and responsibility to many subordinate chiefs of departments. Such men are able to find as full and free expression as parts of a great business as they would have been able to get as heads of smaller independent establishments.

As to the great body of the workers, their position is but slightly altered. Whether their employer is a millionaire or not does not affect their work or their position. They commonly find in the great corporations, better masters, more permanent positions, and more certain pay than in smaller businesses. Their various unions, long since fully organized, will look after their interests, and will be as likely to meet with just and fair consideration at the hands of great corporations as at the hands of great combinations of corporations, which have already been formed to offset the unions. A strike has just as much power to stop the earnings of one great corporation as of a dozen smaller ones, for even trusts live by earnings.

Again, the attack on millionaires because of their alleged greed and sordidness is entirely beside the mark. The modern millionaire is the very antithesis of the ancient or mediaeval miser, who isolated his hoard from the world and gloated over it in private. The modern millionaire, in every normal case, has really no special interest in money, commonly possessing but little of it, and being best pleased when he has least on hand. His interest is creative, and is akin to that of the scientific enthusiast, the statesman or the artist. Each must have means of expression, but their interest centres, not in the means, but in the ideal to be realized. But it may be said, the millionaire monopolizes so much means, and crowds so many others out of the field of self-realization, that many must forego that which is the highest object of human life. To this the answer must be both yes and no. Yes, as far as regards the number who can find in business alone a large and full field for the expression of their higher qualities. No, as regards the increasing opportunities for finding other outlets for the higher life. One of the special evils which has resulted from the free competition of American business in the past has been the complete absorption of so much talent in the rush and stress of business competition, much of it being wasted in the process. In the changes which are at present taking place in the economic life an increasing check is being put upon miscellaneous and wasteful competition, and, incidentally, upon the opportunity and attraction for men to make business the whole object of life.

As already pointed out, there will still be much scope for expression, even within the larger corporations. But while income is derived from invested capital, greater freedom from business care and anxiety will result, with corresponding opportunity and inducement to find one's creative and realizing expression in other lines.

It is inevitable that, for lack of sufficiently definite and recognized standards of the higher life, we shall have to pass through a stage of frivolous and abortive experiment on the part of many wandering souls vainly seeking adequate expression. Here there will be much room for sympathetic and constructive criticism.

In the face of the criticism which is commonly bestowed upon men of wealth, the attitude of the intelligent freeholders of towns and cities towards them, is of interest. Let it be rumoured that a millionaire or wealthy corporation might possibly invest a large amount of capital in any of our towns or cities. Do we find the citizens holding up their hands in dread, or the newspapers filled with protests and warnings at the thought of such a grasping, monopolizing power coming into their very midst? Oh no! there are rejoicings and mutual congratulations on all hands. Indeed, they will not merely welcome this terrible engine of oppression without any handicap, but, rather than lose it, in proportion to its size and power, they will offer freedom from taxation, free land, free power, if they have it, and increase their own burden of taxation to give a bonus in cash. Need it be said, in the face of such characteristic tendencies, that the millionaire is in no immediate danger of extinction?

Unlike the prophet, the millionaire is chiefly honoured in his own locality and among his own people. So far as he is in danger from active hostility, it is from legislative bodies which cater to abstract popular prejudice. Yet these bodies are so irrational in their methods, that with one hand they hold out bonuses, privileges and protection in business for those who are capable of taking advantage of them, being most naturally the millionaires, and with the other they threaten with destruction all who dare to successfully take advantage of them.

Another mighty objection to the millionaire is that in him we have the embodiment of that terrible bogey, the one man power. This really means the dominance of men of exceptional capacity, force and power. As a matter of fact the world never has got on, and never will get on without the one man power, that is, without leadership in every department of life. Wherever it has been necessary to get rid of a one man power that had become intolerable, another one man power has been called in to do the work. The characteristic change in this line, from ancient to modern times, has been from vague and general leadership to discrete and special leadership, with corresponding development of organization to keep the leaders in contact and harmony with each other. Mere abstract prejudice against one man power is vain and meaningless. It all depends on the one man; he may be a statesman or a demagogue, an independent business man or a shark. As to which we are to have will depend very much upon our character as a community.

The millionaire, at any rate, will abide with us. He may not be a saint above all men, but neither is he unique as a sinner. His rise has been natural and inevitable. He is simply the latest expression of a development which has been in process for more than a century past. The question which now faces us is not, shall men of great wealth and power be permitted to exist, but what kind of men should they be? In what spirit and with what sense of responsibility shall they exercise their rights and fulfil their obligations?

In the gradual solution of this question there is ample scope for the critical exercise of public opinion. But to claim respect the criticism must be enlightened and sympathetic.

THE REV. WILLIAM CAVEN

William Caven (1830-1904) was principal of Knox College, the Presbyterian theological college within the University of Toronto, from 1873 until his death. He strode onto the public stage in 1890 as one of the leaders of the English-Canadian agitation against ultramontanism. He served as the first president of the Equal Rights Association. The following article, which explains the association's program, represents the calm inner core of the hurricane that raged at the time over Jesuits, language, and schools.

The Equal Rights Movement

The designation Equal Rights almost explains itself. It suggests that all classes of people should be treated alike by the body politic. Race and creed should not be taken into account, but all should be dealt with according to the same measures: none should be favoured, and none placed under disabilities because they are French, German or English, or because they are Roman Catholics, Protestants, or Jews. No one can object to this statement or take the ground that Equal Rights should not be accorded to all. But the Equal Rights Association may be opposed on two grounds; either that Equal Rights are already established so that there is nothing to complain of—nothing to reform, or that Equal Rights so-called are not Equal Rights but something else. The Equal Rights movement is certainly shown to be unnecessary and mischievous if either the one or the other proposition can be sustained.

The Equal Rights Association originated in the opposition offered to the Jesuits' Estates Act, passed by the Legislature of Quebec in 1888.* In the correspondence with Rome, which is incorporated in the preamble of this famous Act, the Premier of Quebec asks permission of the Pope to sell certain Government properties, known as the Jesuit Estates, and the Pope grants permission to sell, under condition that the proceeds should be disposed of with his sanction. Large numbers of persons in Ontario, Quebec and other Provinces of the Dominion were shocked at legislation which not only recognized a moral claim on the part of the Jesuits to these estates, and endowed them with public funds, but placed, or seemed to place, the allegiance of a British Province at the feet of the Roman Curia—recognizing by implication, as it distinctly did, the superiority of the Canon Law to that of the Empire. The feeling of opposition to this Act of Quebec was greatly intensified by the unseemly haste with which the Dominion Government declared its allowance of it, and by the overwhelming vote by which the House of Commons refused to ask the Government to apply the veto.†

Had this been the only instance in which the strong hand of Ultramontanism had been felt in Provincial or Dominion affairs, little more might have been heard of it, beyond the indignant protest which was raised in many quarters. But the Jesuits' Estates Act had the effect of bringing home to men more than anything which had recently occurred, the ascendancy which a powerful and well-organized ecclesiastical body had attained in the politics of

Canada. It could hardly be disputed that the Church of Rome had it in her power to make or mar the fortunes of political parties, that she was ready on proper occasion to exercise this power, and that in consequence she was regarded by the parties with a subserviency which degraded not only them but the politics of the country, and even in some degree threatened its liberties. It was sufficient proof of this to remember that no election passed in the Protestant Provinces without the keenest competition for *the Catholic vote*—an expression which of itself bears witness to a disturbing element in the community; while in the Catholic Province of Quebec the parties were in equally keen competition for the especial favour of the Church. With the professional politicians it had become an instinct to court the Church of Rome.

The Equal Rights movement sees no adequate remedy for the evil referred to except in so defining the provinces of Church and State that the one shall be clearly discriminated from the other, that neither shall be under special temptation to seek favour from the other, and that the Church shall have to depend entirely upon its own resources in doing its own work. 'We deem it essential to the peace and highest welfare of our country and to the maintenance of good government that the line between the civil and ecclesiastical authorities should be clearly defined and should be respected in all legislation and administration, both of the Dominion and the several Provinces thereof. While the Church is entitled to entire freedom and to protection in its own domain, which embraces all that is purely spiritual, the State must have full control in all temporal matters; and it cannot, without abrogating its just authority, ask or accept permission from any ecclesiastical person or organization, or from any extraneous body whatever, to exercise its own functions and perform its own duties.' These words, which are the fourth article in the platform of the Equal Rights Association, express the central principle of the Association and of the movement which it represents. Churches must not under any pretext receive public moneys to aid them in their proper work; nor must they, under colour of doing work which is beneficial to the State, draw upon the public treasury. Their adherents must provide the means for carrying on all their operations. If the work for which in any case they claim assistance from the State is properly the business of the State, let the State attend to it, and if it is their own work let them do it on their own charges. To say that this work is beneficial to the State is no good argument for public aid, because all true work done by any class of people, in any connexion, is profitable to the whole community. The view here set forth is in no way allied to irreligion, and implies no failure to recognize the inestimable benefits which the Christian religion has conferred upon civil society.

The great majority of those who zealously hold it believe that the State—the community—is under unspeakable obligations to the Christian faith, and that the Christian Church in the humble discharge of her high duties is indeed a great public benefactor. But they also hold that any arrangement which, on the one hand, tempts the Church to lean upon secular favour, or, on the other hand, encourages the politician to regard the Church as an instrument which he may use for his own ends, should be declined in the interests of both Church and State. The question as to the teaching of the New Testament regarding the constitution and maintenance of the Church lies entirely beyond the scope of the present statement; though, were it here proper, we might easily show that the duty of supporting the Church and diffusing the Christian faith is definitely laid in Scripture upon those who profess that faith.

Our principle therefore cuts off all endowments, subsidies, or grants of any kind made to any particular religious denomination, or to a variety of denominations concurrently; and in this way it would avoid serious evils of which Canada has too much experience, the undue influence of churches in politics and the subserviency of political parties to ecclesiastical power.

It will hence be seen how completely they who regard the Equal Rights movement as an anti-French and anti-Catholic crusade have failed to comprehend its meaning. Regrettable things will be said in connection with any movement which enlists considerable numbers in its support; for all men are not wise; but to cite sporadic utterances of a harsh or senseless character about Frenchmen or Roman Catholics, as if this were the sufficient condemnation of the Equal Rights Association, is to trifle with a great question. Let all uncharitable language be severely condemned, and all rabid persons of every class muzzled if possible, but let the very important questions which the Equal Rights Association has brought forward be considered without prejudice, upon their merits. They *must* indeed be considered; for whatever be the merits or demerits of the Equal Rights movement, it has made it impossible to keep these questions away from public view.

The present writer confesses his anxiety that a proper intellectual and moral perspective should be observed in discussing matters which are cognate to the central principle of Equal Rights, and especially that the subject of the French language should be handled with delicacy, and only in so far as it directly affects that principle. The general question of promoting homogeneity in the Dominion, though quite important, is not specially before the Equal Rights Association.

It must not be imagined that the Equal Rights Association seeks to terminate at once, and in some violent way, what is peculiar in the institutions and customs of Quebec. With Quebec as a Province the Equal Rights Association of Ontario has indeed little directly to do. The Association will gladly see its influence tell upon that Province, but it will not forget the rights which are properly guaranteed to Provinces under the Constitution, and will not attempt anything so foolish as to seek, perforce, the complete assimilation of social and political conditions throughout the Provinces of the Dominion. But the system of Quebec must not claim to be national in the broader sense, so that its special features should be reproduced in the new territories and provinces. No vindication of such claim can rest upon anything which does not involve contravention of the fundamental principle of separation between Church and State. It is almost unnecessary to say that when Mr Mercier in his recent pamphlet* taunts the Equal Rights people with the inconsistency of Protestantism in maintaining tithes in England while pronouncing against them in Quebec he makes no point against them; for the Equal Rights Association does not profess to represent Protestantism throughout the world, or indeed anywhere, and its members— almost without exception I should suppose—would condemn a tithe system or fabrique system enforced by law wherever it may exist.

A word respecting the application of Equal Rights principles to Separate

Schools. These schools are established in order that the Roman Catholic children may escape a danger to which it is alleged they are exposed in the Common School, and may be thoroughly indoctrinated in the tenets and observances of their faith. In our school law provision is made for the establishment in certain circumstances of Protestant Separate Schools also, but so little has advantage been taken of this provision that practically it is of no account. For the purposes of this argument Separate Schools may be identified with Roman Catholic Separate Schools. The objection, then, to such Schools from the Equal Rights point of view, is that they use public funds in the special service of a Church, and for teaching definitely and in detail, the peculiarities of a Church. The principle of the Equal Rights Association would not be more certainly violated by giving public money for the endowment of a church, or for its annual expenditure. This is so clear that it only needs to be stated, and to state it is, to Equal Rights men, to condemn it.

The question of abolishing the system of Separate Schools is, in the opinion of the Equal Rights Association, one which is properly open to discussion. In the British North America Act, which guarantees these Schools, the Association cannot recognize any such character of inviolability that no attempt may be made, by constitutional methods, for its improvement; nor can they admit that its provisions as to Separate Schools are more sacred than the rest of the instrument. No people can permanently renounce the right to revise or improve their constitutions without at the same time renouncing their liberty; nor can any valid reason be given why the subject of education should, in the Confederation Act, be committed to the Provinces under restrictions which do not apply to any other subject, and more especially why Ontario and Quebec should be placed under bonds from which the other Provinces are free. The Equal Rights Association believe that the existence of Separate Schools in Ontario is a violation on a large scale of a principle which should be consistently applied and acted on; that it will be impossible, even were it desirable, to prevent the question of abolition of these Separate Schools from coming up for discussion; and they do not doubt that, whatever the issue may be, nothing will be done to imperil the rights of the minority in Quebec any more than those of the minority in Ontario, in Manitoba, or in any other Province. To argue, as many do, that because in the Province of Quebec, where a strictly denominational or ecclesiastical school system exists, the minority are allowed dissentient schools, therefore in Ontario, where we have an undenominational Public School system, provision should also be made for Separate Schools, is to overlook an essential point of difference in the two systems. But obvious as this is, the Equal Rights Association in Ontario will doubtless seek to act in concert with their friends in Quebec and elsewhere, and will do nothing rashly while endeavouring to bring forward a question which all who have given attention to the educational movement on this continent must regard as uncommonly important. It is quite unnecessary to say that the Equal Rights Association is perfectly aware that the Imperial Parliament alone can modify or give permission to modify the British North America Act.

HENRI BOURASSA

Henri Bourassa (1868-1952) was the great spokesman of Canadian national-ism at the turn of the century, though it is only in retrospect that English Canadians have seen him in this light. A grandson of Papineau, Bourassa was first elected to the House of Commons in 1896, and every door seemed open to the talented and charming young man. But when in 1899 Laurier, under pressure from Ontario and Maritime imperialists, decided to send a contingent of Canadian troops to fight against the Boers in South Africa, Bourassa broke with his leader. In the first selection below, 'The French-Canadian in the British Empire' (1902), Bourassa explains his position to the British Empire, through the medium of a monthly review published in London. The second selection is the program of the Canadian Nationalist League which was founded in 1903 by Olivar Asselin (1874-1937), Omer Héroux (1876-1963), and Armand Lavergne (1880-1935), slightly younger admirers and lieutenants of Bourassa. The third selection was written in 1912 in response to English-Canadian criticism. It shows Bourassa, by this time founder and editor of Le Devoir, *in exasperation, warning that English Canadians do not see under what form the real danger of Americanization lies and how it can be effectively avoided.*

The French-Canadian in
the British Empire

The present feeling of the French-Canadian is one of contentment. He is satisfied with his lot. He is anxious to preserve his liberty and his peace. . . . Upon any proposed modification of the constitutional system of Canada he is disposed to look with distrust, or at least with anxiety. He cannot forget that all changes in the past were directed against him, except those that were enacted under such peculiar circumstances as made it imperative for the British Government to conciliate him. He asks for no change—for a long time to come, at least. And should any change be contemplated, he is prepared to view it, to appreciate its prospective advantages and inconveniences, neither from a British point of view nor from his own racial standpoint, but to approach the problem as it may affect the exclusive interests of Canada. He has loyally accepted the present constitution; he has done his ample share of duty by the country; and he feels that he is entitled to be consulted before any change is effected.

How thoroughly and exclusively Canadian the French-Canadian is should never be forgotten by those who contemplate any change in the constitutional or national status of Canada. This is so patent a fact, so logical a consequence of historical developments, that nothing short of absolute ignorance or wilful blindness can justify the language of those who talk of drawing him either by persuasion or by force to a closer allegiance to the Empire. As a matter of fact, he constitutes the only exclusively Canadian racial group in the Dominion. A constant immigration from the British Isles has kept the English-speaking

Canadians in close contact with their motherlands; so that even now they still speak of the 'Old Country' as their 'home', thus keeping in their hearts a double allegiance. On the soil of Canada, his only home and country, all the national aspirations of the French-Canadian are concentrated. 'Canadian' is the only national designation he ever claims; and when he calls himself 'French-Canadian', he simply wants to differentiate his racial origin from that of his English, Scotch, or Irish fellow citizens, who, in his mind, are but partially *Canadianised.*

When he is told that Canada is a British country, and that he must abide by the will of the British majority, he replies that Canada has remained British through his own loyalty; that when his race constituted the overwhelming majority of the Canadian people, Canada was twice saved to the British Crown, thanks to him and to him only; that he has remained faithful to Great Britain because he was assured of certain rights and privileges; that his English-speaking fellow citizens have accepted the compact and should not now take advantage of their greater numerical strength to break the agreement; that when settling in Canada, new-comers from the British kingdom should understand that they become citizens of Canada, of a Confederacy where he has vested rights, and should not undertake to make the country and its people more British than Canadian.

Of all political evolutions which Canada might undergo—Independence, Annexation to the United States, British Imperialism, Annexation to France—the two latter are undoubtedly those that the French-Canadian would oppose most strenuously.

Independence is to his mind the most natural outcome of the ultimate destinies of Canada. But so long as the present ties are not strengthened he is in no hurry to sever British connection. He realises that time cannot but work in favour of Canada by bringing to her population and wealth, and that the later she starts on her own course the safer the journey.

As to his relations with the land of his origin, I have already explained how the French-Canadian has come to be separated from his European kinsman, not only by political secession, but by racial differences. . . .*

The love of the French-Canadian for his European kinsman is purely moral and intellectual. It is even more inclined towards the national soul of France and the productions of her national genius, than towards Frenchmen individually. This is strongly exemplified by the slight sentiment of distrust manifested by the French-Canadian to the new-comer from France, from the South of France especially. They soon get along very well. But the first movement is not one of warm sympathy, as might be expected from two brothers meeting after a long separation.

Of course the absolute innocuousness of the French-Canadian's love for France depends a great deal on the common sense of the English-speaking majority. If the Anglo-Canadian has enough judgment and sense of justice, as he undoubtedly has, to allow his French-Canadian neighbour freely to speak his mother-tongue, both in public and in private life, and teach his children that same language; if he allows him to keep his traditions and develop his national aspirations, and even to give free expression to his platonic love of France—if the Anglo-Canadian does not require the French-Canadian to entertain such sentiments for England as are only born of blood and flesh, and to accept new ties which neither moral nor legal obligations impose upon him—there is not the slightest apprehension to be felt from this very peculiar double allegiance of the French-Canadian—intellectual and moral allegiance to France, political allegiance to Great Britain—because both are altogether subordinate to his exclusive national attachment to Canada.

Now, apart from his instinctive reluctance to contemplate any political evolution, what are the feelings of the French-Canadian with regard to Imperial Federation or any form of British Imperialism?

First, as may be naturally expected, sentimental arguments in favour of British Imperialism cannot have any hold upon him. To his reason only must appeals on this ground be made. That the new Imperial policy will bring him, and Canada at large, advantages that will not be paid by any infringement on his long-struggled-for liberty, he must be clearly shown.

Towards Great Britain he knows that he has a duty of allegiance to perform. But he understands that duty to be what it has been so far, and nothing more. He has easily and generously forgotten the persecutions of the earlier and larger part of his national life under the British Crown. He is willing to acknowledge the good treatment which he has received later on, though he cannot forget that his own tenacity and the neighbourhood of the United States have had much to do with the improvement of his situation.

In short, his affection for Great Britain is one of reason, mixed with a certain amount of esteem and suspicion, the proportions of which vary according to time and circumstances, and also with his education, his temperament, and his social surroundings.

Towards the Empire he has no feelings whatever; and naturally so. The blood connection and the pride in Imperial power and glory having no claims upon him, what sentiment can he be expected to entertain for New Zealand or Australia, South Africa or India, for countries and populations entirely foreign to him, with which he has no relations, intellectual or political, and much less commercial intercourse than he has with the United States, France, Germany, or Belgium?

By the motherland he feels that he has done his full duty; by the Empire he does not feel that he has any duty to perform. He makes full allowance for the blood feelings of his English-speaking partner; but having himself, in the past, sacrificed much of his racial tendencies for the sake of Canadian unity, he thinks that the Anglo-Canadian should be prepared to study the problems of Imperialism from a purely Canadian standpoint. Moreover, this absence of racial feelings from his heart allows him to judge more impartially the question of the relations between Canada and the Empire.

He fully realises the benefits that Canada derives from her connection with a wealthy and mighty nation. He is satisfied with having the use of the British market. But this advantage he knows that Canada enjoys on the very same terms as any other country in the world, even the most inimical to Britain. From a mixed sense of justice and egotism he is less clamorous than the British Canadian in demanding any favour, commercial or other, from the motherland, because he has a notion that any favour received would have to be compensated by at least an equal favour given.

His ambition does not sway him to huge financial operations. Rather given to liberal professions, to agricultural life, or to local mercantile and industrial pursuits, he is more easily satisfied than the English-speaking Canadian with a moderate return for his work and efforts. He has been kept out of the frantic display of financial energy, of the feverish concentration of capital, of the international competition of industry, which have drawn his English-speaking fellow citizen to huge combinations of wealth or trade; and, therefore, he is not anxious to participate in the organisation of the Empire on the basis of a gigantic co-operative association for trade. He would rather see Canada keep the full control of her commercial policy and enter into the best possible trade arrangements with any nation, British or foreign.

He is told that Canada has the free use of British diplomacy, and that such an advantage calls for sacrifices on her part when Britain is in distress. But considered in the light of past events, British diplomacy has, on the contrary, cost a good deal to Canada. So far the foreign relations of Canada, through British mediation, have been almost exclusively confined to America. That the influence and prestige of Great Britain were of great benefit to Canada in her relations with the United States is hardly conspicuous in the various Anglo-American treaties and conventions in which Canadian interests are concerned.

Not only did the American Republic secure the settlement of nearly all her claims according to her pretensions, but Canadian rights have been sacrificed by British plenipotentiaries in compensation for misdeeds or blunders of the British Government. . . .

So much for the past. When he considers the present and the future, the French-Canadian does not see any reason why he should enter into a scheme of Imperial defence.

The argument that if Canada stands by the Empire, the Empire will stand by Canada, cannot have much weight with him; and his objections on that ground are founded both on past events and on prospective developments. In the South African War he has witnessed an application of the new doctrine. Of the expenditure of that war he has been called upon to pay his share—a small one if compared with that of the British Kingdom, but a large one when it is remembered that he had no interest whatever in the contest, and no control over the policy which preceded the conflict, or over its settlement. Should the principle of military Imperialism predominate, he foresees that he may find himself involved in wars occasioned by friction between Australia and Japan, between New Zealand and Germany, between Great Britain and France in Europe, or between Great Britain and Russia in Asia. He does not see any eventuality in which the Empire may be called upon to help Canada.

He is ready now, as he was in the past, to support a sufficient military force to maintain internal peace and to resist aggression on the territory of Canada. But these eventualities are most unlikely to occur in the near future. The enormous area as well as the vast resources of the country offer such opportunities to the care and activity of its population, that social struggles are almost impossible in Canada for many years to come. Foreign invasion, from the United States excepted, is most improbable. The Canadian territory is easy to defend against attacks on her sea borders, which would offer great difficulties and little benefit to any enemy of the Empire. Moreover, from a purely Canadian standpoint such occurrences are most unlikely to happen. Left to herself Canada has no possible cause of conflict with any other nation but the United States. On the other hand, by entering into a compact for Imperial defence, she may be involved in war with several of the strongest Powers. Therefore, as far as concerns any country outside America, the French-Canadian feels that the scheme of Imperial defence brings upon him new causes of conflict not to be compensated by any probable defensive requirements.

It is worth while mentioning here one possible conflict in which, if Imperialism carries the day, the racial problem of Canada might cause serious trouble. Although happily checked by a large interchange of material interests, the possibility of a war between France and Great Britain is not altogether removed. Were such a conflict confined to these two Powers, the French-Canadian could be counted upon to stand loyally neutral. Should even the French navy, by the most improbable of war fortunes, attack the coast of Canada, the French-Canadian could be relied upon for the defence of his country. But should the principle of Imperial solidarity obtain, were Canada called upon to contribute to an Anglo-French war in which she had no direct interest, the French-Canadian would no doubt resent most bitterly any such contribution in men or money as could be voted by the Federal Parliament. This would no longer be the defence of his home—which he is prepared to undertake even against France—it would mean his contributing to the slaughter of his own kith and kin in a quarrel which was foreign to him. It would hurt the French-Canadian in that most peculiar and sentimental love for the French national soul which I have already mentioned.

There remains to be dealt with the eventuality of a war with the United States. Rightly or wrongly, the French-Canadian is inclined to think that, in order to avert such a calamity, Great Britain would even go to the length of abandoning all British rights in America. And should British sentiment and British policy undergo such a change as would warrant Canada in counting upon the armed help of the Empire against the United States, the French-Canadian entertains some doubt as to the possibility of keeping up the struggle and carrying it to a successful issue.

Should the most sanguine expectations be realised; should the American Navy be annihilated even as a defence force; and were the British Navy to succeed in blockading and bombarding the American ports—the only effective blow which might be struck at the enemy—nothing could prevent the American army from occupying the central portion of Canada, and probably invading most of her territory. Canada would therefore, at all events, be the sufferer in the fight. Moreover, her ways of transportation from the Western grain-growing country would be interrupted; and whilst the Americans would get from their untouched territory unbounded resources of food supply, the British people would be at once deprived of American and Canadian breadstuffs. This alone, in spite of any military success in other ways, would force Great Britain to accept the terms of the American Republic.

Another point to be considered with reference to an Anglo-American War is the fact that there are now as many French-Canadians living under the star-spangled banner as under the Union Jack.* Many of those migrated Canadians have become as loyal and devoted citizens of the American Republic as their brothers have remained loyal and devoted citizens of Canada. Although prepared to do his full duty in the defence of his land, the prospect of his becoming the murderer of his own brother is sufficient to prevent the French-Canadian from exposing Canada and the Empire to any war with the United States.

From all those considerations the French-Canadian concludes that Canada has never been, and never will be, the cause of any display of Imperial strength, with the single exception of a possible encounter with a nation that he is not desirous of attacking, and against which, in his mind, the Empire would be either unwilling or incapable of defending him. He does not therefore feel bound to assume military obligations towards any other part of the Empire.

The stronger Canada grows in population and wealth, the slighter will be the dangers that may threaten her security, and the greater her contribution to the welfare and glory of the Empire. The French-Canadian thinks therefore that the best way in which he can play his part in the building up of the Empire is not by diverting the healthiest and strongest portion of its population from the pursuits of a peaceful and industrious life and sending them to fight in all parts of the world. He does not believe in fostering in Canada the spirit of militarism. He is only anxious to make his country attractive and prosperous by keeping aloof from all military adventures.

Indifferent as he is to commerical Imperialism, hostile as he is to military Imperialism, the French-Canadian cannot be expected to wish for any organic change in the constitution of Canada and to look favourably upon any scheme of Imperial Federation.

For years he fought to obtain full control of his laws, of his social system, of his public exchequer. With the principles of self-government, of self-taxation, of direct control over the legislative body, no other citizen of the British Empire is more thoroughly imbued than he is. His local organisation, in Church, educational or municipal matters, is still more decentralised and democratic than that of the English provinces of Canada. He likes to exercise his elective franchise and to keep as close as possible to the man, the law and the regulation that he votes for. He cannot view with a favour a scheme by which any power that has heretofore been exercised by his own representative bodies may pass under the control of some Council sitting in London.

There remains to be considered the question of annexation to the United States.

As I have stated, left to himself, the French-Canadian is not eager for a change. He requires nothing but quietness and stability in order to grow and develop. He is satisfied with and proud of his Canadian citizenship. But should a change be forced upon him by those who aspire to a greater nationality, he would rather incline towards Pan-Americanism.

For a long time annexation to the United States was most abhorrent to the French-Canadian. In fact, when an agitation in that direction was started by several leading English-speaking Canadians, his resistance proved to be the best safeguard of the British connection. But should his past fidelity be now disregarded, and Canadian autonomy encroached upon in any way, should he be hurried into any Imperial scheme and forced to assume fresh obligations, he would prefer throwing in his lot with his powerful neighbour to the South. His present constitution he prizes far above the American system of Government; but if called upon to sacrifice anything of his Federal autonomy for the working of the Imperial machinery, he would rather do it in favour of the United States system, under which, at all events, he would preserve the self-government of his province. Should Imperial re-organisation be based on trade and financial grounds, he would see a greater future in joining the most powerful industrial nation of the world than in going into partnership with the British communities; and this sentiment is gaining greater force from the present influx of American capital into Canada. The fact that the union of Canada and the United States would bring again under the same flag the two groups, now separated, of his nationality has no doubt greatly contributed towards smoothing his aversion to annexation.

I have so far analysed the sentiments of the higher classes among the French-Canadian people, of those who control their feelings by historical knowledge or by a study of outside circumstances, political, military or financial. If I refer to the masses, mostly composed of farmers, I may say that they entertain similar feelings, but instinctively rather than from reflection. The French-Canadians of the popular class look upon Canada as their own country. They are ready to do their duty by Canada; but considering they owe nothing to Great Britain or any other country, they ask nothing from them. Imbued with a strong sense of liberty, they have no objection to their English-speaking fellow countrymen going to war anywhere they please; but they cannot conceive that Canada as a whole may be forced out of its present situation. They let people talk of any wise or wild proposal of Imperialism; but if any change were attempted to be imposed on them, they would resist the pressure, quietly but constantly.

To sum up, the French-Canadian is decidedly and exclusively Canadian by nationality and American by his ethnical temperament. People with world-wide aspirations may charge him with provincialism. But after all, this sentiment of exclusive attachment to one's land and one's nationality is to be found as one of the essential characteristics of all strong and growing peoples. On the other hand, the lust of abnormal expansion and Imperial pride have ever been the marked features of all nations on the verge of decadence.

The Program of the Nationalist League

WHEREAS

It is reasonable to believe that Providence in giving Canada to England wished it to become familiar, by this conquest, and then by the usage of parliamentary institutions, with the enjoyment of liberty;

The Canadian people, in the usage of these institutions, have shown up to now, a greater and greater aptitude for self government; the self governing colonies of Great Britain pay her sufficient tribute in giving her, for military purposes, access to their ports and the use of their communication system; and that the mother country, despite this tribute and despite our voluntary preservation of the colonial tie in 1775 and 1812, has imposed, on several occasions, onerous and humiliating sacrifices, notably in its agreements with the United States;

Without denouncing a political state which nevertheless has compelled us to undergo two American invasions, we note the necessity of opposing any tightening of the colonial tie because, above all, of the incompatibility of interests between an old European monarchy and those of a young democratic American country;

In fiscal matters, it would be dangerous for Canada to grant England a permanent title to particular favors, as well as to undertake permanent engagements with her;

The interest and security of Canada demand that it not participate in the military organization of Great Britain;

WHEREAS ALSO

For the maintenance and prosperity of Confederation, the federal power must respect the rights which the authors of the Constitution of 1867 wished to guarantee provinces and minorities, and consequently must only operate where the provinces have common interests;

Respect for the autonomy of the provinces leads necessarily to the modifying of financial relations between the two powers;

WHEREAS FINALLY

The federal and provincial governments, while inviting the co-operation of foreign capital in the development of our natural resources, must, by sound internal policies, assure Canadians the possession of their heritage and the development among them of the national spirit,

THE UNDERSIGNED

constitute themselves into an association under the name of Canadian Nationalist League and undertake to work for the realization of the program* enunciated below:

I. For Canada, in its relations with England, the largest measure of political, commercial and military autonomy compatible with the maintenance of the colonial tie.

II. For Canadian provinces, in their relation with the federal power, the largest measure of autonomy compatible with the maintenance of the federal tie.

III. For all of Confederation, the adoption of a policy of exclusively Canadian economic and intellectual development.

I
RELATIONS OF CANADA WITH GREAT BRITAIN

1. POLITICAL AUTONOMY:

(a) Absolute maintenance of the political liberties which belong by right to all self-governing colonies of Great Britain and which the Constitution of 1867, in the opinion of its authors, guaranteed Canada.

(b) Opposition to all participation of Canada in the deliberations of the British Parliament and all permanent or periodical Imperial councils.

(c) Consultation with Parliament on the timeliness of participating in extra-ordinary conferences of countries of British allegiance and total publicity of the deliberations and decisions of these conferences.

(d) Absolute liberty to regulate our immigration from the standpoint only of our interests.

(e) The tabling at each Parliamentary session of all correspondence or official documents exchanged since the last session between the Canadian government and the Colonial Office or the governments of other British colonies.

(f) In the case of constitutional conflict between the federal government and provincial governments, the direct invoking of the judgement of the Privy Council. In all other cases, the restriction of appeals to provincial tribunals for provincial laws and to federal tribunals for federal laws.

(g) The right of representation at all international congresses where Canadian interests would be involved and consultation with Parliament on the timeliness of taking advantage of this right.

2. COMMERCIAL AUTONOMY:

(a) Absolute right to make and break [*de faire et de défaire*] our commercial treaties with all countries, including Great Britain and her colonies.

(b) Freedom to choose agents who will negotiate Canadian commercial interests directly with foreign chancellories.

3. MILITARY AUTONOMY:

(a) Abstention from any participation by Canada in Imperial wars outside of Canadian territory.

(b) Resistance to all recruiting efforts by England in Canada.

(c) Opposition to the establishment of a navy school in Canada with the help and for the benefit of the Imperial authority.

(d) Direction of our militia and our military schools in times of peace as in times of war, from the standpoint only of the defence of Canadian territory. Absolute refusal of all leaves demanded by an officer for the purpose of taking part in an Imperial war.

(e) The command of the Canadian militia by a Canadian officer chosen by the Canadian government.

II
RELATIONS OF THE PROVINCES
WITH THE FEDERAL POWER

1. Absolute maintenance of the rights guaranteed to the provinces by the Constitution of 1867 according to the intention of its authors. Respect for the principle of the duality of languages and the right of minorities to separate schools.

2. Modification of the base of federal grants to provinces by the following means:

(a) Abolition of the special grant destined for the maintenance of the legislatures and the proportional increase of the *per capita* grant.

(b) Determination of the *per capita* grant for each province according to the population recorded at the last census.

3. Administration of criminal justice by the federal government and at its cost.

4. Nomination of judges to civil tribunals by provincial governments.

III
DOMESTIC POLICIES

1. Determination of our customs policy from the standpoint only of Canadian interests.

2. Abolition of the system of state grants to private enterprises (railways, marine transport, etc.). Participation by the state in these enterprises (if it is essential to the public good) in the capacity of shareholder only and under the same conditions as other stockholders or in the capacity of a privileged creditor.

3. More efficient exercise, by the government, of its right to set the transportation rates and to determine the proposed lines and terminals of the railroads.

4. Adoption by the provinces of a more active policy of colonization and one more in harmony with their needs. Exclusive jurisdiction by ministers of colonization of the sale of land for agricultural purposes.

5. A more equitable sharing, between the different parties of [*parties de*] Confederation, of the money voted by the federal Parliament for the purposes of immigration and colonization.

6. The substitution for the actual system of permanent alienation of our hydraulic forces or water power, a system of renting by auction, by long-term leases.

7. Immediate reform of our system of forestry exploitation with a view of assuring the conservation of our forests as a source of public wealth. Annual publication of a statement indicating:

(a) The concessions of land and cutting rights made during the year with their conditions.

(b) The total extent of forests being cut and those of virgin forests with specifications as exact as possible about the species of wood, sites, etc.

8. Development in school of a patriotic teaching suitable to giving the pupil a more correct notion of the beauty of our history and the resources of our country.

9. A more efficient regulation of the operations of insurance companies, mutual benefit associations, industrial and financial societies in general, and the operations of the stock-market.

10. Adoption of suitable laws for the development in Canada of a literary and artistic output. Adhesion of this country to international agreements on literary property and the rights of authorship.

11. A more strict application of existing labor legislation and the adoption of new laws suitable for guaranteeing the security of work and the liberty of association.

The Spectre of Annexation

If preservation of Canada from absorption by the United States be sincerely desired, elementary precautions should be taken: the danger should not be exaggerated; its real and permanent causes should be investigated, instead of imaginary ones being invented; and efficient means of averting the peril should be thoughtfully sought.

In their fight against reciprocity [last year], the Jingoes did the very opposite; and they are now preparing to repeat their mistake [in order] to rush Canada into naval contributions. . . .

Precisely because we [Nationalists] remain utterly indifferent to party success, and irrevocably attached to the defense of our ideals, we see in the possibility of the absorption of Canada by the United States a real danger, the most permanent of all perils that threaten the permanency of the Canadian Confederation. Hence we look upon any false or exaggerated appeal to yankeephobism as an increase in the danger.

By way of throwing light on that very point, for the benefit of all, Imperalists or others, who wish as sincerely as we do to preserve the British connection and the unity of Canada, although they may favour methods and policies less efficacious, in our eyes at least, than our own, it seems to me most opportune to analyse with the utmost frankness the marked evolution that has taken place in the mind of the French Canadian, on the question of Annexation.

In this short study, I do not intend to express mere Nationalist thoughts or feelings, but to define as impartially as possible the various opinions that are beginning to shape themselves in many French-Canadian minds, their growing instincts and tendencies, and the results that may accrue therefrom.

French-Canadians have been the staunchest and most constant opponents of annexation to the United States. This is now a truism in history. At a time when they held in their hands the fate of the Colony, they refused to join hands with the rebels in the English colonies; they resisted the appeals of Lafayette and of France herself; they shed their blood for the defense of the British flag and institutions. Later on, they persistently opposed all annexationist movements and every fiscal or administrative policy capable of strengthening the centripetal force of the great American Republic. But they are beginning to doubt the utility of their efforts. Especially they ask themselves what they have gained by their constant loyalty to the British Crown and their unswerving devotion to the unity of Canada. . . .

Where does [the French Canadian] find himself one hundred and forty years after his defense of Quebec against Arnold and Montgomery, one hundred years after the Battle of Châteauguay, seventy years after the unjust provisions of the Union Act of 1841? Above all, where is he forty-five years after the birth of the Federal régime, offered to him as a remedy to all his grievances and the solution of the racial problem—that régime which, after twenty-five years of existence, was defined by its principle framer, Sir John A. Macdonald, as having established 'absolute equality of rights' between both races, in matters 'of language and religion, of property and of persons'?

It has all ended in his being told that, in law and in fact, his rights are confined to the Province of Quebec, as those of the Indians to their reserves. His language, one of the two official idioms of the country, is excluded from teaching in nearly all the public schools for the support of which he pays his taxes. He is now threatened with a still closer restriction of the very meagre place given to the French language in his own separate and bi-lingual schools in Ontario.* The extraordinary efforts to which he is forced, in order to secure a partial usage of that same language in all the public utilities organised by the various legislatures of his country, and subsidised from the public chest in which his share of contribution falls constantly, are qualified and denounced as rebellious and demogogic.

One must hold strange delusions on the gullibility of the French Canadians, to dare put into print, in the year of grace 1912, what the *Star* published, a few days ago: 'Assimilated by the American Union . . . we will lose . . . our power to shelter the French language and the Roman Catholic religion'.†

That nonsensical argument has been made frequently, in varying terms and on many occasions. It was resorted to in the fight against reciprocity. French Canadians do not bite at that bait; and it is high time this should be known. What is going on in English-speaking Canada they follow attentively. They know equally well the conditions under which their migrated compatriots live in the United States. . . .

What about public education, religious teaching at school, or separate schools? In what respect, on these grounds, does the situation of French Canadians and Roman Catholics, in the United States, differ from that of French Canadians and Roman Catholics in those English provinces of Canada where separate schools do not exist or have been abolished? In this only, that in the United States, French Canadians and Roman Catholics never had any special rights, whilst, in a large portion of Canada, they have been robbed of what they possessed. Yet those rights had been guaranteed in law and by the most solemn pledges of Canadian statesmen, and, what should have been still more binding, by the debt of gratitude toward them incurred by the British Crown and English-speaking Canada.

In Ontario, the only province where, because only of insuperable legal obstacles, the constitutional basis of Catholic education has not yet been destroyed, the French-Canadian minority, and all other Roman Catholics, had to endure violent and repeated attacks against their denominational schools. Now they are threatened, as regards the teaching of their maternal language, by an odious régime, the like of which could be found only in Prussian Poland.

That brings us to the language question. To speak today of the 'shelter' given in Canada to the French idiom, and certain to be lost by annexation to the United States, is but the raillery of ignorance or bad taste. The legal use of the French language once existed in Manitoba and in the North West Territories. It has been suppressed with the complicity of the Parliament of Canada. In none of the English provinces does the French language hold today the slightest legal privilege, or find any broader or more hospitable 'shelter' than in the American Republic. In several of these provinces, and notably in the most important, Ontario, use of that language,—most perfect of modern times, vernacular of diplomacy and science, knowledge of which is necessary to any cultured man,—is opposed by an odious and grotesque coalition of prejudice, hatred, hostility and ignorance, the like of which could not be found in the wildest States of the American Republic, where brigandage and Lynch Laws are supreme. The silly trash printed in some of the Ontario daily papers would put to shame the weekly editors of New Mexico and Oklahoma.

'But', it may be replied, 'for all that, the French language remains official in the Federal Parliament. That privilege would never be preserved under the American constitution'. Does anyone really believe that such a privilege will long be prized by the French Canadians, if reduced to a literal translation of ill-worded laws, official reports, and parliamentary rantings?

Thanks to the incredible ignorance of English-speaking statesmen, magistrates, barristers, civil servants,—with the exception of some of those who live in the Province of Quebec,—the use of the French language has almost totally disappeared from parliamentary debates, as from proceedings and pleas before the Supreme Court, the Exchequer Court, and the Railway Commission.

But what is still more characteristic, is the hostility or indifference shown by most English-speaking Canadians of all classes, toward the maternal language of one-fourth of their fellow-citizens, who constitute the most ancient group of the population of Canada,—that group which has undergone the heaviest sacrifices for the maintenance of Canadian unity and the preservation of the rights of the British Crown in America.

The sole University of Harvard, in the United States, does more for high French culture than all of the English-speaking universities of Canada, with the exception of McGill. French is more frequently heard, and better spoken, in well educated circles in Boston, New York or Washington, than in Toronto, or even in the English-speaking sets of Montreal, in population the fifth French centre of the world, in the very heart of this province of Quebec, where the Anglo-Protestant minority enjoys the most privileged situation ever granted to a religious or national minority. . . .

Let us now consider the peculiar situation of the French Canadians in the Quebec 'reserve'. Traders in loyalty and preachers of imperialism never fail to remind us, with more insistence than courtesy or historical accuracy, of the 'extraordinary privileges' enjoyed by the French Canadians. . . . [They tell us]: 'Shed your blood for the Empire and pour your money into the imperial chest; help us in defending the neutrality of Belgium, in saving France and crushing Germany. Endure silently all humiliations in Ontario and the West, —they are but the moderate price you pay for the extraordinary "privileges" you enjoy, and especially for the most glorious of all, that of being citizens of a vaster empire than has been, and upon which the sun never sets. Should you refuse to worship our Gods, you will fall into the abominable American Republic, the Gehenna where there can be for you but tears and gnashing of teeth.' . . .

This perpetual vaunting of the British Empire and unceasing denunciation of the 'iniquitous' American Republic have brought [the French Canadian] to closer comparisons. In the process of observation, he gradually gives himself to that inborn instinct which leads all independent minds to resist the imposition of admiration and worship, and to look with growing interest upon persons or objects continually offered to his execration.

To the mind of the French Canadian, the question above put to enthusiastic Imperialists [if Canada were annexed to the US, which of the rights, usages, customs, laws, codes, or charters existing today in Quebec would be abrogated, curtailed, or modified in any way?] comes naturally every time a new assault is made against the exclusiveness of his Canadian patriotism. In the double sphere of law and fact he looks for an answer: and what does he find?

In one single clause of the American constitution reference is made to what he regards as his natural inheritance. It is in the first of the Additional Articles, which bears that '*Congress shall make no law respecting an establishment of religion, or prohibiting the free exercise thereof*'.

In this he finds nothing to make him shudder; first, because the Catholic Church is not 'established' in Quebec, at least in the sense meant by the framers of the American constitution; and second, that clause touches only on the powers of Congress, and interferes in no way with State jurisdiction.

As to the teaching of any religion or language at school, as to school laws in general, or the use of languages in legislatures or State courts, there is no reference whatever in the American constitution. Therefore, all those questions remain, in virtue of the Xth Additional Article, within the exclusive jurisdiction of States.

As a matter of fact, under that [tenth amendment], the Province of Quebec and its legislature would enjoy a much larger measure of autonomy in the American Union than under the constitution of Canada.*

Let us summarise.

The traditional horror of the French Canadian for Annexation has almost totally disappeared: he has ceased to look upon it as the worst danger to his creed and nationality. He has found out that the pledges of equality of rights, of an equitable allotment of privileges and burdens, given to him by the Fathers of Confederation, have hardly been kept up. Above all, he is forced to acknowledge that his English-speaking fellow-citizens do not entertain ardent feelings of gratitude towards him, nor even a spirit of justice. Finally, he is beginning to ask himself if he was not duped into the bargain.

'But', it may be objected, 'this is a regular plea in favour of annexation, or at least a theory to demonstrate that the French Canadians are prepared to accept annexation.'

It is neither one nor the other.

First, my personal sentiments I leave out of this study. For various motives, I am still more British and less American than the majority of my fellow-citizens, either of British or of French origin. What I have endeavoured to do is simply to bring into synthetic form, scattered opinions, accidental observations, intermittent impressions, which I have gathered, these late years, in most diverse circles. The sentiments growing therefrom are still incoherent. They have not yet coalesced into the form of a constant mentality or a continuous current of opinion. But they are gradually coordinated in that direction. As the atoms of a gaseous substance are solidified under high pressure, so the separatist feelings of the French Canadians may grow, thanks to ultra-imperialist appeals, the repeated kicks they receive in several of the English provinces, and the stupid efforts made to keep them enclosed in their Quebec 'reserve'. Whether that deep and still unperceived evolution shall be accelerated, retarded or stopped, depends entirely upon the foresight and goodwill of the English-speaking majority in Canada. . . .

Really, the French Canadian is amazed at the attitude of his English-speaking fellow citizens. Of the sincerity of their patriotism and the genuineness of their love for the motherland, he, at times, doubts seriously. Their thunderous asseverations of loyalty he cannot reconcile with their stupefying blindness in the face of the real dangers that threaten the unity of Confederation, and still less with their persistency in letting the peril grow, and even in accelerating its progress. . . .

'*Let Canada be saved from American conquest, the consequence of German supremacy*'.

Why do you not seek first to guard yourselves against the universal contagion of American ideals, morals and mentality, with which your family life, your intellectual and social atmosphere are already permeated? This moral absorption, the prelude of political domination, is more to be dreaded than the catastrophes predicted by the howling dervishes of Imperialism.

Just test yourselves!

Americans you already are by your language, your nasal accent, your common slang, your dress, your daily habits; by the Yankee literature with which your homes and clubs are flooded; by your yellow journals and their rantings; by your loud and intolerant patriotism; by your worship of gold, snobbery and titles.

Americans you are precisely by what constitutes the deepest line of cleavage between both our races: your system of so called 'national schools', a servile copy of the American model, under which your children's mind, passing through the same intellectual roller, is formed or rather deformed to the perfect imitation of little Yankees—whilst we have remained faithful to the old British principle of respect to the liberty of conscience of both father and child.

In all those spheres, French Canadians have been better preserved from American contagion, thanks to their language, their French speech, to Canada the safest of national preservatives, which some of you so foolishly endeavour to eradicate from our country.

Unfortunately, in the sphere of public life, where we live side by side with you, but where you dominate by your numbers and language, you are americanising us as thoroughly as yourselves.

'*Let British institutions be saved*', say you.

Granted; but so much is worth the spirit, so much the letter, so much the soul, so much the body. The spirit that gives life to national institutions and determines their character is to be found in public morals, in the mentality of statesmen, politicians and publicists. These are the sources from which the national spirit springs and in which it takes its nature and tendencies.

In their external fabric, Canadian institutions are but partially British. Our federal régime is largely imitated from the American constitution. Moreover, the inner soul of our national life has passed through a period of deep evolution, and so becomes more and more every day a simple replica of American civilisation,—with this difference, that in the United States, public morals and administration have made marked progress in reform, whilst in Canada their degradation is still increasing.

Americans we are by the despotism of party machines, by the abominable abuse of patronage, by the sway of corporations and bosses, by the venality of our politicians, by the pest of log-rolling and lobbying in our parliaments, by the boodling with which our public bodies, federal, provincial or municipal, are infested, by the quick disappearance of the laws of honour from finance, from trade transactions, and even from the practice of liberal professions.

A few years ago, in a private conversation, a high official of one of the most important Canadian railway companies stated that the parliament at Ottawa was the most 'costly' of all the legislatures with which he had to deal in America. That prices have gone down since I doubt very much.

We are fast approaching the day when, as fifteen or twenty years ago in the United States, it will be forbidden to any man careful of his honour and reputation to aspire to representative functions. No one, unless possessed of ample wealth, will be able to satisfy the mob's cupidity without accepting dishonourable help; and how can the honourable wish to associate with a pack of crooked politicians?

In the social and economical order, where do we stand in Canada? Canadian labour organisation is practically in the hands of American Unions. American capital is invading our industries, and grasping our forests, water powers and public lands. Speculation in the American stock-exchange is fed by the savings of our banks, to the deep detriment, in times of crisis, of Canadian trade. A large portion of our means of transportation are but the 'adjuncts' of American railways.

To radically stop that process of economical penetration may be impossible. That Canada finds in it considerable material advantage nobody denies. But in our eyes, national safety is more than material wealth; and some effort should be made to diminish at least the direst consequences of that economical conquest.

On several instances, nationalist 'demagogues' have called the attention of public powers to that menace. Statesmen laughed and shrugged their shoulders. Some of the stoutest patriots of today even struck very nice bargains with the invaders. Countless are those staunch loyalists, who dream of nothing but war and slaughter on behalf of Britain, but who are always ready to sell any part of the national patrimony, provided they get their commission.

When they writhe with anguish at the sole thought of the danger to be incurred by Canada in case we sold a few bales of hay to the Americans, or when they entreat us to go help and sink German ships in order to 'save our institutions',—it is our turn to shrug our shoulders and laugh at the comedians.

'Let our national character be preserved'.

Very well, but how can we believe in the sincerity or lucidity of those who see nothing but threats in the Black Sea, the Mediterranean or the North Sea, but who obstinately shut their eyes on a peril growing in the midst of Canada, from Lake Superior to the Rockies.

The same people who wish now to entangle us in all imperial wars and difficulties, have either favoured or tacitly accepted a criminal immigration policy, thanks to which Manitoba, Alberta and Sakatchewan are fast becoming foreign to the older provinces in population, habits, traditions, aspirations, requirements, and social and political ideals. This means that the formidable influence of heterogeneous human forces deepens still further the line of cleavage between East and West, already so profoundly marked by differences in climate, soil and production. In order to check the force of segregation and help in the work of unification, we French Canadians have offered our aid in endeavouring to plant through those immense territories outposts from the old population of Quebec, so as to reproduce there, as far as possible, the traditional and basic conditions of Confederation, and oppose to the invasion of American language, morals and traditions, the bulwark of French language, morals and traditions.

How were such efforts and attempts received?

All sorts of obstacles and vexations were raised against us.* The importation of Galicians, Doukobors, Scandinavians, Mormons, or Americans of all races, was more encouraged than the settlement of French Canadians or the immigration of French-speaking Europeans, whom we could have easily assimilated. To preserve Canada from the danger of being 'Frenchified', as he boldly stated, a deputy-minister of the Interior was allowed, without the slightest blame, to claim from England the 'graduates' of jails and workhouses and proffer a helping hand to the human derelicts gathered up by the Salvation Army and the Church Army. Steamship and railway companies, subsidised by the Federal exchequer, which receives contributions from French Canadian as well as from other rate-payers, bring immigrants from the slums of Liverpool to Winnipeg, at a lesser cost than the hardy sons of Quebec and other eastern farmers must pay for transportation to Manitoba.

Within a few years, French Canadians in the West were deprived of their schools, of the official recognition of their language, and of all that could have contributed in attracting them to the settlement of that national domain, one-third of it paid for by their money. When, standing on the constitution of Canada and the solemn pledges of the most eminent statesmen who made Confederation, they demanded justice, this was the brutal rebuff: 'You are less numerous than we are in the West; you are there outnumbered by the Mormons. Besides, this is an English country. If you are not satisfied, then stay in your "reserve", or get out of the Dominion'.

In Ontario, their increase is denounced as a national peril. 'Ontario does not want a France of Louis the Fourteenth', wrote not long ago a missionary in the columns of the Toronto *Globe*. Presumably, Sicilians with their knives, Polish Jews and Syrians are nearer to the heart of that apostle.

After all that, can anyone wonder if the French Canadian no more feels the thrill of joy or pride when he hears of 'Canadian unity', 'British institutions', or 'flag worship'? . . .

STEPHEN LEACOCK

Students heave a sigh of relief when they get to Stephen Leacock (1869-1944): at last, a Political Scientist. Leacock headed the department at McGill from 1908 until his retirement in 1936. He was well known as a writer and speaker on contemporary politics as well as the author of a textbook, Elements of Political Science *(1906; 2nd ed., 1921), which was widely used for over a generation, and a better money-earner than any of his other books, successful though they were.*

The first essay below was published in a monthly review in 1907, shortly before Leacock embarked on a globe-circling lecture tour to promote Imperial Federation. (Note the population predicted for the year 2000: the English were to practise revanche des berceaux?*) 'The Apology of a Professor' was written in 1910 and reprinted, slightly revised, in* Essays and Literary Studies *(1916).*

Greater Canada: An Appeal

Now, in this month of April [1907], when the ice is leaving our rivers, the ministers of Canada take ship for this the fourth Colonial Conference at London. What do they go to do? Nay, rather what shall we bid them do? We—the six million people of Canada, unvoiced, untaxed, in the Empire, unheeded in the councils of the world—we, the six million colonials sprawling our over-suckled infancy across a continent—what shall be our message to the motherland? Shall we still whine of our poverty, still draw imaginary pictures of our thin herds shivering in the cold blasts of the North, their shepherds huddled for shelter in the log cabins of Montreal and Toronto? Shall we still beg the good people of England to bear yet a little longer, for the poor peasants of their colony, the burden and heat of the day? Shall our ministers rehearse this worn-out fiction of our 'acres of snow', and so sail home again, still untaxed, to the smug approval of the oblique politicians of Ottawa? Or, shall we say to the people of England,'The time has come; we know and realize our country. We will be your colony no longer. Make us one with you in an Empire, Permanent and Indivisible.'

This last alternative means what is commonly called Imperialism. It means a united system of defence, an imperial navy for whose support somehow or other the whole Empire shall properly contribute, and with it an imperial authority in whose power we all may share. To many people in Canada this imperialism is a tainted word. It is too much associated with a truckling subservience to English people and English ideas and the silly swagger of the hop-o'my-thumb junior officer. But there is and must be for the true future of our country, a higher and more real imperialism than this—the imperialism of the plain man at the plough and the clerk in the counting house, the imperialism of any decent citizen that demands for this country its proper place in the councils of the Empire and in the destiny of the world. In this sense, imperialism means but the realization of a Greater Canada, the recognition of a wider citizenship.

I, that write these lines, am an Imperialist because I will not be a Colonial. This Colonial status is a worn-out, by-gone thing. The sense and feeling of it has become harmful to us. It limits the ideas, and circumscribes the patriotism of our people. It impairs the mental vigor and narrows the outlook of those that are reared and educated in our midst. The English boy reads of England's history and its glories as his own; it is *his* navy that fought at Camperdown and Trafalgar, *his* people that have held fast their twenty miles of sea eight hundred years against a continent. He learns at his fire-side and at his school, among his elders and his contemporaries, to regard all this as part of himself; something that he, as a fighting man, may one day uphold, something for which as a plain citizen he shall every day gladly pay, something for which in any capacity it may one day be his high privilege to die. How little of this in Canada! Our paltry policy teaches the Canadian boy to detach himself from the England of the past, to forget that Camperdown and Copenhagen and the Nile are ours as much as theirs, that this navy of the Empire is ours too, ours in its history of the past, ours in its safe-guard of the present.

If this be our policy and plan, let us complete our teaching to our children. Let us inscribe it upon the walls of our schools, let us write it in brass upon our temples that for the Navy which made us and which defends us, we pay not a single penny, we spare not a solitary man. Let us add to it, also, that the lesson may bear fruit, this 'shelter theory' of Canada now rampant in our day; that Canada, by some reason of its remoteness from European sin and its proximity to American republicanism, is sheltered from that flail of war with which God tribulates the other peoples of the world, sheltered by the Monroe Doctrine, by President Roosevelt and his battleships, sheltered, I know not how, but sheltered somehow so that we may forget the lean, eager patriotism and sacrifice of a people bred for war, and ply in peace the little craft of gain and greed. So grows and has grown the Canadian boy in his colonial status, dissociated from the history of the world, cut off from the larger patriotism, colourless in his ideas. So grows he till in some sly way his mind opens to the fence-rail politics of his country side, with its bribed elections and its crooked votes—not patriotism but 'politics', maple-leaf politics, by which money may be made and places and profit fall in a golden shower.

Some time ago Theodore Roosevelt, writing with the pardonable irresponsibility of a Police Commissioner of New York and not as President of the United States, said of us here in Canada, that the American feels towards the Canadian the good-natured condescension that is felt by the free-born man for the man that is not free. Only recently one of the most widely circulated of American magazines, talking in the same vein, spoke of us Canadians as a 'subject people'. These are, of course, the statements of extravagance and ignorance; but it is true, none the less, that the time has come to be done with this *colonial* business, done with it once and forever. We cannot in Canada continue as we are. We must become something greater or something infinitely less. We can no longer be an appanage and outlying portion of something else. Canada, as a *colony,* was right enough in the days of good old Governor Simcoe, when your emigrant officer sat among the pine stumps of his Canadian clearing and reared his children in the fear of God and in the love of England—right enough then, wrong enough and destructive enough now. We cannot continue as we are. In the history of every nation as of every man there is no such thing as standing still. There is no pause upon the path of progress. There is no stagnation but the hush of death.

And for this progress, this forward movement, what is there first to do? How first unravel this vexed skein of our colonial and imperial relations? This, first of all. We must realize, and the people of England must realize, the inevitable greatness of Canada. This is not a vain-glorious boast. This is no rhodomontade. It is simple fact. Here stand we, six million people, heirs to the greatest legacy in the history of mankind, owners of half a continent, trustees, under God Almighty, for the fertile solitudes of the west. A little people, few in numbers, say you? Ah, truly such a little people! Few as the people of the Greeks that blocked the mountain gates of Europe to the march of Asia, few as the men of Rome that built a power to dominate the world, nay, scarce more numerous than they in England whose beacons flamed along the cliffs a warning to the heavy galleons of Spain. Aye, such a little people, but growing, growing, growing, with a march that shall make us ten millions to-morrow, twenty millions in our children's time and a hundred millions ere yet the century runs out. What say you to Fort Garry, a stockaded fort in your father's day, with its hundred thousand of to-day and its half a million souls of to-morrow? What think you, little river Thames, of our great Ottawa that flings its foam eight hundred miles? What does it mean when science has moved us a little further yet, and the wheels of the world's work turn with electric force? What sort of asset do you think then our melting snow and the roaring river-flood of our Canadian spring shall be to us? What say you, little puffing steam-fed industry of England, to the industry of Coming Canada. Think you, you can heave your coal hard enough, sweating and grunting with your shovel to keep pace with the snow-fed cataracts of the north? Or look, were it but for double conviction, at the sheer extent and size of us. Throw aside, if you will, the vast districts of the frozen north; confiscate, if you like, Ungava still snow-covered and unknown, and let us talk of the Canada that we know, south of the sixtieth parallel, south of your Shetland Islands, south of the Russian Petersburg and reaching southward thence to where the peach groves of Niagara bloom in the latitude of northern Spain. And of all this take only our two new provinces, twin giants of the future, Alberta and Saskatchewan. Three decades ago this was the 'great lone land', the frozen west, with its herds of bison and its Indian tepees, known to you only in the pictured desolation of its unending snow; now crossed and inter-crossed with railways, settled 400 miles from the American frontier, and sending north and south the packets of its daily papers from its two provincial capitals. And of this country, fertile as the corn plains of Hungary, and the crowded flats of Belgium, do you know the size? It is this. Put together the whole German Empire, the republic of France and your England and Scotland, and you shall find place for them in our two new provinces. Or take together across the boundary from us, the States of Maine, New Hampshire, Vermont, Massachusetts, Rhode Island, and Connecticut— all the New England States and with them all the Middle States of the North— New York, New Jersey, Pennsylvania, Delaware, Ohio, Indiana, Michigan, Illinois, and Wisconsin, till you have marked a space upon the map from the Atlantic to the Mississippi and from the Ohio to the lakes—all these you shall put into our two new provinces and still find place for England and for Scotland in their boundaries.

This then for the size and richness of our country. Would that the soul and spirit of its people were commensurate with its greatness. For here as yet we fail. Our politics, our public life and thought, rise not to the level of our opportunity. The mud-bespattered politicians of the trade, the party men and party managers, give us in place of patriotic statescraft the sordid traffic of a tolerated jobbery. For bread, a stone. Harsh is the cackle of the little turkey-cocks of Ottawa, fighting the while as they feather their mean nests of sticks and mud, high on their river bluff. Loud sings the little Man of the Province, crying his petty Gospel of Provincial Rights, grudging the gift of power, till the cry spreads and town hates town and every hamlet of the country side shouts for its share of plunder and of pelf. This is the tenor of our politics, carrying as its undertone the voice of the black-robed sectary, with narrow face and shifting eyes, snarling still with the bigotry of a by-gone day. This is the spirit that we must purge. This is the demon we must exorcise; this the disease, the canker-worm of corruption, bred in the indolent securities of peace, that must be burned for us in the pure fire of an Imperial patriotism, that is no theory but a passion. This is our need, our supreme need of the Empire—not for its ships and guns, but for the greatness of it, the soul of it, aye for the very danger of it.

Of our spirit, then, it is not well. Nor is it well with the spirit of those in England in their thoughts of us. Jangling are they these twenty years over little Ireland that makes and unmakes ministries, and never a thought of Canada, jangling now over their Pantaloon Suffragettes and their Swaddled Bishops, wondering whether they shall still represent their self-willed Lords nose for nose in the councils of the Empire or whether they may venture now to scale them down, putting one nose for ten. One or ten, what does it matter, so there is never a voice to speak for Canada? Can they not see, these people of England, that the supreme English Question now is the question of Canada: that this Conference of the year of grace 1907 might, if it would, make for us the future of the Empire? Or will they still regard us, poor outlying sheltered people of Canada, as something alien and apart, sending us ever of their youngest and silliest to prate in easy arrogance of 'home', earning the livelihood their island cannot give, still snapping at the hand that feeds them?

And what then can this Colonial Conference effect after all, it is asked? Granting, for argument's sake, the spirit of the people that might prove it, our willingness to pay, their willingness to give us place and power, what can be done? Hard indeed is the question. Hard even to the Ready Man in the Street with his glib solution of difficulties; harder still to the thoughtful; hardest of all to those who will not think. For if we pay for this our Navy that even now defends us, and yet speak not in the councils at Westminster, then is that Taxation without Representation; straightway the soul of the Anglo-Saxon stands aghast; the grim deaths-head of King John grins in the grave, while the stout ghost of old Ben Franklin hovers again upon our frontier holding in its hand the proffer of independence. But if you admit us to your councils, what then? Ah, then indeed an awful thing befalls! Nothing less that the remaking of your constitution, with a patching and a re-building of it, till the nature-growth of precedent and custom is shaped in the clumsy artifice of clause and schedule, powers and prohibitions, measured and marked off with the yard-stick of the *ultra-vires* attorney. This surely is worse than ever. This perhaps you might have done, save for the bare turn of a majority, for Irksome Ireland. But for Uncomplaining Canada, not so.

So there we stand, we and you, pitched fast upon the horns of a dilemma. You cannot tax us, since you will not represent us. We cannot be represented because we will not be taxed. So we stand stock still, like the donkey in the philosophic fable, balanced between two bales of hay, nibbling neither right nor left. So are we like to stand, till some one of us, some of you and us, shall smite the poor donkey of our joint stupidity there where it most profits that a donkey shall be smitten, and bid it move!

Yet is the difficulty perhaps not impossible of solution. The thing to be achieved is there. The task is yours to solve, men of the council table. Find us a way whereby the burden and the power shall fall on all alike; a way whereby, taxed, we shall still be free men, free of the Imperial citizenship, and your historic constitution unshattered in the progress. Is it then so difficult? We come of a race that has solved much, has so often achieved the impossible. Look back a little in the ages to where ragged Democracy howls around the throne of defiant Kingship. This is a problem that we have solved, joining the dignity of Kingship with the power of democracy; this, too, by the simplest of political necromancy, the trick of which we now expound in our schools, as the very alphabet of political wisdom. Or look back to where the scaffolds of a bigot nation run with blood for the sake of rival creeds that know not yet the simple code of toleration, to be framed now in an easy statute with an artful stroke of a pen. Have we done all this and shall we balk at this poor colonial question? At it then, like men, shrewd representatives of Ottawa and Westminster, trained in the wisdom of the ages. Listen not to those who would block the way with a *non possumus* on this side, a *non volumus* on that. Find us a way, shew us a plan, a mere beginning if you will, a widow's mite of contribution, a mere whispering of representation, but something that shall trace for us the future path of Empire.

Nor is guidance altogether lacking in the task. For at least the signs of the times are written large as to what the destiny of Canada shall *not* be. Not as it is—not on this *colonial* footing, can it indefinitely last. There are those who tell us that it is best to leave well alone, to wait for the slow growth, the evolution of things. For herein lies the darling thought of the wisdom of the nineteenth century, in this same Evolution, this ready-made explanation of all things; hauled over from the researches of the botanist to meet the lack of thought of the philosopher. Whatever is, is: whatever will be, will be—so runs its silly creed. Therefore let everything be, that is: and all that shall be, shall be! This is but the wisdom of the fool, wise after the fact. For the solution of our vexed colonial problem this profits nothing. We cannot sit passive to watch our growth. Good or bad, straight or crooked, we must make our fate.

Nor is it ever possible or desirable that we in Canada can form an independent country. The little cry that here and there goes up among us is but the symptom of an aspiring discontent, that will not let our people longer be colonials. 'Tis but a cry forced out by what a wise man has called the growing pains of a nation's progress. Independent, we could not survive a decade. Those of us who know our country realize that beneath its surface smoulder still the embers of racial feud and of religious bitterness. Twice in our generation has the sudden alarm of conflict broken upon the quiet of our prosperity with the sound of a fire bell in the night. Not thus our path. Let us compose the feud and still the strife of races, not in the artificial partnership of an Independent Canada, but in the joint greatness of a common destiny.

Nor does our future lie in Union with those that dwell to the southward. The day of annexation to the United States is passed. Our future lies elsewhere. Be it said without concealment and without bitterness. They have chosen their lot; we have chosen ours. Let us go our separate ways in peace. Let them still keep their perennial Independence Day, with its fulminating fireworks and its Yankee Doodle. We keep our Magna Charta and our rough and ready Rule Britannia, shouting as lustily as they! The propaganda of Annexation is dead. Citizens we want, indeed, but not the prophets of an alien gospel. To you who come across our western border we can offer a land fatter than your Kansas, a government better than Montana, a climate kinder than your Dakota. Take it, Good Sir, if you will: but if, in taking it, you still raise your little croak of annexation, then up with you by the belt and out with you, breeches first, through the air, to the land of your origin! This in all friendliness.

Not independence then, not annexation, not stagnation: nor yet that doctrine of a little Canada that some conceive—half in, half out of the Empire, with a mimic navy of its own; a pretty navy this—poor two-penny collection, frolicking on its little way strictly within the Gulf of St Lawrence, a sort of silly adjunct to the navy of the Empire, semi-detached, the better to be smashed at will. As well a Navy of the Province, or the Parish, home-made for use at home, docked every Saturday in Lake Nipigon!

Yet this you say, you of the Provincial Rights, you Little Canada Man, is all we can afford! We that have raised our public charge from forty up to eighty millions odd within the ten years past, and scarce have felt the added strain of it. Nay, on the question of the cost, good gentlemen of the council, spare it not. Measure not the price. It is not a commercial benefit we buy. We are buying back our honour as Imperial Citizens. For, look you, this protection of our lives and coast, this safe-guard from the scourge of war, we have it now as much as you of England: you from the hard-earned money that you pay, we as the peasant pensioners on your Imperial Bounty.

Thus stands the case. Thus stands the question of the future of Canada. Find for us something other than mere colonial stagnation, something sounder than independence, nobler than annexation, greater in purpose than a Little Canada. Find us a way. Build us a plan, that shall make us, in hope at least, an Empire Permanent and Indivisible.

The Apology of a Professor

I know no more interesting subject of speculation, nor any more calculated to allow of a fair-minded difference of opinion, than the enquiry whether a professor has any right to exist. *Prima facie,* of course, the case is heavily against him. His angular overcoat, his missing buttons, and his faded hat, will not bear comparison with the double-breasted splendour of the stock broker, or the *Directoire* fur gown of the cigar maker. Nor does a native agility of body compensate for the missing allurement of dress. He cannot skate. He does not shoot. He must not swear. He is not brave. His mind, too, to the outsider at any rate, appears defective and seriously damaged by education. He cannot appreciate a twenty-five-cent novel, or a melodrama, or a moving-picture show, or any of that broad current of intellectual movement which soothes the brain of the business man in its moments of inactivity. His conversation, even to the tolerant, is impossible. Apparently he has neither ideas nor enthusiasms, nothing but an elaborate catalogue of dead men's opinions which he cites with a petulant and peevish authority that will not brook contradiction, and that must be soothed by a tolerating acquiescence, or flattered by a plenary acknowledgment of ignorance.

Yet the very heaviness of this initial indictment against the professor might well suggest to an impartial critic that there must at least be mitigating circumstances in the case. Even if we are to admit that the indictment is well founded, the reason is all the greater for examining the basis on which it rests. At any rate some explanation of the facts involved may perhaps serve to palliate, if not to remove, demerits which are rather to be deplored than censured. It is one of the standing defects of our age that social classes, or let us say more narrowly, social categories, know so little of one another. For the purposes of ready reckoning, of that handy transaction of business which is the passion of the hour, we have adopted a way of labelling one another with the tag mark of a profession or an occupation that becomes an aid to business but a barrier to intercourse. This man is a professor, that man an 'insurance man', a third— *terque quaterque beatus*—a 'liquor man'; with these are 'railroad men', 'newspaper men', 'dry goods men', and so forth. The things that we handle for our livelihood impose themselves upon our personality, till the very word 'man' drops out, and a gentleman is referred to as a 'heavy pulp and paper interest' while another man is a prominent 'rubber plant', two or three men round a dinner table become an 'iron and steel circle', and thus it is that for the simple conception of a human being is substituted a complex of 'interests', 'rings', 'circles', 'sets', and other semi-geometrical figures arising out of avocations rather than affinities. Hence it comes that insurance men mingle with insurance men, liquor men mix, if one may use the term without afterthought, with liquor men: what looks like a lunch between three men at a club is really a cigar having lunch with a couple of plugs of tobacco.

Now the professor more than any ordinary person finds himself shut out from the general society of the business world. The rest of the 'interests' have, after all, some things in common. The circles intersect at various points. Iron and steel has a certain fellowship with pulp and paper, and the whole lot of them may be converted into the common ground of preference shares and common stock. But the professor is to all of them an outsider. Hence his natural dissimilarity is unduly heightened in its appearance by the sort of avocational isolation in which he lives.

Let us look further into the status and the setting of the man. To begin with, history has been hard upon him. For some reason the strenuous men of activity and success in the drama of life have felt an instinctive scorn of the academic class, which they have been at no pains to conceal. Bismarck knew of no more bitter taunt to throw at the Free Trade economists of England than to say that they were all either clergymen or professors. Napoleon felt a life-long abhorrence of the class, broken only by one brief experiment that ended in failure. It is related that at the apogee of the Imperial rule, the idea flashed upon him that France must have learned men, that the professors must be encouraged. He decided to act at once. Sixty-five professors were invited that evening to the palace of the Tuileries. They came. They stood about in groups, melancholy and myopic beneath the light. Napoleon spoke to them in turn. To the first he spoke of fortifications. The professor in reply referred to the binomial theorem. 'Put him out,' said Napoleon. To the second he spoke of commerce. The professor in answer cited the opinions of Diodorus Siculus. 'Put him out,' said Napoleon. At the end of half an hour Napoleon had had enough of the professors. 'Cursed idealogues,' he cried; 'put them all out.' Nor were they ever again admitted.

Nor is it only in this way that the course of history has been unkind to the professor. It is a notable fact in the past, that all persons of eminence who might have shed a lustre upon the academic class are absolved from the title of professor, and the world at large is ignorant that they ever wore it. We never hear of the author of the *The Wealth of Nations* as Professor Smith, nor do we know the poet of *Evangeline* as Professor Longfellow. The military world would smile to see the heroes of the Southern Confederacy styled Professor Lee and Professor Jackson. We do not know of Professor Harrison as the occupant of a President's chair. Those whose talk is of dreadnoughts and of strategy never speak of Professor Mahan, and France has long since forgotten the proper title of Professor Guizot and Professor Taine. Thus it is that the ingratitude of an undiscerning public robs the professorial class of the honour of its noblest names. Nor does the evil stop there. For, in these latter days at least, the same public which eliminates the upward range of the term, applies it downwards and sideways with indiscriminating generality. It is a 'professor' who plays upon the banjo. A 'professor' teaches swimming. Hair cutting, as an art, is imparted in New York by 'professors'; while any gentleman whose thaumaturgic intercommunication with the world of spirits has reached the point of interest which warrants space advertising in the daily press, explains himself as a 'professor' to his prospective clients. So it comes that the true professor finds all his poor little attributes of distinction—his mock dignity, his gown, his string of supplementary letters—all taken over by a mercenary age to be exploited, as the stock in trade of an up-to-date advertiser. The vendor of patent medicine depicts himself in the advertising columns in a gown, with an uplifted hand to shew the Grecian draping of the fold. After his name are placed enough letters and full stops to make up a simultaneous equation in algebra.

The word 'professor' has thus become a generic term, indicating the assumption of any form of dexterity, from hair-cutting to running the steam shovel in a crematorium. It is even customary—I am informed—to designate in certain haunts of meretricious gaiety the gentleman whose efforts at the piano are rewarded by a *per capita* contribution of ten cents from every guest—the 'professor'.

One may begin to see, perhaps, the peculiar disadvantage under which the professor labours in finding his avocation confused with the various branches of activity for which he can feel nothing but a despairing admiration. But there are various ways also in which the very circumstances of his profession cramp and bind him. In the first place there is no doubt that his mind is very seriously damaged by his perpetual contact with the students. I would not for a moment imply that a university would be better off without the students; although the point is one which might well elicit earnest discussion. But their effect upon the professor is undoubtedly bad. He is surrounded by an atmosphere of syco-phantic respect. His students, on his morning arrival, remove his overshoes and hang up his overcoat. They sit all day writing down his lightest words with stylographic pens of the very latest model. They laugh at the meanest of his jests. They treat him with a finely simulated respect that has come down as a faint tradition of the old days of Padua and Bologna, when a professor was in reality the venerated master, a man who wanted to teach, and the students disciples who wanted to learn.

All that is changed now. The supreme import of the professor to the students now lies in the fact that he controls the examinations. He holds the golden key which will unlock the door of the temple of learning—unlock it, that is, not to let the student in, but to let him get out—into something decent. This fact gives to the professor a fictitious importance, easily confounded with his personality, similar to that of the gate keeper at a dog show, or the ticket wicket man at a hockey match.

In this is seen some part of the consequences of the vast, organised thing called modern education. Everything has the merits of its defects. It is a grand thing and a possible thing, that practically all people should possess the intellectual-mechanical arts of reading, writing, and computation: good too that they should possess pigeon-holed and classified data of the geography and history of the world; admirable too that they should possess such knowledge of the principles of natural science as will enable them to put a washer on a kitchen tap, or inflate a motor tire with a soda-syphon bottle. All this is splendid. This we have got. And this places us collectively miles above the rude illiterate men of arms, burghers, and villeins of the middle ages who thought the moon took its light from God, whereas we know that its light is simply a function of π divided by the square of its distance.

Let me not get confused in my thesis. I am saying that the universal distribution of mechanical education is a fine thing, and that we have also proved it possible. But above this is the utterly different thing—we have no good word for it, call it learning, wisdom, enlightenment, anything you will—

which means not a mechanical acquirement from without but something done from within: a power and willingness to think: an interest, for its own sake, in that general enquiry into the form and meaning of life which constitutes the ground plan of education. Now this, desirable though it is, cannot be produced by the mechanical compulsion of organised education. It belongs, and always has, to the few and never to the many. The ability to think is rare. Any man can think and think hard when he has to: the savage devotes a nicety of thought to the equipoise of his club, or the business man to the adjustment of a market price. But the ability or desire to think without compulsion about things that neither warm the hands nor fill the stomach, is very rare. Reflexion on the riddle of life, the cruelty of death, the innate savagery and the sublimity of the creature man, the history and progress of man in his little earth-dish of trees and flowers—all these things taken either 'straight' in the masculine form of philosophy and the social sciences, or taken by diffusion through the feminised form literature, constitute the operation of the educated mind. Of all these things most people in their degree think a little and then stop. They realise presently that these things are very difficult, and that they don't matter, and that there is no money in them. Old men never think of them at all. They are glad enough to stay in the warm daylight a little longer. For a working solution of these problems different things are done. Some people use a clergyman. Others declare that the Hindoos know all about it. Others, especially of late, pay a reasonable sum for the services of a professional thaumaturgist who supplies a solution of the soul problem by mental treatment at long range, radiating from State St, Chicago. Others, finally, of a native vanity that will not admit itself vanquished, buckle about themselves a few little formulas of 'evolution' and 'force', co-relate the conception of God to the differentiation of a frog's foot, and strut through life emplumed with the rump-feathers of their own conceit.

I trust my readers will not think that I have forgotten my professor. I have not. All of this digression is but an instance of *reculer pour mieux sauter.* It is necessary to bring out all this back-ground of the subject to show the setting in which the professor is placed. Possibly we shall begin to see that behind this quaint being in his angular overcoat are certain greater facts in respect to the general relation of education to the world of which the professor is only a product, and which help to explain, if they do not remove, the dislocated misfit of his status among his fellow men. We were saying then that the truly higher education—thought about life, mankind, literature, art—cannot be handed out at will. To attempt to measure it off by the yard, to mark it out into stages and courses, to sell it at the commutation rate represented by a college sessional fee—all this produces a contradiction in terms. For the thing itself is substituted an imitation of it. For real wisdom—obtainable only by the few—is substituted a nickel-plated make-believe obtainable by any person of ordinary intellect who has the money, and who has also, in the good old Latin sense, the needful assiduity. I am not saying that the system is bad. It is the best we can get; and incidentally, and at back-rounds it turns out a by-product in the shape of a capable and well-trained man who has forgotten all about the immortality of the soul, in which he never had any interest any way, but who conducts a law business with admirable efficiency.

The result, then, of this odd-looking system is, that what ought to be a thing existing for itself is turned into a qualification for something else. The reality of a student's studies is knocked out by the grim earnestness of having to pass an examination. How can a man really think of literature, or of the problem of the soul, who knows that he must learn the contents of a set of books in order to pass an examination which will give him the means of his own support and, perhaps, one half the support of his mother, or fifteen per cent of that of a maiden aunt. The pressure of circumstances is too much. The meaning of study is lost. The qualification is everything.

Not that the student finds his burden heavy or the situation galling. He takes the situation as he finds it, is hugely benefited by it at back-rounds, and, being young, adapts himself to it: accepts with indifference whatever programme may be needful for the qualification that he wants: studies Hebrew or Choctaw with equal readiness; and, as his education progresses, will write you a morning essay on transcendental utilitarianism, and be back again to lunch. At the end of his course he has learned much. He has learned to sit—that first requisite for high professional work—and he can sit for hours. He can write for hours with a stylographic pen: more than that, for I wish to state the case fairly, he can make a digest, or a summary, or a reproduction of anything in the world. Incidentally the *speculation* is all knocked sideways out of him. But the lack of it is never felt.

Observe that it was not so in Padua. The student came thither from afar off, on foot or on a mule; so I picture him at least in my ignorance of Italian history, seated droopingly upon a mule, with earnest, brown eyes hungered with the desire to know, and in his hand a vellum-bound copy of Thomas Aquinas written in long hand, priceless, as *he* thinks, for the wisdom it contains. Now the Padua student wanted to know: not for a qualification, not because he wanted to be a pharmaceutical expert with a municipal licence, but because he thought the things in Thomas Aquinas and such to be things of tremendous import. They were not; but he thought so. This student thought that he could really find out things: that if he listened daily to the words of the master who taught him, and read hard, and thought hard, he would presently discover real truths—the only things in life that he cared for—such as whether the soul is a fluid or a solid, whether his mule existed or was only a vapour, and much other of this sort. These things he fully expected to learn. For their sake he brought to bear on the person of his teacher that reverential admiration which survives faintly to-day, like a biological 'vestige', in the attitude of the college student who holds the overcoat of his professor. The Padua student, too, got what he came for. After a time he knew all about the soul, all about his mule—knew, too, something of the more occult, the almost devilish sciences, perilous to tackle, such as why the sun is suspended from falling into the ocean, or the very demonology of symbolism—the AL-GEB of the Arabians—by which $X + Y$ taken to the double or square can be shown after many days' computation to be equal to $X^2 + 2XY + Y^2$.

A man with such knowledge simply *had* to teach it. What to him if he should wear a brown gown of frieze and feed on pulse! This, as beside the bursting force of the expanding steam of his knowledge, counted for nothing. So he went forth, and he in turn became a professor, a man of profound acquirement, whose control over malign comets elicited a shuddering admiration.

These last reflections seem to suggest that it is not merely that something has gone wrong with the attitude of the student and the professor towards knowledge, but that something has gone wrong with knowledge itself. We have got the thing into such a shape that we do not know one-tenth as much as we used to. Our modern scholarship has poked and pried in so many directions, has set itself to be so ultra-rational, so hyper-sceptical, that now it knows nothing at all. All the old certainty has vanished. The good old solid dogmatic dead-sureness that buckled itself in the oak and brass of its own stupidity is clean gone. It died at about the era of the country squire, the fox-hunting parson, the three-bottle Prime Minister, and the voluminous Doctor of Divinity in broadcloth imperturbable even in sobriety, and positively omniscient when drunk. We have argued them off the stage of a world all too ungrateful. In place of their sturdy outlines appear that sickly anaemic Modern Scholarship, the double-jointed jack-in-the-box, Modern Religion, the feminine angularity of Modern Morality, bearing a jug of filtered water, and behind them, as the very lord of wisdom, the grinning mechanic, Practical Science, using the broadcloth suit of the defunct doctor as his engine-room over-alls. Or if we prefer to place the same facts without the aid of personification, our learning has so watered itself down that the starch and consistency is all out of it. There is no absolute sureness anywhere. Everything is henceforth to be a development, and evolution; morals and ethics are turned from fixed facts to shifting standards that change from age to age like the fashion of our clothes; art and literature are only a product, not good or bad, but a part of its age and environment. So it comes that our formal studies are no longer a burning quest for absolute truth. We have long since discovered that we cannot know anything. Our studies consist only in the long-drawn proof of the futility for the search after knowledge effected by exposing the errors of the past. Philosophy is the science which proves that we can know nothing of the soul. Medicine is the science which tells that we know nothing of the body. Political Economy is that which teaches that we know nothing of the laws of wealth; and Theology the critical history of those errors from which we deduce our ignorance of God.

When I sit and warm my hands, as best I may, at the little heap of embers that is now Political Economy, I cannot but contrast its dying glow with the generous blaze of the vainglorious and triumphant science that once it was.

Such is the distinctive character of modern learning, imprint with a resigned agnosticism towards the search after truth, able to refute everything and to believe nothing, and leaving its once earnest devotees stranded upon the arid sands of their own ignorance. In the face of this fact can it be wondered that a university converts itself into a sort of mill, grinding out its graduates, legally qualified, with conscientious regularity? The students take the mill as they find it, perform their task and receive their reward. They listen to their professor. They write down with stylographic pens in loose-leaf note books his most inane and his most profound speculations with an undiscriminating impartiality. The reality of the subject leaves but little trace upon their minds.

All of what has been said above has been directed mainly towards the hardship of the professor's lot upon its scholastic side. Let me turn to another aspect of his life, the moral. By a strange confusion of thought a professor is presumed to be a good man. His standing association with the young and the history of his profession, which was once amalgamated with that of the priesthood, give him a connexion at one remove with morality. He therefore finds himself in the category of men—including himself and the curate as its chief representatives—to whom the world at large insists on ascribing a rectitude of character and a simplicity of speech that unfits them for ordinary society. It is gratuitously presumed that such men prefer tea to whiskey-and-soda, blindman's buff to draw poker, and a freshmen's picnic to a prize fight.

For the curate of course I hold no brief. Let him sink. In any case he has to console him the favour of the sex, a concomitant perhaps of his very harmlessness, but productive at the same time of creature comforts. Soft slippers deck his little feet, flowers lie upon his study table, and round his lungs the warmth of an embroidered chest-protector proclaims the favour of the fair. Of this the ill-starred professor shares nothing. It is a sad fact that he is at once harmless and despised. He may lecture for twenty years and never find so much as a mullein stalk upon his desk. For him no canvas slippers, knitted by fair fingers, nor the flowered gown, nor clock-worked hosiery of the ecclesiastic. The sex will have none of him. I do not mean, of course, that there are no women that form exceptions to this rule. We have all seen immolated upon the academic hearth, and married to professors, women whose beauty and accomplishments would have adorned the home of a wholesale liquor merchant. But the broad rule still obtains. Women who embody, so St Augustine had told us, the very principle of evil, can only really feel attracted towards bad men. The professor is too good for them.

Whether a professor is of necessity a good man, is a subject upon which I must not presume to dogmatise. The women may be right in voting him a 'muff'. But if he is such in any degree, the conventional restrictions of his profession tend to heighten it. The bursts of profanity that are hailed as a mark of business energy on the part of a railroad magnate or a cabinet minister are interdicted to a professor. It is a canon of his profession that he must never become violent, nor lift his hand in anger. I believe that it was not always so. The story runs, authentic enough, that three generations ago a Harvard professor in a fit of anger with a colleague (engendered, if I recall the case, by the discussion of a nice point in thermo-dynamics) threw him into a chemical furnace and burned him. But the buoyancy of those days is past. In spite of the existence of our up-to-date apparatus, I do not believe that any of our present professoriate has yielded to such an impulse.

One other point remains worthy of remark in the summation of the heavy disadvantages under which the professor lives and labours. He does not know how to make money. This is a grave fault, and one that in the circumstances of the day can scarcely be overlooked. It comes down to him as a legacy of the Padua days when the professor neither needed money nor thought of it. Now when he would like money he is hampered by an 'evoluted' inability to get hold of it. He dares not commercialise his profession, or does not know how to do so. Had he the business instinct of the leaders of labour and the master manufacturers, he would long since have set to work at the problem. He would have urged his government to put so heavy a tax on the import of foreign professors as to keep the home market for himself. He would have organised himself into amalgamated Brotherhoods of Instructors of Latin, United Greek Workers of America, and so forth, organised strikes, picketed the houses of the college trustees, and made himself a respected place as a member of industrial society. This his inherited inaptitude forbids him to do.

Nor can the professor make money out of what he knows. Somehow a plague is on the man. A teacher of English cannot write a half-dime novel, nor a professor of dynamics invent a safety razor. The truth is that a modern professor for commercial purposes doesn't know anything. He only knows parts of things.

It occurred to me some years ago when the Cobalt silver mines were first discovered that a professor of scientific attainments ought to be able, by transferring his talent to that region, to amass an enormous fortune. I questioned one of the most gifted of my colleagues. 'Could you not,' I asked, 'as a specialist in metals discover silver mines at sight?' 'Oh, no,' he said, shuddering at the very idea, 'you see I'm not a metallurgist; at Cobalt the silver is all in the rocks and I know nothing of rocks whatever.' 'Who then,' I said, 'knows about rocks?' 'For that,' he answered, 'you need a geologist like Adamson; but then, you see, he knows the rocks, but doesn't know the silver.' 'But could you not both go,' I said, 'and Adamson hold the rock while you extracted the silver?' 'Oh, no,' the professor answered, 'you see we are neither of us mining engineers; and even then we ought to have a good hydraulic man and an electric man.' 'I suppose,' I said, 'that if I took about seventeen of you up there you might find something. No? Well, would it not be possible to get somebody who would know something of *all* these things?' 'Yes,' he said, 'any of the fourth-year students would, but personally all that I do is to reduce the silver when I get it.' 'That I can do myself,' I answered musingly, and left him.

Such then is the professor; a man whose avocation in life is hampered by the history of its past: imparting in the form of statutory exercises knowledge that in its origin meant a spontaneous effort of the intelligence, whose very learning itself has become a profession rather than a pursuit, whose mock dignity and fictitious morality remove him from the society of his own sex and deny to him the favour of the other. Surely, in this case, to understand is to sympathise. Is it not possible, too, that when all is said and done the professor is performing a useful service in the world, unconsciously of course, in acting as a leaven in the lump of commercialism that sits so heavily on the world to-day? I do not wish to expand upon this theme. I had set out to make the apology of the professor speak for itself from the very circumstances of his work. But in these days, when money is everything, when pecuniary success is the only goal to be achieved, when the voice of the plutocrat is as the voice of God, the aspect of the professor, side-tracked in the real race of life, riding his mule of Padua in competition with an automobile, may at least help to soothe the others who have failed in the struggle.

Dare one, as the wildest of fancies, suggest how different things might be if learning counted, or if we could set it on its feet again, if students wanted to learn, and if professors had anything to teach, if a university lived for itself and not as a place of qualification for the junior employees of the rich; if there were only in this perplexing age some way of living humbly and retaining the respect of one's fellows; if a man with a few hundred dollars a year could cast out the money question and the house question, and the whole business of competitive appearances and live for the things of the mind! But then, after all, if the mind as a speculative instrument has gone bankrupt, if learning, instead of meaning a mind full of thought, means only a bellyful of fact, one is brought to a full stop, standing among the littered debris of an ideal that has passed away.

In any case the question, if it is one, is going to settle itself. The professor is passing away. The cost of living has laid its hold upon him, and grips him in its coils; within another generation he will be starved out, frozen out, 'evolved' out by the glorious process of natural selection and adaptation, the rigour of which is the only God left in our desolated Pantheon. The male school-teacher is gone, the male clerk is going, and already on the horizon of the academic market rises the Woman with the Spectacles, the rude survivalist who, in the coming generation, will dispense the elements of learning cut to order, without an afterthought of what it once has meant.

II
NATIONALISM
AND SOCIALISM

PROPHETS OF THE NEW AGE

Canadian casualties in the first Great War totalled almost a quarter of a million; the dead numbered about sixty thousand. Conservative estimates of the world-wide losses as a result of the war are ten million dead and twenty million wounded. Did this unprecedented carnage serve some providential purpose? Christian Socialists found such a purpose in the great proof the war provided that brotherhood could exist on a huge scale, and that democracy was actually stronger than authoritarianism.

Canada's most famous Christian Socialists were two Methodist ministers, Salem Bland (1859-1950), who taught for fourteen years at Wesley (later United) College in Winnipeg, and J. S. Woodsworth (1874-1942), who later founded the Co-operative Commonwealth Federation (CCF). Bland's remarkable little book, The New Christianity, *appeared in 1920. The following abridgement omits the important chapter on 'An American Christianity,' but its leading idea—'American Christianity believes in the progressive and aggressive amelioration of things. It believes in this life and its glorious possibilities.' —appears in Woodworth's reworking of the Lord's prayer, which was published in the* Grain Grower's Guide, *the Bible of prairie radicalism, in June 1915.*

Salem Bland: The New Christianity

The western nations to-day are like storm-tossed sailors who, after a desperate voyage, have reached land only to find it heaving with earthquakes. In almost every country involved in the great struggle, the war without has been succeeded by a war within.

Of this turmoil, industrial or political as it may be, two things can be said. One is, that no Western people is likely to escape it, and certainly not the peoples of this Continent. The other is, that even in its most confused and explosive forms it is a divine movement. Mistaken, sordid, violent, even cruel forms it may assume. Strange agencies it may utilize. None the less no student of history, no one, at least, who has any faith in the divine government of the world, can doubt that these great sweeping movements owe their power and prevalence to the good in them, not to the evil that is always mingled, to us at least, so perplexingly and distressingly with the good.

If this be so, no clearer duty can press upon all who wish to fight for God and not against Him than to try to discern the good factors that are at work and the direction in which they are moving. This duty is the more urgent since no one can tell when the clamor and the dust may make it very hard to discern either. . . .

The aim of the following discussion is, as the title suggests, twofold:

First, to show that in the unrest and confusion of the civilized nations two principles, above all others, are at work; that these two principles are both of them right beyond question; and that the disturbance and alarm so widely felt are both due to the fact that these principles are finding their way into regions from which they have hitherto been largely excluded—to show, in short, that the whole commotion of the world, in the last analysis, is chiefly due to the overflow of the two great Christian principles of democracy and brotherhood.

Second, to point out the only kind of Christianity which is adequate to meet the situation, or in other words, to describe the Christianity which, we may hope, is taking form. . . .

THE NEW SOCIAL ORDER

The history of the last nine hundred years in one, at least, of its most vital aspects is the history of the development of democracy. Perhaps in no other way can one so accurately discuss and estimate the progress achieved through this almost millennial period than in noting the successive conquests made by that great principle.

The first conquest was in the field of education. Modern democracy began with the rise of universities in the eleventh and twelfth centuries. Education had been the monopoly of the clergy, not, indeed, through any such design on the part of the clergy, but through the ignorance of the Northern race which had overrun Southern Europe and almost extinguished its culture, and through the unsettled and harassed condition of Europe which had delayed the growth of a new culture. It was only the clergy who felt that education was necessary.

It is one of the many inestimable services that the monasteries have rendered the modern world, that they preserved from destruction some of the precious flotsam and jetsam of that Greco-Roman literature which had for the most part been submerged, and that in these quiet retreats there grew up the schools which were to lay the foundations of yet nobler literatures.

Eventually, when a measure of peace came at last to the lands so long in distress and turmoil, the irrepressible impulses of the human soul for knowledge asserted themselves. The youth of Europe, eager to know, flocked in increasing numbers to the teachers who began to be famous, and the university took its rise.

Education placed in the hands of the people the key to other doors. As a natural consequence, democracy found its way into the jealously guarded realm of religion. After innumerable abortive, but glorious and not wasted, struggles for the right of the individual to find his own religion and dispense with ecclesiatical guides and directors, Northern Europe established the principle of democracy in religion in the great revolt known as the Protestant Reformation. That uprising was a very complex movement. Many motives mingled in it, but of these the desire for a purer faith was, probably, on the whole not so influential as the democratic passion for intellectual and religious freedom.

Concurrent with the overflow of democracy into the realm of religion was its overflow into politics. The evolution of political democracy is the distinctive glory of England. It is her contribution to world civilization as that of the Hebrew was monotheism, that of the Greek culture, and that of the Roman organization and law.

The barons, primarily in their own interest, wrested the Great Charter from a King who more recklessly and oppressively than his predecessors played the despot. In the provision of Magna Charta that the King should levy no more taxes without consent of the taxed was found the necessity of the coming together, first of the barons and the spiritual lords, later of the knights of the shire, and finally of the burghers of the towns—separate assemblies which soon coalesced and by their unification formed the English Parliament. English constitutional history from the reign of Henry III to the Revolution of 1688 is the history of the gradual supersession of the crown by Parliament, and of the ascendancy of the elective House of Commons over the hereditary House of Peers. The eighteenth century witnessed the development of Cabinet government; the nineteenth completed the great fabric of political democracy in those Franchise Acts which admitted to participation in the government—

In 1832, the propertied classes of the manufacturing towns;

In 1867, the artisans;

In 1884, the farm labourers;

In 1918, the women.

With these must be mentioned the Act of 1911 which constitutionally and decisively established the ascendency of the popular House over the Peers.

England broke the trail which all other peoples that have accepted democracy have followed. The mobile and logical intelligence of France, slower through historical conditions to snap the feudal bonds, when it was at last aroused, at one bound outstripped England. Not content to limit, it swept away both monarchy and the House of Peers. A still more striking illustration of how the last may be first may yet be yielded by that great half-European, half-Asiatic people, so long, apparently, impenetrable to democracy, but now in the obscure throes of a revolution which despite its initial disorders and excesses, may, it is perhaps possible to hope, give to Russia the high honour of being the first nation to achieve the last conquest of democracy—its triumph in the economic realm. For it would seem impossible to doubt that that final triumph of democracy can be long delayed. Autocracy and aristocracy overthrown in politics cannot stand in economics.

He who will trace a river like the Mississippi from its source, and find it growing in hundreds of miles from a stream that may be waded to a great river a mile in width and a hundred feet in depth, does not need to actually follow the river to its mouth to be assured that it must reach the sea. Such a river cannot be diverted or dammed. Obstructions will only serve to make its current more violent. . . .

In short, nothing will now satisfy the workers but a share in the control [of industry]. The most hopeful scheme of harmony would seem to be some such arrangement as the Whitley scheme which has been officially endorsed by the British Government. The essential features of the Whitley scheme are the organization of all the workers in any industrial area, the organization of all the employers, the creation of joint committees representative of both groups to fix wages and determine conditions of labor. And this is not the end but the beginning. The end, at least of this phase of industrial evolution, would appear to promise to be the disappearance of the capitalistic control of industry. So far as industries are not owned and managed by the community, they will be owned and managed by the workers that carry them on. The revolution will be accomplished when the men of inventive and organizing and directive ability recognize that their place is with the workers and not with the owners. Capitalistic control must pass away. It has, no doubt, played a necessary and useful part in the social evolution. It has shown courage and enterprise. But it has been, on the whole, rapacious and heartless, and its sense of moral responsibility has been often rudimentary. When the managers on whom it depends desert to the side of the workers, it will be patent how little capacity or service is in capitalism, and how little it deserved the immense gain it wrung from exploited labor and skill.

The process may be harder and slower than even the most sober-minded would estimate, or it may be much easier and quicker; but the process has begun, and there can be but one end. Feudalistic industry must follow feudalistic land holding. Feudalistic land-lordism went because the feudal lords were enormously overpaid in proportion to their services. When organizing and directive ability breaks the artificial bond that has associated it with capital, it will be seen how slight is the service capital has rendered and how enormously it has been overpaid.

Management is, of course, entitled to its wages, and under present conditions those wages must be relatively high, for managing ability is not abundant. What might be called the wages of capital have been unjustly high and are destined to fall until no man can afford to be a mere capitalist. To gain a livelihood he will be obliged to develop some productive function.

So long as industry must be maintained on a capitalistic basis, those furnishing the capital are entitled to a fair return on their investment, but the fashion of this capitalistic age passeth away. The control of money and credit is destined to gradually become a function of government.

A check must be placed on the fatal fashion money has of breeding money. Wages of labor, wages of invention, wages of superintendence, are just; profits of capital must grow less and less to the vanishing point.

The bitter conflict between capital and labor over the division of the profits will never be settled. It probably can never be settled. It will cease to be. Capital will cease to be a factor; only labor in the broadly inclusive sense of the term will remain.

The onward march of democracy, then, cannot be staid. It ought not. Democracy is nothing but the social expression of the fundamental Christian doctrine of the worth of the human soul. Democracies had found their way into human life before the revelation of the worth of the human soul in the redemptive work of Jesus Christ, but at their best, as in ancient Greece, they were restricted. Even that most glorious of all non-Christian democracies and, in some respects, most glorious as yet of all democracies non-Christian and Christian, the democracy of Athens, rested on a slave basis and excluded the man not possessing Athenian citizenship. But it was at least a noble anticipation, a sublime, if inconsistent, partial, and evanescent reaching-out after the democracy which Christianity can never be content till it has achieved, a democracy of religion, of culture, of politics, and of industry. The inherent dignity of every human soul must be recognized in every sphere of life. Heirs of God, joint-heirs with Christ—how is it possible to reconcile such august titles with servitude or subjection? A share in the control of church, community, industry is the Divine right of every normal man and woman.

The church of Jesus Christ should not be alarmed at the inundating progress of democracy. She, of all institutions, should not oppose it. It is her child. But even democracy, with its majestic vindication of the worth and dignity of the humblest and least-endowed human soul, is not so distinctively and gloriously the offspring of Christianity as is the principle of brotherhood. The movement towards brotherhood, the great master-passion of our day, is just the overflow of Christianity from the conventionally religious into the economic realm. One might rest the divine claim of Christianity on this irrepressible impulse to overflow.

The ancient heathen faiths, with a few possible exceptions, did not seek to overflow. They asked only a strictly delimited area, definite times, definite places, definite gifts, definite ceremonial observances and regulations. Outside that circumscribed area, life might go on as it would.

Even some forms of Christianity have shown little disposition to overflow. There has long been and still is a type of Christianity which fixes its eye on heaven and abandons earth. It is indifferent and acquiescent in regard to the affairs of this life, with no surge of passion for their purification and ennoblement. . . .

[This] is only the pale bloodless spectre of Christianity. Christianity is a torrent. It is a fire. It is a passion for brotherhood, a raging hatred of everything which denies or forbids brotherhood. It was a brotherhood at the first. Twisted, bent, repressed for nearly twice a thousand years, it will be a brotherhood at the last.

Does Christianity mean Socialism? It means infinitely more than Socialism. It means Socialism plus a deeper, diviner brotherhood than even Socialism seeks. It abhors inequality. It always has abhorred inequality. It seems almost inexplicable that the censors in these days of panicky attempts at suppression of incendiary ideas have not put under the ban such words as these:

> My soul doth magnify the Lord,
> And my spirit hath rejoiced in God my Saviour.
>
> . . .
>
> He hath showed strength with his arm:
> He hath scattered the proud in the imagination of their heart.
> He hath put down the princes from their thrones, and hath exalted
>   them of low degree.
> The hungry He hath filled with good things:
> And the rich He hath sent empty away.
>
> LUKE 1:46-53

or these:

> Let the brother of low degree rejoice in that he is exalted;
> But the rich in that he is made low; because, as the flower of the
>   grass he shall pass away.
> For the sun is no sooner risen with a burning heat but it
>   withereth the grass, and the flower thereof falleth, and the
>   grace of the fashion of it perisheth: so also shall the rich man
>   fade away in his ways.
>
> JAMES 1:9-11

'Nothing is hid,' was the word of Jesus, 'that shall not be made manifest, nor anything secret that shall not be known and come to light.' Many things have been hidden in that extraordinary amalgam that we call historical Christianity. St Paul hid in it his peculiar idiosyncratic contempt of marriage and lack of reverence for women, and these elements worked out in the millennial denial of woman's rights and the abnormalities and tragedies of asceticism. St Paul, again, and the unknown authors of the letter to the Hebrews and the fourth Gospel hid in primitive Christianity the Greek passion for metaphysics, and there emerged that perverse exaltation of dogma and orthodoxy which has, more than any other thing, withered the heart of the Church, smothered its fresh spontaneous life, kindled the infernal fires of heresy-trials and autos-da-fé. But Jesus hid something in historic Christianity, too, something deeper, diviner, mightier than any foreign ingredients added by other hands. Those commingling elements the Christianity of Jesus probably had to take up, test, and eventually reject. The only way, perhaps, in which the real meaning of Christianity could be discovered by men was in contrast with the innumerable and heterogenous adulterations of it. We come to truth, it has been profoundly said, by the exhaustion of error. Humanity cannot apparently be sure of the right road till it knows all the wrong roads as well. So it would certainly have seemed to be with historic Christianity.

But deepest and most vital of all the elements that have found their way into historic Christianity is what Christ hid there—the equality of brotherhood. That hidden element, too, must find its way to the light. Early repressed, driven in, well nigh smothered, it has, nevertheless, never been extinguished, for it is the secret force, the most deeply vital essence of Christianity. . . .

Nothing is more certain than that the human intellect must refuse eventually to acquiesce in that strange, illogical, and inconsistent jumble we call our Christian civilization. Something drives it irresistibly to consistency. The Christianity of Jesus means nothing if it does not mean brotherhood. Brotherhood means nothing if it does not mean a passion for equality. The story is told that when the Duke of Wellington, who, like so many other great soldiers of other times and of our own, was a devout man, was kneeling to receive the Communion in the village Church near his estate, a humble neighbour found himself, to his consternation, kneeling close beside the great Duke. He was rising at once to move away when the Duke put out his hand and detained him, saying, 'We are all equal here.' It was a fine spirit that the Duke showed for the time and in a country such as England was then. But it holds in it explosives of which probably the Duke did not dream. Equal at the table of their Common Lord! Then equal everywhere! Equality everywhere or equality nowhere! The soul of every man who has seen the divine beauty of equality must forever war against all limitations and impairments of it. Even human logic can not permanently tolerate such a fundamental incompatibility and irrationality as religious equality and social inequality sleeping in the same bed. Religious equality has already worked itself out in political equality. Even in aristocratic England the last vestige of political inequality has disappeared. The accepted formula is now—one man, one vote. It may be a harder problem to work out, but economic equality will be worked out to the same conclusion—one man, one share of all the conditions of human dignity and well being. . . .

Just as clear as the incompatibility of Christianity with social inequality is its incompatibility with business competition.

Competition for a livelihood, competition for bread and butter, is the denial of brotherhood. It is the antithesis of the Golden Rule. It is not the doing unto other men as we would that they should do to us. It is obedience to David Harum's parody of the Golden Rule, 'Do unto the other fellow as he wants to do to you, and do it fust.' The essential condition of competition is that always there shall be at least two men after the one contract, two men after the one job, two men after the custom, the patronage, the *clientèle* only sufficient for one. As a consequence, wherever competition exists, the success of one man always involves the failure of another. The man who gets the position knows that another man is suffering. The merchant who captures the trade knows that another must fail. The rule for success, as given by a highly successful business man of America, was, 'So conduct your business that your competitor will have to shut up shop.' The method is essentially disorderly and wasteful. Worse than that, it is inhuman.

It is difficult, indeed, to imagine how a more inhuman method of business could be devised short of methods which no man who had not ceased to be human would tolerate. Inhuman and dehumanizing. How deeply dehumanizing is seen in the effort of Christian men to justify it—the supreme illustration in our day of the morally blinding power of the accustomed, the familiar, and, above all, the profitable, which has made Christian men defenders of competition, of war, of the drink traffic, of the opium traffic, and of slavery.

Business competition to-day is, conceivably, as great an evil as ever intemperance was. Its working is more subtle, more widespread, more deeply destructive.

It hardens men. It dries up their natural and almost inextinguishable kindliness. It demoralizes them. It almost compels them to resort to crooked methods. It subjects them to temptations sometimes virtually irresistible. It presents them with the alternatives of failure and starvation for themselves and their loved ones or the doing of something, not right indeed, but which plenty of others do and which seems imperative. The honorable man has to compete with the dishonorable. The Hydrostatic Paradox of controversy, the Autocrat of the Breakfast Table has told us, lies in this, that as water in two connected tubes, however different their calibre, stands at the same level in both, so if a wise man and a fool engage in controversy, they tend to equality.* The more demoralizing Hydrostatic Paradox of business competition is its deadly tendency to bring the honorable man down to the level of the dishonorable.

It is not always demoralizing. There are men strong enough to maintain their integrity, even sometimes at great risk. But the strain of it, the feverishness of it, the narrowing influences of it, still fewer men escape.

Under the shade and fallen needles of the pine forest, no other vegetation can grow. Under the absorption, the exhaustion, of the fierce business competition of America, little else than business shrewdness, business insight, business knowledge can grow. A thousand seeds of culture, art, music, philanthropy, religion, human fellowship, home happiness die permanently or fail to germinate at all in the American business man. The struggle, like a remorseless machine, seizes him as a young man and works its way with him till it flings him off at the other end of the process, a failure with a dreary old age of dependence and uncertainty, or a successful man broken in health at fifty, to spend the rest of his days in search of health, or with the leisure and the means to develop the old tastes but the tastes themselves atrophied by long and enforced neglect.

In the name of the brotherhood of Christianity, in the name of the richness and variety of the human soul, the Church must declare a truceless war upon this sterilizing and dehumanizing competition and upon the source of it, an economic order based on profit-seeking. . . .

A profit-seeking system will always breed profiteers. It cannot be cleansed or sweetened or ennobled. There is only one way to Christianize it, and that is to abolish it. That is, it may well be believed, the distinctive task of the age that is now beginning, as the abolition of the liquor-traffic was of the age that is closing, and the abolition of slavery of a still earlier age.

This whole present industrial and commercial world, ingenious, mighty, majestic, barbaric, disorderly, brutal, must be lifted from its basis of selfish, competitive profit-seeking and placed squarely on a basis of co-operative production for human needs.

How this tremendous transformation will be eventually accomplished, probably no one of this generation can foresee. All we can see is some initial steps. . . .

The main line of development, however, it seems altogether probable, will be the extension of public ownership, municipal, state or provincial, and national.

There is no diviner movement at work in the modern world. It is emancipating, educative, redemptive, regenerating. 'Whatever says *I* and *mine*,' says one of the wisest and most Christ-like of Medieval Mystics, 'is Anti-Christ.' The converse is equally true. 'Whatever says *we* and *ours*, is Christian.' Public ownership, more extensively and powerfully than other human agency, teaches men to say *we* and *ours*. It teaches them to think socially.

To discredit and attack the principle of public ownership is to discredit and attack Christianity. It would seem to be the special sin against the Holy Ghost of our age. He who doubts the practicability of public ownership is really doubting human nature and Christianity and God. . . .

A LABOR CHRISTIANITY

A new social order is not more imperatively demanded than a new Christianity. Nothing less than this will suffice, nor will anything less be brought into being, in this crisis of transition. For while there are unchanging elements in Christianity, there are, it is equally certain, aspects that are constantly changing.

The devotion to the Lord Jesus Christ, which is the central and determinative principle of Christianity, is the least variable element; the institutions and dogmas by which that devotion is expressed and seeks to act upon the world, are the most variable.

Institutional Christianity is even more variable than dogmatic Christianity. It has varied greatly, is still changing, and its history shows that it is subject to the same influences as fashion the changing social order. This illuminating principle helps us to understand the past and to forecast the future of the Church. . . .

The most significant feature in the social development of the last hundred years has been the patient, persistent, oft-defeated, yet insuppressible struggle of the proletariat of the western world for human rights. The dead weight of the bygone ages was upon it. When had the men and the women who did the rough and necessary work of the world, smoothed the highways, dug the drains, built the houses and the bridges, carried the burdens over the mountains and across the seas, tilled the fields and cared for the herds and the flocks—when had they been other than the despised, ill-paid, ill-housed servants of the classes who through their fighting-power or their money-power could command the services of the toilers? What right had they to overturn the ancient order, an order which history recognized and the Church was willing to consecrate? Against the established order, against religious sanctions, against the combined authority of wealth and rank, against the legislative and military powers of governments, the workers had to carry on their new, uncharted, and desperate struggle unaided and alone. The Universities from their academic heights looked down on it with calm scientific interest. If any feeling was stirred, it was oftener contempt than pity. Even the Church of Christ was, with a few illustrious exceptions, unfriendly or timidly neutral. Nevertheless, in spite of calamitous setbacks, the movement made way against the public opinion of the dominant classes, against hostile legislation, against anarchic injunctions, against police and soldiers, and to-day Labor is the mightiest organized force in the world.

It is enthroned despotically in Petrograd and Moscow above the shattered ruins of the most imposing monarchy of the modern world. It is the strongest element in that welter of confusion and uncertainty to which the most powerful and compactly organized nation of modern times [Germany] has been reduced by its insane ambition, the indignation of mankind, and the justice of God.

Labor is the uncrowned king of Great Britain. Wisely led, there seems no reasonable aim it cannot realize.

In the United States in the Summer of 1916, in a straight issue between Labor and one of the most powerful capitalistic groups, the President and Congress of the United States wisely and justly capitulated to Labor.*

The futility of trying to 'smash the Labor unions' or to arrest the progress of the Labor movement is now sufficiently clear. As well try to smash a forty mile wide Alaskan glacier or arrest its onward march to the sea. Old precedents have lost their authority, old calculations and presuppositions fail or mislead. It is a new age the world is entering. As the determining factor in the social structure of Europe from 800 AD to 1500 was feudalism, and from AD 1500 to 1900 capitalism, so from 1900 onwards to the dawn, it may be, of still vaster changes as yet undescried, the dominant factor will be organized Labor.

If Labor, then, is to be the dominating factor in the age just opening, it becomes a question of deepest interest to discover the principles of the Labor movement.

A full answer to this question would be lengthy and might have elements of uncertainty, but the essential outstanding principles of the Labor movement are neither doubtful nor difficult to determine. They are three:—

1. Every man and every woman a worker.

The Labor movement has no place except for workers. Its essential demand is that every man and woman shall, during the normal working years, make a just contribution to the welfare of the social organism. It is determined that there shall be no place in society for idlers or exploiters. It is the deadly enemy of parasitism in all its Protean forms.

2. *The right of every worker to a living wage.*

This is nothing other than the assertion, in the only form that makes it more than iridescent froth, of the great Christian principle of the worth of the soul. It is a very modest and restricted assertion of that great principle, but it is a more substantial and significant assertion than has been made anywhere else. The Christian doctrine of the infinite worth of the human soul becomes clap-trap where this principle is not admitted.

3. *Union.*

The Labor movement is based on the solidarity of the workers. It abhors competition. It represents the triumph of the we-consciousness over the I-consciousness. It organizes in unions. There have been few things in history that had more of the morally sublime in them than the way in which the individual has been called upon by the Labor movement to risk, not his comfort merely or his advancement, but his livelihood, in defence of some one whom he would never know but with whom he was linked in the sacred cause of Labor.

And these principles of the Labor movement are at the same time the characteristics of the corresponding Christianity of the new age. For, as we found an aristocratic type of Christianity in the aristocratic medieval period, the social conditions demanding the aristocratic organization in Church and State and permitting no other, and as, in the age which succeeded the feudal, a freedom-loving, competitive, individualistic class imposed its character on the social and the ecclesiastical organization, so institutional Christianity will undergo a third transformation and, in a society dominated by Labor organizations, will become democratic and brotherly.

Protestantism must pass away. It is too rootedly individualistic, too sectarian, to be the prevailing religion of a collectivist age. It is passing away before our eyes. Everywhere it reveals the marks of decay or of transformation. It must change or die.

Not to Protestantism, not to Roman Catholicism, belongs the age now dawning, but to a new Christianity which will, indeed, have affinities with them both but still more deeply with the Christianity of Jesus.

This Christianity, indeed, is already here. Like its Master when He came, it is in the world and the world knows it not. It is still immature, undeveloped, unconscious even of its own nature and destiny. It will receive large and valuable contributions from both the great historic forms of Christianity, not improbably from the Eastern, or Greek Christianity, as well. But in promise and potency the coming Christianity is more fully and truly here in the Labor movement than in any of the great historic organizations. Perhaps a more accurate statement would be, that the Labor movement needs less radical change than the great Church organizations to become the fitting and efficient Christianity for the new age.

It needs, in the main, but two great changes.

1. *It must broaden.*

It must open its doors, as the British and Canadian Labor Parties are now doing, to include all kinds of productive work, of hand or brain. It must make room for all who contribute to the feeding, clothing, housing, educating, delighting of the children of men. It must include the inventor, the research scientist, the manager, as well as the manual worker; the men who grow things or who distribute them as well as those who make them; the professional class, who, on their part, must cease to regard themselves as other than men and women of labor. Labor must become, in short, the category to which all belong who really earn their living and do not seek to 'make' more than they earn.

2. *Labor must recognize the Christianness of its own principles.*

I do not say Labor must become Christian. It is profoundly and vitally Christian in its insistence on the right of the humblest man or woman to human conditions of life, in its corresponding denial of the right of any human being to live on the labor of others without rendering his own equivalent of service, in its devotion to the fundamental Christian principle of brotherhood.

The Draft Report on Reconstruction, for example, prepared near the close of 1917 for the Labor party of Britain, is not only the ablest and most comprehensive programme of social reconstruction so far drawn up, but in its aims and methods and spirit it is profoundly Christian, a thousand times more Christian than the ordinary ecclesiastical pronouncement, though the name of Christ does not occur in it. The need is not so much that Labor become Christian, as that it become clearly conscious that it is Christian and can realize itself and win its triumph only on Christian lines.

It is not strange, after all, that among working men should arise the Church which is to give the truest interpretation of Christianity. The Lord Jesus was Himself a working man and brought up in a working man's home; His chief friends and chosen apostles were mostly working men. How can He be fully understood except through a working man's consciousness? The high, the served, the rich, the mere scholars, as such, are not fitted to understand Christianity. Individuals of exceptional character and insight may escape the limitations of their environment and education, but in any large community interpretation the working man's consciousness would seem to be essential. And, on any large scale, Christianity has never found such an expression as the Labor movement promises to give it—so essentially and predominately democratic and brotherly.

Labor and Christianity, then, are bound up together. Together they stand or fall. They come into their kingdom together or not at all. It is the supreme mission of the prophetic spirit at this fateful hour to interpret Labor to itself, that it may not in this hour of consummation miss the path. To turn away from Christianity now would be for Labor to turn away from the throne. But it will not. Mankind is in the grasp of divine currents too strong to be resisted. . . .

THE GREAT CHRISTIANITY

Is it possible for us at this stage to discern at least the outline of the Great Christianity that is to be?* -

Certainly, every great historic form of Christianity has been tried by history and found wanting. As much of primitive Jewish Christianity as refused to merge in the large Catholic Christianity of the Greco-Roman world dried up into an unfruitful, bigoted, and eccentric heresy and perished.

Greek Christianity emphasized doctrine and tore itself by doctrinal disputes into a shattered, helpless welter of vituperative sects, powerless to spread the Gospel, powerless to withstand the Mohammedan—the shame and tragedy of Christian history.

Latin Christianity emphasized the organization and became the enemy of freedom and progress which, with few exceptions, every Roman Catholic people has had to fight and dethrone to escape intellectual and moral decay and death.

Teutonic Christianity has emphasized freedom and the rights of the individual. Like Islam, it has been a fighting faith. And judgment has fallen on it in its loss of unity, its bitter and wasteful sectarian wrangles, and the ferocious strife between labor and capital, the outcome of which may be one of the great tragedies of history.

Protestantism[1] has taught her people to fight for the rights and now is helpless before the selfish conflict of her own children that have learned too well her spirit.

In the great industrial conflict now reaching its height, one may safely prophesy Protestantism will perish—or be transformed.

She has taught her children to think; she has taught them to cherish freedom; she has not taught them to love.

The future belongs neither to Roman Catholicism nor to Protestantism. Roman Catholicism is too aristocratic and distrustful of freedom. The modern man will no more go back to medieval Christianity than to medieval feudalism. There is a drift from Protestantism to-day, but the drift from Roman Catholicism has been far greater. To fulfil its destiny, Roman Catholicism must accept freedom of thought; magnificently democratic as it has been from the beginning in some respects—the chair of St Peter being accessible to the humblest peasant's son—it must accept a deeper and wider democracy.

Protestantism, on the other hand, must become heart-broken over its divisions, religious and social. It must become more brotherly, more lowly, more worshipful, in a word, more childlike.

It is unthinkable that either of these great forms of Christianity will pass away. They will change. They are already changing, and each, as it changes, moves toward the other.

Thought and life move through conflict to unity. Thesis—antithesis—synthesis—that is the great law. The great and, perhaps, inevitable stage of antithesis that has divided Christendom for four centuries is drawing to a close. . . .

It is a lovely and thrilling hope that the twentieth century may prove to be the century of the Great Christianity, the Christianity which will extinguish neither Latin nor Teutonic Christianity but comprehend and blend them, the simple, yet free and varied, democratic, passionate Christianity of all who love the Lord Jesus Christ and seek His Kingdom on the earth, the Christianity which was the first and will be the last. . . .

But something more must be said about the Great Christianity.

It may be that Latin Christianity and Teutonic combined do not represent the full splendor and power of Christianity, and that the drastic social changes which must be carried out in the next quarter of a century, or even in a briefer period, call for the re-inforcement of another race and another sort of Christianity.

The distinctive Greek Christianity of the first five or six centuries made its contribution and passed away with the vanishing of the original and pure Hellenic race. But there is a Greek Christianity which has found a new lease of life and a new home in that race which has largely replaced the Greek in his own home and has diffused itself over most of eastern Europe, the Slavonic. There is a great Christianity which is still called Greek, but which is rather Slavonic Christianity, and which might more narrowly and specifically be called Russian Christianity, after that people who constitute the largest section of Greek Christianity and promise to be the most influential.

It may well be that the Great Christianity which the world so desperately needs will be neither Latin nor Teutonic Christianity nor both in combination, but a blend of Latin and Teutonic and American and Russian Christianity, and it does not seem unlikely that the contribution of the last of the four may be the most precious and vital of them all. Perhaps in the part Russia is destined to play in the next fifty years will be found the most striking example in all history of how it is God's way to choose the foolish things of the world that He may put to shame them that are wise; and the weak things of the world that He may put to shame the things that are strong; and the base things of the world and the things that are despised that He may bring to nought the things that are [exalted?].

The Slav has been the Cinderella of the European sisterhood. Perhaps we might say, the ugly duckling. From a military point of view he has been no match for the Teuton. In the long struggle of the last thousand years between the Teuton and the Slav, the Teuton has nearly always showed himself the stronger. For centuries he has ruled over the Slav. In the industrial arts, in all that pertains to the utilization of natural resources for the material well-being of men, in agriculture and mining and manufacturing and trading, the Slav has been immeasurably more backward. Mastered and oppressed by the Teuton on the West, subjugated for centuries by the Tartar on the East, the Slav has remained until yesterday a people forgotten and despised, shrouded in poverty, ignorance, mystery. And now out of that twilight he has stepped, ignorant, fanatical, and in his ignorance or superstition capable of ferocity, yet essentially the most childlike, the most religious, the most brotherly, the most idealistic of European peoples. What other people call their country, what the Russian calls his—*holy* Russia?

The peoples of the West, especially the Teutonic or the Anglo-Saxon, are weak where they are strong. It is their practicalness that has given them their high place; it is their practicalness which keeps them from the highest. It is hard for them to believe in a Holy City. If they do believe in it, they do not care to seek it till they are sure of a practicable road. But the Slav instinctively believes in a Holy City, and only needs to be told where it is to be found to set out forthwith over rivers, bogs, and rugged mountain ranges.

And it is just these things the Western world needs in this crisis—the spirit of the little child, the spirit of brotherhood, the sense of the pre-eminence of religion, the idealism that will risk everything for a dream.

The first movements of the awakened Russian may be unsteady. His new found freedom may act on him with intoxicating, almost deranging power. But they know little of the real Russian soul who dread the liberation of that long-prisoned soul and its free play on the Western world.

In the material ground-work of our civilization, its farming, its mining, its building of steamships, of railroads, of modern cities, the Teutonic races have taken the lead. They have builded the house. Now, it may be, when the finer problems arise of living in the home in harmony and helpfulness and in a high and holy spirit, it is the Slav who, in his turn, will take the lead. The Greek, the Italian, the Frank, the Spaniard, the Anglo-Saxon have successively held the premier place. The day of the Slav may now be dawning.

Nor yet is our forecast of the Great Christianity complete. It may be that there awaits us, though in a more distant future, a still more striking illustration of how God chooses for honor the despised things of the world. Of all races the most despised, the most oppressed, has been the African, and that not for generations or centuries but for millenniums. Europe, Asia, and America have all made Africa their servant. The dark Continent stands pre-eminent in suffering and in service. But it is in suffering and in service that He, too, the Coming King, has been pre-eminent. One reason why Africa has been the hunting ground of the slaver from immemorial times is because in the African nature immemorially and inextinguishably is the readiness to serve. All other races love to rule; some of them, like the Latin and the Teutonic, have been intensely proud, greedy of power, and averse from service. The African race is the one race which has by nature the spirit of Him who came not to be ministered unto but to minister. The African race, too, is of all races the most childlike, the most care-free, the one most ready to delight in simple things and the things of to-day. The white race, in comparison, are old, vigilant, suspicious, anxious, care-worn. There is no question which, in these respects, is nearest the ideal of Jesus. The greedy, ambitious spirit of the Western nations, never contented, their delight in to-day always poisoned by the fear or the fascination of to-morrow, is far from the spirit of Jesus. It may be that the white man will yet have to sit at the feet of the black, and that, when Christ is glorified, it will be that race that has, beyond all other races, trodden Christ's path of suffering and service which, beyond all others, will be glorified with Him.

The re-action of the uncounted millions of Asia on Christianity—the contributions of the ancient and deeply experienced brown and yellow races to that religion in which alone they can find their fullest development—is another fascinating subject for enquiry and speculation; but these influences, potent and inescapable as they promise to be, fall outside the limits of the period considered by this book.

AUTHOR'S NOTE

[1] It is, perhaps, scarcely necessary to remark that Protestantism is here being compared, not with Roman Catholicism, but with ideal Christianity. Roman Catholicism, too, has been a fighting faith, and in the appalling century and a half of religious wars that set in with the Protestant Reformation it was the older faith that first resorted to force.

J.S. Woodsworth: Thy Kingdom Come

Otherworldly religion is rapidly becoming a thing of the past. Our hymns still tell us that 'there is a happy land, far, far away', but most of us are really not so much concerned with that 'beautiful isle of somewhere' as we are in making Canada a country in which our children can live happy and noble and useful lives. Nowadays it would be a very abnormal child indeed who could say, 'I want to be an angel and with the angels stand, a crown upon my forehead, a harp within my hand.' Most healthy children would much prefer to skip and play ball with a happy group of school fellows. Some weary pilgrims may sigh for the rest of 'the sweet bye and bye'. Most sturdy Christians are happiest when they are up and doing 'with a heart for any fate'. Let me in this connection quote a totally different kind of song which occurs to me. It is included in the collection used by the Industrial Workers of the World. While doggerel of the worst kind, it hits off the situation very well. Undoubtedly the needy no longer want the consolation of a 'sweet bye and bye':

> Long haired preachers come out every night;
> Try to tell us what's wrong and what's right;
> But when asked how about something to eat
> They will answer with voices so sweet:
>
> *Chorus*:
> You will eat bye and bye
> In that glorious land above the sky;
> Work and pray, live on hay,
> You'll get pie in the sky, when you die.

Of course that is shocking—that is why we quote it! Too long the church has emphasized the future and neglected the present. How we have managed so long to make otherworldly the plain and simple and homely teachings of Jesus is a mystery. The petition 'give us each day our daily bread' has been interpreted as a prayer for spiritual strength or mystical communion or sacerdotal needs, instead of the simple, natural, childlike prayer for the daily necessaries of life.

The petition 'thy kingdom come'—how we have twisted and expounded and spiritualized and futurized it! How does it read—'Thy kingdom come, thy will be done on earth as it is in heaven.' Surely that is simple. As one American journal puts it, 'Thy kingdom come, as in heaven, *so in Brownsville*.' That may sound sacrilegious, but Jesus was constantly shocking the false reverence and piety of the professed religious people of his day. Religion is not a cult. It is simply everyday living.

'Thy kingdom come', not in some future state in some far off world, and not in some vague way all over the universe, but thy kingdom come right here in Canada, in Manitoba, in Winnipeg, in Brownsville, in my own township.

What would that really mean? Several years ago the Governor-General was visiting one of our Western towns. The city fathers, wishing to create as good an impression as possible, undertook to put on a campaign to beautify the city. They cleared away the refuse; they paved some of the streets; they tore down some unsightly buildings; they repainted the public buildings; they put in new street lights; they decorated the stores—all for the Governor-General!

Our task is to make over this old world into God's kingdom; a wholesome, happy place for men and women and little children. The plague-spots must be cleaned out; the dark places must be made light; the crooked places straight and the rough places smooth. After all, is not that just what the old prophets taught a thousand years ago? But we have 'spiritualized' their teaching into an unreal philosophy. Is not that what Jesus taught? But primitive Christianity has, through the ages, become so hidden beneath ecclesiasticism that we have obtained at best a very false idea as to what it really is. But in our day, Jesus has been rediscovered and his teachings shine forth with new meaning. Think what it means to transform even a single district! Until a few years ago the Panama Canal zone was a death-trap. The French engineers were compelled to abandon the digging of the canal because of the fearful ravages of yellow fever. Then scientists discovered that yellow fever was caused by a germ carried by a certain kind of mosquito. The remedy was clear. Get rid of the mosquito and you get rid of yellow fever. The sanitary engineers were called in and set to work with a will. What a glorious fight against the powers of evil! Garbage was collected and burned; food was screened; marshes were drained; petroleum was poured over the ponds, the breeding-places of the mosquito; the sick were isolated and cared for; a hundred precautions were taken; with what result? Within a few years the whole region became one of the most healthful districts in the world, what someone has described as 'an international health resort'.

That is the sort of thing that must be done, not in many districts, but in all. It is, however, not merely sanitation that must be attended to. There are great economic and moral and social evils that must be abolished. Further, it is not merely a case of getting rid of the weeds. Good grain must be cultivated in their place. Clean, wholesome recreation, satisfying labour, stimulating associations—all these must find a place in the renewed world. This means that business and politics and amusement must be made over.

What a change must come in the programmes of the churches and other agencies interested in the bringing in of God's kingdom!

Some years ago, when in charge of a mission located in a poor district in North Winnipeg, I was called upon to conduct the funeral of one of the children of the neighbourhood. We came to the cemetery; there was a long row of tiny baby graves; a number were fresh made, as scores of babies were being carried off during the hot weather. Here was the grave into which we were to lower the little body, and beyond it were a number of half-dug graves; their future occupants were not yet dead, but the grave diggers knew they were coming—disease was rampant, and they were keeping ahead of their work.

I read the well-known service, 'For as much as it hath pleased Almighty God, in His wise Providence, to take out of the world the soul of the deceased . . .' And in my heart I said: 'That is not true.' I knew what had killed the baby—it was bad milk and bad housing. It was not fair to blame God for that of which we were guilty. It was not fair to tell the people that that was what God was like.

Next winter at a theatre meeting that I had instituted on Sunday evenings, we had one evening devoted to public health. The City Health Officer gave a lecture on how disease could be prevented. This was illustrated by means of moving pictures which showed how the fly developed, how it flew from the decaying refuse to the sugar bowl or from a spittoon to the baby's feeding bottle. It was a horrible exhibition—one saw snakes all night after it; but it was tremendously effective. Even the poor foreigners who could not understand English could understand the pictures.

But my church friends were shocked. Here was I, a minister of the Gospel, who had degenerated until I was running a moving picture show in a theatre on Sunday evenings! Well, to tell the truth, I sometimes was almost shocked at myself. But there came back to me the scene at the graveside the summer before. This was how the matter presented itself to me. If it was my religious duty to read the funeral service over the body of a dead baby, was it not as much my religious duty to try to save the babies alive?

Our church reports tell how many funerals the minister has attended during the year; I have never yet seen a report which told how many people's lives the minister had saved. 'Ah,' you say, 'the church's task is to save souls.' But in the church of the future, saving souls will, more and more, come to be understood as saving men and women and children. At least in this world souls are always incorporated in bodies, and to save a man you must save him body, soul and spirit. To really save *one* man you must transform the community in which he lives. No man lives, or can live, to himself.

So we have a bigger problem than we had imagined and one that is very practical: the making of good roads; the getting rid of weeds; the improvement of stock; the providing of a ball ground; the higher education of the young people; a square deal for the stranger; better laws and better administration of law—all these are essentially religious, all are surely part of the work of bringing in the kingdom of God in your home district.

This, of course, does not mean that the church must make roads or provide ball grounds or give agricultural education or go in for politics or engage in co-operative enterprise. The church as an organization should, as a rule, keep out of these things. The church is not the only agency for the bringing in of the kingdom. Each agency has its own peculiar functions. Those of the church would seem to be to interpret, to inspire and to guide.

FRANK H. UNDERHILL

Frank Underhill (1889-1971), one of the bellwethers of Canadian politics, started out as a 'North York Presbyterian Grit'. After studying at Oxford, he taught history at the Universities of Saskatchewan and Toronto. In 1933 he wrote the first draft of the Regina Manifesto and thus ranks as one of the founders of Canadian socialism. He was also, however, one of the finest examples of Canadian liberalism, and after his retirement from teaching in 1955 he was named curator of Laurier House in Ottawa, a Liberal patronage appointment.

For more than twenty years Underhill contributed regularly to The Canadian Forum. *The first selection below is his column, 'O Canada', from the December 1929 issue. The second selection, his 1946 Presidential Address to the Canadian Historical Association, could serve as an introduction to the present anthology, for it deals with a question that weighs heavily on the minds of students of Canadian political thought: why have we Canadians had relatively little to say about the deeper problems of our civilization?*

O Canada,
Our Land of Crown Corporations

An honest attempt to enumerate the points in which our Canadian civilization differs from that of the United States is apt to be almost as brief as the famous essay upon snakes in Ireland. The underlying conditions which have determined the character of the two peoples are so similar. Each is a nation made up of the descendants of Europeans who came and settled in an empty continent that possessed almost unlimited natural resources; the history of each has consisted of the process of exploring and exploiting a half-continent. The factors in their history which have made for differences count for little compared with this fundamental economic similarity. That one of them in the course of its growth had a violent quarrel with the mother-country and severed its political connection while the other grew up to independence without any such political breach is relatively unimportant; and it would be recognized as such by everybody were not our minds dominated by too much study of political history and too little study of social and economic history. It was not the Declaration of Independence which made the Americans a separate people, it was the Atlantic Ocean; and Canada is on the same side of the Atlantic. Most of the superficial differences between the two people on which our good patriots are wont to dwell are due simply to the fact that the Americans have filled up their part of the continent more rapidly than we have ours. They are today more highly industrialized and urbanized than we are. The pace with which they have gone through the revolutionary social changes of the last century has resulted in the restlessness, the volatility, and the riotous exuberance of American life compared with which our Canadian decorum seems either dull or dignified, according to the point of view of the observer. But the pace of our Canadian life is quickening. We shall soon have little to learn from them in the art of getting rich quick.

The most distinctive feature of our Canadian life, one would think, should be our experience in building up a new nationality in the North American environment out of the two races, French and English. Yet, when one gets away from the rhetoric of the *bonne entente* orators, one is puzzled to say what particular quality in our life can be singled out as due to our bi-racial experience. The two races have never coalesced, have never understood one another or tried to understand one another. When they do come into contact each shows its worst side to the other. The French, so we are told, have a native folk literature and art which is a real contribution to the culture of North America; but the only Frenchman most of us ever see is the aggressive Quebec cleric or the jobbing politician at Ottawa. And when they picture to themselves the typical English Canadian he bears a strong resemblance to the Toronto Orangeman. The two races have never solved the most elementary problem of living together, that of education. Contact with each other has only served to accentuate and harden the intolerant qualities of each. They live together in an uneasy balance of power, and we seem as far today as ever from the time when 'Canadian' and *'Canadien'* will mean the same thing. That French-Canadian civilization is different from that of the United States is obvious. But its only effect upon us English Canadians has been to strengthen the qualities which make us like the Americans.

If we are to look for anything distinctively Canadian then, it must be found in the way in which we have handled the social and economic questions which arise in the process of exploiting the resources of our half of the continent. And here one does observe some features in our life which do not appear south of the line. We have not given ourselves up entirely to the unrelieved capitalistic individualism of our American neighbours. In such enterprises as the Ontario Hydro, the Canadian National Railways, and the provincial telephone systems of the West we have experimented in another method of providing public services than that of trusting to the private capitalist in search of profit. Their success has implanted pretty firmly in the minds of a good many Canadians at least a belief in the virtues of the public ownership and operation of public utilities which seems to be entirely lacking in the United States. But the fight for the Hydro in Ontario and for the National Railways in Canada at large is still too recent for anyone to delude himself into an optimistic faith that the cause of public ownership is won in this country. The greatest fights are still in the future. It is still possible to manipulate politics at Ottawa so that the publicly-owned railway is at a disadvantage in competing with the private one for branch lines in new territory. And the enormous development of hydro-electric power which will take place in the next generation makes one strain one's eyes rather anxiously for a second Beck [Sir Adam Beck, first chairman of Ontario Hydro] who shows no signs of appearing. Have the Canadian people sufficient alertness as to the future to save themselves from the gigantic Super Power Trust into which the Americans are rushing with such joyous abandon at present? If they have not, it will not make much difference ultimately whether the management of the trust is located in Montreal or in New York. There is no real difference, except in names, between being controlled by a Holt [Sir Herbert Holt, president of the Royal Bank] and being controlled by a Morgan [J. Pierpont Morgan, American financier]. And nothing is more certain than that the Morgan of the next generation will gobble up the Holt of the next generation. The best defence of a distinct Canadian nationality is to make sure that these great strategic public services shall be owned and controlled by the people themselves.

When one moves among Americans one is struck by their fatalistic attitude toward these problems of the relation of the public to its public services. One meets plenty of individuals who would like to imitate our Canadian public ownership enterprises, but the idea that it is possible for the American people in its collective capacity to stir itself out of the slumber into which it has been lulled by persistent private ownership propaganda is accepted by everyone as visionary. That democratic political machinery can be utilized as a fruitful method by which the people can provide for their own future is a faith which has almost died out among intelligent Americans. One of the hopeful things about Canada is that we have not yet come to this complete despair about our politics, and that enterprises like the Ontario Hydro and the National Railways show that we are still capable of using our political machinery for constructive purposes. But when the people of the pivotal province of Ontario go through a general election in which millions of words are wasted on prohibition and hardly a word is said on either side about the St Lawrence Waterway, one begins to wonder whether that particular community is capable of providing for its future.

It is to the Canadian West that one must turn when one looks for a people who have shown that capacity for tackling their common problems in common which is presupposed in all democratic theory. The Hydro in Ontario was too exclusively the work of one man of genius. It has aroused a great pride in the people of Ontario but their experience with it has been too largely passive, and whether they have the positive ability to carry on in the spirit of Beck is still in question. On the prairie the farmers are working out for themselves a genuine co-operative community. They have refused to acquiesce in the exploitation to which agriculture has been subjected over all the rest of the continent. They have organized to sell their own products and will soon be organized to buy co-operatively all that they need to buy. The most hopeful thing about the whole movement is that, with the exception of Mr H.W. Wood [president of the United Farmers] of Alberta, it has as yet produced no great outstanding leader. It is still throwing up leaders from all sides as they are needed, a fact which shows how really popular it is and how deeply it has its roots in the life of the people. Whatever one may think about their political theories, there can be no question that the prairie farmers have rescued their provincial politics from the atmosphere of futility which pervades our Eastern provinces; and they are probably right in thinking that no healthy political life is possible in a community which has not emancipated itself from the meaningless bickering of the two old political parties. One is sometimes alarmed at the amount of revivalism which the Western farmers work into their co-operative undertakings. Past experience on this continent has gone to show that messianic prophecy does not mix well with plain business honesty and common sense. But their movement is the most hopeful thing in Canadian life at present. . . .

Some Reflections on the Liberal Tradition in Canada

'The reader is about to enter upon the most violent and certainly the most eventful moral struggle that has ever taken place in our North American colonies. . . . That I was sentenced to contend on the soil of America with Democracy, and that if I did not overpower it, it would overpower me, were solemn facts which for some weeks had been perfectly evident to my mind.' So wrote Sir Francis Bond Head in his *Narrative*,[1] the famous apologia for the policy of his governorship of Upper Canada. The issue as he saw it, and as his contemporaries in Canada saw it, was not merely whether the British North American colonies were to set up a responsible form of government; it was the much deeper one of whether they were to follow the example of the United States and commit themselves to achieving a democratic form of society. And good Sir Francis appealed with confidence to all right-thinking property-owning Englishmen against what he termed 'the insane theory of conciliating democracy' as put into practice by the Colonial Office under the guidance of that 'rank republican', Mr Under-Secretary Stephen. No doubt, if the phrase had been then in use he would have accused Stephen, and Lord Glenelg and Lord Durham, of appeasement. In rebuttal of Durham's criticisms of the Upper Canada Family Compact he wrote:

> It appears from Lord Durham's own showing that this 'Family Compact' which his Lordship deems it so advisable that the Queen should destroy, is nothing more nor less than that 'social fabric' which characterizes every civilized community in the world. . . .'The bench', 'the magistrates', 'the clergy', 'the law', 'the landed proprietors', 'the bankers', 'the native-born inhabitants', and 'the supporters of the Established Church' [these were the social groups which Durham had defined as composing the Family Compact] form just as much '*a family compact*' in England as they do in Upper Canada, and just as much in Germany as they do in England. . . . The '*family compact*' of Upper Canada is composed of those members of its society who, either by their abilities and character, have been honoured by the confidence of the executive government, or who by their industry and intelligence, have amassed wealth. The party, I own, is comparatively a small one; but to put the multitude at the top and the few at the bottom is a radical reversion of the pyramid of society which every reflecting man must foresee can end only by its downfall.[2]

Sir Francis' statement is as clear and as trenchant an enunciation of the anti-democratic conservative political philosophy of his day as could be quoted from the American conservatives who were fighting Jacksonian Democracy at this same time or from the English conservatives who were fighting the Reform Bill or Chartism. As we all know, this 'moral struggle' over the fundamental principles on which society should be based, which Sir Francis correctly discerned as representing the real meaning of the Canadian party strife of the 1830s, was to be decided against him and his tory friends. The century since his *Narrative* was published has been, in the English-speaking world at least, a period of continuously developing liberal and democratic movements. Liberalism has merged into democracy. Today the people of Canada are recovering from the second world war within a generation in defence of democracy. Presumably, considering the sacrifices we have shown ourselves willing to make for the cause, we Canadians cherish passionately the liberal-democratic tradition which is our inheritance from the nineteenth century. Presumably, the growth of liberal-democratic institutions and ideas in our political, economic, and social life is one of the main themes in our Canadian history, just as it certainly is in the history of Great Britain and the United States, the two communities with which we have most intimately shared our experience.

Yet it is a remarkable fact that in the great debate of our generation, the debate which has been going on all over the western world about the fundamental values of liberalism and democracy, we Canadians have taken very little part. We talk at length of the status which our nation has attained in the world. We have shown in two great wars that we can produce soldiers and airmen and sailors second to none. We have organized our productive resources so energetically as to make ourselves one of the main arsenals and granaries of democracy. We have achieved political autonomy and economic maturity. But to the discussion of those deep underlying intellectual, moral and spiritual issues which have made such chaos of the contemporary world we Canadians are making very little contribution.

Our Confederation was achieved at the very time in the nineteenth century when a reaction was beginning to set in against the liberal and democratic principles which, springing from eighteenth-century Enlightenment, had seemed up to that moment to be winning ever fresh victories. The liberal nationalism of the early part of the century was beginning to turn into something sinister, the passionate, exclusive, irrational, totalitarian nationalism that we know today. The optimistic belief in human equality and perfectibility was beginning to be undermined by new knowledge about man provided by the researches of biologists and psychologists. At the same time technological developments in mass production industries were building up a new social pyramid with a few owners and managers at the top and the mass of exploited workers at the bottom; and new techniques of mass propaganda still further emphasized this division of mankind into élite and masses. The freedom which our Victorian ancestors thought was slowly broadening down from precedent to precedent seemed to become more and more unreal under the concentrated pressure of capitalistic big business or of the massive bureaucratic state. In such surroundings, the liberal spirit does not flourish. And the more reflective minds of our day have been acutely aware that the mere winning of military victories under banners labelled 'liberty' or 'democracy' does not carry us very far in the solving of our deeper problems.

Canada is caught up in this modern crisis of liberalism as are all other national communities. But in this world-debate about the values of our civilization the Canadian voice is hardly heard. Who ever reads a Canadian book? What Canadian books are there on these problems? What have we had to say about them that has attracted the attention of our contemporaries or has impressed itself upon their imagination? In the world of ideas we do not yet play a full part. We are still colonial. Our thinking is still derivative. Like other peoples Canadians have of late expended a good deal of misdirected energy in endeavours to export goods without importing other goods in return. But we continue to import ideas without trying to develop an export trade in this field. We are in fact, as I have said, colonial. For our intellectual capital we are still dependent upon a continuous flow of imports from London, New York, and Paris, not to mention Moscow and Rome. It is to be hoped that we will continue to raise our intellectual standards by continuing to import from these more mature centres, and that we will never try to go in for intellectual autarchy. But international commerce in ideas as well as in goods should be a two-way traffic at least and preferably it should be multilateral. . . .

Now it seems to me—and this is more or less the main theme of the present rambling discursive paper—that this intellectual weakness of Canada is a quality which shows itself through all our history. In particular it is to be discerned in that process of democratization which is the most important thing that has happened to us, as to other kindred peoples, during the last hundred years. When we compare ourselves with Britain and the United States there is one striking contrast. Those two countries, since the end of the eighteenth century, have abounded in prophets and philosophers who have made articulate the idea of a liberal and equalitarian society. Their political history displays also a succession of practical politicians who have not merely performed the functions of manipulating and manoeuvring masses of men and groups which every politician performs, but whose careers have struck the imagination of both contemporaries and descendants as symbolizing certain great inspiring ideas. We in Canada have produced few such figures. Where are the classics in our political literature which embody our Canadian version of liberalism and democracy? Our party struggles have never been raised to the higher intellectual plane at which they become of universal interest by the presence of a Canadian Jefferson and a Canadian Hamilton in opposing parties. We have had no Canadian Burke or Mill to perform the social function of the political philosopher in action. We have had no Canadian Carlyle or Ruskin or Arnold to ask searching questions about the ultimate values embodied in our political or economic practice. We lack a Canadian Walt Whitman or Mark Twain to give literary expression to the democratic way of life. The student in search of illustrative material on the growth of Canadian political ideas during the great century of liberalism and democracy has to content himself mainly with a collection of extracts from more or less forgotten speeches and pamphlets and newspaper editorials. Whatever urge may have, at any time, possessed any Canadian to philosophize upon politics did not lead to much writing whose intrinsic worth helped to preserve it in our memory.

At least this is true of us English-speaking Canadians. Our French-speaking fellow citizens have shown a much greater fondness and capacity for ideas in politics than we have; but their writings, being in another language, have hardly penetrated into our English-Canadian consciousness.

We early repudiated the philosophy of the Manchester School; but in the long history of our Canadian 'National Policy' it is difficult to find any Canadian exposition of the anti-Manchester ideas of a national economy, written by economist, business man, or politician, which has impressed itself upon us as worthy of preservation. Our history is full of agrarian protest movements, but the ordinary Canadian would be stumped if asked to name any representative Canadian philosopher of agrarianism. And the most notable illustration of this poverty of our politics at the intellectual level is to be found in the fact that while we were the pioneers in one of the great liberal achievements of the nineteenth century—the experiment of responsible government, which transformed the British Empire into the Commonwealth, and which has thrown fresh light in our own day on the possibility of reconciling nationalism with a wider international community—even in this field, in which our practical contribution was so great, there has arisen since the days of Joseph Howe no Canadian prophet of the idea of the Commonwealth whose writings seem inspiring or even readable to wider circles than those of professional historians.

This seeming incapacity for ideas, or rather this habit of carrying on our communal affairs at a level at which ideas never quite emerge into an articulate life of their own, has surely impoverished our Canadian politics. Every teacher of Canadian history has this fact brought home to him with each fresh batch of young students whom he meets. How reluctant they are to study the history of their own country! How eagerly they show their preference for English or European or (if they get the chance) for American history! For they instinctively feel that when they get outside of Canada they are studying the great creative seminal ideas that have determined the character of our modern world, whereas inside Canada there seem to be no ideas at issue of permanent or universal significance at all. I can myself still remember the thrill of appreciation with which as a university freshman I heard a famous professor of Greek[3] remark that our Canadian history is as dull as ditchwater, and our politics is full of it. Of course, there is a considerable amount of ditchwater in the politics of all countries; my professor was more conscious of it in Canada because he missed here those ideas which he found in the politics of classical Greece. And as far as I have been able to observe, young students of this present generation are still repelled by Canadian history because they find in it little more than the story of a half-continent of material resources over which a population of some twelve million economic animals have spread themselves in a not too successful search for economic wealth. . . .

This general failure of our Canadian politics to rise above a mere confused struggle of interest groups has been no doubt due to a variety of causes. In the middle of the twentieth century it is rather too late for us to keep harping on the pioneer frontier character of the Canadian community as the all-sufficient answer to criticism. The young American republic which included a Jefferson and a Hamilton and a Franklin, not to mention many of their contemporaries of almost equal intellectual stature, was a smaller and more isolated frontier community than Canada has been for a long time; but it was already by the end of the eighteenth century the peer of Europe in the quality of its political thinking and was recognized as such. We still remain colonial in the middle of the twentieth century.

One reason for our backwardness, and the reason which interests me most at the moment, has been the weakness of the Radical and Reform parties of the Left in our Canadian history. A healthy society will consist of a great majority massed a little to the right and a little to the left of centre, with smaller groups of strong conservatives and strong radicals out on the wings. If these minority groups are not present in any significant force to provide a perpetual challenge to the majority, the conservatives and liberals of the centre are likely to be a pretty flabby lot, both intellectually and morally.

For this weakness of the Left in Canada, the ultimate explanation would seem to be that we never had an eighteenth century of our own. The intellectual life of our politics has not been periodically revived by fresh drafts from the invigorating fountain of eighteenth-century Enlightenment. In Catholic French Canada the doctrines of the rights of man and of Liberty Equality Fraternity were rejected from the start, and to this day they have never penetrated, save surreptitiously or spasmodically. The mental climate of English Canada in its early formative years was determined by men who were fleeing from the practical application of the doctrines that all men are born equal and are endowed by their Creator with certain unalienable rights amongst which are life, liberty and the pursuit of happiness. All effective liberal and radical democratic movements in the nineteenth century have had their roots in this fertile eighteenth-century soil. But our ancestors made the great refusal in the eighteenth century. In Canada we have no revolutionary tradition; and our historians, political scientists, and philosophers have assiduously tried to educate us to be proud of this fact. How can such a people expect their democracy to be as dynamic as the democracies of Britain and France and the United States have been?

Then also it has never been sufficiently emphasized that our first great democratic upheaval a hundred years ago was a failure. In the United States, Jacksonian Democracy swept away most of the old aristocratic survivals and made a strong attack upon the new plutocratic forces. The Federalists disappeared; and their successors, the Whigs, suffered a series of defeats at the hands of triumphant Democracy. But the Canadian version of Jacksonian Democracy represented by the movements of Papineau and Mackenzie was discredited by the events of their abortive rebellions. And Canada followed the example of Britain rather than of the United States. Responsible government was a British technique of government which took the place of American elective institutions. Our historians have been so dazzled by its success that they have failed to point out that the real radicals in Canada were pushed aside in the 1840s by the respectable professional and property-owning classes, the 'Moderates' as we call them; just as the working-class radicals in Britain, without whose mass-agitation the Reform Bill could not have been passed, were pushed aside after 1832 for a long generation of middle-class Whig rule. The social pyramid in Canada about which Sir Francis Bond Head was so worried in 1839 was *not* upset; and after a decade of excitement it was clear that the Reform government was only a business men's government. When Baldwin and LaFontaine were succeeded by Hincks and Morin this was so clear that new radical movements emerged both in Upper and in Lower Canada, the Grits and les Rouges.

Now in North America the essence of all effective liberal movements—I assume in this paper that liberalism naturally leads towards democracy—must be that they are attacks upon the domination of the community by the business man. This was what the Democratic party of Jackson and Van Buren was. As

Mr Schlesinger has recently been pointing out in his brilliant book, *The Age of Jackson*,[4] the effectiveness of the Jacksonians was due to the fact that their leading ideas about the relations of business and government came primarily not from the frontier farmers of the West but from the democratic labour movements in the big cities and their sympathizers amongst the urban intellectuals. Jefferson had been mainly interested in political democracy; Jackson tackled the problem of economic democracy in a society becoming increasingly industrialized. The social equality of the frontier has never given agrarian democrats a sufficient understanding of the problems of a society divided into the rich and the poor of an urban civilization. Here we seem to come upon an important explanation for the weakness of all Canadian radical movements from the 1830s to the end of the century. They were too purely agrarian. The only force that could ultimately overcome the Hamiltonians must, like them, have its base of operations in the cities.

Mr Schlesinger has also pointed out that American conservatism was immensely strengthened when it transformed itself from Federalism to Whiggism. In the 1830s, as he puts it, it changed from broadcloth to homespun. 'The metamorphosis revived it politically but ruined it intellectually. The Federalists had thought about society in an intelligent and hard-boiled way. The Whigs, in scuttling Federalism, replaced it by a social philosophy founded, not on ideas, but on subterfuges and sentimentalities.'[5] But the Whigs learned the techniques of demagogy from the Jacksonians and set out to guide the turbulent new American democracy along lines that would suit the purposes of business. Surely we should remark that exactly the same metamorphosis took place just a little later in Canadian conservatism. The clear-cut anti-democratic philosophy of Sir Francis Bond Head and the Family Compact Tories was as obsolete and out-of-place in the bustling Canada of the 1850s as Federalism had been in the United States in the 1820s. The Macdonald-Cartier Liberal-Conservative party was American Whiggism with a British title. (And no doubt the British label on the outside added considerably to the potency of the American liquor inside the bottle.) The Liberal-Conservatives had made the necessary demagogic adjustments to the democratic spirit of the times; they had a policy of economic expansion to be carried out under the leadership of business with the assistance of government which was an almost exact parallel to Clay's Whig 'American System'. But there was no Jackson and no Jacksonian 'kitchen cabinet' in Canada to counter this Liberal-Conservatism.

The Grits and les Rouges did not quite meet the needs of the situation. What Rougeism, with its body of ideas from the revolutionary Paris of 1848, might have accomplished we cannot say; for it soon withered under the on-slaught of the Church. Grittism in Upper Canada was originally a movement inspired by American ideas, as its early fondness for elective institutions and its continuing insistence on 'Rep by Pop' show. But Brown's accession tended to shift the inspiration in the British direction. Brown himself became more and more sentimentally British as he grew older. Moreover, as publisher of the *Globe*, he was a business man on the make, and Toronto was a growing business centre. As Toronto grew, and as the *Globe* grew, the original frontier agrarianism of the Grits was imperceptibly changed into something subtly different. As early as January 3, 1857 the *Globe* was declaring: 'The schemes of those who have announced that Toronto must aspire no higher than to be "the Capital of an Agricultural District" must be vigorously met and overcome.' Brown defeated the radicals from the Peninsula in the great Reform convention of 1859, and by 1867 Grit leaders were more and more becoming urban business and professional men. A party which contained William McMaster of the Bank of Commerce and John Macdonald, the big wholesale merchant, was not likely to be very radical. Oliver Mowat, a shrewd cautious lawyer, was about to take over the direction of its forces in Ontario provincial politics; and its rising hope in the federal sphere was Edward Blake, the leader of the Ontario equity bar. Moreover, as Brown's unhappy experiences with his printers in [the strike of] 1872 were to show, the Reform party under *Globe* inspiration found difficulty in adjusting itself to the new ideas which industrialism was encouraging in the minds of the working class. Blake and Mowat, who dominated Canadian Liberal thinking after Brown, were not American democrats or radicals so much as English Whigs in their temperament, their training, and their political philosophy. For political equality and liberty they were prepared to fight; economic equality did not move them very deeply. And the same might be said about Laurier who succeeded them.

Another point worth noting is the effect of British influences in slowing down all movements throughout the nineteenth century in the direction of the democratization of politics and society. Inevitably, because of geographical proximity and the mutual interpenetration of the lives of the two North American communities, the urge towards greater democracy was likely to appear in Canada as an American influence; and since the survival of Canada as a separate entity depended on her not being submerged under an American flood, such influences were fought as dangerous to our Canadian ethos. Sir Francis Bond Head and the Tories of his time habitually used the words 'democratic' and 'republican' as interchangeable. Every Canadian movement of the Left in those days and since has had to meet accusations of Americanism, and in proving its sound British patriotism it has been apt to lose a good deal of its Leftism. Canadian Methodism, for example, widely influenced by its American connections, was on the Reform side of politics until the Ryerson arrangement in the 1830s with the British Wesleyans put it on the other side.

When we get down to the Confederation period no one can fail to see how markedly the British influence gives a conservative tone to the whole generation of the Fathers. Later Canadians have had to reflect frequently on the sad fact that the 'new nationality' was very imperfectly based upon any deep popular feeling. It has occurred to many of them, with the wisdom of hindsight, that Confederation would have been a much stronger structure had the Quebec Resolutions received the ratification of the electorate in each colony in accordance with American precedents. But the British doctrine of legislative sovereignty operated to override all suggestions that the people should be consulted; and Canadian nationality has always been weak in its moral appeal because 'We the People' had no formal part in bringing it into being.

Similarly British example was effective in delaying the arrival of manhood suffrage in Canada till towards the end of the century, though the Americans had adopted it in the early part of the century. The ballot did not become part of Canadian law until sanctioned by British precedent in the 1870s. The

Chancery Court which had long been a favourite object of radical attack in Upper Canada remained intact until jurists of the Mother Country had amalgamated the equity and common law jurisdictions there. And that strange constitutional device, the Canadian Senate, with its life appointees, was slipped into our constitution with the plea that appointment by the Crown was the British way of doing things. John A. Macdonald must have had his tongue in his cheek when he presented this Senate as a protector of provincial rights, its members being appointed by the head of the very federal government against which provincial rights were to be protected. In the privacy of the Quebec Conference, when they were constructing the second chamber, he had remarked to his fellow delegates: 'The rights of the minority must be protected, and the rich are always fewer in number than the poor.'* One wonders what George Brown or Oliver Mowat, the Grit representatives, must have said at this point, or whether the secretary, who caught Macdonald's immortal sentence, failed to take down their comments. Generally speaking, the notable fact is that in all this era of constitution making, and of constitution testing in the decades just after 1867, the voice of democratic radicalism was so weak.

On the other hand, when Britain began to grow really democratic towards the end of the nineteenth century, her example seemed to have little effect upon Canadian liberalism. The two most significant features in internal British politics since the 1880s have been the rise of industrial labour to a share of power both in the economic and in the political fields, and the growing tendency towards collectivism in social policy. We are only beginning to enter upon this stage of development in Canada today. Throughout it has been the conservative trends in English life that we have usually copied. And one of the few sources of innocent amusement left in the present tortured world is to watch the growing embarrassment of all those professional exponents in Canada of the English way of doing things, now that the English way threatens to become less conservative.

Of course, the great force, by far the most important force, weakening liberal and democratic tendencies in Canada after 1867 was the rush to exploit the resources of a rich half-continent. This was the age in American history which Parrington has called 'The Great Barbecue'.

> The spirit of the frontier was to flare up in a huge buccaneering orgy. . . . Congress had rich gifts to bestow—in lands, tariffs, subsidies, favors of all sorts; and when influential citizens had made their wishes known to the reigning statesmen, the sympathetic politicians were quick to turn the government into the fairy godmother the voters wanted it to be. A huge barbecue was spread to which all presumably were invited. Not quite all, to be sure; inconspicuous persons, those who were at home on the farm or at work in the mills and offices were overlooked. . . . But all the important people, leading bankers and promoters and business men, received invitations. . . . To a frontier people what was more democratic than a barbecue, and to a paternal age what was more fitting than that the state should provide the beeves for roasting? Let all come and help themselves. . . . But unfortunately what was intended to be jovially democratic was marred by displays of plebeian temper. Suspicious commoners with better eyes than manners discovered the favoritism of the waiters, and drew attention to their own meager helpings and the heaped-up plates of the more favored guests.[6]

Parrington's description fits the Canadian situation also, though our barbecue did not get going in full force till after 1896. In the first generation after Confederation, Canadian Liberals wandered mostly in the deserts of opposition because they could not produce any policy which could match in attractiveness the economic expansionism of the Conservatives. They criticized the extravagant pace of Conservative policy, they denounced the corruption of the Macdonald system, they pointed with true prophecy to the danger of building up great business corporations like the CPR which might become more powerful than the national government itself. But the spirit of the Great Barbecue was too strong for them. And when finally they did come into office under Laurier they gave up the struggle. The effort to control this social force of the business-man-on-the-make was abandoned. Their moral abhorrence of the methods of Macdonald gave place with a striking rapidity to an ever deepening cynicism. 'You say we should at once set to reform the tariff', Laurier wrote to his chief journalistic supporter after the victory of 1896. 'This I consider impossible except after ample discussion with the business men.'[7] And until he made the fatal mistake of reciprocity in 1911, the Liberal government was conducted on the basis of ample discussion with the business men.

It is easy to say that this was inevitable in the circumstances of the time. And indeed the remarkable fact about the Canada of the turn of the century is the slowness of other social groups in acquiring political consciousness and organizing movements of revolt against government by business men. American populism was only faintly reflected amongst Canadian farmers until the 1920s. The Progressive movement which helped to bring Theodore Roosevelt and Woodrow Wilson to the White House seemed to cause few repercussions north of the border. Everybody in Canada in those days was reading the popular American magazines as they carried on the spectacular campaigns of the muckraking era against the trusts. But this fierce attack next door to us against the domination of society by big business stirred few echoes in Canadian public life. Our Canadian millionaires continued to die in the odour of sanctity. Canadian liberalism in the Laurier era was equally little affected by the contemporary transformation of the British Liberal party into a great radical social-reform movement.

What seems especially to have struck visitors from across the ocean was the absence of any effective labour movement in Canadian politics. Both André Siegfried from France and J. A. Hobson from England remarked upon this phenomenon in the books which they published in 1906. 'When the workers of Canada wake up,' said Hobson, 'they will find that Protection is only one among the several economic fangs fastened in their "corpus vile" by the little group of railroad men, bankers, lumber men and manufacturing monopolists who own their country.'[8]

The Great Barbecue was still in full swing when these observers studied Canada. As I have said already, liberalism in North America, if it is to mean anything concrete, must mean an attack upon the domination of institutions and ideas by the business man. In this sense Canadian liberalism revived after 1918, to produce results with which we are all familiar. Amongst those results, however, we can hardly include any advance in the clarity or the realism of the liberal thinking of the so-called Liberal party, however much we may be compelled to admire its dexterity in the practical arts of maintaining itself in office. In the realm of political ideas its performance may be correctly described as that of going on and on and on, and up and up and up. But I am now touching upon present-day controversies. And, whatever latitude may be allowed to the political scientist, we all know that the historian cannot deal with current events without soiling the purity of his scientific objectivity.

In the meantime Canadian historians must continue to study and to write the history of their country. I have devoted these rambling remarks to the subject of political ideas because I have a feeling that Canadian historiography has come to the end of an epoch. For the past twenty or thirty years, most of the best work in Canadian history has been in the economic field. How different groups of Canadians made their living, how a national economy was built up, how the Canadian economy was integrated into a world economy, these topics have been industriously investigated; and we have been given thereby a new and a deeper understanding of the basis of our national life. The climax in this school of activity was reached with the publication of the Carnegie series on Canadian-American relations and of the various volumes connected with the Rowell-Sirois Report.

The best work in the Carnegie collection is for the most part on the economic side. And the volume, published during the past year, which crowns the series—Professor Bartlet Brebner's *North American Triangle*—can hardly be praised too highly for the skill and insight with which the author brings out the pattern of the joint Canadian-American achievement in settling the continent and exploiting its economic resources, and with which he explains the practical working of our peculiar North American techniques and forms of organization. But it is significant that he has little to say about the intellectual history of the two peoples, about education, religion, and such subjects; and especially about the idea of democracy as understood in North America. Materials from research on the intellectual history of Canada were not, as a matter of fact, available to him in any quantity. Volume I of the Rowell-Sirois Report is likewise a brilliant and, within its field, a convincing exercise in the economic interpretation of Canadian history. But it is abstract history without names or real flesh-and-blood individuals, the history of puppets who dance on strings pulled by obscure world forces which they can neither understand nor control; it presents us with a ghostly ballet of bloodless economic categories.

The time seems about due for a new history-writing which will attempt to explain the ideas in the heads of Canadians that caused them to act as they did, their philosophy, why they thought in one way at one period and in a different way at another period. Perhaps when we settle down to this task we shall discover that our ancestors had more ideas in their heads than this paper has been willing to concede them. At any rate, we shall then be able to understand more clearly the place of the Canadian people in the civilization of the liberal-democratic century which lies behind us.

AUTHOR'S NOTES

1 Sir Francis Bond Head, *A Narrative* (London, 1839), 64. [Reprinted in the Carleton Library in 1969 with an introduction by S.F. Wise and notes by William Lyon Mackenzie.]

2 *Ibid.*, 464.

3 Maurice Hutton, Principal of University College in the University of Toronto.

4 A. M. Schlesinger, jun., *The Age of Jackson* (Boston, 1945).

5 *Ibid.*, 279.

6 Vernon Louis Parrington, *Main Currents in American Thought*, III, *The Beginnings of Critical Realism in America* (New York, 1930), 23.

7 Laurier to Willison, the editor of the *Globe*, 29 June 1896 (in the Willison papers in the Public Archives of Canada).

8 J. A. Hobson, *Canada Today* (London, 1906), 47. [The book by Siegfried is *The Race Question in Canada*, which was reprinted in the Carleton Library in 1966 with an introduction by Underhill.]

THE REGINA MANIFESTO

The Regina Manifesto, the Magna Charta of Canadian democratic socialism, was adopted at the second convention of the Co-operative Commonwealth Federation (CCF), the progenitor of today's NDP, in Regina in July 1933. It became a kind of Holy Writ, for it was the source of philosophic inspiration during the early years of the movement. The Manifesto explains what Canadian socialists understood by such key terms as planning, socialization, federalism, nationalism, freedom, and justice. Like the first great charter, which gave the barons their rights, this one too is susceptible to a class analysis: it is the Magna Charta of the planners.

It would be stretching a point simply to attribute the Manifesto to Frank Underhill, who did not even attend the convention that summer. But he was not unhappy with the relatively minor changes and additions that the delegates made to his draft.

The CCF is a federation of organizations whose purpose is the establishment in Canada of a Co-operative Commonwealth in which the principle regulating production, distribution and exchange will be the supplying of human needs and not the making of profits.

We aim to replace the present capitalist system, with its inherent injustice and inhumanity, by a social order from which the domination and exploitation of one class by another will be eliminated, in which economic planning will supersede unregulated private enterprise and competition, and in which genuine democratic self-government, based upon economic equality will be possible. The present order is marked by glaring inequalities of wealth and opportunity, by chaotic waste and instability; and in an age of plenty it condemns the great mass of the people to poverty and insecurity. Power has become more and more concentrated into the hands of a small irresponsible minority of financiers and industrialists and to their predatory interests the majority are habitually sacrificed. When private profit is the main stimulus to economic effort, our society oscillates between periods of feverish prosperity in which the main benefits go to speculators and profiteers, and of catastrophic depression, in which the common man's normal state of insecurity and hardship is accentuated. We believe that these evils can be removed only in a planned and socialized economy in which our natural resources and the principal means of production and distribution are owned, controlled and operated by the people.

The new social order at which we aim is not one in which individuality will be crushed out by a system of regimentation. Nor shall we interfere with cultural rights of racial or religious minorities. What we seek is a proper collective organization of our economic resources such as will make possible a much greater degree of leisure and a much richer individual life for every citizen.

This social and economic transformation can be brought about by political action, through the election of a government inspired by the ideal of a Co-operative Commonwealth and supported by a majority of the people. We do not believe in change by violence. We consider that both the old parties in

Canada are the instruments of capitalist interests and cannot serve as agents of social reconstruction, and that whatever the superficial differences between them, they are bound to carry on government in accordance with the dictates of the big business interests who finance them. The CCF aims at political power in order to put an end to this capitalist domination of our political life. It is a democratic movement, a federation of farmer, labor and socialist organizations, financed by its own members and seeking to achieve its ends solely by constitutional methods. It appeals for support to all who believe that the time has come for a far-reaching reconstruction of our economic and political institutions and who are willing to work together for the carrying out of the following policies:

1. PLANNING

The establishment of a planned, socialized economic order, in order to make possible the most efficient development of the national resources and the most equitable distribution of the national income.

The first step in this direction will be the setting up of a National Planning Commission consisting of a small body of economists, engineers and statisticians assisted by an appropriate technical staff.

The task of the Commission will be to plan for the production, distribution and exchange of all goods and services necessary to the efficient functioning of the economy; to co-ordinate the activities of the socialized industries; to provide for a satisfactory balance between the producing and consuming power; and to carry on continuous research into all branches of the national economy in order to acquire the detailed information necessary to efficient planning.

The Commission will be responsible to the Cabinet and will work in co-operation with the Managing Boards of the Socialized Industries.

It is now certain that in every industrial country some form of planning will replace the disintegrating capitalist system. The CCF will provide that in Canada the planning shall be done, not by a small group of capitalist magnates in their own interest, but by public servants acting in the public interest and responsible to the people as a whole.

2. SOCIALIZATION OF FINANCE

Socialization of all financial machinery—banking, currency, credit, and insurance, to make possible the effective control of currency, credit and prices, and the supplying of new productive equipment for socially desirable purposes.

Planning by itself will be of little use if the public authority has not the power to carry its plans into effect. Such power will require the control of finance and of all those vital industries and services which, if they remain in private hands, can be used to thwart or corrupt the will of the public authority. Control of finance is the first step in the control of the whole economy. The chartered banks must be socialized and removed from the control of private profit-seeking interests; and the national banking system thus established must have at its head a Central Bank to control the flow of credit and the general price level, and to regulate foreign exchange operations. A National Investment Board must also be set up, working in co-operation with the socialized banking system to mobilize and direct the unused surpluses of production for socially desired purposes as determined by the Planning Commission.

Insurance Companies, which provide one of the main channels for the investment of individual savings and which, under their present competitive organization, charge needlessly high premiums for the social services that they render, must also be socialized.

3. SOCIAL OWNERSHIP

Socialization (Dominion, Provincial or Municipal) of transportation, communications, electric power and all other industries and services essential to social planning, and their operation under the general direction of the Planning Commission by competent managements freed from day to day political interference.

Public utilities must be operated for the public benefit and not for the private profit of a small group of owners or financial manipulators. Our natural resources must be developed by the same methods. Such a programme means the continuance and extension of the public ownership enterprises in which most governments in Canada have already gone some distance. Only by such public ownership, operated on a planned economy, can our main industries be saved from the wasteful competition of the ruinous over-development and over-capitalization which are the inevitable outcome of capitalism. Only in a regime of public ownership and operation will the full benefits accruing from centralized control and mass production be passed on to the consuming public.

Transportation, communications and electric power must come first in a list of industries to be socialized. Others, such as mining, pulp and paper and the distribution of milk, bread, coal and gasoline, in which exploitation, waste, or financial malpractices are particularly prominent must next be brought under social ownership and operation.

In restoring to the community its natural resources and in taking over industrial enterprises from private into public control we do not propose any policy of outright confiscation. What we desire is the most stable and equitable transition to the Co-operative Commonwealth. It is impossible to decide the policies to be followed in particular cases in an uncertain future, but we insist upon certain broad principles. The welfare of the community must take supremacy over the claims of private wealth. In times of war, human life has been conscripted. Should economic circumstances call for it, conscription of wealth would be more justifiable. We recognize the need for compensation in the case of individuals and institutions which must receive adequate maintenance during the transitional period before the planned economy becomes fully operative. But a CCF government will not play the role of rescuing bankrupt private concerns for the benefit of promoters and of stock and bond holders. It will not pile up a deadweight burden of unremunerative debt which represents claims upon the public treasury of a functionless owner class.

The management of publicly owned enterprises will be vested in boards who will be appointed for their competence in the industry and will conduct each particular enterprise on efficient economic lines. The machinery of management may well vary from industry to industry, but the rigidity of Civil

Service rules should be avoided and likewise the evils of the patronage system as exemplified in so many departments of the Government today. Workers in these public industries must be free to organize in trade unions and must be given the right to participate in the management of the industry.

4. AGRICULTURE

Security of tenure for the farmer upon his farm on conditions to be laid down by individual provinces; insurance against unavoidable crop failure; removal of the tariff burden from the operations of agriculture; encouragement of producers' and consumers' co-operatives; the restoration and maintenance of an equitable relationship between prices of agricultural products and those of other commodities and services; and improving the efficiency of export trade in farm products.

The security of tenure for the farmer upon his farm which is imperilled by the present disastrous situation of the whole industry, together with adequate social insurance, ought to be guaranteed under equitable conditions.

The prosperity of agriculture, the greatest Canadian industry, depends upon a rising volume of purchasing power of the masses in Canada for all farm goods consumed at home, and upon the maintenance of large scale exports of the staple commodities at satisfactory prices or equitable commodity exchange.

The intense depression in agriculture today is a consequence of the general world crisis caused by the normal workings of the capitalistic system resulting in: (1) Economic nationalism expressing itself in tariff barriers and other restrictions of world trade; (2) The decreased purchasing power of unemployed and under-employed workers and of the Canadian people in general; (3) The exploitation of both primary producers and consumers by monopolistic corporations who absorb a great proportion of the selling price of farm products. (This last is true, for example, of the distribution of milk and dairy products, the packing industry, and milling.)

The immediate cause of agricultural depression is the catastrophic fall in the world prices of foodstuffs as compared with other prices, this fall being due in large measure to the deflation of currency and credit. To counteract the worst effect of this, the internal price level should be raised so that the farmers' purchasing power may be restored.

We propose therefore:

(1) The improvement of the position of the farmer by the increase of purchasing power made possible by the social control of the financial system. This control must be directed towards the increase of employment as laid down elsewhere and towards raising the prices of farm commodities by appropriate credit and foreign policies.

(2) Whilst the family farm is the accepted basis for agricultural production in Canada the position of the farmer may be much improved by:
- (a) The extension of consumers' co-operatives for the purchase of farm supplies and domestic requirements; and
- (b) The extension of co-operative institutions for the processing and marketing of farm products.

Both of the foregoing to have suitable state encouragement and assistance.

(3) The adoption of a planned system of agricultural development based upon scientific soil surveys directed towards better land utilization, and a scientific policy of agricultural development for the whole of Canada.

(4) The substitution for the present system of foreign trade, of a system of import and export boards to improve the efficiency of overseas marketing, to control prices, and to integrate the foreign trade policy with the requirements of the national economic plan.

5. EXTERNAL TRADE

The regulation in accordance with the National plan of external trade through import and export boards.

Canada is dependent on external sources of supply for many of her essential requirements of raw materials and manufactured products. These she can obtain only by large exports of the goods she is best fitted to produce. The strangling of our export trade by insane protectionist policies must be brought to an end. But the old controversies between free traders and protectionists are now largely obsolete. In a world of nationally organized economies Canada must organize the buying and selling of her main imports and exports under public boards, and take steps to regulate the flow of less important commodities by a system of licenses. By so doing she will be enabled to make the best trade agreements possible with foreign countries, put a stop to the exploitation of both primary producer and ultimate consumer, make possible the co-ordination of internal processing, transportation and marketing of farm products, and facilitate the establishment of stable prices for such export commodities.

6. CO-OPERATIVE INSTITUTIONS

The encouragement by the public authority of both producers' and consumers' co-operative institutions.

In agriculture, as already mentioned, the primary producer can receive a larger net revenue through co-operative organization of purchases and marketing. Similarly in retail distribution of staple commodities such as milk, there is room for development both of public municipal operation and of consumers' co-operatives, and such co-operative organization can be extended into wholesale distribution and into manufacturing. Co-operative enterprises should be assisted by the state through appropriate legislation and through the provision of adequate credit facilities.

7. LABOR CODE

A National Labor Code to secure for the worker maximum income and leisure, insurance covering illness, accident, old age, and unemployment, freedom of association and effective participation in the management of his industry or profession.

The spectre of poverty and insecurity which still haunts every worker, though technological developments have made possible a high standard of living for everyone, is a disgrace which must be removed from our civilization. The community must organize its resources to effect progressive reduction of the hours of work in accordance with technological development and to provide a constantly rising standard of life to everyone who is willing to work. A labor code must be developed which will include state regulation of wages, equal reward and equal opportunity of advancement for equal services, irrespective of sex; measures to guarantee the right to work or the right to maintenance through stabilization of employment and through employment insurance; social insurance to protect workers and their families against the hazards of sickness, death, industrial accident and old age; limitation of hours of work and protection of health and safety in industry. Both wages and insurance benefits should be varied in accordance with family needs.

In addition workers must be guaranteed the undisputed right to freedom of association, and should be encouraged and assisted by the state to organize themselves in trade unions. By means of collective agreements and participation in works councils, the workers can achieve fair working rules and share in the control of industry and profession; and their organizations will be indispensable elements in a system of genuine industrial democracy.

The labor code should be uniform throughout the country. But the achievement of this end is difficult so long as jurisdiction over labor legislation under the BNA Act is mainly in the hands of the provinces. It is urgently necessary, therefore, that the BNA Act be amended to make such a national labor code possible.

8. SOCIALIZED HEALTH SERVICES

Publicly organized health, hospital and medical services.

With the advance of medical science the maintenance of a healthy population has become a function for which every civilized community should undertake responsibility. Health services should be made at least as freely available as are educational services today. But under a system which is still mainly one of private enterprise the costs of proper medical care, such as the wealthier members of society can easily afford, are at present prohibitive for great masses of the people. A properly organized system of public health services including medical and dental care, which would stress the prevention rather than the cure of illness should be extended to all our people in both rural and urban areas. This is an enterprise in which Dominion, Provincial and Municipal authorities, as well as the medical and dental professions, can co-operate.

9. BNA ACT

The amendment of the Canadian Constitution, without infringing upon racial or religious minority rights or upon legitimate provincial claims to autonomy, so as to give the Dominion Government adequate powers to deal effectively with urgent economic problems which are essentially national in scope; the abolition of the Canadian Senate.

We propose that the necessary amendments to the BNA Act shall be obtained as speedily as required, safeguards being inserted to ensure that the existing rights of racial and religious minorities shall not be changed without their own consent. What is chiefly needed today is the placing in the hands of the national government of more power to control national economic development. In a rapidly changing economic environment our political constitution must be reasonably flexible. The present division of powers between Dominion and Provinces reflects the conditions of a pioneer, mainly agricultural, community in 1867. Our constitution must be brought into line with the increasing industrialization of the country and the consequent centralization of economic and financial power—which has taken place in the last two generations. The principle laid down in the Quebec Resolution of the Fathers of Confederation should be applied to the conditions of 1933, that 'there be a general government charged with matters of common interest to the whole country and local governments for each of the provinces charged with the control of local matters in their respective sections.'

The Canadian Senate, which was originally created to protect provincial rights, but has failed even in this function, has developed into a bulwark of capitalist interests, as is illustrated by the large number of company directorships held by its aged members. In its peculiar composition of a fixed number of members appointed for life it is one of the most reactionary assemblies in the civilized world. It is a standing obstacle to all progressive legislation, and the only permanently satisfactory method of dealing with the constitutional difficulties it creates is to abolish it.

10. EXTERNAL RELATIONS

A Foreign Policy designed to obtain international economic co-operation and to promote disarmament and world peace.

Canada has a vital interest in world peace. We propose, therefore, to do everything in our power to advance the idea of international co-operation as represented by the League of Nations and the International Labor Organization. We would extend our diplomatic machinery for keeping in touch with the main centres of world interest. But we believe that genuine international co-operation is incompatible with the capitalist regime which is in force in most countries, and that strenuous efforts are needed to rescue the League from its present condition of being mainly a League of capitalist Great Powers. We stand resolutely against all participation in imperialist wars. Within the British Commonwealth, Canada must maintain her autonomy as a completely self-governing nation. We must resist all attempts to build up a new economic British Empire in place of the old political one, since such attempts readily lend themselves to the purposes of capitalist exploitation and may easily lead to further world wars. Canada must refuse to be entangled in any more wars fought to make the world safe for capitalism.

11. TAXATION AND PUBLIC FINANCE

A new taxation policy designed not only to raise public revenues but also to lessen the glaring inequalities of income and to provide funds for social services and the socialization of industry; the cessation of the debt creating system of Public Finance.

In the type of economy that we envisage, the need for taxation, as we now understand it, will have largely disappeared. It will nevertheless be essential during the transition period, to use the taxing powers, along with the other methods proposed elsewhere, as a means of providing for the socialization of industry, and for extending the benefits of increased Social Services.

At the present time capitalist governments in Canada raise a large proportion of their revenues from such levies as customs duties and sales taxes, the main burden of which falls upon the masses. In place of such taxes upon articles of general consumption, we propose a drastic extension of income, corporation and inheritance taxes, steeply graduated according to ability to pay. Full publicity must be given to income tax payments and our tax collection system must be brought up to the English standard of efficiency.

We also believe in the necessity for an immediate revision of the basis of Dominion and Provincial sources of revenue, so as to produce a co-ordinated and equitable system of taxation throughout Canada.

An inevitable effect of the capitalist system is the debt creating character of public financing. All public debts have enormously increased, and the fixed interest charges paid thereon now amount to the largest single item of so-called uncontrollable public expenditures. The CCF proposes that in future no public financing shall be permitted which facilitates the perpetuation of the parasitic interest-receiving class; that capital shall be provided through the medium of the National Investment Board and free from perpetual interest charges.

We propose that all Public Works, as directed by the Planning Commission, shall be financed by the issuance of credit, as suggested, based upon the National Wealth of Canada.

12. FREEDOM

Freedom of speech and assembly for all; repeal of Section 98 of the Criminal Code; amendment of the Immigration Act to prevent the present inhuman policy of deportation; equal treatment before the law of all residents of Canada irrespective of race, nationality or religious or political beliefs.

In recent years, Canada has seen an alarming growth of Fascist tendencies among all governmental authorities. The most elementary rights of freedom of speech and assembly have been arbitrarily denied to workers and to all whose political and social views do not meet with the approval of those in power. The lawless and brutal conduct of the police in certain centres in preventing public meetings and in dealing with political prisoners must cease. Section 98 of the Criminal Code which has been used as a weapon of political oppression by a panic-stricken capitalist government, must be wiped off the statute book and those who have been imprisoned under it must be released. An end must be put to the inhuman practice of deporting immigrants who were brought to this country by immigration propaganda and now, through no fault of their own, find themselves victims of an executive department against whom there is no appeal to the courts of the land. We stand for full economic, political and religious liberty for all.

13. SOCIAL JUSTICE

The establishment of a commission composed of psychiatrists, psychologists, socially-minded jurists and social workers, to deal with all matters pertaining to crime and punishment and the general administration of law, in order to humanize the law and to bring it into harmony with the needs of the people.

While the removal of economic inequality will do much to overcome the most glaring injustices in the treatment of those who come into conflict with the law, our present archaic system must be changed and brought into accordance with a modern concept of human relationships. The new system must not be based, as is the present one, upon vengeance and fear, but upon an understanding of human behaviour. For this reason its planning and control cannot be left in the hands of those steeped in the outworn legal tradition; and therefore it is proposed that there shall be established a national commission composed of psychiatrists, psychologists, socially-minded jurists and social workers whose duty it shall be to devise a system of prevention and correction consistent with other features of a new social order.

14. AN EMERGENCY PROGRAMME

The assumption by the Dominion Government of direct responsibility for dealing with the present critical unemployment situation and for tendering suitable work or adequate maintenance; the adoption of measures to relieve the extremity of the crisis such as a programme of public spending on housing, and other enterprises that will increase the real wealth of Canada, to be financed by the issue of credit based on the national wealth.

The extent of unemployment and the widespread suffering which it has caused, creates a situation with which provincial and municipal governments have long been unable to cope and forces upon the Dominion government direct responsibility for dealing with the crisis as the only authority with financial resources adequate to meet the situation. Unemployed workers must be secured in the tenure of their homes, and the scale and methods of relief, at present altogether inadequate, must be such as to preserve decent human standards of living.

It is recognized that even after a Co-operative Commonwealth Federation Government has come into power, a certain period of time must elapse before the planned economy can be fully worked out. During this brief transitional period, we propose to provide work and purchasing power for those now unemployed by a far-reaching programme of public expenditure on housing, slum clearance, hospitals, libraries, schools, community halls, parks, recreational projects, reforestation, rural electrification, the elimination of grade crossings, and other similar projects in both town and country. This programme, which would be financed by the issuance of credit based on the national wealth, would serve the double purpose of creating employment and meeting recognized social needs. Any steps which the Government takes, under this emergency programme, which may assist private business, must include guarantees of adequate wages and reasonable hours of work, and must be designed to further the advance towards the complete Co-operative Commonwealth.

Emergency measures, however, are of only temporary value, for the present depression is a sign of the mortal sickness of the whole capitalist system, and this sickness cannot be cured by the application of salves. These leave untouched the cancer which is eating at the heart of our society, namely, the economic system in which our natural resources and our principal means of production and distribution are owned, controlled and operated for the private profit of a small proportion of our population.

No CCF Government will rest content until it has eradicated capitalism and put into operation the full programme of socialized planning which will lead to the establishment in Canada of the Co-operative Commonwealth.

CANON LIONEL GROULX

*According to some historians, the movement that Lionel Groulx (1878-1967)
founded in 1903, the Association Catholique de la Jeunesse Canadienne-
Française (later the Action Française, and still later the Action Nationale), was
the nursery for contemporary Quebec nationalism. Its confusion of religion
and politics, they say, was carried into every walk of French-Canadian life
by the heady indoctrination the young élite received as it passed through its
ranks.*

    *Groulx was ordained in 1903. Between 1906 and 1909 he studied in
Fribourg, Rome, and Paris. After teaching literary and philosophical subjects
at the classical college in Valleyfield, he became in 1915 the first occupant of a
chair devoted to Canadian history at the University of Montreal. His lectures
and writings transformed French Canadians' understanding of their past and
focused their discontent with Confederation. He received many honours during his lifetime, and his death was marked by an official day of mourning and a
state funeral. Groulx was evidently a great success as an educator. In the first
selection below, from his* Mémoires, *he discusses his teaching methodology.
The second selection is the complete text of an address that Groulx presented
to an association of patriotic youth in 1936, when he was at the height of his
influence.*

Methods of Education

I have often been asked: Where did you find the main elements of your
teaching method?

    I was never aware of any method that was my own. I had adopted the
natural, normal method of the Christian faith. I had borrowed the elements of
my method from the Gospels, but perhaps also, without quite knowing it, from
my great masters, the leaders of French Catholicism in the mid-nineteenth
century. They had revealed to me the magnificent nobility of the soul that lives
its faith ardently. Montalembert's *Letters* and those of Léon Cornudet,
Lacordaire's *Letters*, those of Abbé Perreyve to young people, and Ozanam's
letters to his young friends did the rest*. . . . I would add that, left almost
entirely on my own, among colleagues who counted few real teachers, I was
soon led to seek and then to forge for myself a doctrine of education. Necessity
compelled me, forcing me to respond to the demands of young people of rare
quality. Besides, it seems to me that a priest can always count on certain
insights or inspirations from Divine grace. In this arduous task, I try to obtain
the collaboration of teachers and prefects—a threefold collaboration that, managed with tact and discretion, makes it possible to focus on the character or
behaviour of a student the many different kinds of information indispensable to
the educational process. I take on the task of talking to each of my own students
[*mes dirigés*] in my room once a week for the older ones, once a fortnight for
the younger. I see them during the recreation periods at appointed times. As
their numbers grew, the task quickly began to get much heavier. All the same,

how many solid joys this ministry brings me! It takes some effort to bring a college student to the resolute conquest of his freedom and his personality. His whole formation as a man and a Christian is at stake; above all else, he must get through the crisis of puberty victoriously. His determination is the key to that victory. Equally arduous is the attempt to construct in a youngster's head a coherent and engaging spiritual doctrine, and to teach him to live in accordance with the duties of his station in life, his daily life. Oh! I do not deny that the stubborn resistances rooted in weakness or juvenile fickleness, and above all the irretrievable losses, cause the priest frequent anguish. What mother or father could suspect that such anguish exists? Who could suspect the acute anxieties of spiritual paternity? To ward off, so far as possible, such losses, during my whole time at Valleyfield I took on the task of writing regularly to all my young penitents during the vacations. Quite a heavy burden. But how many consoling letters and how many joys it will have brought me! And what an intoxicating and exalting spectacle, to see the growth of an adolescent in the conquest of his purity and in his supernatural manhood! What consolations the soul of a priest can take in the return of a poor child who seemed corrupted and depraved for ever, irremediably lost to the Christian ideal! I have known these sorts of joys; God has sometimes given me the opportunity to do so. Even today [writing about 1954] I consider them among the sweetest and most valuable of my life.

To get back to the subject, my method (if I even dare speak of method) was simplicity itself. It consisted of working out in the minds of these youngsters, little by little, a doctrine of the Christian or supernatural life, the main elements of which I had borrowed from Father [Charles] de Smedt and a little volume by the author of *La Perfection chrétienne par la pratique progressive de la confession et de la direction* (I am not sure of this general title nor of the title of the little volume: *Fondements de la perfection chrétienne*). The hard part is to adapt this doctrine to different ages. In such instances the simplest thing, I believe, is to call upon the help of God and to count on nothing else. My experience, in any case, has shown me that it is possible to interest young people, and even to involve them deeply and passionately, in this magnificent intellectual construct that is Catholic dogma and morality—as easy as interesting them in some literary question or scientific problem. There remained the ascetic side of the doctrine. I used to insist a great deal—and one will not be at all surprised by this—on the natural virtues of man. Indeed, I never stopped repeating that the supernatural is built only on a healthy and well-balanced natural life. I would tell them that the slightest fault in the base of the personality can bring about its dissolution. My doctrine on this question of asceticism thus remained quite simple. I taught my young people the religion of the duties of one's station. I taught them to seek Christian perfection in the small duties of their college life and nowhere else. The sad thing is that too many young people do not see the possible grandeur of their life. They dream. They dream of great actions for the future. They do not doubt that great actions are within their reach and that they can perform them from the time they are youths, still in college. Thus I content myself with reminding them that what counts, in the last analysis, is not the material dimensions of an act, but the intensity of faith and love that goes into it. I tell them, and then I repeat it, that a humble college student who fulfilled scrupulously the requirements of his daily life, with some supernatural insight, would be a true saint; that one is not a Christian only in chapel, after all, but that properly cultural actions are meant to vitalize and reinvigorate those that have to do with the duties of one's station, while the latter in turn react beneficially upon the former, and that together they give life a solid and magnificent unity. My demands for restraint thus come down to having them practise the duties of their station within the framework of the college regulations, leaving nothing out; accepting the demands for discipline, study, religious observances, demands and minutiae that can seem constraining and annoying, but which if they are to be observed require an act of will, a conscious plan of life, a victory over one's instincts, one's carelessness, one's whims. The regulations had not been invented to persecute them or to annoy them, but to form men and Christians. I used to exhort them, therefore, to conform to them with faith and courage. To cultivate one's mind, to be stamped with a BA, was not the whole of one's aim. Still more necessary was to forge one's will and to conquer one's freedom; then, above all, by these means to make oneself, in every aspect of oneself, a Christian. I used to show them, therefore, the powerful assistance in this regard that the college regulations, with all their apparently annoying details, could provide, since to observe them required an effort, a sacrifice, and in short, an act of will. I requested them then to get up in the morning as soon as the bell or the clock rang, and to resist the impulse to snuggle into their pillows. I asked them to observe silence everywhere that it was required and to observe it especially when the master on duty had turned his back. I asked them to line up in a disciplined way, solidly planted on their two legs, not slouching nonchalantly at odd angles. In the study hall, I beseeched them to do their written work first, and to learn their lessons before plunging into their general reading, and not the reverse. In chapel I counselled them not to introduce fantasies into their acts of piety, above all not in their communions, and, for example, not to go to communion only those days when they were told to do so, but to remember that every communion made in the state of grace can only do great good for the soul and please our Lord greatly. And so on. And after many trials of the experiment, I can say that it is easy to win a student—youngster, adolescent, or young man—to this asceticism. They let themselves be swept up in the hope of shaking off instinct and their whims, of mastering their constitution, of thus conquering their freedom, of giving themselves a personality truly their own, and of standing out from the greyness of their surroundings. And when one adds to these motives of a natural order the more elevated motives of supernatural life—to please God, to do his divine will, to develop in oneself the seeds of one's baptism, to let the sublime transformations of grace be achieved; for the sake of God, to attain spiritual manhood, in this way to live the life of an apostle, to offer one's little sacrifices for one's comrades who need them and for the improvement of the moral climate around oneself, to win souls for Jesus Christ, to lost oneself in the greater life of the universal Church—one may and must go that far—I contend that the well-formed soul of a child takes easily and joyfully to these vast perspectives, if only one knows how to shape these great truths to the receptivity of each student. One will see even these children and adolescents enflamed with sacred ardour. And I am writing this remembering what I was able to observe any number of times. I added to these natural and supernatural means one other that always seemed to me extraordinarily effective: the reading of books of a moral or spiritual nature—lives of saints, lives of great Catholics and their letters and diaries. Nothing is more valuable, to my mind, in combatting the influences of a too-often mediocre milieu, than to place the student in the company of these great souls. Some colleagues and I put together a library of these sorts of books. There was something in it for every age. We had them read. I begged my own students to read at least one a month, without letting it interfere, to be sure, with the other readings required by their studies. This method is not to be disdained. Many times I observed that a normal youngster cannot resist the sovereign influence of these great friendships. After two or three years of living in this select company, the soul is turned from its course and won to a nobility of thought and sentiment that will never leave it.

Shall I go on in this vein? So often, young priests have asked me what to read, how to prepare themselves for the terrible trade of educator. Allow me then to spend a little more time on this. Where did I find the substance, the body of this doctrine of education? A moment ago I indicated some of my sources. To those I must add my philosophical and especially my theological studies. All the same, I cannot keep from noting the spiritual poverty in which, even after 1900, a young priest floundered, especially a young educator aspiring to acquit himself decently in his undertaking. Where was one to find a true master in a position to teach? There was not even a normal school for secondary teaching. In the seminary one rarely sees professors, particularly professors of the basic doctrines, pausing to indicate the benefit or practical lesson to draw from such and such a divine truth—the benefit for one's own interior life, for the exercise of the priestly ministry, in particular, for preaching or counselling individuals. Even on the retreats for priests, how rare it is to encounter a preacher, a man of doctrine and virtue, who instructs you and really moves you. Moreover, for these preachers, even the most far-seeing, the educator does not exist. One preaches only for the parish priest, even in a province where the clergy carries the appalling responsibility, directly or indirectly, for all teaching and the whole of education. The fundamentals of my doctrine of education I gathered bit by bit, in fragments, as I said, from the *Letters* of Lacordaire and de Perreyve to young people, from the works of Father M.-S. Gillet, and from the lives of some saints and the biographies of some great lay apostles. I often read and meditated on the life of Father Lacordaire by Chocarne. Nothing of what had then been published on Ozanam escaped me. And how I searched for a Life of Christ, an attractive and revealing one to put into the hands of my young people! Thus, as one can see, we were no great psychiatrists, nor even psychologists. To be honest, such of that type as I have happened to hear since then on radio or on television, holding forth on education, have brought me more tears than consolation for my youthful misery, so impoverished have they seemed intellectually. Psychologists they are without any true philosophy or psychology, and to boot, deprived of any sense of Christianity, completely unaware of that deep and shrewd psychology of the great masters of Catholic spirituality. No, we were only humble educators who took our inspiration from theology, the Gospels, and traditional spirituality. It was from having observed the influence of these examples or these lives of great apostles on myself that I came to press them so insistently on my own students, adapting them to each individual, the same books, the same narratives. . . .

Tomorrow's Tasks

MY YOUNG FRIENDS:

First, allow me to confess my intention: I mean to give this talk a decidedly didactic turn. Your generation is realistic and practical; you say you are tired of speeches; that you are starved for specifics. Specifics, many of them hard, are what I wish to offer you.

I
DUTIES TO CULTURE

Let us establish an initial point of reference: French Canadians constitute a nationality. This is true both in fact and in law, and to my mind it must be held incontestable, even if it causes fits in some quarters. As a second reference point, I will assert that for us the idea of nationality evokes, above all, the idea of culture. Our nationalism, in short, is based on one fundamental conviction: the value of French culture. Our consciousness of being French, our pride in being French, our desire to remain so—these are the foundations both of our national ideology and of the feeling that corresponds to it. For us, being French means belonging to that kind or category of the Latin mind that has assimilated, perhaps better than any other has, the Greek and Roman cultures and drawn from them a lofty humanism—one that is broad and sound, the best balanced of any in the modern era, if we are to believe the historians; one, in any case, that far surpasses the humanism of the ancient cultures, because of its Christian idealism.

These two initial points indicate a primary duty: the obligation of opting in favour of our culture. In French Canada there is a crisis or, more precisely, a problem of cultures that may be expressed as follows: can we and should we remain entirely, exclusively French? And if we both can and should, what attitude should we take in regard to Anglo-Saxon culture? How much of that culture must we accept? What proportion of it? To resolve this problem, let us first recognize the limits of any nationalism in the spiritual order. In what sense is nationalism or commitment to nationality a limitation? In what sense is it not, nor can it be? It is a limitation inasmuch as no people can renounce its deepest being, its native genius, its own personality, without diminishing and even destroying itself. For every people, this genius is what it lives by, what gives it the power to act and to enrich itself. In other words, if there is a French genius, an English genius, a German genius, and if what constitutes each one is some specific element consubstantial with the people in whom it is incarnated, this people cannot renounce what is the foundation, the form, and the dynamism of its spirit without dealing itself a mortal blow. That would mean a loss of balance, a violent dislocation. Does nationality therefore imply a kind of hermeticism, isolation, spiritual closure? The genius of a people is not something fixed or static; it is a reality that is essentially dynamic, capable of infinite evolution and enrichment. In order for it to be both legitimate and possible to limit oneself to one's own, one's own would have to enjoy the singular privilege of containing all human good. Now, literature, art, and science do not belong to any single nationality, any more than they take a single form of expression. To refuse any form of beauty, any intellectual treasure other than that of one's own nation would be to isolate oneself, to will the way a plant would if it were to exhaust the soil it grew in without ever renewing it. Not only *should* no people dispense with others; in fact, it is not in the power of any people to condemn itself to such isolation.

What is the solution? In a word, for a people to appropriate, to assimilate, all that it possibly can of human truth and human beauty while remaining fundamentally itself. In other words, to assimilate without being assimilated, to convert the goods of others into blood and nourishment without letting others rob us of our blood and nourishment. For us, therefore, if we are not to cease altogether to be, the solution comes down to taking in only as much of the Anglo-Saxon language and culture as we are capable of assimilating: as much as offers us the possibility of enrichment, and no more. Certainly, we must firmly refuse to take the attitude of an intellect in bondage, more inclined to submit than to react. The amount of Anglo-Saxon culture to accept varies, needless to say, with the capacity for assimilation, a capacity that itself varies with each person's age and degree of culture, as well as the social class to which he belongs. And here we are forced to make a primary observation: the most serious threat to the future of the French spirit in us derives from the aberration that French Canadians are steeped in the Anglo-Saxon language and culture in inverse proportion to their capacity to assimilate them. They get a bigger dose in elementary school than in secondary school, and more in secondary school than in university.

Now a second duty to culture becomes clear: *National Education*. To maintain an attitude of healthy independence in regard to the other culture and to ensure that every act of assimilation becomes an enrichment for us, one primary condition is essential: we must be French, vigorously and completely French. No one will deny this self-evident truth: only assimilators assimilate.

How will we become assimilators? There is only one method, one way: through national education. For us national education is imperative; only those who are wilfully blind can fail to see its urgency and necessity. Our situation presents no resemblance to that of the old nations descended from ancient fatherlands or civilizations: in these national entities the culture of centuries fills the air, warming and invigorating the people as naturally as the sun. If it is true that we are born French, it is no less true that, because of the constant pressure exerted by certain historic and geographical realities, we cannot remain French without effort and struggle. For us, to be French by instinct or French by habit is to die as Frenchmen. Only one way is viable: to be French by resolve. Which is to say that we cannot remain ourselves without national education.

I will explain. It is not enough to be within reach of a magnificent spiritual treasure, to have been placed at birth in a certain moral climate, a certain current of intellectual life. It is still necessary to appropriate that treasure, to breathe in that air, to bathe oneself in that invigorating current. It is not enough to possess the language of clarity if we speak it obscurely, if all we get of it—at school and in our colleges—are formless rudiments and an anaemic understanding. It is not enough to proclaim ourselves the intellectual descendants of Pascal, Racine, and Bossuet if our young men and women enter their humanities courses without ever having read in full one tragedy of Corneille or Racine, without ever having opened their eyes on the 'immortal jottings' of Pascal. It is not enough to possess an incomparable history if all our children possess of it are vague, sketchy outlines, if the greatest features of our past remain the ones that are the least known to our people. A simple reflection in passing: how sad it is to think that, as models of heroism for our children, we have to call on figures like Guesclin, Bayard, Jean-Bart, and Joan of Arc, and that of all the heroes and heroines who fill the past of New France, not one is really well known.

The national education that would remedy these problems I myself would define as a taking-possession of our cultural treasure, a taking-possession to be achieved through instruction, through education, and, above all, through the atmosphere of the school (elementary school, college, and university). To put our French souls in possession of all the cultural treasures of France and our original share in them—this is indeed a strict duty for our teaching institutions. It is the only way for us to be French and to remain so. A question of life and death! And that is why there is also no escaping the duty of ensuring that the policy of national education is victorious in our province. Young people must be ready to fight for this great idea. For alas, extraordinary as it may seem, there are many minds hostile to this very reasonable and vital necessity. You young people will have to conquer minds that are mummified; dulled by routine; opposed to any change, any effort; minds that do not want to be forced to bestir themselves and work. You will have to conquer minds that are light and superficial, lacking horizons, incapable of seeing what is happening in their country, in America; minds that are convinced they can live forever like goldfish in their little glass bowl. You will have to fight the defeatists for whom there is nothing left to do but lie down; who, because they themselves are dead, are terrified of the living. You will have to fight the politicians and the pedagogue-politicians—there are some of these—for whom any expression of national spirit is synonymous with a spirit of independence: a fearful thing for the partisan conformist. Finally, you will have to fight the false doctrinaires for whom any nationalism is a bogy, a heresy; who denounce us as a people of nationalist 'extremists' because sometimes when we are stepped on, when we are robbed and starved, we do not cry out or rage, but politely say: pardon me!

Now a third duty toward culture: the *creation of a civilization*. Of course I am not advocating national education as an end in itself, or simply as a means of acquiring culture. And this leads us to a third duty: to ensure that once that culture is acquired, it will serve to transcend itself and reach its full natural flowering: a civilization. By 'civilization' I mean the imprint of the spirit on nature, or its finest addition to nature. 'The world is a workshop where human intelligence labours,' said Father Delos, 'and the artefact that comes out of it is civilization.'* Or, if you prefer, let us call civilization, in the highest sense of the word, the humanization of our surroundings and of the national environment. In this light the word takes on a special kind of clarity. A work of sculpture, of architecture, of painting, is something belonging to nature, but this nature is one that has been spiritualized, transfigured by the art that is added to the physical face of the country, making it more beautiful. What is great music but an outburst of sound, except that those sounds have been humanized, orchestrated, organized into poems, to join with the murmuring songs of our forests, our streams, and our fields? A work of literature is another kind of beauty, one even closer to the spirit, because its embodiment is the very language of the intelligence. A beauty that passes from person to person, it enchants, uplifts, and thereby enhances both the humanism of the race and the quality of the milieu. A social order founded on justice and charity, a political order that strikes the right balance between authority and liberty—these too are creations of civilized people. A simple farm—shall I say it?—through its arrangement and architecture can become a work of French civilization.

But why this work of civilization in the first place? Because it is essential for nations to enrich each other culturally. We owe it to ourselves to give other nations as much as we have borrowed from them. Above all, we owe it to ourselves and to our children to be constantly improving our national milieu. We owe it to ourselves to be ceaselessly purifying, ordering, and embellishing it, so that, more and more, we may find in it both our human good, and, through that very process itself, our good that goes beyond this world. Let us never forget that what gives nationality its basis in right is its special capacity to provide us with the human good and, consequently, the super-human good as well. The richer, the healthier, the more civilized the national or cultural milieu is, the greater the chance for the loftiest blossoms of humanity to grow there; the greater the opportunity for the Catholic spirit itself to flower.

Nevertheless, we must return to the fundamental reality: to create an original literature, art, or civilization, one that is individual, uniquely our own, recipes are not enough: *first we must be.* Another truism to imprint on our minds: only creators are capable of creating. I often hear you young people complain of our mediocrity of spirit, the rough, unpolished character of our intellectual and artistic output. Let us not wait for the revival of the life of the mind among us, nor for literary prizes or competitions, important as these things are. We will have an art, a literature, the day when, through the improvement of our instruction and education, by the vigorous, resolute taking-possession of our culture, all our culture, we cease to be a shadow of a people, a shadow of Frenchmen, a shadow of human beings, and stand out as great French Canadians—that is, as great human beings.

II
Second Series of Duties:
DUTIES TOWARDS THE SUPPORTS OF CULTURE

To be! To be ourselves. To be vigorously! Is it so easy? I see two formidable obstacles in our path, two enormous problems that have not yet been resolved: one economic, the other political. Let us begin with the economic problem.

1. The Economic Problem

First, let us recall one principle, one very elementary truth. If nationality has the value and plays the role we have assigned it, and if, like everything that is human, it is mixed with the carnal and the temporal, it follows that material good must be subordinated to this higher good of a spiritual order. Thus it is impossible to conceive of any sound ordering of the economy that would not take nationality into account, or, worse still, that would endanger national values and rob the cultural environment of a significant part of its beneficial activity.

Now, it may well be that at this very moment one of the gravest threats to national values, perhaps even to our chance of *being*, comes from the economic order in this province. Let us examine the situation.

For a people to have the potential to be, vigorously, and the capacity to create a work of civilization, that people—everyone agrees—requires a certain quantity of material goods, a certain social order, a certain freedom of mind. More concretely, it needs a middle class capable of mental labour, with the time and the means to devote itself to the task. Talent needs ample opportunity to break through and develop, especially when it surfaces, as it so often does, in impoverished surroundings. These conditions are unrealizable in circumstances of widespread poverty and material deprivation.

Are we free of this kind of poverty? First, we suffer from one fundamental and very grave disorder, symptomatic of an extremely abnormal situation: the great levers of economic life are not in our hands; the great sources of wealth in our own province evade us. Eighty per cent of the province's population is lorded over, enslaved, by a small group of exploiters, kings of finance, who make up a mere 6 per cent, perhaps, of the total. Hence we have a proletariat that is excessive and constantly growing, and a portion of which is close to slavery. To anyone observing us in spiritual and social terms, what do we look like? Like the head of a dwarf on the body of a giant. Worst of all, the economic dictatorship is infecting us with incurable social ills. The same disorder invariably leads to a distressing 'inferiority complex' among the working masses and even the rural population. The sickness is growing, and its real name is this: destruction of faith in the national genius. It is a fatal, epidemic illness, and no cordon sanitaire can contrive to check it. A population of poor people facing a handful of very wealthy people will always envy that minority; and, envious as they are, they will attribute to them marvellous qualities and great prestige. Thus there is nothing surprising in the morbid penchant for anglicization among our people; a penchant we see in the common man but which is just as pronounced in the bourgeois and the nouveau riche; a penchant that is painfully evident across the whole face of our country. Nor has the foreigner been alone in giving an English air to the highways and towns of our province. We have contributed to it ourselves, with a dazed unconsciousness that astonishes the foreigner himself.

The same sickness has given rise to the grave deviation of our teaching system, with its increasing orientation, especially in the cities, towards Anglo-Saxonism. The conflict of cultures has come to a crisis, and the outcome is turning against us. The people have come to the point where they find a kind of mystical virtue in knowing English. I have said it before: establish an Anglo-Catholic school in every village in Quebec, and the French schools will be emptied. Madness, yes, but are our poor people really so much to blame? This educational anglomania, let us be honest enough to admit it, is in large part a consequence and a function of Anglo-American economic domination. It is to be hoped that as we return to a more normal state of affairs, the English fetish will fade. One can even foresee a day when anglophones will find themselves obliged to learn French in order to get a job in Quebec. But as long as the major employers are English; as long as most business is transacted in English; and as long as our people believe this situation to be normal, natural, and legitimate, how can we blame them for attaching a disproportionate importance to knowing English? Who, moreover, is not aware that our leaders have aggravated the disastrous effect of this economic domination with advice and teaching that would amount to instruction in treason, were it not basically the work of simpletons? Everywhere they turn, the people are told that what they need above all to succeed in life is not intelligence, not character, not work, but English, always more English. What am I saying? Instead of preaching knowledge of English as a temporary necessity, as, above all, a means of emancipation and conquest; instead of exhorting our people to free themselves from economic servitude in order to free themselves from linguistic servitude, most of our so-called leaders—lacking all sense of national mystique and infatuated with the most depressing kind of *bonne-ententisme**—have been teaching us and persuading us to accept the yoke of foreign domination as natural and legitimate.

The same disorder gives rise to the deflection of politics and its progressive turning against us. In democratic states particularly, it is the natural tendency of the financial powers to aim at subjugating political power. This they believe to be the most effective way of expanding their privileges and, above all, maintaining their dictatorship. The result, my young friends, is that the expression 'not to be master in one's own house' can have several meanings for a people. There is no economic servitude that is not accompanied by other forms of servitude, of the most dangerous kind.

The Remedy, the Duty

What is the remedy? What is our duty? I have no small or easy answers to propose to your generation. All I can offer you is a heroic duty, a duty that is urgent and, I venture to say, tremendous, gigantic. Above all, though, urgent. We cannot wait any longer. To ask us to be patient, to play at resignation, to accept our present servitude for yet another generation, is to ask us to commit suicide. We cannot wait any longer, for what the times require is not simple rectification of the situation, but a reversal, or, as you sometimes say, a 'revolution'—which is in no way intended to imply anarchic violence. At all costs, we must change our role from that of servants to that of masters. It is no longer a question of changing the car's steering wheel, of repairing a windshield-wiper or a tire. The whole car must be rebuilt from scratch. Another image, if you prefer: in our province the engine pulling the economic train does not belong to us. It goes where it pleases. In fact, for French Canadians the train is going backwards and the engine is crushing us, brutally. What we must do is jump into the engine, take the controls, and ensure that the train goes in our direction.

How? By what programme of action? It would be the role of an economic council to lay out the programme. And it would be up to the politicians, in particular, to see it executed. Our problem is such that political intervention is a necessity. To hold the people alone responsible for their situation and leave it to them to cure themselves seems to me the final injustice, when you realize that in fact it is the masters of our political and economic life who, by failing to take national values into account in our life, have brought the present disorder to pass. Do you want a task within the reach of everyone? Give the people their confidence back; make them see that there is no fate irrevocably condemning them to this slavery. Our people may have their faults; they may have their troubles. They are still as healthy as any other people. They are as intelligent as any other people. They still have as much taste for hard work as any other people, at least the best—the majority—do. They possess resources that have made millionaires of others. Other peoples with greater problems, starting from worse situations, today know what resurrection and the will to power are. What do we lack? Above all, a mystique of effort. Let the schools and the colleges stop mass-producing all those spineless wonders, those drawing-room dandies I have already deplored as an insult to a Catholic education. To strengthen the souls of our sons and daughters, let us drill into their heads as a watchword, an obsessive *leitmotif*, this phrase: *To be masters in our own house*. Let the walls of every classroom proclaim the greatness of this aim, and in ten years a new race of French Canadians will have appeared, a race resolved to take possession of its province.

Another task within the reach of everyone would consist in making the people understand the relations between economic and national concerns. The *Buy at Home* programme can help, provided it does not stop at the sales counter, but is inspired by a broad education of the national consciousness. The concern is always the same: to change ideas in order to change actions and facts. If there is confusion and disaster on this lower level, it is primarily the result of disorder and betrayal above, in minds and spirits. Again, in the name of economic and national requirements, we must instil in the younger generation the creed of competence; we must train technicians. Do we have enough for major industry, big business, high finance, top management? Fighting off foreign dominance is not the whole issue, it is not even the main issue. Are we capable of taking its place?

There is another task that can be tackled immediately: to put an end to proletarianization. For a hundred years and more, the conquest of land in our province has not kept pace with the birth-rate. The reason for this imbalance is that the land is not accessible enough. Therefore we must work to conquer all the land that can be colonized, and aim for a new disposition of the older farmland.

Fourth, we must return politics to its proper role—a significant one, as we noted a moment ago. It cannot do everything. But it can do a great deal. After all, it is politics that makes economic legislation (commercial, industrial, financial); it is politics that is responsible for defining the law and protecting it. Now, the politicians must understand this: we are at the point of what is known as legitimate defence. At the same time, young friends, remember that in no country in the world, particularly in no parliamentary or democratic country, has politics ever been able to bring the financial powers to heel without being powerfully assisted, if not forced, to do so.

2. The Political Problem

For us, moreover, the political problem presents itself with quite unusual acuteness. I am not discussing, for the moment, the question of pre-eminence between the political and the national. Should the political take precedence over the national? Or vice versa, the national over the political? Suffice it to remember that, far from being strangers to one another, the two are closely interdependent. What is the role of the political? To secure the common good. Now, if nationality is what we have defined it as—a part of the spiritual good of the community—it becomes a large part of the common good, and even a means of attaining the common good. Thus the politician is duty-bound to draw his inspiration from nationality; he is not permitted to ignore it; he must do what it is in his power to do to ensure the flowering of the national culture, in order to allow the members of the nation to realize their full humanity.

A number of very simple, very logical conclusions follow from this, though I admit that our intellectual cowardice confers on them a daring gravity. First: if a geographically and politically delimited country contains 2,500,000 French Canadians, making up four-fifths of the total population; if this country is the country of these four-fifths and is legally its fatherland, by right of first and perpetual occupation and by historic right; if this population possesses significant cultural riches that are indispensable to the acquisition of its human good, I say that, for that population, a national State is a legitimate postulate [un postulat de droit légitime]. Equally legitimate is the proposition that the politics of this province should be primarily French-Canadian. Well! We want a national economy, a national culture, a country with a French face, and we claim it is our right. Is any of this realizable if our population and our country are not governed for their own ends?

I would add, furthermore, that there is nothing new in this idea of a French State. It is in the direct line of our history. Ever since 1774, it has been in the process of realization. Every schoolboy who has grasped a simple series of facts—(1) the implications of the Quebec Act, representing, according to an English-Canadian historian, the accession, the judicial consecration, of French-Canadian nationalism; (2) the implications of the parliamentary constitution of 1791, [that is,] the creation of a French province, the deliberate creation of a French State by the Imperial parliament; (3) the implications of La Fontaine's position in 1842, when he accepted the union of the two Canadas only on a federal basis—the simplest schoolboy, I tell you, who notes the significance of these historic dates, will acknowledge what is obvious: our little people's persistent, victorious striving for an ever more complete national autonomy, for the attainment of its political personality. This is the trend of our history. Such is its direction, or else it has none.

For the rest, the hypothesis is no longer an hypothesis. The French State in the province of Quebec has existed since 1867 on the basis of positive constitutional law. It is an undeniable fact which we must tirelessly continue to impress on our foggy, enfeebled colonial brains. It is we, French Canadians, who are primarily responsible for the federal form of the Canadian state. Confederation was achieved primarily by us and for us. And we demanded these federal institutions not, to my knowledge, in the name of economic and political interests, but above all in the name of our national interests. Reread the documents of the period: the fact is unquestionable. Another unquestionable fact: all our associates of 1867 agreed to our demands, and so did the Imperial Parliament. Once again, as so often before, I cite the words of Lord Carnarvon: 'Lower Canada is jealous, as she is deservedly proud, of her ancestral customs and traditions; . . . and will enter this Union only upon the distinct understanding that she retains them.'* What more does one want? What was their motive for consenting, in 1867, to the resurrection of our province, which had been politically extinct since 1841? On the other hand, what was the supreme argument proposed by our political leaders, at that turning point in history, to make us accept the new regime? On both sides it was understood and proclaimed that Confederation would reinstate us as masters of our province and its policy, ready to determine our own destiny. In fact, we are not demanding any kind of constitutional upheaval when we speak of a French State. To create this State would not require changing one iota of the constitutions that govern us. We are simply asking that what our political leaders did not do in 1867—whether from cowardice or from want of intelligence—be done today. Instead of a State that, in so many areas, masquerades as neutral or cosmopolitan, we are asking for a State that, while respecting the rights of everyone, also remembers to govern for the nationals of this province, for the majority of the population that is French-Canadian.

This political conception could not be more legitimate and, I will repeat, consistent both with justice and with our history. Little wonder if it terrifies so many fine members of the bourgeoisie, when you reflect that, despite having studied their country's history in the books we all know so well, and for two or three generations, so many of these good people have only the most microscopic understanding of it, and have never grasped its main lines. These are the kind of French Canadians that are tolerated, and they have chosen to be of this kind; narrow, restricted centralists to boot, these unfortunate people do not realize that their attitude in itself constitutes the strongest possible argument against Confederation. For if it is criminal and revolutionary in 1936 to demand what could and should have existed sixty-nine years ago, is any more overwhelming evidence required to prove that the federal regime has made us a politically degenerate race?

The Objections

Let us examine the objections of these gentlemen a little more closely. Is such a State possible, they ask, in a province with a mixed population? Why not? In what way does the presence of minorities, in most countries in the world, prevent those countries from giving their politics a national character? Take any point on the globe and put on it a country inhabited by a population that is 80 per cent Jewish, or Polish, or Irish. Then ask any ten-year-old schoolboy whether the politics of that country is Jewish, or Polish, or Irish. You will not have to wait long for his answer, for it is only in countries like Quebec, inhabited by an immature race, that such simple realities are called into question. In what respect, moreover, is a politics with a national character necessarily a politics of injustice, incapable of making room for minority rights? On the contrary, in my opinion the establishment of a French State in Quebec at this moment would usher in, along with a French-Canadian politics, a politics of supreme justice. In the economic and social domain, for example, it would not perpetuate the solution of the [English] minority, which, as it is imposed on us, becomes a supremely unjust and dangerous solution—unjust and dangerous to the highest degree, because it disorganizes our social order and in the end denationalizes us. On the contrary, our solution would constitute a move toward justice and peace for the simple reason that it would seek to restore the balance. The real question is whether, in effect, a minority of exploiters, making up perhaps 6 per cent of the population—for not all anglophones are exploiters—has the right to prevent 2,500,000 people, roughly 80 per cent of the population of the province, from living in freedom and dignity. The question is whether it is even within the power of this 6 per cent to perpetuate their dictatorship. Is it not in the interest of the profit-making minority itself, therefore, to accept a just solution by peaceful means, rather than to let itself drift inevitably towards another solution—assuming it is true that a people will not accept an unacceptable regime, a regime that threatens its very destiny, for long? Of course I am well aware that these questions are difficult; but experience also teaches us that ignoring difficult questions does not solve them, and that if by chance time heals many wounds, it is equally true that it rubs salt in a good many more.

Second Objection

Is a French State possible within Confederation? Here we must define our position with regard to the institutions of 1867. Let us not confuse two very different questions, one of fact and one of right: the solidity or durability of federal institutions, [and] their suitability to our needs, to our essential life, and, as a consequence, their right to demand our allegiance.

The Question of Fact

Does Confederation have any chance of lasting? Shall I tell you what worries me, regarding its future? It is not primarily the much-discussed absurdity of its geographic conflicts, the sectioning from east to west that suggests at least four groups of future states. Nor is it the country's geometric form: a vast longitudinal stretch of land, much of it neither fertile, nor habitable, nor easily travelled. This long stretch of land is in complete contrast to the American quadrilateral, all of which is habitable, where channels run from east to west and west to east, north to south and south to north, strengthening one another as they cross. This explains the extreme difficulty of economic exchanges between Canada's two extremities. Suppose that for some reason—the decline of Europe, say, or the events now underway in the Far East—the centre of the world were to shift tomorrow to the Pacific: the geographic sectioning of our country would then be even more obvious than it is today. The Pacific would naturally become the magnetic pole for the life and economy of the western provinces, while the provinces of the centre and the east would either be forced to look to the south, or continue to live under the influence of Europe—there being little likelihood that the upheaval of the Old World would put an end to it altogether.

The real and present danger to Confederation, however, the most disturbing one, comes from elsewhere: I mean the weakness of the will to live together shown by the provinces and their populations. We all know that there are two elements that constitute a nation. The first we may call, to use the philosophers' terms, the material element: ethnic and cultural similarities, a common heritage of memories, pride, and traditions. The second element is the principal or essential one: the will to live together, a will that, being founded on physical and spiritual similarities, seeks to promote the flowering of the cultural heritage. And what does this will to live together come down to, in Canada? First we must recognize that, by its very nature, the federal regime presupposes a restrained and limited collective will. Nothing could be further removed from the robust, positive will common to unitary States, in which every autonomous or particularized element bows before the unrivalled sovereignty of the State. In a federal State, those who unite consent to live together only for precise objectives, in limited domains.

Observe, moreover, the rather feeble motives that gave rise to this collective will in Canada. To grasp this fragility, let us compare the birth of Canada with the birth of the American federation. At the time when the latter was organized, we find a coalition of young colonies at war with their parent State who unite for what they hold to be an absolute condition of life and liberty. At the beginning of their political and national union, our neighbours thus knew the potent stimulant of the struggle against foreign oppression and together shared great dangers, great sufferings, and great hopes—collective passions that do more than anything else can to arouse the consciousness of a nation.

There was nothing of that sort in Canada. Upper and Lower Canada turned towards a new federation in 1864 because the union of 1841 was no longer tolerable to either of them. The Maritime provinces joined the federal pact for simple economic reasons, as did British Columbia. Such motives, one must admit, are apt to produce rather loose, almost artificial ties. No doubt fear of the United States played some part in the provinces' banding together. But the danger was more distant than imminent, and it did not provide a decisive motive.

What, therefore, has the Canadian confederation lacked up until now? It has lacked the great trial, the shared suffering that cements these kinds of unions. We have had national crises, but they have been divisive rather than unifying. Violations of rights, grievous injustices, have set us against one another. The dangers and crises that have agitated us have always come from within, never from outside. On these grounds alone, we might well be excused from believing in the infinite duration of Confederation. Everyone may think as he likes on this point, of course. Especially since the only means of strengthening the will to live together in Canada so far devised—the centralization of powers, and the growth in the strength of the central authority—leads to an end directly contrary to the one intended. Surely it would be utopian to expect to rule the entire world by the same political institutions; in the same way, taking into account certain distinctions, it is a dangerous fantasy to try to impose a governmental centralization tending continually towards uniformity on a country as vast and diverse as Canada.

The Question of Right

Fragile political construction that it is, is Confederation at least beneficial to us? If not, are we forbidden to break our commitments of 1867? No doubt there are several ways of posing this problem, and some of them may even be wrong.

It is the firm opinion of some school metaphysicians, who contemplate reality from the height of Sirius, that Confederation is not a contract at all, since there were no true contracting parties. Whence they draw this argument: because the province of Quebec was judicially incapable of being a party to the contract, it is so tightly bound by the Imperial law of 1867 that it cannot legitimately break the union. Interesting as these speculative questions may be, they count for little in the present debate. For we strongly doubt that they are taken very seriously by the new generation of French Canadians who feel their spiritual life threatened. No political institution has the right to prevent a group of human beings from obtaining its own good. No province, no nationality is obliged to accept being governed against itself. If Confederation is to endure, it must not overstep its role, and it must prove its utility. The young people of Quebec are telling anyone who cares to listen: 'Either we live freely and prosperously as masters of our own economic and spiritual life within Confederation, or we will leave. We were not created and brought into the world to allow a few gentlemen in the federal capital to forge laws of servitude against us, nor to allow a troop of civil servants, maintained at our expense, to harass us.' The same young people go on to add: 'We have said goodbye to French colonialism and to English colonialism. We refuse to become a colony of Ottawa.'

To ward off the spectre of separatism, others evoke the touching image of the French minorities scattered across the Dominion. They say it would be a crime to abandon our brothers. Certainly we must not broach such an emotional question lightly. All the same, let us remind our dispersed brothers that, for seventy years, everything has conspired to give them grounds to complain, with infinite reason, of the impotence of the federal institutions to protect their rights. No one in Canada has assessed the terrible moral dissolution of their Quebec compatriots under the federal regime with a more lucid and grieving eye than they have. Indeed, we have not spared them any occasion for deploring our cowardice in the face of violations of minority rights, our supreme indifference to any kind of national solidarity. Well, frankly, do our minority brothers think an autonomous French State, a true source of culture, of a robust and radiant life, could serve them any worse? For the rest, let us not forget that separation would not mean abandonment, nor does it intend to put itself forward as such. At most it presents itself as a resignation to the inevitable. When one cannot save everything, one saves what one can. And it would serve nothing for all to perish together on the pretext of helping one another.

Putting these false problems aside, let us address the real ones, the problems posed by the painful reality of the present itself:

1. Is it still possible for us to attain our common good, our human good as a French nation, within Confederation?

2. If we were to leave Confederation, would we be capable of being self-sufficient, of providing our people with the good that is *civilization*?

3. Would our exit from Confederation be such a blow to our current political associates as to put their own good in danger? For example, what would become of the Maritime provinces, thrown into isolation by our separation?

Let me state a doctrinal principle borrowed from Father Louis Lachance, in his luminous book *Nationalisme et religion*: 'As long as it is not established that a political order has become unjust, and especially as long as it is not evident that it could be replaced by another better adapted to provide a nation with its human good, justice requires support for that order.'*

In the light of this doctrine, let us try to answer the three questions posed a moment ago:

1. Is it really federal institutions that have prevented and even now prevent the existence in Quebec of a French State, a State that, duly created in its time, could not have failed to provide us with our human or cultural good? Or, if this State does not exist, is it rather the fault of men? Each of us, on our own, can think of three or four ethnic groups (the English, for example, or the Jews) who, placed in the same situation we are, would have made themselves firmly at home in defiance of the constitutional impediments; who in any case would never have allowed Confederation to turn against them. People speak of the impediments or infringements [on our affairs] of the federal government. Do they think that if, immediately following 1867, Quebec had organized itself into a French State, one that was firmly and frankly autonomous, Ottawa's encroachments would not have encountered an impassable barrier here? Would our federal politicians have been able to do what they did in the capital? But, someone will ask, today, in 1936, isn't it a pipe-dream to hope things can be set right? Certainly—I make no secret of it—the evidence provided by sixty-nine years of political experience is disturbing. To hope that French Canadians as we know them will show more courage and national feeling in Ottawa tomorrow than they have since 1867; to hope that even here, in their own province and in their own politics, they will make the leap of liberation, is evidently to nurse a very large illusion. Therefore I grant you that, given our present race of French Canadians, a race morally weakened by more than half a century of false orientation and lack of concern, Confederation can only be fatal to our nationality. But would it be the same with a new race—I mean a race invigorated by intensive national education, one that had regained a steadfast attachment to its cultural heritage, a heightened sense of its destiny? I would like to see a more compelling demonstration that such recovery is impossible.

2. Masters of neither our economic life nor, as a fatal consequence, our political life, with a cultural life that is still anaemic, would we be a viable State? Incapable of overcoming the obstacles, real or imagined, to our national realization posed by the central power, would we be up to assuming the many and formidable risks of independence? Would we be in a better position to be self-sufficient, to provide our nationals with their human good, than we are

within Confederation? It may be that the answer is yes, but here too I would like to see an irrefutable demonstration.

3. It is obvious that Quebec separatism demands that a solution first be found for the problem of the three Maritime provinces that would be forced out of the Canadian state by our leaving. For the rest, I recognize that the constitution of a [new] Dominion or an independent State does not in any way mean— as so many simpletons are pleased to say or write—isolating ourselves from international or even American or Canadian life. To ascribe to separatists the intention of erecting a Great Wall around French Canada, forcing us into the narrow, secret life of a termite colony—such a hypothesis is simply laughable. It is not in the power of any people to isolate itself. Having left Confederation, we could not be strangers to it. Our highest interests would compel us to reach an understanding, if only on commercial matters, to continue to live among the peoples of this planet.

CONCLUSION

Our one certain duty, in which there is no risk of either mistake or wasted effort, is to work toward the creation of a French State in Quebec—within Confederation if possible, outside it if not. Therein lies the means of attaining our human good and perhaps, if it is not too late, of reforming Confederation. Young people seek real work, redeeming work. They want us to stop glorifying our national genius by words alone. Here is a task equal to their highest dream and of which they can make a masterpiece of French reason.

All the same, young people, remember: a French State will not create itself without help. Ideas travel, but only on condition that they find carriers. The worst enemies of the French State, those most hostile to the idea—you can see it already—will not be the ones you would have thought; they will be your own French-Canadian compatriots. Long enslavement, political and national, has bent our backs, accustomed us to servitude, made us a hesitant, pusillanimous nationality. Before our people can find the simple courage to accept their future, they need re-education, both political and national.

Do not let yourselves be swayed, therefore, by the faint-hearted who will say: 'Have your French State if you want it; but don't talk about it.' That would be to forget the role key ideas play in organizing the life of a people, their value as ideal and impetus. It would mean demanding from the people a long, immense effort, while refusing them the stimulus, the mystique, that can elicit that effort.

No more should you let yourselves be deceived by the outcry of those interested parties who would charge you with racism or an aggressive nationalism. [The creation of] a French Canada would not be directed against anyone. It would be quite simply—and I will never stop repeating this—the act of a people that has rediscovered the direction of its history. It would be the work of builders whose first thought would be to act in a highly civilized way. Wishing to add a French part to the choir of American nations, they would want the score for that part to be, for the glory of human culture, both original and beautiful. Who could find fault with such an ambition? It would be an extraordinary thing if in this province, all ethnic groups had the right to go about their business, and we did not have the right to go about ours; if all others had the right to their destiny, and only the country's oldest, most authentic sons were prevented from realizing themselves. Young people, to fulfil your destiny there is no need to devote yourselves to a labour of hatred, an intemperate nationalism. Hatred is anti-Christian, and its effect is negative. Working against others often makes one forget to work for oneself. Hating others is not enough to shake off their domination. It would be better for us to stop hating ourselves. Therefore I am not asking you to conquer by violence. I am asking you to conquer by using the arms of French-Catholic youth: probity, intelligence, work, tenacity, generous daring. I will even say this: do not rush anything. Be patient. Forge the instruments of the future State slowly and solidly. Let it come into the world piece by piece, each one fitting harmoniously into the next, just as the armour of Minerva was assembled, long ago, on the anvil of the divine blacksmith.

Finally, do not let yourselves be deceived by those great minds among us who find these concerns, these provincial dreams, petty and unimportant, and seek to replace them with their own transcendant centralist dream. Since when do we measure the works of men by the standard of latitudes and longitudes? To work toward the survival of a great Canada—which, after all, we are not renouncing—is to work for the growth and endurance of a political and economic entity; in short, for a material greatness. 'Canada exists solely for political reasons', [André] Siegfried has recently written. But if it is granted that a Catholic people and country represent a value of a higher order; and if, despite our shortcomings and troubles, as a result of historic causes it happens that we embody, here in our land, Catholic spirituality and vitality as no other people does, then to work towards the creation of a French State, towards a climate of liberty for the flowering of human personality and Christian civilization—what is this, in short, but to give our labour and our life an incomparable end: the survival of one of the highest spiritual realities on this continent?

- Call of the young during 30's to realities.
- put education with induce french history & culture
- Must regain control of their political & economic world.
- must achieve perpetuation of French culture either with or within confed. They confed was clearly not yet worked.
- questions if supernatures the answer.

ANDRÉ LAURENDEAU

André Laurendeau (1912-68) was editor of Le Devoir *from 1948 to 1963, when he became co-chairman of the Royal Commission on Bilingualism and Biculturalism, the position he held at the time of his death. As a young man he had been the fiery leader of the Ligue pour la Défense du Canada, which had been formed in 1942 to oppose Mackenzie King on conscription, and of its successor, the Bloc Populaire. He served one term, from 1944 to 1948, in the Legislative Assembly of Quebec and directed* L'Action nationale *from 1937 until 1953. A prolific writer, with three plays and a novel to his credit in addition to innumerable essays and editorials, Laurendeau embodied the kind of Quebec nationalism that was compatible with federalism. The following selection appeared in* L'Action nationale *in 1951 as the last of a series to which four authors contributed on the theme of 'directives nationales'.*

The Conditions for the Existence of a National Culture

What is it that makes us French Canadians? Is it a matter of race? No race is biologically pure and, despite our common origins, we know that we do not constitute a race in the proper sense of the word. Is it the State? No; other Canadians live within the same State; the Canadian State could disappear without our changing our mode of being. Nor could it be a religion, essentially universal, whose beliefs we share with three or four hundred million other men.

Is it language? In large part, yes. Languages are not simply collections of signs; in their vocabularies, their turns of phrase, and their syntactic forms they express a particular genius, and language is a phenomenon that runs very deep in man. Of course it would be wrong to confuse the spirit of a language with its materiality; even so, it does contain certain attitudes, and an elementary psychology. In short, the French language distinguishes us, sets its seal on our milieu, and links us to all those who speak it. But as a treasure common to four or five different peoples, it is not enough to identify us specifically.

Is it history? That term usually evokes images of famous figures, but it is the substratum I am thinking of: the wealth of experiences, lived through collectively, that have imprinted a stable character on our people; the social forces that, acting in time and space, have built our milieu and thus conditioned our being. This living part of history, this active presence of the past among the living, embraces the factors listed above and expresses itself through our national culture.

We will examine what national culture is more precisely in a moment: arising out of history, it distinguishes a people and, as soon as it becomes conscious and voluntary, transforms that people into a nation. (I am speaking, of course, of national culture, not the personal culture of an individual.) But before tackling definitions, I would like to offer an example.

II

I will choose a basic institution: the family. Let us look at it not as the preacher, the moralist, or the history text would, but as it is lived, as it is passed on among us; in this light, the family is a part of our national culture.

Among us a respect for life at once primitive and religious has survived: hence our families are large, even in the cities. Marriage being considered a sacrament—and 'sacrament' implies 'sacred'—when people marry they understand that it is forever. Like all people, they will sometimes cheat; but they will know that they are cheating. Thus fidelity will be a basic rule—even if the rule is frequently broken, even if the quality of feelings deteriorates to the point where quarrels appear to be the only constant. The bonds are made of steel; they magnify the humble spouses, attaching them to a common task, which is the family.

The result is an inner security, an atmosphere of warmth and abundance. In general, families are well centred; their members are bound to one another and yet open to the world of other families; and within themselves they exercise firmness, but without excess. Nevertheless, the hand of authority can weigh heavy. Despite absences, the father remains the head. The mother devotes herself to endless household tasks. The home has lost a few of its rituals, but still keeps a good many; in particular, it enjoys large gatherings and the holidays that both make them possible and ensure that they are festive.

Several of these traits could be found elsewhere. But nowhere else do they appear together with the particular coloration and tonality they have here; an equal blend of austerity, cheerfulness, and good-fellowship. Only the rigorous analysis of the sociologist or the intuition of the artist could give us the complete picture: consider, for a past that is already legend, *Maria Chapdelaine*, or the motherly characters re-created by Gabrielle Roy, or *Tit-Coq*, that bastard in love with the family.

We get married for good. We have many children. The home is cheerful: these are so many basic notions we have *lived*, the results of a history that goes back a very long way. The Christianity that inspired them may no longer be alive in a given family; nevertheless, they will be practised spontaneously. To a certain extent, the adult behaves as he saw his parents behave; he repeats the actions and attitudes to which he bore witness. Thus an element of our national culture is passed on within the home.

My picture is a little idyllic. In the cities, the French-Canadian family is undergoing a crisis; the bonds that used to unite it are loosening. Surpassed by an élite above it, dishonoured below among the rich and the poor [*dans la grande bourgeoisie et le sous-prolétariat*], despite everything this conception of the family retains a powerful hold on us, even in emancipated circles. Compare it with family life in the US as described in *La Civilisation américaine* by Willis D. Nutting, a sympathetic witness, and you will see how distinctive our way of living a marriage still is in America.

III

M. Minville said last month[1] (and, in *Notre question nationale*, Father Richard Arès, S.J., clarifies the same concepts): 'What sociologists today call national culture is the body of rational and spiritual values belonging to a specific group: mores, customs, traditions, belief, laws, and institutions.' These values live in and through man, who 'receives in his innermost personality the deposit of the cultural wealth that identifies him and enables him to participate—by the simple fact that he lives, thinks, and acts—in the endless rebuilding of the nation . . .' The ethnic environment is 'the centre to which the child is spontaneously attuned from one generation to the next, by the simple fact that he grows up within it and is subject to its influence every day . . .'

We have just seen how this phenomenon arises within a family. It seems less strong in a period when mores are changing rapidly, putting parents in direct opposition to their children. But even when there is a struggle between two forms of social constraint—one coming from within, the other imposed from outside—the influence of the family will remain predominant for a long time, because it was the first to imprint itself in the depths of the new being.

IV

But our home life was only an example. Of what does our cultural wealth consist? First there are the cultural minutiae, which have to do with external life yet which influence the sensibility of the people in a certain society. They range from the famous *ceinture fléchée* [a woven belt] that so many of our countrymen think of when we talk about national culture, to crafts or popular folklore, to the sort of songs and dances that distinguish a nation, making it coarse or refined. We should not go into mourning too soon, but neither should we believe that these things are eternal; styles of dress, for example, can disappear, taking picturesque elements with them, without destroying anything important. We must not mistake the residue of a dead past for culture.

On a higher level we find mores, living traditions that, if they have a certain universality, are projected into institutions and laws. A people's hospitality, its taste for adventure, its individualism, its sense of family, its absence of initiative—all these may be manifestations of a popular culture. Quebec's 'little catechism', in itself, is not a custom; but that the catechism has been taught for centuries, and bears its fruit in social behaviour, is indeed among the mores of a nation.

—Now, here two dangers are always lurking. A nation, while continuing to believe in the same basic truths in which its mores are steeped, may receive from the outside and be influenced by other mores, inspired by another way of thinking; and in the long run it risks believing what it lives, and thus of gradually turning its back, almost without realizing it, on its traditional beliefs. Or else in losing that faith or holding it less vigorously, it may continue to act from habit along the same lines as before, but its own mores become somehow foreign, a kind of dead weight that the nation dimly aspires to rid itself of. We are living in the midst of this double danger.

Finally, on a level above national culture properly speaking, which is constantly evolving, there are the achievements of civilization, its highest objective manifestations. These are the great works of art and thought. They establish intellectual traditions and nourish them. In them people of every age recognize themselves, and at the same time learn to go beyond themselves, since all truly great works are universal.

V

But perhaps it is time to tackle the subject that has been entrusted to me. It speaks of cultural directives. We have devoted ten minutes to exploring the word 'culture'. Now for the other one.

Directives: what does that mean? Must one play the magician, flash thunder and lightning, prophesy traditional verities, and consider oneself invested with a mission? Something more modest, surely, is expected. When the question is one of culture, even in the particular sense I have defined, the 'directives' must not be too inflexible. A 'director' of conscience is not a tsar of production. Wherever we find it, even imprisoned in flesh or in a social mechanism, the spirit must be allowed its chance at freedom, its potential for flight.

All those, Canadians or foreigners, who have approached the problems of French-Canadian culture have defined it by three terms that may be worn out from repetition, but nonetheless remain true: this culture, they say, is French; of Catholic inspiration; and rooted in Canada. Thus a great body of religious thought, a great human tradition, and a particular geographic setting provide the three basic elements of its structure. Except that when we repeat this, simple minds take it that we mean to enclose our culture in a straitjacket, or at least force it into a suit as rigid as medieval armour. They imagine a Catholic shirt, *fleur-de-lis* breeches, and shoes of Canadian leather. A slightly simplistic vision . . .

Like most of you, I have children. I would like to give them a religious and humane education according to a doctrine I believe right, neither too lax nor too obtrusive. I may miss the mark. And I may succeed. But if I do succeed, I have no idea what they will be—because an intelligent education aims to make them become what they are; and how can we know what they are before they have become it? 'These strangers who come out of us . . . ', Mauriac calls them, somewhere, these beings who are flesh of our flesh . . . Why? Because, being alive, they are mysteries.

This same mystery exists for the nation, which is also alive. Alive: that is to say, plastic, subject to influences; but with a life of its own, capable of dominating influences or combining them in some dynamic way. I do not know, therefore, what the nation and its culture will be in fifty or a hundred years; no doubt both would astonish us if we were there to judge of their fruits. That does not alter the fact that our conscious choices will have influenced them—just as in the family circle, our attitudes and principles, despite everything, serve to orient our children.

The function of the teacher is limited; it is valuable to the extent that it recognizes its limits. But within this circle its effects are profound. That is why, without believing in a summary cultural *dirigisme*, we must find orienting principles, establish some rules, and if it appears necessary, bring all our weight to bear in a certain area in order to act upon the nation.

VI

Now, we have been talking all this time about *French-Canadian* culture, the *French-Canadian* nation, and we have not even mentioned Canadian culture, or the Canadian nation. Is this a case of oversight or fanaticism?

The answer is far more simple. In all intellectual honesty, I still do not know what people mean when they talk about Canadian national culture—or, by way of consequence, the Canadian nation. If national culture is what we have said it is, there can be no Canadian culture at this time; and if there is no Canadian culture there is no Canadian nation, since the nation is first and foremost a cultural phenomenon.*

But surely Canada exists? Most certainly. There is a Canadian State, a society, and a political regime to which we owe complete allegiance. The government exercises its authority over a vast territory made up of different regions, each of which communicates more naturally with the adjoining American region than with its Canadian neighbour—Quebec more easily with New England, Toronto with the Great Lakes region, Halifax with Boston, Winnipeg with Minneapolis, Vancouver with Seattle—than does Montreal with any other provincial capital. Thus geography is a factor more of disintegration than of unity, opening the door to a foreign culture rather than encouraging the development of a common culture.

On its own, economic life would tend to establish itself along geographic lines, and it is only through constant effort that all these parts hold together. Consider, despite our railroads, the direction in which so many of the natural resources of each province go (those the United States needs, at least). Let us acknowledge the strength of the economic ties already established; however, they do not suffice to engender a culture.

Is there a beginning of a Canadian culture? Possibly: we do not yet know what direction history will take. For the moment there is not much to the idea; it is a vague outline that the future may perhaps enrich, centuries from now; but it carries no compelling force.

Between the English and the French in Canada there are, of course, many points of contact: first of all, because they are human beings; then because, as Western peoples, they share the same spiritual origins: Greece, Rome, and the Bible. But these origins are too distant, shared with too many other peoples, too faintly felt, for them to serve as cement for cultural unity. England and France are both part of Europe, but there is no more an Anglo-French culture than there is a Hispano-Germanic one, despite the rulers they had in common for so long. Similarly in Canada, after two centuries of cohabitation there is no Anglo-French culture. When the two cultures came together they were already formed, individualized, adult. They have borrowed from one another (we accepted the parliamentary system, for instance), in the same way that adults influence one another, without substantially altering their inner unity. To obtain a real fusion, and hence a Canadian nation, would require either that one of the two cultures swallow up the other, or that both together pass through a dark age—as after the fall of the Roman Empire—in which everything would be called into question, and the languages themselves might pass through the refining fire of a vital and profound experience.

Not only is there nothing of the kind taking place, but I believe, along with Prof. F. G. Stanley of Kingston, that the fusion of cultures is 'neither possible, nor desirable'. We would not lightheartedly embark on such a hazardous adventure without knowing where it would lead. Moreover, there is a regrettable tendency in America towards unification: regrettable because its centre lies outside Canada; it is the *American Way of Life*; in other words, the homogenizing influence of the United States puts in question the very existence of both Canadian cultures.

Faced with this mortal danger, we in Canada must develop a friendship between our cultures; and it is an important task, to work towards this friendship, the true unity of the Canadian people. But to develop a truly Canadian culture would be impossible, for it would mean destroying our only real safeguards at the root.

VII

From this follow two practical consequences of a general nature: one political, the other economic.

'As a cultural entity,' as M. Minville pointed out, 'hence by nature neither economic nor political, the nation is obliged, simply in order to survive, to take both economic and political action, and thus to confront the State and demand from it certain attitudes.'

In the political order, we must deal with the federalism of the Canadian State. It is federal for several reasons, one of the most important being the duality of cultures. From this must be derived a definite orientation: wherever the State has anything to do with culture (education in any form, internal social organization, popular culture), the latter should depend on the provincial State rather than the federal—that is, it should revolve around the State that is closest to the people, the one in which, in one province at least, we are free to give ourselves the judicial framework best suited to our culture. I will not dwell on this point, its immediate consequences having already been drawn.[2]

In the same way our national culture encounters economic reality on a daily basis. It will have to seek to obtain not absolute economic independence, which is a dangerous illusion, but economic autonomy, 'which enables a people to employ its own labour force in an economy that is directed in accordance with its own spirit and organized with an eye to the best use of its territory'. M. Minville explored this idea last month.

VIII

Let us now consider popular culture in French Canada, specifically *entertainment*; let us examine a few of its more significant tendencies. This is where we will again find the mortal danger mentioned a moment ago: the *American Way of Life*, which I am not confusing with the higher aspects of American civilization—aspects, often admirable, that our own élites would do well to contemplate.

Entertainment with intellectual or artistic pretensions includes, first, the reading material of the masses: the big newspaper, the tabloid, comics, magazines, and digests. These represent the triumph of the image over the idea, of the facile notion over substantial thought. The American prototype dominates even in our own publications: for you do not change the spirit of comics in translating them from slang to barbaric French, or in producing servile copies or imitations of Tarzan, sports heroes, or Hollywood stars.

The radio inundates our people's homes with booming waves of sound. At prime time, on the top stations, three elements predominate: quizzes so stupid as to make one weep, soap operas—which too often bring even the old newspaper serial down another notch—and popular songs. Of course the most popular songs are almost always the ugliest, most unwholesome ones. Radio-Canada, for the most part, makes a noble effort to raise standards, but even these are falling to a remarkable level of vulgarity and platitude.[3]

Then there is the cinema. Another American annex. Now, it appears that one-third of the Canadian population goes to the movies once a week. In one Montreal high school, according to a recent poll, 36.6 per cent of the 500 students see one film a week, one-quarter see two, 7.6 per cent see three; in all, 71 per cent go to the movies on a weekly basis. The favourite film is the worst kind: the musical.[4] And before long we will have television, bringing the show right into our homes.

Let us return now to our urban French-Canadian family and its way of living family life. For at least twenty years, it has been going to the local cinema from two to four times a month. The films it sees come primarily from Hollywood (even in England, 70 per cent of the films shown are American, and in France 75 per cent are). Since the last war, the family has developed a passion for the comics, and the comics are almost all American imports. If it prides itself on its 'intellectual' curiosity, it opens a digest, which nine times out of ten is *Reader's Digest*, another American concoction. Just about all of its younger members will learn about love from the radio, in the school of Luis Mariano and Georges Guétary.*

Twenty years of this. Do you think the substance of our national culture has not been altered among the parents? And what is one to say about the children, with so little experience to protect them?

This phenomenon is almost universal, of course. The *American Way of Life*, in its lowest form, is rolling over the countries not enslaved by the USSR. But other people's ills do not cure our own. It is less harmful in countries with an old civilization, which enjoy the additional protection of distance. Here, we face the threat of becoming an enclave of US popular culture.

Let us resist negative reflexes, anachronistic fulminations against new inventions and forms of art. But let us also realize that the problem is extremely difficult: if we are inundated with foreign products, it is because those products are cheap, in both senses of the word. Mass production has invaded the realm of entertainment, and the French-Canadian market is very small. So I have no ready-made solutions to offer. What I am passing on to you is my alarm.

We French-Canadian nationalists, are we not wasting time on secondary issues when this one should be galvanizing us into action? Do we not keep an eye—stubbornly vigilant and sometimes hair-splitting—on England for any political or economic wrong she might do Canada, while the enormous, numbing presence of the US leaves us cold and absent-minded? Without slackening either our attitudes or our quest for political independence, is it not time we realized that the balance of power has shifted, and that, on some levels, we should perhaps reverse our alliances? Canadians who want to stay French and Canadians who hate hyphenation, will we not all be melted together in the same pot by a superior power? Will our children or grandchildren not wake up one day in a Canada that will no longer be Canadian?

Governments have little liking for disinterested action. But will the provincial government of Quebec, which is responsible for French-Canadian culture, not judge it necessary to launch a major inquiry into the current evolution of this culture, and its gradual contamination by a foreign, and in some respects enemy, culture? (Let us not forget that religious and moral factors are often involved.) A serious non-partisan inquiry, which might be conducted by the universities, could lead to practical conclusions, and then individual citizens and groups could put their shoulders to the task.

If once again this government, like its predecessors, prefers to concentrate on mines, roads, and bridges, other associations could combine their efforts to measure the distance travelled in twelve years—from the fateful year of 1939, when a movement already underway for half a century broke over us, like the waters of some tremendous flood.* Educators at all three levels possess considerable powers of investigation. Professional organizations and certain national groups as well have important forces and financial means at their disposal. They could pool their resources, under the direction of a few intellectuals, take some soundings to get a true picture of the situation, and from that deduce a conscious cultural policy.

Our political perils have not disappeared—far from it—but they have ceased to be the most serious ones we face. The economic revolution is more frightening, because of its social and cultural repercussions. For in a French Canada that has been urbanized and proletarianized, it is no doubt through popular culture that the blows rain down most heavily. They are easy to take, and they do not arouse the anger that educational persecution does. But their softness itself is a trap. They attack the soul of the nation, infiltrating into the deepest aspects of our private lives. The time has come to rediscover the fervour we have expended, when necessary, in civic and educational struggles in the past, and to devote it to the development of a popular culture that is in tune with ourselves.

IX

Similar problems arise at the higher level. We find them in our educational system, about which there are growing suspicions.

For lack of time, let us confine ourselves to what sets us particularly apart in America: secondary education and its extension into university.†

First off, we run into a question of a practical sort. There is nothing more stupid than a practical problem that is not resolved in good time: some day it will get its revenge by wreaking havoc with the whole system. The problem is this: we are part of a continent where public schools offer a free education, up to the university level, to everyone who wishes and is able to pursue it, and where the courses are integrated from one level to the next.

Now, where does the student go at the end of our system of primary schooling? It leads pretty well nowhere, and doubt has been cast on its value. In addition, the *cours classique*, conceived as a single programme of seven or eight years' duration, cannot be abandoned without wasting almost all of the time already devoted to it: and it is offered only in private institutions, which must demand tuition fees.

Three difficulties result. (1) The failures are so many that records are no longer kept of the young people who must leave the *cours classique* before reaching the baccalaureat; the proportion of rejects must be fearsome—I would not even dare mention the unofficial figures I have been given, they seen so excessive. These students, the majority, who have embarked on secondary education but have failed to reach port, have lost time and money and are left disoriented. We must, if it can be done without destroying the nature of the humanities course, build greater flexibility into the system. Such reforms have been demanded, sometimes very bluntly, for at least thirty years, and the force of these demands is growing constantly.

(2) In many cases, despite the generous assistance available, it is still the wealth of the father that determines the vocation of the son or daughter. The bourgeois family, on account of its preconceived ideas or snobbery, will keep its boy in college, while the intelligent son of a working man will risk missing his vocation. In large part, secondary education remains the privilege of money—while for our Anglo-Protestant countrymen the first four years are open to all. In the past people suffered more flagrant inequalities in silence; but times have changed, and here too the demands are increasing, just as they have for all forms of social security; I would add that these seem to me well-founded. It is scandalous that money should impose its own brazen law, condemn human values to remain undeveloped, and plunge into bitterness all those who see their destiny shattered.

(3) Finally, our secondary colleges are poor; all of them are finding it difficult to make ends meet. The tuition fees they must in fact demand, which shut out some gifted children, are still insufficient to allow the colleges to provide the school premises, the equipment, and, sometimes, the specialized teachers whose value they are the first to recognize. Our teachers are almost always overworked, and invariably underpaid. As a result, despite the authorities' wishes, we must do without lay teachers, who require more reasonable salaries. Now, the establishment of a lay as well as a clerical intellectual élite is essential for our society. It is essential for our universities—for the two major cultural faculties that should be their first priority: the faculties of letters and philosophy, and all their offshoots. Almost everywhere except here, university professors are recruited from the ranks of secondary teachers; conversely, secondary teaching provides posts for the best students from the university faculties. In order to make a living, some young lay teachers today must exile themselves from either their speciality or their country; there are no places here for many of our arts graduates [*licenciés ès lettres*]; they leave and teach French to young Americans. Meanwhile, we will learn a little more English . . . What fun!

You do not expect me to offer you a complete programme of reform. Besides, I recognize that I do not have the technical competence. But I will say this: for all kinds of reasons, the *cours classique* must undergo certain adjustments that will leave its essential nature intact but that will permit it to fit better into our society. We do not exist for its sake, but it for us; hence it is not *a priori* untouchable.

Instead of waiting for some irresistible movement from outside to come in and impose total revolution, the educators themselves, it seems to me, must take the lead in reform and at the same time establish its limits. This is what the most perspicacious among them want anyway.

The question of money will arise—and thus the question of state support. Once again we will face the eternal problem, for primary schools and universities alike: how to receive equitable favours from the State without becoming its slave? I do not intend to solve that problem this evening. . . . But if the solution does not exist, does that mean that we must sacrifice our universities and specialized schools to the State?

Another question presents itself: that of the substance of our secondary studies, the whole question of the humanities.

X

What are the classics of a people? They are the works in which the harmony between the artist or writer, on the one hand, and the nation, on the other, is realized at a level deep enough that, even in very different eras, the nation can recognize itself in its essentials. They are also those works that go beyond the nation and attain the universal.

Need it be said? Our culture lacks this crowning glory. It is in the French classics that we find it—and through the French classics we are carried to the roots of Western civilization. And that is one of the reasons why we have made ample provision for the humanities in our secondary teaching. I hasten to add that this was a wise decision.

The *cours classique* is above all, perhaps, a method, a kind of intellectual gymnastics, an attitude of mind. Hence its value. One can spend six years of one's life practising these exercises (no doubt some of the most formative ever devised), retain no more than a vague memory of the authors one has studied, and nevertheless have received a great benefit. The humanities presuppose prolonged contact with the great authors, but they are not literary studies first and foremost. These remarks will provide the context for the observations to follow.

The *cours classique* is also, however, a return to the original sources of our culture: perhaps we should take a different metaphor, and rather than surface springs, imagine those artesian wells that cannot be reached without digging deep into the earth, drilling through rock.

Now, our young people have been doing their humanities for many years; for many years they have devoted long hours to the study of philosophy. Do you find that this enormous effort has produced satisfactory results, works showing the effect of such a long and close acquaintance? Studies of grammar, studies of texts; and on a higher level, criticism and interpretation of texts, monographs, research works or popularizations . . . I look for all these, and I find extraordinarily little. We content ourselves with French textbooks and no doubt are right to do so, for our own attempts were sometimes pathetic. We study the textbooks rather than the texts themselves. With few exceptions, this kind of study more closely resembles routine drudgery than it does an ardent quest for human truth.

The result is that young people are less and less consumed by the fire of humanism; I would venture to say they are not enflamed at all, that they are barely lukewarm, and that most of the time you will find them listless and bored. Speaking of films in a recent article in *Cité libre*, Pierre Juneau writes: 'It would be interesting to analyze the few studies that have been done on the penetration of movies into this province, particularly among young people. Performing this simple task leads to some disturbing questions: thus when they are free, when they can choose their own intellectual nourishment, the same people who have been taught the virtues of Esther and Andromaque opt for Betty Grable and Esther Williams. This indicates a terrible discrepancy between the values imposed by our official education and the values that people spontaneously adopt for themselves. Moreover, this same discrepancy can be seen in personalities, between the values that are learned and must be consciously upheld, and the values according to which one actually lives.'* In large part it has always and everywhere been so; but the distance between the objects of spontaneous admiration and the study programme used to be less pronounced. What worries me today is that this discrepancy exists among the student élite, and that it looks very like a divorce.

It is always dangerous to generalize, and I know that these judgements are unfair to certain teachers. But a study recently showed us that the adolescents in our colleges seldom read the classics, that they complain they were not introduced to the great authors soon enough—to those *Great Books* a new American school has been discovering with amazement these past few years. What they are lacking is an impassioned initiation into the masters that, paradoxically, they have been obliged to study for so long. Those old texts bore them—and I am talking about the ones who have enough literary curiosity to stay awake; they remember Racine, Corneille, Molière, or Pascal as old greybeards, writers of dusty texts that no longer seem to carry any message. They have not sensed the eternal freshness of these masters, their human value, or their fundamental harmony with our national culture.

What has led to this situation? The atmosphere in which young people now live? The still inadequate education of a number of teachers? The solitude of the best, and their weariness at keeping up the creative effort in an environment that is indifferent? The absence of stimulation, being cut off from university teaching? The long time during which this university teaching did not exist? Certainly there has been a lack of rivalry, of exchanges, of the enrichment provided by faculties devoted to liberal studies [*la recherche désintéressée*]? To put it bluntly, we are suffering from having been deprived of a university education in letters and philosophy.

But this is fundamental! When we talk about secondary education, we extol the poetry of the classics programme; our boys and girls suffer the prose. Habit and routine sometimes make for a very weary handling of these treasures, and then young people turn away in disgust. We can hardly count on them, in future, to defend—except from vanity—the value of an education very little of which, often, they have understood.

Now, I have explained myself very badly if the preceding remarks have led you to believe that I put a low value on the humanities. Not only do I hold their formative value in the highest esteem, but on the more modest level of national culture, I recognize them as a key element in our cultural edifice.

We must at all costs renew them, refresh them, rediscover their deep value. Research and our own writings must bring them to life. Neither in letters nor in philosophy can we be content with others' thought forever. It is essential that the universities provide study centres, sources of knowledge, powerful stimuli; and that there be more circulation between higher education and secondary education.

It would be a grave injustice not to recognize the progress that has been made recently in these two faculties. But to the impatient external observer, how slow this progress seems, how hindered by impediments of all kinds the efforts of the best appear to be, how limited and problematic their influence. . . . The absence of great liberal institutions [*facultés désintéressées*] in Montreal and Quebec has often been deplored, for they would be unique in North America and could therefore attract thousands of foreign students. That would be a practical justification for the work to be pursued. But how much closer to the heart, and the heart of the question, is the other justification: it is not for others that we need it, but for ourselves! It is essential that some people examine the foundations of our culture. For even in an age when, perhaps, a new civilization is being founded, in which prodigious scientific discoveries are altering not only scientific concepts but the whole social and economic organization of the planet—even today the great books remain great, and they have never finished delivering us their message. They remain a marvellous school of personality.

XI

For in fact that is where these reflections have been leading. The great duty is to be oneself, to become oneself fully, one's best self—to deepen oneself while keeping in harmony with oneself.

If we had time to explore the other areas of culture—understood this time in its intellectual sense—artistic creation, scientific research, the training required for the major professions—in the end we would come back to the same conclusion: the need to be, and in order better to be, to remain in harmony with the most basic elements of our existence, both individual and collective.

It would also be necessary to examine the question of cultural exchanges, since being oneself has never implied closing oneself to others; nowhere is 'isolation' more unthinkable than in the realm of the spirit. And here I would point out the necessity of maintaining close relations with France; we never doubted this before, but with the fantastic development of American power and with the decline in the political prestige of France, this assumption has been called into question in more than one quarter; but never has the necessity been more real. It implies not subjugation, but much interchange, bonds of affection, a mutual confidence based on a more complete truth. Then there is the connection with Latin-America. And the friendship of other Canadian cultures. Remember that we are small and weak, threatened by a neighbour diffusing a virulent poison; we know that we cannot be self-sufficient. Being ourselves, therefore, requires that we choose our influences, that among those from the United States we accept the very best—that there are such is indisputable—and balance them with others that share a spiritual kinship with us.

In short, what we have been discussing, at length and inadequately, are the conditions for the existence of a national culture. Except for the stateless (and even then!) every being carries the mark of a particular culture. The richer it is, the more it nourishes him. Behold him as an adult. Now, if his destiny transcends that of the common run, let him depart on his own mysterious personal journey. He will make it on his own strengths, together with those he has received from his environment, and wherever he goes he will take with him something of his origins. In return, if he attains some prominence, his long journey will have an effect on the nation, adding to it some new and precious element.

On the one hand, then, is the compost from which we have sprung, and on the other the summits we wish to scale. If we aspire to maintain both, to reconcile one with the other, are we trapping ourselves in a contradiction? Must we betray nationality in order to attain humanity? Is it asking too much to want to slight nothing: neither the cultural past to which we feel ourselves tied—and more than tied—so conditioned by it that we carry it with us in all our undertakings and intend to preserve it—nor the other glories, the foreign ones that properly speaking are not foreign at all, since they too are the work of man, and as such invite our respect and our love . . . ?

In a man capable of reflection, I believe that this duality is productive. It requires a tension in his being, a constant search for a rich equilibrium.

In the same way, as the old image has it, the elm seeks security and nourishment deep in the earth, hanging on with all the strength of its roots. But it stretches its branches up and out, towards the sky.

AUTHOR'S NOTES

[1] *L'Action nationale*, May 1951.
[2] Me Antoine Rivard, 'Pour servir la cause canadienne-française', *L'Action nationale*, February 1951.
[3] Let us note, however, that of all forms of popular entertainment, radio is the least dominated by the American influence, and a field in which strenuous efforts are being made.
[4] *Cahiers d'action catholique*, February 1950, summarized by Pierre Juneau in *Cité libre*, February 1951.

III
HIGH-TECH
POLITICS

GEORGE GRANT

George Grant (b. 1918) is Canada's outstanding political thinker. Although he is often labelled a 'Red Tory', the name does little to clarify his distinctive amalgam of toryism, liberalism, socialism, and nationalism. Like any real thinker, he is not easily categorized. Grant's early writings—mainly articles published in academic quarterlies—are represented here by an address he presented at the Couchiching Conference in the summer of 1955.

The Minds of Men in the Atomic Age

I don't intend tonight to discuss whether we are going to be blown up or whether the human race is going to be sensible enough to survive. Whether we are going to destroy ourselves by Intercontinental Ballistic Missiles or slowly corrupt the very basis of our animal existence—I do not know. At this conference I've noticed so far an assumption that all is well if only we escape these external menaces. General Phillips talked of the horrors of atom war and asked are we going to sacrifice the happy and free life we have now. When there was talk of underdeveloped countries—it was just assumed that what the West had to give these countries was an unreserved blessing. That is if all the world became one big prosperous suburb like those in Toronto or Detroit or Manchester—then all would be well. Last night Mr Parkinson and the other speakers talked of the dynamic economy of expansion—a polite word for the boom—and just assumed that naturally this was to be taken as an undisputed good. But can these assumptions be made? Have we such a wonderful society in Canada and the States? Is the great problem of our world how we can escape simple animal destruction as General Phillips said—or is the question what is there about the human race that makes it worthwhile that it should survive? I can imagine a prosperous society, without war, of healthy animals adjusted to worshipping their machines which could be so disgusting that one could will that it should be destroyed.

Therefore what I want to talk about is the quality of mind or soul (for these two words mean exactly the same thing) which exists on this continent. In other words, if we aren't smashed in an all-out fight with the Asiatics, what kind of society is developing here at home?

The great fact of Canada to-day—indeed the great fact of the whole modern world—is that we are now living in the mass scientific society and this is something totally new in the experience of the human race. All the forms of our life—sexual, economic, political, artistic, moral and above all religious—must be seen within this new situation—the world of the big city, automation and the atom.

When I want to think of what the mass society is, and how much it has come to be in Canada I think of Mr E. P. Taylor's Don Mills development in the north of Toronto. Thousands of comfortable simple homes thrown up within a year from which hundreds of white collared workers go forth to the new clean factories and offices. A community whose centres are an enormous Dominion store and Brewers warehouse—(they should put a spire on this warehouse)—a community where families are co-operative enterprises to get the latest in electrical equipment and where children in mass schools are taught to be adjusted to their total life situation, watch the same television programmes, drink the same drinks and go charging around in the same over-powered automobiles, the bumpers of which are now decorated with phallic symbols. Now of course, not all Canada is the mass world yet. But gradually and surely we move towards it. For instance the farm community, as it once existed, is bound slowly to disappear—for even if people are farmers by profession they must become more and more town people with the automobile, the radio and television, the machine and mass education. Indeed of one thing we may be certain, the economy of organised obsolescence, and high returns for the salesman, the broker and the engineer, public technical education and social standardisation, mass stimulated sexual life and mass popular entertainment, this is the world which must find an ever fuller incarnation in Canada. I do not know what forms of the human spirit this new world will produce—but one thing I do know—no sensible person can believe that the same kind of people are going to come out of this environment as came out of the old Canadian towns and farms.

Now there is no doubt that the mass society is here to stay—unless the bombs really start falling. Nor have I any doubt about the great good it has brought. It is obviously good that women should have automatic washing machines; it is almost as good that we men should have cars. The fact that machines do our work means we have more free time and human freedom requires this time. In the old days leisure was something reserved for the privileged. Now it is open to more and more and surely what we need for ourselves we must see as necessary for others and this possibility of leisure for all does involve the machine. Even modern medicine, however much of a sacred cow it has become, we must judge as good. Let anyone who has a child in pain doubt that. Indeed at the profoundest level we must welcome the mass scientific society, despite all its horrors. For it has put us in a new relation to nature. We can now as never before choose to make our world, to use nature and abuse her, but less than ever before need we submit to her as necessity. For instance, with advances in contraception chastity is less motivated by fear and becomes an open decision of the spirit.

But let us also be certain what a terrible price is being paid over all North America for the benefits of the mass society. And what that price is can easily be stated. Economic expansion through the control of nature by science has become the chief purpose of our existence. It has become the goal to which everything else must be subordinated, the God we worship. Indeed for the last three hundred years there have been a band of thinkers telling men to worship the world. Now at last in North America this has become the dominant religion, which shapes our society at nearly every point. What is wrong with this religion? The plain fact that man's real purpose in life is not this. The goal of human existence is not to be found in the world of nature—but in freedom. Indeed, to be a man at all and not just an animal who looks like a man but is not, is to strive to become free. And a free man is a person who is not ruled by fear or passion—or the world around him—but by the eternal world of truth and goodness which is there to be realized by every thought and action in our lives.

The freest of all men once said: 'I have overcome the world.' And this is what life is for, to overcome the world, as we live in it deeply.

This is our human destiny, because our environment of nature depends upon an absolute environment—call it if you will God—and to live in the presence of that absolute and to judge the world by it, is what it is to be free. I do not mean by this that a free man will turn away from the world in aloof isolation—after all the man I have called freest lived in no ivory tower—but met the world most directly on a cross—but what I do mean is that the free man is he who does not abandon himself to the mood of his age—but who lives at the point where the passing moments of his life are met by the urgent present of the eternal. That is not to be a sheer animal or, worse, a machine.

Therefore, the price we have paid for the expanding economy is that by making it God men turn away from their proper purpose in this life. There is nothing wrong with automobiles and washing machines, but they must be known as simply means—means to richness of life for individuals and society.

But the expanding economy is no longer a means to us—a means for the liberation of the spirit—it has become an end in itself and as such is enslaving us. It so sets the tone and pattern of our society that the standards it imposes close people off from knowing what life is for. Look at the wives of our executives; look at the young men in the sack suits who have taken the vow to success; look at the girls in Woolworth's selling all day till they are exhausted and then being peddled a dream of heaven from Hollywood and NBC. The boom world creates like an aura its own standard of success—of what really matters in life—and that aura lies over everything, choking people with the fear of failure in terms of those standards, and cuts us off from any truer vision of life.

If you want to see just how much the expanding economy has become our God read a book called 'Canada's Tomorrow'. It is an account of a conference the Westinghouse company called together [in 1953] to discuss the future of our country. Leaders of all kinds from business and labour and government, from the universities and science and journalism were present. Well, the unanimous report of that conference was just more and more of the expanding economy—more trade, more production, more scientific research, more people. Its motto was the bigger the better; or size is greatness. The book should have been called 'The Messiah Machine; or What Mr C. D. Howe Wants for Canada's Tomorrow'.* There was no attempt to look at what all the expansion is for or what kind of people are produced by such a world. It was just taken for granted that the true happiness of persons is always to be found in short term economic gain. No questions of quality were asked; only questions of quantity. No ultimate questions were asked at all. If this is Canada's tomorrow, count me out of it.

And why I mention this book is that the people at this conference were the leaders of Canada—the men who are making our society and whose thoughts about our future are therefore really important. If these people think this way, this is the kind of Canada we are going to have. For let's have no soft democratic soap. It is the powerful and the influential who shape the short term destiny of a country. If this 'the bigger-the better' spirit prevails among these educated leaders, it gradually shapes all of us. Brantford and Kitchener can be but pale shadows of Toronto.

One comic side of this conference 'Canada's Tomorrow' was that though there was the usual talk about the dangers of communism and Russia, the kind of society outlined at it, doesn't seem very different from the society the Russian leaders are building for their people. If a conference of this sort had been called among Russian managers and university presidents and officials, the pattern of Soviet Tomorrow would probably have been very much the same. The same quantitative judgment of success. There must be places very much like the Don Mills development outside Moscow at the moment—less comfortable now—but they'll soon be equally comfortable and equally adjusted.

Indeed one of the communist myths which most of our business men and government leaders wholeheartedly accept—though they would loathe it to be known as a Marxist myth—is seek ye first the kingdom of the boom and all shall be added unto you. What they say is that economic development must come first and it will inevitably bring in its trail the pursuit of truth and beauty. Indeed the very words 'truth and beauty' are seldom used now to denote realities, but rather a confused blend of sentiment and culture. Nice for those who have the time, but less real than the 'hard facts of life'—'the business of living'. Just as it takes a while for the new rich to learn to spend their money with taste, so it will take time for culture to flower in our new rich society. The frosting of the cake is put on last. Like much Marxist theory this is so much liberal illusion. What should be perfectly obvious is that if you pursue economic prosperity at the expense of everything else, what you will get is economic prosperity at the expense of everything else.

To see our minds in the atomic age, it is particularly necessary to look at our schools, our universities and our churches. For the schools, the universities and the churches are the chief institutions which can lead men to freedom in the truth. Love and art, thought and prayer are after all the activities which distinguish men from the other beasts and it is the school, the university and the church upon which we are chiefly dependent for stimulation of these activities. Our political and economic institutions have a function which is largely negative—they exist to prevent bad things happening: the schools and universities and churches have the positive role, they exist to stimulate the good.

Now our schools have been going through a terribly difficult period. When I criticise them I do not mean to lay all the blame on any particular shoulders. All of us, our ancestors and ourselves are corporately involved in the guilt of what our schools have become. The mass democratic society has insisted on mass education. This, of course, has been the only possible and right course. But let us have no doubt that this process has meant a falling away of quality. What has happened is that the schools have been trying to carry on their job in a society which by and large does not think that education is important. What parents in the mass society are interested in is that their children should be fitted for success and adjustment, not educated. And what has been particularly sad is that so many educational administrators have not only given in to that pressure but have accepted the philosophy of worldly success and adjustment as a true account of what the schools are for. This is where I agree one hundred percent with Hilda Neatby.* The acceptance by so many educationalists of the philosophy of John Dewey has in general meant the surrender by the teacher and the school of their proper function. If you say with Dewey that the intellect is solely a servant of social living, then you are saying that human beings have no transcendent purpose beyond society—no need for liberation of the mind. Indeed such liberation is now no longer considered even a respectable goal. How can it be, since it is almost the exact opposite of the adjustment which the psychologists and the progressive educators teach us to aspire to? Nowadays, who really minds about prejudices, illusions, myths and superstitions, as long as they are the right ones, the socially acceptable ones, the mentally healthy ones, the good Canadian ones? Does not Dewey tell us that truth is what works?

What is meant by successful democratic living is conformity to the lowest common denominator of desire in our society. With such a philosophy the schools exist to pander to that mediocrity of desire—rather than to lead children to know what is truly worth desiring. No wonder—school teaching is a despised and underpaid profession. Teachers are seen as servants of the desires of the multitude.

To go a step downward, the surrender of the universities to the boom spirit is overwhelming. I watch it every day of my life. Universities are now places where young people can insure their entrance into the prosperous part of society by learning some technique and where staff employees (once known as professors) increase the scope of some immediately useful technique. Intellect is respected, if at all, as a tool which can help one to do certain things in the world more efficiently. It is no longer valued for its relation to its proper object, truth. For there is no truth which it concerns us to know, there is only the truth with which we are concerned to do things. Indeed the three powerful forces in our society, business, government and the democratic many all have used their power to kill the university as a place of truth seeking and turn it into a successful technological institute.* The business men who rule our universities, naturally see them as places to perpetuate in the young the desires of the market place and of competition. Governments break down the balance of the university by encouraging those studies useful for defence and prosperity. It would be foolish for instance to blame the government for setting up the National Research Council—an institution perfectly valid in itself—but let us face the consequences of its existence for the university and the nation. It means we are channelling our ablest students into a narrow training in physical science and this will mean finally a nation which knows how the physical world works and knows nothing else and believes there is nothing more to know but this. Perhaps the disappearance of the liberal university was an inevitable accompaniment of the expanding economy but let us not fool ourselves as to what this disappearance means to the kind of world that is coming into existence.

Last and saddest we come to the churches. Let me say immediately that when I speak of the churches I speak only of my own tradition, the Protestant. And here we come to the heart of the matter. For what men believe to be ultimately true is what makes them what they are and through them their society. And Protestantism is the basic issue because North America has been more deeply formed by Protestantism than by any other influence. Indeed, the central riddle of our history is why Protestantism, centred as it was on a great affirmation of freedom and the infinite, has been the dominant force in shaping a society which is now so little free and so little aware of the infinite. To answer that riddle is not possible here, but what must be said clearly is that whatever the present outward success of Protestantism, it is faced by a deep inward failure. That inward failure is seen in the fact of its surrender to become a tame confederate of the mass secular society. The ideal minister has become the active democratic organiser who keeps the church going as a place of social cohesion and positive thinking à la Norman Vincent Peale. If he can promote building, increase organisation, provide inspiration on Sunday and convince young people that there are more socially acceptable activities than sex and drinking he is a success. Best of all, if he knows a little empirical psychology, he will understand that when a church member gets into real spiritual difficulties he should be sent to a psychiatrist (the man who can really get things done in the world of the spirit). What is however wrong about it, is that it is a soft substitute for the real work of the church, which is to teach people through thought and prayer and worship, to seek the ultimate truth, and to live by it. In my opinion to this their real job the Protestant churches are largely indifferent.

I do not want to be pessimistic, but when asked to give a diagnosis, one must be honest. Nothing has done us more harm in Canada than that aura of self-congratulation with which we surround ourselves. 'This great country of ours' or 'the Kitimat and democracy'* routine which now goes the rounds in pulpits, service clubs and political platforms. 'Take what you want', said God, 'take it and pay for it.' Let us not doubt what we have wanted, what we have taken and how we are paying for it.

Of course, this is not to say that we can or should turn back from the technological society. What I am saying is that the great job in Canada now does not lie in further economic expansion and quantitative progress, but in trying to bring quality and beauty of existence into that technological world—to try and make it a place where richness of life may be discovered. And of course some people in Canada are realizing this in their lives right now. I think of a brilliant architect who is not interested in making a fortune but in seeing how the city of Toronto can be more than an efficient machine of sewers and super-highways, rather a place in which human beings can lead a good life. I think of ministers who are making their churches places of adoration rather than issuers of eternal insurance policies. I think of the man who runs a small garage where the repairing of cars is made a work of excellence and interest rather than greed. I think of young people who have the courage to be school teachers when to the world it is a mark of their failure. I think of people in broadcasting and TV who use all their intelligence and integrity to see that these instruments are used for the dissemination of truth. I think of artists who give themselves to reality and beauty rather than quick financial success. I think of philosophers who practice the presence of God.

Whether freedom and love will be realized into the technological world who can tell? Or will our society pour into its emptiness the bare idea of pleasure in all its manifold, fascinating and increasingly perverted forms—till force and mediocrity come entirely to rule us?

I do not want to be pessimistic. However, what is certain, beyond doubt, is that whether we live at the end of the world or at the dawn of a golden age or neither, it still counts absolutely to each one of us that in and through the beauty and anguish, the good and evil of the world, we come in freedom upon the joy unspeakable.

DAVID LEWIS

The 1950s were the era of 'the end of ideology'. The Soviet experiment had failed; the Western capitalist societies, with their mixed free-enterprise economies, were prospering; the Labour party in Britain had been defeated in the general elections of 1951 and 1955; and socialism everywhere seemed to be in the doldrums intellectually as well as electorally. Many leading members of the CCF thought that the party's fortunes might be improved by abandoning the Regina Manifesto, with its strident demand for an end to capitalism, and adopting a program more in tune with the times. It was against this background that David Lewis (1909-81) delivered the speech reprinted here. One of the founders of the party, he had served from 1937 to 1950 as its National Secretary, and in 1955 was its National Chairman. Lewis was later to become national leader of the NDP (1971-5).

A Socialist Takes Stock

In view of my official position as National Chairman of the CCF, I should emphasize immediately that what I say here this evening represents my own thoughts and opinions and is not necessarily official party policy. I am confident, from my knowledge of the CCF and its personnel, that most of the opinions I shall express are shared by a majority of our members and by a majority of the National Executive and Council. But, in fairness, it should be understood that my remarks have not even been seen, let alone approved, by any of my colleagues on the National Executive or Council and that they are, therefore, made on my own personal responsibility.*

SOCIALIST ENDS

Democratic socialism has always proclaimed five major ends and four major means. There are, of course, other ways of stating the ends and of combining them into a smaller or greater number. Equally, there are other ways of stating the means. But no matter what words and particular combination are used, the following are the ends and the means which have motivated and inspired the great labour and democratic socialist movement the world over and throughout the years.

What are the ends which socialism seeks to achieve? They are, broadly, the following:

1. *A classless or egalitarian society within the borders of a nation.* Socialists have proclaimed as their goal a society from which exploitation of man by man and of class by class or of group by group will be eliminated; where every person will have an equal opportunity to share in a rich and varied life and to develop his talents, whatever they may be, to the full, both at work and during leisure hours. This—the classless society based on equality—is the major aim of democratic socialism.

2. *Equality among all nations, regardless of colour, race, or economic*

standard. We strive for a world based on the brotherhood of man from which the practices of imperialism and the ignominy of colonialism will disappear; a world in which the more advanced economic societies will assist the less developed ones without the price in human exploitation which has characterized overseas expansion in the last centuries. We want a classless world society based on universal brotherhood.

3. *Human freedom everywhere.* The socialist dream is of a society in which the worth and dignity of every human being is recognized and respected, where differences of origin, of religion and of opinion will not only be tolerated, but accepted as desirable and necessary to the beauty and richness of the human mosiac.

4. *Economic and social security.* Socialists seek not only equality of opportunity but a constant advance in the opportunities offered and available to mankind; not only a fair division of the cake, but a constantly larger cake. Socialists long ago recognized that modern technological advance has made possible, and will increasingly make possible, an economic standard of living from which material suffering, economic want and the oppression of insecurity can disappear. We know, of course, that meeting the economic needs of mankind will not by itself create the life for which the human spirit strives. But we also know that if we can break the prison walls built by economic pressures and insecurities, the human spirit will be released and our moral and cultural values enriched by new and greater opportunities.

5. *A lasting peace based on freedom and equality within nations and freedom and equality among nations.* This end is today shared by all men of goodwill the world over, but socialists have always been among the leaders searching for peace, long before the threat of nuclear weapons frightened many sleeping consciences into a fretful awareness of the horrors of war.

These aims—an egalitarian society, a world free from imperialism, freedom, social security and peace—have inspired and continue to inspire socialist thought and action. Let me say immediately that I am well aware that some of these aims are shared by democratic non-socialists. There are many people in Canada and elsewhere who hold other social philosophies, but who also genuinely believe in human freedom and in peace. However, some of the aims which I have described are held by socialists only and all of them together form the fabric of democratic socialist philosophy and do not form the fabric of any other political philosophy.

People who support the capitalist society as a desirable social system believe in a class society and not in a classless one; they believe in inequality and not in equality; they believe in the right of one nation to make profits at the expense of another, just as they believe in the right of one group within a nation to make profits at the expense of the rest; they believe in the right of the sons and daughters of the rich to have greater opportunities than those of the poor; and even as regards freedom they place the rights of property above those of human beings or, at least, on an equal footing. All these concepts the socialist passionately rejects.

At the other extreme, those who believe in the Communist society reject in practice all of the aims of socialism, despite their deceitful words and slogans. In every communist land there has been established a new, but no less evil class society. The elite of the communist party, the membership of that party, the civil service in government as well as in the party, the secret police, and the army, form a class or classes which are the top of a social pyramid as clearly defined as the pyramid of wealth to which we are accustomed and, if anything, much more oppressive and evil in its consequences. It is unnecessary to remind you that the communist state stifles freedom and enthrones uniformity and conformity as the absolute duty of every citizen. Domination by the chief communist state over other nations and states, rather than equality among nations, has been the communist practice, particularly during the last decade, and the brotherhood of man is derided by communists as a sentimental, decadent, bourgeois idea. The communist society has become a new type of class society, based on force and dedicated to world domination.

Thus even a brief analysis of the major social philosophies heard in the market place of world ideas today, shows that though proponents of capitalism do believe in some form of freedom and peace and although communist protagonists do advance social services such as health and education, only the democratic socialist fully believes in and fights for all of the aims which I have outlined and which together comprise the elements of a morally desirable society.

SOCIALIST MEANS

What means has the socialist proposed for building the road to this society? Briefly, they are, I think, the following:

1. We must emphasize, first, the determination of the socialist to pursue at all times *only democratic procedures* and to base his actions on the consent of the people freely expressed. To use any form of dictatorship to achieve so-called desirable ends is a perversion of our basic ideas of freedom and will in practice also pervert the ends. We reject the cynical proposition that the ends justify the means, if for no other reason than that the means shape the ends. An evil means will much more likely lead to an evil end, than to a desirable one. Therefore, the democratic socialist condemns the use of dictatorial methods anywhere at any time and is determined to achieve his ends by democratic means only.

2. *A constant and continuing improvement in the existing standards of living and in the social services provided by the state.* The democratic socialist has not taken the position that the worse conditions are, the easier it will be to persuade people of the need for fundamental change. Whether that is true or not, it is thoroughly immoral and inhuman. The democratic socialist has, therefore, always fought for all day-to-day improvements in the life of the people: for desirable labour legislation, unemployment insurance, old age pensions, family allowances, pensions for widows and orphans, the rehabilitation of those who are physically handicapped, improved housing, improvements in the educational system, the elimination of corruption in government, progress in democratic procedures and machinery, improvement of the judicial system, protection for civil liberties and civil rights of individual citizens,

protection of the farmer's income and the equity in his land and produce, protection of labour's right to strike and to build powerful free trade unions, pre-paid national health insurance, financial assistance for higher education and measures to assist and enrich the cultural and artistic life of the country. All these things we have not put on a shelf to wait for the coming of socialism. On the contrary, we have pressed for them and fought for them throughout the years; we want them now and we welcome measures to implement them whatever the complexion of the government which puts them into effect and even though they offer much less than they should.

3. The third means which the socialist has proposed, and when he has had the chance, has used, is that of *social planning*. The socialist rejects the capitalist theory that an unregulated law of supply and demand should control the destinies of a society and its members. He believes that it is both necessary and possible for society collectively to plan at least its economic future and to regulate the production and distribution of goods and services so as to achieve an expanding economy of full employment and a fair share for all members of society. Both the last war and the immediate post-war years have clearly demonstrated that without such planning socially desirable objectives are not automatically reached and that social planning is possible without encroaching on freedom and without bending democratic procedures.

4. The fourth means which the socialist has proposed is that of *public ownership*, whether it be ownership by the state,—federal, provincial or municipal,—or ownership by a collectivity of citizens in the form of co-operatives, credit unions or the like. There are three main reasons behind the socialist belief in public ownership.

REASONS FOR PUBLIC OWNERSHIP

First and foremost, that the modern concentration of wealth and property places too much power, both economic and political, in the hands of too few people or, what is even worse, in the hands of giant corporations which, by their very nature, are without heart and without soul. A corporation is merely a legal entity, concerned exclusively with ledger sheets and financial statements, with profit and loss accounts, with efficiency and the accumulation of ever-increasing assets and with extension of its economic power regardless of the consequences to society as a whole. Such vast power, the socialist argues, cannot intelligently be left uncontrolled to a few people and to non-human agencies such as the modern corporation and, still less, the modern monopolistic corporation.

Secondly, nationalization has been proposed by socialists because the job of social planning is made more difficult by the power of private corporations and would be made much easier by public ownership of the key levers in the economy.

Thirdly, the growth and power of private corporations have imposed on society a standard of values which perverts the best ideals of man. Wealth has become the major mark of success and he who dares inquire into the ways used to accumulate that wealth and to question the ethics employed, is a wild-eyed agitator. All the precepts of the highest human morality expressed in religion or in the philosophies of great men are ignored even when they are praised, and perverted even while they are proclaimed in high-sounding phrases. Human co-operation, tolerance, charity, humility, sympathy, the idea that one is his brother's keeper, the notion that one owes a duty to live his life without hurting anyone else and the concept that one's rights are no higher than those of any other person,—all these moving human ideals are derided and ignored by the daily practices of capitalist behaviour. And this attitude stems directly from the hungry drive for ever larger accumulations of wealth, of profits and of private power.

ENDS AND MEANS

It has been necessary to outline briefly the objectives which motivate socialism and the means which socialism proposes to use in order that the discussion of the tool of public ownership may be framed in the proper context. It is obvious that the important thing about socialism is its objectives. Indeed, that is the important thing about any social philosophy. The means by which one may try to achieve his objectives are necessarily secondary to the ends.

Among democratic socialists there is, and always has been, agreement about the ends. On the other hand, there is, always has been and probably always will be, disagreement about the means to be used at any given time. This disagreement is desirable as well as inevitable if it is recognized as disagreement on means only and if there is tolerance in the family. When people mistakenly identify the means with the ends, the disagreement becomes bitter and unreasonable.

Perhaps first among socialist controversies is the question of the extent to which the tool of public ownership can or should be used by socialists in modern society. The disagreement on this issue really dates back to the very first discussions of socialism, but it has been sharpened and [made] more acute in the last quarter of a century. And it has been thus sharpened for several reasons which derive from the experiences which societies have had in the past twenty-five or so years.

Until fairly recently it had been accepted by most socialists as axiomatic that nationalization of industry would automatically bring with it greater social and political freedom and a release from the obstacles to the widest liberty which private economic power produces. Place the ownership of the economy in the hands of the people through their government, the argument ran, and you will automatically remove the evil influence and power of private corporations and simultaneously give the workers unheard-of freedom. It was also accepted by many socialists as axiomatic that a country in which private capitalism has been abolished will automatically and necessarily be a country of peace, a country which will have no reason to want aggression against or domination over other lands.

PUBLIC OWNERSHIP NO PANACEA

The developments in the Soviet Union in particular, and in other communist states as well, have completely shattered both these assumptions and have shown them to have been and to be entirely false. In the communist societies all wealth, or almost all wealth, has been taken over by the state. But, instead of greater freedom, there is actually no freedom at all. The power of the private corporation has been replaced by the totalitarian power of the Communist party and state over the lives of the workers, farmers and every other section of the community. Far from releasing the wells of liberty, the concentration of economic and political power in the communist state has poisoned them altogether. That experience is conclusive that public ownership alone does not guarantee freedom; that political and social freedom,—the foundation-stone of any desirable society,—is not dependent only on the form of ownership in the economy.

Similarly, we have learned from the actions of the Soviet Union since the end of the war and from the military structure of communist society as a whole, that there are pressures towards aggression and war other than economic ones and that the lust for power and the zeal of fanaticism are at least as powerful forces endangering peace as economic competition and conflicts.

In short, the comfortable generalizations of the early socialists have been proven by history to be false, or only partially valid, although they were genuinely and well meant. Socialists can, therefore, no longer regard nationalization as an automatic panacea for all ills, but must regard it merely as one tool that is available in appropriate circumstances for the furtherance of socialist ends.

OTHER CONTROLS

The experience of the Scandinavian countries, the history of the Roosevelt era in the United States and developments during the last war, have all shown that there are available in the modern economy tools of control and of planning which can be effectively applied without actually replacing private with public ownership in all spheres. We have in the past quarter century, and particularly in the past fifteen years, learned more about economic planning and control than society had experienced in the previous century and a half of modern capitalism. The use of fiscal and financial policies to influence the volume and direction of investment, to redistribute income, and to stimulate purchasing power, has been demonstrated as a practical tool for economic planning, at least in periods when there is no major depression. How effective and fair the use of the tool has been is another matter. That depends on the user and not on the tool.

In all modern societies there is growing up a considerable body of social welfare legislation which produces what are known as 'transfer payments'. These,—unemployment insurance benefits, old age pensions, family allowances, farm support payments and the like,—provide a constant stream of purchasing power into the hands of large sections of the people. The payments are, of course, grossly inadequate and one of the things for which socialists fight is an increase in them. However, whatever their level, whether more or less adequate, they represent a sizeable flow of purchasing power into the hands of consumers and obviously constitute a cushion against loss of purchasing power through loss of earnings.

To these transfer payments from the state must be added the pension and welfare plans, and the more recent guaranteed annual wage, which are being won over the bargaining table by organized labour. The growth of such plans adds to the cushion against the loss of purchasing power which the people have always experienced from time to time under capitalism.

PREREQUISITES FOR NATIONALIZATION

The consequences of these experiences are clear. For one thing, they make the need for public ownership a great deal less urgent in some fields and they make the appeal of public ownership a great deal less attractive to the average citizen. The question of the citizens' support for public ownership is not merely one of votes at election time; it goes much deeper than that. If you agree with my premise that socialists like ourselves are determined to implement our programme democratically, it follows that we cannot do so except it have the consent of a majority of the people.

The experiences of labour and socialist governments in Scandinavian countries, in Great Britain, in Australia and New Zealand, and in our own Saskatchewan, have also taught us two other things about public ownership. The first is that in order to make public ownership successful, it is necessary to have skilled personnel at the executive and management levels as well as a skilled production force, and that to train the required personnel takes time and effort.

Secondly, we have learned that nationalization of an industry does not immediately remove, although it substantially lessens, the conflicts in short-term interests between labour and management. I recall the pithy remark of a British Miners' leader who addressed a CCF National Convention some years ago to the effect that it is much easier to socialize an industry than it is to 'socialize' its workers. To develop the necessary techniques, attitudes and relationships which will remove such conflict and will produce a greater identity of interests between the workers in an industry and the public management of it also takes a great deal of time and effort.

Furthermore, these experiences have thrown up practical problems of democratizing the management and control of a publicly-owned industry, the relationship of such industry to the actual machinery of government and similar questions which, until a dozen or so years ago, had merely been the subject of theoretical disputation.

In short, recent experiences have shown to the thoughtful, open-minded socialist that nationalization even of monopolistic and key industries must be planned and timed so as to coincide with public understanding of its need, the availability of the necessary personnel and the development of the necessary relationships within the industry and between it and the state.

The present disagreements on the value and extent of nationalization as a tool toward the socialist objective all stem, in my view, from the experiences over the past quarter century, and more particularly over the past decade. The opinions range all the way from a refusal to acknowledge or even to recognize any of the experiences as facts, to the rejection of public ownership altogether as a useful socialist tool. I suspect that the truth, as usual, lies somewhere between those two extremes.

It cannot be the purpose of this talk to attempt to lay down any definitive policy for public ownership. For one thing, the major intent of my discussion is to persuade you, if I can, that it is a mistake to lay down a definitive programme since the programme must necessarily change from period to period in the light of changing economic and political facts. Moreover, I am free to admit that the experiences I have discussed are still too recent to justify any final conclusions. There are, however, certain principles which necessarily flow from the analysis which I have attempted to make and which I present to you for further study and discussion.

Public ownership should be recognized by us as a means or as a tool to be used wherever the circumstances make it necessary and only to the extent that it is necessary. It remains and is an important tool and one that can be defended by the highest social and moral principles. It remains the most effective tool for breaking the greedy stranglehold on the life of the nation held by huge corporations and [for] restoring to the people the resources which are their birthright and the wealth which they have produced.

NEVER TOTAL NATIONALIZATION

It follows from what has been said that the democratic socialist today should continue to reject any suggestion of total nationalization. In fact, of course, he has always rejected it and has always emphasized that he is concerned with public ownership only of the key economic levers of society. Nevertheless, the idea is still abroad that socialists intend eventually, if not now, to socialize everything. I, as one socialist, have no such intention and it is my firm belief that neither the CCF in Canada, nor its sister parties in Great Britain and all other free countries, has such an intention or ever has had. Public ownership in a democratic society and under a democratic socialist government will never cover more than a part of the economy and only that part the public ownership of which is essential for the welfare of the people. The time is long overdue when this should be frankly stated without qualification and without apology.

It is not possible to lay down ahead of time the principles which should govern the question as to when and whether any industry should be socialized. There are, however, some general criteria which may be suggested. From what has been said, it is clear that one factor would be the place of the industry in the economy, its importance to other industries and the extent to which the rest of the economy is dependent on it. Another factor would be the monopolistic character of the industry and whether it was part of a price or other combine. A third consideration would be the industry's efficiency, its treatment of its employees and its attitude toward the public welfare. Finally, a government would have to decide whether it was equipped to handle the industry efficiently, whether it had the necessary personnel to operate it satisfactorily for the benefit of the people.

In short, the advantages of socialization would be carefully weighed against any possible disadvantages. If the health of the economy required it and if the welfare of Canada would be advanced by it, then socialization should follow without fear or favour.

THE FIGHT AGAINST GIANT CORPORATIONS

In any case, it is clear that the battle against the inhuman power of giant corporations, whether monopolistic or semi-monopolistic, must continue unabated. The evils of the concentration of wealth are still with us. The insecurity of millions of people whose very life is dependent on such corporations and their policies is still around us. The injustice and the misery flowing from unreasonable inequalities of income are everywhere in the land for anyone with open eyes and heart to see and to weep over.

Even cold statistics make this clear. At this time of relatively full employment, some 83% of our wage earners make under $3,000 per year. If you convert this amount into real wages, taking 1939 as a basis, you have 83% of our wage earners making only slightly more than $1,600 per year, or just over $30 per week, in terms of 1939 purchasing power of the dollar. The reverse of this is equally staggering. Only 1% of our wage earners which, by the way, include executives from the president down as well as the workers on the line, earn $6,000 a year or more.

The farmers are in a similar position and, if anything, even more insecure. For a few years following the war the farmers' net income reached reasonable proportions, particularly in 1951 and 1952. In 1954, however, their income dropped to half of what it was in 1951 and to only a little more than half of what it was in 1945.

In short, the examples just given merely serve to illustrate statistically what everyone can see around him in our country. Certainly the insecurity of our people is nowhere as great as it was in the 1930s. But inequality and insecurity, slums and unnecessary disease, lack of opportunity for many children and intolerable hardships in illness and old age, as well as sizeable unemployment among able-bodied workers, are still with us and all around us even in the best of years.

THE REAL STRUGGLE

At the same time our gross national product continues to climb, the expansion of the economy continues to provide ministers of the Crown with lyrical phrases and every year corporate profits reach greater heights. It is, therefore, obvious that the battle of the common man against the privileged groups in our society and against the large corporations within it remains important and urgent. Socialists must continue to stand in the forefront of that battle. The aim of increasing equality and decreasing the power of those at the top of the economic and social pyramid remains as necessary and desirable as it ever was.

Thus, the aims and policies of socialism, properly understood and stated, remain the only democratic answer to the basic problems of our society. Nor is it valid to assume that the present so-called prosperity of North America will continue forever without interruption. It can continue and even expand, but not without planning.

THE DANGERS AHEAD

For one thing, our present economy is geared to large defence expenditures. If international relations should, as we all hope, improve and lead either to an international agreement on armaments or to substantial reductions in defence expenditures in any other way, the effect on the stability of the economy is bound to be immediate and disastrous unless alternative uses for the released resources are provided in advance.

Furthermore, we have for two or three years had depressed areas in our economy. The coal, textile and agricultural implement industries are outstanding examples. Perhaps the greatest danger lies in our farm situation. The income of our farmers has fallen to depression levels. There are still unused surpluses of grain from 1953; the 1954 crop has hardly begun to move and the 1955 harvest is piled up without, even, the necessary storage space. If this situation lasts much longer, the farmers' reserves will disappear entirely with serious depressing effects on the rest of our economy. Wise planning is again essential.

Above all, we seem to be on the threshold of an industrial revolution to dwarf all previous ones. It is popularly termed 'automation'. All examples of the present technological revolution indicate that within a relatively few years thousands and thousands of workers will be thrown out of employment by new machines and new processes. What is socially significant about the present development is that white collar workers in offices and service industries will be hit just as hard, if not harder than plant workers. Unless we are prepared to plan for the transition, we are bound to have increasing unemployment as the technological development accelerates, with consequent dislocation and widespread hardships.

All this is becoming particularly urgent for Canada because we are rapidly becoming an economic colony of the United States. An increasing and alarming share of our natural resources is in the hands of American corporations which milk our economy without regard to Canada's future. The capitalists in our land, and their political parties, encourage this development, for they are as interested as their American counterparts in a 'fast buck' without regard to the social consequences for the Canadian people.

EQUALITY IS SOCIALIST WATCHWORD

It follows from what has been suggested throughout, that henceforth democratic socialism should emphasize its objectives in clear and rousing terms, rather than permit itself to be constantly on the defensive about the means which it proposes to use. Capitalist governments have found it necessary, sometimes unavoidable, to use the tool of public ownership. It is true that when they have used it, they have treated it with the contempt and the distrust which non-believers always show in such circumstances. Capitalist governments have also been forced to use the tool of a progressive advance in social welfare measures. Here it is also true that they have given with closed fist, rather than open hand, only so much as the vote-getting tacticians considered it necessary at any given time. Most of them do not really believe in the welfare society but have learned that welfare measures have become so popular that it would be political suicide to ignore them. For this socialists rightly take a great deal of the credit. Capitalist governments in the war era and in the years immediately following the war, were forced to use the tools of planning and controls to some extent. Again, their use was grudging and discriminatory, because they did not believe in it, but they used it. What I am trying to say is that the use of these tools, which were first made popular by socialists, does not make a Liberal or a Conservative into a socialist, nor does the failure to use one of the tools in a given set of circumstances make a socialist less a socialist.

The big and real difference between the socialist and the non-socialist lies in the philosophy of society, the social objectives which each respectively has. The second big and real difference is the kind of political instrument which each of them forges: the difference between the political party financed and controlled by a small group at the top of the pyramid and the party financed and controlled by the large masses at the bottom.

These are the real and lasting differences. The modern democratic socialist should proclaim his aims loudly and passionately. The equality of man is the socialist watchword; the moral struggle against injustice and inequality is the socialist's duty; to be a strong and powerful voice for the common man against the abuse and oppression of the privileged minority is the socialist's function; and to forge an ever finer and higher standard of values and a richer pattern of life and behaviour is the socialist's dream.

Some of his objectives and his aspirations the socialist shares with citizens of other political beliefs and orientation. Surely that is a good thing. To that important extent, the socialist work has already succeeded. But it is my profound conviction that no person who consciously and knowingly supports and defends the present system of society as a desirable basis of human life and relationships, can possibly understand the world around him or embrace the moral principles and social ends which democratic socialism alone proclaims.

W. L. MORTON

In the 1950s extreme conservatism was no more popular than extreme social-ism was. In 1959 William Morton (1908-80), who taught Canadian history at the University of Manitoba, equated conservatism with cognizance of human fallibility and thus the need for authority and tradition. His definition empha-sizes loyalty, continuity, and organic growth—more or less what Laurier had in mind when he spoke of 'the charm of habit'. Morton quickly classifies Macdonald's conservatism—'inspired through Elgin by the Peelites of the Pittite tradition'—and casts a hurried glance at the close but ambivalent relation between conservatism and liberalism since the middle of the last century. He seems unaware, however, of any special affinities between conservatism and either nationalism or socialism, affinities that were soon to be discovered as a result of the romance between nationalism and socialism. A group of Young Conservatives comprised the first audience for Morton's address.

Canadian Conservatism Now

Dr Johnson, that great Tory, once remarked that the devil was the first Whig. He meant, of course, that Satan was the first to rebel against constituted authority. If you ask yourself who the first Tory was, let me advise you to hesitate and draw back. Whoever the first Tory may have been, he was, we may be sure, respectful of authority. For one of the first principles of a conservative is respect for authority; not for authority merely as the right to command, but for authority as the expression of that law and order, and that civil decency without which society dissolves in anarchy.

And the next first principle is a similar respect for tradition, for that which is handed down from the experience of the race, or the wisdom of our ancestors. This is not ancestor worship, but merely the realization that, important as the individual is, he is what he is largely in virtue of what he is by blood and breeding, and of what he has absorbed, consciously or unconsciously, formally or informally, from home, church, school, and neighbourhood. He subscribes, in short, to Burke's definition of the social contract as a partnership in all virtue, a partnership between the generations, a contract not made once for all time, but one perennially renewed in the organic processes of society, the birth, growth, and death of successive generations.

Authority and tradition, then, are cornerstones of conservative belief. And the quarry from which they are dug is a particular belief about the nature of man. To the theologian this is the belief in original sin, the belief, that is, that man by his nature is imperfect, and is to be made perfect only by redemp-tion and grace. In philosophic terms, it is a denial of the fundamental liberal and Marxist belief that human nature is inherently perfectible, that man may realize the perfection that is in him if only the right environment is created. And, I need not tell you, this belief in human fallibility, or the other belief in human perfectibility, are what unmistakably and for all time separate the conservative from the liberal.

The belief in human imperfection need not, of course, be derived only from Christian theology. It is present by implication both in Stoicism and in Aristotle's *Politics*.

It is because he knows that the individual man is weak, imperfect, and limited that the conservative believes that men need to be sustained by authority and guided by tradition, the formulated experience of society.

This human need of fellowship, of the support of the church, or of the Aristotelian *polis*, gives rise, of course, to the next fundamental conservative principle. That is Loyalty. Loyalty is the instinct to do for others what is expected of one, it may be by one's superiors, it may be by one's fellows, it may be by one's inferiors. So important in the conservative creed is this great principle that Lord Hugh Cecil once defined conservatism as simply 'loyalty to persons'. He meant, of course, that the conservative not only regards loyalty as a cardinal virtue, but that he gives loyalty not to institutions or abstractions, but to persons, not to the Crown but to Queen Elizabeth, not to the Conservative party but to John Diefenbaker. But if loyalty is a personal matter, it is also a peculiarly conservative thing, for the conservative prefers the concrete to the abstract, and persons to ideas.

Finally, the conservative holds firmly to the need for continuity in human affairs. He does so because he believes in what Coleridge calls the Principle of Permanence in society. But today's conservative believes in permanence while recognizing the fact of change in human affairs. But change should come, he firmly believes, by way of organic growth, not by deliberate revolution or skilful manipulation. The good society of the conservative ideal, the society which would be just and admit of the good life, would not be static. It would change, but it would change as insensibly as a child grows, or as a river runs. Such change leads to the continuity that makes permanence possible.

The conservative, that is, is devoted to actual life, with all its imperfections. That is why, when the Whig is extinct and the Liberal as rare as the whooping crane, the Conservative continues perennial. He lives for the simple, organic things, children, dogs, the elm on the skyline, the water lapping at the rock. He is interested in family; he instinctively wants to know who your people were and where you come from. He sees society as persons knit by kinship and neighbourhood. And he endows society and nation with the same sense of organic life, and believes that men in their particular communities are members one of another.

That is how I define the conservative.

If that definition will serve to hint at the main characteristics of conservatism, I should now like to ask what are the particular qualities of Canadian conservatism? I raise the question, not because I profess to be able really to answer it, but only because I think it important to raise it. For the difficulty is that, if one has read something of the literature of conservatism, one is likely, in discussing Canadian conservatism, to talk in terms of English and continental philosophy and history.

This I hold to be one of the many faults of the late John Farthing's rare and precious little book, *Freedom Wears a Crown*.* Every thoughtful conservative would do well to read it, but it is caviare to the general, and it is, in my opinion, too much concerned with the English and the Anglican origins of conservatism. Canadian conservatism is of broader origin than Farthing suggests.

To discuss Canadian conservatism in these terms is not only to be unjust, it is to be historically inaccurate. I am all too prone to commit their error myself, because of my own descent and education. Yet it is important to realize that Canadian conservatism is of more than English origin, important though that is, and that it is a blend of so many strains of conservatism that it possesses a distinct national character.

Allow me briefly to touch on these various strains.

There is first of all the French Catholic tradition, that of the old *bleus* which at the touch of ultramontanism became the ultranationalist creed of the *castors*. Not only are there profoundly conservative qualities in Roman Catholicism itself, Catholic thinkers like de Maistre in the nineteenth century elaborated a body of conservative philosophy flatly opposed to the doctrine of popular sovereignty. In Quebec this strain of conservative thought worked itself out, superficially not so much as an anti-democratic movement as a cultural isolationist one. For Quebec, majority rule has meant English rule. Perhaps its chief manifestation today is [Premier] Duplessis' opposition to centralization.

So far as my observation goes, Canadian Roman Catholicism outside Quebec has been little influenced by Catholic conservative thought. The curious capture by the British Liberal party under the leadership of that errant Tory, William Ewart Gladstone, of the role of defender of minorities, has, I believe, led many Canadian Roman Catholics to ally themselves with the Liberal party. I cannot believe that this purely historical and quite unphilosophical connection can last much longer, indeed, I would suppose it to be far advanced in dissolution.

The next strain of Canadian conservatism was that of the Loyalists. We tend to forget that the Loyalists were for the most part Americans of two to three generations descent. Their political ideas were therefore influenced by, if not born of, American political experience. There is, to my knowledge, no full statement of the political ideas of the Loyalists. One must largely infer it. But one thing is clear. Though called Tories, they were not original Tories, or Jacobites, in any sense. They accepted the Revolution Settlement of 1688 as the basis of the constitution. In what then did their Toryism consist?

The answer, I think, is very interesting, and extraordinarily relevant to the circumstances of our own day. They not only accepted the Revolution Settlement, they accepted the constitution which evolved out of it, a constitution which was so largely the work of Tory votes. That was the constitution of the three divided powers of king, courts, and parliament, each checking and balancing the other, so that the authority of government was maintained while the liberty of the subject was assured, that greatest miracle wrought by the English political genius. The Loyalists of the American colonies, that is, refused to see the king struck from the constitution, to be replaced by an elected democrat; they refused to see the legislature devour the executive and override the courts; they refused, in Chief Justice William Smith's famous phrase, to see 'all America abandoned to democracy'.* How right they were. When they had been defeated and driven into exile, what they feared came to pass under the first American constitution, the ultra-democratic Articles of Confederation. Then the men who had driven them out had to set up in the Constitution of 1788, a constitution any Loyalist could have accepted, a constitution, in fact, largely carried by former Loyalist votes, a conservative constitution which testifies to their sagacity to this day.

The third strain of Canadian conservatism is that drawn from what Keith Feiling calls the Second Tory party. The first, or Jacobite, Tory party died with Queen Anne and since 1745 has been as dead as Queen Anne. But there were also Revolution or Hanoverian Tories and, despite the capture of the first two Hanoverian kings by the Whig party, and the writing of English history in Whig terms by Macaulay and the Whig school, I cannot see why there should not have been. For the Revolution Settlement was as much a Tory as a Whig settlement. The constitution of checks and balances of the glorious Revolution is merely an elaboration of the Tudor-Tory ideal of Clarendon, which was the basis of the Restoration.

The events and personalities which led to the creation of the Second Tory party were the failure of the Young Pretender in 1745, which ended the Jacobite danger and the old Whig game of smearing the Tory party as Jacobite; the accession of George III, who was not content to be a party king; and the tremendous personality of William Pitt. Pitt was a new man; he did not belong to one of the great Whig connections; he was not content to be a client of a Whig patron. He found his way to power by two landmarks; one was the power of the Crown, which he respected as no Whig magnate did, the other was the support of the city of London, which he won by fighting a war for colonial and Indian commerce. This tradition he passed on to two remarkable men, the Earl of Shelbourne, the founder of British Canada, and his son, the younger Pitt. When in 1784 George III turned in desperation to Pitt for rescue from Fox and North, Pitt had only a small following of Pittite Whigs. But this readiness to deliver the king from the control of the Whigs rallied to him in Parliament the Tories, the country gentlemen, the King's friends. To them were rallied in the nation the moneyed cohorts of the city and the great body of the squirearchy. In a few brief years Pitt had created a party which, only partly Tory to begin with, became wholly so under the shock of the French Revolution.

These were the men who framed the Constitutional Act of 1791. Their purpose was to give Canada, French as well as Loyalist Canada, the British constitution in all its balanced perfection, confident that the liberty it conferred would ensure the loyalty of those who enjoyed that liberty. Such was the essence of their Toryism, that liberty was the product of, and could be the product only of, constitutional government. It could not be, Burke had taught them, the product of the sovereignty of the people, still less of a theoretical liberty, equality, and fraternity. Of these, they felt if they did not know, the more men had of one the less men had of the others.

It was under such a constitution in the United Kingdom that Pitt created that great tradition of enlightened administration which, using legislation as little as possible, in the hands of the Pittite Tory succession, Canning, Peel, and Gladstone, made government a marvellously efficient instrument of the political will of the community and created that tradition of able and honest civil service without which the welfare state today would be a morass of cost and corruption.

Part of this Pittite Toryism was of Scots and Irish origin. Here I speak with scant knowledge. But Scottish Toryism is of an old and honourable descent.

It goes back to Montrose. It drew the broadsword with Dundee. It reappeared in the Earl of Bute, George III's mentor and minister, a name slowly being cleared of Whig calumny as that of the man who broke the Whig system. In Pitt's day Henry Dundas, and in another sphere Sir Walter Scott, carried on the tradition, and, of course, it was to transform Canadian politics at the touch of that famous Peelite Conservative and Scot, James Bruce, Earl of Elgin and Kincaird.

To the Tory tradition Ireland contributed not only the majestic name of Burke before the Union, but also those of Castlereagh and Wellington after. Both countries, with England, sent a steady stream of English, Scots, and Irish Tories to Canada after Waterloo to reinforce the Loyalists there.

Canadian conservatism, derived from these many strains, took its Canadian form, of course, in the struggle for responsible government. In none of its periods is Canadian history so much in need of re-examination. In no other period is Liberal mythology more blatant and more virulent. Since the days of the Whig historians J. C. Dent and William Kingsford, Canadian historiography has celebrated the winning of responsible government as a Liberal triumph hardly won against the powers of Tory darkness. It is time this documented nonsense was dusted off. And one doesn't need new documents to ask, who called the French and English reformers first to office but that arch-Tory, that scholar of Christchurch and friend of Castlereagh and Canning, who but Sir Charles Bagot? And who conceded the practical working of responsible government in Canada but that former Tory, that Peelite Conservative, that political mentor of John A. Macdonald, the Earl of Elgin?

The struggle for responsible government, it is becoming evident, was not a struggle between valiant and outnumbered Reformers and Tory citadels manned by the arch-reactionaries of the Family Compact. Many Reformers, such as Papineau and Mackenzie, would have nothing to do with responsible government. They wanted the American elective system. Most Tories, those who were not office holders, were prepared to accept some measure of responsible government. They were doubtful about how far the governor's prerogatives should be reduced, they were concerned to maintain the British connection, and they were definitely afraid of the excesses of party government and a spoils system. But the only questions were how much responsible government, and by what stages it was to be introduced. That there were ultra-Tories like brave old Sir Allan MacNab proves nothing except that all parties have extremists, and that all parties can be condemned by identifying them with their extremes.

From this period emerged the Liberal Conservatism of John A. Macdonald, a conservatism inspired through Elgin by the Peelites of the Pittite tradition. It was a conservatism which through responsible government had come to terms with democracy in Canada, and was prepared to move with the times when the need for change was proven. Since that time, if I am not mistaken, the essential principles of Canadian conservatism have not changed. It has remained traditional and constitutional, progressive and pragmatic. It has concerned itself with sound administration of existing laws rather than the forming of new laws, and with economic development rather than political reform.

If the principles of Canadian conservatism have not substantially changed in the last century, what role is there for these principles in mid-twentieth century?

To answer that, one must ask what are the main features of the mid-twentieth century? I would suggest that they are four.

The first I would term the transformation of agrarian societies into industrial ones, a transformation now at work in every quarter of the globe, and nowhere more actively than in Canada. Since the fifth millennium BC, the civilized world has lived on the peasant; now there are to be no more peasants, and the farm is to be power-mechanized.

The second I would call the fantastic but practical results of scientific research, with all their consequences in increased output, new products, new sources of supply, and rapid obsolescence of plants and skills. In the wonders of science, nothing is impossible but peace and quiet, and nothing is permanent but change. Whirl, as the Greek philosopher remarked, is King.

The third I would describe as the enormous acceleration of the pace of social change. Conditioned though we are to it, this rate of change puts a terrible stress upon the traditional norms of civilized society. Our moral behaviour is greatly dependent on habits, and when we have to change our habits, we are all too likely to shed our morals in the process.

Finally, there is what I would call the end of philosophic individualism, or the extinction of the true liberal. The radical survives, and the socialist, but the liberal who was an individualist, a rationalist, and an internationalist—who was also, be it acknowledged, at his best a humanitarian, and a man of generous instincts and magnanimous mind—that kind of liberal is gone with the top hat and the frock coat. The world is the poorer for his going, and it behoves conservatives to remember that they are in fact his residuary legatees, and that the liberal spirit now finds almost its sole dwelling place in conservative minds. This is a trust not to be ignored.

If these are the major economic and social changes of our time, what practical consequences have they in Canada?

There are first of all the problems which arise from the multiplication of abundance—the ever-varying social standards which result from a rapidly rising and diffusing standard of living; industrialization, urbanization, unionization of labour; agricultural surpluses and the anaemia of rural life.

With these come the consequences of obsolescence of plant and skills, the dislocation of old industrial patterns, of social ways and of personal lives by the compulsive mobility of the labour force at all levels.

Offsetting these, and in many ways a response to the same consequences of the main forces of our times, are the welfare state, the bureaucracy necessary to work that state, and the steady abdication of Parliament in the face of the complexity of the new collectivist and bureaucratic society.

There is also in response to these forces, as well as a result of legal changes, the steady corporatization, if I may coin an ugly word, of our society. I refer not only to commercial and industrial corporations. I include the growth of labour unions and cooperatives. Our society is becoming ever less individualistic and ever more corporate, if not collectivist.

That reminds one, of course, of the socialist change [claim?], namely, that by central planning productivity can be increased and the good life realized.

With that challenge, one recalls the Communist menace to liberty, to tolerance, and to civility.

All these are, I believe, immediate and actual things, and if so, they are undoubtedly very serious things. They are not things, I suggest, to be faced without a philosophy and without a program.

What then is a conservative philosophy for our times and circumstances? I wish that I could phrase one with sufficient wisdom and adequate eloquence. I cannot, but neither can I avoid the challenge to do so now.

That philosophy, as Russell Kirk reminds us in the new American conservative review, *Modern Age*, must rest on absolute values, the established norms of our western tradition, both secular and Christian. The relativism of the liberal thinkers of our times must be shunned for the moral infection it is.

It must remember that such values do not practically exist outside of or beyond persons. It follows, therefore, that people are themselves of absolute value; they are never means to any end whatever; they are, themselves, as they exist, the test of justice, of the good life, and of all social and economic values.

But as persons they never exist in isolation. Man, said Aristotle, is a political animal, a being who lives in a *polis*, a social order. Men are always members of some group. The conservative philosophy will always cherish all human association—the family, the church, the municipality, the province, the nation.

Because that philosophy has persons as its test of values, it will be mindful of their unfailing weaknesses, their proneness to error, to crime, and to sin. But it will also be mindful of how, by the authority of tested institutions, the educative force of tradition, and the mutual support of loyalty, men can be made better than they naturally are, more wise, more brave, more gracious.

It will insist, finally, following the lead of those restorers of learning, Hilda Neatby in this country and Allan Bestor in the United States, that among men as endowed by nature there can be no equality, if there is to be liberty in men to realize what is in them.* But a conservative philosophy will rest assured that there can be justice. Justice is that each should have his own and that each should be what it is in him to be. It will also never doubt that there can be something now almost forgotten, a sense of honour. This men can possess only when they know what they stand for, and what is expected of them. This is possible only in a society which recognizes merit, which makes duties the preface to rights, and which makes rights a trust to be discharged, not an opportunity to be exploited.

Such a philosophy would also honour intelligence. John Stuart Mill said the Conservative was 'the stupid party'. It was a typical Liberal jibe, and sounds, for Mill, surprisingly like the honourable member from Bonavista-Twillingate.† And it is true that the Conservative is likely to prefer the promptings of the heart to the dictates of the head. May it always be so. But no party can survive without brains, as no party can long continue without vision. One thing that is wrong with Canadian Conservatism today is that too many of its brains are in its boots, that is, in the youth and ranks of the party. Time will correct this, but you must note, gentlemen, that nearly one year is gone, and only three are left. It is not much time for reflection, or for shaking the brains out of the boots.

Finally, that philosophy will stress the need for continuity of development, for time to mature, to test and to adapt, whether it be ideas or hospitalization schemes.

A sound philosophy should always admit of being reduced to a practical program. Can such a program, applicable to present circumstances in Canada, be deduced from the above attempt to sketch a Conservative philosophy for our time? I believe so, and here is my statement of it:

1. The frank and loyal acceptance of the welfare state, in order to keep it one humanely administered for people, for people who matter as people. For the welfare state is not in any conflict with Conservative principles, of which *laissez faire* and rugged individualism are no part.

2. The reflective development of social and financial policies which will strengthen the family, preserve our local institutions, and enable the provinces to discharge their functions under the constitution.

3. The restoration of the balance of the constitution by assuring the continued impartiality and independence of the Queen's representative; by strengthening the Senate by appointment of Senators by the provinces, with a suspensive veto by the Senate on legislation of the Commons; by dropping reference to the dangerous and improper idea of the electoral mandate; by recreating the tradition of ministerial and parliamentary independence; and by these changes reducing the now extravagant power of the Office of Prime Minister.

4. The improvement of government by setting administration above legislation; by re-capturing the spirit of the rule of law; by the institution to the courts of appeals of all cases from the decisions of administrative boards [*sic*]; by re-placing the onus of proof on the Crown in all criminal trials.

5. The maintenance in foreign policy of the national interest by all possible forms of international association—the Commonwealth, the United Nations, and, in special but limited undertakings, the United States, in order that by organic relationships national independence and international obligation may be reconciled and made mutually supporting.

6. The massive support of the able in education and of research in all fields of knowledge.

7. The re-valuation of democracy, by a citizenship ceremony uniform for all conferrings of citizenship; by the forfeiture of the franchise for repeated non-use; by the encouragement of people of first-rate ability and genuine distinction to seek public office by election or to accept it by appointment.

8. The cultivation of our traditions by systematic encouragement and public patronage of the arts, letters, and history.

9. The creation of a Canadian system of honours that merit may be recognized and distinction acknowledged without the present recourse to the farce of the QC, or to the overworked honorary doctorate.

You will note that I do not ask anyone pass a law, except to reform the Senate. I do ask that conservatives should have a definite concept of government, that they should endeavour to substitute enlightened administration for hasty law-making and stop the diarrhoea of legislation which now drains Parliament of its vitality. I ask them to realize that our constitution has been reduced to a plebiscitary democracy, which only awaits a television Caesar who has discarded the liberal democratic tradition our past and present leaders honour, to sweep away the few remaining safeguards against the play of unrestrained will in our government. Above all, I would ask them, I would ask you, to think. Without vision a party perishes; we have seen that happen. But without ideas a party not only dies; it becomes a mockery and after derision stalks defeat.

For Conservatism to be defeated today would be a tragedy. For we are witnessing not merely a series of electoral victories. We are witnessing a great Conservative resurgence. Conservatism is the only alternative to Communism. Liberalism, if anything, has by its encouragement of class war by unrestrained competition prepared the way for it. Socialism at best innoculates against it. Only Conservatism can fight it philosophically, for only Conservatism, as a political creed, denies the basic postulates of Communism, its materialism and its utopianism, and points to a way of life in which the material is infused with the ideal, and the ideal with the human and the possible.

Not to think now, to lose the contest for want of clarity of thought and firmness of conviction, would be not only a tragedy. It would be a betrayal, of past, of future, of the soul of man.

NATIONALISM AND SOCIALISM

Syntheses effect miracles, a wise man once said, and a minor miracle of this sort occurred in French Canada around 1960, when separatist nationalism and Marxist socialism first came together. The event transformed French-Canadian nationalism, prepared the way for the Parti Québécois, and soon had a profound impact on the political thought of English Canada. The following selections provide two introductions to the ideas behind this synthesis. The first is an anonymous letter to the editor of Cité libre *published in 1961. The second is an article by Paul Chamberland (b. 1939), known today as a poet, but who was then also a scholar and one of the leaders of the 'shouting signpainters' who published* parti pris, *the chief theoretical organ of the New Left in Quebec, from 1963 to 1968. Chamberland's scholarly career was short: he began a doctoral dissertation at the Sorbonne, but during the excitement of May 1968 put his theory of freedom into practice and destroyed the completed manuscript. The article below appeared in the second issue of* parti pris, *in November 1963.*

Letter from a Nationalist

Montreal, 13 December 1960

SIR:

It seems to me there are questions, if not more urgent (let's try to be objective), at least more important in another way than whether the Jesuits will get their university before the Dominicans, or whether the Sisters of Providence will do better with the sale of their land than the Grey Nuns with theirs. And these questions, the painful ones, seem to be systematically ignored by *Cité libre*—no doubt because they pose the real problems. *Cité libre*: what does that mean?* Freedom in the city, of course, but also and above all, I think, it means freedom of the city. Freedom in the city we have—little enough, let's face it, but it does exist. The proof is the very existence of *Cité libre*, which would be inconceivable under Franco or in a 'people's democracy'.

But what does *Cité libre* do with this troublesome freedom? Most of the time it is content (I am being unfair, of course) to take a few shots at the clergy and to publish—without endorsing it—a letter that can only be described as powerful and courageous from one Pierre Charbonneau on the right to freedom of thought. Fine. But isn't that taking the long way round to the problem, as they say? It is simply a matter of telling the clergy a few things that should have been said a long time ago. If they had been, the force of events would not have driven us to call for rather more serious measures. Let's not fool ourselves: everything in a society is connected, and there comes a time when the forces of oppression, of every kind, are so inextricably linked that it is useless to think of breaking one string and leaving the knot intact. It is in these exceptional periods of its history that a people, through those voices that are in a position to express it, shows the stuff it is made of. And the gordian knot that must be cut just happens to be tied in the umbilical cord of French Canada.

Like everyone else, I observe that our culture and our language are going to the dogs, that our economy is going to the Americans or the English Canadians (our official statistics speak modestly of 40-per-cent Canadian ownership—consoling, isn't it?—but they do not specify the microscopic percentage of this 40 per cent that goes to the citizens of what is virtually the richest province in the country). I observe that the foreign policy for which Ottawa makes us responsible in the eyes of the world responds to neither our aspirations nor the needs of the planet. I observe that military waste is increasing international tensions that are already unbearable. I observe that the unemployment situation in this country and especially in Quebec is not improving. I observe that the government's immigration policy has always been detrimental to us, and that its result has been to reduce our influence within a confederation to which we have been loyal for close to one hundred years. I observe that the state radio and television network (which belongs to us, the people—one of the few things that are our own) is bound hands and feet by Ottawa and given over to advertising and therefore to the capitalist oppressor. I observe . . . I observe . . . Enough observations. The cause is clear. Justice and happiness will not come to us from Ottawa. Nor will freedom.

THE DYNAMISM OF HISTORY

Two measures alone are capable of signifying freedom for the French-Canadian citizen. Sooner or later, they are inevitable (no one can fight the dynamism of History, of universal History, indefinitely; in the end, even President de Gaulle realized it in the case of Algeria). These measures are:

1. Absolute independence for Quebec;
2. The establishment of a regime based on socialism (a socialism adapted to our national character).

I would add that these two measures are so closely linked that they form a single reality; they are nothing more than two phases in a single process of collective and individual liberation. Our learned political intelligentsias, in agreement for once, have always been mysteriously allied—at our expense—against these measures ('reconciling the social and the national', as they so oddly put it, has always struck them as something somehow beyond the power of human reason, a kind of squaring of the circle, a way for lovers of political puzzles to pass the long winter evenings). What they do not see is that, on the contrary, separating the two makes both meaningless (and therefore unattractive). How could it be otherwise? Independence for Quebec without some degree of socialization is laughable, for it is hard to see what practical advantages it would give French Canadians to have their own state if it was controlled economically from outside. In the same way an Ottawa-based socialism—which is unthinkable, because it would imply a systematic centralization—would simply put control of the whole nation's economy in the hands of a government over which we, as a minority, have no effective influence. It would be tantamount to putting us so directly under Ottawa's thumb that no improvement in our welfare could compensate for it. Juggle your sophisms all you like, you cannot escape these two facts. And the French-Canadian people, which paradoxically has always refused to accept either 'salvation' (nationalism or socialism) *in isolation*, is well aware of it.

Yet we French Canadians are the only members of the present confederation who can call for the establishment of socialism with some justification (and therefore some chance of success). Why? Because we are the only real proletarians in this hybrid, utterly artificial nation wishfully known as the Canadian nation. The fact that we have been colonized and exploited is clear enough. Let's leave the figures aside. All you have to do is look at a map of the second largest French city in the world, Montreal, with its strangely English face. To the west, clinging to the side of the mountain, the well-to-do English Canadian bourgeoisie; to the east, the little people, the needy, the lowly—ourselves, the Canadians of French origin. But we are so accustomed to shocking situations, we live our lives so completely within them, that we do not see them any more. And that is the greatest scandal of all—the habituation, which means that we accept the scandal as a given, which means that those who call for simple justice look like fanatics or visionaries even to the self-styled champions of liberty whose sole preoccupation is supposed to be justice. There is no room for half measures where justice and liberty are concerned. There is no room for a respect for others that holds back because of what others will say. 'What would our English Canadian compatriots say? They are so full of British *fair play*—imagine, they let us live! Besides, they have such a clear conscience, it would hurt their feelings.' What I say is this: as long as our English-Canadian compatriots have a clear conscience, we should have a guilty one, for it is our cowardice that allows them their clear conscience.

THE RIGHT TO LIVE

There is a people here demanding to live, to live in peace with the world, and it *has the right* to do so. Since when does a nation not have the right to live as one? Is it asking too much? Is it unjust to anyone else? Would our liberty, the full development of our society [*notre épanouissement*], be incompatible with that of the other inhabitants of this land of America? If so, let us commit suicide right now—we are keeping the world from turning, we are a danger to the human race, we are not worthy of existence. For it comes down to the same thing: either we have a right to exist or we do not. I know some people who find the second alternative seductive—let us assimilate as fast as possible, they say, let us unite ourselves with the soul of America (which according to them can be nothing but Anglo-Saxon); we have 'survived' long enough in our glass jar with its stale smell of rotting jansenism. This position is defensible. But it is not mine. It does have the merit of frankness, a merit lacking in the intermediate positions to which we have been subjected for a hundred years—including your own, gentlemen of *Cité libre*. Are you concerned about the bastardization of our educational methods and the language we speak? There is only one solution: we must become conscious of our national dignity. As long as the language of administration, of business, of 'the interests' is English, nothing can be done to give French its right value. That is where they are more realistic than you are, gentlemen, less utopian. As long as you accept the idea of French remaining a language of culture, however good your intentions, French will lose ground, and our literary works will be doomed to failure before they are even born. Let us close the frontiers and proclaim unilingualism—the next day French will be worth its weight in gold. How do you expect our educational system not to suffer when it is asked to perform the impossible feat of preparing citizens for an Anglo-Saxon struggle by French means alone? We should not be surprised that American textbooks are well on the way to taking over our universities (up to 80 per cent in some of our ultra-French, ultra-Catholic faculties), and Anglo-American models exercise an ever-increasing influence on the forms of our secondary and university teaching. Soon we too will have our own 'Faculties of Arts' in every college, starting after Belles Lettres [the equivalent of Grade 12], or else, our colleges having become 'high schools', our universities will become nurseries for bachelors. And we will not even have earned the credit for inventing any of this—we will have stolen it, lifted it, followed the path of least resistance, all the while denying the values and categories that are the reflection of our own thought.*

INDEPENDENCE

Whether we like it or not, I repeat, our cultural, economic, and political interests—not to mention our ethnic, geographic, and historic realities—differ from those of English Canada. Why not face it? I have indicated the two routes open to us, between which it is absolutely necessary that we choose: assimilation or independence. I believe the second responds to our deepest aspirations better than the first does, while at the same time conforming, in my view, with the dynamism of History: that is why it is my choice. The status quo is nothing more than a slow, gradual defeat, and all those who support it, whether in good faith or in their own interests, I call reactionaries. In the past, when might took precedence over right and the powerful made the law, nationalism may have been a doctrine of the political right (and even so it would have been necessary in many cases to substitute for *nationalism* the word *imperialism*, a term that applies precisely to the enemies of our independence). Today—and from now until the era of internationalism that we all hope and pray for, but which isn't going to arrive tomorrow—the movement is nationalism: we must pass through the national phase while there is still time, while the world's sympathy is finally focusing on those peoples who are demanding emancipation. Afterwards we will be ready to make all the concessions and sacrifices that may be required to assure unity among nations. But one cannot sacrifice what one has never possessed, give what one does not have. We were a colony before 1760, and we have remained one ever since. We have paid more than enough tribute to the right of the strongest. We deserve independence.

Socialism is independence in action. Individual liberty is rightly arranged after the attainment of national liberty. Since everything now is beyond our control, we must use new political structures to take back what belongs to us. This position is not doctrinaire. The word 'socialism' simply reflects a concern for human beings over property. But if it shocks a few timid souls, let us find a new term for our purposes, one that will signify our liberation from the many subtle forces that hinder our full development, both material and moral. We are oppressed by the clergy, they say. Of course, but I mistrust what everyone (I mean every thinking person) says, because it is usually easy and only half-true. When we are ill we are quick to blame the organ we know to be the weakest and most vulnerable, for if it were another one—then it might be really serious. And it must not be (for all that we write in *Cité libre* and wear the badge of liberty on our sleeve, there are some risks we must not take): it must not be *really* serious, so serious as to imply greater risks than we can reasonably assume. Thus the diagnosis is determined by the courage (or the lack of courage) of the doctor. *Cité libre* has come so far: fine, granted. But a static freedom—even before one has acquired it, when one is still demanding it—is no longer freedom: rather it becomes a comfort—the delightful comfort, for the intellectual, of agreeable non-conformity. Intellectuals, you are the doctors of this nation—but please, stand aside. I concede that the clergy is in league with the economic powers that are strangling us; I concede that its chief concern is not the preservation of French but religious proselytism (that is to be expected; one would have to be a quarrelsome type indeed not to allow it that right); I concede that it is opposed to the non-denominational school (put yourself in its position); but all of this, once again, is the result of the system that makes us the slaves of a politics that by nature resists any movement (before 22 June) or whose movement is essentially determined by a cowardly opportunism (since 22 June)*—and let us note that it is only in a reactionary state that hospitalization insurance, as desirable as it may be, threatens anyone's interests. Start the machine in motion and the clergy will move with the rest. It is not really the clergy that keeps Mr Lesage from doing something—he would sooner cover himself with shame and ridicule by calling conferences among provinces that do not recognize the existence of their own French minorities, although some are larger than the English minority in Quebec. (Is that justice, Mr Lesage? Is that British *fair play*? Permit me to laugh—but these things are so obvious and so familiar that no one laughs at them any more; rather, they sometimes draw tears from those who have more gift for feeling than for making money.) Again, it is not the clergy (that would be too easy) that prevents Mr Lesage from giving us a Ministry of Education which would establish standards for all educational institutions supported by public funds. It is the system as a whole, the same system that makes us the vassals of the capitalist lords. A Ministry of Education would be an attack on the rights of sacrosanct private enterprise—in the field of education.

As long as the state bows to the powers that be rather than to the people it is supposed to represent, there is nothing to be done. Change the point of view, against the strong (in other words, take a good sharp turn to the left) and you will see our most obstinate Monsignors take a deep breath and put on a new face, for no one is strong except through the weakness of others, particularly of governments. These are truisms, I admit—but unfortunately that is what we have come to. We want to correct one thing, improve another, and then we think everything will look after itself; we have done our duty and we can sleep in peace. But things never take care of themselves, and as long as we draw back from the essential, nothing has been done. Let us focus our efforts on the essential, and we will have all the rest into the bargain.

THE NEW [DEMOCRATIC] PARTY

The New Party? I do not trust it. From the start, by its very nature it makes French Canadians the slaves of a politics that denies their existence as such. Oh, you will hear them indignantly denouncing American interference in our economy and preaching nationalism on the Canadian scale (that is allowed), and a few of our brave trade-unionists will be dazzled by it and taken in. But what's the difference for a French Canadian, faced with the choice of being eaten like a hot dog by the Americans or like roast beef (more classy, I admit) by the *Canadians*? If this New Party were genuinely socialist (which it does not even pretend to be) it would never dream of forming a 'Quebec wing'. The first plank of its platform would be independence for Quebec. And for that there is no need even to be socialist: all it takes is to have a minimal sense of humanity and of history.

In 1967 we will celebrate the centennial of the Canadian Confederation. We will hear the same familiar speeches on national unity, the national unity whose costs we have been paying for a hundred years (for unity is expensive, and who pays if not the weakest?—this law is inescapable). At the same time we will continue wallowing in our pious wishes, our bilingual cheques (I myself have always refused to place my pride in a cheque), in our Châteaux Maisonneuve (castles in Spain!), in our miserable requirements for census statistics forms* (if they give in, it will be a favour; who wants to live on favours?), in hearing French in the Commons, in the National Museum, in Montreal Airport . . . No more! Never again! It's too little! We are worth more than a cheque, bilingual or not!

In 1967, if God wills it—and above all if we will it—we shall celebrate our independence. We shall celebrate it without pettiness (and without animosity towards the former Canadian Confederation, if it comes to that point), in joy and brotherhood, remembering the little patriot—the twenty-year-old law student who mounted the scaffold in 1838 on the order of the colonial power. The poor kid was so unwilling to die that he cheated the executioner the first time, and the last sound he heard on earth, the last echo of his country, was the cry of the horrified crowd calling for mercy. We do not want to die either; we are as unwilling as he was and we deserve death no more than he did. That blood, his and the other unknown patriots', must not have flowed in vain. We do not want to die, but we can no longer be satisfied with half-survival, with death on the instalment plan. What we aspire to is a complete life. We want to hear our own voice at the United Nations, not Mr Diefenbaker's or Mr Green's. We want to play the role in the world that should have been Canada's, but that Canada could not, in the nature of things, play, given all its economic and political entanglements. We want to bring a new, generous voice—a voice different from that of the trusts—into the world of today. We want to live both for ourselves and for others. It is not just a question of economic and cultural interest, it is a question of honour, pride, and dignity.

This may be our last chance. Will we once again prove unequal to our destiny?

I do not want to believe it.

Sincerely,
G.C.†

Paul Chamberland:
Cultural Alienation and National Revolution

French-Canadian nationalism is the normal, if not predictable, expression of a culture whose overall design has been put in question all the more subtly as it has been given the funds necessary to treat itself to mythical compensations.

HUBERT AQUIN *

FREEDOM AND REVOLUTION

Revolt is the metaphysical condition of *freedom*. All freedom must triumph over a fate.

The slave becomes aware of his total being through the anguish he feels facing the threat of death, the power of which is embodied in his master. He decides that his master must die because he himself has trembled at the prospect of his own death. *Revolution* deploys this movement of human negativity through concrete historical situations. It realizes, in the facts, the *freeing* [*la libération*] of mankind. Revolution is man going beyond himself as freedom towards the world (which is the site of his future), freeing himself from the real oppressions that tend to chain him to what he *is* and reduce him to the condition of a *thing*.

Above all, revolt is individual or, more precisely, subjective in nature. It is the phase of the pure consciousness of self, when freedom affirms itself in the abstract, as an absolute. An individual in revolt will affirm himself as freedom, as negativity, in decisions and behaviour aimed at complete suppression of the established *values* that define his situation in the world. The absolute character of his refusal simply reflects the unconditioned affirmation of his freedom. But revolt is so total only because, being a phase, it conceals a radical impotence to actually transform the situation that determined it. The nihilist, that is, the person who has hardened in his revolt, can exist only by maintaining, to give purpose to his refusal, the realities or values against which he defines himself. Unless he is brought to a halt by insurmountable obstacles (brute natural forces, for example), the man in revolt cannot persist in his attitude without bad faith; because in his refusal he already comprehends the real powers he could use to actually suppress what oppresses him.

The collectivity too can revolt and harden in its attitude of revolt. Then it becomes aware of itself as an oppressed collectivity. It discovers that it is free, that is, capable of refusing the order imposed on it; but, either from ignorance of the real causes of its oppression or from inability to overcome them, it settles into mere consciousness of its misfortune; and if from despair or exasperation it sometimes moves to concrete actions—demonstrations or riots—it never gets beyond the stage of disorderly and ephemeral uprisings.

Individually or collectively, revolt is a failure of freedom because it does not recognize the *objective conditions* of oppression and, consequently, the *effective means* that might allow it to overcome this oppression in reality. It destroys itself as an unhappy subjectivity, cut off from its power.

The superiority of revolution over revolt consists in its objective knowledge of the conditions of oppression and the means of overcoming them. The revolutionary goes beyond himself as pure negativity in relation to his oppressor and his order of values. The man in revolt, by withdrawing into pure subjectivity, blinds himself because he believes that the abstract and total affirmation of his liberty is essential. Disdainfully, he leaves it to his oppressor to exercise mastery and power over the concrete conditions of existence in the real world. But what he judges to be inessential—the world and values of the oppressor as essence and affirms himself *as man* in political, social, and revolt. Revolt is blind inasmuch as it misunderstands its true essence, namely, the power and the world of the oppressor. To exist in fact as freedom and going-beyond, man must unveil the world, make himself exist in concrete relations to being, through historical tasks and undertakings.

The revolutionary negates the world and values of the oppressor, but by going beyond the phase of pure negativity to destroy in fact, in the order of concrete multiplicity, the world and values of the oppressor. He negates the oppressor as essence and affirms himself *as man* in political, social, and cultural tasks. He realizes his freedom by eliminating the oppressor's values. The revolutionary represents the phase of a new *positivity*. He appropriates the real world and gives himself objective being in nature. He makes himself exist as subject of the world and of history.

Revolt is essentially *individualist*. And individualism constitutes a failure of freedom: it is the freedom of the 'private' man [*l'homme privé*], deprived [*privé*] of his human relation to the other. Just as the individual can exist as such only in relation to the object, so the individual can achieve his freedom only if he links himself to the other, and each one to all—only if he acknowledges the freedom of the other. Revolution is *intersubjectivity*.

Man is a *social being* as much as an individual one. Sociality and individuality exist only in relation to each other, and this dialectical relation defines man as freedom and going-beyond towards the world, towards his future.

Individualism is not the only form of separation that alienates mankind; it is indeed a secondary, derivative form. The profound reasons why man is 'deprived' of himself lie in his alienation from the *social structures* that escape his control, as realities that have been fetichized or made into things. This alienation is rooted in man's opposition to himself through the group, class, national, and racial conflicts that rob both the individual and the collectivity of complete control and enjoyment of all the goods produced by man. Freedoms destroy one another.

Moved by both the consciousness he has, as a social being, of his freedom and by the precise knowledge of the concrete obstacles he has to overcome to liberate himself, the revolutionary begins and completes—starting from the particular situation in which he is acting—the liberation movement that must bring man closer and closer to his freedom, his total being. He is aware of the real limits of his action: he appreciates that he is working for the liberation of a particular people, class, or nation. He has no use for a complete and definitive revolution that does not exist outside the minds of stridently unhappy subjectivities. He acts in a concrete time and place. He makes himself exist at the heart of human misery and conflict. He knows that he must oppress some particular group in order to free another one. He knows that the world of men is a *world of violence*, and that only struggle, armed or unarmed, really makes history. If he makes use of violence and combat, it is only to overcome, one by one, the situations that engender violence and combat. If he suppresses the oppressor, it is to liberate the oppressed, and if oppression must follow upon oppression, he knows that the one does not simply replace the other, but rather hastens the historical process leading to the disappearance of all antagonism.

Social struggles arise from the contradictions that set men against each other and man against himself. Only the suppression of alienating situations can put an end to struggles, and the only way of attaining that goal is active involvement in the heart of these struggles. Violence can be met only by violence, even if it is the 'non-violence of the strong' represented by Gandhi or the American blacks. Whoever refuses, from humanitarian scruples, all forms of struggle and preaches a unilateral pacifism is taking his stake out of the game, and by abstaining is favouring the existing oppression. The idealism of the *silent*, of the mystics of non-violence, in the end serves the reactionary elements that perpetuate the seeds of violence.

QUEBEC ON THE BRINK OF LIBERATION

Up to this point we have sketched a metaphysical description of the dialectical process of revolution. Now, a revolution is above all a particular revolution: a concrete historical act that, arising from a situation experienced and acknowledged as 'critical' and oppressive, aims at eliminating the real conditions that have brought this situation about. The revolution is first of all that of a unique collectivity at one moment in its history. In the history of societies, there are revolutionary 'moments', periods when social equilibrium conceals an actual disorder, felt by those undergoing it to be intolerable. It presents itself to the oppressed class, group, or nation as something that must be dissolved and replaced by a superior order. The violent and sudden character of the revolution is the result of the absolute antagonism between oppressors and oppressed. The revolution can be accomplished only through the suppression of the former and the rise of the latter.

The revolutionary 'moment' does not impose itself at one time rather than another because of a simple determinism in social practice, but rests at one and the same time on the real conditions of the oppression and the degree of consciousness of the oppressed. Revolution is no longer the instinctive revolt of a group, but the coherent praxis by which this group breaks free of the contradictions that are tearing it apart.

Today in Quebec we are living through a revolutionary 'moment' that is making our history more irreversible than ever before. More precisely, we are living through a period I would describe as pre-revolutionary: on the one hand, Quebec society has, since the end of the Duplessis era, been undergoing a crisis that has affected the nation's structures and its very existence; on the other hand, individual and collective movements of various kinds reveal an overall effort by the nation to overcome the obstacles impeding its growth and completion. A brief survey verifies this. The 'Quiet Revolution' of the Lesage government, with its nationalization of hydro-electric power, its 'great charter' on education, its bold demands on the central government; the lay movement, the rise of *indépendantisme*, with its dramatic manifestations—the terrorism of the FLQ, Marcel Chaput's hunger-strike, the protest at the Place des Arts*—all these sometimes disparate elements indicate the gravity of the crisis and, parallel thereto, the awareness it is arousing among the most progressive elements in the nation.

Quebec is entering a new era, and this statement reflects the objective conditions of our situation. Everyone is talking about revolution in a rather facile way. To do so is to abuse the term, but this abuse is significant nonetheless, for it reveals an obscure awareness that there is a true revolution to be accomplished.

Now revolution does not spring forth from a people as fruit does from a tree: it is not the result of some mechanical interplay of inhuman causes. The distance that separates 'pre-revolution' from revolution can be crossed only through a conscious collective movement, which can be commenced, directed, and borne only by individuals who expressly *desire* the revolution, starting from a situation that *objectively establishes* the necessity for the revolution. A revolution, once set in motion, exposes the *mystifications* that hide oppression from the oppressed. It lays bare the social antagonisms perpetuating the social imbalance, and forces the oppressing class or group, including their collaborators, to take refuge in *reaction*.

One may wish to defuse a social or political crisis by introducing a show of more or less radical reforms in order to facilitate or even accelerate the group's evolution. This is the position represented by the 'Quiet Revolution' of the Lesage government, or even the national revolution sought by people who desire political independence without promoting the social changes that give meaning and scope to this national revolution.

Whenever the social and political situation is the result of a relation of oppression between two collectivities, it cannot be overcome and transformed to respond to the interests of the oppressed group through changes that, important as they may be, perpetuate the fundamental antagonism that defines this situation. 'Reformism' is merely a defensive weapon in the hands of the rulers and accomplices of the regime, intended to protect their interests and to perpetuate their grip on the rest of the collectivity. *Reformism is the enemy of revolution.*

NATIONALISM AND SOCIAL REVOLUTION

Today in Quebec we discern, despite the confusing appearance of things, an alignment of social and political forces characteristic of a pre-revolutionary situation. The revolution here clearly has a *national countenance*; it is even a nationalist type of revolution. It aims at the liberation of the French-Canadian nation in Quebec, which is oppressed by the English-Canadian nation, represented by Ottawa, and at the full development [*l'épanouissement*] of Quebec society in response to the needs and the daily life of its members and groups.

The misunderstanding arises as soon as we have stated the problem of *nationalism* and its resolution in a national revolution that would bring about the independence of Quebec. *The majority of independantists and anti-separatists* base their respective options on the existence and value of a *national sentiment* that either justifies or does not justify a nationalist revolution. The former are moved by pride or fanaticism, the latter by concern for 'realism' or simply bad faith. The 'sentimental' argument leads to confusion; whence the weakness of the *indépendantistes* in relation to their adversaries.

A revolution cannot be brought about in the name of a sentiment, however powerful and legitimate it may be. National sentiment, like any other community sentiment, reflects the objective conditions of the national situation. In Quebec national sentiment is violently assertive, which makes it a kind of nationalism. *Nationalism reveals a profound alienation of the nation*, and this alienation is brought about by the contradictions and constraints afflicting the nation. Revolution must base itself on these contradictions in order to suppress them.

If the national revolution were achieved in the name of nationalism alone, it would risk, under cover of independence, perpetuating the conflicts whose resolution requires independence as a first step. Independence would be a failure, diverted from its course by the pressure of a blind ideology. Moreover, certain anti-separatists are set in their attitudes by fear of just such mystification. Or rather they fear that nationalism as sentiment may blind the national consciousness to its real problems. They fear neglect, in the separatist movement, of the concrete social and political tasks involved in a national revolution; they turn against the idea of independence precisely from concern for the social undertakings that the development of the nation requires.

We think that both of these attitudes equally fail to understand the complexity of the situation. We consider that *national liberation cannot be dissociated from the solution of the nation's social, economic, and political problems*. The only way of 'going beyond' nationalism lies in starting and completing the national revolution. This revolution, to be effective, can only be social.

One must pay attention here to the national sentiment that gives some form to the consciousness of the Quebec community, as confused as its features may be. Our social problems can be resolved effectively only through a struggle for national liberation, for these problems are entangled in our condition as a dominated people, 'colonized' by Ottawa. This the people sense, whatever the Lesage government, *Le Devoir*, *La Presse*, and *Cité libre* may claim to the contrary. The bad faith of our élites will not deceive us much longer. On the contrary, we think that the national sentiment so disparaged by our federalists of every colour is the decisive element that can raise the majority of the nation to social consciousness, providing it finds leaders who have the frankness and audacity to channel nationalism to this end.

The revolution can only be nationalist, and, being national, it must transform radically the structures of Quebec society. Independence is not reducible to a declaration of territorial sovereignty. The revolution, national in its form, will be social only if it seeks to destroy the powers of oppression alienating the majority of the nation: capitalism—American, Anglo-Canadian, and even French-Canadian. The survival of these alienating structures would only cast the nation into an equally odious form of 'neo-colonialism'.

THE INSTRUMENTS OF REVOLUTION

A revolution is above all *political*: the exercise of power establishes the domination of one class over another, or of one group over another. The oppressed collectivity must take political power away from the oppressors. The Quebec nation will free itself by taking from the Canadians (Ottawa) all political power over Quebec. Moreover, this revolution will be real in so far as it is carried out for the benefit of the majority of the nation: the working classes. The national revolution must not be confiscated by a native bourgeoisie. For the working classes it must signify the mastery of their future.

The reality of the revolution resides in the relationship of the productive forces. A revolution is first realized at the level of economic structures, appropriation of which assures the mastery of social and human reality. When we say that Quebec must be the master of its natural resources and its entire economy, we should add that this mastery must be exercised by the majority of the nation, that is, the workers. Otherwise, '*maîtres chez nous*' will remain pure mystification: it will in fact justify the bourgeois élites' domination over the whole of the nation. National revolution must not mean the creation of a national capitalism perpetuating class conflict in new forms.

Revolution is above all political and economic. It can be brought about only through a sudden and radical transformation of society, acting first at the level of the infrastructure (economic) and the superstructure (political) that secures the power of the economically dominant class. The meaning of the revolution, however, consists in the concern for fundamentally transforming the conditions of human existence and for making man progress towards his total realization. Social liberation seeks to liberate, not abstract man, but the concrete man of everyday life.

Leaving aside, in this article, political and economic forms of alienation, which call for precise revolutionary tasks, we wish to concentrate rather on criticizing another form of alienation: *cultural alienation*. This alienation is found at a well-defined level of social practice and requires a specific effort of criticism and recovery [*désaliénation*]. To be sure, total revolutionary praxis must remain organic, for it aims at the simultaneous destruction of all forms of alienation; recovery on the cultural plane is impossible without implementing a parallel political and economic revolution. It must be conceived in the perspective of a total revolution and carried out in the achievement of that revolution. The differentiation of tasks that the revolution requires simply reflects the different levels of social reality.

RACISM AND XENOPHOBIA

Hubert Aquin, in his remarkable essay 'La Fatigue culturelle du Canada français' (*Liberté*, no. 23, May 1962), offers a penetrating critique of our national misfortune. We do not wish to re-examine the sociology of our cultural crisis here. By concentrating on a criticism of Quebec's cultural alienation, we wish in particular to analyse the *myths* and the *ideologies* that mystify the consciousness of the Québécois and come between his being and his consciousness to hide the objective conditions of his alienation. More precisely, in this article we wish to clarify the tasks of a demystifying criticism.

The national revolution is not being brought about in the name of a mystique—instinctive, messianic, or racist. We have seen that the contemporary national sentiment reflects an objective situation brought about by a foreign (Anglo-Canadian) oppression and the internal contradictions in our society caused by this domination. Our colonized intellectuals greatly fear reflexive bursts of 'mass' instinct; they reject the national liberation movement, having identified it with a simple-minded *xenophobia*. When the first bombs explode, they cry, 'After them!', and refuse to see, in the violence carried out by certain representatives of the younger generation, a *normal human reaction* arising out of impatience and exasperation, a reaction 'motivated' by a situation whose evils their elders, through defeatism and inertia, help to perpetuate.

Hatred of the oppressor has nothing to do with xenophobia or racism. Only in bad faith could one confuse these two attitudes. The xenophobe or the racist refuses to acknowledge the foreigner as an equal, sharing a common humanity; into his relations with the other he introduces the separation and antagonism that preserve the seeds of violence. Hatred of the oppressor is just the opposite: in his hatred, the oppressed shows his refusal to consider himself a thing in relation to the oppressor. He demands that the latter recognize him as his equal in humanity and that he do so concretely, in the realities of political, economic, social, and cultural life. Hatred of the oppressor evinces the refusal of the xenophobia, more or less acknowledged, on the part of the oppressor. The violence of the oppressed seeks to suppress the bonds, *imposed by violence*, that enslave him to the oppressor. This 'counter-racism' can be lived only as a form of racism. It could not be otherwise in a situation that imprisons the mind of the oppressed within a racist framework. But in truth this counter-racism aims precisely at suppression of the 'racist' situation.

It is up to the clear-thinking men of the nation to lead national consciousness from the stage of instinctive nationalism to a deliberate will for social liberation. Our established intellectuals have understood nothing of the *Créditiste** and terrorist phenomena. They consider these sudden outbursts of the oppressed nation as simply irrational or puerile. This attitude saves them from really understanding the vicissitudes of national discontent. Instead, they prefer to speculate on civil liberties and good relations with Ottawa.

A CRITIQUE OF EVERYDAY LIFE IN QUEBEC

When we speak of cultural alienation, we should pay particular attention to such phenomena as Caouettism and the FLQ. As forms of revolt, they reveal the real conflicts that define the present situation of the nation. Our critique of cultural alienation is not aimed directly at Quebec's social institutions and structures; by sifting through myths and ideologies, it aims at demystifying the alienated everyday life of the Québécois. In the last analysis, national revolution seeks to redeem [*désaliéner*] the everydayness [*la quotidienneté*] of the members of the nation.

Everydayness is distinguished from culture inasmuch as the latter term specifically designates the social forms of behaviour, symbols, customs, and knowledge. The concept of everydayness designates the individual's lived experience of cultural 'patterns'. Everydayness designates, as Henri Lefebvre has written, 'a level of social reality'. It includes all superior activities (political, economic, scientific, artistic, etc.) in so far as it is the soil that nourishes them and the reality in which they find meaning and value. Everyday life is defined primarily as an area for man's appropriation, not so much of external nature, as of his *own nature*—as a functional zone dividing the *dominated sector* of life from the *undominated sector*—as a region where goods meet needs transformed, to a greater or lesser degree, into desires. It is 'a mixture of nature and culture, of history and experience, of the individual and the social, of the real and the unreal, a place of transition and of meeting, of interference and conflicts, in short, a *level* of reality.'[1]

Every revolution must be brought about in the name of the *man with needs*. The redemption [*désaliénation*] it promotes and realizes must reach the concrete man, and his realization, through the *dialectical process of need-work-enjoyment*. Thus national revolution in Quebec must be directed to transforming the Québécois in his daily life, in the network of the real and experienced conditions of his existence. Ending enslavement to the Anglo-Canadian nation constitutes the first step on the road to total revolution.

Men's daily lives differ according to the class to which they belong. This means that they reflect, in the most trivial aspects of experience, the balance or imbalance that sets classes against one another in the capitalist regime of production. There is the daily life of the politician, the university professor, the industrialist, the specialized worker, the white-collar worker, the blue-collar worker, and the housekeeper. Analytical reason will establish the different characteristics of these types of daily life, but in so doing it risks giving a false idea of the complexity of the situations it studies, for, starting from the elements revealed through analysis, it reconstructs a mosaic of heterogeneous experiences. The dialectical understanding of 'everyday experiences' must show their reciprocity, their relation as difference and contradiction. The critique of daily life deals with the overall structures of society.

Apart from the nation's internal contradictions, *everyday life in Quebec* reflects the colonialist alienation brought about by 'Canadian' domination. This alienation modifies radically all other forms of social alienation, and consequently has a global effect on the everyday life of the Québécois. It is in the fabric of his actual life, in his daily activities, that the Quebec French Canadian suffers from his condition as one who is dominated, politically, economically, and socially. National liberation seeks, among other tasks, to liberate the everyday life of the man who lives here from the contradictions relating to the colonial regime.

MYTHS AND IDEOLOGIES

A Québécois will experience his situation as a 'colonized' being in different ways according to the class to which he belongs. The tangle of internal (class) antagonisms and external ones (between nations) is reflected, with infinite shadings, in the myths and ideologies that keep the individual from seeing the contradictions of the society in which he lives. Thus the clerico-bourgeois élite, because of its relative domination over the whole of the nation, will be able to provide itself with selfish and illusory compensations. Its privileges as a petty dominator bring it closer to the side of power, the more easily so as it maintains its hold on the rest of the nation because of the masters' might. Its more or less acknowledged servility will hide under the mask of a collaboration judged indispensable to the nation's survival and prosperity. The ideologies of this 'élite' will strive to ensure that the nation as a whole remains docile.

In the complexity of national myths and ideologies we can discern two classes: the first consisting of the ideologies that justify the colonial situation, and the second of the compensatory ideologies and myths of revolt that reveal the failure of the national consciousness in its desire for liberation. Of course the ideologies of power and the myths of liberation can penetrate one another. Power can cunningly confiscate the incipient forms of national revolt for its own benefit and integrate them into its ideology. This is all the easier as the movements of revolt, if they show a deep subjective consciousness, have a poor understanding of the objective conditions of national subjugation, and can satisfy themselves with compensations as tempting as they are ephemeral. Power can play at liberation, and the name of this game is reformism. The similarity between Lesage and Duplessis lies in their both being puppet-kings [*leur position de roi nègre*].

A DEMYSTIFICATION

To sum up, we might say that a critique of cultural and, especially, everyday life in Quebec calls for numerous measures that in the end must all interconnect: the contributions of the different human sciences serve their common goal only when they are integrated in a dialectical vision of man and history. We have drawn attention to myths and ideologies. We have attempted to bring to light their common factor: the 'colonialist' situation of Quebec. It is not enough to *know* how the Québécois live and think; above all, we must *demystify* the everyday man we find here; in the current pre-revolutionary context the urgency of this critique of myths and ideologies is proportionate to the total *praxis* of the revolution underway. Demystification is a practical weapon in the hands of the oppressed class or nation. It seeks the destruction of the values imposed by the dominant class in order to know itself and to create itself [*se faire exister*] in the light of its true needs and desires.

Every ideology reflects the economic structures of a society and in turn influences the evolution of that society. In the economic and political structures of Quebec society we have recognized two levels of oppression directed against the working majority: foreign oppression and local oppression, two levels joined by a link of subordination: 'colonial' domination consecrates and even brings about the ascendancy of the national petty bourgeoisie. (It does not create the latter, of course: if we had been free, we would have had a national bourgeoisie that no doubt would have given the nation a more dynamic economy . . . but we do not have to go on discussing possibilities that history did not choose.)

The critique of myths and ideologies seeks to expose the double oppression that affects the working class of Quebec. It serves no purpose to analyse them *for themselves*: their meaning and their truth are to be found only in the objective contradictions alienating the majority of the nation.

This demystification is a gigantic task. Even an initial analysis of the different myths and ideologies requires the framework of several articles. Here we shall content ourselves with an enumeration that can constitute the program for a series of articles. It would be necessary to consider each ideology in turn, highlighting its traits and appearances, tracing its relations to other ideologies, and showing how it justifies (as an ideology of power) or hides (as a myth of revolt) the oppression exercised against the nation as a whole.

Myths and ideologies that justify national oppression:

Traditionalism: agriculturalism and the 'revenge of the cradle'. Messianic and racist nationalism (a French Catholic Quebec in an Anglo-Saxon and

Protestant—pagan—America: Canon Groulx.) Theocratic clericalism. The *'cours classique'* reserved for an élite. Loyalty to the Crown of England (an *Ersatz* of divine-right monarchism and the alliance of Throne and Altar against the baneful influence of the French Revolution). This is the ideology of Quebec's traditional clerico-bourgeoisie. It justifies both 'colonial' domination and the ascendancy of the clergy and the liberal petty bourgeois, an ascendancy guaranteed, moreover, by colonial domination. Industrialization, urbanization, and the rise of a national industrial bourgeoisie compromise many traditional values going back to a society of a rather simple rural type.

Pan-Canadianism (symbolized by *Mr Vanier and his wife**). Federalism or neo-federalism. Biculturalism. An ideology that in part fights against traditional messianic nationalism but basically justifies the same interests: those of the national bourgeoisie. Represented by the major information media such as *Le Devoir* and *La Presse* (whose director, straight-faced, claims impartiality regarding the national news); reviews such as *Cité libre*; and, despite 'nationalist' appearances, the Lesage government.

Abstract humanism. Universalism. Parliamentary democratism. The objectivism of the universities. Unilateral pacifism. The mysticism of non-violence . . . Ideologies in so far as they legitimize ignorance, scorn, avoidance, and neutrality regarding the national problem. Myths of the 'colonized intellectual', which contribute to the preservation of colonial domination.

Among the myths of revolt:

The *individualism* of the intellectuals. 'Competencies' or personal success as a substitute for the true national success that would be the independence of Quebec.

The *revolt* of the artists: from Saint-Denys Garneau to Borduas. Unhappy and sterile negativity; from refusal to exile, solitude, and seclusion. Myths of the 'inner life'; dualism; absolute and proud destitution. Exemplary 'private' lives (which push to the limit the 'deprivation' of the everyday life of the Québécois).

Caouettism, or rejection of the 'national élites', whose instruments of political domination are the 'old parties'. An embryonic form of revolt and of a growing consciousness on the part of Quebec's working class (Caouette's supporters represent a false right, just as, conversely, *Cité libre* represents a pseudo-left).

In the same way we would also have to distinguish the ideological elements in certain movements that, since the end of the Duplessis era, have channelled the progressive forces of the nation: the MLF, the RIN, the PRQ, the FLQ, the MDN, and the PSQ.†

For as many numbers as may appear, *parti pris* intends to continue the task of demystification and critique of everyday life in Quebec. This is a complex endeavour, which if it is to be done successfully requires many different analyses of the situation. We cannot accomplish this alone. Thus we hope to find among our readers many co-workers who will participate in our modest effort towards an effective and authentic national and social revolution.

AUTHOR'S NOTE

[1] Henri Lefebvre, *Critique de la vie quotidienne*, II (Éditions de l'Arche, 1961), 50-2.

PIERRE ELLIOTT TRUDEAU

Pierre Elliott Trudeau (b. 1919) represented political authority in Canada from 1968 to 1984. He was our philosopher king.

Reconciling liberty with authority is an old conundrum, usually avoided by practical politicians. Trudeau perceived the elements of a solution in popular sovereignty and representative government; and being, as it were, a recent convert to the democratic faith, he defended it with greater clarity and resolve than most of his generation. 'Advances in Politics' is an abridgement of Les Cheminements de la Politique, *a series of articles written for a weekly newspaper in 1958 and republished in book form in 1970. 'Nationalist Alienation' was the first of Trudeau's anti-separatist articles in* Cité libre; *it appeared in March 1961 and was in part a response to the anonymous letter that began the previous section. The writer of that letter suggested closing the frontiers; Trudeau, by contrast, calls for open frontiers as the basis for democratic politics.*

Advances in Politics

We can only think of Plato and Aristotle in grand academic robes. They were decent fellows, like others, laughing with their friends; and when they diverted themselves with writing their Laws *and their* Politics *they did it for their own amusement. This was the least philosophical, the least serious, part of their lives; the most philosophical part was to live simply and quietly. If they wrote of politics, it was as if to make rules for a lunatic asylum. And if they made a show of speaking of great affairs it was because they knew that the madmen they were talking to thought they were kings and emperors. They entered into their principles in order to mitigate as far as possible the damage done by their madness.*

PASCAL*

We are going to be governed whether we like it or not; it is up to us to see to it that we are governed no worse than is absolutely necessary. We must therefore concern ourselves with politics, as Pascal said, to mitigate as far as possible the damage done by the madness of our rulers.

The first—almost the only—question to ask is: how does it happen that one man has authority over his fellows?

Sermons and worthy books are always talking of respect for the human personality and of the inviolability of conscience. In the context of our Christian civilization, those phrases have no meaning unless all men are regarded as fundamentally free and equal, each man being of infinite value in himself, bound only by his own conscience; from which it must follow that neither authority nor obedience ought to be taken for granted. If my father, my priest, or my king wants to exert authority over me, if he wants to give me orders, he has to be able to explain, in a way that satisfies my reason, on what grounds he must command and I must obey.

This is not the place to go into the natural and supernatural sources of authority within the family and the Church. But whence comes authority in civil and political society? It is extraordinarily important to know this. For even the priest, collecting his tithes or building his church, can do so only under the sway of the civil power. You cannot marry or bring children into the world or educate them without conforming to the laws of the state. Neither the owner of a factory nor the president of a club nor the headquarters of a union can exercise the least authority except within the legal framework determined by the government. You can neither buy a newspaper, nor take a tram, nor live in your house, nor beat your wife (or your husband), nor baptize your children unless the law ratifies your action and weighs its import.

What, then, is the source of the astonishingly universal law that gives so much power to our political leaders? The question engrossed the first philosophers thousands of years ago, and it is still a question.

Some take the easy way out by reiterating that authority comes from God. They omit to explain why God conferred it on a Stalin or a Hitler; or why, in our democracies, God would choose to express himself through the intermediary of electoral thugs and big campaign contributors.

According to others, authority is founded on force. To quote Pascal again, 'unable to make justice strong, we make strength just'.* This explanation is inadequate too. For no man or group of men can impose authority on a population against its will. When injustice reaches a certain point, even soldiers and policemen refuse to obey—as witness the French, Russian, Chinese, Indo-Chinese, and other revolutions.

Still others invoke natural law, affirming that authority rests on the nature of things. Like the divine explanation, this is an abstraction; while it is not false, it fails to explain the contradictory variety of forms of authority and law. In certain societies it is the grandfather who rules, in others it is the mother, in still others the queen's eldest son. Slavery is illegal here; elsewhere it is allowed. One country sanctions divorce, another forbids it altogether. Two years ago the Padlock Law governed us in Quebec, today we are free of it.† 'The nature of things', then, is no great help in explaining how it is that Maurice [Duplessis] can give orders to Pierre, and why something permitted here is forbidden elsewhere. . . .

Some philosophers have tried to explain [the authority possessed by certain leaders and certain laws over the mass of people] by a kind of contract among the members of society, delegating authority to some of them. This notion has its attraction, bringing into our inquiry as it does the idea of consent: A has authority over B because B agrees to it. The obvious difficulty is that such a contract is an abstract idea, never having in fact been signed. In reality, man is born into society without having been consulted, and he has very little choice but to go on living in it.

Let us see, then, where our discussion has led us. On the one hand we say that all men are brothers, that is to say equals. But on the other hand wherever we look, in whatever country we may be, we see that the great majority are subject to a small number of superiors who make the law for them. As Rousseau said, 'Man is born free, yet everywhere he is in chains. . . . How did this change come about?'°

To reconcile these contradictions and unravel our difficulties, we must begin by observing that society is a given fact for man. We cannot know if there has ever existed, or will ever exist, a species of man who does not live in society but courses the woods like a lone wolf. What we do see is that wherever men live they in fact live in society and depend on a social order. Not even the criminal can escape this order, for his ignorance of the criminal code and his dislike of prison do not prevent his subjection to those institutions. The nomad, the hermit, and the gypsy also depend on the social order on whose fringes they think they live; for there is no territory in the world that does not fall under the dominion of some sovereign power. The hermit's cave, whether he likes it or not, is regulated by the laws of possession and property. The gypsy cannot tell your fortune without liability under the law of contract. And I have watched the nomads of the Asiatic steppe being required to pay duty to the Afghan treasury when their migrations took them into the Khyber Pass.

The human being, then, lives in the framework of society; and life in society cannot be pictured without subjection to an established order—that is, a government. It is in this sense that one can say that authority, philosophically speaking, comes from God or from the nature of things, since God has created man with a nature that compels him to live in society: subject, that is, to politics. Political authority comes from God in the same sense as the queen's authority in a beehive comes from God.

But we are not bees, nor are we ants, and that is why this answer by itself is not enough. Men stay free because *no one* is fully vested by God or nature with authority to rule his fellows. James I of England wrote big books to prove that he was king by divine right; he believed that his son Charles I could be too, but that did not prevent the English from cutting off his head. Louis XVI of France and Tsar Nicholas II of Russia ended their careers in much the same manner. And in democracies political parties and prime ministers that thought themselves eternal have been sent packing by the people, and will be again.

Human societies, then, differ from the beehives in that men are always free to decide what form of authority they will adopt, and who will exercise it. And it really is men who have the responsibility of taking these decisions—not God, Providence, or Nature. In the last analysis any given political authority exists only because men consent to obey it. In this sense what exists is not so much the authority as the obedience. . . .

One can . . . say that the power of governments rests on a psychological disposition on most people's part to believe that it is *good* to obey and *bad* to disobey.

Why is this belief so universal? Partly because the majority seek only their own comfort and pleasure: when these ends are assured, they ask no more than to conform to a given social order and to obey political masters who work to maintain that order. Few men are aroused by an injustice when they are sure of not being its victims themselves. That is why the newspaper *Vrai* has so much trouble in convincing people that Coffin was the victim of a judicial murder;* or that a poor devil of an orphan ought to be let out of Bordeaux jail where he has languished *without trial* for eleven months.

Also, the multitude's psychological disposition to obey is fostered by all who exercise authority in any form—for these have a strong sense of their mutual interdependence. In the family, in the school, in the parish, or at work, blind obedience is preached as a virtue: in this way one can be confident of bringing up a good little people that will cause no trouble.

As long as authority does not pass all bounds of stupidity and incompetence it is sure to hold its position. Mr Duplessis, for instance, constantly teaches us that we must not criticize the authority he exercises: firstly because this authority comes from God, and secondly because he rules in the name of the Province and the 'race', values that none but a perverse spirit could assail. Thus, a few weeks ago, our prime minister declared that the powers given to the provincial supreme court were not to be criticized because the former chief justice of that court was the father of the Archbishop of Quebec, Mgr Roy!

In saying this Mr Duplessis was trying to prove to us that all authority is interconnected and indivisible. The blessing of bridges, hospitals, and universities, accompanied by great political demonstrations, is based on a similar piece of trickery.

We see then that governments and the majority of the governed concur in decreeing the immutability of the established order. It remains true, however, that most of the authorities claiming divine right, and most of the laws called natural, are the artificial products of education. Men believe that it is good to obey such people and such laws because these men were born and brought up in a civilization in which they were taught that it was natural.

In the civilization next door, though, men obey utterly different laws, believing just as strongly that this is good and true and natural. 'Truth on this side of the Pyrenees,' said Pascal, 'error on the other.' And he recognized clearly that the surest way of provoking rebellion was to make people think about the injustice of established laws and customs. 'The art of opposition and revolution is to upset established customs, tracing them to their source to point out their lack of authority and justice.'*

There is nothing wrong with doing this; on the contrary, it is often the only way to re-establish justice and liberty among men. For society is made for man; if it serves him badly he is entitled to overthrow it. The purpose of living in society is that every man may fulfil himself as far as possible. Authority has no justification except to allow the establishment and development of a system that encourages such fulfilment.

It follows that when authority in any form bullies a man unfairly, all other men are guilty; for it is their tacit assent that allows authority to commit the abuse. If they withdrew their consent, authority would collapse. . . .

Tyrants always claim that their social order is founded on the common weal, the welfare of the race; but they reserve the right to define this welfare themselves, and their laws require the citizens to act accordingly. Now to credit one or several leaders with superior knowledge of what particular set of actions is best for everyone is to call in question the very basis of social morality. For the only good action, of real moral value, is a voluntary action, chosen by the enlightened thinking of the person who performs it.

It is the duty of citizens, therefore, to examine their consciences on the quality of the social order they share and the political authority they acknowledge.

If the order is rotten and the authority vicious, the duty of the citizen is to obey his conscience in preference to that authority. And if the only sure way of reconstituting a just social order is to stage a revolution *against tyrannical and illegal authority*—well, then, it must be done.

So when you teach the people to obey authority, you ought to add that it is possible to disobey it with an equally good conscience. If you did so you would find, on the one hand, that the rulers would grow rather more respectful towards the governed; on the other, that the latter would become more sensitive to the notions of liberty and justice.

It follows from all this that no government, no particular régime, has an absolute right to exist. This is not a matter of divine right, natural law, or social contract: a government is an organization whose job is to fulfil the needs of the men and women, grouped in society, who consent to obey it. Consequently the value of a government derives not from the promises it makes, from what it claims to be, or from what it alleges it is defending, but from what it achieves in practice. And it is for each citizen to judge of that. . . .

Such a doctrine must obviously be applied prudently and circumspectly or we shall have anarchy. One citizen will refuse conscription because he conscientiously believes that war is evil. Another will defraud the treasury because he thinks taxes are too high and undermine the family. A third will ignore the closing hours of bars, or the speed limit, because he thinks these laws antiquated and out of date. In this way, with everyone arrogating to himself the right to judge each law that inconveniences him, sooner or later everyone will be living in a state of constant lawless disorder; eventually strength, audacity, and guile will usurp the place of law, and the life of man will be, in the words of Hobbes, 'solitary, poor, nasty, brutish, and short'.*

So, even though it is the duty of citizens to make conscientious judgements on the value of laws and the integrity of rulers, it would be a mistake to conclude that every citizen is automatically entitled to break the laws and get rid of the leaders he dislikes. Assassination of tyrants, though authorized by Canon Boillat of Saint-Maurice Abbey, and civil disobedience, though invoked this week by His Eminence Cardinal Léger, are clearly exceptional measures, to be undertaken only as a last resort against illegitimate and tyrannical governments.†

And it is precisely to avoid the necessity of such violence and disorder that most civilized peoples provide mechanisms whereby citizens can fight against laws they disapprove of without going outside the law or becoming conscientious objectors or political martyrs. . . .

Our study of politics leads us, then, to pose this problem: what régime, or what system, gives the maximum guarantee against oppression? Given these terms of reference, our investigation can dispense with a comparative study of various forms of government. True, a monarchy can offer more continuity than a republic, and a dictatorship gives (temporary) guarantees of order that a democracy cannot match. But that is not our problem. In itself it is of little importance to purge our souls of violence; what matters is to make it useless by seeing to it that liberty always has peaceful means of expressing itself.

A possible reply here would be that it is conceivable that a benevolent despot might rule wisely, establish a just order for all his subjects, and leave them enough freedom of expression. Would such a régime not be based on the consent of the people?

Yes, this is conceivable. But such consent clearly could not be taken for granted. A mechanism would have to be provided to allow the people to express their opinions freely on the excellence of the régime and the wisdom of the despot. There would also have to be some device to ensure that the despot would abdicate if opinion went against him. And finally a means would have to be invented to designate, peacefully, a successor whom the people would agree to obey. But clearly such a régime would no longer be called a despotism; it would have borrowed the actual mechanism of democracy.

And it must be recognized that democracy is the form of government we are looking for. It is the system in which popular consent is most methodically sought; it is the one that allows the people to choose and dismiss their rulers as peacefully as possible. . . .

The detractors of democracy are wrong . . . in equating this form of government with anarchy, disorder, and impotence. The democratic state is a strong state; but its strength, being based on agreement, can be exerted only in the direction desired by the consensus of citizens.

Now, what is it that the citizens desire? That is the question that every democratic govenment must ask itself constantly. And it is in this respect that the democratic state, better than any other, turns to account the creative liberty of people living in society. For if it is to establish an order that citizens will agree to support, the state must go further than merely investigating their needs; it must also encourage them to demand what they consider just. In this way democracy becomes a system in which all citizens *participate* in government: the laws, in a sense, reflect the wishes of the citizens and thus turn to account the special wisdom of each one; the social order to some extent embodies all the wealth of human experience that the citizens possess.

In such a state the liberty of citizens is an end in itself. The authorities don't think of it as an annoying phrase; on the contrary, they want it, and encourage it as the surest guide to the common good.

And that defines just how remote from the democratic spirit are the political *mores* of Quebec. With very few exceptions, and at any level of authority you care to pick, you find only distrust of freedom and hostility towards its exercise. . . .

[But] the truly democratic state is bound to encourage the exercise of freedom among its citizens so that, by listening to them, it may learn better what paths to follow to attain the common good.

That is why certain political rights are inseparable from the very essence of democracy: freedom of thought, speech, expression (in the press, on the radio, etc.), assembly, and association. Indeed, the moment these freedoms suffer the smallest restraint, the citizens have lost their full power to participate in the organization of the social order. And so that each citizen may feel the benefit of the inalienable right to exercise his liberties—in spite of anyone, in spite of the state itself—to these rights two more must be added: equality of all before the law, and the right not to be deprived of one's liberty or one's goods without recourse to a trial before one's peers, under an impartial and independent judicial system.

The rights listed in the last paragraph are so basic that they are regarded in democratic philosophy as inalienable—that is, to assure the effective participation of all citizens in the development of public policy, these rights must remain vested in each citizen independently of the laws. To guarantee that they will remain beyond the reach of the state, many democratic constitutions have felt the need to include a 'bill of rights', treating these rights as in some sense anterior to the very existence of the state.

This is not, alas, the case with us. However, the fact that Canada is a federal country, in which sovereignty is shared between a central government and provincial governments, has enabled the Supreme Court to invalidate certain laws as infringing on civil liberties. Thus the court annulled the laws diminishing the freedom of the press in Alberta several years ago; and, more recently, the padlock law restricting the diffusion of political ideas and the bylaw restricting the diffusion of religious ideas (in the Jehovah's Witnesses affair).* In a similar context, the court also invalidated the Labour Relations Board's action in revoking the certification of the Teacher's Alliance without giving the parties a hearing. . . .

At the end of this first series of articles, which is based on the Declaration of Principles of the Rassemblement,† democracy appears as the logical outcome of a policy aimed at preventing tyranny, avoiding violence, doing justice to all, encouraging the full flowering of personality, and turning to account the creative liberty of every citizen.

That is not to say that democracy is a perfect form of government: you just have to look around you . . . What holds us to democracy is not that it is faultless but that it is less faulty than any other system. If the people use their sovereignty badly, the remedy is not to take it away from them (for to whom could we hand it over who would offer a better guarantee for *all* citizens?), but rather to educate them to do better. To be precise, democracy is the only form of government that fully respects the dignity of man, because it alone is based on the belief that all men can be made fit to participate, directly or indirectly, in the guidance of the society of which they are members.

However, we must refrain from making undue claims for democracy; that would be the best way to discredit it. For instance, democracy does not claim that majority rule is an infallible guide to *truth*. Nor does it claim that the average citizen is capable of resolving the extraordinarily complicated problems that face modern governments.

As for majority rule, the fact must be faced that it is a convention, possessing simply a practical value. It is convenient to choose governments and pass laws by majority vote, so that those who exercise authority can feel assured of having more supporters than opponents—which is in itself some guarantee that the social order will be upheld. It is true that from one point of view the majority convention is only a roundabout way of applying the law of the stronger, in the form of the law of the more numerous. Let us admit it, but note at the same time that human groupings took a great step towards civilization when they agreed to justify their actions by counting heads instead of breaking them.

And this must be added. Democracy genuinely demonstrates its faith in man by letting itself be guided by the rule of fifty-one per cent. For if all men are equal, each one the possessor of a special dignity, it follows inevitably that the happiness of fifty-one people is more important than that of forty-nine; it is normal, then, that—*ceteris paribus* and taking account of the inviolable rights of the minority—the decisions preferred by the fifty-one should prevail. But the majority convention has only a practical value, I repeat. Democracy recognizes that one person may be right and ninety-nine wrong. That is why freedom of speech is sacred: the one person must always have the right to proclaim *his* truth in the hope of persuading the ninety-nine to change their point of view.

On the second claim falsely attributed to democracy, the point is that parliamentary democracy does not require a decision from its subjects on each of the technical problems presented by the complicated art of government in the modern world. It would be a delusion to look to a vote of the citizens to settle the details of, for example, a fiscal policy, a war budget, or a diplomatic mission. The citizen as a group can judge such measures only by their effects— real or apparent—on the happiness of the group.

That is why modern democracies hardly ever resort to the plebiscite— which requires each citizen to decide on what is often too technical a question. In contrast, the electoral system asks of the citizen only that he should decide on a set of ideas and tendencies, and on men who can hold them and give effect to them. These sets of ideas and men constitute political parties, which are indispensable for the functioning of parliamentary democracy.

But the study of parties, and of their responsibilities in the democratic education of citizens and in the guidance of the nation, opens up a new direction for our [advances] . . .

Nationalist Alienation

It is a fact: from the beginning there has been a tendency at *Cité libre* to consider Quebec nationalists as alienators.

We were painfully aware of Quebec's inadequacies in every area—of the need to dismantle the superstructures, to secularize civil society, to democratize politics, to penetrate the economic realm, to relearn French, to get the ignoramuses out of the universities, to open our borders to culture and our minds to progress.

We instinctively disbelieved our nationalists' claim to the effect that virtually all our backwardness was 'the fault of the English'; but we did not want to go on discussing it interminably.

Whether the conquest was or was not at the root of all our ills, whether the English were or were not the most perfidious occupying force in human history, *hic et nunc* the fact remained that the French-Canadian community had all the tools necessary for regeneration: through the Canadian constitution, the state of Quebec was capable of exercising the broadest powers over the soul of French Canadians and the land in which they lived—the largest and richest of all the provinces in Canada.

As a consequence, what to us seemed more urgent than discussing the role others played in our misadventures was that the community should make effective use of the powers and resources put at its disposal in 1867. For it was not doing so.

We have grown up—and our fathers before us, and their fathers before them—in a provincial state whose basic policy has been to alienate all the best and most accessible of our resources and to abdicate all jurisdiction over the social organization and intellectual orientation of French Canadians. This policy was not imposed on us by 'the English' (read: all those who do not belong to our own ethnic group), although they have managed to take good advantage of it; it has been imposed on us by our own clerico-bourgeois élites. These élites have always tried to keep us from accepting the notion of a state whose function it would have been to play an active role in the historic process and to turn the community's energies to the general good.

These élites have called their anti-democratism by a series of very different names—the struggle against liberalism, against modernism, against freemasonry, against socialism. Nevertheless, in every case it was a matter of protecting class and caste interests against a civil power whose only concern would have been the general interest. Obviously I am not suggesting that the clergy and the bourgeoisie claimed to be looking out for anything but the common good; but they believed that they alone were capable of defining it, and hence they wanted no part of a democratic state that would have had some reality outside themselves, or of politicians who would have been able to exercise some authority at odds with their own.

In such circumstances, we at *Cité libre* considered it more urgent to prod our people out of their indolence, to rehabilitate democracy, and to attack our clerico-bourgeois ideologies than to go looking for guilty parties among the English. That is why the *Cité libre* team and those who have been our faithful collaborators seemed animated by a common purpose: to lead French Canadians to assume their own responsibilities. It was towards that end that we directed our writing and our actions, each in the area where he felt most useful: education, religion, politics, economics, the labour movement, journalism, literature, philosophy, etc.

As much as anyone, I imagine, the friends of *Cité libre* must have suffered the humiliations to which our ethnic group was subjected. But however great the external attack on our rights may have been, our own negligence in exercising them was greater still. For example, it seemed to us that the contempt for the French language shown by the English never equalled in either depth or stupidity the contempt of those among us who spoke it and taught it so abominably. Or another instance: the attacks on the educational rights of French Canadians in the other provinces never seemed as shameful and odious as the narrowness, incompetence, and lack of foresight that have always characterized educational policy in the province of Quebec, even though here we possessed all those rights. And it was the same in every area where we claimed injury: religion, finance, elections, the civil service, and so on.

Thus we at *Cité libre* saw nationalism as a form of alienation because it was alienating, in hostilities and recriminations, the intellectual and physical energies vital to our own national rehabilitation. In fighting the Other it was alienating the forces we needed, a thousand times over, to combat those primarily responsible for our general indigence: our so-called élites.

And among the nationalists, the separatist faction seemed to us to be pushing this alienation to the point of absurdity. The people they were ready to call to the barricades for a civil war had never even taught itself to use its constitutional weapons boldly and clear-headedly: witness the uninterrupted mediocrity of our representatives in Ottawa. The separatists were calling for heroism (for the economic and cultural 'liberation' of Laurentia would have meant a general drop in both our material and our intellectual standard of living) from people who did not even have the courage to deprive themselves of American comics or to turn out for French movies. Finally, with criminal inconsistency, by closing the frontiers the separatists would inevitably put full sovereign power in the hands of the very same élites responsible for the abject condition from which the separatists were promising to rescue us.

Today, it is true, the separatists and nationalists are beginning to present themselves as socialists, and they would respond that in *their* Laurentia those in power would not be the old élites but the socialists. But they are never able to demonstrate how this trick would be accomplished. How could a people long subject to clerico-bourgeois superstructures succeed in ridding itself of the same simply by taking them as allies in its fight against the English?

Either the nationalists ally themselves with the traditional forces to fight the English, in which case they will be keeping the reactionary side in power; or else they attack the traditional powers, in which case they will be too busy to think of fighting the English at the same time.

This is what we at *Cité libre* realized. For we found it absurd to think that French Canada would become more democratic, more socialistic, more secular, and more modern by closing in on itself and leaving itself with no other support against a hostile world than its antiquated traditions and reactionary ideologies.

But refusing to close the frontiers does not mean abolishing them. And *Cité libre* has never been either centralist or *bonne-ententiste*: reread our articles supporting the direct tax imposed by Mr Duplessis and objecting to the federal grants to the universities, for example.* We did not believe, in effect, that French Canadians would reach political maturity by leaving it to others to exercise their rights.

If I had to sum up our position in one paragraph, then, I would say that we have been seeking to make the state of Quebec a reality; and since the federal constitution has given us ample powers towards that end, we have regarded the nationalist movements as diversionary activities. In effect, to excuse French Canadians from having exercised their ample constitutional powers so little and so badly, the nationalists have been busy trying to show that these powers should have been even more ample! Thus the Other has invariably been found guilty of holding back powers that we had neither the intention nor the capacity nor the intelligence to exercise in any case.

* * *

In its January issue, *Cité libre* noted the 'remarkable rebirth of Québec nationalism', and proposed to define its position once again. In February, the magazine published a clear and accusatory piece in which Jean-Marc Léger declared that 'a left that aspires to be anti-national or a-national is untrue to its vocation.'

In the present article I have tried briefly to show why, in my opinion, *Cité libre* has believed and continues to believe that the best way to serve the French-Canadian community is to mistrust the nationalist ideology. 'When their adulterated ideology was made flesh, it bore the rotten fruit known as the Union Nationale'[1]: so wrote Guy Cormier in the first issue of *Cité libre* (June 1950).

Of course I have not been able to do full justice to nationalist thought in this brief sketch—nor to my own, for that matter. But it is a matter of marking positions in a debate that will continue. Next month *Cité libre* will publish an article by Guy Cormier in which he will take another look at the arguments against nationalism that he put forward eleven years ago. And in the *Tribune libre* section below, the reader will find an open letter on nationalism signed G. C.

In closing, allow me a few remarks regarding this letter. I know the author, a serious and responsible man. On looking into it, I realized that his observations have the support of a strong group of the younger separatist intellectuals, who reject the nationalism both of *Le Devoir* (and of Jean-Marc Léger) and of the magazine *Laurentie*, the one as being too faint-hearted, and the other as too far behind the times.

On this occasion, I had the surprise of discovering that many people think the reason *Cité libre* is not separatist is that it lacks courage ('. . . risks one cannot reasonably assume, . . . lack of courage', and so forth). And G.C., for his part, is so convinced that separatism is a dangerous position to take that he asks us to respect the anonymity of his letter—in short, he is counting on the remnant of courage he grants us that his letter will reach our readers.

I write this not in irony but to emphasize that perhaps this is the angle from which one must try to explain the rebirth of nationalism in the younger generation. Perhaps they believe that clericalism and traditionalism in Quebec are mortally wounded, and they are mocking the cowards at *Cité libre* who persist in attacking such aged and toothless lions. Seen from this perspective, nationalism would appear to be the only important fight left for them, one that the young would be drawn to inasmuch as it represents a perilous escapade against the English.

In that case I congratulate the young on their courage, but not on their lucidity. In our province, out-of-date traditionalism still has the strength to devour a few adversaries, and clericalism (even on the part of the laity) still has sharp claws. I will give only one example, but it is convincing. When, in his letter, G. C. writes that 'it is not the clergy that prevents Mr Lesage from giving us a Ministry of Education', he is rejecting the testimony of Mr Lesage himself! In fact, in December the latter declared on television that the state had only a supportive role to play in the area of education, this being essentially the responsibility of the Church and of parents. This nonsense, universally accepted among us but nonetheless false philosophically, will no doubt long continue to justify the chaotic development, and especially the absence of development, in the whole educational sector in the province of Quebec. During this time every diocese and every community (Jesuits at the forefront, and why shouldn't they take advantage of it?) will appeal to the theology of Mr Lesage to establish their university, and G. C. will continue to find it ' the fault of the English' that French Canadians do not have an educational policy.

In believing that all the internal enemies are in their death throes, the young nationalists not only lack realism: the better to resist the English, they are led logically to strengthen the established interests and positions at the heart of the French-Canadian community. This is to say that the young generation is becoming essentially conservative, and I can see no more frightening proof of it than G.C.'s appeal to 'Close the frontiers'.

* * *

Twenty-five years ago nationalism succeeded in putting all the energies liberated by the economic crisis of the 1930s at the service of reaction. At all costs, we must prevent neo-nationalism from likewise alienating the forces born in the post-war period, which are now being sharpened by a new unemployment crisis.

Open the frontiers! This people is dying of asphyxiation!

AUTHOR'S NOTE

[1] We hardly need ask what kind of fruit Jean Drapeau's party would give us: the strong man of today's nationalism has just told the private bills committee that he would prefer a police state to one dominated by the underworld. Not I: for I have laws on my side to put an end to the reign of crooks; against the police and the dictatorship they would support, I have nothing but my freedom, which I would very soon lose.

AN APPEAL FOR REALISM IN POLITICS

This manifesto, in which a group of young Montreal intellectuals proposed to replace most of the panaceas then in vogue among politicians, was published in Cité libre *and* The Canadian Forum *in May 1964. It was the result of regular meetings and discussions between the signatories during the previous academic year. The French version bore the title 'Pour une politique fonctionelle': when, in June 1964, Trudeau advised us that if we had to get emotional about something, we should get emotional about functionalism, this is what he had in mind to stir our blood. It is a good example of what is sometimes called technocratic liberalism; note especially the section on Human Capital.*

I
TO EVERY CANADIAN

We are a group of citizens strongly opposed to the present state of affairs in Canada generally, and in our province in particular. We condemn the indifference of the public and private sectors of our society in the face of many pressing problems. We declare our disagreement with most of the panaceas at present in vogue among our politicians.

Canada, to-day, is a country in search of a purpose. Emphasis on regional interests and the absence of leadership from the central government risk the utter disintegration of the Federal State.

In the Province of Quebec, the 'Quiet Revolution'—while it has a number of achievements to its credit—has nonetheless been limited to a mere waving of symbols in many sectors, and, in others, has come to a complete halt, already exhausted. The reform movement appears to be on the verge of becoming compromised, of deviating badly. Emotional cries often drown out the voice of reason, and racial appeals take the place of objective analyses of reality.

In the present context of Canadian politics, it is necessary above all else to reaffirm the importance of the individual, without regard to ethnic, geographic or religious accidents. The cornerstone of the social and political order must be the attributes men hold in common, not those that differentiate them. An order of priorities in political and social matters that is founded upon the individual as an individual, is totally incompatible with an order of priorities based upon race, religion or nationality.

This, then, is a manifesto. It is an affirmation of faith in man, and it is on the basis of human criteria that we demand policies better adapted to our world and our times. This is our only motivation. Of 'appeals to pride and dignity', we care for none other.

II
THE TASKS

Human resources are limited. Work abounds that requires every bit of available energy. On the basis of the criteria just enunciated, the following are some of the most pressing tasks, set out in such a way as to reveal the point of view from which each question can best be seen. It is not pretended that complete solutions are presented here; these can be formulated later in relation to each of the problems analysed.

A. Unemployment

Between 1957 and 1964, there was a considerable increase of unemployment in Canada.* During this period, from 13% to 16% of the Canadian unemployed lived in the Maritime Provinces though these provinces contained scarcely 10% of the labour force. Unemployment in Quebec varied between 35% and 37%, although our province held only 28% of the labour force.

Whether measured in terms of lost production or human misery, the socio-economic costs of such a situation are frightening. Our politicians occasionally talk about unemployment, but neither the Federal nor the Provincial authorities have ever categorically declared that they would assume the responsibility of fixing the problem. In fact, the country awaits from all levels of government the elaboration of a new and adequate policy. Among other things, it is inconceivable that politicians should continue to dread budgetary deficits and that, even when resorting to them, they should continue to pay homage to the sacred cow of a balanced budget. Similarly, if the information media were truly aware of the problem, they would treat it otherwise than by the occasional back-page when official statistics are published, otherwise than by a passing mention in reports of election speeches or trade-union meetings.

Here, as elsewhere, the intellectual élite and bourgeoisie—who in our society are largely responsible for its political orientation—have become completely introverted and persist in dissociating themselves from the population generally. Where unemployment is concerned, this withdrawal is encouraged by an apparently new phenomenon. It used to be that in times of accentuated unemployment, everyone's income tended to decrease. The situation to-day is that, while the standard of living of the unemployed diminishes, that of the working population actually continues to increase. Thus, there is now a tendency that must ultimately lead to the formation of two societies, each unfamiliar with the needs of the other.

Policies appropriate to the reduction of unemployment encounter not only the inertia and opposition of powerful groups, but are also frustrated to a considerable degree by the nationalism of the Canadian Government. The order of priorities dictated by nationalist ideologies leave little room for the expansionist policies necessary to reduce unemployment. In effect, such policies would require either a readjustment of the external value of the dollar or a strong injection of foreign capital. Because devaluation and large scale investment from abroad are found to be unacceptable from the nationalistic point of view, the government rejects truly expansionist measures and relies upon ineffectual expedients.

B. The Distribution of Wealth

The present distribution of wealth and income among the various social groups and diverse regions of Canada is plainly unacceptable.

There are in Canada several instances of an inequitable distribution of wealth and income. Thus, in the Province of Quebec, the majority of the rural population (including farmers, fishermen and forest workers) lives in economic conditions totally unacceptable when compared to the general standards in Canada. The same applies to a large fraction of the citizens of the Maritime Provinces.

No government has ever had the courage to vigorously attack these problems; society has been generally content to do little more than ameliorate the more shameful manifestations of the situation. For instance, mobility is one of the indispensable conditions to the achievement of maximum yield from human capital—as, indeed, it is for any other form of capital; nonetheless, one can search in vain for any dynamic policies aimed at encouraging such mobility. Obviously, the solution to this problem is neither easy nor fast, but what is especially revolting is that such a situation seems to be classed as a minor difficulty by virtually all our politicians and information media.

C. The Administration of Justice

Justice is one of the worst administered social functions in our society.

Our penal system belongs to the middle ages. Our laws are so made that they tend mainly to punish the culprit, seldom to rehabilitate him. They look for vengeance and not for correction. The law carries the marks of legislators who are far behind the times. These texts, replete with legendary complexities and contradictions, are applied by tribunals that tend to look to the letter of an old fashioned penal philosophy.

Frequently people are arrested, detained and interrogated on the slightest suspicion and in a highly illegal manner.

Accused persons often have to defend their liberty against the whole weight of the judicial apparatus without the assistance of a lawyer and against prosecutors to whom victory is sometimes more important than justice. At times, injustice is compounded by the perjured testimony of corrupt policemen. The condemned are then fed into an almost antediluvian penitentiary machine whose degradation and vice respect neither innocence, nor weakness, nor even youth.

As for the Civil law, in our Province, we are subject to a Code that for over a hundred years we have vaunted as the cornerstone of our society. If this claim is true, then it must be said that our society rests at least in part on rather weird foundations. A great many sections of the Code are out-of-date and whole chapters are ultra vires of the Provincial Government. For the past ten years successive groups have been assigned, one after the other, to modernize the Code; yet even today this vital work has hardly begun. The situation is even worse in the case of the Code of Civil Procedure. As long ago as 1945, its revision was designated as a matter of urgent necessity but so far little has been done. Similarly, in the case of other statutes, there has not been a revision since 1941 and the previous revision before that was in 1925. By comparison, Ontario revised its statutes in 1937, 1950, 1960; British Columbia in 1936, 1948, 1960. In fact, of all the provinces excepting Quebec, Prince Edward Island is the most in arrears, having last revised its Statutes in 1951. Quebec is thirteen years behind that.

These laws are pleaded before tribunals that are both antiquated and inadequate. At the present time there is, for Montreal alone, a backlog of more than 17,000 cases before the Superior Court. Many of these cases have been waiting three or even five years. The effect of such delay is often to deprive the litigant of his witnesses, if not also of his rights. The whole situation is aggravated by lawyers who allow themselves all kinds of delays despite the law. To these defenders of right, slowness is, indeed, a weapon professionally effective and financially rewarding. Justice has become iniquitous in two respects: it is too slow and too expensive. Legal aid cannot even begin to cope with the situation.

The whole mechanism of judicial administration must be reworked and brought up-to-date. Though this is the responsibility of government, more particularly of Provincial Government, it is surely not too much to expect some leadership from the Bench and Bar which, after all, should be somewhat concerned with the administration of justice. For example, let them examine the law to root out ineptitude or retroactive effect. Let them look to the workings of justice with an eye to more speed and less cost. Let them reconsider the whole domain of Administrative Law, now so riddled with confusion and arbitrariness. Among other things, let them attack the problems arising from school and municipal legislation which is now in such chaos. Let them do something about a Declaration of Human Rights or the institution of an ombudsman to assist citizens who may be caught up in the complexities of administration.

For how much longer will justice be considered as something far removed and inaccessible to the average citizen? Against such limited 'justice' and those who dispense it, there are centuries of resentment already accumulated. Our Province looks pretty ridiculous in so clamoring for a new constitution for the country, while at the same time showing so outrageously its inability in bringing up-to-date its own laws.

D. Human Capital

Our society devotes too little of its resources to the development of human capital. It is, of course, true that more money is being spent on education and health today than ever before. But, it is still not enough when one considers what high returns accrue from each dollar invested in this form of capital. For example, in the United States—a country which generally invests more in human capital than we do in Canada—the cure of a tubercular patient has been estimated to yield a return, in terms of real production, of 700 percent per year. Smaller, but nonetheless impressive, returns have been calculated for investments in education, mobility, inventiveness and other types of human capital.

All the same, it is not sufficient to merely increase the sum of moneys set aside for a certain type of human capital: equally important is the precise choice of the technique or technology in which to invest. It does not make sense, for instance, to invest in education, if the teaching programs and methods are obsolete; for the goal of a realistic policy in education is not only to increase the number of students in the schools but, at the same time, to augment the total sum of knowledge in the community.

The problems of education are, at present, much debated. In this debate, we must not forget the adults who have not sufficient access to means of education adapted to their ages and conditions. The benefits of free schooling are paid for by generations of people now at work. To deny these people a share of what they pay for is iniquitous.

E. Adaptation

The growth of an individual's income, or even of a family's income is largely determined by ability to adapt to new technologies, new jobs, new products and new ways of life. Those who can foresee and adjust to changes are the ones who will enjoy the most rapid increase in living standards.

But, rare indeed are those who have the opportunity and ability to rapidly adapt themselves to new circumstances. This is partly due to the fact that the individual and the family often feel helpless when confronted with situations beyond their control or understanding. In part, it is also the result of feelings of insecurity engendered by changes in methods of production, in employment and in ordinary day-to-day living.

Whether by himself or as part of a group, the individual often has no other recourse but to oppose the innovations going on about him. While such a reaction no doubt reduces his feelings of insecurity and uncertainty, it also reduces his income.

A realistic policy on the family must seek to solve the difficult problems of adaptation posed by modern society. The implementation of such a policy rests largely with the Government. Indeed, faced by obvious and pressing necessity, a bare beginning has been made in retraining workers displaced by industrialization and automation, and in informing them of employment opportunities. However, in general, Canada's main distinction in this domain is the lack of courage and absence of thought given to it by intellectuals and politicians alike.

F. Health

Government and the medical professions tend to forget that sickness is still quite capable of suddenly destroying without warning the economic well-being of a great many people. Certainly, hospital insurance has solved some important aspects of this problem, but it has not solved them all. At a time when religion and magic are less and less able to replace real medicine, the cost of medical care and drugs is still far beyond the means of a great many people. For many families, even a short sickness can mean years of financial difficulty.

Political parties have talked and talked about health insurance, but those Governments in power do not seem very concerned about actually doing something about it. Similarly, despite certain initiatives by professional bodies, the medical people more often than not prefer to maintain the status quo in this matter.

During the past twenty years, our society has made some effort to participate in the great universal upsurge in medical science. Many of our doctors have been able to go abroad to study the most recent methods and discoveries.

Unfortunately, the community organization of hospital and university services has not kept abreast of these developments. The chasm between scientific advances on the one hand, and community organization and facilities for medical research and services on the other, has been further widened by the sudden launching of a scheme as far reaching and socially important as hospital insurance. The resulting stress is cracking open the lay and clerical empires that have heretofore considered health as their private fiefs.

Surely it is self-evident that only the vigorous initiative of government, of the medical profession, of all the people concerned, and the support of large investments of public funds, will be able to cope with the health needs of the entire population throughout the whole country.

G. Federalism

We believe in federalism as a political structure for Canada. However, we are not satisfied with the evolution of Canadian Federalism in a number of areas. As this subject is being discussed ad nauseam nowadays, the mention of one typical area will be quite sufficient.

In those domains which the Constitution has given to the jurisdiction of both Ottawa and the Provinces, it is evident that plans must be developed jointly. Sharing could also be introduced, if necessary by constitutional amendment, in cases where the establishment of joint plans would permit the population to benefit from important external economies. But, one thing is certain: the kind of haphazard political expediency which has inspired so many sharing schemes and federal subsidies for so long has got to stop.

Whatever may be the division of responsibilities between the Provinces and the central authority, each must have a share of fiscal powers in proportion to the duties entrusted to it by the Constitution.

H. Political Leadership

We deplore the absence of leadership in political affairs. Public figures, federal and provincial, do not provide the people with a clear idea of the direction in which they want the country to go. They appear to be the toys of the communications media and of their ghost writers.

In leadership, there must be the courage to promote the structural changes that are necessary, the ability to propose to the people precise and intellectually acceptable objectives in a given order of priority, and the strength to gain for these objectives the voluntary support of the populace.

But, our political leaders want to be all things to all men. They propose goals so vague and incoherent that the voters can never be sure of the relationship between what is said today and done tomorrow. Instead of explaining in plain terms the problems they face or the policies they propose, our politicians fall back on propaganda loaded with emotional slogans. So it was with a part of the political campaign on nationalizing electricity in the Province of Quebec.* So it is now when we are told that 'we owe it to ourselves to have a steel industry'—as though it were simply a matter of pride and without any need to publish the studies on the subject. We may well wonder if we are not being led down the garden path.

Democratic progress requires the ready availability of true and complete information. In this way people can objectively evaluate their Government's policies. To act otherwise is to give way to despotic secrecy. Yet, despite this fact, in many areas it is extremely difficult—if not impossible—for the people to make well-informed political judgments. For example: what means did the people have to evaluate the cost and advantages of the World Exposition in 1967, including the choice of the site, before irreversible decisions had been taken?

The opposition parties must accept their share of the responsibility for keeping the public so little and so badly informed. The Opposition is supposed to force the Government to define their policies and to furnish the public with all relevant information. The Opposition is supposed to proclaim the true problems of the people, for it is the conscience of the Government. Whole sections of society could be completely ignored if the opposition prostitutes its function for the sake of short-term political advantage.

At the same time, however, the present state of our parliamentary mechanism is such that the Opposition, even when it is vigilant, is virtually helpless in the face of the resources available to the Government. The system must be reformed to give the opposition at state expense the tools which are necessary for it to fulfill its important and true role.

I. Other Problems

In the foregoing sections, we have briefly set out eight problems which appear to us to be of prime importance today. There are, however, a great many other difficulties which require immediate and popular attention.

Thus, there are problems—unrecognized in many areas—of improving the physical environment in rural and urban centers. Public hygiene is still in an elementary stage; the degree of air and water pollution is almost disastrous.

In a great many provincial ministries and municipal governments, public administration is still makeshift and rudimentary, if not in fact completely lawless.

Planning—particularly, state planning—is widely talked about. The central government and the provinces give every appearance of working resolutely in this direction. But in practice we must recognize the great difficulty and little success that these governments are having in the co-ordination of their own activities and in their own budgeting, which, after all, are the first steps necessary to any organized planning. With so much talking and so little doing, it is only fair to ask if all this 'planning' will ever produce anything other than inter-governmental and inter-departmental disputes, if it will ever contribute to the increase of anything but confusion.

Transportation and communication is one of the areas in which planning is particularly needed. Yet, we dare political leaders to define their plans for the development and coördination of the various means of transportation—highways, airways, railways and seaways—in Canada.

Aid to under-developed countries has been the subject of many declarations by political figures but Canada's contribution in this domain is still far below what our Country could easily afford. The comments we have made about the distribution of wealth in Canada are equally applicable to the distribution of wealth and income throughout the world.

As regards National Defence, there are two points that seem to require urgent attention. First, that our Government seems incapable of defining a clear and coherent National Defence policy is alarming. Second, the lack of information about defence matters released to the public is very worrying and could prove to be a serious setback to democracy in our Country. The excuse of 'state secret', so often a cloak for administrative ineptitude and confusion, can also hide base servility.

In international trade, we must gradually but resolutely work toward free exchange. In this connection, the way in which Canada has been trying to get around her international commitments is a cause for real concern. For examples one need only think of our system of quotas on the importation of Japanese textiles or of our policy of subsidizing the exportation of automobile parts.

Should the need for a higher level of public morality be added to this list? Examples of public corruption are too numerous and too well-known to be listed here; yet it is essential to the proper functioning of democracy that each citizen be convinced that honest government is attainable.

III
NATIONALISM

Face to face with these problems we choose the free flow of economic and cultural life. We reject the idea of a 'national state' as obsolete.

The presence within a state of many ethnic groups poses problems of speech and culture which must be dealt with in their proper place. Let there be no doubt that we are against the discrimination practiced by those who would have the English language as the only means of communication. But that is not to say that language should be a standard governing all politics. The future of a language depends upon the dynamism of those who speak it.

To use nationalism as a yardstick deciding policies and priorities is both sterile and retrograde. Overflowing nationalism distorts one's vision of reality, prevents one from seeing problems in their true perspective, falsifies solutions and constitutes a classic diversionary tactic for politicians caught by facts.

Our comments in this regard apply equally to Canadian nationalism or French-Canadian nationalism. Whether it be the Hon. Walter Gordon's first budget in June, 1963,* or the rulings of the Board of Broadcast Governors on Canadian content,† or the intolerance current among 'white Anglo-Saxon Protestants', or the present notion of a 'State of Quebec' and the economic salvation of French-Canada, it is always the same problem. We are not any more impressed by the cries in some English circles when American financiers buy Canadian enterprises, than we are by the adoption in the Province of Quebec of economic policies based upon the slogan 'maîtres chez nous'.

Separatism in Quebec appears to us not only as a waste of time but as a step backwards. That separatist nationalism would deliver but a purely juridical or formal sovereignty. The problem of real independence would remain untouched.

Our view of nationalism is not at the present time shared by many of the middle class élite. But, then again, nationalistic policies in Canada or in

Quebec are generally advantageous to the middle class though they run counter to the interests of the majority of the population in general, of the economically weak in particular.*

IV
THE CONSTITUTION

The derangement resulting from nationalism is particularly revealed today by the exaggerated importance given by our leading citizens to constitutional problems.

Constitutional problems in Canada are far from being so serious or so important as some would have us believe. The obstacles to economic progress, to full employment, to an equitable welfare scheme, or even to the development of French culture in Canada, are not principally the result of the Canadian Constitution. The restraints are not juridical but social and economic in nature. It is an exaggerated conception of the power of the written word that believes that these restraints will be wiped away as a result of mere constitutional change, whatever its magnitude. The so-called building of a new constitutional structure is as futile as a huge game of blocks and the effort devoted at the present time to debating such a reform takes up a great deal of energy that could be profitably spent in solving much more urgent and more fundamental problems in our society.

The real constitutional debate—if it should ever take place—must be removed from the emotional context in which it is at present enmeshed. The language being used by a great many political figures and commentators is clearly alarmist. The prophets of a 'last chance' and the makers of ultimatums risk creating the dangers they profess to fear. Grand declarations about ending Confederation betray in those who make them a narrow and myopic view of the nature of our political institutions.

V
CANADA

We refuse to let ourselves be locked into a constitutional frame smaller than Canada. Our reasons are of two kinds.

First, there is the juridical and geographical fact called Canada. We do not attach to its existence any sacred or eternal meaning, but it is an historical fact. To take it apart would require an enormous expenditure of energy and gain no proven advantage. It would be to run away from the real and important tasks that lie ahead. To want to integrate it into another geographical entity would also be, it seems to us, a futile task at the present time, even though such a development might appear in principle to conform to the natural course of the world's evolution. More important at the present time than any question of juridical boundaries is the opening of the cultural frontiers of Canadian society.

In fact—and this is our second reason—the most valid trends to-day are toward more enlightened humanism, toward various forms of political, social and economic universalism. Canada is a reproduction on a smaller and simpler scale of this universal phenomenon. The challenge is for a number of ethnic groups to learn to live together. It is a modern challenge, meaningful and indicative of what can be expected from man. If Canadians cannot make a success of a country such as theirs, how can they contribute in any way to the elaboration of humanism, to the formulation of the international political structures of tomorrow? To confess one's inability to make Canadian Confederation work is, at this stage of history, to admit one's unworthiness to contribute to the universal order.

If this country is to work, federalism must be preserved and refined at all cost. Of course, a federal political system has some inconveniences. It tends to multiply the points of strain in the body politic—arguments about fiscal powers are an example. Such a system can also be inefficient—conflicts of jurisdiction have, at times, delayed in Canada the implementation of policies that were socially desirable.

But, on the other hand, this form of constitution has great advantages for a country such as ours. The nature of the country, its geography, its ethnic diversity, the variety of its contrasting regional economies, the necessity in a democracy of bringing Government close to the people—these are all factors that favor the decentralization that federalism permits.

VI
REALISM IN POLITICS

The solution of the problems listed at the beginning of this manifesto and the realization in Canada of a true plurality [*pluralisme*] are tasks that, on the political level, can bind our generation together.

The challenge presented to us consists in defining and implementing a policy with precise objectives, practicable and based on the universal attributes of man. To this end, there are certain conditions:

1. We must be more precise in our analysis of situations, more intellectually honest in debate and more realistic in decision.

2. We must descend from the euphoria of all-embracing ideologies and come to grips with actual problems. Planning, for instance, is largely a technical problem, but it is becoming an ideological pass key. We must start to analyse reality and establish priorities in terms of the precise tasks to be accomplished.

3. Worthwhile political action requires a sense of responsibility. This has often been said to gain respect for political institutions from the people. But it must not be forgotten that these norms apply even more stringently to governors than to the governed. The political equilibrium of society is maintained by a delicate mechanism that can easily be fouled by irresponsible acts or declarations from public figures, leaders of industry, labour, ethnic groups, religious organizations and so on.

4. Democratic rule must be maintained at all costs. It is a matter which we will not compromise. The truly democratic traditions have few roots in Canada, where Indians, Métis, Orientals, Doukhobors, Hutterites and dissidents of all kinds have been victimized one after the other by the intolerance of the majority. Quebec itself is just emerging from past regimentation and authoritarianism. We will fight any action that tends to erode fundamental liberties and democratic institutions.

It is subject to these conditions that we wish to work for the good of the community.

(signed)
THE COMMITTEE FOR POLITICAL REALISM*

Albert Breton	Marc Lalonde
Raymond Breton	Maurice Pinard
Claude Bruneau	Pierre E. Trudeau
Yvon Gauthier	

STATEMENT ON MULTICULTURALISM

Official multiculturalism tests the ingenuity of those who would describe it. It is a touchstone of contemporary liberalism, here and elsewhere. Its ancestry might be traced far into our past, but it became something quintessentially Canadian only in 1962, at the end of 'The New Treason of the Intellectuals', when Pierre Trudeau strove to imitate the greatness of Thucydides, who was able to visualize a world in which Athens would be no more. Multiculturalism has three main elements: a non-racist immigration policy designed to maintain the lively diversity of Canadian society; official encouragement, through generous subsidies, for cultural activities that express that diversity; and official disapproval, increasingly forceful and effective, of any public expression of the private tensions that naturally flourish in cities like Montreal, Toronto, or Vancouver. In short, multiculturalism promises to solve the problems it first creates. The following official statement, made by Prime Minister Trudeau in the House of Commons in October 1971, emphasizes the second element of the policy. The style of the statement suggests that it emanated from the bowels of the bureaucracy that was soon to be dispensing the subsidies.

Mr Speaker, I am happy this morning to be able to reveal to the House that the government has accepted all those recommendations of the Royal Commission on Bilingualism and Biculturalism* which are contained in Volume IV of its reports directed to federal departments and agencies. Honourable members will recall that the subject of this volume is 'the contribution by other ethnic groups to the cultural enrichment of Canada and the measures that should be taken to safeguard that contribution'.

Volume IV examined the whole question of cultural and ethnic pluralism in this country and the status of our various cultures and languages, an area of study given all too little attention in the past by scholars.

It was the view of the royal commission, shared by the government and, I am sure, by all Canadians, that there cannot be one cultural policy for Canadians of British and French origin, another for the original peoples and yet a third for all others. For although there are two official languages, there is no official culture, nor does any ethnic group take precedence over any other. No citizen or group of citizens is other than Canadian, and all should be treated fairly.

The royal commission was guided by the belief that adherence to one's ethnic group is influenced not so much by one's origin or mother tongue as by one's sense of belonging to the group, and by what the commission calls the group's 'collective will to exist'. The government shares this belief.

The individual's freedom would be hampered if he were locked for life within a particular cultural compartment by the accident of birth or language. It is vital, therefore, that every Canadian, whatever his ethnic origin, be given a chance to learn at least one of the two languages in which his country conducts its official business and its politics.

A policy of multiculturalism within a bilingual framework commends itself to the government as the most suitable means of assuring the cultural freedom of Canadians. Such a policy should help to break down discriminatory attitudes and cultural jealousies. National unity if it is to mean anything in the deeply personal sense, must be founded on confidence in one's own individual identity; out of this can grow respect for that of others and a willingness to share ideas, attitudes and assumptions. A vigorous policy of multiculturalism will help create this initial confidence. It can form the base of a society which is based on fair play for all.

The government will support and encourage the various cultures and ethnic groups that give structure and vitality to our society. They will be encouraged to share their cultural expression and values with other Canadians and so contribute to a richer life for us all.

In the past, substantial public support has been given largely to the arts and cultural institutions of English-speaking Canada. More recently and largely with the help of the royal commission's earlier recommendations in Volumes I to III, there has been a conscious effort on the government's part to correct any bias against the French language and culture. In the last few months the government has taken steps to provide funds to support cultural educational centres for native people. The policy I am announcing today accepts the contention of the other cultural communities that they, too, are essential elements in Canada and deserve government assistance in order to contribute to regional and national life in ways that derive from their heritage yet are distinctively Canadian.

In implementing a policy of multiculturalism within a bilingual framework, the government will provide support in four ways.

First, resources permitting, the government will seek to assist all Canadian cultural groups that have demonstrated a desire and effort to continue to develop a capacity to grow and contribute to Canada, and a clear need for assistance, the small and weak groups no less than the strong and highly organized.

Second, the government will assist members of all cultural groups to overcome cultural barriers to full participation in Canadian society.

Third, the government will promote creative encounters and interchange among all Canadian cultural groups in the interest of national unity.

Fourth, the government will continue to assist immigrants to acquire at least one of Canada's official languages in order to become full participants in Canadian society.

Mr Speaker, I stated at the outset that the government has accepted in principle all recommendations addressed to federal departments and agencies. We are also ready and willing to work co-operatively with the provincial governments towards implementing those recommendations that concern matters under provincial or shared responsibility.

Some of the programmes endorsed or recommended by the Commission have been administered for some time by various federal agencies. I might mention the Citizenship Branch, the CRTC and its predecessor the BBG, the National Film Board and the National Museum of Man. These programmes will be revised, broadened and reactivated and they will receive the additional funds that may be required.

Some of the recommendations that concern matters under provincial jurisdiction call for co-ordinated federal and provincial action. As a first step, I have written to the First Ministers of the provinces informing them of the response of the federal government and seeking their co-operation. Officials will be asked to carry this consultation further.

I wish to table details of the government's response to each of the several recommendations.*

It should be noted that some of the programmes require pilot projects or further short-term research before more extensive action can be taken. As soon as these preliminary studies are available, further programmes will be announced and initiated. Additional financial and personnel resources will be provided.

Responsibility for implementing these recommendations has been assigned to the Citizenship Branch of the Department of the Secretary of State, the agency now responsible for matters affecting the social integration of immigrants and the cultural activities of all ethnic groups. An Inter-Agency Committee of all those agencies involved will be established to co-ordinate the federal effort.

In conclusion, I wish to emphasize the view of the government that a policy of multiculturalism within a bilingual framework is basically the conscious support of individual freedom of choice. We are free to be ourselves. But this cannot be left to chance. It must be fostered and pursued actively. If freedom of choice is in danger for some ethnic groups, it is in danger for all. It is the policy of this government to eliminate any such danger and to 'safeguard' this freedom.

I am tabling this document, Mr Speaker, but it might be the desire of the House to have it appended to *Hansard* in view of its importance and long-lasting effect.

GAD HOROWITZ

Gad Horowitz (b. 1936), who teaches political science at the University of Toronto, was one of the most interesting and influential writers on the left in English Canada during the 1960s. The selections reprinted below were origi-nally published in Canadian Dimension *between 1965 and 1967. The first is a summary and criticism of George Grant's* Lament for a Nation *(1965), which linked nationalism and socialism for English Canadians and revived the very nationalism it said had died. The second is from a discussion of another book then widely debated, John Porter's* The Vertical Mosaic *(1965), which demon-strated that not all Canadians are middle class. The third is the practical summation, delivered the month before the centennial celebrations, of the Hartz-Horowitz analysis of conservatism, liberalism, and socialism in Canada.*

Tories, Socialists and the Demise of Canada

English Canada is not merely a fragment of the American culture. There are significant differences between the English-Canadian and American ways of life. English Canada is being Americanized; the un-American characteristics of Canada are disappearing, but they are not yet gone. They can be retained by an effort of intellect and of will. An intellectual effort is necessary to make us fully conscious of our un-Americanism and of its value. An effort of will is necessary to do the things required for the preservation of English-Canadian distinctiveness, to pay 'the price of being Canadian'.

What is un-American about English Canada can be summed up in one word: British. The American society was the product of a 'liberal' revolution, and it has remained monolithically 'liberal' until the present day. English Canada's dominant ideology has always been a liberalism quite similar to the American but there has also been a Britishness about English Canada which has expressed itself in two ideologies each of which is 'alien,' beyond the pale of legitimacy, in the United States. These two ideologies are 'conservatism' and 'socialism'.

By 'conservatism' I mean not the American conservatism which is nine-teenth century liberalism, but toryism—the British conservatism which has its roots in a pre-capitalist age, the conservatism that stresses prescription, author-ity, order, hierarchy, in an organic community. By 'socialism' I mean not the American New Dealism which is nineteenth century liberalism with a pseudo-socialist tinge, but socialism properly so-called—the socialism which stresses the good of the community as against possessive individualism; equality of condition as against more equality of opportunity; the co-operative common-wealth as against the acquisitive society.

English Canada was founded by British Loyalists, rejects of the American revolution. Their purpose was to build in Canada a society which would be not liberal like the American but retain certain important conservative characteristics of British society. Their influence has been crucial and pervasive. Many students of Canada have noted that English-Canadian society has been powerfully shaped by tory values that are alien to the American mind. The latest of these is Seymour Martin Lipset (*The First New Nation*), who stresses particularly the relative strength of what he calls 'elitism' (the tendency to defer to authority) in Canada.

A few observers, again including Lipset, have noticed that Canada differs from the United States in yet another respect: Our socialism has been much stronger than that of the United States. South of the border, socialism is 'alien'; but in English Canada it has been a legitimate element of the political culture—not un-Canadian, but one of the ways of being Canadian. The presence of a relatively strong, legitimate socialism in Canada has been explained primarily as a result of the waves of British immigration beginning late in the nineteenth century. This explanation is not wrong; it is true that American socialism was borne primarily by Continental European immigrants who sloughed off their socialism in the process of Americanization, while Canadian socialism was borne primarily by British emigrants who did not have to slough off their socialism as part of a 'Canadianization' process, since they came as Britons to British North America. But the explanation is incomplete, because it ignores the oft-ignored relationship between toryism and socialism.

Socialism and liberalism are almost always placed together on the political spectrum, on the left, opposed to toryism, on the right. This is a legitimate approach, but it is one-sided. It stresses certain ideas that socialism and liberalism have in common (especially egalitarianism) when they are contrasted with toryism. But it is also true that socialism and toryism have certain things in common when they are contrasted with liberalism. I refer especially to their common orientation towards the collectivity. Indeed, it can be argued that socialism has *more* in common with toryism than with liberalism, for liberalism is possessive individualism, while socialism and toryism are variants of collectivism.

The liberal sees life in society as a competition among individuals; the prize is individual 'achievement' or 'success'; equality is equality of opportunity in the struggle for success. The individual is thought of as self-determining, autonomous, rather than a *member* determined by the class and community of which he is a part. It is *because* the socialist has a conception of society as *more* than an agglomeration of competing individuals—a conception much closer to the tory view of society as an organic entity—that he rejects the liberal idea of equality as inadequate. Socialists disagree with liberals about the essential meaning of equality *because* socialists have a tory conception of society.

In a society which thinks of itself in liberal terms, a society which has not known toryism (a society like the United States) the demand for equality will express itself as left-wing liberalism. It will be pointed out that all are not equal in the competitive struggle. The liberal government will be required to assure greater equality of opportunity, and perhaps a welfare floor so that no one will fall out of the race. In a society which thinks of itself as a community of classes rather than an aggregation of individuals, the demand for equality will take a socialist form: at its most extreme, it is a demand for the *abolition* of classes so that the good of the *community* can truly be realized.

Once we have recognized this, we are in a position to entertain the suggestion that the presence of *both* toryism and socialism in English-Canada is no
coincidence. The presence of one is related to the presence of the other: where
one is found, the other is likely to be found. The relationship can take two
forms, positive and negative, both of which exist in Canada:

1. Since toryism is strongly present in the political culture, at least part of
the leftist reaction *against* it will be expressed in its own terms: that is, in terms
of *class* interests and the good of the community as an organic entity (socialism)
rather than in terms of the individual and his vicissitudes in the competitive
struggle (liberalism).

2. Since the tory and socialist minds have some crucial assumptions,
orientations, and values in common, there is a positive affinity between them.
From certain angles they may appear not as enemies, but as two different
expressions of the same basic ideological outlook. This helps to explain the
Canadian phenomenon of the *red tory*. At the simplest level, he is a tory who
prefers the socialists to the liberals, or a socialist who prefers the tories to the
liberals, without really knowing why. At a higher level, he is a conscious
ideological tory with some 'odd' socialist notions (R. B. Bennett, Alvin
Hamilton) or a conscious ideological socialist with some 'odd' tory notions
(Eugene Forsey). At the very highest level, he is a philosopher who combines
elements of socialism and of toryism so thoroughly in a single integrated
Weltanschauung that it is impossible to say that he is a proponent of either one
or the other. Such a red tory is George Grant of McMaster University, author
of *Lament for a Nation: The Defeat of Canadian Nationalism* [1965].

George Grant is a tory, a scion of the Loyalists. The nation he laments is the
British-Ontarian nation which is now being absorbed into the culture of Michigan and New York. The dying values he mourns are the values of stability,
order, tradition. He does not care for the United States because it is liberal. He
loves dying Canada because it is conservative. The death of Canada, he says,
is the death of conservatism. It is an inevitable death; conservatism, and
therefore Canada, are impossible in the modern world.

George Grant is also a socialist, a radical critic of the power elite of
corporate capitalism, who would replace this society of competition and inequality with the co-operative commonwealth. He mourns the dying values of
tradition and order, but also mourns the unborn value of equality. The Grant
who writes *Lament for a Nation* is the same Grant who wrote the keynote
article ('An Ethic of Community') in *Social Purpose for Canada*. The Grant
who dedicates his new book to the Drew-loving columnist Judith Robinson
and the Roblinite Conservative Derek Bedson is the same Grant who was an
intellectual founding father of the New Democratic Party.*

For Grant, socialism is a variant of conservatism. Socialism, like conservatism, uses 'public power to achieve national purposes. The Conservative
party . . . after all, created Ontario Hydro, the CNR, the Bank of Canada,
the CBC . . . .'† And he reminds us that the tory founders of Ontario Hydro
wrapped themselves in the Union Jack to keep the development of electric
power out of the hands of grasping private enterprise.

To Grant socialism, like conservatism, is a teleological philosophy: it is based on a doctrine of good, or happiness, a conception of an essential human nature which men are either prevented from realizing, or made to realize, by their social arrangements. Such a conception involves the notion that 'there are ways of life in which men are fulfilled and others in which they are not'. It therefore implies the restraint of certain forms of human freedom, the discipline of certain human passions, which prevent the realization of the good life in the good society. Conservatism is 'essentially the social doctrine that public order and tradition, in contrast to freedom and experiment, were central to the good life.' Socialism is 'the use of the government to restrain greed in the name of social good.' It appeals to the conservative idea of social order against the liberal idea of freedom.

Liberalism, on the other hand, is the doctrine of open-ended progress. It has no conception of an essential human nature which *ought* to be realized; it denies any conception of good which imposes limits on our freedom to make anything we want of our human nature. It does not tolerate the limitation of human action by any idea of good. In the nineteenth century it liberated individuals to exploit one another on the free market without governmental restraint; the passion emancipated was the passion of greed. In the twentieth century it takes the form of unchecked technological progress, *mastery* of human and non-human nature becomes an end in itself. Liberal ideology is the 'end of ideology'—experimentation in the shaping of society is to be uninhibited by any preconceived notion of good. Good is whatever technological progress happens to produce. Liberal freedom is the 'freedom to change any order that stands in the way of technological advance.' The passion emancipated is the passion to innovate. Automation, for example, is not controlled in order to prevent evil. Nor is it used to create a good society. It is allowed to take its course. The liberal is not willing to stop it, to control it, or to use it for good; he is willing only to make some gestures of alleviation of the suffering it creates, after the fact.

Conservatism in both its pre-capitalist and socialist forms blocks progress with its old-fashioned pre-conceived ideas of good; therefore, says Grant, it is doomed. Nothing can stand in the way of technological advance. Canada is worth preserving because its culture contains illiberal, un-American streams of toryism and socialism. But Canada cannot be preserved because 'end of ideology' technological liberalism, based in the United States, inevitably 'universalizes' and 'homogenizes', eliminates all differences, destroys what it cannot absorb. All 'indigenous' cultures must fall before the all-consuming international liberal (American) culture.

For Grant, the disappearance of English Canada is primarily the result of a change in the economic motivations of our corporate elite and their bureaucratic allies. The Canadian economy once consisted chiefly of the extraction of raw materials for export to Europe together with some secondary industry operating behind high tariff walls. The economic elite of Montreal and Toronto were the pillars of toryism, of nationalism, and of the British connection. The nation was safe because the economic motives of the elite were served by their nationalist-tory-British ideology. Their economic and ideological motives coincided so as to make Canada possible.

Two events occurring more or less simultaneously broke the connection between economic and ideological motivation:

1. Britain ceased to be a world power. She was no longer a powerful economic force pulling trade eastward, nor a powerful cultural and political force providing an 'alternative pull' to that of the United States.

2. The American economy began to expand into Canada. The Canadian capitalists found that they could 'make more money by being the representatives of American capitalism and setting up branch plants.' 'The wealthy rarely maintain their nationalism when it is in conflict with the economic drive of the day.' 'Capitalism is, after all, a way of life based on the principle that the most important activity is profit-making. That activity led the wealthy in the direction of continentalism. They lost nothing essential to the principle of their lives in losing their country. . . . When everything is relative to profit-making, all traditions of virtue are dissolved, including that aspect of virtue known as love of country.'

Once the tie between economics and ideology was broken, the economic elite began to lose its toryism, its Britishness, and its nationalism. 'The wealthy of Canada ceased to be connected with their British past.' The 'older Canadianism disappeared first in Toronto and Montreal, cities that once prided themselves on being most British.' The Canadian economic elite 'developed into a northern extension' of the American, looking 'across the border for its final authority in both politics and culture.' American control need not express itself in the form of direct pressure, for 'the dominant classes of Canada see themselves at one with the continent.' American capital 'incarnates itself as an indigenous ruling class.' Canada becomes an extension of American society, for 'branch plant economies have branch plant cultures.'

These changes coincided with a shift of the economic elite's political weight from the Conservative to the Liberal party. The immediate cause of the shift was R. B. Bennett's red tory programme of social legislation. But the business-Liberal alliance was solidified by the Liberals' readiness to serve as the 'political instrument of the Canadian establishment'. The policy of the alliance was to facilitate the expansion of the American economy into Canada. King and Howe presided over the disappearance of English Canada. The Liberal, the 'anti-national' party, 'openly announced that our resources were at the disposal of continental capitalism.'

Some of the old pro-British ruling class maintained the strength of the Conservative party in Ontario for a while, and the old ideology is *still* alive in certain segments of the Conservative party, but it is sputtering to its death. For the Conservative wealthy, like the Liberal wealthy, cannot resist the 'economic drive of the day'. The continentalist elite now expresses itself through *both* the Liberal party and the anti-Diefenbaker wing of the Conservative party. Ontario Conservatism is becoming Americanized.

The Diefenbaker phenomenon is the last gasp of a confused, bewildered Canadian nationalism, rooted in the small towns which are slowest to adjust themselves to a changing society. Diefenbaker's heart was pure, says Grant, his nationalism strong and genuine. His sincerity is proved by his behavior in the Defence Crisis of 1963,* when he sacrificed political advantage to make 'the strongest stand against satellite status that any Canadian government ever attempted', and 'maintained that stand even when the full power of the Canadian ruling class, the American government, and the military was brought to bear against him. . . . It took the full weight of the North American establishment to bring him down.' In manuscript, the subtitle of Grant's book was not 'The Defeat of Canadian Nationalism', but 'In Defence of John Diefenbaker'. Grant is 'saddened by the failure of Diefenbaker', but 'sickened by the shouts of sophisticated derision at his defeat.' Those who mocked him and destroyed him are the establishment, 'the wealthy and the clever' whose real loyalty is to the 'homogenized culture of the American Empire'. They hated him because his conception of Canada as a sovereign state was incompatible with their allegiance to the United States.

According to Grant, Diefenbaker failed to produce feasible nationalist policies because he was confused. He wanted an independent Canada, but didn't know how to go about making one. Grant recognizes that after the second world war, the only feasible nationalist policy for Canada was socialism. Reversal of the process of Americanization demanded 'concentrated use of Ottawa's planning and control'. If Diefenbaker had been a *realistic* nationalist, he would have appealed 'over the heads of corporation capitalism to the masses of Ontario and Quebec' with a socialist programme. In order to do this, he would have had to realize that the corporation elite were 'basically anti-national'. But he did not realize this. He tried to make a nationalist appeal to the very forces which had opposed his leadership because they feared his populism—the established classes of Ontario, the Donald Flemings. He tried to live with them. These men, whose philosophy was hardly that of the fair share, could tolerate Diefenbaker's *populism* as a nuisance, but when he showed his *nationalist* teeth in the Defence Crisis, they knew that he must be destroyed.

Diefenbaker rendered himself ineffective not only by attempting an alliance with the corporate, anti-national forces in his own party, but by combining his populism with the free enterprise ideology of Canada's small towns. Clearly, Diefenbaker the free-enterpriser was incapable of using the power of government to reverse the Americanization process. This failure, since it was linked with his failure to solve the problem of unemployment, lost him the support of Canada's urban masses. And finally, Diefenbaker seals his doom by failing to connect his nationalism with the nationalism of French Canada, by making enemies of two brands of un-Americanism that could have been allies. So, abandoned by rulers and ruled, English and French, Diefenbaker is pushed back to the rural English Canada which still has warm memories of a British North American past.

Grant's message seems to be that English Canada is dying because the only remaining nationalists—Conservatives of the Diefenbaker stripe—are tied, despite their populism, to a free-enterprise ideology which prevents them from using socialist policies for nationalist reasons.

What then of Canada's social democrats? Why does Grant not look to them for the socialist-nationalist policies which alone can save Canada? Part of Grant's answer is that Canada's socialists are not nationalist enough, that they do not understand the need for a strong link between nationalism and socialism. They are 'good-natured utopians', themselves somewhat affected by the pull of continentalism, too much inclined to play the role of 'left-wing allies of the Liberals'.

But Grant's primary reason for his lack of faith or hope in Canadian socialism is that he lacks faith and hope, period. He believes that the 'homogenization' of all un-American 'indigenous cultures' is inevitable *because* technological progress is inevitable. (I will argue that this is a *non sequitur*). His determinism is overpowering, his pessimism uncompromising. Not only English Canada, but French Canada (despite the socialist policies of Lévesque and his followers), Britain herself, and *all* un-American cultures the world over must inevitably be absorbed into an American world-culture. He has no hope that socialist policies can save English Canada because he has no hope that they can save cultures with a much *stronger* will to survive and a much *more* distinctive culture than those of English-Canada. Technology is all-powerful and all-absorbent and Technology is America. Socialism and conservatism both have notions of the good; technology refuses to be limited by any preconceived idea of good; therefore socialism and conservatism, and the cultures which embody them, insofar as they embody them, are anachronisms doomed to disappearance.

But Grant's pessimism is unreasonable. It is unreasonable because it *identifies* the inevitability of technological progress with the inevitable failure of any attempt to control and use it for human purposes. It *assumes* that progress is *entirely* incompatible with any ideology but liberalism because liberalism alone gives it complete freedom. Must it have *complete* freedom? It assumes that no society can be both progressive technologically and un-American in significant aspects of its ideology and social structure. *Must* Yugoslavia and Sweden and Japan and Australia all end up as replicas of the United States? Surely there are grounds for arguing that they need not. Many cultures are becoming modernized, and in *that* sense Americanized, more like the United States than they were before; but these cultures, because they have histories which differentiate them from the United States, will remain in significant respects un-American. English-Canada *may* be such a culture. A conservative should realize that Americanization does not work on a *tabula rasa*. The past cannot be entirely erased. Grant's doctrine of inevitability is unreasonable, finally, because all arguments of inevitability are dubious and ought therefore to be avoided both in prognoses and in programmes of action.

Grant's tory fatalism has sucked the life out of his socialist humanism. In lamenting for Canada and for socialism as if they were already dead, he betrays the Grant who wrote 'An Ethic of Community'.

British toryism and socialism are *present* in English Canada, but the dominant element in our political culture has always been liberalism. Toryism and socialism may not be strong *enough* to withstand Americanization-Liberalization. Granted. But even if the disappearance of English Canada turns out to be inevitable, that is no reason to give up the fight. Nothing can be *known* to be inevitable until it happens. Grant himself makes the following distinction between the ways in which English and French Canada will disappear: 'The French . . . will at least disappear . . . with more than the smirks and whimpers of their English-speaking compatriots—with their flags flying, and indeed, with some guns blazing.' There is, then, a difference between going down fighting and going down smirking. But the danger of Grant's pessimism is that it encourages smirking rather than fighting. Why give up the fight unless you know for certain that it is lost?

Grant's pessimism and determinism exude death. They ought to be rejected. Once they are rejected, he has a vital lesson to teach Canadian social democrats. The lesson can be put in the form of three crucial points:

1. The existence of Canada was, in the past, guaranteed by the nationalism of our economic elite. They have abandoned nationalism, and are therefore twice cursed: for being an economic elite and for being anti-national. If Canada is to remain in existence, the nation building role must now be played by forces other than those of entrenched wealth—popular forces with democratic socialist leaders who know where they are going. *English Canada needs a Lévesque.*

2. Canadian socialists must resist such 'end of ideology' temptations as those evinced in certain portions of the liberal manifesto *The Prospect of Change.* * The difficulties of implementing social democratic ideals, the necessities of compromise in day to day politics, the dictates of practical wisdom must not be allowed to dim the vision of the co-operative commonwealth. Socialist equality, not mere liberal equality of opportunity, must remain the *ultimate* objective of socialists if they are to resist liberalization.

3. Canadian socialists must become wholehearted nationalists. This involves a recognition that they have—for certain purposes—more in common with uncorrupted conservative nationalism of the Howard Green-Alvin Hamilton type than with Americanized Liberals and Liberalized Conservatives.

Canadian socialism can become the only political force in Canada that combines both nationalisms with a readiness to implement the only type of policy which can save both nations. In English and French Canada as in all small nations, socialism and nationalism require one another.

English Canada is not worth preserving unless it can be different from the United States. Our British past provides the foundations for building on the northern half of this continent a social democratic order (let Grant call it conservative if he wishes) *better* than the liberal society of the United States. A tory past contains the seeds of a socialist future.

Mosaics and Identity

Among the many themes developed by John Porter in his impressive pioneering study of power in Canadian society [*The Vertical Mosaic*] there is one which ought—more than any other—to be taken up for intensive discussion among all 'liberally minded Canadians'. This theme is the argument Canada *could* develop a more democratic way of life but is prevented from doing so by the absence of a 'creative politics', i.e., a democratic class struggle, a left-right polarization. Porter argues that this creative politics does not come into being because of the absence of a strong national identity over and above the ethnic and regional particularisms of Canada. . . .

Porter himself does not elaborate this argument sufficiently, and his reviewers ignore it entirely. Nevertheless, it is the most important of his arguments, because it exposes the causes of the Canadian malaise, reveals the dilemmas we would like to ignore, confronts us with choices we do not want to make. . . .

A functioning democracy requires a well developed sense of national community, a feeling on the part of ordinary people that they are part of that community, that they have a sacred right and duty to participate in its affairs, that it is obliged to respond to their demands, in other words the feeling of a citizen rather than that of a subject.

Canadians do not have this feeling about their country because their strongest identifications are with their regions and ethnic groups rather than with Canada. This is clear enough with regard to English-French relations, but it is also true with regard to English Canada. The French Canadian identifies primarily with French Canada. The English Canadian identifies himself most strongly neither with Canada nor with English Canada but with his ethnic group—British, Ukrainian, etc.—and with his region—Maritimer, Westerner, etc.

Two interrelated factors are responsible for this situation, both of which are alluded to by Porter. The first is the colonial and exclusive mentality of the British charter group; the second is the presence of the French in the confederal partnership.

The British of Canada, unlike those of the United States, did not see themselves as the founding element of an entirely new nation. They saw themselves as Britons in North America; they retained their identifications with England, Scotland and Wales. They therefore made no conscious effort to integrate new ethnic groups into a new Canadian nation. The new groups were left alone, permitted and even encouraged to follow the British example, that is, to retain their identifications with their homelands. Canada was a purely political, not a national or cultural entity. It consisted of a number of ethnic groups, politically united through allegiance to the British Crown.

The presence of a self-conscious nationalistic French element played a very important part in giving rise to this situation and in sustaining it. If the French were to be left outside the British community, logic and justice required that other ethnic groups be treated similarly. If Quebec were to be left alone, logic and justice required that other provinces be left alone. In short, the French presence meant that the 'national' community and its government must be weak, its symbols and slogans empty of content. It meant that the national community did not have enough power to integrate even its English speaking elements.

This situation has changed recently in two ways: The British charter group has lost most of its Britishness, so that the sense of a shared connection with Britain and with British traditions which once linked British Columbians, Manitobans, Ontarians, and Nova Scotians has now nearly disappeared. And the French charter group has finally insisted once and for all that it is not an ethnic group like the others and that Quebec is not a province like the others.

The British revolt against the father opened up two possibilities: Americanization, and movement towards a genuine Canadian amalgam. The latter approach is well illustrated by Diefenbaker: One Canada, primary identification with the nation, equal status for all ethnic groups, no hyphenation. But the

French do not want to be amalgamated. One Canada is left high and dry. The possibility of amalgamating the *English* speaking regions and ethnic groups into one nation is not taken up because 'logic' and 'justice' continue to require that *all* Canadian particularisms receive roughly equal treatment. In other, more realistic, words, our national politicians are afraid to challenge the professional ethnics and the provincial empire builders who perversely demand for their groups a status similar to that of the French. The continuation of our strong emphasis on regional and ethnic differentiation perpetuates fragmentation, prevents the emergence of any clear Canadian *or* English Canadian identity, and leaves the door wide open for Americanization. We are not facing the dilemma. Instead of giving the French alone a special status, we are disintegrating the country by giving all ethnic groups and provinces special status. Canada may never be a national community because of the French presence. English Canada can be a national community, but only if our image of Canada is transformed from a political union of provinces and tribes into a political union of two national communities, one English and one French. We must have the courage to combine *accommodation* of the French particularism with *resistance* to intra-English particularisms.

Porter condemns our beloved 'mosaic' primarily because it is vertical. When the British left the 'other' ethnic groups alone instead of trying to build them into a new national community, these 'others' were frozen in their original economic occupations and social statuses. The absence of a national identity sustains stagnation in our politics *and* inequality of opportunity in our economic and social life. Assignment to social roles continues to be based on ethnicity. Here is a dilemma which the professional ethnics and all mosaic celebrators refuse to face. Ethnic segregation cannot easily be combined with equal opportunity for the members of different ethnic groups.

Most mosaic celebrators take the line that the very nothingness of Canada is its most praiseworthy characteristic. 'How wonderful to live in a country that has no flag.' How wonderful to live in a non-nationalistic nation, a nation that is not a nation, 'a land of many cultures'. How wonderful to be left alone, not to be pressed into any moulds. How wonderful to escape the conformitarian pressures of a US-style melting pot.

When this way of talking is not fake, it is literally nihilistic. It ignores the dark side of the mosaic, the side exposed by Porter. Furthermore, it combines exaggeration of the cultural *uniformity* of the United States with exaggeration of the cultural *diversity* of English Canada. Ethnic segregation does not necessarily preserve genuine cultural diversity. The forces of assimilation can and do operate as powerfully on the segregated immigrant groups of Canada as they do on the less segregated immigrant groups of the United States. In both countries, cultural diversity and assimilation coexist. In both countries, immigrant groups, though they retain partially separate communities and cultures for a very long time, adopt the ways of life and thought of the English speaking charter groups. The groups that have been in Canada for a long time are just as assimilated, in this sense, as the groups that have been in the United States for a long time. In Canada, however, assimilation has not levelled the barriers of social segregation—it has not eroded ethnicity as a criterion for assignment of social status—to the same extent as in the United States. Canada has cultural diversity with segregation, the United States has cultural diversity without segregation. That is an oversimplification, but it is aimed at the truth of the matter. The other factor which truly differentiates the Canadian mosaic from the American situation is the absence of a Canadian or English Canadian identity. As immigrant groups assimilate in the United States, they are *also* integrated into a general national community. They acquire a strong identification with the American nation. Here they assimilate culturally without being integrated into a unifying national community. It is this absence of a strong Canadian or English Canadian loyalty, combined with the example of French Canada, which enables ethnic spokesmen to demand for their willingly assimilating 'constituents' a status similar in principle to that of English and French Canada.

I would rather be a Jew in the United States than a Jew in Canada. The Jews of Canada are more ghettoized, but their cultural life as Jews is thinner. Their participation in the general national culture is also less profound in Canada than in the United States. The ghettoization of the ethnic communities of Canada stifles me, and I suspect it stifles all non-British non-French Canadians except those who make the nurturing of particularism a professional career in the Senate and elsewhere.

Our image of the United States as a melting pot is very much overdrawn. A Jewish community and a Jewish culture are so powerfully present in the United States that Canadian Jews, even though they are more recent arrivals, and in spite of the 'protection' of the mosaic, look south of the border for community leaders, for rabbis, and for ideas. Most American Jews identify strongly with the Jewish community; *at the same time* they are very American. They have powerful feelings of commitment to and participation in the American national community. Canadian Jews, on the other hand, feel themselves to be not so much a *Canadian* Jewry as an extension of American Jewry. It should be evident that this relatively weak identification with *Canada* is not the result of a strongly felt Jewish particularism. It is, rather, a natural reaction to the *absence* of any real Canadian community with which one can identify.

I suspect that this is equally true of the other immigrant groups: They remain in their ghettoes; at the same time, they assimilate: English becomes their language, the ways of the English-speaking become their ways. But they do not acquire a strong identification with the Canadian nation, because there is none, except in the political sense. The whole ideology of the mosaic came into being not so much to justify cultural diversity as to justify the absence of a national community embracing that diversity. We have only the pluribus, not the unum. The mosaic ideology is not needed to preserve the diversity; it is a weak and often insincere apology for the absence of unity. What differentiates us from the Americans is not our cultural diversity—they have it too—but our failure to develop a national community. That is the meaning of the 'mosaic'. . . .

The ethnic politicans' pretensions to semi-equal status with the French and English must be rejected, just as the provincial politicians' pretensions to equal status with Quebec must be rejected. These pretensions have no solid bases of support in the ethnic and provincial constituencies. The French Canadians of Quebec want to be a nation in an autonomous province. The Ukrainians of Manitoba do not want to be a nation; the people of British Columbia do not want their province to be autonomous. The ethnic and regional particularisms of English Canada are neither powerful nor self-sustaining; they are artificially stimulated by self-seeking politicians; they are almost wholly parasitic growths on the genuine, deeply felt, self-sustaining autonomist impulse of Quebec. If an overarching English Canadian national community existed, the ethnic and regional particularisms would evaporate, with no regrets and little nostalgia.

When the mosaic celebrator thanks the Lord for Canada's exemption from the conformitarian pressures of the American melting pot, he is confusing a very important issue. It is true that the US enforces conformity to a greater degree than Canada, but that conformity, is *ideological*, not cultural. American liberalism is all-engulfing; non-liberal ideologies are excluded from the pale of legitimacy. Liberalism is Americanism; other 'isms' are un-American. But *cultural* conformity of the same type does not exist. I return to the Jewish situation because it is the one with which I am familiar. Jewish parochial schools exist in the United States—cultural diversity. But in these schools the cult of Americanism is taught—ideological uniformity.

The development of an English Canadian national identity does not require that we impose a single set of social and political values on our society. The United States is not the only model of a nation. Most countries manage to combine national identity with ideological diversity. Our terrified equation of nationality with uniformity is irrational. . . .

The mosaic preserves nothing of value. It is literally nothing. It is the *absence* of a sense of identity, the *absence* of a common life which can be shared by the English-speaking regions and tribes of Canada.

The mosaic 'preserves' only political stagnation, inequality of opportunity, culturally meaningless ghettoization, and Americanization. In the absence of a Canadian identity, we identify—all of us, though to varying degrees—with the American national community. Its media absorb us. Through the American media, John Kennedy became the first President of Canada. Through the media, we participate vicariously in the affairs of the American community, without power over those affairs. Through the media the causes of American radical youth become the causes of our radical youth, automatically, without regard to the differences between the American and Canadian situations. Complete annexation of the Canadian mind will be accomplished in a few decades. Political independence will be left to us—but for what purpose?

Porter recognizes that galloping Americanization prevents the development of national identity and creative politics in Canada. The American media, he says, 'contribute substantially to "Canadian" values and to the view of the world held by Canadians. . . . It is difficult under these conditions for a society to provide itself with a distinct structure of values or with an image of itself as a distinct society.' A large part of the responsibility for this situation is assigned to the English Canadian intelligentsia. It is, says Porter, conservative, apolitical, disinclined to 'articulate a consistent set of defensive values'.*

If the situation can be saved, and that is of course extremely doubtful, English Canadian intellectuals, like those of other under-developed nations plagued by tribalism, must become self-conscious nation builders, as 'survivance' conscious as the Québécois. Two huge obstacles will probably rule out this development. The first is our distaste for 'imposing' a single 'uniformity' on the 'diversity' of English Canada. The second is our even stronger distaste for building a 'Chinese wall' along the forty-ninth parallel to 'isolate' ourselves from American influences. But our assumption that there can be no English Canadian nation unless these distasteful things are done is false.

There is no need to ' impose' anything on anyone. If we can find a way of retarding Americanization, the fragmented elements of English Canada will come together of their own accord; they are, after all, elements of one society, speaking one language, and bound together in one federal union. All that is needed is the will to create something new here, and something different from what the Americans have created. I would like that something new to be a social democracy, but there are other possibilities. Let one hundred flowers bloom. Something definite can grow out of the confusing mix that is English Canada. It *would* grow without any kind of coercion if not for the overpowering presence of pre-existing American models available for imitation in every area of existence. The problem of Americanization, then, must be faced; without chauvinism, but also without a fake, self-effacing, embarrassed cosmopolitanism. . . .

On the Fear of Nationalism

Canada is, and has always been, a relatively stable and peaceful society. Our political tradition, in its substantive content and even more in its rhetoric, has emphasized above all, the themes of moderation. The tradition may have served us well in the past, but it must now be transcended if Canada is to survive. Let us not mince words; survival is the issue. The fear of political annexation is not realistic: but the prospect of total economic and cultural integration into American society, is real and immediate.

Our political and intellectual elites, true to the Canadian tradition, are moderately concerned about the impending demise of their country, and moderately determined to do something to prevent that demise, on condition that whatever is done, be moderately done. This moderation will be the death of us. One of the sources of contemporary moderation is a genteel fear of *nationalism* that pervades the English-Canadian establishment. The continentalist elements of establishment use this fear of nationalism cynically, in the interest of the greater American nationalism of which we are a part.

Simultaneously, in order to draw the teeth of Canadian nationalism they produce a counterfeit-nationalism of their own, a centennial-nationalism which amounts to no more than a local boosterism: What a wonderful country this is, how lucky we are to be citizens of this blessed land, how proud we are to be Canadians, let's stop running ourselves down, we have a magnificent future, and so on. In this way, nationalist emotion is drained off to be expressed in harmless flag-waving and in sentimental pap, with no more impact on the process of Americanization than the self-glorification of a small town Chamber of Commerce. American society is broad and flexible enough to accommodate innumerable local patriotisms, from Hawaii to Puerto Rico, so long as they are American.

But there are also elements of the establishment which are not continentalist, which might be prepared to do something if it were not for their genuine fear of nationalism. Americanization, they would agree, is an evil which we ought to avoid if we can, but nationalism is an even greater evil—it is the malevolent force which has bathed the world in blood.

The moderate view is that Canadian nationalism would be more harmful to Canada and to the world than the Americanization of Canada. This view is false because it is based on a model of nationalism which is not applicable to Canada. The nationalism that has bathed the world in blood, is not the nationalism that seeks to prevent the integration of Canada into American society.

There are, to begin with, crucial distinctions to be made among the nationalism of expansionist great powers, the nationalism of small states struggling to preserve some degree of independence and the nationalism of colonized people seeking self-determination. The first of these is never justifiable. The other two, nearly always are. Canadian nationalism is clearly that of the small state: our relationship with the United States is analogous to the relationship of Finland with the Soviet Union. The Americans and the Soviets need not fear conquest by the Canadians and the Finns. The Canadians and the Finns are no threat to their great neighbours. The shedding of blood is simply not in this picture. Second of all, there is a difference between the nationalism that disrupts established states and the nationalism that preserves or consolidates existing states. Examples of the disruptive type are the nationalisms that destroyed the Austro-Hungarian Empire and the nationalisms that today threaten to destroy and dismember India and Nigeria. These nationalisms, though they are often justifiable reactions to alien domination, are usually accompanied by bitter chauvinistic hatred of neighbouring peoples and often result in the shedding of blood. The mutually antagonistic chauvinisms of *English* and *French* Canada, are potentially analogous to those of Austro-Hungary, India and Nigeria. The *intra*-Canadian nationalist extremisms which threaten to tear this country apart are correctly feared, not only by our moderates, but by all Canadians with the exception of a fringe of separatists and a fringe of Orangemen. But the Pan-Canadian nationalism which seeks to preserve a Canadian state in some form, and to prevent the digestion of both English- and French-Canadian societies by the United States, is an entirely different matter.

Canada exists. The nationalism that preserves its existence, is not disruptive.

Third, there is a difference between racist nationalism and other types of nationalism. This is a distinction which should require no elaboration. Canadian nationalism has nothing to do with race, nothing to do with blood and soil. The Canadians, far from being a master race, are not even a *Volk*. Canadian nationalism does not lead to Auschwitz. It simply leads away from Washington.

Finally, there is a difference between what might be called doctrinal and non-doctrinal nationalisms. A doctrinal nationalism perceives the nation as the embodiment of a specific set of values, such as Communism, Liberalism, Catholicism and fascism. This leads it to relate to the outside world in a paranoid manner. The values incarnated in the nation may be viewed as the unique possession of the nation—a treasured possession, which can only be tarnished and mutilated by contact with the outside world. If this is the case, the nation will be *isolationist*—in a sense, it will turn in on itself and shun the outside influences as a potential corruptor. Another possibility for doctrinal nationalism is the view that the nation's [values] have universal unique validity, and that the nation has a special mission to impose these values on the rest of the world by force, by persuasion, or by forceful persuasion. This is the *messianic* subtype of doctrinal nationalism.

Within its own borders, doctrinal nationalism imposes a rigid ideological conformity. The only legitimate ideology is the national ideology. Adherents of other ideologies are, at best, barely tolerated deviates and at worst, witches to be burned at the stake. I have of course, been describing the nationalism of the United States. The doctrine of its nationalism is liberalism, individualism, 'democratic capitalism'. To adhere to a different ideology is to be un-American, a deviate or a witch. To be a citizen of another country, is to be either a corrupter to be shunned or an infidel to be converted. Of all contemporary 'free world' nationalisms, the American variety most closely approximates the ideal type of doctrinal nationalism. It is therefore ironic, in the extreme, that our Canadian moderates quake with terror at the prospect of a Canadian nationalism causing our society to turn in on itself, isolating itself from outside influences and pressing all Canadians into a single ideological mould. It is ironic because only Canadian nationalism can *prevent* these things from happening, as we are absorbed into the American mind, and it is in large part, the obtuseness of our moderates that prevents Canadian nationalism from happening.

Canadian nationalism cannot be doctrinal. On the contrary, its purpose must be to preserve on the northern half of this continent, a society which does not share the liberal conformitarianism, the isolationism and the messianism of the United States.

What is the doctrine of Canadian nationalism? The moderates cannot answer this question, because there is no such doctrine. There is no *unique* set of Canadian values which is to be preserved from corruption by outsiders and/or imposed on them by forceful persuasion. Certainly Canadian nationalists are anxious to diminish the economic and cultural influence of the United States in Canada—not in order to preserve some unique set of Canadian national values, but in order to preserve the *possibility* of building, in this country, a society which is *better* than the Great Society. It needn't be uniquely Canadian as long as it isn't a copy of the United States. It could be anything. It could be a replica of Sweden, or if you like, of North Korea, Albania or Ireland, or Spain or Yugoslavia, or Cambodia, or all of them. The point is not to preserve *all* aspects of Canadian society which differentiate it from the American simply because they are *uniquely ours*, but to preserve those distinctive aspects of Canadian society which make it *better* than American society and above all, Canada's freedom of action to *become something*—who knows what it will be—different from Flint, Michigan. If the United States were Utopia, I would not be a Canadian nationalist; but the United States is not Utopia. It is a fully formed, highly integrated national community, with clearly defined ways of thought and behaviour. Americans have *chosen* their direction in every sphere of life. They are stuck with Americanism. We can be different, precisely because we are a muddle, nothing definite. Roads which are closed to the Americans, may be open to us. Some of them may lead to a *better* society than theirs—better, not because it is distinctively Canadian, but simply *better*.

Dare we try to come closer to Utopia, or must we imitate *American* models *all* the time, in *every* way?

This is a Diefenbaker cliché, but it is true, Canadian nationalism is not 'anti-Americanism' necessarily in a sense of hatred of all things American just because they're American. There is much we can learn from the United States. The leaders of the Soviet Union themselves have sometimes admitted as much; it is nothing to be ashamed of. There is much to be learned, but it should be *intended* learning for our purposes, not automatic imitation, not unconscious absorption.

The problem of Americanization can be faced without chauvinism, but also without a fake, self-effacing, embarrassed cosmopolitanism. It can be faced; without building Chinese walls, without 'restricting the free flow of ideas'. It can be faced positively, by taking control of our economy into our own hands *and*, this is just as important, releasing our production and distribution of ideas from a dam of *market* forces, by assigning a very high priority to the subsidization of Canadian cultural production of all sorts, on a scale very much larger than anything contemplated at the moment. By cultural production, I mean not only the arts, but anything that can be published or broadcast. The use of the state for nation building purposes is not a new idea in Canada. We need a National policy not of cultural tariffs and taxes, but of cultural bounties and subsidies.

The purpose of Canadian nationalism is not to close Canada to the world, but to open Canada to the world by keeping out of the United States. The fears of our moderates are entirely groundless.

NATIONALISM AND SOCIALISM

Socialism is internationalist. It looks forward to the establishment of the republic of mankind, a world in which inequality among nations will be abolished together with every other form of useless and unjust inequality. It looks forward to the withering away of the nation-state and perhaps of the state itself.

But this dream may never be realized. Certainly it will not be realized in our lifetime, and it most assuredly will not to be brought one centimetre closer to realization by the absorption of Canada in the United States. Canadian socialists who are also Canadian nationalists, have been accused of abandoning and betraying socialism and even of converting it into its opposite, which is of course, national-socialism. This is libel. Canadian socialists are nationalists *because* they are socialists.

If the United States were socialist, at this moment, we would be continentalists at this moment. If the possibilities of building a socialist society were brighter in the United States than in Canada, or as bright, we would not be terrified by the prospect of absorption. We are nationalists because, as socialists, we do not want our country to be utterly absorbed by the *citadel of world capitalism*.

We are nationalists, not in the sense that we want to keep Canada forever out of all future mergers of nations, but in the sense that we want to keep Canada out of the *United States* in the foreseeable future. We are nationalists because we believe that something new can be created here—something different from what the Americans have created—and that something new might be a social democracy.

The point of our nationalism is not to preserve a Canadian identity no matter what it might be, but to create a Canadian identity that measures up to a socialist vision of the good society.

A Canadian socialism which did not fight continentalism, would be betraying itself. There will be no socialism in a Canada which is being absorbed into the United States. Therefore, there can be no Canadian socialism without Canadian nationalism. It is as simple as that.

Canadian nationalists who are not socialists have equally valid principled grounds for their nationalism. They are *not* nationalists simply because Canada is here, Canada is ours, Canada is wonderful and must be preserved forever, no matter what. They are nationalists *because* they are liberals, or pacifists, or tories.

The Canadian liberal might want to stay out of the United States because he is offended by America's betrayal of its own liberal ideology in the sphere of foreign relations and in the spheres of civil liberty and race relations. He might believe that an independent Canada could come closer to achieving the American dream of Liberalism.

The Canadian pacifist might want to stay out of the United States because he does not want to be part of a society that sends lively young men to slaughter and be slaughtered, to give and receive violent death in the rice paddies. The Canadian tory might want to stay out of a society in which the masses are given to excesses of violence and intolerance, noblesse oblige is nowhere to be found, tradition is a dirty word and individual greed rides roughshod over all feelings of community.

Is there room, then, for a common front of Canadian nationalists of all political parties and all ideological persuasions?

The socialist answer must be: in the long run, only socialism can preserve Canadian independence, because only socialism can decisively and fully eliminate the power of the 'international' corporations over the Canadian economy. In the short run, however, a common front is not only possible, but essential. Socialism is a minority ideology in this country. It will not halt the tide of continentalism by itself in the immediate future, and the tide must be halted in the *immediate* future. There is much that can be done, short of socialism to halt the tide, if not reverse it. A common front to *halt* the tide—a Canada sufficiently independent to develop a socialist majority—then the reversal of the tide; that must be the socialist programme. A common front to halt the tide must be the programme of all Canadians who do not want to be stuck with Americanism.

THE POLITICAL ECONOMY TRADITIONS

There are two Canadian political economy traditions: the orthodox neo-classical and the critical neo-Marxist. The first is represented here by John Dales (b. 1920), whose essay 'Protection, Immigration, and Economic Nationalism' (1966) is a little masterpiece of economic analysis. Dales taught in the department of political economy at the University of Toronto from 1954 to 1982. The second tradition is best represented by Kari Levitt (b. 1923), who teaches at McGill University. The distinction between growth and development that Levitt popularized in Silent Surrender *(1970) is the key contribution of neo-Marxist dependency theory to our politics. The following excerpts have been heavily edited to link together the main passages on her original theme.*

John Dales: Protection, Immigration and Canadian Nationalism

The use of the term 'national policies' by Canadians to describe certain governmental policies designed to promote economic growth in Canada suggests, and is perhaps often meant to suggest, that these policies also tend to promote nationalist sentiments among the citizenry. In what follows I take a particular case—our long-standing policy of tariff protection for manufacturing—and ask whether its probable economic effects (which are themselves a matter for dispute) are likely to have promoted Canadians' pride in their country. An analysis of protection is thus my major theme, but this inquiry leads to the subject of immigration, and in a final section of this paper I offer a brief and inadequate commentary on Canadian immigration policy, another of our historic 'national policies'.

I have a very unsophisticated understanding of nationalism, and define it simply as the pride that the citizens of a country take in their own and their fellow citizens' achievements in all aspects of life—social, political, cultural, technological and economic. National pride, I think, can be *affected* by economic policies. But I want to stress at the outset that I do not believe that growth policies can *create* a nation. I feel obliged to make this curious confession because Canadian historians, politicians and journalists almost always get carried away when they are discussing Canada's 'national policies' and end up by leaving the impression that without them there would be no Canada, and therefore no nationalism to discuss. I reject this view. I am prepared to believe that the existence of Canada may be explained on the basis of geography, political decisions, military events, or historical evolution—on almost any basis, indeed, *except* economic policy. My own view is that the community we now call Canada was founded in 1608 by Champlain and has had a continuous existence distinct from other communities on this continent ever since; in this I take it that I am being conservative, since most histories of Canada start with

Cabot in 1497, and some with Leif the Lucky four or five hundred years earlier. In brief, I take the *existence* of Canada and Canadian nationalism to be independent of Canada's economic policies. My procedure is to try to identify the economic effects of Canadian tariff and immigration policies, and then to ask whether these effects are such as to enhance or to detract from Canadians' pride in their social, political and cultural achievements.

THE TARIFF

I begin with protectionism and ask the straighforward question: How has Canada's tariff policy, now eighty years old, affected Canadian economic development? The answer to that question certainly lies buried somewhere in the historical record; the trick is to find it.

It seems sensible to begin our search by consulting a typical example of each of two types of intellectual guidebooks: those written by Trade Theorists, and those written by Economic Historians. Both guides, we find, give us explicit instuctions about how to approach our problem and how to track down the answer to it: indeed both take us into their confidence and tell us what the answer is, so that our own quest at first seems superfluous. When we begin to compare the two books, however, we soon find that each gives a rather different version of where we should look for our answer, how we should go about finding it, and what it will look like when we do find it. Like other guide books, we reflect, these have their mystifying aspects; indeed it is hard to believe that their authors are describing the same tour, and difficult to suppress the suspicion that neither of them has actually made the trip himself.

The Trade Theorist's *Guide* is very elegantly written. We are told, first, to find a country that exchanges goods with other countries on a regular basis, but that never allows either immigrants or emigrants to cross its national boundaries, and absolutely prohibits any export or import of capital. This sounds a little strange, and no country that we know of seems quite to meet all the specifications. (The *Guide* seems to anticipate our difficulty, for it adds, not very helpfully, that if we cannot find such a country, we should imagine it.) After this initial difficulty, however, the rest is clear sailing. We are told that without a tariff the country exports goods that it can produce efficiently, that is to say at low cost, and imports goods that it could only produce inefficiently, i.e., at high cost. Let the country now impose a tariff on imports that is sufficiently high to induce some of the labour and capital within the country to give up making things they can produce efficiently and start making things they can produce only inefficiently, namely commodities that used to be imported. The natural result of this system is that the country will experience a decline in its economic well-being. Its National Income will fall, and National Income per head, since the number of heads remains unchanged, will also fall in the same proportion. So there we have our answer! Apparently that old rascal Sir John A. Macdonald reduced both our National Income and our Standard of Living. The astonishing thing is that he somehow managed, at the same time, to win our undying gratitude for what he proudly called his National Policy.

As we lay down the Trade Theorist's *Guide* we are bothered by this last thought. Was Macdonald really the master confidence man that the *Guide* implies him to have been? Can millions of Canadians have been so wrong, for so many years, about their beloved National Policy? After all what country doesn't follow a protectionist policy? Doubts creep in, and indeed on making enquiries of seasoned travellers we find that no one takes the T.T. *Guide* seriously as a practical handbook. Curiously, however, it commands almost universal respect, even reverence. This reverence seems to derive partly from the *Guide's* antiquity—it dates from the eighteenth century—and partly from the fact that no one has ever been able to find any error in it. 'It is completely useless, but it is also completely right', say the experienced travellers, 'and for that reason ought to be preserved; every young traveller should read it.' 'Curious reasoning', we reflect, as we turn to the Economic Historian's *Guide*, universally recommended as the most useful book for intending tourists.

'Curious reasoning', we murmur, as we read in the E.H. *Guide* that Canada's National Policy provides dividends for owners of CPR common stock, and protects Canada's territorial integrity—by which the author seems to mean something akin to Canada's virginity. We cannot undertake to unravel these tangled skeins—we are in search of economic effects, not territorial integrity—and we are about to discard the E.H. *Guide* as irrelevant to our purpose when our roving eye picks up the occasional sentence that seems to relate to the argument of the T.T. *Guide*. Indeed the Economic Historians seem to agree with the Trade Theorists that protection has lowered the Standard of Living in Canada, though they seldom stress the point; characteristically, when the reduction in the per capita income *is* mentioned it is identified as 'the price of being a Canadian', a phrase which shows that the author is at least aware that virginity involves foregone earnings. We read further and notice with interest that on another point the E.H. *Guide* disagrees violently with the T.T. *Guide*: Macdonald's National Policy, the Historians say, far from reducing Canada's National Income, has greatly increased it. Even though they do not bother to support their view by logical argument, they obviously believe that our glorious (if inefficient) secondary manufacturing industry has been a net addition to, rather than a subtraction from, our other simple-minded activities of hewing logs and hauling water.

This disagreement is indeed very interesting. True, the Economic Historian's case has not been argued; but that doesn't mean it isn't arguable. And then there *was* that mystifying preliminary instruction in the T.T. *Guide* about either finding a very special sort of country or else imagining it. There is room for thought here. Perhaps Macdonald was right after all, and the T.T. *Guide* wrong, which would explain why it is reputed to be completely useless. Or perhaps Macdonald was partly right, and the T.T. *Guide* partly right, and therefore not so useless as the worldly-wise believe.

I have tried elsewhere to provide a reasoned resolution of the main disagreement suggested by the metaphor of the two *Guides*.[1] Let me summarize my position in three points. First, the odd character of the country that the Trade Theorist talks about, results from his assumption that labour and capital are internationally immobile. This assumption, which implies that a protectionist policy can have no effect on a country's supplies of productive factors, is highly unrealistic in the Canadian case, and is probably unrealistic for all countries; it is responsible for the Trade Theorist's conclusion that a tariff reduces *both* a country's National Income *and* its National Income per capita. I think that it is this assumption, and its related conclusion, which more than anything else has discredited trade theory in the eyes of policy-makers. The main purpose of the Canadian tariff, and perhaps most other tariffs, was to increase the number of jobs in the country in order to prevent emigration and promote immigration of both labour and capital. Policy-makers might have paid some attention to a theory that *proved* this result to be impossible, but they quite understandably ignored one that merely *assumed* it to be impossible.

Second, when the extreme assumption of zero factor mobility is replaced by assumptions that are realistic in the Canadian case (and probably in most other cases) the trade model yields the conclusion that a protectionist policy does increase a country's population and its supply of capital, and *does* increase its National Income; in this respect, then, economic analysis that employs a model appropriate to the Canadian case confirms the Economic Historian's view that protected industry in Canada is an addition to, rather than a subtraction from, unprotected production.

Third, the conclusion of the authorized trade model that a tariff reduces a country's National Income per capita is also a conclusion of my unauthorized model. A country is bound to reduce the average output of a man-year of work if it insists on producing inefficiently within its national borders what could be procured more cheaply abroad; the strength of a wine is reduced whether you keep its volume constant and substitute water for alcohol, or whether you simply increase its volume by adding water.

My answer to the question of what the National Policy has meant for Canada is therefore that it has *increased* our National Income and *reduced* our Standard of Living. In asking you to accept these conclusions, at least for the purposes of the present discussion, I doubt very much that I am asking you to accept anything that you don't already believe. You know that the prices of manufactured goods in Canada are considerably higher than the prices of the same, or better goods in the United States, and that this burden on your pocket-book could be removed if the Canadian tariff were removed. Moreover, I doubt that anyone here believes that if the tariff were removed all the supplies of labour and capital at present employed in protected industries in Canada would be able to find employment, at incomes they were prepared to accept, in other sectors of the Canadian economy. Yet that is what trade theory asks you to believe. I think that removal of the Canadian tariff would be followed by emigration from Canada (or less immigration to Canada) of both labour and capital—though I doubt that the emigration would be on a large scale. I suspect that you share these views, both as to the direction and the magnitude of the effects of tariff removal.

In my opinion, therefore, the choice between protectionism and free trade is a choice between a larger National Income with a lower Standard of Living on the one hand, and a lower National Income with a higher Standard of Living on the other. I confront you with this choice. It is a hard choice, both in the sense that it has to be made, and in the sense that reasonable men may differ about how it should be made. Our protectionist policy, and most of our other national policies, from Northern Visions to automobile parts, have opted for size at the expense of quality—for a larger National Income at the expense of a higher Standard of Living. In the remainder of this Section, I want to present the case for the other view, the argument that a high Standard of Living is to be preferred to a big National Income.

I opt for a high Standard of Living because I am an economist, and I would not be an economist if I didn't accept the ethical implications of economics. Let me therefore meet head on the oft-repeated charge that the Economic Ethic is a materialistic ethic. Materialism, it seems to me, is more a desire for bigness in total magnitude than in average magnitude—more the pursuit of a Big National Income than of a High Standard of Living. Let me remind you that no proposition in economic science relates to the maximizing of total size. When an economist speaks of 'maximizing total profits' or 'maximizing total utility', he is using a convenient contraction for the full phrase, 'maximizing total profits (utility) that can be derived from a *given quantity of resources*'. The goal of the economic game is more clearly described as the maximization of profit (utility) *per unit of resources available*. The point is that economics has nothing whatever to say about maximizing total income by means of increasing 'the resources available'. (A study of economics is irrelevant for such institutions as churches, political parties and some trade unions, which seek to maximize a total magnitude, i.e. their membership.) The Economic Ethic is an ethic of proportion, not an ethic of size; it lauds the household, or the community, that makes the best use of its talents, not the household, or the community, that owns, or amasses, the most talents. I therefore fling the 'Materialist' charge back into the teeth of the self-styled Canadian Nationalists. They, not I, want a Big Canada. I get no satisfaction whatever from the knowledge that automatic transmissions for automobiles are now produced in Canada. I see our protectionist policy as a materialistic policy of Bigness, and I reject it as such *because* I am an economist.

And now to nationalism. I suggest that at least three effects of our National Policy—two of them economic and the other political—have been seriously detrimental to our national life. First, as we have seen, protectionism in all its forms reduces a nation's National Income per capita, i.e., the Standard of Living of its citizens. Artificially reduced incomes will be unacceptable to people who have high productive capabilities, and who are therefore likely to emigrate; those whose capabilities match the rewards available will have no complaint. In brief, by opting for a *larger* Canadian economy, supporters of the protectionist policy, the professional Nationalists, are opting for a reduction in the *quality* of Canadian economic life. It is hardly astonishing that most observers find Canadians, after almost three generations of protectionism, to be economically less aggressive than Americans.

Second, low incomes lead to low savings per capita and low domestic capital formation per capita. Since protectionism reduces domestic capital formation per capita, we can easily see why the proportion of foreign capital to total capital in Canada is unusually high—a situation which Nationalists publicly deplore in the strongest terms at every opportunity, but which is nevertheless of their own making. More important in my view is the likelihood that low domestic capital formation will show up most obviously in a low per capita level of *social capital*—by which I mean such things as museums, libraries, parks, universities, and public buildings that are show pieces rather than large economy-size boxes. I suggest that if Canadian incomes are some thirty per cent below American levels, the level of social capital per capita in Canada is a good deal more than thirty per cent below American standards. I further suggest that this discrepancy is not unrelated to Canadian protectionism, and is indeed one of the saddest manifestations of that sacrifice of quality for quantity that the National Policy involves.

Finally, there is the political cost of the tariff. It is confidently maintained by all and sundry in Canada, that the tariff has benefited Ontario and Quebec, and hurt all other parts of the country. This contention seems to me to be the utmost economic nonsense—the tariff raises the price of an automobile in Ontario as much as it raises the price of an automobile in Moncton, and if it raises the 'National Income' of Ontario relative to that in Saskatchewan this fact is of no interest to me either as an economist or as a resident of Ontario—but the fact that it is economic nonsense, does not mean that it is not political dynamite. It might seem that the tariff, if it raises the population of Ontario and Quebec, would at least give those provinces a political advantage by increasing their representation in Parliament. But it also gives the other provinces a wonderful argument, on grounds of equity, for special compensation. The result is an appalling collection of crutches designed to compensate the alleged losers: freight rate acts; floor prices; transport subventions; gold-mining subsidies; equalization payments; and so on and on. Federal politics in Canada often seems to be a confused game of regional blackmail in which the victims believe they should bribe others to participate in a game in which they, as well as everyone else, are losers. It is no consolation to reflect that the bribe probably hurts the receiver at least as much as it hurts the giver; part of the public license to be inefficient given by the tariff to manufacturing industry in Ontario is used to allow the continuation of an inefficient coal mining industry in Nova Scotia, and Nova Scotia seems to consider this distortion of its production pattern to be partial compensation for the tariff-created distortion of its consumption pattern. The economist must be humble in the face of political complexities. But it does seem that political deals, consummated in the name of equity, add insult to the original injury inflicted by the tariff. At the very least, the arranging of deals designed to equalize the regional burden of the tariff greatly complicates the political process which, especially in a federal state, is complicated enough to begin with. The National Policy, bequeathed to us by Macdonald, ought to be dismantled, if only in the interest of reducing political frictions and simplifying Canadian politics.

IMMIGRATION POLICY

The Canadian tariff, I have argued, has tended to increase Canada's population by promoting net immigration. By lowering the Canadian standard of living, it is true, the tariff has undoubtedly led to emigration from Canada, especially to the emigration of native Canadians who are both skilled and economically aggressive, and therefore highly mobile. This loss, however, has been offset by the immigration to Canada of skilled and professional Europeans who could not, because of American immigration quotas, emigrate to the United States, and who therefore took the 'second best' alternative of emigrating to Canada. In addition, the extra jobs created in Canada by the tariff have attracted both skilled and unskilled workers to the country, so that on balance protectionism has fostered net immigration.

But of course the tendency of the tariff to increase immigration will only be effective if Canadian immigration *policy* permits the increase to occur, and if a supply of immigrants is continuously available. During most of this century these conditions have been fulfilled. Canada has persistently sought as large an immigration as possible, subject only to the condition that the rate of inflow will not create or aggravate domestic unemployment problems. Policy, therefore, has consisted largely of controlling the *timing* of the inflow—and also of ensuring that the immigrants come from the 'right' countries.[2] Until recently, moreover, the supply of immigrants available to Canada has normally been in excess of the numbers that Canada has been willing to admit. Canada has therefore not lacked for immigrants, despite the fact that Canadian incomes have been substantially lower than American incomes. During the past forty years the main explanation for this situation is probably to be found in *American* immigration policy, which has prevented large numbers of Europeans from entering the United States, and thereby deflected them to Canada.

How has our policy of 'all the immigration the labour market can absorb' affected our economy? 'It expands the market and promotes growth', says the businessman, and since immigrants both eat and work the case may be granted; immigration certainly increases the National Income. 'It tends to keep down wages', says the union man (to which the businessman might well reply, *sotto voce*, 'so much the better, if it does'), but this contention cannot be either accepted or rejected out of hand; because immigration affects *both* the supply *and* demand sides of the labour market, its effect on National Income per capita remains in doubt.

So long as a country is expanding geographically and new resources are being opened up, so that more new job opportunities are being created than can be filled by the growth of the domestic labour force, immigration cannot be a threat to existing living standards; the alternative to immigration would simply be unutilized resources. In Canada the end of this period of 'extensive growth' must be dated not later than 1930. Once the 'frontier' is closed, economic progress depends primarily on technological advance, and 'extensive growth' is replaced by 'intensive growth', that is to say, by improved utilization of both natural resources and human resources. Under the conditions of *intensive* growth, an excess demand for labour results not from *more* job opportunities but from *better* job opportunities; in the absence of immigration the excess demand will be extinguished by 'upgrading' the existing labour force and increasing incomes to pay for the additional skills. But a policy of 'all the immigration the market can absorb' may seriously distort this process and even short-circuit it altogether. Skills may be imported, in which case the domestic labour force will not be upgraded, or upgraded more slowly than it otherwise would have been. Even if the 'upgrading' process is not adversely affected by immigration, the competition of skilled immigrants for the better job opportunities that intensive growth creates will tend to keep the domestic *price* of skill low—and thus, incidentally, foster the emigration of those skilled people who are allowed into other countries where a higher remuneration is paid for skill.

I conclude, therefore, that the union man's view is correct. Within a context of intensive growth, economic advance depends primarily on techno-logical improvement, and technological improvement, in order to be trans-lated into economic growth, demands a complementary improvement of the labour force. Large scale immigration tends to be an alternative to the upgrad-ing of the domestic labour force, and also tends to reduce the domestic remu-neration for skill, whether domestically produced or imported; on both counts immigration therefore tends to reduce (or rather to slow down the rate of increase in) the standard of living of the domestic labour force.

It turns out, then, that both the businessman and the union man are correct. Immigration does increase National Income, but it also reduces National In-come per capita. The conclusion is identical to that reached in the earlier discussion of the tariff. Both our protectionist policy and our immigration policy are 'Big Canada' policies; they increase the 'quantity' of our economic life (the size of the National Income) at the expense of its 'quality' (the level of the National Income per person).

Though I have stated these conclusions dogmatically, I do not hold them dogmatically. I am all too aware of how little we know about the actual effects of our 'national policies', despite all that has been written about their intended effects; until social scientists in Canada stop venerating our national policies and begin to analyze them, *any* conclusion about their actual effects must be viewed as tentative and unproved. It is particularly astonishing that so little effort has been made to study the effects of Canada's immigration policy; because immigration policy is the one major area in which Canadian economic policy has differed dramatically from American economic policy, one would have thought that a study of its effects might be expected to throw light on some of the distinctive features and problems of the Canadian economy. Let us hope that our lethargy in this field of research will be dispelled by Professor John Porter's recent volume, *The Vertical Mosaic*, for in this study Porter makes immigration policy a central feature of his analysis of Canadian society. My earlier remarks have drawn heavily on Porter's work, especially on his argument that heavy immigration has retarded the upgrading of our domestic labour force. More generally, Porter suggests that by relying on immigration to provide an important part of our skilled and professional manpower require-ments we have tended to let our educational system fall into disrepair; the alarm engendered by this thesis has not been allayed by subsequent publica-tions of the Economic Council of Canada which present statistical evidence of serious short-comings in our educational performance.

It may be, too, that recent changes in the setting in which our immigration policy has operated during the past half century will force us to pay more attention to the subject in the future. Rapid economic progress in Europe has greatly reduced the incentive for Europeans to move to North America, and in the past few years Canada has experienced great difficulty in attracting skilled labour from Europe. Moreover, the recent revision of American immigration policy, which will become fully effective in 1968, has replaced the old nativity quotas with a list of priorities based on kinship and skill. One result of the new legislation is likely to be a modest increase in total immigration to the United States; another is that skilled and professional people will find it easier than in the past to be admitted to the United States, so that Canada will in the future face stronger competition from the United States for this class of immigrant.[3] In brief, the days when the Department of Immigration could always count on a large supply of European labour anxious to emigrate to Canada are already past, and will probably never return. Faced with the disappearance of the historic basis of our immigration policy, we probably have only two alternatives.

One is to continue our present policy of 'as much immigration as we can manage' by switching our source of supply from Europe to the Orient. *The Globe and Mail* has been a strong proponent of this policy: 'The bulk of immigration has so far come from Europe, but, with improved living conditions there, this source is showing signs of drying up. Canada, therefore, needs to look elsewhere for immigrants, and the obvious place to look is the Orient.'[4] The Ontario Government actively considered the same policy late in 1964 when it offered to create an airlift for skilled workers from Hong Kong if Ontario companies would guarantee them jobs.[5] Union leaders objected to the scheme, which seems to have been directed primarily to the provision of skilled workers for some parts of the textile industry, and urged instead that in-plant training programmes (for which government grants are available) should be instituted in order to upgrade the existing labour force. The Government airlift did not materialize; and it is doubtful whether any in-plant training (which is still rare in Ontario) resulted directly from the unions' plea. Nevertheless the incident throws into sharp relief the conflict between immigration and investment in education that John Porter has identified as a major feature of Canadian society.

The other alternative, then, is to give up our Big Canada immigration policy, and instead to give first priority to the improvement of our existing labour force. Under this policy, our Immigration Rule would be almost the reverse of the present Rule. No immigration into an occupation would be allowed unless it was proved to the satisfaction of the Minister of Immigration that wages in that occupation were rising considerably more rapidly than wages generally—for example, that wages in the occupation in question had risen 10% or 15% more than wages in all occupations during the previous calendar year. By making such a relative increase in wages a pre-condition for immigration into that occupation we would provide an incentive to upgrade the existing labour force, and prevent immigration from removing that incentive. (In protected industries, incidentally, the requirement that wages rise *relatively* more than general wages *before* immigration would erode the degree of protection afforded protected manufacturers by the tariff, and would therefore reduce the expansion of protected—that is to say, inefficient industry. This is exactly what we want to happen; by reducing the expansion of inefficient industry we increase the productivity of industry generally!)

One result of this policy would be a sharp reduction in immigration. It will be objected that such a policy is illiberal, and that the present policy is liberal and humane because it allows immigrants to Canada to raise their standard of living. But if, as has been argued, the present policy *prevents an increase* in the standard of living of the existing labour force, how can one balance this effect against an *increase* in the standard of living of the immigrants? Since resident and immigrant must count the same, there is no solution to this problem—unless one argues that the immigrant starts from a lower standard of living than the resident and should therefore weigh more heavily than the resident in the scales of justice. This latter argument contends that Canadians, being rich, should share their wealth with those foreigners who emigrate to Canada, but not with those foreigners who stay at home. But there are many 'share the wealth' schemes, of which immigration is only one. Another possibility is for present Canadians to maximize their income per capita, and then to tax themselves for foreign aid so as to leave themselves with a standard of living after taxes that is as low as they please. The tax revenues, given as foreign aid, could benefit *all* foreigners—both those who would have emigrated to Canada under the present immigration policy and those who would have stayed at home. In brief, it is not at all clear that the longstanding American policy of severely restricted immigration plus massive foreign aid is necessarily any less 'liberal' than the present Canadian policy of massive immigration plus severely restricted foreign aid.

Thus our examination of both tariff and immigration policy, the two major prongs of Canada's historic 'national policy' has revealed that in each case Canadians have opted for Bigness, at the expense of the quality of national life. Indeed, it is the crux of the matter that the latter alternative has hardly been considered. Today Big Canada policies remain the quintessence of appeals made by the most vocal Canadian nationalists. It is surely time that this view be questioned by those whose national pride derives from the quality of the national performance, rather than from the mere size of the cast.

AUTHOR'S NOTES

1 J. H. Dales, 'The Cost of Protectionism with High International Mobility of Factors' *The Canadian Journal of Economics and Political Science*, XXX (November 1964), 512-25.

2 Canadian policy has probably been as discriminatory in terms of national origins and colour of skin as the American policy based explicitly on nativity. I avoid discussion of the ethics of immigration policy since the topic is irrelevant to the present argument.

3 Canadians who were born abroad and could not in the past be admitted to the United States may now find that they can be admitted. Native-born Canadians who emigrate to the United States are now to be counted in an annual quota of 120,000 immigrants from independent countries of the Western Hemisphere. More important, perhaps, the new law required 'that no Western Hemisphere immigrant could be admitted unless the Secretary of Labor determined that he would not replace a worker in the United States and that his employment would not adversely affect the wages and working conditions of individuals in the United States who were similarly employed.' *Congressional Quarterly* (8 Oct. 1965), 2037.

4 Editorial page, 29 July 1963. Similar editorials appeared in the issues of 9 May, 25 September and 16 November 1963; and 9 March, 26 June and 15 September 1964.

5 See *The Globe and Mail*, 26 November 1964. 12.

Kari Levitt: Silent Surrender

Canada was discovered, explored and developed as part of the French, and later the British mercantile system. It grew to independence and nationhood in a brief historical era in which goods, capital and people moved in response to economic forces operating in relatively free, competitive international markets. Present-day Canada may be described as the world's richest underdeveloped country. Its regression to a state of economic and political dependence cannot possibly be attributed, as is fashionable in some quarters, to an unfavourable endowment of resources. Nor can its present lack of independent dynamic be laid at the door of a traditional culture. Thus we are forced to seek the explanation of underdevelopment and fragmentation in the institutions and processes of modern society. We suggest it is to be found in the dynamics of the New Mercantilism of the American international corporation.

[The logic of competition drives local firms to become national, and national firms to become multinational: only by expansion can the modern firm capture the profits from its expertise in product-innovation and want-creation. The branch plants of these multinational corporations penetrate the markets and transform the cultures of their host countries. They eventually monopolize the technical and managerial resources of the hinterland; the personnel of the corporations become, in effect, citizens of private corporate empires. American business is the vanguard of this development, and Canada is the best example of what results. But before examining Canada's hinterland economy, we must clarify what is meant by economic development.]

ECONOMIC DEVELOPMENT

It is almost axiomatic to equate development with wealth and high income, and underdevelopment with poverty and low income. For this reason Gross National Product per head is widely used as an indicator of economic development. On such a scale Canada is more highly developed than the United Kingdom, France or Germany, and Venezuela is more highly developed than Japan. While there is evidently a relationship between economic development and income growth, we suggest that a more basic explanation of development and underdevelopment must be sought outside the factors normally termed 'economic'. Here it is useful to turn to the work of one of the few modern economists who declined to concern himself with income growth or capital formation. In Joseph Schumpeter's writings development is defined exclusively in terms of endogenous entrepreneurial initiative and innovation.

By 'development', therefore, we shall understand only such changes in economic life as are not forced upon it from without but arise by its own initiative, from within. Should it turn out that there are no such changes arising in the economic sphere itself, and that the phenomenon that we call economic development is in practice simply founded upon the fact that the data change and that the economy continuously adapts itself to them, then we should say that there is *no* economic development. By this we should mean that economic development is not a phenomenon to be explained economically, but that the economy, in itself without development, is dragged along by the changes in the surrounding world, that the causes and hence the explanation of the development must be sought outside the group of facts which are described by economic theory.[1] . . .

In Schumpeter's world profit derives from the deliberate introduction of innovation by the entrepreneur. Profit is thus created by his 'will and action'. Entrepreneurs are distinguished from 'capitalists', who are merely rentiers who lend funds and receive interest. Capitalists have money; entrepreneurs have wits, and these they use to create situations of a type which result in venture profit. . . . Entrepreneurs innovate and entrepreneurial profit is a 'quasi-rent' accruing to the temporary monopoly created by the innovator. An innovation, in the Schumpeterian sense, consists of the introduction of a new process of production, a new or improved commodity or service, the opening up of a new market, the securing of a new source of supply, [or] the introduction of new methods of business organization, including the creation or destruction of market monopoly positions through mergers. In this scheme of things innovation implies economic development and economic development cannot take place without innovation: 'without development there is no profit, without profit no development.'[2] Profit is the result of innovation and the origin of the accumulation of wealth. . . .

Unlike Marx's capitalist who makes profit from exploiting labour in the production of standard commodities for a competitive market, Schumpeter's entrepreneur may or may not be a producer. The innovating entrepreneur primarily creates situations in which the selling price of his product exceeds the cost of producing and marketing it. Profit is a surplus to which there corresponds no liability. The forerunner of the modern entrepreneur is the old-time mercantile trader who sold glass beads and similar articles to African tribesmen: 'The principle of the matter is that a new commodity is valued by purchasers much as gifts of nature or pictures by old masters, that is its price is determined without regard to cost of production.'[3]

It is now widely acknowledged that what gives the United States the capacity to compete in world markets despite its high wages is its ability to produce a steady flow of new products.[4] Competition by product-innovation is of course not confined to the export market. Rather, the reverse is true: the technique of product-differentiation and product-innovation was developed by the American firm in the context of its domestic market and subsequently carried into the world economy by foreign trade and direct investment.

Because there are no total substitutes for new products they will be bought even if they are considerably more expensive than the older less sophisticated products.[5] These 'quasi-rent' are temporary monopoly profits which can be secured against competition by imitators only by creating a business organization which generates a perpetual stream of innovations. It is inherent in the logic of this Schumpeterian view that markets are never perfect, knowledge is never certain, and that any steps taken to reduce the risk to the producer in securing the necessary inputs at the prices he has estimated they will cost and selling the planned output at the prices he has estimated he can obtain, will make profit more certain and enduring. . . .

The corporations have mastered the techniques of manipulating our personal and social requirements in the interests of their private imperatives of survival; they can make people buy things they don't really want and produce things nobody else really needs. As Professor Johnson has pointed out, in the opulent or affluent society real scarcity has been succeeded by contrived scarcity and the successful functioning of our economy depends on reiterating the contrivance. Increasing income implies the gratification of ever less and less essential wants. The margin of want-satisfaction tends to move from the physical to the psychological and sociological—the psychological becomes necessities, while the luxuries are psychiatric. The decision-taking structure becomes ever more bureaucratic. Labour itself becomes a produced means of production, an item of human capital equipment. The universities become factories for the production of capital goods.[6] . . .

As Professor Williams noted forty years ago, the entrepreneur of modern industry is concerned with his industry and its products, not with political geography. An ever-increasing array of basic industries spread across political frontiers.

> They represent in some cases the projection by one country into others of its capital, technique, special knowledge along lines of an industry and its market, as against the obvious alternative of home employment in other lines. They represent, in other cases, an international assembly of capital and management for world enterprises ramifying into many countries. They suggest very strikingly an organic interconnection of international trade, movements of productive factors, transport, and market organization.[7]

The organic relationships noted by Williams are formed primarily through the process of direct foreign investment. And the pioneers of this new mercantilism are undoubtedly the American corporations which have, within the last twenty years, transformed the international economy.

[The great majority of economists see nothing disturbing in these trends. In particular, they regard direct foreign investment as a stimulant to economic growth and development; they claim that it creates no problems that the host country cannot deal with by legislation. Canadian economists have generally used their authority to promote integration into the American economy. Efforts to discourage takeovers or to repatriate some of the foreign-controlled sectors of Canadian industry have been decried as misguided nationalism, likely to benefit greedy and lazy Canadian capitalists at the expense of the Canadian consumer.]

The argument advanced by Canadian economists for continental integration rests on the neo-classical static theory of 'comparative advantage'. It concludes that lower tariffs would benefit Canada by encouraging further specialization in efficient resource extraction and discouraging inefficient manufacturing. The argument totally misses the point. It fails to provide an effective answer to the concern that economic integration with the United States, in the context of an economy dominated by branch plants and subsidiaries, will weaken internal integration within Canada, will perpetuate the 'technology gap', and deprive this country of the 'dynamic comparative advantage' accruing to indigenous technological advance and innovation. Professor Harry Johnson does not seem to grasp that the case for economic nationalism, as presented here, is *not* the case for tariff protection of industry but rather the case for the protection of local entrepreneurial initiative, whether public or private, particularly in the strategic 'new technology' industries. Policies directed towards the protection of Canadian enterprise against penetration by US direct investment will have to be complemented by a lowering of Canadian tariffs on commodity imports from all sources.

The case against further Canadian integration with the economic-political–political-military power complex based in the United States cannot be countered by trotting out the tautological propositions of international trade theory. These dogmas are based on institutional assumptions which take account neither of the competitive strategy of the modern multinational corporation nor of the political relationships between these corporate giants and their home government. [The branch plants of an American multinational are not independent profit-maximizing firms whose shareholders happen to be non-resident, but organic parts of a production and marketing organization whose major decisions are taken with respect to the viability, security, expansion and ultimately the global profitability of the enterprise as a whole. A branch plant is the intrusion into the Canadian social and economic fabric of a tightly-controlled and private corporate enterprise. Its profits help to finance American political and military expenditures abroad, and it is protected, in turn, by the political and military strength of the American government.] Moreover, the abrogation of sovereignty implicit in the branch-plant economy may yet prove to carry substantial economic cost. In the contemporary world, in which innovation in technology and in social organization is a critical factor in the capacity of a country to utilize her resources and the ability to decide what will be produced and to whom it will be sold, the branch-plant nature of Canada's economy is likely in the not-so-long run to involve a serious loss in the material quality of living. Historical experience of the past century indicates that the key to economic strength lies in the creation of a cultural, social and political milieu which favours indigenous initiatives. This is an area of social science about which we know very little. There is no *a priori* reason to believe, however, that contemporary improvements in communication and the increased interdependence of the world have diminished the ability of smaller countries to achieve a high standard of living by adopting policies which protect their populations from cultural and economic absorption into the super-empires. On the contrary, it may well turn out that countries much poorer than Canada can escape from poverty and unemployment only by deliberately blocking further penetration by the multinational corporations. In the Canadian context, the further continental integration of industries that are for the most part branch plants and subsidiaries of American corporations accelerates the erosion of freedom of choice in economic policy. This may yet prove to be very expensive for Canada. . . .

HINTERLAND ECONOMY

It is widely believed that countries benefit from metropolitan direct investment because they thereby acquire entrepreneurship as well as funds. This, so the argument runs, compensates for the weakness of the local entrepreneurial class and introduces the necessary 'know-how' of modern industrial techniques into the hinterland economy. In the course of time, it is argued, the presence of modern enterprise will impart managerial and technical skills to the population and local entrepreneurship will be stimulated.

Branch-plant development, however, results in the erosion of local enterprise, as local firms are bought out and potential local entrepreneurs become the salaried employees of the multinational corporation. [The executives of branch plants are managers, not entrepreneurs. They dispose of funds, equipment and personnel within the means allocated to them. They do not formulate policy, they administer it.] Enterprises which remain locally-owned tend to be marginal in the sense that they are small, or inefficient, or operate in industries which do not lend themselves to corporate organization. Exceptions to this pattern include publicly-owned or controlled enterprises or firms which have established an early technological lead over the metropolitan concerns.

The entrepreneur, operating in a well-developed branch-plant economy, is increasingly confronted with an organizational and institutional complex which presents him with a choice either of joining his resources with those of the international corporation, as a salaried employee, or contenting himself with a very limited role.

In the mineral resource industries, independent enterprises face a situation where the large established corporations control the terms of sale of raw materials. For independents, markets are uncertain, prices too low to cover costs, and for these reasons their capacity to borrow funds is limited. Their activities tend, therefore, to be of the riskier kind—drilling, prospecting, exploration, operation of marginal mines in abnormal market conditions, and sub-contracting for work where large companies enjoy the stronger bargaining position. Ironically, success increases the risk. At the point where a venture succeeds in reaching the threshold beyond which it could become really profitable, it discovers that the doors to entry are opened only by coming to terms with those already inside.

The nature of manufacturing industry makes entry very much easier, but independent entrepreneurs have less security against loss than do branch plants. The latter can charge back losses against parent companies, which can offset them against profits earned on their exports to subsidiaries and against royalties and fees received. The existence of the branch-plant firm is thus justified even where its profits are small or negative. The disadvantage of the local firm is even greater where incentive programs are biased in favour of foreign concerns.

It is to be noted that entrepreneurship does not bear any simple relationship to high levels of income, or to high levels of education. Canada, as well as some countries of Latin America and some Caribbean countries today, has higher levels of per capita income than prevailed in the metropolitan countries during the heyday of private accumulation. They have far higher levels of per capita income than contemporary Japan, where private and public entrepreneurship is highly developed.

The lack of entrepreneurship in countries where branch-plant economy has taken root has sometimes been explained in terms of religious or ethnic factors. The superficial nature of all these explanations is best illustrated by the case of Canada. The relative decline in local entrepreneurship in contemporary English-speaking Canada as compared with the late nineteenth and early twentieth century has occurred in a period of rising income, rising educational attainment and within a framework of 'modern' culture and institutions.

One of the few economists who has suggested that branch-plant economy may be as much the cause as the result of a lack of indigenous entrepreneurship is Dr Stephen Hymer. Although addressed to the Canadian case, the following observation may well have general validity:

> The large volume of foreign investment in Canada seems to suggest a shortage of Canadian entrepreneurs. But which is cause and which is effect? We usually think of foreign investment as a consequence of a shortage of domestic entrepreneurs, but perhaps the former has helped to create the latter.
>
> Suppose, in the extreme case, Canada forbade all foreign direct investment. This would certainly slow down the flow of technology and create a gap between techniques used in Canada and the best available technique elsewhere. What would happen then? Through time the gap would grow and there would be an increasing incentive for Canadians to learn how to breach it. Might not this stimulate a growth of Canadian entrepreneurship? Once over their initial learning period, might not Canadian entrepreneurs be able to stand on their own feet? The shortage of entrepreneurs in Canada might disappear and with it the need for so much foreign investment.[8]

A branch-plant economy dependent on imported technology is assured of a perpetual technological backwardness *vis-à-vis* the metropolis. Furthermore, dependence is addictive and the dynamics of dependence are cumulative. Countries with indigenous entrepreneurship and with consumption and behavioural patterns differing from those of the metropolis relinquish a potential advantage in production for domestic and foreign markets, when they permit branch-plant economy to take over indiscriminately and on a large scale.

These tendencies become more pronounced to the degree that product and technological innovation play an increasingly important role in international competition. The advantages of temporary monopoly acquired by manufacturers in some nations by producing new products or differentiating old ones have been offered as explanations for the pattern of trade in manufactured goods. This 'technology-gap' theory coincides with the argument we have been presenting throughout this book, that advantages accrue to countries to the extent that they are innovators and not takers of technology. The importance of maintaining distinctive consumption and cultural patterns in encouraging the development of indigenous innovation has received less attention. It is noted in the literature, however, that there is a tendency for exporters of manufactured goods to find markets in countries where income levels are similar. Resistance to the importation of metropolitan values and consumption patterns, and barriers to the absorption of a country's intellectual, scientific and managerial resources into the world of the multinational corporation, force the country to develop its own resources of entrepreneurship.

Obviously products developed on the basis of particular climatic, geographical and cultural factors, or traditional skills and crafts, have an advantage similar to that accruing to the 'temporary monopoly' acquired by producing new products or differentiating old ones. Obvious examples are small aircraft developed for use in the Canadian north, the small-scale automobiles of Europe, the glassware of Czechoslovakia, the wood-working industries of Scandinavia, or the many Italian industries developed on the basis of excellence of artistry in design.

Indigenous entrepreneurship can 'learn by doing'. It has been pointed out that the dynamic economies resulting from indigenous technological innovation are of particular importance for countries of limited size, and further that they are irreversible in that a nation, having acquired them, will not lose them. The importance of these factors is best illustrated in countries which are relatively poor in resources but, perhaps for that reason, rich in resourcefulness. Examples include Japan, Switzerland, Israel, the Scandinavian countries. Branch-plant economy destroys the mobilizational basis of indigenous entrepreneurship. Direct investment produces growth, but not development:

> The main weakness of direct investment as a development agent is a consequence of the complete character of its contribution. As it brings enterprise, management and technology to the country, it may inhibit the emergence and formation of local personnel and local institutions to perform these essential functions. Insofar as this happens foreign investment does not help the country to advance itself towards self-sustaining development. . . . Direct investment increases production and income, expands employment, creates jobs of higher productivity, augments tax revenues and raises foreign exchange receipts or reduces foreign exchange payments. The country receives benefits but not as a result of its own initiative and effort; and the production facilities created do not belong to the country nor are they run by it. . . . For the above-mentioned reasons, direct foreign investment can be depended on to play an important role in development but not a decisive one; that must be played by local entrepreneurs.[9]

The most direct expression of technological dependence in branch-plant economies is found in the relative absence of research facilities in these countries. Technological and innovational activity is concentrated in the research laboratories, boardrooms and academic centres of the metropolitan countries. Where research is carried out in hinterland countries, it tends to be limited to the modification of products developed in the metropolitan country to special conditions in particular hinterland countries.

Professor Chandler has suggested that a country's investment in research and the development of the technical skills and equipment that can handle a range of products is a far more meaningful indicator of economic strength than is the output of steel, or meat, or automobiles.[10] Skilled personnel are attracted to the metropolitan industrial and academic centres by high salaries, superior facilities and the fact that the professionals involved have internationalized [internalized?] the values of the metropolitan society. By means of the 'brain drain', the brightest and ablest people from lower-income countries swell the technological resources of private international business empires.

Similar processes are at work with respect to managerial skill. The following account of company policy, provided by the Procter and Gamble Company, illustrates the point:

> When Procter and Gamble moves into a country for the first time, it has to bring in a skilled top-management team, already developed. The initial cadre goes about building an organization in depth. Just as soon as local talent can be developed, it is. Of the American group in Canadian Procter and Gamble in 1947, only two of us are left. The others have gone to Geneva, to Venezuela, to Cincinnatti, and elsewhere. More important, from the organization they built, we have taken cuttings. Today the General Manager of Procter and Gamble in France is a Canadian; the General Manager in Morocco is a Canadian; the General Manager in Mexico is a Canadian; and the man responsible for all our business in the 'outer Seven', including Britain is a Canadian. The important thing is that in the total organization they were neither helped nor hampered by their nationality.

These Canadians have become citizens of an international corporate empire. Their professional and management skills have been harnessed to the service of some particular international company. Meanwhile there is much wailing that Canada is short of managerial talent.

Although the total savings generated by the activities of branch-plants are considerable, the access to these savings by local enterprise is limited. The major part of the contribution which the branch-plant sector makes to national income comes in the form of wages and salaries and government revenue. The overwhelming part of profit income, whether distributed or retained, accrues as factor income to shareholders of the parent corporation or to the corporation itself and makes no direct contribution to national income. The branch-plant economy thus chokes the development of local capitalists and inhibits the development of a local capital market. . . .

[SOME CONCLUSIONS]

Twenty years of unprecedented intake of American capital, technology, know-how and marketing connections have probably resulted in increased income and employment. Direct American investment has not, however, secured the basis of continued growth. Indeed, there has been a regression in Canada's economic position relative to other equally industrialized countries. The author of a survey of recent trends and patterns of Canadian trade concluded that 'Canada's position resembles more closely that of a less developed nation than that of other developed countries.'[11]

The golden days of easy export earnings have long passed. The resource boom which fed the income-generating process of the fifties and attracted the heavy inflow of direct investment in secondary manufacturing is largely played out. In the sixties the trend of US direct capital flow is towards expansion of manufacturing facilities in the rich and growing markets of Europe. The honeymoon is over, and the realization is dawning that the heavy intake of direct investment and the consequent loss of economic control has restricted Canada's freedom of action in a highly competitive world economy.

In the key sectors of the Canadian economy, decisions concerning what is to be produced, where it is to be sold, from whom supplies are to be purchased and what funds are to be transferred in the form of interest, dividends, loans, stock-purchases, short-term balances, charges for management, research or advertising services, and so on, are made externally in accordance with considerations of global strategy of foreign corporations. Nor is dependence confined to decisions transmitted through parent-affiliate links. For Canada, freedom of action has been progressively restricted by a proliferation of commitments—both formal and informal—arising from bilateral arrangements with the government of the United States. In this manner the free market is being replaced by internal transfers within multinational corporations. Correspondingly, intergovernmental relationships resemble increasingly those of the old mercantilist systems. Although the country is richer, the Canadian economy is less flexible than it has been in the past. The instruments of public policy are constrained by umpteen commitments made in exchange for 'special favours'.

In the private sector there is little entrepreneurship and technological dynamism. The share of crudely processed materials in exports has not diminished significantly. Imports of manufactured goods as a percentage of domestic production have increased. Technological dependence is greater than ever and unequalled by any other industrialized country. In a world in which competition places a premium on innovation and entrepreneurship, imitative technology is reflected in a high cost structure and lagging productivity. The capital market is distorted in the sense that Canadian savings cannot find attractive equity investments in Canada, while large proportions of savings generated in Canada are not available to other sectors of the economy because they accrue in the form of retained earnings and depreciation allowances of foreign-controlled corporations. The structure of ownership and control is such that there are barriers to the flow of Canadian savings to finance new Canadian enterprise. Technology-oriented industries are firmly in the hands of foreign corporations. As the Watkins Report observes: 'Power accrues to nations capable of technological leadership, and technical change is an important source of economic growth.[12]

AUTHOR'S NOTES

[1] Joseph A. Schumpeter, *The Theory of Economic Development*, trans. R. Opie (Cambridge, Mass.: Harvard University Press, 1949), 63.

[2] *Ibid.*, 154.

[3] *Ibid.*, 135.

[4] See for example D. B. Keesing, 'Impact of Research and Development on United States Trade', *Journal of Political Economy*, 75 (1967), 38-48.

[5] All the work on the 'product cycle' and international trade is highly relevant to our argument. In a useful summary article of the work of Professor Raymond Vernon, it is observed that 'in the early stages of the product life cycle the consumer is frequently not very much concerned with price. Success comes to the manufacturer who can quickly adjust both his product designs and market strategy to consumers' needs which are just beginning to be well-identified.' See L. T. Wells, jun., 'A Product Life Cycle for International Trade', *Journal of Marketing*, 32 (July 1968), 2.

[6] H. G. Johnson, 'The Political Economy of Opulence', in Johnson, *The Canadian Quandary* (Toronto: McGraw-Hill, 1963), 236-52.

[7] J. H. Williams, *Postwar Monetary Plans* (New York: Alfred A. Knopf, 1944), 144-5.

8 Stephen Hymer, 'Direct Foreign Investment and the National Economic Interest', in *Nationalism in Canada*, ed. Peter Russell (Toronto: McGraw-Hill, 1966), 198.

9 Dr Felipe Pazos, 'Organization of American States', in *Capital Movements, Proceedings of a Conference Held by the International Economic Association*, ed. J. H. Adler (Toronto: Macmillan, 1967), 196-7.

10 Alfred D. Chandler, *Strategy and Structure: Chapters in the History of the Industrial Enterprise* (Cambridge, Mass.: M.I.T. Press, 1962), 395.

11 B. W. Wilkinson, *Canada's International Trade: An Analysis of Recent Trends and Patterns* (Montreal: Canadian Trade Committee, 1968), 17.

12 *Foreign Ownership and the Structure of Canadian Industry*, Report of the Task Force on the Structure of Canadian Industry (Ottawa: Privy Council Office, 1968), 35.

RENÉ LÉVESQUE

René Lévesque (b. 1918) was a journalist and broadcaster before he won election to the Quebec National Assembly in 1960. He became the most nationalist member of the 'équipe de tonnerre' that directed the Quiet Revolution under Jean Lesage. When the Quebec Liberal party, deeply divided, rejected his constitutional proposals in 1967, he left it to found the Mouvement Souveraineté-Association and the Parti Québécois. From the outset there was widespread support in academic, journalistic, and bureaucratic circles for Lévesque's concept of political independence combined with economic association, but the Parti Québécois had to wait until 1976 before taking power. The following selection is the first part of An Option for Quebec, *which was published in 1968.*

A Country That Must Be Made

Vive le Québec libre!
CHARLES DE GAULLE*

For my part I believe in the quality of small nations: here is where common values have a chance to sink deep roots.

FERNAND DUMONT†

I

We are *Québécois*.

What that means first and foremost—and if need be, all that it means—is that we are attached to this one corner of the earth where we can be completely ourselves: this Quebec, the only place where we have the unmistakable feeling that 'here we can be really at home'.

Being ourselves is essentially a matter of keeping and developing a personality that has survived for three and a half centuries.

At the core of this personality is the fact that we speak French. Everything else depends on this one essential element and follows from it or leads us infallibly back to it.

In our history, America began with a French look, briefly but gloriously given it by Champlain, Joliet, La Salle, La Vérendrye. . . . We learn our first lessons in progress and perseverance from Maisonneuve, Jeanne Mance, Jean Talon; and in daring or heroism from Lambert Closse, Brébeuf, Frontenac, d'Iberville. . . .

Then came the conquest. We were a conquered people, our hearts set on surviving in some small way on a continent that had become Anglo-Saxon.

Somehow or other, through countless changes and a variety of regimes, despite difficulties without number (our lack of awareness and even our ignorance serving all too often as our best protection), we succeeded.

Here again, when we recall the major historical landmarks, we come upon a profusion of names: Étienne Parent and Lafontaine and the Patriots of '37;

Louis Riel and Honoré Mercier, Bourassa, Philippe Hamel; Garneau and Édouard Montpetit and Asselin and Lionel Groulx. . . . For each of them, the main driving force behind every action was the will to continue, and the tenacious hope that they could make it worth while.

Until recently in this difficult process of survival we enjoyed the protection of a certain degree of isolation. We lived a relatively sheltered life in a rural society in which a great measure of unanimity reigned, and in which poverty set its limits on change and aspiration alike.

We are children of that society, in which the *habitant*, our father or grandfather, was still the key citizen. We also are heirs to that fantastic adventure—that early America that was almost entirely French. We are, even more intimately, heirs to the group obstinacy which has kept alive that portion of French America we call *Québec*.

All these things lie at the core of this personality of ours. Anyone who does not feel it, at least occasionally, is not—is no longer—one of us.

But *we* know and feel that these are the things that make us what we are. They enable us to recognize each other wherever we may be. This is our own special wave-length on which, despite all interference, we can tune each other in loud and clear, with no one else listening.

This is how we differ from other men and especially from other North Americans, with whom in all other areas we have so much in common. This basic 'difference' we cannot surrender. That became impossible a long time ago.

More is involved here than simple intellectual certainty. This is a physical fact. To be unable to live as ourselves, as we should live, in our own language and according to our own ways, would be like living without an arm or a leg—or perhaps a heart.

Unless, of course, we agreed to give in little by little, in a decline which, as in cases of pernicious anaemia, would cause life to slip slowly away from the patient.

Again, in order not to perceive this, one has to be among the *déracinés*, the uprooted and cut-off.

II

On the other hand, one would have to be blind not to see that the conditions under which this personality must assert itself have changed in our lifetime, at an extremely rapid and still accelerating rate.

Our traditional society, which gave our parents the security of an environment so ingrown as to be reassuring and in which many of us grew up in a way that we thought could, with care, be preserved indefinitely; that 'quaint old' society has gone.

Today, most of us are city dwellers, wage-earners, tenants. The standards of parish, village, and farm have been splintered. The automobile and the airplane take us 'outside' in a way we never could have imagined thirty years ago, or even less. Radio and films, and now television, have opened for us a window onto everything that goes on throughout the world: the events—and the ideas too—of all humanity invade our homes day after day.

The age of automatic unanimity thus has come to an end. The old protective barriers are less and less able to mark safe pathways for our lives. The patience and resignation that were preached to us in the old days with such efficiency now produce no other reactions than scepticism or indifference, or even rebellion.

At our own level, we are going through a universal experience. In this sudden acceleration of history, whose main features are the unprecedented development of science, technology, and economic activity, there are potential promises and dangers immeasurably greater than any the world ever has known.

The promises—if man so desires—are those of abundance, of liberty, of fraternity; in short, of a civilization that could attain heights undreamed of by the most unrestrained Utopians.

The dangers—unless man can hold them in check—are those of insecurity and servitude, of inhuman governments, of conflicts among nations that could lead to extermination.

In this little corner of ours, we already are having a small taste of the dangers as well as the promises of this age.

A Balance Sheet of Vulnerability

The dangers are striking enough.

In a world where, in so many fields, the only stable law seems to have become that of perpetual change, where our old certainties are crumbling one after the other, we find ourselves swept along helplessly by irresistible currents. We are not at all sure that we can stay afloat, for the swift, confusing pace of events forces us to realize as never before our own weaknesses, our backwardness, our terrible collective vulnerability.

Endlessly, with a persistence almost masochistic, we draw up list after list of our inadequacies. For too long we despised education. We lack scientists, administrators, qualified technical people. Economically, we are colonials whose three meals a day depend far too much on the initiative and goodwill of foreign bosses. And we must admit as well that we are far from being the most advanced along the path of social progress, the yardstick by which the quality of a human community can best be measured. For a very long time we have allowed our public administration to stagnate in negligence and corruption, and left our political life in the hands of fast talkers and our own equivalent of those African kings who grew rich by selling their own tribesmen.

We must admit that our society has grave, dangerous, and deep-rooted illnesses which it is absolutely essential to cure if we want to survive.

Now, a human society that feels itself to be sick and inferior, and is unable to do anything about it, sooner or later reaches the point of being unacceptable even to itself.

For a small people such as we are, our minority position on an Anglo-Saxon continent creates from the very beginning a permanent temptation to such a self-rejection, which has all the attraction of a gentle downward slope ending in a comfortable submersion in the Great Whole.

There are enough sad cases, enough among us who have given up, to show us that this danger does exist.

It is, incidentally, the only danger that really can have a fatal effect upon us, because it exists within ourselves.

And if ever we should be so unfortunate as to abandon this individuality that makes us what we are, it is not 'the others' we would have to blame, but only our own impotence and resulting discouragement.

The only way to overcome the danger is to face up to this trying and thoughtless age and make it accept us as we are, succeeding somehow in making a proper and appropriate place in it for ourselves, in our own language, so that we can feel we are equals and not inferiors. This means that in our homeland we must be able to earn our living and pursue our careers in French. It also means that we must build a society which, while it preserves an image that is our own, will be as progressive, as efficient, and as 'civilized' as any in the world. (In fact, there are other small peoples who are showing us the way, demonstrating that maximum size is in no way synonymous with maximum progress among human societies.)

To speak plainly, we must give ourselves sufficient reason to be not only sure of ourselves but also, perhaps, a little proud.

III

Now, in the last few years we have indeed made some progress along this difficult road of 'catching up', the road which leads to the greater promise of our age.

At least enough progress to know that what comes next depends only on ourselves and on the choices that only we can make.

The enticements toward progress were phrases like 'from now on', or 'it's got to change', or 'masters in our own house', etc.*

The results can be seen on every side. Education, for us as for any people desirous of maintaining its place in the world, has finally become the top priority. With hospital insurance, family and school allowances, pension schemes, and the beginnings of medicare, our social welfare has made more progress in a few years than in the whole preceding century; and for the first time we find ourselves, in many of the most important areas, ahead of the rest of the country. In the economic field, by nationalizing electric power, by creating the SGF, *Soquem*, and the *Caisse de Dépôts*† we have taken the first steps toward the kind of collective control of certain essential services without which no human community can feel secure. We also, at last, have begun to clean up our electoral practices, to modernize and strengthen our administrative structures, to give our land the roads that are indispensable to its future, and to study seriously the complex problems of our outmoded municipalities and underdeveloped regions.

To be sure, none of this has been brought to completion. What has been done is only a beginning, carried out in many cases without the co-ordination that should have been applied—and far too often in circumstances dictated by urgency or opportunity. All along the way there have been hesitations and, God knows, these still exist. In all these accomplishments mistakes have been made and gaps have been left—and whatever happens, even if we do a hundred times as much, this always will be so.

No One Will Do It For You

But in the process we have learned certain things, things which are both simple and revolutionary.

The first is that we have the capacity to do the job ourselves, and the more we take charge and accept our responsibilities, the more efficient we find we are; capable, all things considered, of succeeding just as well as anyone else.

Another is that there is no valid *excuse*, that it is up to us to find and apply to our problems the solutions that are right for us; for no one else can, much less wants to, solve them for us.

Yet another thing we have learned—and perhaps the most important: 'The appetite comes with the eating.' This is a phenomenon we can see everywhere as soon as a human group decides to move forward. It is called the 'revolution of rising expectations.'

This is the main driving force at our disposal for continued progress. We must calculate its use as precisely as possible, to avoid costly diversions; but even more we must take care not to stifle it, for without this we shall experience the collective catastrophe of an immobilized society, at a time when those who fail to advance automatically retreat, and to a point which can easily become one of no return.

In other words, above all we must guard against loss of impetus, against the periodic desire to slow down, against the belief that we are moving too quickly when in reality—despite a few wanderings—we are just beginning to reach the speed our age demands. In this, a nation is like an individual: those who succeed are those who are unafraid of life.

The fact is that we are condemned to progress *ad infinitum*.

Not only are we just beginning, but we shall always be just beginning, as far as we can see ahead. On the horizon are further changes and adaptations; on the horizon is the hope that we will be wise enough to make the right choices, with the courage and vitality called for by the ceaseless pursuit of progress and the acceptance of every challenge on the way.

IV

On this road where there can be no more stopping are a number of necessary tasks which must be attended to without delay. Neglecting them would endanger the impetus we have acquired, perhaps would slow it down irreparably.

And here we encounter a basic difficulty which has become more and more acute in recent years. It is created by the political regime under which we have lived for over a century.

We are a nation within a country where there are two nations. For all the things we mentioned earlier, using words like 'individuality', 'history', 'society', and 'people', are also the things one includes under the word 'nation'. It means nothing more than the collective will to live that belongs to any national entity likely to survive.

Two nations in a single country: this means, as well, that in fact there are *two majorities*, two 'complete societies' quite distinct from each other trying to get along within a common framework. That this number puts us in a minority position makes no difference: just as a civilized society will never condemn a little man to feel inferior beside a bigger man, civilized relations among nations demand that they treat each other as equals in law and in fact.

Now we believe it to be evident that the hundred-year-old framework of Canada can hardly have any effect other than to create increasing difficulties between the two parties insofar as their mutual respect and understanding are concerned, as well as impeding the changes and progress so essential to both.

It is useless to go back over the balance sheet of the century just past, listing the advantages it undoubtedly has brought us and the obstacles and injustices it even more unquestionably has set in our way.

The important thing for today and for tomorrow is that both sides realize that this regime has had its day, and that it is a matter of urgency either to modify it profoundly or to build a new one.

As we are the ones who have put up with its main disadvantages, it is natural that we also should be in the greatest hurry to be rid of it; the more so because it is we who are menaced most dangerously by its current paralysis.

Primo Vivere

Almost all the essential tasks facing us risk being jeopardized, blocked, or quietly undone by the sclerosis of Canadian institutions and the open or camouflaged resistance of the men who manipulate them.

First, we must secure once and for all, in accordance with the complex and urgent necessities of our time, the safety of our collective 'personality'. This is the distinctive feature of the nation, of this majority that we constitute in Quebec—the only true fatherland left us by events, by our own possibilities, and by the incomprehension and frequent hostility of others.

The prerequisite to this is, among other things, the power for unfettered action (which does not exclude co-operation) in fields as varied as those of citizenship, immigration, and employment; the great instruments of 'mass culture'—films, radio, and television; and the kind of international relations that alone permit a people to breathe the air of a changing and stimulating world, and to learn to see beyond itself. Such relations are especially imperative for a group whose cultural connections in the world are as evident and important as ours.

Our collective security requires also that we settle a host of questions made so thorny by the present regime that each is more impossible than the next. Let us only mention as examples the integrity of Quebec's territory, off-shore rights, the evident inacceptibility of an institution like the Supreme Court, and Quebec's need to be able to shape freely what we might term its internal constitution.

That collective personality which constitutes a nation also cannot tolerate that social security and welfare—which affect it daily in the most intimate ways—should be conceived and directed from outside. This relates to the oft-repeated demand for the repatriation of old-age pensions, family allowances, and, when it comes into being, medicare.

By the same token, and even more so, it relates to the most obvious needs of efficiency and administrative responsibility. In this whole vast area there are overlapping laws, regulations, and organizations whose main effect is to perpetuate confusion and, behind this screen, to paralyze change and progress.

The Madhouse

Mutatis mutandis, we find similar situations with equally disastrous results in a multitude of other areas: the administration of justice, jurisdiction in fields such as insurance, corporations, bankruptcies, financial institutions, and, in a general way, all economic activities which have become the most constant preoccupations of all men today and also the aspect of society in which modern states have seen their sphere of action grow most dramatically in the last couple of generations.

On this point, here is how the CSN, the FTQ, and the UCC* describe the situation in their joint memorandum to the Quebec Legislature's Constitutional Committee:

> The fact that certain economic tools belong to the federal government, while other powers whose exercise also influences economic life belong to the provinces, creates a difficult problem in the rational planning of economic activity in general. Thinking in terms of a more advanced socialization than that we know today, this situation, along with opportunity given one government to thwart the actions of others, may lead to conflict, and is in any case of such a nature that it could, at these two levels of government, result in impotence in attacking the economic problems of the country with any kind of resolution or efficiency. Any duplication of institutions should be avoided, moreover, if it leads to a duplication of costs. This situation should demand our attention all the more urgently because of the fact that already (for example, in agriculture) laws and regulations at the two levels of government, and especially their application, because of their overlapping, their duplication, their superimposition or their lack of co-ordination, cause many grave difficulties and are often more prejudicial to the citizens involved, especially those of Quebec in view of our lagging behind in a number of areas.

Here again let us limit ourselves to citing the minimums established by the most complete studies of recent years. And so, back to those three organizations and the way in which they define these minimums in the cautious conclusion of their memorandum:

> The Quebec government should exercise its powers by giving direction to the economy, rationalizing its marginal industries, developing secondary industry, etc. The government of Quebec should promote an economic policy frankly favourable to its own population and more demanding *vis-à-vis* the capitalist interests, for it is not enough only to appear to govern in favour of the people in this sector. In particular, the Quebec government must obtain the greatest advantages and royalties it can possibly extract from the exploitation of natural resources, taking account of the reasonable limits of this kind of policy. Activity just as intense and equally devoted to the interests of the people must spread through all departments responsible for economic matters, notably agriculture, industry, and commerce, and so forth.

This outline, which is necessarily incomplete ('and so forth'), hints at a program immediately acceptable to everyone, but it poses at once the question of means.

A Strong State

How can it be carried out? Let us mention only what is clearly obvious. Order must be re-established in the chaos of a governmental structure created at a time when it was impossible to foresee the scientific and technical revolution in which we now are caught up, the endless changes it demands, the infinite variety of things produced, the concentration of enterprises, the crushing weight that the greatest of these impose on individual and collective life, the absolute necessity of having a state able to direct, co-ordinate, and above all humanize this infernal rhythm.

In this up-dating of political structures that are completely overtaxed by an economic role they cannot refuse to play, the action demanded of the Quebec government, to be specific, would require at the very least new jurisdictions over industrial and commercial corporations, fiduciary and savings institutions, and all the internal agencies of development and industrialization, as well as the power to exercise a reasonable control over the movement and investment of our own capital.

So as not to belabour the obvious, we shall mention only for the record the massive transfer of fiscal resources that would be needed for all the tasks this State of Quebec should undertake in our name—not counting the tasks it already has, tasks that daily grow more out of proportion to its inadequate means: i.e., the insatiable needs of education, urban problems without number, and the meagreness or tragic non-existence of the tools of scientific and industrial research.

Very sketchily, this would seem to be the basic minimum of change that Quebec should force the present Canadian regime to accept in order to reach both the collective security and the opportunity for progress which its best minds consider indispensable.

We could certainly add to the list. But nothing could be struck from it easily.

For us, this is, in fact, a true minimum.

V

But we would be dreaming if we believed that for the rest of the country our minimum can be anything but a frightening maximum, completely unacceptable even in the form of bare modifications or, for that matter, under the guise of the constitutional reform which certain people say they are willing to proceed with.

Not only the present attitude of the federal government, but also the painful efforts at understanding made by the opposition parties and reactions in the most influential circles in English Canada all give us reason to expect that our confrontation will grow more and more unpleasant.

From a purely revisionist point of view, our demands would seem to surpass both the best intentions displayed by the 'other majority' and the very capacity of the regime to make concessions without an explosion.

If we are talking only of revision, they will tell us, our demands would lead to excessive weakening of that centralized state which English Canada needs for its own security and progress as much as we need our own State of Quebec. And they would be right.

And further, they could ask us—with understandable insistence—what in the world our political representatives would be doing in Ottawa taking part in debates and administrative acts whose authority and effectiveness we intend so largely to eliminate within Quebec.

If Quebec were to begin negotiations to revise the present frame of reference, and persisted in this course, it would not be out of the woods in the next hundred years. But by that time it is most likely that there would be nothing left worth talking about of the nation that is now trying to build a homeland in Quebec.

During the long wait we would soon fall back on the old defensive struggle, the enfeebling skirmishes that make one forget where the real battle is, the half-victories that are celebrated between two defeats, the relapse into divisive federal-provincial electoral folly, the sorry consolations of verbal nationalism and, above all, ABOVE ALL ELSE—this must be said, and repeated, and shouted if need be—above all the incredible 'split-level' squandering of energy, which certainly is for us the most disastrous aspect of the present regime.

And as for this waste of energy, English Canada suffers from it, too. And there, too, the best minds have begun to realize this fact, let there be no doubt of that.

Two Paralyzed Majorities

For the present regime also prevents the English-speaking majority from simplifying, rationalizing, and centralizing as it would like to do certain institutions which it, too, realizes are obsolete. This is an ordeal which English Canada is finding more and more exhausting, and for which it blames the exaggerated anxieties and the incorrigible intransigence of Quebec.

It is clear, we believe, that this frustration may easily become intolerable. And it is precisely among the most progressive 'nationalist' groups in English Canada, among those who are concerned about the economic, cultural, and political invasion from the United States, among those who are seeking the means to prevent the country from surrendering completely, that there is the greatest risk of a growing and explosive resentment toward Quebec for the reasons mentioned above. And these are the very men among whom we should be able to find the best partners for our dialogue over the new order that must emerge.

We are seeking at last to carve out for ourselves a worthy and acceptable place in this Quebec which has never belonged to us as it should have. Facing us, however, a growing number of our fellow-citizens of the other majority are afraid of losing the homeland that Canada was for them in the good old days of the Empire, when they at least had the impression that they were helping to rule, and that it was all within the family. Today the centres of decision-making are shifting south of the border at a terrifying rate.

In this parallel search for two national securities, as long as the search is pursued within the present system or anything remotely resembling it, we can end up only with double paralysis. The two majorities, basically desiring the same thing—a chance to live their own lives, in their own way, according to their own needs and aspirations—will inevitably collide with one another repeatedly and with greater and greater force, causing hurts that finally would be irreparable.

As long as we persist so desperately in maintaining—with spit and chewing gum or whatever—the ancient hobble of a federalism suited to the last century, the two nations will go on creating an ever-growing jungle of compromises while disagreeing more and more strongly on essentials.

This would mean a perpetual atmosphere of instability, of wrangling over everything and over nothing. It would mean the sterilization of two collective 'personalities' which, having squandered the most precious part of their potential, would weaken each other so completely that they would have no other choice but to drown themselves in the ample bosom of 'America'.

VI

We think it is possible for both parties to avoid this blind alley. We must have the calm courage to see that the problem can't be solved either by maintaining or somehow adapting the *status quo*. One is always somewhat scared at the thought of leaving a home in which one has lived for a long time. It becomes almost 'consecrated', and all the more so in this case, because what we call 'Confederation' is one of the last remnants of those age-old safeguards of which modern times have robbed us. It is therefore quite normal that some people cling to it with a kind of desperation that arises far more from fear than from reasoned attachment.

But there are moments—and this is one of them—when courage and calm daring become the only proper form of prudence that a people can exercise in a crucial period of its existence. If it fails at these times to accept the calculated risk of the great leap, it may miss its vocation forever, just as does a man who is afraid of life.

What should we conclude from a cool look at the crucial crossroads that we now have reached? Clearly that we must rid ourselves completely of a completely obsolete federal regime.

And begin anew.

Begin how?

The answer, it seems to us, is as clearly written as the question, in the two great trends of our age: that of the freedom of peoples, and that of the formation by common consent of economic and political groupings.

A Sovereign Quebec

For our own good, we must dare to seize for ourselves complete liberty in Quebec, the right to all the essential components of independence, i.e., the complete mastery of every last area of basic collective decision-making.

This means that Quebec must become sovereign as soon as possible.

Thus we finally would have within our grasp the security of our collective 'being' which is so vital to us, a security which otherwise must remain uncertain and incomplete.

Then it will be up to us, and us alone, to establish calmly, without recrimination or discrimination, the priority for which we are now struggling feverishly but blindly: that of our language and our culture.

Only then will we have the opportunity—and the obligation—to use our talents to the maximum in order to resolve without further excuses or evasions all the great problems that confront us, whether it be a negotiated protective system for our farmers, or decent treatment for our employees and workers in industry, or the form and evolution of the political structures we must create for ourselves.

In short, this is not for us simply the only solution to the present Canadian impasse; it also is the one and only common goal inspiring enough to bring us together with the kind of strength and unity we shall need to confront all possible futures—the supreme challenge of continuous progress within a society that has taken control of its own destiny.

As for the other Canadian majority, it will also find our solution to its advantage, for it will be set free at once from the constraints imposed on it by our presence; it will be at liberty in its own way to rebuild to its heart's desire the political institutions of English Canada and to prove to itself, whether or not it really wants to maintain and develop on this continent, an English-speaking society distinct from the United States.

—and a New Canadian Union

And if this is the case, there is no reason why we, as future neighbours, should not voluntarily remain associates and partners in a common enterprise; which would conform to the second great trend of our times: the new economic groups, customs unions, common markets, etc.

Here we are talking about something which already exists, for it is composed of the bonds, the complementary activities, the many form of economic co-operation within which we have learned to live. Nothing says that we must throw these things away; on the contrary, there is every reason to maintain the framework. If we destroyed it, interdependent as we are, we would only be obliged sooner or later to build it up again, and then with doubtful success.

Now, it is precisely in the field of economics that we feel the pinch most painfully. In our outmoded constitutional texts and governmental structures, we flounder hopelessly over how to [divide] between our two states the powers, the agencies, and the means for action.

On this subject any expert with the slightest pretension to objectivity must certainly endorse the following statement by Otto Thur, Head of the Department of Economics at the University of Montreal (in a special edition of *Le Devoir*, June 30, 1967): 'It is not the wording of a constitution that will solve problems [in the field of economics], but rather enlightened and consistent action, which brings about a progressive betterment of existing reality.'

It seems to us, given a minimum of wisdom and, of course, self-interest—

which should not be beyond the reach of our two majorities—that in the kind of association we are proposing we would have the greatest chance of pursuing jointly such a course of 'enlightened and consistent action' worth more in economic affairs than all the pseudo-sacred documents with their ever-ambiguous inflexibility.

Such an association seems to us, in fact, made to measure for the purpose of allowing us, unfettered by obsolete constitutional forms, to pool our stakes with whatever permanent consultation and flexible adjustments would best serve our common economic interests: monetary union, common tariffs, postal union, administration of the national debt, co-ordination of policies, etc.

And nothing would prevent us from adding certain matters which under the present system have never had the advantage of frank discussion between equals: the question of minorities, for one; and also the questions of equal participation in a defence policy in proportion to our means, and a foreign policy that might, if conceived jointly, regain some of the dignity and dynamism that it has lost almost completely. [1]

We are not sailing off into uncharted seas. Leaving out the gigantic model furnished by the evolution of the Common Market, we can take our inspiration from countries comparable in size to our own—Benelux or Scandinavia—among whom co-operation is highly advanced, and where it has promoted unprecedented progress in the member states without preventing any of them from continuing to live according to their own tradition and preferences.

Making History Instead of Submitting To It

To sum up, we propose a system that would allow our two majorities to extricate themselves from an archaic federal framework in which our two very distinct 'personalities' paralyze each other by dint of pretending to have a third personality common to both.

This new relationship of two nations, one with its homeland in Quebec and another free to rearrange the rest of the country at will, would be freely associated in a new adaption of the current 'common-market' formula, making up an entity which could perhaps—and if so very precisely—be called a Canadian Union.

The future of a people is never born without effort. It requires that a large number of 'midwives' knowingly make the grave decision to work at it. For apart from other blind forces, and apart from all the imponderables, we must believe that basically it is still men who make man's history.

What we are suggesting to those who want to listen is that we devote our efforts, together, to shape the history of Quebec in the only fitting direction; and we are certain that at the same time we shall also be helping the rest of the country to find a better future of its own.

AUTHOR'S NOTE

[1] In this paragraph some people have felt obliged—and others have hastened—to find a far-too-strict limitation imposed on Quebec's sovereignty. This would indeed be true if we proposed really to include Defence and External Affairs in the areas of actual association. These two are among the most important means through which a people

can express its personality. But such is not our proposal. The highly conditional form in which it is couched, and the suggestion of preliminary studies, seem to us to indicate clearly enough that we were referring to the possibility of agreements which *might* be reached, agreements that would be strictly limited in nature (e.g., joint general staffs? Certain common agencies abroad, such as commercial representatives?), which should not *a priori* be excluded in the free development of countries which are neighbours and partners. This is the sort of thing we had in mind below when we speak of these two distinct societies which 'have a crying need now to give each other some breathing space, and to rediscover themselves, freely and without prejudice, creating little by little new points of contact as the need arises.'

THE WAFFLE MANIFESTO

The most important manifestation of the New Left in English Canada was the Waffle movement within the NDP ('If we're going to waffle, I'd rather waffle to the left than waffle to the right'). It developed in the late sixties, against the backdrop of Trudeaumania, the war in Vietnam, and growing concern about American ownership of Canadian industry. The goal of the Wafflers was an independent socialist Canada; they hoped to convert the NDP to their more radical brand of socialism. Their Manifesto, the work of political economists James Laxer (b. 1941) and Mel Watkins (b. 1932), was presented as Resolution 133 at the party's biennial convention in Winnipeg in 1969. It was opposed by the old guard, led by David Lewis and his son Stephen, who argued that it would put the NDP into an ideological strait-jacket. Although the Wafflers had been eliminated as a distinct faction within the party by 1972, their ideas have continued to have some influence on Canadian politics to this day.

Our aim as democratic socialists is to build an independent socialist Canada. Our aim as supporters of the New Democratic Party is to make it a truly socialist party.

The achievement of socialism awaits the building of a mass base of socialists in factories and offices, on farms and campuses. The development of socialist consciousness, on which can be built a socialist base, must be the first priority of the New Democratic Party.

The New Democratic Party must be seen as the parliamentary wing of a movement dedicated to fundamental social change. It must be radicalized from within and it must be radicalized from without.

The most urgent issue for Canadians is the very survival of Canada. Anxiety is pervasive and the goal of greater economic independence receives widespread support. But economic independence without socialism is a sham, and neither are meaningful without true participatory democracy.

The major threat to Canadian survival today is American control of the Canadian economy. The major issue of our times is not national unity but national survival, and the fundamental threat is external, not internal.

American corporate capitalism is the dominant factor shaping Canadian society. In Canada American economic control operates through the formidable medium of the multi-national corporation. The Canadian corporate elite has opted for a junior partnership with these American enterprises. Canada has been reduced to a resource base and consumer market within the American empire.

The American empire is the central reality for Canadians. It is an empire characterized by militarism abroad and racism at home. Canadian resources and diplomacy have been enlisted in the support of that empire. In the barbarous war in Vietnam Canada has supported the United States through its membership on the International Control Commission and through sales of arms and strategic resources to the American military-industrial complex.

The American empire is held together through world-wide military alliances and by giant monopoly corporations. Canada's membership in the American alliance system and the ownership of the Canadian economy by American corporations precludes Canada's playing an independent role in the world. These bonds must be cut if corporate capitalism, and the social priorities it creates, is to be effectively challenged.

Canadian development is distorted by a corporate capitalist economy. Corporate investment creates and fosters superfluous individual consumption at the expense of social needs. Corporate decision-making concentrates investment in a few major urban areas which become increasingly uninhabitable while the rest of the country sinks into underdevelopment.

The criterion that the most profitable pursuits are the most important ones causes the neglect of activities whose value cannot be measured by the standard of profitability. It is not accidental that housing, education, medical care and public transportation are inadequately provided for by the present social system.

The problem of regional disparities is rooted in the profit orientation of capitalism. The social costs of stagnant areas are irrelevant to the corporations. For Canada the problem is compounded by the reduction of Canada to the position of an economic colony of the United States. The foreign capitalist has even less concern for balanced development of the country than the Canadian capitalist with roots in a particular region.

An independence movement based on substituting Canadian capitalists for American capitalists, or on public policy to make foreign corporations behave as if they were Canadian corporations, cannot be our final objective. There is not now an independent Canadian capitalism and any lingering pretensions on the part of Canadian businessmen to independence lack credibility. Without a strong national capitalist class behind them, Canadian governments, Liberal and Conservative, have functioned in the interests of international and particularly American capitalism, and have lacked the will to pursue even a modest strategy of economic independence.

Capitalism must be replaced by socialism, by national planning of investment and by the public ownership of the means of production in the interests of the Canadian people as a whole. Canadian nationalism is a relevant force on which to build to the extent that it is anti-imperialist. On the road to socialism, such aspirations for independence must be taken into account. For to pursue independence seriously is to make visible the necessity of socialism in Canada.

Those who desire socialism and independence for Canada have often been baffled and mystified by the problem of internal divisions within Canada. While the essential fact of Canadian history in the past century is the reduction of Canada to a colony of the United States, with a consequent increase in regional inequalities, there is no denying the existence of two nations within Canada, each with its own language, culture and aspirations. This reality must be incorporated into the strategy of the New Democratic Party.

English Canada and Quebec can share common institutions to the extent that they share common purposes. So long as Canada is governed by those who believe that national policy should be limited to the passive function of maintaining a peaceful and secure climate for foreign investors, there can be no meaningful unity between English and French Canadians. So long as the federal government refuses to protect the country from American economic and cultural domination, English Canada is bound to appear to French Canadians simply as part of the United States. An English Canada concerned with its own national survival would create common aspirations that would help to tie the two nations together once more.

Nor can the present treatment of the constitutional issue in isolation from economic and social forces that transcend the two nations be anything but irrelevant. Our present constitution was drafted a century ago by politicians committed to the values and structure of a capitalist society. Constitutional change relevant to socialists must be based on the needs of the people rather than the corporations and must reflect the power of classes and groups excluded from effective decision-making by the present system.

A united Canada is of critical importance in pursuing a successful strategy against the reality of American imperialism. Quebec's history and aspirations must be allowed full expression and implementation in the conviction that new ties will emerge from the common perception of 'two nations, one struggle'. Socialists in English Canada must ally themselves with socialists in Quebec in this common cause.

Central to the creation of an independent socialist Canada is the strength and tradition of the Canadian working class and the trade union movement. The revitalization and extension of the labour movement would involve a fundamental democratization of our society.

Corporate capitalism is characterized by the predominant power of the corporate elite aided and abetted by the political elite. A central objective of Canadian socialists must be to further the democratization process in industry. The Canadian trade union movement throughout its history has waged a democratic battle against the so-called rights or prerogatives of ownership and management. It has achieved the important moral and legal victory of providing for working men an effective say in what their wages will be. At present management's 'right' to control technological change is being challenged. The New Democratic Party must provide leadership in the struggle to extend working men's influence into every area of industrial decision-making. Those who work must have effective control in the determination of working conditions, and substantial power in determining the nature of the product, prices, and so on. Democracy and socialism require nothing less.

Trade unionists and New Democrats have led in extending the welfare state in Canada. Much remains to be done: more and better housing, a really progressive tax structure, a guaranteed annual income. But these are no longer enough. A socialist society must be one in which there is democratic control of all institutions which have a major effect on men's lives and where there is equal opportunity for creative non-exploitative self-development. It is now time to go beyond the welfare state.

New Democrats must begin now to insist on the redistribution of power, and not simply welfare, in a socialist direction. The struggle for worker participation in industrial decision-making and against management 'rights' is such a move toward economic and social democracy.

By strengthening the Canadian labour movement, New Democrats will further the pursuit of Canadian independence. So long as Canadians' economic activity is dominated by the corporate elite, and so long as workers' rights are confined within their present limits, corporate requirements for profit will continue to take precedence over human needs.

By bringing men together primarily as buyers and sellers of each other, by enshrining profitability and material gain in place of humanity and spiritual growth, capitalism has always been inherently alienating. Today, sheer size combined with modern technology further exaggerates man's sense of insignificance and impotence. A socialist transformation of society will return to man his sense of humanity, to replace his sense of being a commodity. But a socialist democracy implies man's control of his immediate environment as well, and in any strategy for building socialism, community democracy is as vital as the struggle for electoral success. To that end, socialists must strive for democracy at those levels which most directly affect us all—in our neighbourhoods, our schools, our places of work. Tenants' unions, consumers' and producers' cooperatives are examples of areas in which socialists must lead in efforts to involve people directly in the struggle to control their own destinies.

Socialism is a process and a programme. The process is the raising of socialist consciousness, the building of a mass base of socialists, and a strategy to make visible the limits of liberal capitalism.

While the programme must evolve out of the process, its leading features seem clear. Relevant instruments for bringing the Canadian economy under Canadian ownership and control and for altering the priorities established by corporate capitalism are to hand. They include extensive public control over investment and nationalization of the commanding heights of the economy, such as the key resources industries, finance and credit, and industries strategic to planning our economy. Within that programme, workers' participation in all institutions promises to release creative energies, promote decentralization, and restore human and social priorities.

The struggle to build a democratic socialist Canada must proceed at all levels of Canadian society. The New Democratic Party is the organization suited to bringing these activities into a common focus. The New Democratic Party has grown out of a movement for democratic socialism that has deep roots in Canadian history. It is the core around which should be mobilized the social and political movement necessary for building an independent socialist Canada. The New Democratic Party must rise to that challenge or become irrelevant. Victory lies in joining the struggle.

CHARLES TAYLOR

One of Canada's most eminent philosophers, Charles Taylor (b. 1931) has published important books on Hegel and on the philosophy of scientific explanation. Now teaching political science at McGill University, he has also taught philosophy at the University of Montreal and had visiting appointments at Oxford and the Institute for Advanced Study in Princeton. During the 1960s he was a vice-president of the NDP, a frequent contributor to Canadian Dimension, *and one of the most prominent supporters of the Waffle Manifesto. He quickly retracted his support, however, and helped to draft an alternative statement, 'For a United and Independent Canada', which its detractors dubbed the 'Marshmallow Manifesto'. Taylor's one book on Canadian politics,* The Pattern of Politics *(1970), is a straightforward argument, along familiar lines, for class conflict rather than consensus. But he broke new ground the following year in the essay reprinted here, which argues that socialists have been as deluded as capitalists in expecting great good from the further conquest of nature through technology.*

The Agony of Economic Man

In the coming years the thought and program of socialism will have to be worked out afresh. Of course, socialism is always rethinking itself, but the present transformation will have to be the most far-reaching in the past century—since the appearance of *Das Kapital* in 1867.

The occasion for this rethinking is a breakdown of one of the props of our civilization, a prop of capitalist civilization to be sure, but one on which socialists counted for the transition to a higher form of society. This breakdown can perhaps best be thought of as a crisis of legitimacy, a crucial weakening of the set of beliefs, practices, and collective representations that help to hold society together. Of course, modern western societies—like all societies beyond the most primitive—have been held together by a variety of legitimating ideas. Nationalism has been one such powerful idea, and no one can claim that it is on the wane. But one of the most important foundations of legitimacy has been the self-image of modern industrial society as a vast productive engine based on creative work, disciplined and rational effort, and the division of labour.

We are so used to this idea that we fail to notice it. Above all, we fail to appreciate how unprecedented it is in human history. It is not that previous societies have not had some shadowy notion of their economic organization, but no society before the rise of modern commercial-industrial civilization has ever founded its sense of its own fundamental value on this economic organization (or even on an idealized version of what it is supposed to be). The idea would have appeared grotesque to earlier civilizations. For the Greeks, the 'economic' was concerned with the maintenance of life, a pre-condition for politics, which was what really distinguished human society from that of gregarious beasts. To be concerned one's whole life only with the economic was to be in effect a slave. In the Middle Ages what was important in society was that its hierarchical order reflected and connected with the order of things in the universe.

Modern society singled itself out in that its paradigm justifying self-image was that of a productive association bent on transforming the surrounding natural world to meet the needs and fulfil the ends of man. So powerful was this justifying image that moderns were impelled to project it onto other, earlier civilizations. Thus, for Marxism, the real motive force of change in history has always been the tensions within the economic organization of societies. Nascent nineteenth century anthropology interpreted primitive magic as a first, muddled attempt at technological control of the environment. Even today American political science gives us theories of 'development' which assume the universality of our modern economic based categories.

The malaise of our time arises partly from the fact that this justifying image has rather suddenly ceased to justify in the eyes of a growing number of people. The image of a society dedicated to constantly increasing production, to greater and greater prodigies of technology, suddenly seems tawdry and senseless. The constant rise in the GNP goes along with an increasing demand for consumer goods, so that increasing social wealth seems to have no impact on the pool of poverty and material want which persists in contemporary industrial society. Seen in the light of humane priorities, we appear to be running as fast as possible in order to stand in the same place. And, to cap it all, this accelerating squirrel-wheel threatens to precipitate an ecological crisis which could be fatal.

This type of criticism of modern society is pretty standard stuff on the left these days. But its implications are not really thought through, and to do so properly requires much more than some minor retouching of socialist theory. To begin with, two facts have failed to register with their full impact: that the decline of its economic justifying image really could threaten our civilization with breakdown, and that socialism has traditionally defined itself in terms of its own version of the productive society, hence its own economic justifying image. It cannot just shrug off the challenge implicit in the fact that all such economic images are under attack today.

The fact that many young people are dropping out today reflects a much more serious threat to present society than could be concluded from the number of drop-outs. To some extent, this fact is instinctively felt by everyone, but the nature of the threat is misidentified. That a number of young people choose to live a life outside the circuit of the regular job, cellular family, gradual increase in consumption level—this by itself poses no great problem. Our society is rich and productive enough to carry a leisure class of this kind, particularly one which makes such limited material demands: the resources commandeered by one millionaire playboy would probably supply two or three hippie communes.

The threat which dropping out represents for society is usually understood as a threat of contagion, of increasing numbers: what would happen if all or most young people do it? But this is not very likely. There are still substantial rewards in the system and substantial sacrifices which have to be made to stay out of it. So dropping out is likely to remain limited to a minority and, even for them, to a limited period of their lives in most cases. More fundamentally, the act of dropping out presupposes a square society not only to give material support but also to give a psychological point to the action. In its very nature, it has to be a minority affair.

The sense of threat is really based on the fact that drop-outs dramatize something that everybody feels: that a life integrated in the productive system is not one of ultimate value. The hostility of the square comes from the fact that the hippy arouses in him and in all those around him something very disquieting—a sense of doubt. This is disquieting not only because it calls into question the purpose of square life—an unpleasant experience in itself—but also because it is felt to question the whole basis of social cohesion, and it undoubtedly does. Modern industrial society has developed by undermining and sapping the strength of the traditional foundations of solidarity: the sense of religious community, of primary group loyalty, of allegiance to age-old authority. These foundations now tend to appear to moderns as 'irrational', that is, as obstacles to the 'rationalized' organization of things for the sake of production. Of course, modern society is very far from having made a clean sweep of such 'irrational' ideas. Rather, one such idea, nationalism, is a child of the modern age and has grown to unparalleled proportions in our own day. But the gap opened by the decline of traditional foundations has had to be partly filled by the economic self-image of industrial society itself. The reason for playing one's part according to the rules was no longer that all authority comes from God, or that life outside one's community was inconceivable. It was that one was part of a vast engine of production based on peaceful negotiation and a disciplined, rational division of labour. To reject this idea would be to jeopardize this great enterprise, source of welfare, happiness, dignity for all.

The ideologues of the Enlightenment and their successors thought of this justification as founded on rational self-interest, and thus qualitatively different from the traditional foundations of solidarity which preceeded it. With industrial civilization man at last comes to the age of reason, where he no longer needs childish ideologies and myths to motivate sensible, ordered behaviour. But this claim to a monopoly on rationality is another ethnocentric illusion. The simple calculation of pleasures and pains was never enough to motivate allegiance to society, but rather the great spiritual prestige of the enterprise of production itself.

Now that this prestige is waning we can see this more clearly. Industrial civilization, having brought men to an unprecedented degree of interdependence, requires an unprecedented level of co-operation. But interdependence does not by itself breed solidarity, as it should according to the philosophy of enlightened self-interest. It is terribly vulnerable to breakdown and paralysis which can be provoked by an indefinite number of small minorities. Without a widespread sense of solidarity the whole of our system is in grave danger of breakdown.

Hence the feeling of danger inherent in the phenomenon of dropping out goes beyond the fear that large numbers may follow this example. It is rather that the weakening prestige of the productive enterprise, which dropping out illustrates, threatens breakdown in all sorts of ways: for example, in a paralysis bred of many sided intransigence, or in mass passivity before the take-over bids of small minorities. The hippy provokes disquiet as a symbol of society's destruction rather than as its agent.

Socialist writers and thinkers have recognized these signs of incipient breakdown, and generally they rejoiced in them. But this rejoicing has been a little premature, for the full significance of such a breakdown hasn't yet registered. In part this is because it is believed by socialists that any failure of capitalist society must lead to the advance of socialism. But on examination this belief turns out to be almost totally devoid of rational foundation. There already is a clear historical example of a failure of capitalist society which did not result in socialism, but rather in something incomparably worse than its starting point: fascism. The only reason for faith in the inevitability of socialism is a naive Enlightenment belief in the certainty of progress and the goodness of human nature.

In fact, what usually follows a breakdown in one of the essential foundations of solidarity is a dramatic increase in the only alternative instrument of social cohesion—force. Periods of declining legitimacy are periods of rapid expansion in government by force and also in violence. That is why the important transitions in our history have usually been marked by periods of strife and rule by force, which we often call revolutions. These historical precedents form the basis for a terribly fallacious argument widely espoused by writers on the left today: we are enjoined not to be too worried by the increasing violence in our society since the revolutions out of which modern democracy grew were also accompanied by violence. But to be reassured by this argument one has already to believe that some great step forward is in gestation, and no evidence is offered for this beyond faith in progress. Why should one not just as logically conclude that, since the conquests of Hitler and Genghis Khan were accompanied by violence, we must be sinking back into barbarism? It would be more realistic to hold that both alternatives, socialism and barbarism, are possible, and that neither is foreordained. Which alternative comes about depends on a number of things, but perhaps in part on what kind of socialist alternative is offered.

Socialism in its present definitions is closely tied up with the economic self-image which it has borrowed from capitalist civilization. Perhaps it would be truer to say that both visions spring from the same civilization, born of the Enlightenment and the growth of industrial society. A really adequate socialist alternative has to be rethought from the ground up.

The socialist economic vision of society is not identical with the capitalist one. In fact, traditional socialism incorporates some strands of the romantic rebellion against the economic vision. But this synthesis is an unstable one; it is a synthesis in wish only, and it cannot withstand the test of practice. This can best be illustrated from the case of Marxism, which after a hundred years still remains the basis of the most coherent and influential conceptions of socialism. On one hand, Marxism offers a vision of socialism as the fulfilment of the productive vocation of capitalism. Socialism will overcome the contradictions of capitalism, the forms of which have become fetters which prevent the immense productive powers of human society from giving their full measure. This has remained a theme of socialist rhetoric for over a century, that capitalism is inherently inefficient and wasteful, that socialism is ultimately the only rational organization of the economy.

This critique is not simple and univocal: it can mean that capitalism is inefficient in its own terms; or it can mean that socialists are applying a different standard of efficiency—effectiveness in meeting real human need—as against abstract production targets, growing profits, greater potential armaments production, and so on. In practice, socialists have usually meant both, though the accent has varied from context to context. But insofar as the second, more fundamental criticism is salient, we have gone beyond a simple reliance on the economic model; production is now seen as undertaken for the sake of some higher goal, at least potentially.

The question of the re-definition of socialism in our time turns on the definition of that higher goal or goals and the relation of the productive organization of society to it. And here traditional socialism is full of half-clarities and wishful thinking. Basically there are two answers, neither of them satisfactory. Both can be found in Marxism, which here as elsewhere retains its predominant influence.

The first answer is that in socialist or communist society, the distinction between productive work and creation will disappear. All production will take on the intensity, the freedom, the self-expressive power, the playfulness of artistic creation at its most untrammeled. Production will not thus be just a means, which has usurped the role of an end, as many people now experience it in capitalist society, a senseless squirrel-wheel. It will merge with intense self-fulfilment, with the true end of life.

But this perspective is unfortunately as implausible as it is attractive. Artistic creation itself is only free and untrammeled at privileged moments; these moments pre-suppose long hours and months of disciplined work. Even so, we would gladly settle for a world in which all productive labour could have the same creative goal and motivation as the work of artists does today. But although much could be done to relieve men from drudgery and to heighten the significance of many jobs for those who hold them by increasing their participation in the direction of the whole enterprise, it would be utopian to look forward to a society in which there was no more labour which was not an antechamber to creation.

This hard fact is the basis of the second answer of traditional socialism to the alienation of productive labour: that socialist society will profit from technological advance and investment to reduce the hours of work dramatically, thus liberating men for free, creative activity. This answer accepts the continued distinction between creation and productive labour; it proposes to reduce one, perhaps ultimately to the vanishing point, at the expense of the other. We can see this solution as offering in a sense a return to the Greek polis, as it was idealized by its most fortunate citizens: a life of creative action and of full participation in public life. But where with the Greeks the material basis for this life of creative leisure was assured by slave labour, in the future socialist society machines would fill the helot role.

This is probably the most commonly held view among socialists today who are concerned with the shape of a future socialist society; and it is a perspective which many non-socialists also espouse at least in part. It looks deceptively simple: we just apply our increasing productive power to liberating men from drudgery and we open a new era of human history. We truly relegate production to a subordinate role, and one to which we need give less and less time, in order to devote ourselves to the true ends of life.

This idyllic prospect ignores certain stubborn realities. To begin with, we have to admit that we are not proceeding in this direction at all, that the immense wealth and productive power accumulated to date has not served to liberate more and more people for a life of creative leisure. On the contrary, we are probably the hardest working civilization in history. It is true that we have reduced the work week from the horrendous sixty to seventy hours that it was in the last century to more humane proportions. But reductions in the work week today do not usually mean significant reductions in the number of hours worked, but rather an increase in the number of workers for whom overtime is paid. And many people feel obliged to moonlight and thus still work sixty or seventy hours.

Why? The quick answer, which raises all the questions, is that we are absorbing our increased productivity in more and more refined consumer goods. With each rise of productive potential something new is invented which we feel we must have, and the race for this product, together with the efforts of those who haven't yet obtained the last wave of inventions, keeps the squirrel-wheel turning.

The standard socialist response is to lay the blame at the door of the contemporary corporate capitalist system and its essential ancillary of consumer management. But the elements of truth in this charge easily distract attention from the crucial illusion underlying it. The corporate system is built on this endless drive for consumer goods; it provides its focus, determines its pace, and above all entrenches its priorities in the decisions which shape the development of the economy. The corporate system has entrenched the power of these priorities, but it does not itself create these priorities, they do not exist only because of the power of manipulation. Any movement which wishes to change our economic goals in a fundamental way must fight the present hegemony of the large corporation over our society, but the corporation is not the only prop on which this consumer civilization rests. To believe that it is means accepting a naive, demonological, manipulative view of history. No institution creates the spiritual conditions for its own existence; it may intensify them, give them permanence, but it does not bring them into being.

The simple answer which lays the drive for consumer goods at the door of the corporate system cannot be taken seriously. Another equally simple answer is given by apologists for the present system: that men naturally want to possess things, and that given a productive potential which increases indefinitely there will naturally and inevitably follow a desire to possess which also increases indefinitely. Any other view of human nature, it is implied, is naively altruistic.

One does not need to have a wildly altruistic vision of man to question this theory. Men have desired prosperity throughout the ages and, given the chance, riches. But this wealth has not always, or even most often, been defined so exclusively in terms of the possession of things, in particular things, many of which have no intrinsic beauty. The problem of the ends of life cannot be so easily settled. Even if one concedes that men generally desire wealth, the important problems reappear when one tries to define what the life of a wealthy man consists in: and in particular, is wealth desirable because it is the only basis for a life of creative leisure, or is it desirable because it permits an increasing variety of possessions?

Once we set aside both vulgar socialism and corporate apologetics, we have to admit that we have not begun to understand the background to our endless propensity to consume, although such understanding has become an essential part of any adequate socialist theory. We cannot hope to change this propensity without an understanding of it, and we cannot hope to build a socialist society, one founded on more humane priorities, or one in which endless production would not be an end in itself, unless we can bring our urge to consume back into sane proportions.

I cannot claim to have the key to this mystery, but I think it is time that we engaged in some basic speculation about this problem as an indispensable prelude to more sober analysis. In this regard, there are a couple of hypotheses which seem worth exploring. First, we find it very hard to redirect our productive powers from endless consumption to creative leisure because in fact these powers are much less our servants than we like to think. The analogy with ancient Greece might again be appropriate here. Slave labour emancipates the free for other pursuits, but it subjects them to other servitudes, those which are inseparable from life in a slave society: the brutality, the abuse of power, the perpetual fear of revolt. The same is possibly true of our technological civilization. It requires us to acquire certain skills, submit to certain disciplines, integrate ourselves in certain forms of organization, adopt certain attitudes to change, and some of these requirements may be intensified as we try to substitute automated production for human labour.

The picture of machines as the pliant servants of humanity with all options open is more a childish dream of omnipotence than a realistic prospect. Machines are extensions of our own powers, but as such they require that we be moulded to operate them effectively. The mere hardware of a modern economy is nothing without the work discipline, the bureaucratic culture, the habits of innovation which make it operational. This is not to say that we must accept holus-bolus theories of technological determinism which paint a picture of inexorable development of a society dominated by machines. Socialists have rightly been sceptical of such theories. But they are no more schematic and implausible than the theories of human omnipotence. The interesting, and useful enterprise is to identify the limited but significant degrees of freedom which a technological society allows us.

Our endless drive to consume is not accidentally connected to a society founded on the economic justifying image described above. A society which sees its ultimate significance in being a productive engine of unparalleled power must celebrate this by continually renewed tangible expression of this power. It must in some form or other glorify its products. The consumer society which we live in is one variant of this glorification. The society renews itself by recurrently giving birth to an array of 'new', freshly designed, supposedly improved products. With the renewal of our consumer durables, we are being sold renewed potency, happiness, a way of life. The hypothesis I am putting forward is that this apotheosis of the compleat consumer is not just an adventitious creation of the advertising-man, it is closely bound up with our basic images of our society and of its ultimate value.

Of course, the glorification of our products doesn't have to take the form of the consumer society. We can also glorify our collective products. This seems to be the path taken by orthodox Soviet Marxism. Here, too, society is defined economically, but the accent is on the collective achievements of 'the people', prodigies of productive growth, technological wonders, targets met. Even capitalist societies have taken up this celebration of collective effort, as with the American moon shot.

This is a fatally inadequate vision of socialism. To substitute the glorification of collective products for that of individual products is to remain with the same economic image of society. But it is this image which is losing the allegiance of contemporary man. If socialism is to provide a creative alternative to the decay of capitalist civilization, it could not choose a worse or a more ineffective model.

Additional corroboration of this fact comes from the history of communist societies themselves. They can only maintain the pace of collective endeavour by rigid control from the top. There is pressure within these societies from the base to give more emphasis to consumer goods. This pressure, to be sure, has a very different meaning in a society where things which are by any reckoning essentials are in short supply. But one cannot help suspecting that if consumer demand in these countries were given its head it would show the same endless, insatiable character that it has here.

The collective celebration of productive power has not worked in communist societies. They do not seem to command autonomously the allegiance and enthusiasm to sustain themselves in a less repressive climate. This suggests another connection between modern economically defined society and the drive for consumption. The collective celebrations of this society do not call forth a deep response in men. Only when a modern community defines itself as a nation do its collective acts and symbols strike a deep chord. Modern nationalism is powerful as a public religion; the modern cult of production is not. Hence the public environments of modern industrial societies tend to be drab, if not positively injurious. The centres of modern industrial cities exercise an immense force of repulsion on their citizens, which itself contributes to their degradation. There is thus a powerful drift in modern society towards privatization, the creation of a private space of happiness and personal meaning. The products in which our society celebrates its power thus tend to be private consumption goods.

Seen from another angle, the connection is this: the cult of production projects a vision of man as dominating, transforming the surrounding world and enjoying the fruits of this transformation. It is because we place ultimate value on this form of human life that we are ready to make production the central function of modern society. But, in order to participate in this cult, individuals have to have some tangible part in the process of transforming/

enjoying. The problem is that just being part of a vast production team, even one which realizes some important achievement, is too abstract; the connection with the end result is too tenuous. The ethos of modern society stresses dominance, control; but the man in the production line feels much more controlled than controlling. It has been a constant theme of socialist aspiration to remedy this by some form of workers' participation in management. But unless some formula of this kind can transform the worker's relation to the whole process of production, the only way in which the average man can have a sense of control is as a consumer, a possessor of things, one who enjoys the fruits of production. This is the only universally available mode of participation in the cult of production. Hence the poor in contemporary affluent societies suffer not just from material deprivation, but from a stigma. They are excommunicated, as it were, from the dominant cult of modern society.

The drive to consumption is therefore no adventitious fad, no product of clever manipulation. It will not be easy to contain. It is tied up with the economic self-image of modern society, and this in turn is linked to a set of powerfully entrenched conceptions of what the value of human life consists in. This is why it is not realistic to treat the infra-structure of technological society as an instrument which we can use at will for any ends we choose. Rather, as long as technological society is held together and given its legitimacy and cohesion by this economic self-image, it will tend to remain fixed on its present goals, the perpetual increase in production and the ever-widening bonanza of consumption. If we are to build a society with radically different priorities, one which will not be driven by this mania of consumption, then we have to evolve a different foundation for technological society, a quite different self-definition to serve as the basis of its cohesion.

This is no easy matter. We might at first be encouraged by the fact that the economic justifying image is losing its grip, but by itself this is no cause for rejoicing. This breakdown could simply render technological society more unlivable in that the only basis for its cohesion would be the widespread use of force. There is no providence, no ineluctable force, which assures us that the breakdown of the cult of production must be followed by another viable foundation for a technological society. Whether this is so or not depends on a number of things, but partly on what is offered as a socialist alternative.

The preceding discussion should allow us to measure a little better what is involved in rethinking socialism for our time. For socialist thought has to tackle this central problem of evolving a different foundation for technological society if the socialist alternative is to be fully relevant to our time. To date the socialist tradition is woefully inadequate to this task. As an alternative to the cult of production it offers mainly the idyll in which productive labour is swallowed up in artistic creation, or the hope that labour can be almost entirely done away with, liberating man for leisure. But the first prospect is impossible; and the second is offered without any idea of how we can overcome the obstacles to it. Without a genuine alternative to the economic image, socialism in the West will be condemned either to offer alternative variants of the cult of production, which will certainly be ignored, or to stand by inactive in the foolish hope that any destruction of the present order will inaugurate a socialist era.

But what would be involved in elaborating such a genuine alternative? I cannot claim to have the answer. But one or two things can be said about what such an alternative would have to be.

The economic model has at its centre the notion of man as producer, as transformer of nature. Man is pure agent. Its Achilles heel is that this offers men a goal which is ultimately empty. The drive to increase production starts with certain goals—to overcome poverty, to provide education for the masses and freedom of choice. But as the production oriented society takes over, it sets its own priorities, and these end up being those of production for its own sake, a glorification of the products. When the hold of this image wanes men have the feeling that this vast and diversified activity is to no purpose, that it is all dressed up with the most prodigious means, yet with nowhere to go. Hence the dominant feeling in this period of decline of the economic image is one of emptiness. The challenge to the current model is coming from young people who cannot find a satisfactory identity in its vision of the future. It offers no form of life which makes sense.

The failure of the economic model is the condemnation of all models of human society which are based purely on an image of man as agent. Man is also a being to whom things happen, to whom things occur, who sees, hears, and feels. There is a genus of human activities in which what happens to us, or what we simply observe, is given human meaning for us, not changed for our purposes, but taken in, understood, interpreted. For the ancients, the most important of these activities was contemplation: for Aristotle this was the highest activity of man. But in modern time this contemplative function, whereby we take in and come to terms with reality, has been largely assumed by art. One of the signs of malaise in our civilization is that much of contemporary art is infected by the disease of the surrounding social reality, that it tries, half desperately, to become pure action, and wants to escape the exigencies of attentiveness.

In our present society the priorities governing the uses of technology and its development are almost entirely dominated by the goals of production. In an alternative society, they would be dominated, although not so one-sidedly, by a contemplative aspiration. In our present society our man made environment and artifacts are designed chiefly for some function, and then secondarily for 'aesthetic appeal'. But we rarely think of them in terms of what they express about our vision of things. They do indeed express something, but this is the latent, the forgotten dimension. Exactly the opposite is the case, for instance, with Chartres cathedral, to take a very spectacular example. There beauty and function are secondary to statement. Of course it is out of the question that there be another such total, confident statement in our day. We are more tentative, but we have not ceased wondering, imagining, thinking, in short, contemplating. It is just that we have abandoned one of our paradigm languages. We have let our architecture, and our world of useful objects, go dumb.

A civilization which recovered contemplation would have very different priorities in technology. The rage for obsolescence makes sense in our society because functional objects must be frequently replaced. But expressive objects are kept as long as possible, if they really speak. The priority would be not on serviceable materials and objects but on those which could be lived with for a long time. In such an alternative society, learning would not be confined to a preparatory phase but would be a major occupation for great numbers of people, who would return to it for prolonged periods at different points in their lives. This means that the society would commit a great part of its resources to supporting disinterested, non-functional study.

No one can say whether an alternative mode of technological society, principally organized around the goals of contemplation, would really be viable, whether it could claim men's allegiance as the productive model did in its hey-day and still does for many today. But only some such alternative can provide a creative denouement to the crisis which our contemporary capitalist civilization is entering. That such an alternative would have to be socialist—that is, based on planning and a high degree of common ownership—must be obvious, but the converse is not true: socialism does not necessarily offer this kind of alternative.

We therefore need a rewriting of socialist theory as complete and far-reaching as that of Karl Marx a hundred years ago. The greatest of socialist theories then was born out of an acute sense of crisis. Perhaps we will be lucky enough to repeat this exploit once more.

PIERRE VADEBONCOEUR

*Pierre Vadeboncoeur (b. 1920), a personal writer given to extreme but illumi-
nating formulations, is the most reflective voice of French-Canadian nationalism at present. Like Pierre Trudeau a graduate of the élite Collège Jean-de-
Brébeuf, Vadeboncoeur worked for many years as a legal adviser to the
Confédération des Syndicats Nationaux. During the 1950s he was one of the
main contributors, along with Trudeau and Gérard Pelletier, to Cité libre, but
during the 1960s his cheminement took a different direction from theirs. In
1974 René Lévesque wrote that Vadeboncoeur's work deserved not just to be
read but to be studied, for he was a master.*

*The selections below, taken from the first eight sections of Un génocide en
douce, were written in June and July 1976. In the ninth section Vadeboncoeur
says that the scourge of our epoch is a certain kind of limited and superficial reasonableness about politics—a narrow determination to carry through
logically, without regard to sentiment or emotion, a few simple, abstract
principles. Intuition, he suggests, must compensate for this aberration of
reason; we must listen for the intimations of deprival, striving to distinguish
between what is merely personal and what belongs to man as man.*

Gentle Genocide

We know as yet only dimly what the future holds for the people we are. Among
peoples who are not asleep, national peril gives effective warning of the
dangers into which individuals risk being plunged by the defeat of their country—
individuals, their families, and their posterity. Vigilant nations have the ability
to perceive politics in this way, as if they saw things that the limited horizons of
the individual rarely permit him to discern on his own. They feel them coming,
as if by an indispensable complementary consciousness—sharper, with a broader
grasp of facts, more sensitive to the consequences of certain movements in
history. This collective awareness is usually immediate and infectious. It puts
men, ordinarily so myopic and pedestrian, instantly on the alert. This is the result
of centuries of experience. The hasty judgements of individuals cannot hold
out against this general perception; they yield before it as if before a deeper
instinctive knowledge. The strength of the nation and its will to exist protect it
against the inadequacy of individual viewpoints concerning the future of the
nation and the individuals of which it is composed. Well in advance, the nation
foresees the collapse of its own people and refuses it.

A healthy nation represents a superior form of group. Groups, be they
countries, parties, trade unions, even villages or professions, have organs to
which individuals connect their own powers of judgement and foresight. The
isolated individual, by contrast, using his own quibbling, forgetful little brain,
is apt to minimize the meaning of events.

In many modern societies the individual has been diminished by a shattered culture that tends to break the individual himself down into fragments.
As a result, he often can no longer comprehend events except as an individual,

and shuts out more than ever the collective understanding of things. Being thus ever more limited as a person, he also increasingly deprives himself of the means of perception resulting from a real sense of belonging to certain collectivities that, over the centuries, had become almost natural, and that gave him an immediately intelligible and unified sense of the complexity of coming changes. Today the individual, disconnected in this way, is less capable of grasping certain warnings of history. To be sure, some new groups claiming a social vocation have appeared, but they are of little help in dealing with the problems that concern us here.

The most necessary truths usually reach us in the form of echoes; otherwise they remain inaudible. There are social forms that act as sea-shells do, storing up the deepest and most salutary sounds, which they alone can transmit for the world at large to hear. Today this has been practically forgotten, because the West never ceases reducing the individual to his own thoughts and systematically destroying the means of relating to others.

The consequence is obvious. Morally, the West is squandering itself in extremely harmful directions. This is no longer a matter of adults alone; the West has put its young people into the furnace of disintegration. Youth entered the furnace freely; how could it so otherwise? At a certain moment it thought it could begin everything anew, starting from luminous intuitions. Hopes were raised that in my own shortsightedness I shared, though with some reservations and apprehension. But these explorations did not give rise to any new relatedness. Thus we have young people now tormented—to the point of defeat, in some cases—by the growth within them of the spirit of nihilism, rejecting one thing after another; and they are more completely abandoned to this spirit than any other group, for young people are fresh, unfettered, and at the mercy of the general lack of direction. The West continues dissolving into individuals, the hollowest [elements] of its substance, tiny, infinitesimal beings living in a state of suspension. For it is to these, in the final analysis, that Western society has given the keys to speech. Social revolution, with a temporary success that cannot be denied, attempts a collective recovery of consciousness, but the limits of political discourse are soon clear enough—being a part, as it is, of all that can be discussed today without circumlocution, and thus subject to the deleterious effects of our reasoning. Its very nature makes examination essential, so much the more as politics is easily corrupted.

II

Capitalism has blossomed in a culture that no longer contains any final authority [*parole suprême*] and is therefore able to tolerate anything. It was in this void, in which anything could be done and into which anything could be thrown, that capitalism set itself to amassing material junk and destroying inheritances. It did not content itself with merely piling up objects; through economic activity, so close to man and so determining a factor in his life—hence at every instant of the day and in every human choice—it effected an insidious separation of the elements of the whole.

It is obvious that capitalism is independent of all principles, and that simple humanism, for example, would mean its destruction. Ask capitalism a single important spiritual question—ask insistently—and if it does not succeed in either destroying the question or driving it back, it will die. Raise the problem of ecology, which is also a great cultural problem, and suppose for a moment that ecological thought were powerful enough to bar its further progress: capitalism would collapse overnight. Ask it another question—I shall take at random the first one that comes to mind, the idea that Moravia discussed in his famous essay on Mao's China:* namely, the inevitability and healthfulness of poverty for the human race. Capitalism is intrinsically incapable of reasoning about this fundamental idea, unless it be for the purpose of dividing the world into an infinite mass of starving wretches [*miséreux*] dominated by a stuffed minority. Capitalism cannot conceive of *poverty* and necessarily substitutes for it the notion of *misery*, just as it turns well-being into the corrupt notion of the seizure of goods by powerful minorities. Moravia's conception of poverty, were it strong enough to prevail, would overthrow capitalism immediately. Capitalism is not based, and absolutely cannot be based, on a philosophical and geo-political conception [that values] poverty; it can proceed only from the idea of enrichment. This idea is completely compatible with the idea and the fact of misery; indeed, the latter is the inevitable accompaniment to the former: economic misery, social misery, and eventually the misery of the human race as a whole, for the consequences of the idea of enrichment for the future condition of humanity will be disastrous—as becomes clear the moment one considers the depletion of natural resources, for example, and the devastation of the environment. A realistic philosophy of the future cannot be reconciled with capitalism and the idea of enrichment. If enlightened concern for the future really did prevail in human thought, capitalism would not last two days. It continues to last, for the moment, because it can lead us to catastrophe without the general population's realizing it. The condition of its subsistence is that it be able to continue leading humanity to ruin. Capitalism can go on only so long as humanity keeps moving towards a precipice. Capitalism is incompatible with the management of human poverty. Moreover, it must be agreed that socialism, under the influence of capitalism and its concept of enrichment, is caught in the same rut, the same impossibility, the same unconsciousness, the same crime. The poison of the concept of enrichment is spreading everywhere, and it affects collectivities just as clearly as it dominates small minorities of monopolists. Up to a certain point, I am myself, in the reality of my own life, a willing victim. But capitalism, throughout the world, is the power that maintains the madness of the will to enrichment. It is a disjointed political and economic activity in a disjointed spiritual and philosophical universe. . . .

Capitalism, a destructive principle in society, destroys everything in society that it touches. Wherever the nation does not serve its purposes, or shows signs of not serving them just as it would wish, it exercises a solvent action on the nation, as one sees in France, or a destructive one, as is clearly the case in Quebec.

Capitalism itself prepares the ground for its insidious total conquest. Long before, the West had, through its philosophical activity, already introduced a principle for the dissolution of wholes, leaving the individual to some subjectivist presumption, I know not what, that made collective syntheses most unlikely. Socialism arose on these ruins, fortunately, but that good fortune is still problematic, for collectivism, perhaps out of Western atavism, has difficulty reuniting the human things in a larger synthesis—as people like Garaudy and the great Russian protesters are no doubt aware.* The thought of a great many Quebec Marxists is yet another example of this, a sectarian thought that, on the whole, is as limited in its humanism as in its politics—as marked by its philosophical thoughtlessness as by its practical incompetence (this latter somewhat surprising in a movement devoted to political action). But capitalism eliminates even the need to rebuild, to the extent that it distributes its material products.

Nothing can ever do more than capitalist materialism to atomize the human race, because [in the triumph of capitalism] the individual's relations to things of immediate usefulness will have swallowed up all his other relationships. Through the attractiveness of the objects it spreads throughout the world, capitalism prepares its own ground, razing the obstacles it faces, as in germ warfare, destroying the recuperative powers of a humanity stricken with indifference, unconcern for politics, and forgetfulness.

As a nation, clearly, we have formidable enemies. From within, capitalism is exerting a deleterious influence on us, as I have just said, and it is doing so all on its own, without anyone's having thought much about it. Moreover, it is directing a precise, considered, and resolute strategy against us from the outside.

III

In America capitalism is at present the vehicle of history, and, in modern circumstances, history has acquired an unprecedented power at the very time when it was surrounding us. We had paid little attention to what was happening. Suddenly the opposing forces were there, at a moment when we ourselves had forgotten the nation. In a period of thirty years we took on Western scepticism and capitalist materialism, traversing two centuries of history in a flash. This time was far too short, given the enormity of these changes, for us to develop anything to put in the place of what was being destroyed with such catastrophic speed. We are one of the few Western countries in which the liquidation of the past was so rapid as to prevent the assimilation of new experiences and the maturing of replacement values. We have scarcely had the time to recall, even briefly, such former realities as the nation, realities that the precipitous movement of history has not erased and that, objectively, subsist. But in our modern revolution, the novelties attracted so much attention that everything that was not new disappeared into a shadowy realm where it seemed only a memory. This effect was all the more disastrous as the revolution we were undergoing caused the disappearance of more than half of our culture: the religion that had contained our conception of the world, our morality and our spirituality, in which every aspect of our existence was reflected. Although obviously important to consider, the question now is not the objective worth of this culture; the important thing is that once there was a culture, and now it has almost disappeared. . . .

IV

Our situation resembles that of a man who has lost his home in some disaster.

He sits outside in the midst of the furniture strewn about on the ground. A curious people, who likewise lost their religion in the space of a day, without struggle or heartbreak, the way one might forget about old letters already lost in the attic. A people exposed, with no possessions, not even a roof over their heads. History pulled them off their farms and out of their homes. They had no real political property. They had something else. Their country had existed as long as they maintained it in their homes, on adjoining strips of land, in parishes that had names. Yet history has seen to it that this country is now nothing more, so to speak, than an immense construction site to which a name had to be given, one that formerly had no symbolic value—*le Québec*—as if to create a dwelling place in an anonymous city.

Le Québec—a modern notion, not unattractive as a project and a symbol— takes the place of a flesh-and-blood reality that seemed secure only yesterday. Today it is the name of a tomorrow, whereas the land, long divided up and possessed as a heritage, was something present, an immediate political truth that sustained centuries of national existence. These are not the same things, and the difference highlights the precariousness of our present situation. The idea of Quebec, a political country, was formed just as we were losing our real property, our physical country. It was born in the Depression, our first great urban and industrial crisis. (The separatist movement first became visible during those years.) We had begun to mass together in the cities. The idea resurfaced in the 1950s, when the rural exodus had radically reduced the importance of the peasant class. French Canadians had by then almost finished uprooting themselves. They no longer had a homeland, a *patrie*, and even this word fell out of use with the disappearance of the thing itself. The concept of a homeland will be revived only after a political country has been created, just as the past will speak to us again only when we start building a national future.

(I should warn the reader here that the following pages will be judged grim and gloomy. I am going to attempt to describe a situation that, at a certain level, is no less dark. I warn the reader that in order to examine one particular truth I shall be obliged to isolate it from the rest, rather the way a scientist studying an object focuses his attention on certain aspects of it and temporarily disregards others. During this whole operation, therefore, I shall ignore almost completely another facet of reality, namely, the nationalist rebirth of the Québécois. In any case, the vigour of this renaissance in part depends on how penetrating an insight we can attain into our present situation, about which the least that can be said is that it does not guarantee us a future.)

No past, no homeland—these are gaping holes in our language and our feelings. What reality vanished, that its absence could thus stop the flow of a certain speech? The fragility of our political as well as our religious culture must have been great indeed. Had this double culture been slowly withering away as a result of the situation that made our history, for several generations past, something no longer in our charge? Suddenly we no longer remembered even the words. Patriotism, a living awareness of the past, the heartfelt words to express them, do not derive their power from any mere sentimentality. Nor do they receive their energy from the ancient hearths of history. They depend on the energy of the present. Only the value of the present can revive the value of the past, and the opposite is hardly ever the case. . . .

That there should be so little relation between the fact, on the one hand, of constituting the population of a country, and, on the other, the feeling which that fact normally entails, namely, the feeling of also constituting the substance of that country, its primordial reality, its determining factor—this is very strange. It is abnormal that we feel we have been placed on the surface of this immense land as a population, and yet have no determining relation to it. Necessarily, our possession of it cannot extend very far. To feel like a stranger in one's own home, like a group of immigrants even in a territory where we are the overwhelming majority; to feel that our language is special and private when it is actually the language of the great mass of the people; to see ourselves as different when we are in fact the norm—these are so many unmistakable signs of a break between ourselves and the truth. . . .

We are a people that cannot be evicted, and yet we deny the truth about ourselves, we absent-mindedly ignore the politics of our massive presence, we do not know how to recognize this reality that any other people, it seems, would grasp spontaneously. To conceive of oneself more or less as a simple demographic datum; to find oneself in a place just because one happens to be there; to be a sort of effect of universal history; a group of sedentary wanderers . . . America happened to give Europe two continents free of charge, and in the extreme north, in lands of ice and relative civil tranquillity, colonists from a few French provinces, over some dozen generations, formed a people; yet this people never settled for itself—through any declaration of possession, neither in its soul, nor in the facts—its title to this country. These, I have no doubt whatever, are so many indications of a fault-line running through the foundations of the last two centuries of our history. Substitutes have continually been found, different ones in different periods, for the political ownership of our country by ourselves. The sense of sovereignty, because it lacked support in most sectors of the reality that must underlie general political and economic ownership, has not grown with our numbers. Other things have taken the place of sovereignty: once we possessed land, now we have business and industry, but as wage-earners. Our possessions have become narrowly material and dangerously apolitical, since capitalism began concentrating our attention on consumption.

Politically, the country does not have sufficient hold on us, and we live in it as if we were weightless. This explains, in part, many aberrations, notably the curious fruits of my generation. *Cité libre* was not so much a cause as an effect. The threesome* left Quebec, so far as I could tell, because of a certain propensity for dispersion, without which they would have devoted themselves to governing Quebec in a progressive nationalist spirit. Federalism, moreover, encourages dispersion, making it difficult for our people to find its centre of gravity. Consider the fragility, the incoherence, the rapid turnover, and the verbalism of several political options that have followed one after another, like fads, over the past ten years—are these not simply secondary effects of the situation of a people astonishingly deprived of true political roots? The fearsome revolutionaries organizing celebrations for an imaginary local revolution are no longer counted. A certain political frivolity—quite compatible with conviction in the defence of one's own political inventions—is now the standard in Quebec. The Three Wise Men gave the first contemporary signs of this trend, and they were succeeded by a certain number of the Left. The most arbitrary ideas rise like smoke from these hot little fires—an effect of the quite irresponsible liberty of a people that does not know [what it should know]. In Quebec, it seems to me, ideas are more arbitrary and unfounded than they are elsewhere. Yet if this people remain ignorant, it is because they do not control the essentials of their own domain; true ownership of their property would be constantly bringing them back to their proper business. But we can reflect on this. Through attention and reason we can try to dominate these shifting games; we need not dance every time the band starts to play. We can attempt to get to the bottom of things. But this cannot be done by haphazardly pasting imported words on our reality—a reality we do not take the time to study in the complexity that one realizes it still has, the moment one stops to consider the history, culture, and psychology of the people, and the multiplicity of facts that must be taken into account if we wish to come up with any half-way plausible idea of what we must do and think with regard to the future. In short, we could strive for a thought and strategy with some balance. At present this is the last concern of the most fashionable militants, who, with a little help from their friends in the secret service, follow the current fashion—which is not to think, but simply to shout. . . .

V

We are the first people dispersed (it is hard to say this briefly), so far as their country is concerned, within their country, where they still live and will continue to live. Our situation appears to be unique and unprecedented. There is no connection between the people and the country, reciprocally constituting both. These people do not make the history of their country. They constitute a demographic reality with the strength of a people, but they stand alone, with no other props. The people and the country live separately and apart. Neither one tightens the springs of political action, and as a result both wind down: such is the price of this divorce. The country slips and at the same time, separately and independently, the people slip as well. The two have destroyed their reciprocal defence systems through this dissociation. Recent years have given us many examples of this double desertion, and their parallelism is striking: the amassing of wealth by the multinationals; the accelerated turning-over of this wealth by our government, without this causing a single important political problem; the unreserved consent of the Provincial State to the economic-political invasion of American power; the people's acquiescence in the spirit of consumption and the general liquidation that accompanies it; the fact that the government of Quebec no longer offers even minimal resistance to the whims of the central government; the deliberate ruin, from within, of the sources of our cultural and political identity, as evident in the lack of instruction in history, literature, and language, or in the defects corrupting such instruction, or in the progressive abandonment of the sense of values it can serve. The decay of our nation both corresponds to and complements that of our country, each drifting in isolation along the river of history. For the first time, the political country is no longer defending itself at all; for the first time, the nation (which, through neo-nationalism, is nevertheless making a great effort to recover) is finding that it not only resembles but has in fact become a people being sucked into a void. But for the first time as well, this double resignation corresponds to a third phenomenon that is particularly marked: namely, an Anglo-Saxon and capitalist determination to push the offensive against us so quickly that before very long it will leave us with no further means of effective resistance. This offensive is no joke. *For the first time, we can speak of an attempt at genocide.*

There you have, then, the three elements that certain formidable forces are striving to use to this end. I have no hesitation in believing in the existence of this goal when I see how the traitors are betraying us this time: their acts point immediately in a direction that confirms their treason. Acts reveal intentions. The nature and implications of a traitor's actions clearly reveal the thought of the forces for whom he is acting, and they clearly reveal the reality of those forces. It is quite obvious that the Bourassa government is practising *a policy of cultural dissolution, constitutional resignation, economic alienation, ideological neutralization, and political disorganization for the Québécois people.*

This coherent and cynical policy has only one explanation: it is devoted body and soul to the service of American imperialism. Please remember one obvious point: imperialism does not fool around. The hidden reality of the master's will is clearly discernible through the actions of his servant. Our government is giving itself away through a policy that in every important area follows a single law directed against the Québécois, their power, their integrity, and their interests. From this one must surely conclude that above the State there is a master whose policy is no less precise—which is in fact the same. The master's goals must be at least as systematic, deliberate, logical, and lucid. There is no effect without a cause. Knowing the people involved, I hasten to add that this government is thinking only of the short run, and adapting as best it can from day to day; but it is following a long-range plan, the outlines of which can only really belong to imperialism, and which the pawns in the game could hardly have invented themselves. Besides, as Québécois, why would they have invented such a scheme themselves, for their more limited ends? The great politics of this undertaking, of which we see close up only the day-to-day details, thus unquestionably reveal the work of an incomparably larger hand. Its shadow falls over everything. Could espionage, for example, so powerfully organized that it follows even the thoughts of individuals, exist merely at the instigation and for the benefit of a little provincial government and its local needs? Obviously not. The writing on the wall is in a hand too large for us to have been its only authors. It belongs to a different order from our own. We are being governed, against ourselves, by a universe. . . .

Genocide. A big word. A word that suggests blood and sacrifices. Quite rightly, we cannot see how a sudden, harrowing tragedy could befall us. There is nothing in our history to remind us of the imminence of extermination by force of arms, as has so often occurred in the history of the world. We know nothing about such events, neither from memory nor from fear. World politics are sombre enough to give rise to terrible fears, experienced even unconsciously, but such is not the case for the political situation that is ours alone. In so far as we concern ourselves only with our own nation, we have never seen the future in such an evil light. The words for these things always taste of rhetoric to us, and I have often noticed that in this country one must use them sparingly, if at all. Armed revolution, seizure of power by force, martyrdom, persecution, heroism—expressions of the greatest antiquity, and elsewhere of the greatest currency—in our reality all are just so many sounds corresponding to nothing but fantasies. Here, revolution can mean a profound change, but one spread out over time; unless the word is misused, it cannot mean a single local event, impending and decisive. We have used the word only once in our real history, and then it was attached to the word 'quiet'. Nothing can be more ridiculous than to hear the word 'revolution' chanted to a people who are absolutely determined not to take up arms—or who, more precisely, do not even dream of doing so. For us, such dramatic words are bombastic.

But the word 'genocide'? It belongs to the same family, and yet I use it. Let me explain. I must show how this modern, painless genocide implies essentially the same consequences as more brutal forms of genocide do, but without the risky methods employed elsewhere, in other circumstances. There is no question, here, of using the military to seize land; it can be purchased. There is no question of suddenly taking away all our political power; the nation can be left to decay simply by distracting and systematically misleading it. In the end, it will no longer recognize itself; this process has already begun. All the nation will have left to hang on to will be a few scraps of power. It will have been so penetrated by the surrounding world that the latter will have acquired a power, both in key areas and in the whole, deriving as much from its establishment as from its original force, which will not have decreased—far from it. There is no question of taking any rights away from us; all that is necessary is to gradually make our rights null and void by the steady progression of various real circumstances working against them. The French language will not be forbidden; but it will become superfluous, out of date, defeated. This is obviously the Bourassa policy. . . .

Thus there is a double strategy whose two terms are complementary. On the one hand, don't push things too much, count on time and the status quo of the façade to allow the progressive disintegration of the nation to be carried out in secret, without stirring up any great increases in solidarity, until the day arrives—and that day is not a century away—when this people will have altered its identity even more, practically forgotten many of the questions it is asking today, and lost sight of numerous means by which it can still effectively attempt to lead its life in accordance with its own will. On the other hand, deliberately activate the forces that all by themselves, unguided, simply through the effect of their mass, work against us; then undermine, dissolve, hinder, and anaesthetize as much as possible, for as long as necessary, our powers of recovery; corrupt and distract national opinion, deprive it, as far as possible, of memory and understanding; pave the road for every invader; give up territory, give away property, mortgage our financial future, dispossess the nation, bring in people from outside; continentalize power as much as possible; 'functionalize' political thought—that is, despiritualize it—in every way; in short, hasten the day when, behind the screen of the conservatism of traditional political institutions and their deceptive continuity, one will have succeeded in doing one thing while professing the opposite: act in such a way that this people becomes unrecognizable, disarmed, disoriented, a futile mass historically, a mere shadow of what it was, ripe at last for yielding, for no advantage and with no resistance, to the pressures of history—a history that from then on will be in the hands of those who have taken everything away from us, including our will and the originality of our thought, which includes social and political thought, for the greater benefit of the America of Ford and Meany. The neat and proper little Bourassa, we can see, is a rather nauseating specimen. He undoubtedly has a certain share in some of these lovely schemes.

It is a question of genocide, that much is clear—a slow-motion genocide, on the instalment plan, hypocritical and efficacious, whose final result, as in death, will be no different from that of a violent history, which in this case will not have taken place. We shall die in our beds, but we shall die all the same. The process is underway, and such is the point to which the enemy intends to carry it; for the process conforms to a broad historical trend that, if it is not vigorously opposed, does in fact lead there.

VI

The true extent of this quiet disaster no one has yet measured. One can easily guess the enemy's motives, but one cannot yet foresee well enough the effects our final defeat will have on us. The motives I have in mind are obviously political, which is a way of saying they are economic, imperialist, and capitalist. But they are also cultural and ethnic, and racism simply waits for the opportunity to destroy in a fit of rage whatever it hates. . . .

The Québécois genocide derives not just from imperialism, which is now clear enough, though at first it did not hit us between the eyes; it also derives from racism, which has been so well hidden for decades past that we were able to believe it extinct. The present situation is thus paradoxical: we are on our guard against something that formerly was scarcely visible, while we no longer have the slightest understanding of something else that in earlier times was on everyone's mind.

Yet incidents are occurring in which the wolf shows the tip of his ear. *French Power* (which is in fact neither powerful nor French in its politics) is finding itself driven back or knocked about here and there, notably in the civil service. The fight over bilingualism (which in any case led nowhere, although it did throw a little dust in the eyes of francophones everywhere) has resumed, but in the opposite direction: a mere semblance [of the real thing] was still too much for the English. Now we have the backlash. Moreover, the English-speaking air-controllers and pilots now exemplify the purest traditions of racism.* Even recent immigrants in Montreal, where they are numerous, judge themselves invested, through participation, with the same powers and the same haughty privileges as the actual *Anglais*, and there is no question that they have begun their resistance, not to say conquest. Thus they firmly refuse to speak French to us here in Quebec. This means that they are already encircling us in a move whose probable completion we should expect to come at a time when, on the whole, the main circumstances will be unfavourable to us. I am truly afraid that when that day comes we shall not manage it well. For every society elevates a man, a group, a party, or a people above its competitors as their master. This struggle is not a conversation among philosophers; it is to a great extent the domain of greed, prejudice, and force; and a people like ourselves—who have long had the vocation, so to speak, of defeat, and yet the insolence to subsist all the same—seems to me somehow set apart from all the rest for injustice, unfair judgements, and a career of endless humiliation, as soon as it is no longer anything but what it is. At the end of this road lies the shame that invades a mass of degraded and servile human beings. This psychological dimension is no small matter, even if the treatises on politics hardly mention it—except for the modern works on the victims of colonization whose originality consists in their treatment of this neglected theme.* There will be shame and the culture will dissolve, not just the culture of the past but the actual culture, so to speak, of a true people, a culture inseparable from its reality in the present, a reality that constitutes this people dynamically, from the loss of which the latter cannot recover.

Imperialism and racism thus converge in their efforts to get the upper hand over us. As for racism, it will become apparent only gradually, for it is a secretive urge that really shows itself only when everything is ready for its victory, when it has only to bring out into the open its strange reservations, the hatreds it has suppressed out of cowardice. But hidden racism is no less operative from the outset, and we must understand that it is present and active at a time when superficially our apparent culture seems expressly to exclude it. I have no doubt that it haunts those places where we find ourselves opposed by so much suppressed but still active violence. Is there anyone who does not sense that we are really encircled? . . .

But all this does not stop some geese in the latest brood from augmenting the stock of political nonsense with their latest find, which being the latest is more 'advanced' than all the rest: it seems that we, who feel that a people need not necessarily let itself be proletarianized nationally, and thus in every way, the better to ensure 'the revolution'—a conclusion as grotesque as it is confused—it seems that we are racists! A certain category of definers of the correct line is currently making its presence known by just such judicious pronouncements. One could say that their anathema has come at the right moment: just when the surrounding racism is, for the first time, undertaking operations designed to kill the Québécois people!

We watch these operations as if we were spectators at a show of which we could see only fragments. Journalism lets us glimpse only a few detached images. One would think that our daily life, nothing out of the ordinary, was simply continuing in front of our eyes. Because it lacks perspective, this point of view fools the observer. It shows us things cut up into little episodes, like so many accidental or haphazard events. But there is something radically new in our national life. One fact, which threatens to become the most important of all, follows our arrival in the current of universal history by only a few years. We are not aware of it. At least we have not come to terms with it. What is new is that the major power groups of the continental Right as well as those of the surrounding English-speaking world have arrived most opportunely at the same crossroads we have reached on our own journey; and they have undertaken something never before seen: the clearing of the Quebec crossing that lies before them, on which the nation we are has always constituted an obstacle. They feel the same necessity that we do, but in the opposite direction. Who will control this territory? Who will govern it? Who, in the end, will be sovereign here? . . .

It is obvious that great games follow their own rules. One rule is that the approach of the game's end requires choices that are definitive, complete. In the course of the game, one can lose some advantages and win some, but at the end one either wins or loses the whole thing; one point and the game is over. Now, when it is a game where the question is which side a country will ultimately belong to, one side looks for the means of permanently establishing a nation, while the other seeks the means of effecting a genocide. There is no middle way between these two outcomes, nor, consequently, between these two sets of means, in these ultimate circumstances. Extreme politics—as extreme as the possible outcomes which alone are at issue—are forced on both nationalists and their opponents by the proximity of the game's end and the absolute quality of the stakes, which can no longer be relativized or presented as a matter of degree, as might be the case with a question in the ordinary course of events. There is no extremism in this; rather there are extremes, independent of us and having nothing to do with any radicalism of temperaments. These extremes, unrelated to attitudes, inhere in the event itself. In any case, extremism in attitudes, whether in violence, romantic fantasies, drama, or anything else, works against the antagonist who is weak enough to resort to it. Nationalists and anti-nationalists, we are all making our way towards one or the other of these outcomes, using rather conventional methods. Neither group can choose to do things differently, unless they want to compromise everything. This is what it is so hard to make some frenzied spirits understand. For them, the more one bellows, the more effective one is; the more shocking an idea is, the more obstacles it will overcome. Cunning is the mistress of war; the most subtle intelligence counts for more than half in the arts of war and politics alike.

VII

Faced with the possibility of national collapse and our disappearance as a people, independence will either be attained or it will not be. It will not happen easily, and the odds are against success. People are anxious, questioning, in doubt. Some would like to go into exile; some do it. To borrow a saying from an actress who did leave and now practises her art on the far side of the continent: 'That's it!'

In a quite different sense I repeat my own 'That's it!' There are not two roads between which we can choose quite indifferently, one leading to political sovereignty, the other to a very different state in which our people, who would no longer be a people, would continue existing on its own momentum, flowing henceforth into another universe that could be its own, with no damage and in the fullness of life, which itself would give a fresh start to the individuals who make it up. This is an imaginary vision [*une vue de l'esprit*]. Independence will either be realized or it will not be. It is possible that it may be blocked. It is also possible that we do not want it enough. But in a sense these contradictory possibilities leave me indifferent as problems. We need not stop to consider them, for in fact we have no choice: the failure of the project of independence would be only the beginning of an end that itself would be endless. The tomorrows, in effect, would never end; they would consist of an interminable series of rearguard struggles, individual and collective, shameful ordeals with no future, such that we would have gained nothing, not even peace. We must win once or else always lose. *That's it*. There is no other dilemma.

We do not know what awaits us, since we have never lived it. Besides, we have the promises of the eternal life that for us is in the past. In this respect the impression left by our history is only a bad habit, but it is deeply rooted. The past just gives us the example of a long, quiet train-ride. We were settled in. We have kept intact the mental habits of this state. In a sense, things happened all by themselves, and at the same time they gradually made us into a people. History helped us to build ourselves up, and we had only to let ourselves be carried along by it. That was a very bad school. Up to a certain point, we had nothing to fear. Where would we then have found more dramatic images? Where would we have seen the immense wrong that a twist of fate can inflict on a mass of human beings, causing their historical ruin? These tranquil people do not get agitated. That is understandable. We have never been seriously victimized, even if we had to fight vigorously after the Conquest; but that was a century and a half, if not two centuries ago. We know nothing from experience about being a lost and broken people. That is why a certain element of the Left, who share our ignorance on this subject, boast that they do not care what might happen to the nation. Intellectually, moreover, this Left is pathetically servile, and since their foreign masters waste little time worrying about national or ethnic alienations, passing over them quite arrogantly, the parrots learn nothing at all to repeat from the only teachers they listen to. The reflections of a phonograph are severely limited. But ask a Jew who is concerned about the Jewish condition what ethnic alienation is. Ask the Irish, who have a history. Or, more simply, ask French Canadians in Saint Boniface or Moncton. Better yet, even closer to home, get francophone civil servants in Ottawa to tell you their story; or, if you prefer, French Canadians in the Armed Forces, at least the ones who have not sold out completely, who have not been arse-lickers. There is no racism, there never has been and there never will be. The conclusion is obvious . . .

The truth is that the culture of a people either imposes that people or exposes it. One or the other. The culture of a people, or a group, or a community, their distinctive qualities, their natural solidarity, or simply their biological persistence in a history where they are not wanted, everything that makes them themselves and not like their neighbours, whether it be the language they speak, or their stubbornness, despite everything, in remaining part of the scene, or the fact that they have the particular misfortune of being Jewish, Indian, or even French-Canadian—all these factors, in a condition of inferiority, act as a magnetic pole in relation to everything around them, which acts as the opposing pole and pushes away the former. This makes the people's faults stand out, either those attributed to them or those that have been inculcated in them. These 'inferiors' who wear the badges of deficiency or failure, like the Star of David, are detested, scorned, and constantly put down. How can one think that a dissolution of whatever forces we have left will not result in a defeat that is not temporary but permanent, the essence of which is to make certain communities the everlasting rubbish of history? Against such groups injustice is practised as a kind of sport, something to be enjoyed. No one can make me believe that five million *étranges*, as they used to say in the country, vestiges of a people who used to have an identity, can become nomads of history without suffering as a result. Marked by their origin; exposed to a rejection that, having grown for so long in the past, will bear fearsome fruit; surrounded by the best-equipped rivals, our people will not only feel diminished, but will in fact be so. Will their lot in life be anything other than that which falls impartially to any man beaten by life? I think not. . . .

It would be very wrong to believe that this people will decide to become American overnight, or pure anglophone or anything else that would entirely negate it and yet, paradoxically, preserve our individual faculties, through an historic leap that would allow us to rise again in a new role, with a new personality, in an historical time starting tomorrow. No, there will be no such transposition. The people will carry with them the heavy legacy of their stifled being. There is a law of persistence that holds for the lame as well. There is a law governing the duration of decrepitude that is even less likely to be violated than the law that determines a people's rise to a supreme existence. A people cannot choose between a victory and a defeat that would also be a victory, a different kind of victory. Nor does it have the following choice: between victory and a defeat that would put an end to its career. No, in the case of defeat we must foresee a heart-breaking situation in which a multitude of people would subsist in some vague state of inferiority, without any possible stimulation, a state characterized precisely by its having no end, neither through rebirth nor through extinction. We should take the time to think about this. We will find ourselves facing something formless, amorphous. There will no longer be anything vertical; everything will proceed horizontally. Social purposes [*volontés*] will have been levelled by the advancing continental tide and rendered fruitless by the failure to grasp hold of any political structure; national purposes, obviously, will have fallen into decay, for lack of an object. Each person's goals, for whatever they are worth, will have become highly individual, a trend that will of course be encouraged by the American cultural climate. Yet some are certain that in these conditions, through some miracle, a proletarian revolution will take shape, as heralded by all the words in the red dictionary, terms invented over the past hundred and fifty years; a revolution stirred up by the striking power of slogans, only too many of which may be found in the books describing [the revolutions that] have taken place among peoples who were literally starving to death. Now, it is a very simple matter to observe that no revolution—nor even any noteworthy undertaking, nor even the beginnings of any revolution or noteworthy undertaking—has ever occurred among people who were not integrated nationally either in their goals or in the facts. This, moreover, is why the capitalists take such good care of Canada and Canadian federalism: this country is not a country. To say all this is not to be dishonest or disloyal to socialism; it is simply to state established facts. . . .

The national question [by contrast] can stand on its own. And if one is of my opinion, one will not sacrifice our people on the altar of class struggle, exposing the one for the supposed benefit of the other, for in these conditions the altar would be one on which everything else would be burned at the same time: the nation as well as all the other factors that make Quebec different from America, our national trade unions different from American trade unions, our social thought different from that of the continent, and that also ensure that a more or less restive colony is not the empire but, on the contrary, an obstacle to it. . . .

Nationality is more than nationality; it makes more than a people. In large measure, an indispensable measure, it makes men. The great difference between a French Canadian and a Swede or a Chilean or a Frenchman or a German is not his inborn character—far from it—but his acquired character, which largely depends on the integrity of his nation. Give me a single example of a revolution that did not ennoble the nation concerned. No such example exists. The only time in the past century when we took the trouble of temporarily pulling ourselves together, it was in the name of national progress, and everyone knows the energies that were liberated then. Yet some have the remarkable insight, and no less remarkable good sense, to maintain that there would be no disadvantage in abandoning from the start the superiority that comes from belonging to ourselves; or else they practise the kind of politics that, directly or indirectly, compromises that advantage.

To be right, we are supposed to reason as they do. In vain would I declare a truth with which I am deeply concerned, namely, that capitalism is a horror, that it must disappear, and that it will in any case disappear (though not tomorrow). I would have to do as they do and proclaim a revolution for which the foundations they presuppose have not even been laid. In addition, I would have to compromise this people to which I belong, to the detriment of this people and the benefit of the empire. That is not the way one works. One must learn to work.

At present, the important thing is to succeed in putting the government of the nation in the hands of the *indépendantistes* and attaining the specific goals of independence.

VIII

I would like to express a few other ideas that are perhaps even closer to my view of things. Basically, I will never admit to any decline of the human race; still less to that of a people on whose faces diminution is already visible. I do not see why I should not reject immediately, without asking myself a single question, the diminution to which history seems to have destined the people that are my own. But today one could say that we receive what passes for higher education without undergoing a far more necessary schooling in a primary truth, not at all academic, that we learn from those who need us as we need them. It appears that this generation is thinking and acting without ever having loved anything or anyone. For a man fairly well protected from what is arbitrary and mechanical in most ideas, a hundred bonds already exist before he even begins to think. These bonds tell him imperatively a large part of what he must defend. It was probably this that Camus had in mind when he said that if he had to choose between justice and his mother, he would choose his mother.* Many of the things in this world that we must love, as well as the duties bound to that love, are already given, existentially. Study and philosophy, although they are essential, always threaten to denature us, especially when ideas enter into our mores and practices, becoming living examples with powerful capacities for influence. As far as nationalism is concerned, my *Cité* *libre* period was in part the result of such intellectual artifices. I no longer knew certain things that cannot be learned through speculation, and I had forgotten my country. Beneath the reasons I can cite for taking the side of my country lie others as well. Unlike the former, these cannot be disputed, since they result from inclination and are in a way absolute. What sort of reasoning might be set against someone who decides to help a person in need? I am under no obligation to justify my engagement in a true service. In the case of defending one's homeland, moreover, our era is constantly showing us how well such service answers both the spontaneous desires of the heart and political exigencies. More and more, we see minorities, or colonized peoples, or categories of human beings dominated by certain regimes, or others suffering from cultural dehumanization, defending their liberty and wholeness out of necessity—directly, without any elaborate justifications—because man naturally wants his primary good, and that is all there is to it. At this time when the powers exercised by economic and political empires are being extended out of all proportion, such an affirmation of life needs no justification: it is inscribed in humanity. Virtually everywhere, the striving for liberty is characterized by this quality of elementary necessity. Rather, it is up to those who make learned negative distinctions in this area to offer some explanations. More and more in the world—and this is a sign of the times—we are witnessing a phenomenon whose forms may be many, but whose sources are clear: human beings are fleeing the Machine. Reasoned reasons only come later, in a subsequent state of more articulate consciousness.

I am a nationalist and an *indépendantiste*, basically, for one very simple reason. I am taking charge, as far as I can, as a private individual, of several millions of human beings who are threatened. I do not consult oracles. I do not first ask myself if the choice I am making conforms to dialectical reason. I do not plot graphs, and besides, I might as well admit that I have not the faintest idea what a graph is. All I know is that there is no reason strong enough to forbid someone's standing up for a single human being, specifically the one he has chosen to help. Now, it happens that I do not want to see my compatriots, my world, living in state of humiliation I foresee only too clearly. There is a reason, truly unquestionable, that supports the choice to protect a human being's integrity. If need be, this reason would suffice for me. We may see that it is also, I do not say the best, but the only one that meets the particular menace of our age, in every latitude—the menace of the automatism of history, today's and tomorrow's, and of the greedy, blind, impersonal, cynical perverted, and frightening technocratic, totalitarian imperialist mechanism. It is the mission of weakness to hold firm before this force. This requires a great deal of intelligence. In the Quebec situation, where is the resistance? It is not to be found in any war or mythical revolution. For the moment, it is in the nation and in the movement that allows us to hope it will survive. The success we anticipate is not guaranteed, obviously, but nothing is guaranteed. We must find our direction with difficulty, without preconceived ideas, in a place full of traps. Politics are difficult because they are so uncertain. . . .

GEORGE GRANT

Any study of Canadian political thought must include leisurely reflection on the strengths and weaknesses of Lament for a Nation, *the most influential book by our most interesting thinker. An anthology can do no more than provide some raw materials for such reflection. Here, therefore, it must suffice to point out that the first part of Grant's* Lament, *ostensibly a 'Defence of Mr Diefenbaker', is really a defence of Diefenbaker's Minister of External Affairs, Howard Green, because of his commitment to disarmament and the United Nations, while the second part, the attack on the Liberals, chastises King, St Laurent, and Pearson because their policies promoted the universal and homogenous state, which Grant (following Heidegger and Strauss) thinks will be a tyranny. What Grant means by a tyranny is a political order destructive of human excellence. The two main forms of human vice that he finds characteristic of modern times are clarified in the following selections. The first is a chapter from* Time as History, *a series of lectures published in 1969; the second is from an essay published in 1979.*

Teaching What Nietzsche Taught

I

In the last section of *Thus Spoke Zarathustra*, Nietzsche wrote : 'The hour in which I tremble and in which I freeze; the hour which demands and demands and goes on always demanding: "Who has enough courage for that, who deserve to be the masters of the earth?" ' In the eighty years since Nietzsche stopped writing, the realized fruits of that drive to mastery are pressed upon us in every day of our lives. Capabilities of mastery over human and non-human beings proliferate, along with reactions by both against that mastering. The historical sense comes from the same intellectual matrix as does the drive to mastery. We have been taught to recognize as illusion the old belief that our purposes are ingrained and sustained in the nature of things. Mastery comes at the same time as the recognition that horizons are only horizons. Most men, when they face that their purposes are not cosmically sustained, find that a darkness falls upon their wills. This is the crisis of the modern world to Nietzsche. The capabilities for mastery present men with a more pressing need of wisdom than any previous circumstances. Who will deserve to be those masters? Who will be wise enough? What is wisdom when reason cannot teach us of human excellence? What is wisdom when we have been taught by the historical sense the finality of becoming? What is wisdom, when we have overcome the idea of eternity?

Till recently it was assumed that our mastery of the earth would be used to promote the values of freedom, rationality, and equality—that is, the values of social democracy. Social democracy was the highest political wisdom. It was to be the guaranteed culmination of history as progress. But to repeat: for Nietzsche progress was the doctrine which held men when the conception of history in western Christianity had been secularized by modern philosophy and science. Christianity was Platonism for the people. Platonism was the first rationalism. Its identification of rationality, virtue, and happiness was a prodigious affirmation of optimism. This identification was for the few who could reach it in the practice of philosophy. Christianity took this optimism and laid it open to the masses, who could attain it through trust in the creating and redeeming Triune God. It united the identification of reason, virtue, and happiness with the idea of equality, sustained in the fact that all men were created by God and sought by Him in redemption. By this addition of equality, the rationalism was made even more optimistic. In the modern era, that doctrine was secularized: that is, it came to be believed that this uniting of reason and virtue and happiness was not grounded beyond the world in the Kingdom of God, but was coming to be here on earth, in history. By saying that this union was to be realized here on earth, the height of optimism was reached.

In the last part of *Zarathustra* Nietzsche writes: 'The masses blink and say: "We are all equal.—Man is but man, before God—we are all equal." Before God! But now this God has died.' The modern movements which believe in progress towards social democracy assert the equality of all men and a politics based on it. But the same liberal movements have also at their heart that secularism which excludes belief in God. What kind of reason or evidence then sustains the belief that men are equal?

As for the expectations from the progress of knowledge—that is, the belief that freedom will be given its content by men being open to the truths of science and philosophy—Nietzsche asserts that we have come to the end of the age of rational man. To repeat: the cause of this end is the ambiguity at the heart of science. For Nietzsche, modern science is the height of modern truthfulness and the centre of our destiny. But it is an ambiguous centre, because in the very name of 'truthfulness'—itself a moral value—it has made plain that the values of rationalism are not cosmically sustained. The natural science of Darwin and Newton has shown us that nature can be understood without the idea of final purpose. In that understanding, nature appears to us as indifferent to moral good and evil. We can control nature; but it does not sustain virtue. As for the sciences of man, they have shown us that reason is only an instrument and cannot teach us how it is best to live. In openness to science we learn that nature is morally indifferent, and that reason is simply an instrument.

At the end of the era of 'rational' man, the public world will be dominated by two types, whom Nietzsche calls the last men and the nihilists. The last men are those who have inherited the ideas of happiness and equality from the doctrine of progress. But because this happiness is to be realized by all men, the conception of its content has to be shrunk to fit what can be realized by all. The sights for human fulfilment have to be lowered. Happiness can be achieved, but only at the cost of emasculating men of all potentialities for nobility and greatness. The last men will gradually come to be the majority in any realized technical society. Nietzsche's description of these last men in *Zarathustra* has perhaps more meaning in us and for us than it had for his contemporaries who read it in 1883. 'They have their little pleasure for the day and their little pleasure for the night: but they respect health. "We have discovered happiness", say the last men and blink.' Or again, 'A little poison now and then: that produces pleasant dreams. And a lot of poison at last, for a pleasant death.' Or again, 'Formerly all the world was mad, say the most acute of the last men and blink. They are clever and know everything that has ever happened: so there is no end to their mockery. They still quarrel, but they soon make up—otherwise they might have indigestion'—our intellectuals. The central fact about the last men is that they cannot despise themselves. Because they cannot despise themselves, they cannot rise above a petty view of happiness. They can thus inoculate themselves against the abyss of existing. They are the *last* men because they have inherited rationalism only in its last and decadent form. They think they have emancipated themselves from Christianity; in fact they are the products of Christianity in its secularized form. They will be the growing majority in the northern hemisphere as the modern age unfolds. The little they ask of life (only entertainment and comfort) will give them endurance. This is the price the race has to pay for overcoming two millennia of Christianity.

The end of rational man brings forth not only last men but nihilists. These are those who understand that they can know nothing about what is good to will. Because of the historical sense, they know that all values are relative and man-made; the highest values of the past have devaluated themselves. Men have no given content for their willing. But because men are wills, the strong cannot give up willing.[1] Men would rather will nothing than have nothing to will. Nietzsche clearly has more sympathy for the nihilists than for the last men, because the former put truthfulness above the debased vision of happiness, and in this hold on to the negative side of human greatness. But he has little doubt of the violence and cataclysms which will come forth from men who would rather will nothing than have nothing to will. They will be resolute in their will to mastery, but they cannot know what that mastery is for. The violence of their mastery over human and non-human beings will be without end. In the 1880s he looked ahead to that age of world wars and continued upheavals which most of us in this century have tried to endure.

In parenthesis: if we look at the crises of the modern world through Nietzsche's eyes, and see them above all as the end of two millennia of rational man, we can see that those crises have come to North America later than to Europe. But now that they have come, they are here with intensity. The optimism of rational man was sustained for us in the expectations of the pioneering moment. It was also sustained by the fact that among most of our population our identification of virtue and happiness took the earlier and more virile form which came out of Biblical religion, rather than the soft definition of that identification in the liberalisms of the last men. Among the early majority this was above all Protestant; but its virility was sustained in the Catholicism and Judaism of the later immigrants. In the fresh innocence of North America these religions maintained their force, albeit in primitive form, longer than they did in the more sophisticated Europe. Because the identification of virtue and reason and happiness in these religions was not altogether immanent in its expectations, it held back many North Americans for longer from that banal view of happiness which is the mark of mass liberalism. As these religions provided some protection from the historical sense, they still provided horizons for our willing which saved the resolute from nihilism. At the height of our present imperial destiny, the crisis of the end of modern rationalism falls upon us ineluctably. In Nietzsche's words: 'the wasteland grows'. The last men and the nihilists are everywhere in North America.

For Nietzsche, there is no possibility of returning to the greatness and glory of pre-rational times, to the age of myth and cult. The highest vision of what men have yet been was unfolded in the early Greek tragedies. Here was laid forth publicly and in ordered form the ecstasy of the suffering and knowing encounter of the noblest men and women with the chaos of existing. The rationalism of Socrates smoothed away that encounter by proclaiming the primacy of the idea of the Good, and in so doing deprived men of the possibility of their greatest height. The optimism of philosophy destroyed the ecstatic nobility which had been expressed in the tragedies. But now that rationalism has dug its own grave through the truthfulness of science, there is no returning to that earlier height. The heritage of rationalism remains in its very overcoming. Its practical heritage is that through technique and experimental science men are becoming the masters of the earth. Its theoretical heritage is that men now know that nature is indifferent to their purposes and that they create their own values. Therefore the question for our species is: can we reach a new height which takes into itself not only the ecstasy of a noble encounter with chaos, but also the results of the long history of rationalism? Neither the nihilists nor the last men deserve to be masters of the earth. The nihilists only go on willing for the sake of willing. They assuage their restlessness by involvement in mastery for its own sake. They are unable to use their mastery for joy. The last men simply use the fruits of technique for the bored pursuit of their trivial vision of happiness. The question is whether there can be men who transcend the alternatives of being nihilists or last men; who know that they are the creators of their own values, but bring forth from that creation in the face of chaos a joy in their willing which will make them deserving of being masters of the earth.

It must be said that for Nietzsche this crisis is authentic, because there is no necessity about its outcome. This may be compared with another influential account of the modern crisis, that of Marx. For Marx also, industrial society is at a turning point. The achievements of capitalism have led to the stage where this form of social organization must now be transcended. For Marx, as for Nietzsche, this is a situation which produces widespread and terrible human suffering. But according to Marx, if we have knowledge of the forces now at work, we can know that the crisis will inevitably be transcended. In the midst of the suffering we have that enormous consolation and spur to effort. A net of inevitable success is put under the performers, so that their actions are guaranteed from the ultimate anguish. For Nietzsche there is no such net. The historical sense shows us that we must take seriously the idea that we create history, and that therefore there can be no inevitable outcome. We do not know whether beings will appear who will so overcome themselves that they will deserve to be masters of the earth; we do not know whether the last men will be in charge for centuries and centuries. To repeat: for Nietzsche the net of inevitable progress is a shallow secular form of the belief in God. Just as the historical sense has killed God, it kills the secular descendants of that belief. Indeed the first step in man's self-overcoming is to know that all such nets over chaos are simply comforting illusions. The historical sense teaches us that what happens now and what will happen is radically contingent. (I may be allowed to note that the absence of all nets is a truth that those of us who trust in God must affirm.)

Unfortunately, one of the key words in Nietzsche's answer has been killed amongst us by strangely diverse associations. Most of us on this continent grew up with the comic strips and film cartoons in which the bespectacled newspaper man, Clark Kent, turned into 'Superman', who went zooming through the skies destroying gangsters and enemies of his country. To use the word 'superman' is to think that image—an image from the comics and the Saturday matinee filled with screaming children and popcorn.

The other association is a debased one. The word 'superman' was used by the propagandists of the most disgusting political regime that the western world has yet produced. The Nazis took over this part of Nietzsche's language, so that when people of my generation hear the word 'superman' as used about reality, we conjure up images of those arrogant and sadistic maniacs sweeping their violence and vulgarity over Europe. Because of those events, the word 'superman' has become revolting. Of course, without doubt, Nietzsche would have seen in the Nazis his worst predictions of nihilism and vulgarity combined—predictions which he made particularly about his own people—the Germans.

Indeed as I have watched Leni Riefenstahl's famous documentaries of the Nazi era, particularly her shots of Hitler speaking, I have been aware in Hitler of just that spirit which Nietzsche believes to be the very curse of mankind—the spirit of revenge (that which in Nietzsche's language above all holds back men from becoming 'supermen'—*übermensch*). As one watches Hitler speaking one sees that his effectiveness came from the uniting of his own hysterical self-pity with the same feelings present in his German audience. Life has been a field of pain and defeat for him both privately and publicly, as it has been for the Germans, and he summons up their *ressentiment*. In a political context, Hitler made specific demands; but behind anything specific one feels a demand more universal—a demand for unlimited revenge. This is what Nietzsche says is the very basis for the violence of nihilism. Indeed in his language, the supermen will be those who have overcome in themselves any desire for revenge. As he writes in *Zarathustra*: 'That man may be delivered from revenge: that is for me the bridge to the highest hope.'

(To make a parenthesis about Leni Riefenstahl's films: many people these days seem to place enormous confidence in the electronic media. They see in them the way by which enlightenment can be brought to the majority. Electronic enlightenment will overcome the old anal rationality of print and speech. Those who think this way should ponder these films of Leni Riefenstahl. The art of the film was there used in all its stunning magic. But these films were made to persuade men of the glory of the basest of political regimes. Indeed to watch them is to be presented with Nietzsche's very question: who deserves to be the master of electronics? The last men and nihilists from contemporary television journalism and politics? One would be happier about the McLuhanite cult,* if its members dealt with such questions.)

Both because of the comic strip and because of the Nazis, the word superman cannot be used with seriousness amongst us. But that fact must not prevent us from looking at Nietzsche's question. Who is wise enough for this moment in history? Nietzsche takes the historical sense for granted. He does not speak of the race of men as if they had a nature which is unchanging through the course of history. Man is a bridge between the beasts and something higher than man. As he writes in *Beyond Good and Evil*: 'Man is the as yet undetermined animal.' It is now open to man in the future to become nobler than his past, so that some will come to deserve the present destiny of being masters of the planet. For this deserving, the essential condition is that men overcome the spirit of revenge. Therefore if one wants to understand what Nietzsche means by history, one must look at what he means by revenge.

Desire for revenge has come from the very conditions of human existence. As self-conscious animals men have lived in the chaotic world, experiencing as anguish all its accidents, its terrors, and its purposelessness. Most men have lived in a world in which our instincts are thwarted and twisted from the very moment we enter it. Our wills are continually broken on the wheel of the chaos which is the world. Our response to that brokenness is the will to revenge against others, against ourselves, against the very condition of time itself. 'It is the body which has despaired of the body.' From that despair comes forth the spirit of revenge. The more botched and bungled our instincts become in the vicissitudes of existing, the greater our will to revenge on what has been done us.

Nietzsche was the first to use consistently that description of man which Freud later employed for psycho-analysis. The elemental in man is an 'it'; that is an impersonal chaos of instincts out of which comes forth as epiphenomena, reason and morality. It was once believed that the irrational in man existed to be subordinated to the rational. In Nietzsche this is denied. This does not, however, free us from thinking. It simply means that thinking is carried on over an abyss which it can never fathom. Philosophy is simply the highest form of 'the will to power'. As he writes in *Beyond Good and Evil*: 'There is a point in every philosophy when the philospher's "conviction" appears on the stage—or to use the language of an ancient Mystery:

> Adventavit asinus,
> Pulcher et fortissimus.'*

Nietzsche enucleates with black wit the many forms of revenge which make up for him the very substance of history. In the earliest societies, the victory of the strong over the weak is the victory of those with vigorous instincts over the majority of weak instinct. The weak bring forth from their condition of enslavement the spirit of revenge. The rules of justice come from that spirit. The creditor takes a quantum of revenge from the debtor who cannot meet his debts. As the infliction of pain gives pleasure, the creditor finds his satisfaction in that punishment. In the West, the greatest achievement of the spirit of revenge has been Christianity. In it, the priests, who are those among the ruling classes whose instincts have been most botched and bungled, and therefore desire the greatest revenge, get power by uniting with the weak majority against the strong. They produce a morality which exalts such virtues as altruism, humility, equality, etc. Those virtues necessary anyway for the weak majority are guaranteed to get them revenge, in the next world, if not in this. The priests teach an ascetic morality, telling men that the instincts should be repressed. In the name of this rationalist control, those of strong and noble instinct are held back from their proper authority for the sake of the weak and bungled majority.

Indeed, the will to revenge is turned inward by men against themselves. They punish themselves, not only others. The greed of the self teaches us that if we put aside full living in the name of humility and altruism and asceticism, we will gain an infinite extension of our wills in eternity. Those who transpose their will from this world to the beyond are expressing the most intense will to power from out of their desire for revenge at not being able to express it in this life. For Nietzsche the very idea of transcendence—that time is enfolded in eternity—is produced out of the spirit of revenge by those who because of their broken instincts are impotent to live in the world, and in their self-pity extrapolate to a non-existent perfection in which their failures will be made good. In the language I have used in these lectures, any belief that time cannot be identified with history comes from the broken instincts of men who cannot live greatly in history. For Nietzsche, Plato is the philosophic enemy, because he conceives time as an image, 'the moving image of eternity'. The reality of the 'idea' was invented by Socrates, who wanted to overcome tragedy and who therefore posited that the immediate world was just the moving image of a real eternity. The greatness of Socrates was the greatness of his revenge on tragedy. But philosophy only provided revenge for the few. In Christianity the will to revenge is taken up into a transcendence opened to the majority. As Nietzsche puts it in *The Genealogy of Morals*: 'Then suddenly we come face to face with that paradoxical and ghastly expedient which brought temporary relief to tortured humanity, that most brilliant stroke of Christianity: God's sacrifice of himself for man. God makes himself the ransom for what could not otherwise be ransomed; God alone has power to absolve us of a debt we can no longer discharge; the creditor offers himself as a sacrifice for his debtor out of sheer love (can you believe it) out of love for his debtor.'

Now that Christianity has been secularized, the transcendence of progress has been substituted for the transcendence of God. The spirit of revenge is still at work among the last men and the nihilists. The last men want revenge against anything that is noble and great, against anything that threatens their expectations from triviality. The nihilists want revenge on the fact that they cannot live with joy in the world. Their revenge takes the form of restless violence against any present. As nothingness is always before them, they seek to fill the void by willing for willing's sake. There can be no end to their drive for mastery.

Indeed for Nietzsche revenge arises most deeply in our recognition that all our existing is subject to time's thrall. Everything is enfolded in 'it was', 'it is', 'it will be'. And as we recognize that inescapable temporality in every lived minute, we can will to batter against its inevitable consequences. That is the deepest cause of our revengings. At its simplest, we want revenge against what is present in our present. If we seek to overcome our present by bending our efforts to the building of a future to suit our heart's desire, when that future came we would still be subject to that thrall. At the deepest level, revenge is most engaged against the past. Consciousness always includes within itself 'it was'. Human life would not be possible without some memory. But the will can do nothing about the past. What has happened has happened, and we cannot change it. By the 'it was' of time, Nietzsche means not only our personal past (with its defeats, its enslavements, its tortured instincts), but the past of the race which is opened to us in communal memory, and opened to us as never before by the historical sense. In *Zarathustra* Nietzsche writes: 'To transform every "it was" into "this is what I wanted"'—that alone I could call redemption.' The height is for him *amor fati*. And that love must come out of having grasped into one's consciousness the worst that can be remembered or imagined—the torturing of children and the screams of the innocent.

To deserve to be masters of the earth will be to have overcome the spirit of revenge and therefore to be able to will and create in joy. Nietzsche's image for himself is the convalescent. He is recovering, step by step, from the spirit of revenge. The recovery from that sickness is not simply from the disasters of his own instincts, but the recovery from the long history of revenge in the race. In that history, the greatest revenge against time's 'it was' took the form of belief in the transcendence of a timeless eternity. It pretended to be a redemption of time, but it was in fact an expression of revenge against time. To live on the earth, to be masters of the earth, to deserve to be masters because we can live in joy, requires the act of *amor fati*, held ouside any assertion of timelessness. The love of fate has been asserted in the Greek tragedies, in Plato, and by certain Christians. But this fate was enfolded in a timeless eternity, in an ultimate perfection. For Nietzsche, the achievement of *amor fati* must be outside any such enfoldment. It must be willed in a world where there is no possibility of either an infinite or finite transcendence of becoming or of willing.

For Nietzsche, the possibility of that love of fate is related to his discovery of 'the eternal recurrence of the identical'. This 'discovery' was that as the number of possible combinations of what exists is finite, yet time is infinite; there has already been and will be again an endless recurrence of the present state of affairs, and of every other state possible. As he writes in *Zarathustra*:

> You do not know my abysmal thought— that thought which you could not endure.
> Look at this gateway.—Two paths come together here and no one has ever reached their end.
> This long path behind us goes on for an eternity. And that long path ahead of us—that is another eternity.—
> On the gateway is written its name: 'Moment'.
>
> Must not all things that can run have already run along this path? Must not all things that can happen have already happened, been done, run past?
> And if all things have been here before; what do you think of this moment?
> —Must not this gateway, too, have been here, before?
> And are not all things bound inextricably together in such a way that this moment draws after it all future things? Therefore, draws itself too?
> For all things that can run must also run once again forward along this long path.
> And this slow spider that creeps along in the moonlight, and this moonlight itself and both of us at this gateway whispering together—must we not all have been here before

—and must we not return and run down that other path before us, down that long terrible path—must we not return eternally?
This is what I said and I said it more and more softly: for I was afraid of my own thoughts and reservations.

It is not my business to repeat here all that Nietzsche says about that 'discovery'. It can be found in *Zarathustra* and in his notebooks which have been published posthumously in English under the title *The Will to Power*. Nor is it my task to write here of the objections which have been made against 'the eternal recurrence of the identical'—that is, to discuss the varied thoughts of those who claim that it is not a discovery. However, I can say that in the endurance of that 'discovery' Nietzsche found the possibility of overcoming the spirit of revenge. In that thoughtful enduring was the movement towards the realization of *amor fati*. According to Nietzsche, when men know themselves beyond good and evil, the strong are moved to the violence of an undirected willing of novelty. But from his 'discovery' Nietzsche's nihilism becomes therapeutic, so that he can begin to will novelty in joy. In the recognition of the dominance of time in which no past is past and no future has not yet been and yet in which there is openness to the immediate future—the conception of time as history reaches its height and yet is not hypostasized into a comforting horizon.

II

There is no escape from reading Nietzsche if one would understand modernity. Some part of his whole meets us whenever we listen to what our contemporaries are saying when they speak as moderns. The words come forth from those who have never heard of him, and from those who could not concentrate sufficiently to read philosophy seriously. A hundred years ago Nietzsche first spoke what is now explicit in western modernity. When we speak of morality as concerned with 'values', of politics in the language of sheer 'decision', of artists as 'creative', of 'quality of life' as praise and excuse for the manifold forms of human engineering, we are using the language first systematically thought by Nietzsche. At the political level his thought appears appropriately among the atheists of the right; but equally (if less appropriately) it is on the lips of the atheists of the left. When we speak of our universities beyond the sphere of exact scientific technologies, what could better express the general ethos than Nietzsche's remark: 'Perhaps I have experience of nothing else but that art is worth more than truth.' And of course radical historicism is everywhere in our intellectual life. It even begins to penetrate the self-articulation of the mathematicised sciences.

In such circumstances there is need to read Nietzsche and perhaps to teach him. One must read him as the great clarion of the modern, conscious of itself. If the question of reading Nietzsche is inescapable, the question of whether and how and to whom he should be taught is a more complex matter. It is particularly difficult for somebody such as myself, who in political philosophy is above all a lover of Plato within Christianity. The following story is relevant. A man with philosophic eros was recently asked the rather silly question: 'At what period of time would you best like to have lived?' He answered that he was lucky to have lived in the present period, because the most comprehensive and deepest account of the whole has been given us by Plato, and the most comprehensive criticism of that account has been given us by Nietzsche. In the light of that criticism, one can the better understand the depth of Platonic teaching. That is, one should teach Nietzsche as the great critic of Plato. The difficulty of reading Plato today is that one is likely to read him through the eyes of some school of modern philosophy, and this can blind one. For example, many moderns have in the last century and a half followed Kant's remark in the first Critique that he was combining an Epicurean science with a Platonic account of morality. With such spectacles how much of Plato must be excluded. The great advantage of Nietzsche is that such strange combinations are not present. His criticism of Plato is root and branch. In the light of it the modern student may break through to what the Platonic teaching is in itself.

Nevertheless, the teacher who is within the philosophic and religious tradition, and who also takes upon himself the grave responsibility of teaching Nietzsche, must do so within an explicit understanding with those he teaches that he rejects Nietzsche's doctrine. If I were not afraid of being taken as an innocent dogmatist, I would have written that one should teach Nietzsche within the understanding that he is a teacher of evil. The justification of such a harsh position is difficult, particularly in universities such as ours in which liberalism has become little more than the pursuit of 'value-free' scholarship. This harsh position is clearly not 'value-free'. Moreover, such a position is ambiguous in the light of the fact that I do not find myself able to answer comprehensively the genius who was the greatest critic of Plato. But there is no need to excuse myself. Who has been able to give a refutation of radical historicism that is able to convince our wisest scientific and scholarly friends?

Without such capability, what is it to say that one should teach within the rejection of Nietzsche? Is not this the very denial of that openness to the whole which is the fundamental mark of the philosophic enterprise? Is it not to fall back into that dogmatic closedness which is one form of enmity to philosophy? I will attempt to answer that by discussing Nietzsche's teaching concerning justice. As a political philosopher within Christianity, my willingness to teach Nietzsche within an understanding of rejection, while at the same time I am not capable of the complete refutation of his historicism, turns around my inability to accept as true his account of justice. At least we need have no doubt as to what Nietzsche's conception of justice is, and the consequences of accepting it.

A caveat is necessary at this point in the argument. I am not making the mistake that is prevalent in much condemnation of Nietzsche—namely that there is no place for justice in his doctrine. His teaching about justice is at the very core of what he is saying. To understand it is as fundamental as to understand the teaching concerning 'the eternal recurrence of the identical'. This is said unequivocally in a fragment written in 1885, towards the end of his life as a writer.

> It happened late that I came upon what up to that time had been totally missing, namely justice. What is justice and is it possible? If it should not be possible, how would life be supportable? This is what I increasingly asked myself. Above

all it filled me with anguish to find, when I delved into myself, only violent passions, only private perspectives, only lack of reflection about this matter. What I found in myself lacked the very primary conditions for justice.[2]

This quotation does not give content to Nietzsche's conception of justice. Its nature appears in two quotations from the unpublished fragments of 1884. 'Justice as function of a power with all encircling vision, which sees beyond the little perspectives of good and evil, and so has a wider advantage, having the aim of maintaining something which is more than this or that person.' Or again: 'Justice as the building, rejecting, annihilating way of thought which proceeds from the appraisement of value: highest representative of life itself.'[3]

What is the account of justice therein given? What is it to see 'beyond the little perspectives of good and evil'; to maintain 'something which is more than this or that person'? What is 'the building, rejecting, annihilating way of thought'? What is being said here about the nature of justice would require above all an exposition of why the superman, when he is able to think the eternal recurrence of the identical, will be the only noble ruler for a technological age, and what he must be ready to do to 'the last men' who will have to be ruled. That exposition cannot be given in the space of an article. Suffice it to speak popularly: what is given in these quotations is an account of justice as the human creating of quality of life. And is it not clear by now what are the actions which follow from such an account? It was not accidental that Nietzsche should write of 'the merciless extinction' of large masses in the name of justice, or that he should have thought 'eugenical experimentation' necessary to the highest modern justice. And in thinking of these consequences, one should not concentrate alone on their occurrence during the worst German regime, which was luckily beaten in battle. One should relate them to what is happening in the present western regimes. We all know that mass foeticide is taking place in our societies. We all should know the details of eugenical experimentation which are taking place in all the leading universities of the western world. After all, many of us are colleagues in those universities. We should be clear that the language used to justify such activities is the language of the human creating of quality of life, beyond the little perspectives of good and evil.

One must pass beyond an appeal to immediate consequences in order to state what is being accepted with Nietzsche's historicist account of justice. What does a proper conception of justice demand from us in our dealings with others? Clearly there are differences here between the greatest ancient and modern philosophers. The tradition of political thought originating in Rousseau and finding different fulfilments in Kant and Hegel demands a more substantive equality than is asked in Plato or Aristotle. What Hegel said about the influence of Christianity towards that change is indubitably true. But the difference between the ancients and the moderns as to what is due to all human beings should not lead us to doubt that in rationalist traditions, whether ancient or modern, something at least is due to all others, whether we define them as rational souls or rational subjects. Whatever may be given in Plato's attack on democracy in his *Republic*, it is certainly not that for some human beings nothing is due. Indeed to understand Plato's account of justice, we must remember the relation in his thought between justice and the mathematical conception of equality.

In Nietzsche's conception of justice there are other human beings to whom nothing is due—other than extermination. The human creating of quality of life beyond the little perspectives of good and evil by a building, rejecting, annihilating way of thought is the statement that politics is the technology of making the human race greater than it has yet been. In that artistic accomplishment those of our fellows who stand in the way of that quality can be exterminated or simply enslaved. There is nothing intrinsic in all others that puts any given limit on what we may do to them in the name of that great enterprise. Human beings are so unequal in quality that to some of them no due is owed. What gives meaning in the face of historicism is that willed potentiality is higher than any actuality. Putting aside the petty perspectives of good and evil means that there is nothing belonging to all human beings which need limit the building of the future. Oblivion of eternity is here not a liberal-aesthetic stance, which still allows men to support regimes the principles of which came from those who had affirmed eternity; oblivion of eternity here realises itself politically. One should not flirt with Nietzsche as a flirtation for the purposes of this or that area of science or scholarship, but teach him in the full recognition that his thought presages the conception of justice which more and more unveils itself in the technological west.

AUTHOR'S NOTES

1 Who ever more agreed with St Augustine's dictum 'Quid sumus nisi voluntates?'
2 *Nietzsche Werke* (Naumann, Leipzig, 1904), XIV, 385. This translation and the ones that follow are my poor own. How does one translate properly this polysyllabic language of compounds, into a language which has reached its greatest heights in the use of the monosyllable? How does one not lose both the substance and rhetoric of that immoderate stylist?
3 Nietzsche, *op. cit. Nachgelassene Fragmente*, 1884.

Editor's Notes and Sources

MGR JOSEPH-OCTAVE PLESSIS

'Sermon on Nelson's Victory at Aboukir': from Yvon-André Lacroix, 'Un Français et un Anglais dénoncent la révolution française: deux textes anciens de 1793 et 1799', *Écrits du Canada français*, 30 (1970), 231–54.

Page 2

* Nelson (1758–1805), Great Britain's greatest naval hero, destroyed the French fleet anchored in Aboukir Bay, near Alexandria, at the beginning of August 1798. This naval success (the Battle of the Nile) restored Britain's prestige in the Mediterranean and prepared the way for her victory on land three years later. The French army was in Egypt as the result of a plan hatched earlier in the year by Napoleon, at 28 already the hero of the Italian campaigns. He had argued against a projected invasion of Great Britain and recommended that instead France strike against Britain's eastern empire through Egypt. The Directory accepted this advice and put him in charge of a huge expeditionary force that sailed from Toulon in May. After capturing Malta, it moved on to Egypt, landing at Aboukir at the beginning of July. On 24 July, after crushing the Mamelukes in the Battle of the Pyramids, Napoleon entered Cairo.

† Psalms 115:14, 19 (Douay Bible).

Page 5

* Pius VI (1717–99), who became Pope in 1775, opposed the Civil Constitution of the Clergy (1790) designed to establish a Gallican or state Church; protested the execution of Louis XVI in 1793; and, despite serious differences with the Hapsburgs, sided with the anti-French coalition. In 1797 Napoleon, after stunning victories in northern Italy, moved against Rome, but before reaching the city concluded a peace (the Treaty of Tolentino) with the Pope that deprived him of Avignon, Venaissin, Bologna, Ferrara, and the Romagna, as well as many other treasures. In 1798 civil unrest led to French occupation of Rome, the proclamation of a republic under the rapacious governorship of Marshal Masséna, and the expulsion of the Pope, who died, a prisoner of the French, in August 1799.

† Psalms 73:10.

° Psalms 73:3.

Page 6

* Psalms 36:25.

† Luke 1:71.

° *Arbres de liberté* were 'trees erected temporarily, or planted, during the Revolution as symbols of liberty and fraternity, and later—following a decree (1794) that one should be planted in every *commune*—to commemorate the constitution of 1793.' *The Concise Oxford Dictionary of French Literature*, ed. Joyce M.H. Reid (Oxford: Oxford University Press, 1976), 21.

Page 7

* Psalms 67:3.

Page 8

* Allusions to the Quebec Act of 1774 and the Constitutional Act of 1791 (see *Documents*

of the Canadian Constitution, ed. W.P.M. Kennedy [Toronto, 1918], 132-6, 207-20).
The former revived the whole body of French civil law based on the *Coutume de Paris*; the latter made a representative Assembly, elected on a broad franchise, part of the government of Lower Canada. French civil law differed from English common law in innumerable details, but one difference was crucial because it later became a source of great practical difficulties. Land had been granted in New France in such a way as to establish a complex system of rights and obligations between those who promoted settlement, the *seigneurs*, and those who actually cleared and farmed the land, the *censitaires* (see Marcel Trudel, *The Seigneurial Regime*, Canadian Historical Assocation Booklet No. 6 [Ottawa, 1956]). The English system of land tenure, 'free and common soccage', was by contrast a simple system of private property in land, better adapted to an increasingly commercial and industrial economy. British policy was to preserve seigneurial tenure where it already existed, in the settled part of the province, but to establish the English system in the Eastern Townships.

THE RIGHT REV. JOHN STRACHAN

'On Church Establishment': excerpts from *A Sermon Preached at York, Upper Canada, Third of July 1825, on the Death of the Late Lord Bishop of Quebec* (Kingston, Macfarlane, 1826), and 'Church Establishment' in *The John Strachan Letter Book: 1812-1834*, ed. George W. Spragge (Toronto: The Ontario Historical Society, 1946), 222-3.

Page 10

* Sections 36–42 of the Constitutional Act of 1791 (see previous note) made provision, through grants of Crown lands, for 'the due and sufficient support and maintenance of the Protestant clergy within the [two] Provinces'. One-seventh of Crown lands were to be set aside for this purpose. In 1819 it was decided that the Church of England should manage these grants in Upper Canada and be the sole beneficiary of their sale or leasing.

Page 13

* In a famous 'review' of this sermon, Egerton Ryerson singled out this passage for particularly virulent attack. Condemning it as 'ungenerous, unfounded and false', he went on to observe: 'The Methodist preachers do not value themselves upon the wealth, virtues, or grandeur of their ancestry; nor do they consider their former occupation an argument against their present employment or usefulness. They have learned that the "venerable" Apostles, were once fishermen; that a Milner could once throw the shuttle; and that a Newton was not ashamed to watch his mother's flock. By these examples, and a hundred more, they feel themselves sufficiently shielded from the envious reflections of a bigotted ecclesiastic. They are likewise charged with "preaching the gospel out of idleness".—Does the Dr claim the attribute of omniscience? Does he know what is in man? How does he know they preach "the gospel out of idleness"? Let the Doctor remember that "with what judgement he judges, he shall be judged" (Matt. 7:2). What does the Doctor call idleness? Not the reading of one or two dry discourses every Sabbath: not the preaching to one congregation, with an annual income of 2 or £300. No; this is hard labour, this is indefatigable industry. . . . Who are they then, that preach the gospel out of idleness? Those indolent covetous men who travel from 2 to 300 miles and preach from 25 to 40 times every month. Those who in addition to this visit from house to house, and teach young and old "repentance towards God and faith in our Lord Jesus Christ" (Acts 20:21). Those who continue this labour year after year, and are elevated with the enormous salary of 25 or £50 per annum; these are the men who preach "the gospel out of idleness".—O bigotry!

thou parent of persecution; O envy! thou fountain of slander; O covetousness! thou god of injustice! would to heaven, ye were banished from the earth!' Egerton Ryerson, *Claims of the Churchmen and Dissenters of Upper Canada Brought to the Test* (Kingston, 1828), 40–1.

Page 16

* Presumably a reference to the select committee of the House of Commons, the 'Canada Committee', appointed in May 1828 to investigate the causes of discontent in Lower Canada and to recommend appropriate remedies. The demands of the Lower Canadian Assembly were presented by John Neilson, Augustin Cuvillier, and Denis Viger. The Committee's report, published in July 1828, generally endorsed the claims of the Assembly and by implication condemned the past policies of the British government and the conduct of the Governor, Lord Dalhousie. See Peter Burroughs, *The Canadian Crisis and British Colonial Policy, 1828–1841* (Toronto, 1972), 28–42.

CANADIAN VOICES OF REFORM AND REVOLT

'Papineau on Constitutional Reform': abridgement of the speech of 10 Jan. 1833 in *La Minerve* (Montreal), 21 Jan. 1833; excerpts in *Papineau: textes choisis*, ed. Fernand Ouellet (Quebec: Les Presses Universitaires Laval, 1958), 47–54.

'Baldwin on Responsible Government': excerpts from the 1836 letter to Lord Glenelg, in *Report of the Public Archives for the Year 1923*, ed. A.G. Doughty (Ottawa, 1924), I, 329–37.

'The Six Counties Address': from *The Vindicator* (Montreal), 31 Oct. 1837. The French text appeared in *La Minerve* (Montreal), 2 Nov. 1837.

'Mackenzie's Draft Constitution': excerpts from *The Constitution* (Toronto), 15 Nov. 1837, reprinted in *A Source-book of Canadian History*, ed. J.H. Stewart Reid, Kenneth McNaught, and Harry S. Crowe (Toronto: Longmans Green and Co., 1959), 90–5.

Page 18

* In the summer of 1832 a cholera epidemic struck Lower Canada, evidently transmitted from the British Isles by impoverished emigrants travelling in overcrowded and unsanitary ships. It killed at least 7,000 people (the equivalent of about 100,000 Quebecers today) and was a source of bitter complaints against the British government and British colonists for many years. Epidemics—there was another in 1834—were among the problems associated with the mother country's policy of alleviating its own difficulties by assisting the mass migration of paupers and vagrants.

Page 19

* Sections IV and VIII of the Quebec Act of 1774 in *Documents*, ed. Kennedy, 133, 134.

Page 20

* An allusion to John Locke who in 1669, because of his connection with the first Earl of Shaftesbury, had a hand in framing the *Fundamental Constitutions for the Government of Carolina*. These were 'frankly designed to "avoid erecting a numerous democracy". . . . The political framework proposed was a manorial system; it provided for a legislative assembly balanced between the common people and the nobility in such a way that the power of the commoners should not outweigh that of their betters.' Maurice Cranston, *John Locke: A Biography* (London: Macmillan, 1957), 120.

Page 21

* At an early stage in the debate on the Quebec Bill (the Constitutional Act of 1791), Charles James Fox, the leader of the Whigs in the Commons, expressed his opinion that the Revolution was a blessing to France, and added his hope that in framing a constitution for what had been formerly a French province, the Tory ministers would keep in view those enlightened principles of freedom that were making such rapid progress around the world, and soon would be universal. Later Edmund Burke, in a disorderly altercation that marked the end of his twenty-five-year friendship with Fox and the beginning of his support for William Pitt, reiterated his rejection of the principles underlying the Revolution, saying that the Rights of Man were unfitted to be the foundation of a government for the Canadians or any other people.

Page 26

* Baldwin was in London as the unofficial representative of the Upper Canadian Reformers, who felt themselves aggrieved because their Lieutenant-Governor, Sir Francis Bond Head, had suddenly swung from apparently favouring responsible government to adamantly opposing any sharing of responsibility whatever, even with his Executive Council. Baldwin had requested an interview with the Colonial Secretary, Lord Glenelg, soon after arriving in London in June 1836, but his request had been refused in order not to imply any official endorsement of his complaints or suggestions; Baldwin was therefore forced to communicate with Glenelg in writing. Head (1793–1875), one of the most interesting minor figures in our history, had taken up his duties in Toronto the previous January. His task, as he saw it, was to cure Upper Canada of its political fevers, which he attributed to excessive partisanship and 'strong republican principles [that had] leaked into the country from the United States'. He saw the contenders as 'constitutionalists on the one side, and democrats on the other'; he rejected 'the insane theory of conciliating democracy'; and he did not believe he should behave 'like a republican governor, who, from his cradle, has been brought up to reckon "that all men are born equal"'—that the fabric of human society has neither top nor bottom—that the protection of property of all descriptions belongs to the multitude—and that the will of the mob is the real "law of the land"'. He recognized that 'a monarchy may be mechanically lowered into a republic by an inclined plane, the angle of which may be so acute, that the surface to a common observer appears to be level'. He was impatient: 'I felt perfectly confident that I should very soon [after arriving in Toronto] be able proudly to report that the grievances of Upper Canada were defunct—in fact, that I had veni-ed, vidi-ed, and vic-ied them.' *Sir Francis Bond Head: A Narrative*, ed. S.F. Wise (Toronto: McClelland and Stewart, 1969), 28, 135, 20-1, 124, 22.

† See *Report of the Select Committee . . . Relative to a Responsible Executive Council* (Toronto, 1836). The 'Memorial', dated 18 April 1836, is the last of the documents appended to this report. Originally the 'Report', which reviewed the conduct of Bond Head and reiterated the Assembly's demand for responsible government, was appended to the 'Memorial'.

Page 27

* See the despatch of 5 Dec. 1835 from Lord Glenelg to Head in *Documents*, ed. Kennedy, 412-21.

Page 34

* The Governor, the Earl of Gosford, pursuing his and London's policy of conciliation, had recently appointed nine new Legislative Councillors, six of them French. These

new appointments together with some resignations produced a Council consisting of 18 French and 22 English members. 'Ces nominations ne plaisaient pas toutes aux Patriotes. Les nouveaux conseillers étaient surtout des Chouayens [anti-Patriotes], modérés il est vrai, mais des Chouayens tout de même. Le *Canadien* lui-même critiqua fortement plusieurs choix.' Gérard Filteau, *Histoire des Patriotes* (Montreal: L'Aurore, 1975), 264.

Page 42

* Grattan (1746–1820) was a member of the Irish and British Parliaments who advocated, and briefly secured, both Catholic emancipation and the independence of the Irish Parliament from the English government. Locke (1632–1704), who made important contributions to almost every field of philosophy, is presumably cited here because defenders of the American Revolution drew heavily upon his thought. Sidney (1622–83), the author of *Discourses concerning Government* (1698), was a prominent republican during the English Civil War and was eventually executed for his involvement in a plot against Charles II. Franklin (1706–90), a signatory of the Declaration of Independence and one of the greatest statemen of the American Revolution, had earlier attained European fame as a scientist and writer.

ÉTIENNE PARENT

'The Importance of Studying Political Economy': 'L'Importance de l'étude de l'économie politique' (1846), reprinted in *Étienne Parent, 1802–1874*, ed. Jean-Charles Falardeau (Montreal: Les Éditions La Presse, 1975), 127–43.

Page 43

* See 'Industry as a Means of Survival for the French-Canadian Nationality', in *French-Canadian Nationalism*, ed. Ramsay Cook (Toronto, 1969), 82–91.

Page 50

* J. R. McCulloch, *A Discourse on . . . Political Economy* (Edinburgh, 1824), 86.

† An allusion to the repeal of the complex Corn Laws that had for centuries regulated the import and export of grain. The purpose of these laws was to prevent England from becoming unduly dependent on foreign foodstuffs, but they favoured the landowners and penalized consumers and labourers. Manufacturers argued that they hampered industrialization by protecting agriculture. Following a seven-year mass campaign by the Anti-Corn-Law League, led by the Manchester liberals Richard Cobden and John Bright, the laws were repealed in 1846 by the Conservative government of Sir Robert Peel.

° Saint-Pierre (1658–1743), an influential precursor of the French Enlightenment, anticipated many features of the modern social welfare state run by experts. Perhaps his most far-seeing work, however, was his *Projet de paix perpétuelle* (1713), which argued that wars between states should be outlawed in the same way that wars within them had been—by establishing a confederation of states (or league of nations) able to impose its will, through an international court of arbitration and an armed executive force, upon recalcitrant states. An English translation of the work appeared in 1714; a condensation by Jean-Jacques Rousseau was published in 1761.

Page 51

* McCulloch, *Discourse*, 78–9.

† *Ibid.*, 77.

Page 52

* Jean-Baptiste Say, *Traité d'économie politique*, 6th ed. (Paris, 1841), 46-7, 47-8.

† McCulloch, *Discourse*, 85.

Page 53

* See Vernon C. Fowke, *Canadian Agricultural Policy: The Historical Pattern* (Toronto, 1946), 92-4.

JOSEPH HOWE

'The Organization of the Empire': abridgement of *The Organization of the Empire* (1866) reprinted in *The Speeches and Public Letters of Joseph Howe*, ed. J.A. Chisholm (Halifax: The Chronicle Publishing Co., 1909), 19, 187.

Page 56

* 'These wretched Colonies will all be independent in a few years, and are a millstone around our necks'—so wrote Benjamin Disraeli in 1852. In 1866 he wondered publicly what was the use of 'these colonial deadweights which we do not govern'. Disraeli's scepticism regarding the value of colonies—if not his contempt for them— was widely shared, particularly in Liberal circles. Goldwin Smith's *Empire* letters of 1862-3 (later issued as a book) were perhaps the best presentation of the Little Englanders' arguments for colonial emancipation. See Elisabeth Wallace, *Goldwin Smith: Victorian Liberal* (Toronto, 1957), 19, 187.

Page 57

* In 1764 the British government decided that the Island, recently taken from the French and almost unsettled, would be surveyed and divided into townships of 20,000 acres each, which would then be granted to persons deserving the patronage of the Crown. On 23 July 1767 sixty-seven townships were matched with as many names (deserving military officers, politicians, merchants, and civil servants) by simply drawing the names from a ballot box. Certain conditions were attached to the land grants, but from the very outset most of the proprietors—resident in England, concerned with other business, and shielded by their influence with the Imperial authorities—disregarded their responsibilities with impunity. The resulting conflicts between absentee proprietors, local officials desirous of a share in the spoils, and insecure tenants were the staple of Island politics for more than a century. In 1839 Lord Durham cited them as 'one of the most remarkable instances of evils resulting from profuse grants of land'. *Lord Durham's Report*, ed. C.P. Lucas (London, 1912), II, 241. The problems were ultimately resolved in 1875, when the remaining proprietors were forced to sell their holdings at prices determined by an independent commission.

SIR JOHN A. MACDONALD

'Speech on the Quebec Resolutions': in *Parliamentary Debates on the Subject of the Confederation of British North American Provinces* (1865) (Ottawa: King's Printer, 1951), 25-45.

Page 66

* That is, to adopt the Quebec Resolutions, which may be consulted in *British North America Acts and Selected Statutes, 1867-1962*, ed. Maurice Ollivier (Ottawa, n.d.), 39-49; and *Documents on the Confederation of British North America*, ed. G.P. Browne (Toronto, 1969), 154-65.

† Presumably a reference to Galt's speech of 5 and 7 July 1858, in which he outlined his plan for a federal union of all the British North American colonies. See O.D. Skelton, *Life and Times of Sir Alexander Tilloch Galt* (Toronto, 1920), 219-22.

° G.E. Cartier, J.J. Ross, and A.T. Galt, 25 Oct. 1858, in *Documents*, ed. Browne, 15-19.

Page 74

* '[The government] presented the scheme as a whole, and would exert all the influence they could bring to bear in the way of argument to induce the House to adopt the scheme without alteration, and for the simple reason that the scheme was not one framed by the Government of Canada, or by the Government of Nova Scotia, but was in the nature of a treaty settled between the different colonies, each clause of which had been fully discussed, and which had been agreed to by a system of mutual compromise. . . . It was obvious that unless the scheme were adopted as it had been settled between the different provinces . . . they would have to commence *de novo,* and he [Macdonald] had no hesitation in expressing his belief that if the scheme was not now adopted in all its principal details, as presented to the House, we could not expect to get it passed this century.' *Confederation Debates* (Quebec, 1865), 15.

Page 79

* 'The idea that a man should vote simply because he breathed was ever repellant to Sir John Macdonald's conception of government. I have heard him express the opinion with much energy that no man who advocated universal suffrage had any right to call himself a Conservative. He favoured the extension to single women of the privilege of voting on the same terms as men, his argument being that the exclusion of women otherwise duly qualified was at variance with the theory of a property qualification.' Joseph Pope, *Memoirs of the Right Honourable Sir John Alexander Macdonald*, rev. ed. (Toronto: Oxford University Press, 1930), 616-17.

ULTRAMONTANISM

'The Programme Catholique: The Next Elections': 'Programme Catholique: les prochaines élections' (1871) in Arthur Savaète, *Voix canadiennes: vers l'abîme* (Paris: Arthur Savaète, n.d), II, 100–4.

'Pastoral Letter of the Bishops of the Ecclesiastical Province of Quebec': from *Mandements, lettres pastorales et circulaires des Évêques de Québec*, ed. Mgr H. Têtu et l'abbé C.-O. Gagnon, Nouvelle Série, I (Quebec: Imprimerie Générale A. Côté et Cie, 1889), 320–36; translation in *The True Witness and Catholic Chronicle* (Montreal), 15 Oct. 1875, revised by H.D. Forbes.

Page 94

* This appears to be a direct quotation from a Pastoral Letter of 10 March 1871 from Mgr Laflèche, Bishop of Trois Rivières, commenting on the ninth decree of the Fourth Council of the Bishops of Canada (May 1868), which dealt with honesty in elections. The relevant passage of this decree stated that electors 'sont toujours obligés devant Dieu, et en conscience, de donner leur suffrage au candidat qu'ils jugent avec prudence être réellement honnête, et capable de remplir la charge si importante qui lui est confiée, à savoir, de veiller au bien de la religion et de l'état, et de travailler fidèlement à le promouvoir et à le conserver'. *Mandements, lettres pastorales et circulaires des Évêques de Québec,* ed. H. Têtu and C.-O. Gagnon (Quebec, 1887–90), N.S. I, 28.

† As is well known, terms like 'conservative' and 'liberal' are used in two senses, the

party sense (capital C or L) and the theoretical sense (lower-case c or l). Here and elsewhere I have taken the liberty of introducing capitals not in the original where the sense has seemed to require them.

Page 97

* The dogma of papal infallibility was proclaimed by the first Vatican Council in 1870. In his Pastoral Letter of 1876, 'Concernant le libéralisme catholique, les journaux, etc.', Bishop Bourget summed up its meaning for the laity as follows: *'J'écoute mon Curé; mon Curé écoute l'Évêque; l'Évêque écoute le Pape; le Pape écoute N.S.J.C., qui l'assiste de son divin Esprit, pour le rendre infaillible dans l'enseignement et le gouvernement de son Église.'* Ignace Bourget, écrivain, ed. Adrien Thério (Montreal, 1975), 190-1.

Page 98

* The definition of Catholic liberalism, like that of liberalism itself, is controversial. Bourget offered one explanation of the term in the 1876 Pastoral Letter cited above. In France Catholic liberalism had until recently been best represented by the Comte Charles de Montalembert (1810–70). He was the longest survivor of the brilliant group that had gathered around Félicité de Lamennais (1782–1854) at the time of the second revolt against the Bourbons and had tried, under the banner of *Dieu et liberté*, to combine ultramontanism in religion with republicanism in politics. They founded the journal *L'Avenir* in October 1830, but their defence of the Church against their governments (they viewed the July monarchy as no better than the Bourbons); their objections to Gallicanism among the clergy; their reliance on 'the common sense of mankind'; their acceptance of liberty of the press and of conscience; their stress on the need for regenerating Catholicism; and their outspoken sympathy for every people in a state of revolt gave rise to suspicions of their orthodoxy and soon earned them a condemnation from Rome—the Encyclical *Mirari Vos* of 1832 by Gregory XVI. The condemnation was reaffirmed by Pius IX, especially in *Quanta Cura* (1864), to which was attached a Syllabus of Errors ending with a famous declaration to the effect that 'the Roman pontiff cannot, and ought not to, reconcile himself and come to terms with progress, liberalism, and modern civilisation.' J. B. Bury, *History of the Papacy in the 19th Century*, ed. Frederick C. Grant (New York, 1964), 40. There is a brief analysis of the issues in Guido de Ruggiero, *The History of European Liberalism*, trans. R. G. Collingwood (Oxford, 1927), 173–6. See also *Anticlericalism*, ed. J. Salwyn Shapiro (Princeton, 1967) for an historical survey and a useful collection of documents.

Page 99

* Thomas Aquinas, *Summa Theologica* I-II, 90, 4, c.

Page 102

* Presumably an allusion to the decrees issuing from the Fourth Council of the Bishops of Canada in May 1868. The joint Pastoral Letter of that date (which may be consulted in *Mandements*, ed. Têtu and Gagnon, IV, 617–43) does not discuss the duties of journalists.

Page 105

* There is a diverse literature on the Guibord case, including a useful collection of excerpts from the press, *The Guibord Affair*, ed. Lovell C. Clark (Toronto, 1971). The circumstances are analysed at some length in Mason Wade, *The French Canadians*, rev. ed. (Toronto: Macmillan, 1968), I, 341-53, and in Rainer Knopff, 'Quebec's "Holy War" as "Regime" Politics: Reflections on the Guibord Case', *Canadian Journal of Political Science*, 12 (1979), 315–31.

† The ancient liberties and immunities of the French Church *vis-à-vis* Rome, differently defined at different times, but involving three basic ideas: independence of the king of France in the temporal order; superiority of general councils over the Pope; and the union of king and clergy in France to limit papal intervention within the kingdom. The most famous statement of these liberties was by Pierre Pithou, *Les libertés de l'Église gallicane* (1594), five editions of which were published between 1824 and 1860. *New Catholic Encyclopedia* (New York, 1967), VI, 262-7.

GOLDWIN SMITH

'From His *Reminiscences*': excerpts from Goldwin Smith, *Reminiscences*, ed. Arnold Haultain (New York: Macmillan, 1911), 430–43.

'The Ascent of Man': excerpt from 'The Ascent of Man' (1877) reprinted in *Lectures and Essays* (New York: Macmillan, 1881), 89–96.

'The Political Destiny of Canada': abridgement of 'The Political Destiny of Canada', *Fortnightly Review*, N.S. 21 (1877), 431–59.

Page 109

* 'Canada First' developed from a meeting in Ottawa in the summer of 1868 of five young English Canadians with literary ambitions. United by their disgust with the low partisanship of Canadian politics and their belief in the need to cultivate national feeling, they pledged themselves to put 'Canada first'—above party or personal considerations. But did they do so? Historians have been divided, some saying that their nationalism was merely racial, full of bravado and silly emotion, others implying that they were the paladins of the only viable Canadian nationalism. Their first crusade was on behalf of the acquisition of the Northwest Territory, but unfortunately their infidels were the Métis led by Louis Riel, and the agitation they helped to stir up in Ontario threatened the delicate compromises of Confederation. In January 1874 the group, under the label 'The Canadian National Asociation', issued the following platform:

1. British Connection, Consolidation of the Empire—and in the meantime a voice in treaties affecting Canada.
2. Closer trade relations with the British West India Islands, with a view to ultimate political connection.
3. Income Franchise.
4. The Ballot, with the addition of compulsory voting.
5. A Scheme for the Representation of Minorities.
6. Encouragement of Immigration, and Free Homesteads in the Public Domain.
7. The imposition of duties for Revenue, so adjusted as to afford every possible encouragement to Native Industry.
8. An Improved Militia System, under the command of trained Dominion Officers.
9. No Property Qualifications in Members of the House of Commons.
10. The Reorganization of the Senate.
11. Pure and Economic Administration of Public Affairs.

Canada First: A Memorial of the Late William A. Foster, ed. Goldwin Smith (Toronto, 1890), 8–9. The movement seemed to be on the point of great success in October 1874, when Edward Blake—having had his offer to serve as Prime Minister rejected by the incumbent—briefly embraced their cause (see following note).

† Blake (1833–1912), the second premier of Ontario, in 1873 resigned that office to

become a minister without portfolio in the Mackenzie administration in Ottawa. After only three months he resigned, and in October 1874, in his famous 'Aurora Speech' (reprinted in the *Canadian Historical Review*, 2 [1921], 249-71), he elaborated seven of the eleven points of the Canadian National Association Platform and generally endorsed Canada First's emphasis on the importance of 'a national sentiment'. Blake returned to the Liberal fold in May 1875 and in 1880 succeeded Mackenzie as leader of the party. He led it to defeat in the elections of 1882 and 1887, after which he withdrew from Canadian politics. From 1892 to 1907 he sat as an Irish Nationalist in the British House of Commons, but made little impact on British politics.

Page 110

* Henry Sidgwick, *The Methods of Ethics* (London, 1874).

† Herbert Spencer, *First Principles*, 5th ed. (London, 1884), 396.

Page 111

* Presumably Henry Sumner Maine, whose *Ancient Law* (London, 1861) includes a chapter on 'Primitive Society' in which he suggests that the Homerian Cyclops provide a good model of 'the situation in which mankind disclose themselves at the dawn of their history': 'They have neither assemblies for consultation nor *themistes* [appointed laws], but every one exercises jurisdiction over his wives and his children, and they pay no regard to one another' (*Odyssey*, IX, 112-15).

Page 112

* Possibly an allusion to Spencer, *First Principles*, chs. 2 and 3.

Page 118

* New Brunswick had abolished its separate schools in 1871, and the federal government refused to take remedial action. 'Using as an excuse the danger of infringing provincial rights and thus setting a precedent which might later be turned against Quebec, the ever-temporizing Sir John A. Macondald . . . instead suggested recourse to the courts. Thus the question dragged on for years, envenoming the relations between Church and State and arousing ethnic antagonism.' Mason Wade, *The French Canadians,* rev. ed. (Toronto: Macmillan, 1968), I, 353.

Page 128

* The phrase 'figments and hypocrisies' refers to the forms of monarchy and the idea that they safeguard against corruption and the evils of crude democracy. The preceding three pages, here omitted, developed the theme that the tutelage of a mother country is rarely of any benefit to a colony.

Page 133

* George Cornewall Lewis, *An Essay on the Government of Dependencies* (London, 1841), 239–40.

SIR WILFRID LAURIER

'Political Liberalism': from *Wilfrid Laurier on the Platform*, ed. Ulric Barthe (Quebec: Turcotte & Menard, 1890), 51–80; translation revised by H.D. Forbes.

Page 136

* See above, note * for page 98.

Page 138

* T.B. Macaulay, *History of England*, 8th ed. (London, 1852), I, 97-8.

Page 139

* Apocryphal quotation usually traced to John Philpot Curran but here associated with 'Junius', an eighteenth-century writer of anonymous letters to the London *Public Advertiser* that embarrassed George III and his ministers by their revelations of secret misconduct.

Page 140

* During the 1830s liberal opinion had been divided on the question of tenures. Papineau, the Seigneur of Montebello, had frowned on any tampering with seigneurial rights, but his more radical lieutenants (for example, Robert Nelson) held that the 'feudal' system should be 'abolished, as if it had never existed' and the land turned over to those who had cleared and farmed it. Only in 1854, on the basis of a settlement worked out by Cartier, were seigneurial rights 'commuted' and the *censitaires* enabled to purchase the land they farmed.

Page 143

* G.O. Trevelyan, *The Life and Letters of Lord Macaulay* (New York, 1875), I, 186-8.

Page 144

* Probably a reference to the 23-section electoral manifesto of J.-B.-E. Dorion published in *L'Avenir*, 28 November 1851. See Jean-Paul Bernard, *Les Rouges* (Montreal, 1971), 340-74.

Page 147

* Rough of voice and hard of feature,
Brown-complexioned and fiery-eyed, who
Marches with agile strides,
Takes pleasure in the people's cries, the bloody brawls,
The beating drums,
The smell of powder, the distant peal
Of bells and muffled cannon-fire;
Who take her lovers only among the people,
Offers her broad flank
Only to those as strong as she, and desires the embrace
Of arms red with blood.

Translation by Sally Livingston.

Page 148

* The god, holding his course,
Poured down torrents of light
Upon his obscure blasphemers.

Translation by Sally Livingston. 'The orator has confounded J.B. Rousseau with Lefranc de Pompignan; but the two great lyric poets are so often cited together that the lecturer, who was quoting from memory, may easily be pardoned this *quid pro quo*.' Note by Ulrich Barthe in *Wilfrid Laurier on the Platform* (Quebec, 1890), 74. The lines that Laurier quotes are from Pompignan's 'Ode sur la mort de Jean-Baptiste Rousseau'.

JULES-PAUL TARDIVEL

'On Liberalism': excerpts from *Mélanges*, I (Quebec: Imprimerie de la Vérité, 1887), 310–15, and *Notes de voyage en France, Italie, Espagne, Irlande, Angleterre, Belgique et Hollande* (Montreal: Sénécal, 1890), 87–9.

Page 153

* Matthew 7:20.

Page 155

* Gabriel Garcia Moreno (1821–75), president of Ecuador from 1861 to 1865 and again from 1869 to 1875, is known for his attempt to implement Catholic political theory. His policy is exemplified in the concordat he signed with the Vatican in 1862, which placed education entirely in the hands of the Church, and in the constitution he promulgated in 1869, under which only practising Catholics qualified for citizenship. He was killed by liberal assassins, who split his skull with a machete.

SIR GEORGE PARKIN

'The Reorganization of the British Empire': from *The Century Magazine*, 37 (1888), 187–92.

Page 157

* The Imperial Federation League was established in London in 1884 to promote imperial unity. The unsentimental approach to Empire characteristic of Manchester liberalism had given way, during the 1870s, to a deeper appreciation of the value of colonies. Disraeli's tune had changed from 'Millstones Round our Necks' to 'Jewels in Your Crown'. (The League's object, 'not too plainly put, was quite simple, to get the colonies to contribute to Imperial defence.' A.R.M. Lower, *Colony to Nation*, 4th ed. [Toronto, 1969], 393–4.) Branches of the League were established in Canada and attracted support from those who were proud of their Britishness, eager for Canada to play a larger role on the world stage, impatient with the diversity and provincialism of Canadians, and contemptuous of the small-mindedness of Canadian politicians. The Toronto branch, established in 1887, played a prominent part in the campaign leading up to the election of 1891, which pitted loyalism and imperialism against continentalism. For many years the leading spirit in the Toronto branch was Col. George T. Denison, one of the original protagonists of Canada First (see above, note * for page 109), whose political memoirs, *The Struggle for Imperial Unity* (Toronto, 1909) are worth reading. The first president of the Toronto branch was D'Alton McCarthy. One of the 'Noble Thirteen' who voted to disallow the Jesuits' Estates Act, he is now best remembered for his important contributions to the Manitoba schools and languages question. See Carl Berger, *The Sense of Power* (Toronto, 1970), for an excellent analysis of imperialist thought between 1867 and 1914.

Page 159

* Georges-Etienne Cartier: 'I am an Englishman who speaks French'.

ADAM SHORTT

'In Defence of Millionaires': from *The Canadian Magazine*, 13 (1899), 493–8.

THE REV. WILLIAM CAVEN

'The Equal Rights Movement': from the *University Quarterly Review*, 1 (1890), 139–45.

Page 173

* The Jesuits' Estates problem developed in the late eighteenth century as a result of the successful British policy of gradually suppressing the Jesuit order in Canada. Who was to take over their property? In fact it reverted to the Crown. After 1791 the citizens of the colony, through their Assembly, claimed the Estates as an endowment for education, and in 1831 this claim was formally recognized with the transfer of their management to the Lower Canadian legislature. But in 1773 Pope Clement XIV, acting under pressure from the House of Bourbon, had abolished the Society of Jesus and decreed that their real property should revert to the bishops in whose dioceses it was located. In 1814 Pius VII had restored the Jesuit order, and by the 1860s the Jesuits had re-established themselves in Canada and begun pressing for compensation. During the 1870s and 1880s the question became entangled in the byzantine rivalries of the Montreal (Ultramontane) and Quebec (Gallican) clergy. In 1888 the Liberal Nationalist premier of Quebec, Honoré Mercier, by openly and formally involving the Pope in the negotiations, achieved a final settlement of the question. See J.R. Miller, *Equal Rights* (Montreal, 1979).

† Section 90 of the British North America Act gives the central government the power to disallow any provincial legislation. In 1881 the federal authorities began to use this power to strike down provincial acts contrary to 'sound principles of legislation'. (I am grateful to Robert Vipond for clarification of this point.) Macdonald announced in January 1889 that the Jesuits' Estates Act would not be disallowed. In March the House of Commons supported the government's policy 188 to 13.

Page 175

* Mercier was responding to Robert Sellar's assertions that an outrage was perpetrated whenever 'British courts' in Quebec enforced tithes and that 'as British subjects we have a right to say whether or not the courts of the Empire are to assist in maintaining those demands [of the priests] and in becoming collectors of those assessments.' *Answer of the Hon. Honoré Mercier to the Pamphlet of the Equal Rights Association* . . . (Quebec, 1890), 9, 61–8.

HENRI BOURASSA

'The French-Canadian in the British Empire': abridgement of 'The French-Canadian in the British Empire', *The Monthly Review*, 9 (Oct. 1902), 53–68.

'The Program of the Nationalist League': from Joseph Levitt, *Henri Bourassa and the Golden Calf*, 2nd ed. (Ottawa: Les Éditions de l'Université d'Ottawa, 1972), Appendix; translation revised by H.D. Forbes.

'The Spectre of Annexation': excerpts from *The Spectre of Annexation and the Real Danger of National Disintegration* (Montreal: Le Devoir Printing, 1912).

Page 178

* The present is the second of two articles by Bourassa published in *The Monthly Review* in 1902. The first, which had appeared the previous month, had analysed

French-Canadian history and character, emphasizing that 'most of the settlers of New France came from the western and northern provinces of France . . . regions which had been for centuries in close contact with England. . . . [And they were] severed from the motherland half a century before the modern French nationality was completed [by Napoleon].' *The Monthly Review*, 8 (Sept. 1902), 59–60.

Page 181

* Bourassa exaggerates here. In 1900 there were roughly twice as many French Canadians in Canada as in the United States. See Leon E. Truesdell, *The Canadian Born in the United States* (New Haven, 1943), 60, and Yolande Lavoie, *L'Émigration des Québécois aux États-Unis, de 1840 à 1930* (Quebec, 1979), 45–6.

Page 184

* See Henri Bourassa; 'The Nationalist Movement in Quebec', Canadian Club of Toronto, *Addresses* (Toronto, 1907), 56–64, for an interesting discussion of this program.

Page 188

* In June 1912 the Ontario Department of Education, responding to discontent among Irish Catholics and to an adverse internal report on conditions in its bilingual schools, adopted the infamous 'Regulation 17', which effectively outlawed the use of French as a language of instruction in the elementary schools of the province and placed the bilingual Catholic schools under English Protestant inspectors. The regulation remained in force for fifteen years and caused much bitterness.

† Bourassa's pamphlet, a translation of editorials that had appeared in *Le Devoir*, was provoked by an editorial in the Montreal *Star* of 9 July 1912, which warned of the dreadful calamities that might befall the world should Germany become its overlord because Canada had failed to contribute enough to the strengthening of the British Navy. The list of future woes culminated with the following: 'We will lose our flag, our institutions, our system of government, our judiciary, our power to shelter the French language and the Roman Catholic religion, our industries, our independent development, our name, [and] our place in history.' The complex background to Bourassa's bitterness and sense of deception is presented in Wade, *The French Canadians*, II, 608–26.

Page 190

* The tenth amendment of the American constitution states that 'the powers not delegated to the United States by the Constitution, nor prohibited by it to the States, are reserved to the States respectively, or to the people.' It was the last of the ten amendments that constitute the Bill of Rights and it clarified what was already implicit in the distribution of powers effected by Article I of the constitution.

Page 193

* Bourassa himself at one time raised obstacles and objections. See his speech of 26 July 1899 in the Commons (*Debates*, 1899, III, 8538–42). But a very different attitude is apparent in *Les Écoles du Nord-Ouest* (Montreal, 1905) and subsequent discussions of immigration policy.

STEPHEN LEACOCK

'Greater Canada: An Appeal': from *The University Magazine*, 6 (1907), 132–41, reprinted in *The Social Criticism of Stephen Leacock*, ed. Alan Bowker (Toronto: University of Toronto Press, 1973), 3–11.

'The Apology of a Professor': from *Essays and Literary Studies* (London: John Lane, 1916), 9–37, reprinted in *The Social Criticism of Stephen Leacock*, ed. Bowker, 28–39.

PROPHETS OF THE NEW AGE

Salem Bland, 'The New Christianity': abridgement of *The New Christianity, or the Religion of the New Age* (1920), The Social History of Canada Series (Toronto: University of Toronto Press, 1973).

J.S. Woodsworth, 'The Kingdom Come': from *Grain Grower's Guide*, 30 June 1915, reprinted in *Our Sense of Identity*, ed. Malcolm Ross (Toronto: The Ryerson Press, 1954), 292–6.

Page 215

* Luke 8:17.

Page 216

* Oliver Wendell Holmes, *The Autocrat of the Breakfast-Table*, Riverside Edition (Boston, 1900), 114.

Page 218

* Probably an allusion to the Adamson Act, which provided for an eight-hour day and time-and-a-half for overtime on interstate railways.

Page 220

* The chapter on American Christianity came between the 'divine currents too strong to be resisted' and 'the Great Christianity that is to be'. It surveyed the evolution of Christianity from the standpoint of race, dealing with the Jewish, Greek, Latin, and Teutonic forms of Christianity before presenting American Christianity as 'the most remarkable phenomenon of Christian history . . . since the revolt of the Teutonic peoples [i.e., the Reformation]'. *The New Christianity* (Toronto, 1920), 65.

FRANK H. UNDERHILL

'O Canada, Our Land of Crown Corporations': excerpt from 'O Canada', *Canadian Forum*, Dec. 1929, reprinted in *Forum: Canadian Life and Letters 1920–70*, ed. J.L. Granatstein and Peter Stevens (Toronto: University of Toronto Press, 1972), 66–7.

'Some Reflections on the Liberal Tradition in Canada': abridgement of 'Some Reflections on the Liberal Tradition in Canada' (1946) reprinted in *In Search of Canadian Liberalism* (Toronto: Macmillan of Canada, 1960), 3–20.

Page 237

* *Documents*, ed. Browne, 98.

THE REGINA MANIFESTO

From Walter D. Young, *The Anatomy of a Party: The National CCF, 1932–61* (Toronto: University of Toronto Press, 1969), Appendix A.

CANON LIONEL GROULX

'Methods of Education': excerpt from *Mes mémoires*, I (Montreal: Fidès, 1970), 96–102.

'Tomorrow's Tasks': 'Labeurs de demain' (1936) in *Directives* (Montreal: Les Éditions du Zodiaque, 1937), 95–135.

Page 251

* Montalembert, as noted above (note for p. 98), was the outstanding Catholic liberal

of his generation. He and Léon Cornudet (1808–76), a high civil servant, were lifelong friends, and in 1873 Cornudet published Montalembert's early letters to him, *Lettres à un ami de collège*. In 1884 Cornudet's son published a new edition that included his father's letters to Montalembert. Henri Lacordaire (1802–61) was a Dominican priest, a famous preacher, and a leading Catholic liberal who had collaborated in 1830 with Lamennais on *L'Avenir*. Henri de Perreyve (1831–65), a close friend of Lacordaire, was an Oratorian priest who taught ecclesiastical history at the Sorbonne. Frédéric Ozanam (1813–53), another outstanding Catholic liberal, taught literature at the Sorbonne and is remembered as the founder of the St Vincent de Paul Society.

Page 258

* J.T. Delos, *La Société internationale et les principes du droit public* (Paris, 1929), 79.

Page 260

* An allusion to the *bonne entente* movement that flourished during the 1930s. Its goal was to improve relations between English and French Canadians by increasing each group's understanding of the other. A prominent representative of the movement, Abbé Arthur Maheux, was criticized by Groulx in 'Why We Are Divided' (in *French-Canadian Nationalism*, ed. Cook, 237–56), a response to Maheux's *Pourquoi sommes-nous divisés?* (Quebec, 1943).

Page 263

* *Hansard's Parliamentary Debates*, 3rd series, Vol. 185 (1867), 568. Lord Carnarvon was Colonial Secretary when the British North America Act was drafted. The quoted remark is from his speech on the second reading of the bill.

Page 267

* The last part of this sentence has been loosely translated to accord with the meaning of the one following it in the original: 'Tant qu'il n'est pas avéré qu'il est devenu injuste, et surtout, tant qu'il n'est pas manifeste qu'il puisse être remplacé par un autre plus propre à pourvoir une nation du bien humain, un ordre politique vaut et est objet de justice sociale. La piété maintient l'homme dans les vénérations et les respects qui s'imposent envers les causes de son existence, la justice le courbe aux obéissances nécessaires à la conservation de l'ordre politique: deux vertus aussi admirables l'une que l'autre, la première donnant libre cours ''aux grands sentiments du coeur'', la seconde imposant les prestations indispensables au bien-vivre actuel.' Louis Lachance, *Nationalisme et Religion* (Ottawa, 1936), 191.

ANDRÉ LAURENDEAU

'The Conditions for the Existence of a National Culture': 'Les Conditions d'Existence d'une culture nationale', *L'Action nationale*, 37 (1951), 364–90.

Page 274

* An allusion should be noted here to the Royal Commission on National Development in the Arts, Letters and Sciences which had been appointed in 1949 to investigate, under the chairmanship of Vincent Massey, federal government policy respecting cultural agencies and institutions, including the question of federal aid to universities, and which submitted its report in May 1951. In carrying out its mandate the Commission found it necessary to survey 'the spiritual foundations of our national life.' Its survey was based on the assumption that there did indeed exist an embryonic national tradition in Canada's cultural life. 'Through all the complexities and diversities of

race, religion, language and geography, the forces which have made Canada a nation and which alone can keep her one are being shaped. These are not to be found in the material sphere alone. Physical links are essential to the unifying process but true unity belongs to the realm of ideas. . . . Canadians realize this and are conscious of the importance of national tradition in the making.' *Report* (Ottawa, 1951), 4–5. Laurendeau's reservations on this point are similar to those expressed by Quebec's Royal Commission on Constitutional Problems, the Tremblay Commission, which conducted an equally broad inquiry and published its report in 1956.

Page 276

* Luis Mariano and Georges Guétary were entertainers with many films and million-selling records to their credit. One volume of Mariano's memoirs is entitled *Ma vie et mes amours*.

Page 277

* Presumably an allusion to wartime centralization and the activities of the Royal Commission on Dominion-Provincial Relations, the Rowell-Sirois Commission, which submitted its report in May 1940. Laurendeau may also have had in mind the Quebec provincial elections of October 1939, when the Union Nationale government led by Maurice Duplessis—who campaigned against participation in the war—was defeated by the Liberals led by Adélard Godbout. The federal Liberals under Ernest Lapointe had intervened in the campaign, turning it into a ratification of their pledge that there would be no conscription for overseas service.

† The most distinctive feature of the French-Canadian system of education was the network of private classical colleges that bridged the eight-year gap between primary education, which ended with grade 7, and the specialized graduate faculties of the universities. The colleges offered the equivalent of a four-year high school program emphasizing the ancient and modern languages and literature, followed by four years of university-level work in languages, literature, philosophy, theology, mathematics, and the fundamentals of empirical science. The *baccalauréat* awarded upon successful completion of the second cycle of studies was the basic prerequisite for entrance to the universities proper. The first of these colleges was established in 1635; in 1852, when Laval University was founded, there were 13 of them; and by 1951, when Laurendeau was writing, the number had increased to 95, 71 for men and 24 for women. Each of these colleges was then affiliated with either Laval or the University of Montreal, and together they constituted the undergraduate arts faculties of these universities. The most interesting thing about the colleges was their curriculum, the *cours classique*. The student was not allowed to design his own program of studies within a loose system of electives, but rather was required to follow one basic program, the design of which went back to the Catholic reformation and the educational theories of the Jesuits. Emphasizing, as noted, the classical languages and Catholic philosophy, it was well suited to produce teachers, preachers and lawyers, but ill suited to produce applied scientists—educational psychologists, masters of business administration, biochemists, or engineers. The colleges were, of course, part of a larger system, some of the weaknesses of which Laurendeau notes. That system survived, with only minor modifications, until the mid-1960s, when the 'révolution globale' that Laurendeau feared took place. See Claude Galarneau, *Les Collèges classiques au Canada français* (Montreal, 1978).

Page 280

* Pierre Juneau, 'Le Cinéma canadien: illusions et faux calculs', *Cité libre*, no. 2 (Feb. 1951), 20-1.

GEORGE GRANT

'The Minds of Men in the Atomic Age': from *Texts of Addresses Delivered at the 24th Annual Couchiching Conference* (Toronto: Canadian Institute of Public Affairs, 1955), 39–45.

Page 286

* C. D. Howe (1886–1960) was Minister of Trade and Commerce in the St Laurent government. An American by birth and an engineer by training, he had had a successful academic and business career in Nova Scotia before entering politics as a Liberal in 1935. He was immediately taken into the cabinet and was involved in establishing the CBC and Trans-Canada Air Lines, now Air Canada. During the war, as Minister of Munitions and Supply, he gave strong political direction to the Canadian economy.

Page 287

* The reference is to Hilda Neatby, *So Little for the Mind* (Toronto, 1953), a widely read attack on child-centred progressive education. John Dewey, the American philosopher of pragmatism, was the most influential proponent of such education.

Page 288

* 'Can it be doubted that Canadian universities today exist essentially as technical schools for the training of specialists? They turn out doctors and physicists, economists and chemists, lawyers and social workers, psychologists and agriculturalists, dietitians and sociologists, and these technicians are not being called upon in any systematic way to relate their necessary techniques to any broader whole. Even the traditional humane subjects such as history, the classics and European literature are in many cases being taught as techniques by which the student can hope to earn his living, not as useful introductions to the sweep of our spiritual tradition.' George Grant, 'Philosophy', in *Royal Commission Studies: A Selection of Essays Prepared for the Royal Commission on National Development in the Arts, Letters and Sciences* (Ottawa, 1951), 119-20.

Page 289

* Between 1951 and 1954 a planned community of some 10,000 souls came into being at Kitimat, B.C., 400 miles north of Vancouver—an area previously wilderness. The Aluminum Company of Canada chose Kitimat as the site for a new aluminum smelter (the largest in the world) because of its deep-water anchorage (the bauxite comes from the West Indies) and the availability of vast amounts of hydro-electric power in the vicinity. Harnessing the power involved building the third highest dam in the world and drilling two tunnels, each ten miles long, through a mountain to divert the course of a river. The water dropped 2,600 feet (16 times the drop at Niagara) to turbines having an installed capacity of 2,200,000 horsepower.

DAVID LEWIS

'A Socialist Takes Stock': *A Socialist Takes Stock* (Toronto: Ontario Woodsworth Memorial Foundation, 1955).

Page 290

* Lewis was speaking in October 1955. The 1950 convention of the CCF had resolved that a new statement of democratic socialist principles was needed to replace the Regina Manifesto. Over the next four years a complex consultative process resulted in two drafts that satisfied almost no one. In 1956 a small committee headed by Lewis

produced the draft that was ultimately adopted at the Winnipeg convention of the party in August of that year. In April 1956 the two large trade-union federations, the Trades and Labour Congress (craft unions) and the Canadian Congress of Labour (industrial unions), united to form the Canadian Labour Congress. This opened the way to a closer relation between unionism and socialism. 'From [July 1955] on I gave my attention and my support to the development of a political arrangement which would have the labour movement as its muscle and the CCF philosophy as its guiding spirit.' David Lewis, *The Good Fight* (Toronto: Macmillan, 1981), 441.

W.L. MORTON

'Canadian Conservatism Now': from *Conservative Concepts*, 1 (1959), 7–18, reprinted in *Contexts of Canada's Past: Selected Essays of W.L. Morton*, ed. A.B. McKillop (Toronto: Macmillan of Canada, 1980), 243–53.

Page 302

* This book, incomplete at the author's death in 1954, was edited by Judith Robinson and published in 1957. The editor remarked in her preface that 'a parallel with the work of Simone Weil should not go unremarked'.

Page 303

* Letter to Lord Dorchester, 5 Feb. 1790, in *Documents*, ed. Kennedy, 204.

Page 307

* See above, note * for p. 287.

† Jack Pickersgill (b. 1905), MP for Bonavista-Twillingate, 1953-67: 'If I got elected six times without living there, I see no reason to live there now [that I am retiring].'

NATIONALISM AND SOCIALISM

'Letter from a Nationalist': 'Lettre d'un nationaliste', *Cité libre*, no. 35 (1961), 6–8.

Paul Chamberland, 'Cultural Alienation and National Revolution': 'Aliénation culturelle et révolution nationale', *parti pris*, no. 2 (Nov. 1963), 10–22.

Page 310

* *Cité libre* was a review begun in 1950 by Pierre Trudeau and Gérard Pelletier to provide an outlet for radical criticism of French-Canadian authoritarianism and nationalism, particularly as represented by Maurice Duplessis, the leader of the Union Nationale and Premier of Quebec, 1936-9 and 1944-59. Trudeau's analysis of nationalist thought in 'Quebec on the Eve of the Asbestos Strike' (in *French-Canadian Nationalism*, ed. Cook, 32–48) is the best introduction to the thought of its founders.

Page 313

* See above, note † for p. 277.

Page 314

* An allusion to the provincial election of 22 June 1960, which brought the Liberal party under Jean Lesage to power.

Page 315

* Before July 1962 all cheques issued by the federal government were in English only. This small but significant indication of official unilingualism was long resented by French Canadians, but when the policy was changed it was, as André Laurendeau

remarked, 'too little, too late'. 'Châteaux Maisonneuve' presumably refers to the controversy some years earlier over the naming of the new CNR hotel in Montreal. Although many Montrealers wanted to name it after Paul de Chomedey, Sieur de Maisonneuve, the founder of Montreal, CNR president Donald Gordon decided to call it the Queen Elizabeth. The question of census forms arose when Prime Minister Diefenbaker ordered that the forms for the 1961 census allow people to call themsleves simply 'Canadians', without specifying their family's ethnic origins. This would have meant a drastic drop in the apparent 'French' proportion of the total population, and the move was bitterly and successfully opposed by French-Canadian politicians and editorialists.

† Gilles Constantineau (b. 1933)?

Page 316

* Hubert Aquin, 'La fatigue culturelle du Canada français,' *Liberté*, no. 23 (May 1962), 312. There is a translation in *Contemporary Quebec Criticism*, ed. Larry Shouldice (Toronto, 1979), 54-82.

Page 318

* A small group of young people calling themselves the Front de Libération du Québec (FLQ) placed bombs in mailboxes and public buildings in the Montreal area in April and May 1963. This was the first of several waves of terrorism that climaxed with the October crisis of 1970. Marcel Chaput, as a result of the extraordinary success of his book, *Pourquoi je suis séparatiste* (1961), was for a short time the most prominent spokesman for the independence movement. In July 1963 he began a 33-day hunger strike in an unsuccessful effort to raise money for his branch of the movement. In September 1963 the official opening of Montreal's Place des Arts, a new complex of concert halls, was the occasion for a rowdy nationalist demonstration to protest against the choice of an American as its director.

Page 322

* The Quebec section of the Social Credit party led by Réal Caouette won 26% of the popular vote in Quebec and 26 seats in the 1962 general election. Although the party had been active in the province since the 1940s, it had never before elected any members, and its sudden success was the occasion for much bewildered commentary. Later a consensus developed that its success was to be attributed to Caouette's skill at articulating the economic grievances of the conservative lower classes of rural and small-town Quebec. Cf. Dominique Clift, *Quebec Nationalism in Crisis* (Montreal, 1982), 35-50.

Page 325

* *'Mr Vanier and his wife'*: in English in the original. Georges Vanier (1888-1967), after an exceptionally distinguished military and diplomatic career, served as Governor General from 1959 until his death.

† MLF—Mouvement Laïque de Langue Française; RIN—Rassemblement pour l'Indépendance Nationale; PRQ—Parti Républicain du Québec; FLQ—Front de Libération du Québec; MDN—?; PSQ—Parti Socialiste du Québec.

PIERRE ELLIOTT TRUDEAU

'Advances in Politics': excerpts from *Approaches to Politics*, trans. I.M. Owen (Toronto: Oxford University Press, 1970).

'Nationalist Alienation': 'L'Aliénation nationaliste', *Cité libre*, no. 35 (1961), 3-5.

Page 326

* Pascal, *Pensées*, 533 (Lafuma). Each article in the original series, and each section of the book in which it was later published, carried an epigraph. I have eliminated all of these except for the present one accompanying the second article, with which this abridgement begins.

Page 327

* Pascal, *Pensées*, 81.

† 'In 1956 Frank Scott had successfully challenged the Padlock Law before the Supreme Court. This law had been passed by the government of Quebec in 1937. On the pretext of preventing the incursion of Communism into Quebec, Duplessis had given himself the discretionary power to padlock premises used by organizations alleged to be "communist".' Note by I. M. Owen in the English edition of the book.

° Rousseau, *Social Contract*, I, 1.

Page 328

* An allusion to the trial and conviction, on circumstantial evidence, of Wilbert Coffin for the murder of three American hunters in 1953. Coffin was hanged in 1956. Jacques Hébert (publisher of the weekly in which these articles appeared) later wrote a book, *J'accuse les assassins de Coffin* (1963), in which he argued that the authorities had been more concerned with pinning the murders on someone than on determining Coffin's guilt or innocence. In 1964 a one-man Quebec Royal Commission reviewed the case but upheld the original verdict.

Page 329

* Pascal, *Pensées*, 60.

Page 330

* Hobbes, *Leviathan*, I, 13.

† An allusion to the epigraphs of the preceding section—'When the government is illegitimate and tyrannical, each individual may destroy it by violence. . . . The tyrant makes (unjust) war on each individual; each one has the right to kill him'—and the present one: 'Like the apostles, I would rather obey God than men . . . I condemn these newspapers, and like the Bishop of Prato I am ready to be dragged through the courts rather than be silent.'

Page 332

* 'Persecuted by Mr Duplessis, the Jehovah's Witnesses appealed to the Supreme Court. Mr [Frank] Roncarelli, a Montreal restaurant-owner who was a member of the sect, undertook the expenses of the suit. Mr Duplessis arbitrarily took away his licence to sell alcohol, which was likely to ruin his business. Mr Roncarelli sued the prime minister and was awarded $33,000 damages and costs.' Note by I. M. Owen in the English edition of the book.

† The Rassemblement was an organization established in 1956 to promote 'a movement of education and democratic action'. Its first president was Pierre Dansereau and its vice-president was Pierre Trudeau. Its manifesto is reprinted in *Le manuel de la parole*, ed. Daniel Latouche and Diane Poliquin-Bourassa (Montreal, 1977-9), II, 307-10.

Page 335

* Presumably a reference to 'De libro, tributo . . . et quibusdam aliis' (Oct. 1954) and 'Les octrois fédéraux aux universités' (Feb. 1957), which are reprinted in *Federalism and the French Canadians* (Toronto, 1968).

AN APPEAL FOR REALISM IN POLITICS

From *Canadian Forum*, May 1964, 29–33.

Page 339

* Between 1957 and 1964 the average annual rates of unemployment were 4.6, 7.0, 6.0, 7.0, 7.1, 5.9, 5.5, and 4.7% respectively. At present (summer 1984) the rate is nudging 12%.

Page 343

* See below, note * for p. 392.

Page 345

* Walter Gordon (b. 1906), one of the most prominent economic nationalists during the 1960s and 1970s, was Minister of Finance from 1963 to 1965. His first budget contained a number of provisions to discourage foreign takeovers and to encourage foreign subsidiaries to sell 25% of their shares to Canadian investors. These produced such an outcry that he had to withdraw them almost immediately.

† A new Broadcasting Act was passed in 1958 establishing a Board of Broadcast Governors to supervise both the CBC and private stations. The idea behind this legislation was to permit a private television network to develop, and more than one television station in a given locality, but to require adequate 'Canadian content' in all broadcasting as a condition for a licence. In November 1959 the BBG specified that stations would have to broadcast 45% Canadian content by July 1960 and 55% by April 1962.

Page 346

* Cf. Albert Breton, 'The Economics of Nationalism', *Journal of Political Economy*, 72 (1964), 376–86; and P.E. Trudeau, 'A propos de "domination économique"', *Cité libre*, no. 20 (May 1958), 7–16.

Page 348

* 'The *Forum* is pleased to publish, at the same time as *Citè libre* in Montreal, the following manifesto drawn up by a group of young French Canadian intellectuals (only one is over thirty-five). This manifesto is not a 'French Canadian Manifesto', but a Canadian Manifesto. It is therefore of interest to our readers not merely as a reflection of French Canadian life, but as a challenge to all Canadians. Albert Breton, a graduate of Columbia University, is an Assistant Professor of Economics at the University of Montreal; Raymond Breton, a graduate of Johns Hopkins, in sociology is at McGill. Both Bretons are members of the important Social Research Group, Inc. Claude Bruneau is a lawyer and one-time special assistant to the Hon. Davie Fulton and is now with the legal department of Steinberg's Ltd. Yvon Gauthier is a psychoanalyst, specialist in child psychology, practising in the Department of Psychiatry at Ste-Justine Hospital in Montreal. Marc Lalonde, a graduate of Oxford, is a former assistant professor of Law at the University of Montreal, one-time special assistant to Hon. Davie Fulton, now a practising lawyer and member of the Board of Directors of the Institute of Public Law, University of Montreal. Maurice Pinard, another sociologist, studied at the University of Montreal, the Sorbonne and Johns

Hopkins and now teaches at McGill. Even English Canadians need no introduction to Pierre-Elliott Trudeau, a founder and editor of *Cité Libre*, lawyer, political economist, educated at London School of Economics and Harvard. He is at present with the Institute of Public Law at the University of Montreal. The manifesto was translated into English by Mr P. M. Pitfield.'' Note by Ramsay Cook introducing the Manifesto to readers of the *Canadian Forum*.

STATEMENT ON MULTICULTURALISM

From House of Commons, *Debates*, 1971 (3rd Session, 28th Parliament), VIII, 8545-6 (8 Oct. 1971).

Page 349

* The Royal Commission on Bilingualism and Biculturalism was appointed in 1963 'to inquire into and to report upon the existing state of bilingualism and biculturalism in Canada and to recommend what steps should be taken to develop the Canadian Confederation on the basis of an equal partnership between the two founding races, taking into account the contribution made by the other ethnic groups to the cultural enrichment of Canada and the measures that should be taken to safeguard that contribution.' The final Report of the Commission, in six large volumes, appeared between 1967 and 1970. The blue pages (pp. xv-lii) of volume I, attributed to André Laurendeau, are of particular interest. For an abridgement of the whole report, see Hugh R. Innis, *Bilingualism and Biculturalism* (Toronto, 1973).

Page 351

* The document referred to here, which explained particular policies in greater detail, included the following general remarks: 'The government while responding positively to the commission's recommendations, wishes to go beyond them to the spirit of the Book IV to ensure that Canada's cultural diversity continues.

'Cultural diversity throughout the world is being eroded by the impact of industrial technology, mass communications and urbanization. Many writers have discussed this as the creation of a mass society—in which mass produced culture and entertainment and large impersonal institutions threaten to denature and depersonalize man. One of man's basic needs is a sense of belonging, and a good deal of contemporary social unrest—in all age groups—exists because this need has not been met. Ethnic groups are certainly not the only way in which this need for belonging can be met, but they have been an important one in Canadian society. Vibrant ethnic groups can give Canadians of the second, third, and subsequent generations a feeling that they are connected with tradition and with human experience in various parts of the world and different periods of time.

'Two misconceptions often arise when cultural diversity is discussed.

'(a) Cultural Identity and National Allegiance. The sense of identity developed by each citizen as a unique individual is distinct from his national allegiance. There is no reason to suppose that a citizen who identifies himself with pride as a Chinese-Canadian, who is deeply involved in the cultural activities of the Chinese community in Canada, will be less loyal or concerned with Canadian matters than a citizen of Scottish origin who takes part in a bagpipe band or a highland dancing group. Cultural identity is not the same thing as allegiance to a country. Each of us is born into a particular family with a distinct heritage: that is, everyone—French, English, Italian and Slav included—has an ''ethnic'' background. The more secure we feel in one particular social context, the more we are free to explore our identity beyond it. Ethnic groups often provide people with a sense of belonging which can make them better able to cope with the rest of society than they would as isolated individuals.

Ethnic loyalties need not, and usually do not, detract from wider loyalties to community and country.

'Canadian identity will not be undermined by multiculturalism. Indeed,we believe that cultural pluralism is the very essence of Canadian identity. Every ethnic group has the right to preserve and develop its own culture and values within the Canadian context. To say we have two official languages is not to say we have two official cultures, and no particular culture is more "official" than another. A policy of multiculturalism must be a policy for all Canadians.

'(b) Language and Culture. The distinction between language and culture has never been clearly defined. The very name of the royal commission whose recommendations we now seek to implement tends to indicate that bilingualism and biculturalism are indivisible. But, biculturalism does not properly describe our society, multiculturalism is more accurate. The Official Languages Act designated two languages, English and French, as the official languages of Canada for the purposes of all the institutions of the Parliament and government of Canada; no reference was made to cultures, and this act does not impinge upon the role of all languages as instruments of the various Canadian cultures. Nor, on the other hand, should the recognition of the cultural value of many languages weaken the position of Canada's two official languages. Their use by all of the citizens of Canada will continue to be promoted and encouraged.' *Debates*, 1971, VIII, 8580-1.

GAD HOROWITZ

'Tories, Socialists and the Demise of Canada': from *Canadian Dimension*, 2, no. 4 (May–June 1965), 12–15.

'Mosaics and Identity': excerpts from 'Creative Politics' and 'Mosaics and Identity', *Canadian Dimension*, 3, no. 1 (Nov.–Dec. 1965), 14, and 3, no. 2 (Jan.–Feb. 1966), 17–19.

'On the Fear of Nationalism': from *Canadian Dimension*, 4, no. 4 (May–June 1967), 7–9.

Page 354

* *Social Purpose for Canada*, ed. Michael Oliver (Toronto, 1961), was a venture in social criticism from a 'left-of-centre viewpoint'. It was intended to be a source of ideas for the NDP, as *Social Planning for Canada*, published by the League for Social Reconstruction in 1935, had been for the CCF. It included essays by George Grant, Albert Breton, Pierre Trudeau, and thirteen other contributors. Grant dedicated *Lament for a Nation* to Derek Bedson and Judith Robinson. Bedson was the principal civil servant in the Conservative administration of Duff Roblin in Manitoba; Robinson was a columnist for the Toronto *Telegram*.

In a subsequent letter to *Canadian Dimension* (2:5 [July-Aug. 1965], 30), Grant objected to Horowitz's reference to Robinson as 'the Drew-loving columnist' and his suggestion that she was 'of the capitalist wing of the Conservative Party'. 'If one reads her writing one will see that she stood for "A Tory Socialism". It is indeed a pity that history's most disgusting regime should prevent the use of the phrase "national socialism".'

† This quotation and all subsequent quotations are from *Lament for a Nation*. Grant later summed up the theme of the book as follows: 'the belief that human excellence is promoted by the homogenising and universalising power of technology is the dominant doctrine of modern liberalism, and . . . that doctrine must undermine all particularisms and . . . English-speaking Canada as a particular is wide open to that doctrine.' *Technology and Empire* (Toronto: Anansi, 1969), 69.

Page 356

* The Defence Crisis of 1963 was the climax of the Diefenbaker government's difficulties, internally and externally. It grew out of commitments the government had made in 1958 and 1959 to accept a role in NATO and in North American air defence that required the use by the Canadian armed forces, and the storage on Canadian soil, of American nuclear warheads. Planes and missiles were purchased that would be worthless, or almost so, without the warheads, but when it came time to work out arrangements for their joint control, the government split between supporters and opponents of the policy. The question of nuclear arms, and more broadly the question of Canada's relation to the Western alliance, was a main issue in the 1963 federal election.

Page 359

* *The Prospect of Change*, ed. Abraham Rotstein (Toronto, 1965), was the first publication of the University League for Social Reform, another attempt to revive the old League for Social Reconstruction.

Page 363

* John Porter, *The Vertical Mosaic* (Toronto, 1965), 465, 466, 507.

THE POLITICAL ECONOMY TRADITIONS

John Dales, 'Protection, Immigration and Canadian Nationalism': in *Nationalism in Canada*, ed. Peter Russell (Toronto: McGraw-Hill, 1966), 164–77.

Kari Levitt, 'Silent Surrender': excerpts from *Silent Surrender: The Multinational Corporation in Canada* (Toronto: Macmillan, 1970), 25–30, 32–4, 103–9, 118–19.

RENÉ LÉVESQUE

'A Country That Must Be Made': excerpt from *An Option for Quebec* (Toronto: McClelland and Stewart, 1968), 13–24.

Page 389

* In July 1967 President de Gaulle was to make a five-day state visit to Canada as part of Expo and the centennial celebrations. He arrived aboard the flagship of the French Mediterranean fleet, landed at Wolfe's Cove, and was given a tumultuous reception by a crowd of thousands in the old city of Quebec. The next day he made a triumphal progress in an open car along the old Chemin du Roi from Quebec to Montreal. That evening, speaking to a cheering throng of about 10,000 from the balcony of the Montreal City Hall, he said that he sensed 'the same atmosphere' in Quebec that he had felt 'during the liberation of France in World War II.' He concluded by exclaiming: 'Vive le Québec! Vive le Québec libre! Vive le Canada français! Vive la France!'

† *The Vigil of Quebec*, trans. Sheila Fischman and Richard Howard (Toronto, 1971), 36. The article from which this quotation is taken appeared in *Le Devoir*, 30 June 1967.

Page 392

* *'Désormais'*, *'Il faut que ça change'*, and *'Maîtres chez nous'* were phrases associated with Paul Sauvé, Jean Lesage, and René Lévesque respectively, and more generally with the Quiet Revolution of the early 1960s. The last of the three was the Liberal battlecry in the 1962 provincial elections, in which the main issue was the nationalization of some private power companies to create the contemporary Hydro Québec.

† 'SGF is *la Société Générale de Financement* (General Investment Corporation), an investment, holding, and management company designed to promote business and industry in the province, and financed by both public and private sectors. *Soquem* is *la Société Québécoise d'Exploration Minière* (Quebec Mining Exploration Co.), government-owned and the largest in the province. The *Caisse de Dépôts* is the investment arm of the Quebec Pension Plan.' Note in the English edition of the book.

Page 395

* 'CSN is the *Confédération des Syndicats Nationaux* (Confederation of National Trade Unions) and FTQ is the *Fédération des Travailleurs du Québec* (Quebec Labour Federation). These are the two largest central labour bodies in the province. The UCC is the *Union Catholique des Cultivateurs*, a major farm organization sometimes known in English as the Catholic Farmers' Union or the Farmers' Catholic Union.' Note in the English edition of the book.

THE WAFFLE MANIFESTO

From *Gordon to Watkins to You*, ed. Dave Godfrey and M.H. Watkins (Toronto: New Press, 1970).

CHARLES TAYLOR

'The Agony of Economic Man': from *Essays on the Left*, ed. Laurier LaPierre *et al.* (Toronto: McClelland and Stewart, 1971), 221–35.

PIERRE VADEBONCOEUR

'Gentle Genocide': excerpts from *Un génocide en douce: écrits polémiques* (Montreal: L'Hexagone/parti pris, 1976), 11–59.

Page 419

* Alberto Moravia, *The Red Book and the Great Wall*, trans. Ronald Strom (New York, 1968).

Page 420

* The most prominent Russian dissident at the time was Andrei Sakharov, a distinguished physicist ('the father of the Soviet H-bomb') who in 1975 had been awarded the Nobel Peace Prize for his struggle 'against the abuse of power and violations of human dignity in all its forms, . . . [and] for the ideal of a state founded on the principle of justice for all.' Another well-known dissident was Alexander Solzhenitsyn, who was awarded the Nobel Prize for Literature in 1970 and whose *Letter to the Soviet Leaders* was published in 1974, following his expulsion from the Soviet Union. Roger Garaudy, a leading French Communist politician and intellectual, was evicted from the party in 1970 as a result of his objections to the Soviet invasion of Czechoslovakia in 1968. He is best known for his advocacy of dialogue between Marxists and Christians.

Page 422

* The reference is to Jean Marchand, Gérard Pelletier, and Pierre Elliott Trudeau, who joined the Liberal party and were elected to the House of Commons in 1965. Trudeau and Pelletier were founders of *Cité libre* (see above, note for p. 310), which published many articles by Vadeboncoeur.

Page 426

* An allusion to the wildcat walkouts by pilots and air traffic controllers in June 1976. In the name of safety in the air—an extraordinarily powerful symbol—they opposed the Trudeau government's bilingualism policy and threatened to break the government itself. Their action crystallized the latent hostility of English Canada to bilingualism, produced the resignation of Jean Marchand from the cabinet (because of his opposition to the terms of the agreement ending the walkouts, which was negotiated by the Minister of Transport, Otto Lang), and strengthened the Parti Québécois. Reaction to the crisis suggested that 'public opinion in Canada . . . was fundamentally critical of bilingualism and supported the pilots less because they too understood the safety argument but because the pilots were taking a stand on a fundamental issue.' *Canadian Annual Review of Politics and Public Affairs*, ed. John Saywell (Toronto: University of Toronto Press, 1977), 76.

Page 427

* An allusion to O. Mannoni, *Psychologie de la colonisation* (Paris, 1950), Albert Memmi, *Portrait du colonisé* (Paris, 1957), Frantz Fanon, *Les Damnés de la terre* (Paris, 1961), and related literature, particularly Jean-Paul Sartre, *Réflexions sur la question juive* (Paris, 1946). All these titles have been published in English translations.

Page 431

* Camus made this remark during an informal question and answer session with students at Stockholm University two days after his official acceptance of the 1957 Nobel Prize for Literature. He was pressed by a young Moslem to explain why he spoke out against Soviet oppression in Hungary and not against the French in Algeria. In his reply he said: 'I have always denounced terrorism. I must also denounce a terrorism which is exercised blindly, in the streets of Algiers for example, and which some day could strike my mother or my family. I believe in justice, but I shall defend my mother above justice,' Herbert R. Lottman, *Albert Camus* (New York, 1979), 618. (I am indebted to David Cook for this reference.)

GEORGE GRANT

'Teaching What Nietzsche Taught': excerpts from *Time as History* (Toronto: Canadian Broadcasting Corporation, 1969), 31–43, and 'Nietzsche and the Ancients: Philosophy and Scholarship', *Dionysius*, 3 (1979), 12–16.

Page 437

* An allusion to Marshall McLuhan (1911–80), a professor of English literature at the University of Toronto whose books, popular with media specialists, developed the idea—sometimes attributed to Harold Innis—that 'the medium is the message'. Some claim that McLuhan was the first to recognize that technology has become one of the major factors in human evolution. Cf. *Oxford Companion to Canadian Literature* (Toronto, 1983), 494.

Page 438

* 'The ass arrived, beautiful and most brave.' *Beyond Good and Evil*, sec. 8.

Suggested Readings

Cook, Ramsay, ed. *French-Canadian Nationalism: An Anthology.* Toronto: Macmillan, 1969.

Craig, G.M., ed. *Lord Durham's Report.* Toronto: McClelland and Stewart, 1963.

Crean, Susan, and Marcel Rioux. *Two Nations: An Essay on the Culture and Politics of Canada and Quebec in a World of American Preeminence.* Toronto: James Lorimer, 1983.

Creighton, Donald. *Canada's First Century.* Toronto: Macmillan, 1970.

Dafoe, John. *Canada: An American Nation.* New York: Columbia University Press, 1935.

Grant, George. *Lament for a Nation: The Defeat of Canadian Nationalism.* Toronto: McClelland and Stewart, 1965.

——. *Philosophy in the Mass Age.* Toronto: Copp Clark, 1959.

——. *Technology and Empire: Perspectives on North America.* Toronto: Anansi, 1969.

King, W.L.M. *Industry and Humanity.* Toronto: T. Allen, 1918.

Kroker, Arthur. *Technology and the Canadian Mind: Innis/McLuhan/Grant.* Montreal: New World Perspectives, 1984.

Kwavnik, David, ed. *The Tremblay Report: Report of the Royal Commission of Inquiry on Constitutional Problems.* Ottawa: Carleton University Press, 1973.

Leacock, Stephen. *Essays and Literary Studies.* London: John Lane, 1916.

Lower, A.R.M. *Colony to Nation.* Toronto: Longmans, 1946.

Trudeau, Pierre Elliott. *Federalism and the French Canadians.* Toronto: Macmillan, 1968.

Vallières, Pierre. *White Niggers of America.* Joan Pinkham, trans. Toronto: McClelland and Stewart, 1971.